LEAVING CERTIFICATE HIGHER LEVEL

Active Mat

Book 1

Michael Keating, Derek Mulvany and James O'Lou

Special Advisors:
Oliver Murphy, Colin Townsend and Jim McElroy

FOLENS

Contents

Introduction

Active Maths 4 is a comprehensive **two-book series** covering the **complete Leaving Certificate Higher Level course**. *Active Maths 4* covers all five strands of the new Project Maths syllabus.

- **Book 1** corresponds to **Paper 1** and therefore contains **Strands 3 (Number), 4 (Algebra) and 5 (Functions).**

- **Book 2** corresponds to **Paper 2** and therefore contains **Strands 1 (Statistics and Probability) and 2 (Geometry and Trigonometry).**

Teachers and students will find that they have the new syllabus fully covered.

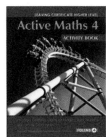

- A separate **free Activity Book** provides a wealth of activities designed to develop students' understanding of each topic in a hands-on way. The textbooks are linked throughout with the Activity Book to introduce topics and emphasise key Learning Outcomes.

Active Maths 4 is packed with student-friendly features:

- It prepares students for the new style of exam question with comprehensive **graded exercises** on each topic and **end-of-chapter revision exercises** include Project Maths-type exam questions based on all material that has been released by the NCCA and SEC.

- **Learning Outcomes** from the new syllabus are stated at the beginning of each chapter.

- Each chapter includes a **You Should Remember** section so that students can check they are fully prepared before starting the chapter.

- A list of **Key Words** at the start of each chapter helps students to consolidate learning. On first occurrence in each chapter, key words are set apart in **Definition boxes** to reinforce the importance of understanding their meaning.

- Clear and concise **Worked Examples** show students how to set out their answers, including step-by-step instructions with excellent diagrams to explain constructions.

- Essential formulae are set apart in **Formula boxes**.

- **Answers** to exercises are given at the end of each book.

  Additional **teacher resources, including digital activities** and **fully worked-out solutions** for the textbooks, will be available online at www.folensonline.ie.

Active Maths 4 allows teachers to meet the challenge of the new syllabus for Leaving Certificate Higher Level, and encourages students to discover for themselves that mathematics can be enjoyable and relevant to everyday life.

> Note: Constructions in Book 2 are numbered according to the NCCA syllabus for Project Maths Higher Level.

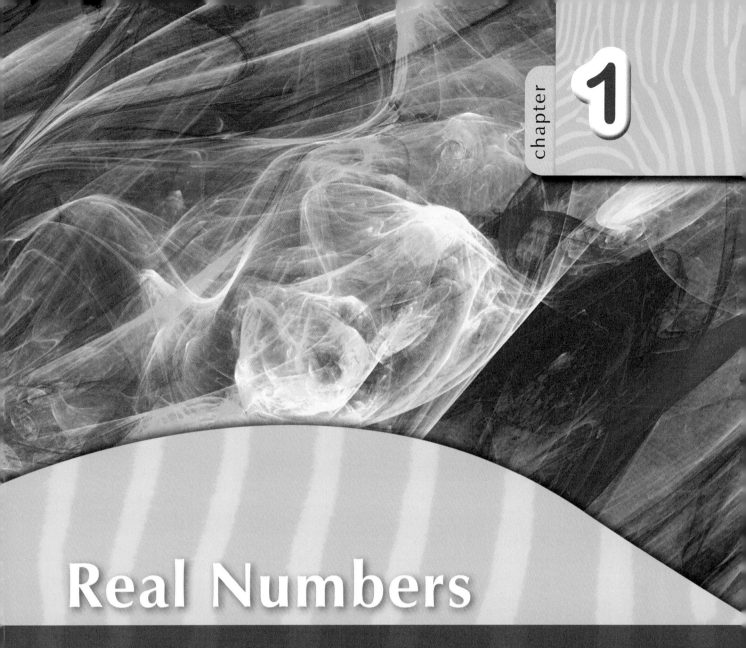

chapter 1

Real Numbers

Learning Outcomes

In this chapter you will learn:

➲ How to define the real numbers

➲ About factors, multiples and prime factors

➲ How to write a whole number as a product of prime factors

➲ The properties of integers

➲ The properties of rational numbers

➲ About rounding and significant figures

➲ How to geometrically construct $\sqrt{2}$ and $\sqrt{3}$

➲ About orders of magnitude and scientific notation

The **real numbers** can be thought of as the set of all numbers that lie along an infinitely long number line.

This is not a very rigorous definition of the **real numbers**. However, it will serve our purposes. The discovery of a proper rigorous definition of the real numbers was one of the most important developments in the mathematics of the nineteenth century. The main contributors to the field were a French mathematician, Augustin-Louis Cauchy (1789–1857), and two German mathematicians, Richard Dedekind (1831–1916) and Karl Weierstrass (1815–1897).

KEY WORDS

■ **Factor**
■ **Multiple**
■ **Prime factor**
■ **Proof by contradiction**
■ **Natural number**
■ **Integer**
■ **Rational number**
■ **Irrational number**
■ **Real number**
■ **Order of magnitude**
■ **Scientific notation**

Augustin-Louis Cauchy (1789–1857)

Richard Dedekind (1831–1916)

Karl Weierstrass (1815–1897)

The natural numbers, the integers, the rational numbers and the irrational numbers are all subsets of the real number system.

1.1 FACTORS, MULTIPLES AND PRIME FACTORS

Natural Numbers

The **natural numbers** are the ordinary counting numbers. The set of natural numbers is an infinite set. This means that the set is never-ending. The letter N is used to label the set of natural numbers.

$N = \{1, 2, 3, 4...\}$

Rationals

Reals

Irrationals

Integers

Naturals

Factors

A factor of a natural number is any natural number that divides evenly into the given number.

For example, all the factors of 24 are $\{1, 2, 3, 4, 6, 8, 12, 24\}$.

As you can see, 1 is a factor of 24 and 24 is a factor of 24.

■ 1 is a factor of every natural number.
■ Every natural number is a factor of itself.

Multiples

> A **multiple** of a natural number is itself a natural number, into which the natural number divides, leaving no remainder.

The multiples of 6 are {6, 12, 18, 24, 30, 36 ...}.

As you can see, the set of multiples is an infinite set, i.e. it goes on forever.

Prime Numbers

> **Prime numbers** are natural numbers that have **two** factors only.

- 7 is a prime number as it has two factors only: 1 and 7.
- 2 is the only even prime number. Its two factors are 1 and 2.
- 11 is the first two-digit prime. Its two factors are 1 and 11.
- 1 is **not** a prime as it has one factor only, itself.
- 0 is **not** a prime as it has an infinite number of factors, and it is not a natural number.

The Greek mathematician Euclid proved that the number of primes is infinite.

Euclid

Natural numbers greater than 1 that are not prime numbers are called **composite numbers**. The first five composite numbers are 4, 6, 8, 9, 10.

The Fundamental Theorem of Arithmetic

> Every natural number greater than 1 is either prime or can be written as a unique product of primes.

The **Fundamental Theorem of Arithmetic** is an important result that shows that the primes are the building blocks of the natural numbers.

The **highest common factor** of two natural numbers, n_1 and n_2, is the largest natural number that divides evenly into both n_1 and n_2.

The highest common factor of 12 and 20 is 4, as 4 is the largest natural number that divides evenly into both 12 and 20.

The **lowest common multiple** of two numbers is the smallest multiple that both numbers share.

The lowest common multiple of 3 and 4 is 12, as 12 is the smallest number that both 3 and 4 divide evenly into.

 **ACTIVITIES 1.1, 1.2**

In Activities 1.1 and 1.2 you discovered how to find the HCF and LCM of two natural numbers, by writing each number as a product of primes.

Ⓡ Worked Example 1.1

Express 240 as a product of prime numbers.

Solution

2	240
2	120
2	60
2	30
3	15
5	5
	1

Start with the lowest prime that is a factor.

$240 = 2 \times 2 \times 2 \times 2 \times 3 \times 5$

$\therefore 240 = 2^4 \times 3 \times 5$

Ⓡ Worked Example 1.2

Find (i) the HCF and (ii) the LCM of 512 and 280.

Solution

Express both numbers as a product of primes.

2	512
2	256
2	128
2	64
2	32
2	16
2	8
2	4
2	2
	1

2	280
2	140
2	70
5	35
7	7
	1

$512 = 2^9$ and $280 = 2^3 \times 5 \times 7$

(i) HCF $(512, 280) = 2^3 = 8$

(ii) LCM $(512, 280) = 2^9 \times 5 \times 7 = 17{,}920$

R Worked Example 1.3

Show that if p is a prime number and p divides evenly into r^2, then p divides evenly into r.

Solution

Let $r = r_1^{\alpha_1} r_2^{\alpha_2} r_3^{\alpha_3} \ldots r_n^{\alpha_n}$, where each r_i is prime and each $\alpha_i \in N$.

Therefore, using the rules of indices:

$$r^2 = (r_1^{\alpha_1} r_2^{\alpha_2} r_3^{\alpha_3} \ldots r_n^{\alpha_n})^2$$
$$= r_1^{2\alpha_1} r_2^{2\alpha_2} r_3^{2\alpha_3} \ldots r_n^{2\alpha_n}$$

If $p \mid r^2$ (p divides r^2), then $p \mid$ one of $r_i^{2\alpha_i}$.

Since each r_i is prime, $\Rightarrow p \mid$ one of r_i.

Hence, p divides $r_1^{\alpha_1} r_2^{\alpha_2} r_3^{\alpha_3} \ldots r_n^{\alpha_n} = r$.

R Worked Example 1.4

Periodical cicadas are insects with very long larval periods and brief adult lives.
For each species of periodical cicada with larval period of 17 years, there is a
similar species with larval period of 13 years.
If both the 17-year and 13-year species emerged in a particular location in 2011,
when will they next both emerge in that location?

Solution

Here we are looking for the LCM of 17 and 13. As both numbers are prime, the LCM of 13 and 17 is
$17 \times 13 = 221$.

Therefore, both species will next appear together in that location in the year 2232.

R Worked Example 1.5

Evaluate (i) 5! and (ii) $5 \times 4!$

Solution

(i) $5! = 5 \times 4 \times 3 \times 2 \times 1$

   $\therefore 5! = 120$

(ii) $5 \times 4! = 5 \times (4 \times 3 \times 2 \times 1)$

   $= 120$

Let n be a natural number.
$n!$, read as n factorial, is the product
of the natural numbers 1, 2, 3 ... n.
We define 0! to be 1.

$5! = 120$
$4! = 24$ } $120 \div 24 = 5$
$3! = 6$ } $24 \div 6 = 4$
$2! = 2$ } $6 \div 2 = 3$
$1! = 1$ } $2 \div 1 = 2$
$0! = x$ } $1 \div x = \textcircled{1} \leftarrow$ to continue the pattern

$\therefore \dfrac{1}{x} = 1$

$\therefore x = 1$

$\therefore$ 0! is defined as being $= 1$.

Infinitude of Primes

There are infinitely many prime numbers. In the next activity you will discover a proof, by contradiction, that this statement is correct.

 ACTIVITY 1.3

Proof by contradiction is a form of proof that establishes the truth of a proposition by showing that the proposition being false would imply a contradiction.

 ## Exercise 1.1

1. Express the following numbers as a product of prime factors:

   (i) 160   (v) 1,155   (viii) 102

   (ii) 273   (vi) 1,870   (ix) 1,224

   (iii) 128   (vii) 10,500   (x) 38,016

   (iv) 368

2. (a) Express each of the following pairs of numbers as the product of prime factors.

   (b) Hence, find the LCM and HCF for each set of numbers.

   (i) 102 and 170   (vi) 123 and 615

   (ii) 117 and 130   (vii) 69 and 123

   (iii) 368 and 621   (viii) 20, 30 and 60

   (iv) 58 and 174   (ix) 8, 10 and 20

   (v) 60 and 765   (x) 294, 252 and 210

3. Let n be a natural number. What is the HCF of:

   (i) n and $2n$ (ii) n and n^2

4. If 3 divides $334,611^2$, explain why 3 must also divide $334,611$.

5. r is an even natural number and s is an odd natural number. The prime factorisations of r and s are:

   $$r = r_1^{\alpha_1} r_2^{\alpha_2} r_3^{\alpha_3} \ldots r_n^{\alpha_n}$$

   $$s = s_1^{\theta_1} s_2^{\theta_2} s_3^{\theta_3} \ldots s_m^{\theta_m}$$

   (i) Explain why one of the primes, $r_1, r_2, r_3, \ldots r_n$ must be 2.

   (ii) Explain why none of the primes, $s_1, s_2, s_3, \ldots s_m$ is 2.

6. Let u be any natural number with prime factorisation,

   $$u = u_1^{\phi_1} u_2^{\phi_2} u_3^{\phi_3} \ldots u_n^{\phi_n}$$

   (i) Explain why none of the primes, $u_1, u_2, u_3, \ldots u_n$ divide $u + 1$.

   (ii) Hence, write down the HCF of u and $u + 1$.

7. Let u be any natural number with prime factorisation:

   $$u = u_1^{\phi_1} u_2^{\phi_2} u_3^{\phi_3} \ldots u_n^{\phi_n}$$

   (i) If u is even, then find the HCF of u and $u + 2$.

   (ii) If u is odd, then what is the HCF of u and $u + 2$.

8. Kate has two pieces of material. One piece is 72 cm wide and the other piece is 90 cm wide. She wants to cut both pieces into strips of equal width that are as wide as possible.

   How wide should she cut the strips?

9. Tom exercises every 14 days and Katie every nine days. Tom and Katie both exercised on March 12. On what date will they both exercise together again?

10. Ms Hoover has 160 crayons and 30 colouring books to give to her students. If each student gets an equal number of crayons and an equal number of colouring books what is the largest number of students she can have in her class?

11. Bart is making a board game with dimensions of 16 cm by 25 cm. He wants to use square tiles. What are the dimensions of the largest tile he can use?

12. Beginning on Monday of each week and running until Friday, *The Breakfast Show* gives away €100 to every 100th caller who gets through to the show. During the week before a Saturday night concert, the show offers two free tickets to the concert for every 70th caller. How many callers must get through before one wins the tickets and the €100?

13. The Ulam numbers, u_n, $n \in N$, are defined as follows:

$$u_1 = 1,$$
$$u_2 = 2$$

and each successive natural number, m, where $m > 2$, u_m is an Ulam number **if and only if** it can be written **uniquely** as the sum of two **distinct** Ulam numbers.

  (i) Explain the words in bold.

  (ii) Why is 5 not an Ulam number?

  (iii) Find the first 10 Ulam numbers.

14. Let n be a natural number. Define the function, F(n) as follows:

$$F(n) = \frac{n}{2} \quad \text{if } n \text{ is even.}$$

$$F(n) = \frac{3n + 1}{2} \quad \text{if } n \text{ is odd.}$$

  (i) Find F(1) and F(2).

  (ii) Explain why F(n) is always a natural number.

  (iii) Consider the sequence:

  n, F(n), F(F(n)), F(F(F(n))) ....

  Construct the first 15 terms of the sequence for each of the following values of n:

  6, 10, 15, 32 and 17.

  (iv) Based on your results make a conjecture about the sequence.

  (v) Test your conjecture for $n = 39$.

15. Consider the finite sequence:

  10! + 2, 10! + 3, 10! + 4, ... 10! + 9, 10! + 10

  (i) How many terms are in the sequence?

  (ii) Explain why none of the terms are prime.

  (iii) Construct a sequence of 20 consecutive natural numbers none of which are prime.

  (iv) Is it possible to have a set of consecutive natural numbers of any given size, that does not contain any prime numbers? Explain.

1.2 INTEGERS AND RATIONAL NUMBERS

The integers are made up of zero and all the positive and negative whole numbers. Mathematicians use the letter Z to represent the set of integers.

$$Z = \{... -6, -5, -4, -3, -2, -1, 0, 1, 2, 3, 4, 5, 6, 7...\}$$

Properties of Integers

■ $a + b$ and $a \times b$ are integers whenever a and b are integers. (Closure property)

■ $a + b = b + a$ and $a \times b = b \times a$ (Commutative properties)

■ $(a + b) + c = a + (b + c)$ and $(a \times b) \times c = a \times (b \times c)$ (Associative properties)

■ $a \times (b + c) = (a \times b) + (a \times c)$ (Distributive property)

■ $a + 0 = a$ and $a \times 1 = a$ for all integers a. (Identity elements)

■ For every integer a, there exists an integer $-a$, such that $a + (-a) = 0$.
  We say $-a$ is the additive inverse of a. (Additive inverse)

Rational Numbers

The letter Q is used to represent the set of rational numbers.

- Rational numbers are also called fractions.
- All integers can be written in the form $\frac{a}{b}$ and hence are rational numbers. For example, $3 = \frac{3}{1}$.

> $Q = \{$Any number that can be written in the form $\frac{a}{b}$, where $a, b \in Z, b \neq 0\}$

- The properties listed for the integers also carry over into the rationals.
- Two fractions are **equivalent** if they have the same value. For example, $\frac{1}{2} = \frac{3}{6}$.
- The **reciprocal** of a fraction is found by turning the fraction upside down (inverting). For example, the reciprocal of $\frac{11}{12}$ is $\frac{12}{11}$.
- Every fraction, with the exception of zero, has a multiplicative inverse. The product of a number and its multiplicative inverse is always 1. The multiplicative inverse of a fraction is its reciprocal. For example, the multiplicative inverse of $\frac{3}{4}$ is $\frac{4}{3}$.

R Worked Example 1.6

Use the properties of the integers to prove that for any integer $a \times 0 = 0$.

Solution

$$0 + 0 = 0 \quad \text{(Identity)}$$
$$\Rightarrow a \times (0 + 0) = a \times 0 \quad \text{(Multiplying both sides by } a)$$
$$\Rightarrow a \times 0 + a \times 0 = a \times 0 \quad \text{(Distributive property)}$$
$$a \times 0 + a \times 0 + (-a \times 0) = a \times 0 + (-a \times 0) \quad \text{(Adding } -a \times 0 \text{ to both sides)}$$
$$a \times 0 + [a \times 0 + (-a \times 0)] = a \times 0 + (-a \times 0) \quad \text{(Associative property)}$$
$$a \times 0 + 0 = 0 \quad \text{(Additive inverse)}$$
$$\therefore a \times 0 = 0 \quad \text{(Identity)}$$

R Worked Example 1.7

Use the properties of the integers to prove that for all integers a and b, $(a)(-b) = -ab$.

Solution

$$(a)(-b) + (a)(b) = a(-b + b) \quad \text{(Distributive property)}$$
$$= a(0) \quad \text{(Additive inverse)}$$
$$\therefore (a)(-b) + (a)(b) = 0$$

Therefore, $(a)(-b)$ is the additive inverse of $(a)(b)$.

But $(a)(b) = ab$ and its additive inverse is $-ab$.

$$\therefore (a)(-b) = -ab$$

R Worked Example 1.8

Use the properties of the integers to prove that for all integers a and b, $(-a)(-b) = ab$.

Solution

$$(-a)(-b) + (-a)(b) = -a(-b + b) \quad \text{(Distributive property)}$$
$$= -a(0) \quad \text{(Additive inverse)}$$
$$\Rightarrow (-a)(-b) + (-a)(b) = 0$$

Therefore, $(-a)(-b)$ is the additive inverse of $(-a)(b)$.

But $(-a)(b) = -ab$ and its additive inverse is ab.

$$\therefore (-a)(-b) = ab$$

Worked Example 1.9

(i) Find the sum of the squares of the four consecutive integers, −2, −1, 0 and 1.

(ii) Show that the sum of the squares of any four consecutive integers is always an even number.

Solution

(i) $(-2)^2 + (-1)^2 + (0)^2 + (1)^2 = 4 + 1 + 0 + 1$

$$= 6$$

(ii) $n, n + 1, n + 2,$ and $n + 3, n \in Z$, are four consecutive integers.

$$\therefore (n)^2 + (n + 1)^2 + (n + 2)^2 + (n + 3)^2 = n^2 + n^2 + 2n + 1 + n^2 + 4n + 4 + n^2 + 6n + 9$$

$$= 4n^2 + 12n + 14$$

$$= 2(2n^2 + 6n + 7) \text{ [an even number as 2 is a factor]}$$

$\therefore$ The sum of any four consecutive integers is an even number.

Exercise 1.2

1. Evaluate each of the following:

   (i) $-8 - 5 + 13$ (iii) $(-5)(-8)$

   (ii) $(2)(-3)$ (iv) $3(4)^2 + 2(4) - 56$

   (v) $\dfrac{3(5-2)^2 - 3(4-2)^2 + 5(3)^3}{(5-2)^2}$

2. Evaluate each of the following, leaving your answers in their simplest form:

   (i) $\dfrac{14}{15} \times \dfrac{3}{8}$ (vi) $\dfrac{1\frac{3}{4} \times 1\frac{2}{3} + \frac{2}{3} \times \frac{5}{6}}{7\frac{1}{2} - 4}$

   (ii) $2\frac{1}{2} \times 5$ (vii) $\dfrac{8.4(19.6 - 12.2)^2}{(14.4 - 12.2)^3}$

   (iii) $1\frac{3}{4} \times 1\frac{2}{3}$ (viii) $\dfrac{\frac{3}{5} - \frac{13}{20}}{\frac{5}{8}}$

   (iv) $\dfrac{1}{2} - \dfrac{1}{8}$ (ix) $3(2.5 - 1.2)^2$

   (v) $\dfrac{2}{3} + \dfrac{5}{6}$

3. Use the properties of the integers to prove that $4 \times -5 = -(4 \times 5)$.

4. Use the properties of the integers to prove that $-3 \times -6 = (3 \times 6)$.

5. Use the properties of the integers to prove that $-5 \times 8 = -(5 \times 8)$.

6. A box contains oranges and grapes. An equal number of the oranges and grapes are rotten. $\frac{2}{3}$ of all the oranges are rotten and $\frac{3}{4}$ of all the grapes are rotten. What fraction of the total number of pieces of fruit in the box are rotten?

7. Alice and Bob share an allotment. The ratio of the area of Alice's portion to the area of Bob's portion is 3 : 2. They each grow vegetables and fruit on the allotment. The entire allotment is covered by vegetables and fruit in the ratio 7 : 3. On Alice's portion of the allotment, the ratio of vegetables to fruit is 4 : 1. What is the ratio of vegetables to fruit in Bob's portion?

8. Three cans of juice fill $\frac{2}{3}$ of a 1 litre jug. How many cans of juice are are needed to completely fill eight 1 litre jugs?

9. A rectangle has a length of $\frac{3}{5}$ units and an area of $\frac{1}{3}$ units². What is the width of the rectangle?

10. In the diagram, the number line is marked at consecutive integers, but the numbers themselves are not shown. The four large red dots represent two numbers that are multiples of 3 and two numbers that are multiples of 5. Which of the black points represents a number that is a multiple of 15? Give an explanation for your choice.

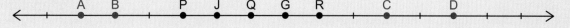

11. The integers from 1 to 9 are listed on a whiteboard. If an additional m 8s and n 9s are added to the list, then the average of all the numbers is 7.3. Find $m + n$.

12. Five square tiles are shown. Each tile has a side of integer length. The side lengths can be arranged as consecutive integers. The sum of the areas of the five squares is 1,815.

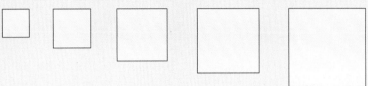

(i) Show that the sum of the squares of five consecutive integers is divisible by 5.

(ii) Find the dimensions of the largest square.

13. Seán has a pile of tiles, each measuring 1 cm by 1 cm. He tries to put these small tiles together to form a larger square of length n cm, but finds that he has 92 tiles left over. If he had increased the side length to $(n + 2)$ cm, then he would have been 100 tiles short. How many tiles does Seán have?

14. A palindromic number is a positive integer that is the same when read forwards or backwards. For example, 31213 and 1237321 are palindromic numbers.

(i) Find the total number of three digit palindromic numbers.

(ii) Determine the total number of palindromic numbers between 10^6 and 10^7.

(iii) If the palindromic numbers in part (ii) are written in order, find the 2,125th number on the list.

1.3 IRRATIONAL NUMBERS

In the right-angled triangle shown, the value for x can be found using the theorem of Pythagoras. Here is the solution:

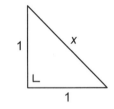

$x^2 = 1^2 + 1^2$

$x^2 = 1 + 1$

$x^2 = 2$

$x = \sqrt{2}$ (as $x > 0$)

Can $\sqrt{2}$ be written as a fraction? This problem preoccupied the ancient Greek mathematicians for many years. Around 500 BC, Hippasus, a follower of Pythagoras, proved that $\sqrt{2}$ could not be written as a fraction. Pythagoras, who did not believe in the existence of irrational numbers, was so enraged by this proof that he had Hippasus thrown overboard from a ship and Hippasus subsequently drowned. Numbers that cannot be written as fractions are called irrational numbers. $\sqrt{2}$ was the first known irrational number.

Hippasus, a follower of Pythagoras

An **irrational number** is a number that cannot be written in the form $\frac{a}{b}$, where a is an integer and b a non-zero integer, i.e. an irrational number is a number that cannot be written as a fraction.

While $\sqrt{2}$ cannot be written as a fraction, it is possible to find an approximation for $\sqrt{2}$. A calculator gives the approximation $\sqrt{2} = 1.414213562$, but this decimal goes on forever with no pattern or repetition.

The rational numbers together with the irrational numbers make up the **Real Number System.**

Proof That $\sqrt{3}$ Is Irrational

To prove: $\sqrt{3}$ is irrational.

The proof of this result is another example of proof by contradiction.

Proof: Assume that $\sqrt{3}$ is rational and can therefore be written in the form $\frac{a}{b}$, $a, b \in Z$, $b \neq 0$.

Also, assume that the fraction $\frac{a}{b}$ is written in simplest terms, i.e. HCF$(a, b) = 1$.

$$\sqrt{3} = \frac{a}{b},$$
$$\Rightarrow 3 = \frac{a^2}{b^2} \text{ (squaring both sides)}$$
$$\therefore a^2 = 3b^2 \qquad\qquad (*)$$

As b^2 is an integer, a^2 has to be a multiple of 3, which means that 3 divides a^2.

If 3 divides a^2, then 3 divides a. (Worked Example 1.3)

$\therefore a = 3k$, for some integer k. Substituting $3k$ for a in (*) gives,

$$(3k)^2 = 3b^2$$
$$9k^2 = 3b^2$$
$$\Rightarrow b^2 = 3k^2$$

As k^2 is an integer, b^2 has to be a multiple of 3, which means that 3 divides b^2.

Therefore, 3 divides b. If 3 divides a and 3 divides b, then this contradicts the assumption that HCF$(a, b) = 1$. This completes the proof.

Constructing $\sqrt{2}$ and $\sqrt{3}$

$\sqrt{2}$ and $\sqrt{3}$ cannot be written as fractions, but can be constructed.

Construct $\sqrt{2}$

1. Let the line segment AB be of length 1 unit.

2. Construct a line m perpendicular to [AB] at B.

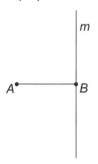

3. Construct a circle with centre B and radius [AB].

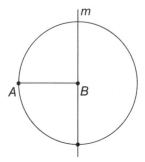

4. Mark the intersection, C, of the circle and m.

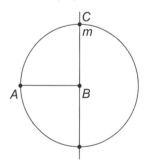

5. Draw the line segment CA.
$$|AC| = \sqrt{2}$$

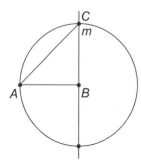

Proof: $|AB| = |BC| = 1$ (radii of circle)

$$|AB|^2 + |BC|^2 = |AC|^2 \quad \text{(Theorem of Pythagoras)}$$
$$1^2 + 1^2 = |AC|^2$$
$$|AC|^2 = 2$$
$$\therefore |AC| = \sqrt{2}$$

Construct $\sqrt{3}$

1. Let the line segment AB be of length 1 unit.

2. Construct a circle with centre A and radius length $|AB|$.

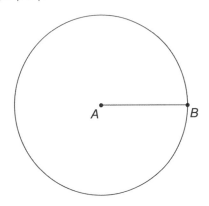

3. Construct a circle with centre B and radius length $|AB|$.

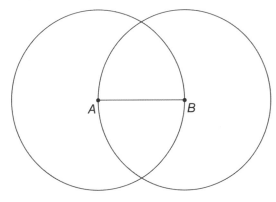

4. Mark the intersection of the two circles as C and D.

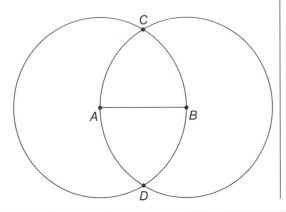

5. Draw the line segment $[CD]$.
   $|CD| = \sqrt{3}$

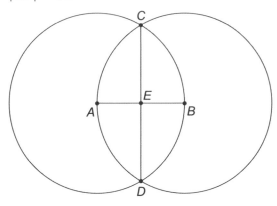

Proof: CD is the perpendicular bisector of $[AB]$ (Construction).

$$\therefore |AE| = |EB| = \frac{1}{2}$$
$$|AC| = |BC| = 1 \quad \text{(Construction)}$$
$$|AE|^2 + |EC|^2 = |AC|^2 \quad \text{(Theorem of Pythagoras)}$$

$$\left(\frac{1}{2}\right)^2 + |EC|^2 = 1^2$$
$$|EC|^2 = 1 - \frac{1}{4} = \frac{3}{4}$$
$$\therefore |EC| = \sqrt{\frac{3}{4}} = \frac{\sqrt{3}}{2}$$
$$|CD| = 2\,|EC|$$
$$= 2\left(\frac{\sqrt{3}}{2}\right)$$
$$\Rightarrow |CD| = \sqrt{3}$$

Exercise 1.3

1. Copy the diagram and use it to show $\sqrt{5}$ on the numberline.

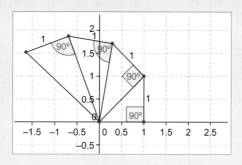

2. Using a diagram similar to that used in Question 1, show $\sqrt{7}$ on the numberline.

3. Prove by contradiction that $\sqrt{2}$ is irrational.

4. π, the ratio of the circumference of a circle to its diameter, is also an irrational number. The British mathematician John Wallis (1616–1703) discovered the following formula for approximating π:

$$\frac{\pi}{2} = \frac{2^2}{(1)(3)} \times \frac{4^2}{(3)(5)} \times \frac{6^2}{(5)(7)} \times \dots \times \frac{(2n)^2}{(2n-1)(2n+1)}$$

   (i) Use the first seven terms of the product to approximate π to four decimal places.

   (ii) Use your calculator to approximate π to four decimal places.

   (iii) Assuming that your calculator has given the true approximation to four decimal places, calculate the percentage error in using seven terms of Wallis' formula (answer to two decimal places).

5. Show that $x = \sqrt{3 + 2\sqrt{2}} - \sqrt{3 - 2\sqrt{2}}$ is a rational number. (Hint: find x^2.)

6. Two quantities are in the golden ratio, if the ratio of the sum of the quantities to the larger quantity is equal to the ratio of the larger quantity to the smaller one. In the rectangle below $a > b$ and $\frac{a+b}{a} = \frac{a}{b}$; therefore, the ratio $a : b$ is the golden ratio.

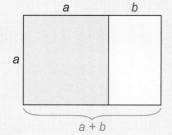

This ratio is a constant and also irrational. It can be shown that the ratio is the positive solution to the equation:

$$r = 1 + \frac{1}{r}$$

   (i) Solve the equation to find the golden ratio.

   (ii) Use your calculator to approximate the ratio to four decimal places.

1.4 ROUNDING AND SIGNIFICANT FIGURES

Rounding to Decimal Places

In geometry, the number of times the diameter of a circle divides into the circumference is called π. We normally substitute 3.14 for π in these calculations. However, 3.14 is just an approximation:

- There are infinitely many decimal places in π.
- π is 3.141592654 to nine decimal places.
- For simplicity, we often write π as 3.14, i.e. to two decimal places.
- Engineers use 3.1416 as an approximation for π.

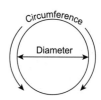

R Worked Example 1.10

Write the following correct to one decimal place:

(i) 2.57   (ii) 39.32

Solution

(i) 2.57

When rounding to **one decimal place**, we look at the **second number after the decimal point**. If this number is 5 or greater, we round up to 2.6. Otherwise, the corrected answer is 2.5. As 7 is the second number after the decimal point, we round up to 2.6.

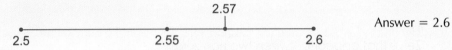

Answer = 2.6

(ii) 39.32

Here, the second number after the decimal point is 2, which is less than 5. Therefore, the number rounded to one decimal place is 39.3.

Answer = 39.3

Significant Figures

The **significant figures** of a number express a magnitude to a specified degree of accuracy.

R Worked Example 1.11

Correct the following numbers to two significant figures:

(i) 3.67765   (ii) 61,343   (iii) 0.00356

Solution

(i) 3.67765

The **first significant figure** in a number is the **first non-zero digit in the number**. In this number, 3 is the first significant figure in the number. We need to correct to two significant figures, so we look at the third significant digit. If this number is 5 or greater, we round up the second digit. The third digit is 7, so the corrected number is 3.7.

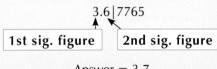

(ii) 61,343

Here, the third digit is 3, which is less than 5. Therefore, the rounded number is 61,000.

Note that all other digits after the rounded digit change to zero.

61,|343

| 1st sig. figure | 2nd sig. figure |

Answer = 61,000

(iii) 0.00356

The third significant digit is 6. Therefore, the rounded number is 0.0036.

0.0035|6

| 1st sig. figure | 2nd sig. figure |

Answer = 0.0036

- Leading zeros are not significant figures. For example, 0.0053 has two significant figures, 5 and 3.
- Zeros that appear between two non-zero digits **are** significant. For example, 503.25 has five significant figures.

1.5 ORDERS OF MAGNITUDE AND SCIENTIFIC NOTATION

When doing calculations, scientists often use very large numbers or very small numbers. For example, the speed of light is about 300,000,000 metres per second.

Very large or very small numbers can be awkward to write down. So, scientists use scientific notation to write down these numbers.

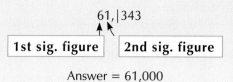

A number is written in **scientific notation** if it is of the form $a \times 10^n$, where $1 \leqslant a < 10$ and $n \in Z$.

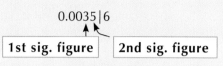

Another name for scientific notation is **standard form**.

R Worked Example 1.12

Write the following numbers in scientific notation:

(i) 725,000,000,000

(iii) 0.0000056

(ii) 980,000

(iv) 0.000000034

Solution

(i) First, note that dividing a number N by 10^n, where $n \in N$, moves the decimal point n places to the left.

For example, $\dfrac{144.25}{10^2} = 1.4425$ (Decimal point moves two places to the left)

$$725,000,000,000 = \frac{725,000,000,000}{10^{11}} \times 10^{11}$$

$$= 7.25 \times 10^{11}$$

(ii) $980{,}000 = \dfrac{980{,}000}{10^5} \times 10^5$

$\qquad\qquad = 9.8 \times 10^5$

(iii) Note that dividing a number N by 10^n, where n is a negative integer, moves the decimal n places to the right.

For example, $\dfrac{0.00146}{10^{-3}} = 0.00146 \times \dfrac{1}{10^{-3}}$

$\qquad\qquad\qquad\quad = 0.00146 \times 10^3 \quad$ (Rules of indices)

$\qquad\qquad\qquad\quad = 1.46 \quad$ (Decimal point moves three places to the right)

$\qquad 0.0000056 = \dfrac{0.0000056}{10^{-6}} \times 10^{-6}$

$\qquad\qquad\qquad = 5.6 \times 10^{-6}$

(iv) $0.000000034 = \dfrac{0.000000034}{10^{-8}} \times 10^{-8}$

$\qquad\qquad\qquad = 3.4 \times 10^{-8}$

Orders of Magnitude

Orders of magnitude are generally used to make very approximate comparisons. If two numbers differ by one order of magnitude, one is about ten times larger than the other.

A number rounded to the nearest power of 10 is called an order of magnitude.

R Worked Example 1.13

By how many orders of magnitude does 345,632 differ from 567,123,423?

Solution

Write both numbers in scientific notation:

$345{,}632 = 3.45632 \times 10^5$ $\qquad\qquad\qquad 567{,}123{,}423 = 5.67123423 \times 10^8$

■ If the decimal number is less than 5, round to 1.

■ If the decimal number is 5 or greater, round to 10.

$\approx 1 \times 10^5$ $\qquad\qquad\qquad\qquad\qquad\qquad\qquad\qquad \approx 10 \times 10^8$

$= 10^0 \times 10^5 \qquad$ Note: $1 = 10^0$ $\qquad\qquad\qquad\qquad\qquad = 10^1 \times 10^8$

$= 10^5 \qquad\qquad\qquad\qquad\qquad\qquad\qquad\qquad\qquad\qquad = 10^9$

$\dfrac{10^9}{10^5} = 10^{9-5} = 10^4$

Therefore, both numbers differ by four orders of magnitude.

1. (a) Write these numbers correct to three decimal places:

    (i) 5.1456   (iv) 62.1235321

    (ii) 7.2983   (v) 23.7654

    (iii) 17.8943   (vi) 0.07893

  (b) Write these numbers correct to two decimal places:

    (i) 1.263   (iv) 21.3

    (ii) 5.9876   (v) 22

    (iii) 21.456   (vi) 0.00391

2. (a) Write these numbers correct to two significant figures:

    (i) 0.00985   (vi) 0.000849

    (ii) 0.00234   (vii) 0.238

    (iii) 0.0125   (viii) 52.00285

    (iv) 0.000000785   (ix) 52.487

    (v) 1.000034   (x) 967,333

  (b) Write these numbers correct to one significant figure:

    (i) 32.14   (iv) 1,698

    (ii) 3.857   (v) 5,965

    (iii) 19,345   (vi) 999

3. Write these numbers in scientific notation:

    (i) 34,000,000   (vi) 0.000032

    (ii) 0.25   (vii) 5,000,000

    (iii) 4,570   (viii) 0.6464

    (iv) 0.0001258   (ix) 532,600

    (v) 7,206   (x) 5,000

4. Write these as decimal numbers:

    (i) 2.65×10^2 (vi) 4×10^{-2}

    (ii) 4.53×10^{-3} (vii) 2.64×10^7

    (iii) 7.2×10^6 (viii) 7.612×10^3

    (iv) 1.7×10^{-5} (ix) 2.76×10^8

    (v) 3×10^2 (x) 3.02×10^{-9}

5. Calculate each of the following, giving your answers as decimal numbers:

    (i) $3.4 \times 10^3 + 2.8 \times 10^3$

    (ii) $5.2 \times 10^9 + 3.5 \times 10^9$

6. The following numbers are written in scientific notation. Rewrite the numbers in ordinary form.

    (i) 2×10^6 (iv) 6.47×10^5

    (ii) 1.69×10^4 (v) 6.12×10^1

    (iii) 2.48×10^3 (vi) 9.43×10^5

7. Write the following in the form $a \times 10^n$, where $1 \leqslant a < 10$, $a \in R$, $n \in Z$:

    (i) 0.000036   (iv) 0.00063

    (ii) 0.0005613   (v) 0.0078

    (iii) 0.0345   (vi) 0.0011

8. Write the following numbers in the form $a \times 10^n$, where $1 \leqslant a < 10$:

    (i) 0.00068   (iv) 0.0000000097

    (ii) 0.0000328   (v) 0.00000056

    (iii) 0.0657   (vi) 0.0030307

9. The following numbers are written in scientific notation. Rewrite the numbers in ordinary form.

    (i) 1.5×10^{-3} (iii) 3.5×10^{-5}

    (ii) 2.54×10^{-4} (iv) 6.67×10^{-6}

10. By how many orders of magnitude do the following numbers differ:

    (i) 868, 932, 145 and 284

    (ii) 453, 987, 312 and 3548

    (iii) 767, 894, 567,000 and 23,000,000

    (iv) 0.1 and 0.00042

    (v) 1.8 and 234

Revision Exercises

1. The German mathematician Christian Goldbach conjectured that every odd positive integer greater than 5 is the sum of three primes. Verify this conjecture for each of the following odd integers:

   (i) 11　(ii) 33　(iii) 97　(iv) 199　(v) 17

2. Two bikers are riding in a circular path. The first rider completes a circuit in 12 minutes. The second rider completes a circuit in 18 minutes. They both started at the same place and at the same time and go in the same direction. After how many minutes will they meet again at the starting point?

3. Use the properties of integers to prove the following:

   (i) $5 \times -3 = -15$　　(ii) $-5 \times -3 = 15$

4. Show that no integer of the form $n^3 + 1$ is prime, other than $2 = 1^3 + 1$.

5. (i) List the smallest five consecutive integers that are composite.

   (ii) Find 10,000 consecutive integers that are composite.

6. Express each of the following numbers as the product of prime factors, and hence, find the LCM and HCF of each pair:

   (i) 68 and 102　　(iii) 104 and 351

   (ii) 69 and 123　　(iv) 123 and 615

7. (a) What fraction when added to $\frac{1}{4}$ gives $\frac{1}{3}$?

   (b) A mathematician states that her children's ages are all prime numbers that multiply together to give 7,429. She also says that two of her children are teenagers.

      (i) How many children does she have?

      (ii) What are their ages?

8. A palindromic number is a number that reads the same forwards and backwards. For example, 52,325 is a palindromic number. All four-digit palindromic numbers have 11 as a prime factor.

   (i) Find the prime factorisations of the palindromic numbers 2,332 and 6,776.

   (ii) Hence, find the HCF and LCM of 2,332 and 6,776.

9. Write the following numbers correct to two significant places:

   (i) 852,233　　　(iv) 0.000054

   (ii) 0.134　　　(v) 652,494

   (iii) 2.00062　　(vi) 0.000814

10. Given a line segment of length one unit, show clearly how to construct a line segment of length $\sqrt{2}$ units.

11. Given a line segment of length one unit, show clearly how to construct a line segment of length $\sqrt{3}$ units.

12. (a) (i) Find the values of the primes p and q, if $p^3 \times 13 \times q = 1{,}768$.

      (ii) Find the values of the primes m and n, if $24 \times m \times n = 3{,}192$.

      (iii) Using your answers to parts (i) and (ii), find the HCF and LCM of 1,768 and 3,192.

   (b) Evaluate the following, giving your answer in scientific notation:

   $$\frac{3\frac{3}{7} \times \left(2\frac{2}{5} + 1\frac{1}{10}\right)}{3 \times 10^4}$$

13. (i) P represents a pointer on a gauge. What is the decimal value shown by the pointer?

   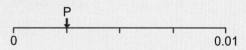

   (ii) A computer shop buys a batch of iPod nanos for €99 each and marks the price up by $\frac{1}{3}$. The goods fail to sell so they are included in the next sale where all prices are reduced by $\frac{1}{4}$.
   What price would you pay for an iPod nano in the sale?

   (iii) John calculates correctly $85 \times 142 = 12{,}070$. **Using this information**, what should his answer be for $12{,}070 \div 850$?

14. Prove that $\sqrt{5}$ is irrational.

15. (i) A single-celled protozoa is about one-tenth of a millimetre in diameter. Write down its diameter in metres, giving your answer in scientific notation.

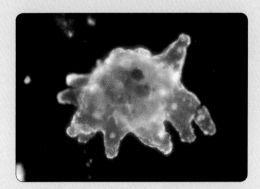

(ii) A bag contains 350 disks. Seán takes four-fifths of the disks out of the bag and divides them into seven equal groups. How many disks are in each group?

16. A man died, leaving some money to be divided among his children in the following manner:

- €x to the first child plus $\frac{1}{16}$ of what remains.

- €$2x$ to the second child plus $\frac{1}{16}$ of what then remains.

- €$3x$ to the third child plus $\frac{1}{16}$ of what then remains and so on.

When all the money was distributed, each child received the same amount of money and no money was left over.

How many children did the man have?

17. The digits 1, 2, 3, 4 and 5 are each used once to create a five-digit number $vwxyz$, which satisfies the following conditions:

- The three-digit number vwx is odd.
- The three-digit number wxy is divisible by 5.
- The three-digit number xyz is divisible by 3.

Determine the six five-digit numbers that satisfy all three conditions.

18. A well known series for the irrational π is:

$$\frac{\pi}{2} = 1 + \frac{1}{3} + \frac{1 \times 2}{3 \times 5} + \frac{1 \times 2 \times 3}{3 \times 5 \times 7} + \frac{1 \times 2 \times 3 \times 4}{3 \times 5 \times 7 \times 9} + \cdots$$

By summing the first 10 terms of the series, find an approximation for π to two decimal places.

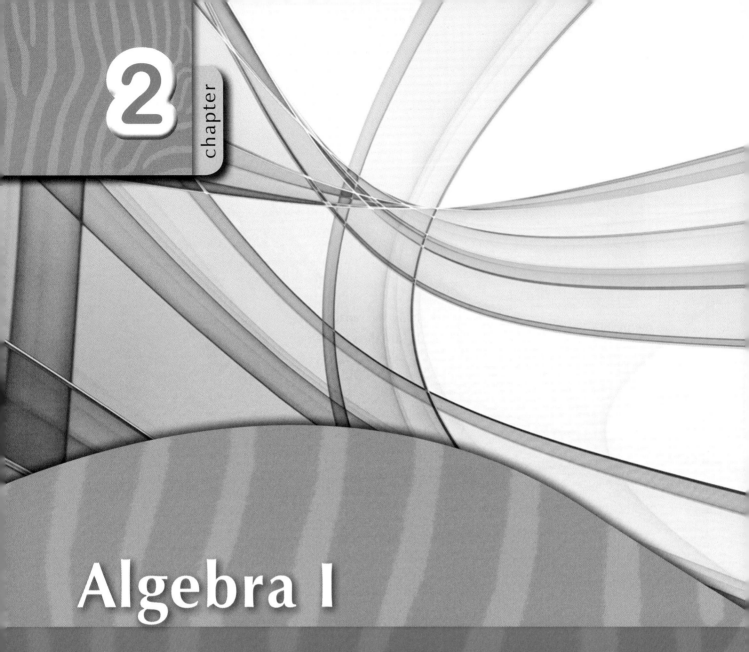

2 chapter

Algebra I

Learning Outcomes

In this chapter you will learn to:

- ➲ Add, subtract, multiply and divide algebraic terms
- ➲ Factorise quadratic expressions
- ➲ Factorise certain cubic expressions
- ➲ Divide algebraic expressions using long division

2.1 EXPRESSIONS

Algebra has many uses, from the design of computer games to the modelling of weather patterns.

To be able to use algebra, we must first understand the rules involved in the basic operations of adding, subtracting, multiplying and dividing algebraic terms and expressions.

YOU SHOULD REMEMBER...

- How to add, subtract, multiply and divide algebraic expressions

KEY WORDS

- Expression
- Term
- Polynomial
- Coefficient
- Pascal's triangle
- Highest common factor (HCF)
- Difference of two squares
- Quadratic trinomial
- Lowest common dominator (LCD)
- Factors

Notation in Algebra

A **variable** is a letter (usually x or y) that represents a number. This number may change or be unknown.

- In $5x$, the variable is x.
- In $20y$, the variable is y.

A **coefficient** is a number or symbol that is multiplying a variable.

- In $5x$, the coefficient is 5.
- In $20y$, the coefficient is 20.
- In x, the coefficient is 1.

A **constant** is a quantity that does not change in value, i.e. a number by itself.

In $10x + 2$, the **constant** is 2.

$12(x)$ is an example of a **term**.

This is written as $12x$.

$x + 5y - 7$ contains three terms:

A constant, a variable or a constant multiplied by a variable are all considered **terms**.

- x (a variable)
- $5y$ (a constant times a variable)
- -7 (a constant)

An **algebraic expression** is an expression that contains one or more numbers, one or more variables, and one or more arithmetic operations.

$5x + 2$ is an **expression**. Other examples of expressions include $x + 3y$, $8y^2$ and $4pr^3 - 7$.

Polynomials have variables that only have whole number powers.

A polynomial in x has the form $a_n x^n + a_{n-1} x^{n-1} + a_{n-2} x^{n-2} + ... + a_2 x^2 + a_1 x^1 + a_0$, where all the coefficients ($a_0, a_1, a_2, ..., a_{n-1}, a_n$) are constants and the powers are non-negative whole numbers.

The **degree** (or order) of the polynomial is equal to the highest power of x.

- A polynomial of degree 1 is called **linear**.
- A polynomial of degree 2 is called **quadratic**.
- A polynomial of degree 3 is called **cubic**.
- A polynomial of degree 4 is called **quartic**.

For example, $5x^6 + 2x^2 - 3x + 7$ is a polynomial in x of degree 6. It has four terms.
The coefficient of x is -3 and the constant is 7.

Addition/Subtraction

When adding or subtracting algebraic terms, we must always remember the following rules:

Algebra Rule: Only terms that have the exact same letter(s) raised to the same power(s) (**like terms**) can be added or subtracted.

Examples:
$5x + 6y + 4x - 3y = 9x + 3y$
$p + 2q + 3p - 4q = 4p - 2q$

Algebra Rule: When adding or subtracting like terms, the powers of the variables do not change but the coefficients do.

Examples:
$20y^2 + 8y^2 = 28y^2$
$xy - 3w^2 + 5xy + 2w^2 = 6xy - w^2$

Multiplying

Unlike when adding or subtracting, in algebra any term may be multiplied by any other term. When we multiply terms, we encounter another set of rules that are important to understand.

Example: $(4x)(5y)$

Algebra Rule: To multiply terms: coefficient × coefficient, variable × variable.

$= (4)(x)(5)(y)$
$= (4)(5)(x)(y)\ldots$ (Commutative)
$= 20xy$

Algebra Rule: When multiplying terms that contain the same variable, we **add** the powers or indices of that variable.

This rule is also written as $a^p a^q = a^{p+q}$.

Example: $(4x^3)(3x^5)$

$= (4)(x)(x)(x)(3)(x)(x)(x)(x)(x)$
$= (4)(3)(x)(x)(x)(x)(x)(x)(x)(x)\ldots$ (Commutative)
$= 12x^8$

Note: We could have written:

$$(4x^3)(3x^5)$$
$$= (4)(3)(x^3)(x^5)$$
$$= 12x^8$$

Important Products

$$x(y + z) = xy + xz$$

$$(a + b)(x + y) = ax + ay + bx + by$$

$$(a + b)(a - b) = a^2 - b^2$$

$$(a + b)^2 = a^2 + 2ab + b^2$$

$$(a - b)^2 = a^2 - 2ab + b^2$$

$$(a + b)^3 = a^3 + 3a^2b + 3ab^2 + b^3$$

$$(a - b)^3 = a^3 - 3a^2b + 3ab^2 - b^3$$

x^2 Worked Example 2.1

Expand and simplify:

(i) $4(2a - b)(a - 5b)$ (ii) $23x - x(2x + 3)^2$ (iii) $(4x - 5)^3$

Solution

(i) $4(2a - b)(a - 5b)$

$4[(2a(a - 5b) - b(a - 5b)]$

$4[2a^2 - 10ab - ab + 5b^2]$

$4[2a^2 - 11ab + 5b^2]$

$8a^2 - 44ab + 20b^2$

(ii) $23x - x(2x + 3)^2$

$23x - x[(2x)^2 + 2(2x)(3) + (3)^2]$

$23x - x[4x^2 + 12x + 9]$

$23x - 4x^3 - 12x^2 - 9x$

$-4x^3 - 12x^2 + 14x$

> This is a polynomial of degree 3.

(iii) $(4x - 5)^3$

$(4x)^3 - 3(4x)^2(5) + 3(4x)(5)^2 - (5)^3$

$64x^3 - 240x^2 + 300x - 125$

Pascal's Triangle

$(a + b)^5$ would take a long time to expand and simplify using the methods employed above. However, by looking at the expansion of $(a + b)^n$ we can spot a pattern that we may be able to use for other expressions ($n \in N$ or $n = 0$).

ACTIVITY 2.1

$(a + b)^0 = 1$

$(a + b)^1 = a^1 + b^1$

$(a + b)^2 = a^2 + 2ab + b^2$

$(a + b)^3 = a^3 + 3a^2b + 3ab^2 + b^3$

$(a + b)^4 = a^4 + 4a^3b + 6a^2b^2 + 4ab^3 + b^4$

$(a + b)^5 = a^5 + 5a^4b + 10a^3b^2 + 10a^2b^3 + 5ab^4 + b^5$

If we examine the powers, we notice that, for $n \geqslant 1$, the power of each term in the expansion add up to the power of the original expression.

$(a + b)^0 = 1$

$(a + b)^1 = a^1 + b^1$

$(a + b)^2 = a^2 + 2a^1b^1 + b^2$

$(a + b)^3 = a^3 + 3a^2b^1 + 3a^1b^2 + b^3$

$(a + b)^4 = a^4 + 4a^3b^1 + 6a^2b^2 + 4a^1b^3 + b^4$

$(a + b)^5 = a^5 + 5a^4b^1 + 10a^3b^2 + 10a^2b^3 + 5a^1b^4 + b^5$

If we highlight $(a + b)^5$:

$(a + b)^5 = a^5b^0 + 5a^4b^1 + 10a^3b^2 + 10a^2b^3 + 5a^1b^4 + a^0b^5$

we notice that the first term is a^5 and then the powers of a decrease by 1 each term and eventually reach zero. Also, the powers of the b start at zero and increase by 1 each term.

Examining the coefficients of each expansion, we notice another pattern.

The next row of coefficients can be calculated by adding the pairs of coefficients from the row above.

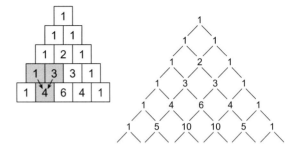

This pattern was first described by the French mathematician Blaise Pascal (1623–1662) and is named in his honour.

In general, using Pascal's triangle in the expansion of $(x + y)^n$:

- There are $n + 1$ terms.
- The coefficients of the first two terms are 1 and n.
- The sum of the powers of x and y in each term is n.

x^2 Worked Example 2.2

Use Pascal's triangle to expand $(x - 2)^3$.

Solution

Note: $(x - 2)^3 = (x + (-2))^3$

From Pascal's triangle we can determine the initial coefficients as:

1 3 3 1

We next fill in the powers of each term.

The x term will start with a power of 3 and decrease to zero.

The (-2) term will start with a power of zero and increase to 3.

$\therefore (x - 2)^3 = (x + (-2))^3 = 1x^3(-2)^0 + 3x^2(-2)^1 + 3x^1(-2)^2 + 1x^0(-2)^3 = x^3 - 6x^2 + 12x - 8$

x^2 Worked Example 2.3

Use Pascal's triangle to expand $(2p + 3)^4$.

Solution

From Pascal's triangle we can determine the coefficients as:

1 4 6 4 1

The $2p$ term will start with a power of 4 and decrease to zero.

The 3 term will start with a power of zero and increase to 4.

$\therefore (2p + 3)^4 = 1(2p)^4(3)^0 + 4(2p)^3(3)^1 + 6(2p)^2(3)^2 + 4(2p)^1(3)^3 + 1(2p)^0(3)^4$

$= 16p^4 + 96p^3 + 216p^2 + 216p + 81$

1. If $p = 3$, $q = -4$ and $r = 7$, find the value of:

   (i) $2pq$

   (ii) $(q + r)^p$

   (iii) $\dfrac{q + p}{2r}$

   (iv) $pqr - q^2$

   (v) $\sqrt{\dfrac{q^2 + rp + r + 4}{\frac{-q}{p}}}$

2. Expand and simplify:

   (i) $3x(x + 4) + 5(3x - 2)$

   (ii) $3(a^2 - b) - (a - 3b)$

   (iii) $12x(3x^2 + 2x + 1) + 5x(2x - 4)$

   (iv) $-y(2y - 3x) - y(xy + 3x)$

   (v) $b(b^2 + 4b + c) - 4c(a^2 + b)$

3. Expand each of the following expressions. For each polynomial, state:

   (a) The degree

   (b) The value of the constant term

   (c) The number of terms

   (d) The coefficient of the x term

      (i) $(x + 2)(x - 3)$

      (ii) $(2x - 5)(3x + 4)$

      (iii) $-x(5x^2 - 3)(2x^2 - 3)$

      (iv) $(x^3 - 4)(2x^2 - 8x + 3)$

      (v) $(11x^4 - 3x^3 + x^2 - 3x + 1)(4x - 7)$

4. Multiply out the following expressions:

   (i) $(5x + 1)(7x + 1)$

   (ii) $(x + 3)(4x - 3)$

   (iii) $5(3s - t)(2t - 1)$

   (iv) $(x - y)(2x + 5y)(3x)$

   (v) $(xy - y)(y - 6xy)(y)$

5. Expand:

   (i) $(3p + 4)^2$

   (ii) $(4y - x)^2$

   (iii) $2(3a - 1)^2$

   (iv) $(a + b)(x + 5)^2$

   (v) $(y + x)^3(2y - 3x)$

   (vi) $3p(p + q)(p - q)$

6. Expand:

   (i) $(3p - 4)(b^2 + 4b + c)$

   (ii) $(b^2 + 4b + c)(4y - x)$

   (iii) $(3a - 1)(a + 3b)(2a + b)$

   (iv) $5(x + y)(x + 4y)(y + x)$

   (v) $(z + x)^2(z - x)^2$

7. Expand:

   (i) $(p + q)^2$

   (ii) $(p - q)^2$

   (iii) $(p - q)(p + q)$

   (iv) $(x - 3)(x + 3)$

   (v) $2x(4x + 3)^2$

   (vi) $(y - 3)^3$

   (vii) $(x + 4)^3$

   (viii) $(2a + 5b)^3$

   (ix) $(p - 8q)^3$

   (x) $(x + y)(x - y)y^2$

8. Expand:

   (i) $(2p - q)(2s + 4r)$

   (ii) $(a - 3b)(a + 3b)$

   (iii) $(4m + 7n)^3$

   (iv) $(9x - 2y)^3$

   (v) $5(2a + 9b)^3$

   (vi) $(x^2 - y^2)(x - y)$

   (vii) $[(a - b)b]^3$

9. Using Pascal's triangle, expand the following polynomials:

   (i) $(a + 1)^4$

   (ii) $(b - 3)^3$

   (iii) $(x + y)^5$

   (iv) $(2a + 3b)^3$

   (v) $(3y - 4x)^4$

   (vi) $(3x - 2y)^5$

10. In a maths competition, a student gets 8 marks for a correct answer, and 3 marks are deducted if the answer is incorrect. One mark is awarded for any question not attempted. If there are 20 questions on the test, write an expression for a student's total mark if the student got x questions correct from a total of y questions attempted.

11. Mark is y years old. In five years' time, Aoife will be twice as old as Mark and Daniel will be two years younger than Aoife is now. Write an expression in y for the sum of their three ages now.

12. Express as a polynomial the area and perimeter of each of the following shapes:

(i)

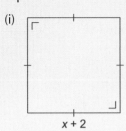

$x + 2$

(ii)

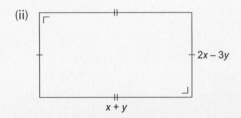

$2x - 3y$

$x + y$

13. An open-topped tank is in the shape of a cuboid. The length of the tank is $(x + 7)$ cm. Its breadth is 3 cm less than its length and its height is 1 cm more than its breadth. Write an expression in terms of x for the volume and surface area of the tank.

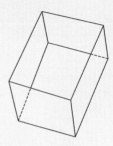

14. Find the value of the coefficient of x^3 in the expansion of $(x + y)^7$.

15. Find the value of the third term in the expansion of $(4a - 5b)^8$.

16. The middle term of the expansion of $(ax + ay)^n$ is $14{,}580x^3y^3$. Find the value of a and the value of n, where $a, n \in N$.

2.2 FACTORISING

Another important skill is that of **factorising** expressions.

> **Factorising** is the reverse of expanding. We turn the given expression into a **product**.

■ **Highest Common Factor**

$x^2 - 3x = x(x - 3)$

■ **Difference of Two Squares**

$4x^2 - 25y^2$

$= (2x)^2 - (5y)^2$ (writing each term as a square)

$= (2x - 5y)(2x + 5y)$

■ **Quadratic Trinomials**

$2x^2 + 13x + 15 = (2x + 3)(x + 5)$

x^2 Worked Example 2.4

Factorise: (i) $49x^2 - 225y^2$ (ii) $3x^2 + 11x - 20$ (iii) $8x^2 - 18x + 9$

Solution

(i) $49x^2 - 225y^2$

Write each term as a square.

$(7x)^2 - (15y)^2$

$(7x - 15y)(7x + 15y)$

(ii) $3x^2 + 11x - 20$

If the constant term is negative, then one factor of 20 is positive and the other is negative

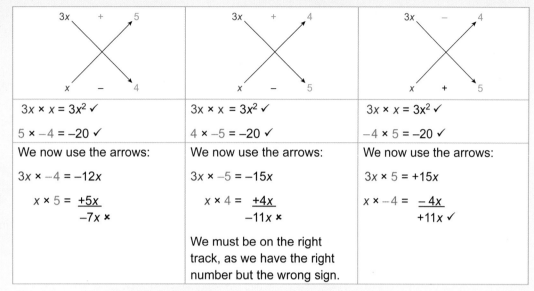

$3x \times x = 3x^2$ ✓	$3x \times x = 3x^2$ ✓	$3x \times x = 3x^2$ ✓
$5 \times -4 = -20$ ✓	$4 \times -5 = -20$ ✓	$-4 \times 5 = -20$ ✓
We now use the arrows:	We now use the arrows:	We now use the arrows:
$3x \times -4 = -12x$ $x \times 5 = \underline{+5x}$ $-7x$ ✗	$3x \times -5 = -15x$ $x \times 4 = \underline{+4x}$ $-11x$ ✗ We must be on the right track, as we have the right number but the wrong sign.	$3x \times 5 = +15x$ $x \times -4 = \underline{-4x}$ $+11x$ ✓

So $(3x - 4)(x + 5)$ are the correct factors.

(iii) We can also use the **Guide Number Method** to factorise quadratic trinomials.

$8x^2 - 18x + 9$

Step 1 Multiply the coefficient of x^2 by the constant.

$8x^2 - 18x + 9$

$8 \times 9 = 72$

Step 2 Find two factors of 72 that add to give the coefficient of the middle term, i.e. −18.

−12 and −6

Step 3 Use the answers from Step 2 to rewrite $8x^2 - 18x + 9$ as follows:

$8x^2 - 12x - 6x + 9$

$4x(2x - 3) - 3(2x - 3)$ 　　　(Factorise by grouping)

$(4x - 3)(2x - 3)$ 　　　(Distributive property)

The factors of $8x^2 - 18x + 9$ are $(4x - 3)(2x - 3)$.

Sum and Difference of Two Cubes

We may also be asked to factorise certain cubic expressions.

 ACTIVITY 2.2

$a^3 + b^3 = (a + b)(a^2 - ab + b^2)$ **Sum of two cubes**

$a^3 - b^3 = (a - b)(a^2 + ab + b^2)$ **Difference of two cubes**

x^2 Worked Example 2.5

Factorise:

(i) $x^3 + 125$ 　　　　(ii) $64p^3 - 27q^3$ 　　　　(iii) $1 + 216w^3$

Solution

(i) $x^3 + 125$

Write each term as a cube.

$(x)^3 + (5)^3$

$= (x + 5)(x^2 - 5x + 25)$

(ii) $64p^3 - 27q^3$

Write each term as a cube:

$(4p)^3 - (3q)^3$

$= (4p - 3q)[(4p)^2 + (4p)(3q) + (3q)^2]$

$= (4p - 3q)(16p^2 + 12pq + 9q^2)$

(iii) $1 + 216w^2$

Write each term as a cube.

$(1)^3 + (6w)^3$

$= (1 + 6w)[(1)^2 - (1)(6w) + (6w)^2]$

$= (1 + 6w)(1 - 6w + 36w^2)$

x^2 Worked Example 2.6

Factorise fully:

(i) $9px^2 + 24px - 9p$

(ii) $5x^3 - 625y^3$

Solution

(i) $9px^2 + 24px - 9p$

First find the highest common factor:

$3p[3x^2 + 8x - 3]$

Now factorise the quadratic:

$3p(3x - 1)(x + 3)$

(ii) $5x^3 - 625y^3$

First, find the highest common factor:

$5[x^3 - 125y^3]$

Now factorise the expression inside the brackets:

$5(x - 5y)(x^2 + 5xy + 25y^2)$

Exercise 2.2

Factorise fully:

1. $4ab^2 - 12ab^3$

2. $7x^2 + 9x + 2$

3. $3y^2 - 4y - 7$

4. $5x^2 + 12x + 4$

5. $x^2 - 3x - 18$

6. $3x^2 + 10x - 8$

7. $2y^2 + 11y - 63$

8. $7x^2 + 2x - 57$

9. $25a^2 - 1$

10. $2x^2 - 9x + 4$

11. $5x^2 + 52x + 96$

12. $64a^2 - 81b^2$

13. $2x^2 - 23x - 12$

14. $4x^2 + 7x + 3$

15. $10y^2 + 27y + 17$

16. $9x^2 + 3x - 2$

17. $9x^2 - 21x + 10$

18. $4y^2 + 23y + 19$

19. $6x^2 + 37x + 45$

20. $36p^2 - 100q^2$

21. $12x^2 + 11x - 56$

22. $8x^2 - 22x + 15$

23. $10x^2 - 4x - 6$

24. $12x^2 - 18x - 12$

25. $48y^3 + 48y^2 + 12y$

26. $16x^2 - 100$

27. $2x^3 - 8x$

28. $6pq^2 + 11pq + 4p$

29. $x^4 - 36x^2$

Factorise fully the following expressions:

30. $x^3 - 27$

31. $p^3 + 8$

32. $x^3 - y^3$

33. $64a^3 - 1$

34. $8a^3 + 27b^3$

35. $125p^3 + 512q^3$

36. $1{,}000x^3 - 729$

37. $343c^3 + d^3$

38. $3x^3 - 648$

39. $128 + 16x^3$

40. $54a^4 + 432ab^3$

Factorise fully the following expressions:

41. $(x + 2)^2 - (x + 3)^2$

42. $x^2 + 2px + p^2$

43. $a^2c^2 - b^2$

44. $x^4 - 25$

45. $a^2b^2 - 2ab + 1$

46. $x^4 - y^4$

47. $(x - y)^2 - 9$

48. $8x^2 - 18xy + 9y^2$

49. $a^4 + a$

50. $a^2 - (b + c)^2$

51. $ab^5 - ab^2$

52. $x^4 - 7x^2 - 18$

2.3 ALGEBRAIC FRACTIONS I: ADDITION AND SUBTRACTION

When adding or subtracting two algebraic fractions, we first find the lowest common denominator (LCD).

x^2 Worked Example 2.7

Write as a single fraction: $\dfrac{2x + 5}{2} - \dfrac{x - 1}{9} - 2$

Solution

$$\frac{2x + 5}{2} - \frac{x - 1}{9} - \frac{2}{1} = \frac{9(2x + 5) - 2(x - 1) - 18(2)}{18}$$

$$= \frac{18x + 45 - 2x + 2 - 36}{18} = \frac{16x + 11}{18}$$

ACTIVITY 2.3

x^2 Worked Example 2.8

(i) Write as a single fraction:

$$\frac{5}{3x - 5} - \frac{2}{4x - 1}$$

(ii) Write $\frac{1}{x - 2} - \frac{1}{x + 2}$ as a single fraction in the form $\frac{b}{x^a - b}$, where $a, b \in N$.

Solution

(i) $\dfrac{5}{3x - 5} - \dfrac{2}{4x - 1} = \dfrac{5(4x - 1) - 2(3x - 5)}{(3x - 5)(4x - 1)}$

$= \dfrac{20x - 5 - 6x + 10}{(3x - 5)(4x - 1)}$

$= \dfrac{14x + 5}{(3x - 5)(4x - 1)}$

> Do not expand the denominator unless required to do so.

(ii) $\dfrac{1}{x - 2} - \dfrac{1}{x + 2} = \dfrac{1(x + 2) - 1(x - 2)}{(x - 2)(x + 2)}$

$= \dfrac{x + 2 - x + 2}{x^2 - 4}$

$= \dfrac{4}{x^2 - 4}$

> Here, the question requires that we expand the denominator.

x^2 Worked Example 2.9

Simplify $\dfrac{5x - 10}{x^2 - 4}$.

Solution

We factorise both numerator and denominator.

$5x - 10 = 5(x - 2)$

$x^2 - 4 = (x - 2)(x + 2)$

$\therefore \dfrac{5x - 10}{x^2 - 4} = \dfrac{5\cancel{(x - 2)}^{\,1}}{\cancel{(x - 2)}(x + 2)}$

$= \dfrac{5}{x + 2}$

x^2 Worked Example 2.10

Simplify $\dfrac{3a^2 - 6a}{2 - a}$.

Solution

$\dfrac{3a^2 - 6a}{2 - a} = \dfrac{3a\cancel{(a - 2)}^{\,1}}{-1\cancel{(a - 2)}_{\,1}}$

$= \dfrac{3a}{-1}$

$= -3a$

x^2 Worked Example 2.11

(i) Express as a single fraction in its simplest form:

$$\frac{2}{x - 1} - \frac{3x - 1}{x^2 - 4x + 3} + \frac{4}{x - 3}$$

(ii) Express as a single fraction in its simplest form:

$$\frac{3}{x - 2} + \frac{2}{2 - x}$$

Solution

(i) $\dfrac{2}{x-1} - \dfrac{3x-1}{x^2-4x+3} + \dfrac{4}{x-3} = \dfrac{2}{x-1} - \dfrac{3x-1}{(x-1)(x-3)} + \dfrac{4}{x-3}$

$$= \dfrac{(2)(x-3) - (3x-1)(1) + 4(x-1)}{(x-1)(x-3)}$$

$$= \dfrac{2x - 6 - 3x + 1 + 4x - 4}{(x-1)(x-3)}$$

$$= \dfrac{3x - 9}{(x-1)(x-3)}$$

$$= \dfrac{3(x-3)^{1}}{(x-1)(x-3)_{1}}$$

$$= \dfrac{3}{x-1}$$

> Not expanding the denominator can allow for reducing of fractions to occur.

(ii) $\dfrac{3}{x-2} + \dfrac{2}{2-x}$

$$= \dfrac{3}{x-2} + \dfrac{2}{2-x} \cdot \dfrac{-1}{-1}$$

$$= \dfrac{3}{x-2} - \dfrac{2}{x-2}$$

$$= \dfrac{3-2}{x-2}$$

$$= \dfrac{1}{x-2}$$

Exercise 2.3

Express as single fractions in their simplest form:

1. $\dfrac{4x-1}{4} + \dfrac{2x-5}{2}$

2. $\dfrac{3x-7}{12} - \dfrac{5x-3}{4}$

3. $\dfrac{x-1}{5} + \dfrac{2x-4}{3}$

4. $\dfrac{7}{4x-5} + 2$

5. $\dfrac{1}{5x} - \dfrac{2}{7x}$

6. $\dfrac{8}{x+1} + x$

7. $\dfrac{3}{x+5} - \dfrac{1}{x}$

8. $\dfrac{5}{x-2} + \dfrac{2}{3x-1}$

9. $\dfrac{1}{3x+5} + \dfrac{3}{2x-1}$

10. $\dfrac{x+y}{3x+3y}$

11. $\dfrac{ab^3}{a^2 b}$

12. $\dfrac{x+y}{x^2-y^2}$

13. $\dfrac{ab+b^2}{a^2-b^2}$

14. $\dfrac{p-q}{q-p}$

15. $\dfrac{x^2-2x}{x-2}$

16. $\dfrac{15x^2+5x}{15x^2+20x+5}$

17. $\dfrac{x^3-8}{x^2+2x+4}$

18. $\dfrac{2x^4-250x}{4x^2-20x}$

19. $\dfrac{x^3+y^3}{x^2-y^2}$

20. $\dfrac{x^4-y^4}{x^2-y^2}$

21. $\dfrac{(p-q)^3}{p^2-q^2}$

22. $\dfrac{x^2-8x+16}{x^2-16} - \dfrac{16x}{16-x^2}$

23. $\dfrac{2x}{x-1} - \dfrac{x}{1-x}$

24. $\dfrac{x+4}{x^2-16} + \dfrac{x-5}{x^2-25}$

25. $\dfrac{1}{x+2} - \dfrac{3}{x-3} + \dfrac{4}{x^2-x-6}$

26. $\dfrac{1}{x^2+3x+2} + \dfrac{4}{x+2} - \dfrac{3}{x+1}$

27. $\dfrac{3}{a-1} - \dfrac{a+1}{a^2-1} + \dfrac{a-1}{a+1}$

28. $\dfrac{a}{a+b} + \dfrac{a}{a-b}$

29. $\dfrac{a+2}{a-2} + \dfrac{a-3}{a+3}$

30. $\dfrac{p+1}{p-1} + \dfrac{p+2}{p-2}$

31. $\dfrac{1}{n+1} + \dfrac{1}{n} + \dfrac{1}{n+2}$

32. $\dfrac{a+b}{a^2-b^2} - \dfrac{a-b}{b^2-a^2}$

33. $\dfrac{a-b}{a^2-2ab+b^2} - \dfrac{a+b}{a^2+2ab+b^2}$

34. Write as a single fraction in the form $\dfrac{a}{x^b-c}$, where a, b and $c \in N$:

(i) $\dfrac{5}{x^2-1} + \dfrac{1}{1-x^2}$

(ii) $\dfrac{3x}{x^2+3x-18} - \dfrac{18}{18-3x-x^2}$

2.4 ALGEBRAIC FRACTIONS II: MULTIPLICATION AND DIVISION

x^2 Worked Example 2.12

Simplify $\dfrac{3x^2 - 27}{4x^2 - 15x + 9} \times \dfrac{4x - 3}{x^2 + 3x}$.

Solution

$\dfrac{3x^2 - 27}{4x^2 - 15x + 9} \times \dfrac{4x - 3}{x^2 + 3x}$

$= \dfrac{3(x^2 - 9)}{(4x - 3)(x - 3)} \cdot \dfrac{(4x - 3)}{x(x + 3)}$

$= \dfrac{3\,\cancel{(x + 3)}\,\cancel{(x - 3)}\,\cancel{(4x - 3)}}{\cancel{(4x - 3)}\cancel{(x - 3)}(x)\cancel{(x + 3)}}$

$= \dfrac{3}{x}$

x^2 Worked Example 2.13

Simplify $\dfrac{x - 5}{x + 1} \div \dfrac{x^2 - 25}{x^2 + 4x + 3}$.

Solution

$\dfrac{x - 5}{x + 1} \div \dfrac{x^2 - 25}{x^2 + 4x + 3}$

$= \dfrac{x - 5}{x + 1} \times \dfrac{x^2 + 4x + 3}{x^2 - 25}$

$= \dfrac{\cancel{(x - 5)}}{\cancel{(x + 1)}} \cdot \dfrac{(x + 3)\cancel{(x + 1)}}{(x + 5)\cancel{(x - 5)}}$

$= \dfrac{x + 3}{x + 5}$

Complex Fractions

Sometimes a fraction's numerator and/or denominator may be a fraction as well. These types of fractions are called **complex fractions**.

For example: $\dfrac{1 + \frac{1}{3}}{\frac{2}{5} + \frac{3}{7}}$  ACTIVITY 2.4

x^2 Worked Example 2.14

Simplify $\dfrac{1 - \frac{9}{x^2}}{2 + \frac{6}{x}}$.

Solution

Numerator: $1 - \dfrac{9}{x^2} = \dfrac{x^2 - 9}{x^2}$

$= \dfrac{(x - 3)(x + 3)}{x^2}$

Denominator: $2 + \dfrac{6}{x} = \dfrac{2x + 6}{x}$

$= \dfrac{2(x + 3)}{x}$

$\therefore \dfrac{1 - \frac{9}{x^2}}{2 + \frac{6}{x}} = \dfrac{(x - 3)(x + 3)}{x^2} \div \dfrac{2(x + 3)}{x}$

$= \dfrac{(x - 3)\cancel{(x + 3)}}{x^2} \times \dfrac{\cancel{x}^{\,1}}{2\cancel{(x + 3)}}$

$= \dfrac{x - 3}{2x}$

Alternative Method

Multiply the numerator **and** the denominator by x^2.

$= \dfrac{1 - \frac{9}{x^2}}{2 + \frac{6}{x}} \cdot \dfrac{x^2}{x^2}$

$= \dfrac{x^2 - 9}{2x^2 + 6x}$

$= \dfrac{\cancel{(x + 3)}\,(x - 3)}{2x\,\cancel{(x + 3)}}$

$= \dfrac{x - 3}{2x}$

Exercise 2.4

For Questions 1 to 19, express as single fractions in their simplest form.

1. $\dfrac{10b^2}{5a^2} \times \dfrac{25a^3}{2b}$

2. $\dfrac{4x}{2y} \div \dfrac{8x^3}{4y^2}$

3. $\dfrac{2}{2x-1} \div \dfrac{4}{4x^2-1}$

4. $\dfrac{x^2+x-2}{x^2+2x-3} \times \dfrac{2x+6}{4x-4}$

5. $\dfrac{4x-4}{x} \div \dfrac{x^2-1}{x^3}$

6. $\dfrac{y^2-64}{y^2-16} \times \dfrac{2y^2-8y}{2y-16}$

7. $\dfrac{2x^2-x-1}{2x^2+x-1} \cdot \dfrac{4x^2-1}{x^2-1}$

8. $\dfrac{8x^2-34x-9}{4x+1} \times \dfrac{3x}{4x^2-81}$

9. $\dfrac{6x^2-20x+16}{4x^2-16x+16} \div \dfrac{9x^2-16}{2x^2+2x-12}$

10. $\dfrac{\frac{4x+3}{x^2-49}}{\frac{16x^2-9}{x-7}}$

11. $\dfrac{\frac{x-y}{xy}}{\frac{5}{xy}}$

12. $\dfrac{\frac{x-5}{x+5}}{\frac{1}{x^2-25}}$

13. $\dfrac{\frac{x}{x+1}+1}{\frac{3}{x+1}}$

14. $\dfrac{1-\frac{1}{x}}{2-\frac{2}{x^2}}$

15. $\dfrac{\frac{x}{x^2-6x+9}}{\frac{5}{(3-x)(x-3)}}$

16. $\dfrac{a-\frac{1}{b}}{1-\frac{1}{b}}$

17. $\dfrac{p+q}{\frac{1}{p}+\frac{1}{q}}$

18. $\dfrac{\frac{x+3}{y-x}}{\frac{x^2+3x}{x^2-y^2}}$

19. $\dfrac{\frac{x^2-y^2}{x^2}}{\frac{x^2+2xy+y^2}{x}}$

20. If $u = x - \dfrac{1}{x}$ and $v = x^2 - \dfrac{1}{x^2}$, show that $u^2(u^2 + 4) = v^2$.

21. If $x = \dfrac{a^3-b^3}{a^3+ab^2}$ and $y = \dfrac{a^3-ab^2}{a^2b+b^3}$, show that $\dfrac{x}{y} = \dfrac{b(a^2+ab+b^2)}{a^2(a+b)}$.

2.5 LONG DIVISION IN ALGEBRA

Another approach to dividing one algebraic expression by another is to use long division.

x^2 Worked Example 2.15

Simplify:

$\dfrac{6x^3 + 5x^2 - 10x + 3}{2x - 1}$

> The numerator is called the dividend.
>
> The denominator is called the divisor.

Solution

$$
\begin{array}{r}
3x^2 + 4x\ \ -3 \\
2x-1{\overline{\smash{\big)}\,6x^3 + 5x^2 - 10x + 3}} \\
-\,(6x^3 - 3x^2) \\
\hline
8x^2 - 10x \\
-\,(8x^2\ -\ 4x) \\
\hline
-6x + 3 \\
-\,(-6x + 3) \\
\hline
0
\end{array}
$$

Arrange the divisor and dividend in descending powers of x.
We divide $6x^3$ by $2x$ to get $3x^2$.

We multiply $2x - 1$ by $3x^2$ to get $6x^3 - 3x^2$ and subtract to get $8x^2$.

Bring down the next term. We divide $8x^2$ by $2x$ to get $4x$.

We multiply $2x - 1$ by $4x$ to get $8x^2 - 4x$ and subtract to get $-6x$.

Bring down the next term. We divide $-6x$ by $2x$ to get -3.

We multiply $2x - 1$ by -3 to get $-6x + 3$ and subtract.

We get a remainder of 0.

$\therefore \dfrac{6x^3 + 5x^2 - 10x + 3}{2x - 1} = 3x^2 + 4x - 3$

> The remainder 0 tells us that $2x - 1$ is a factor of $6x^3 + 5x^2 - 10x + 3$.

ALGEBRA I

x^2 **Worked Example 2.16**

Divide $x^3 - 4x^2 + 3$ by $x - 1$.

Solution

As the x term is missing, we write $0x$ into the expression.

$$
\begin{array}{r}
x^2 - 3x \; - 3 \\
x - 1 \overline{\smash{\big)}\ x^3 - 4x^2 + 0x + 3} \\
-\underline{(x^3 - x^2)} \\
-3x^2 + 0x \\
-\underline{(-3x^2 + 3x)} \\
-3x + 3 \\
-\underline{(-3x + 3)} \\
0
\end{array}
$$

$\therefore (x^3 - 4x^2 + 3) \div (x - 1) = x^2 - 3x - 3$

$x^2 - 3x - 3$ is called the quotient.

Long division is also useful as it can be used to find the other factors of an expression.

Consider the following question: 'Find the prime factors of 30.'

Starting with the smallest prime factor of 30, which is 2, we have:

$30 \div 2 = 15$

Continuing:

$15 \div 3 = 5$

So the prime factors of 15 are 3 and 5.

$\therefore 30 = 2(3)(5)$. Its prime factors are 2, 3 and 5.

Long division in algebra is very similar to finding the prime factors of a positive whole number.

 **ACTIVITY 2.5**

x^2 **Worked Example 2.17**

Show that $x - 4$ is a factor of $12x^3 - 55x^2 + 29x - 4$ and find the other two factors.

Solution

$$
\begin{array}{r}
12x^2 - 7x \; + 1 \\
x - 4 \overline{\smash{\big)}\ 12x^3 - 55x^2 + 29x - 4} \\
-\underline{(12x^3 - 48x^2)} \\
-7x^2 + 29x \\
-\underline{(-7x^2 + 28x)} \\
x - 4 \\
-\underline{(x - 4)} \\
0
\end{array}
$$

There is no remainder, so $(x - 4)$ is a factor.

$\therefore 12x^3 - 55x^2 + 29x - 4 = (x - 4)(12x^2 - 7x + 1)$

$= (x - 4)(4x - 1)(3x - 1)$

$\therefore$ The other two factors are $(4x - 1)$ and $(3x - 1)$.

ALGEBRA I

Exercise 2.5

Simplify each of the following:

1. $(x^3 + 2x^2 - 7x - 2) \div (x - 2)$

2. $(3x^3 + 13x^2 - 18x - 40) \div (3x + 4)$

3. $(6x^3 - 29x^2 + 21x - 4) \div (3x - 1)$

4. $(14x^3 + 33x^2 - 5x) \div (7x - 1)$

5. $(36x^3 - 28x + 8) \div (3x - 2)$

6. $(15x^4 - 11x^3 - 77x^2 + 31x + 42) \div (5x + 3)$

7. Divide $x^3 - 13x - 12$ by $x + 1$.
   Hence, find the other factors.

8. Find the quotient when:
   $4x^4 - 8x^3 - 13x^2 + 2x + 3$ is divided by $2x - 1$.

9. Divide $x^5 - x^4 - 6x^3 - 8x^2 + 8x + 48$ by $x^2 - x - 6$. Hence, fully factorise $x^5 - x^4 - 6x^3 - 8x^2 + 8x + 48$.

10. Show that $x - 1$ is a factor of $2x^4 - 14x^3 + 22x^2 - 10x$.

11. Find all four factors of $36x^4 - 289x^2 + 400$, if $4x^2 - 25$ divides evenly into the quartic expression.

12. Show that $2x + 1$ is not a factor of $6x^3 - 13x^2 - 19x + 12$.
    Give a reason for your answer.

13. Find all four factors of $72x^4 + 18x^3 - 29x^2 - 3x + 2$, if $6x^2 + x - 2$ divides evenly into the quartic expression.

14. Investigate if $g(x) = 3x + 4$ and $h(x) = 5x + 4$ are factors of the function $f(x) = -6x^4 - 29x^3 - 16x^2 + 16x$.

Revision Exercises

1. (a) Factorise the following:

   (i) $x^2 - x - 90$

   (ii) $4x^2 + 4x + 1$

   (iii) $10x^2 - x - 2$

   (iv) $9x^2 - 12xy + 4y^2$

   (v) $14x^2 - 15x + 4$

   (b) Simplify:

   (i) $\dfrac{3a - 9b}{6a - 18b}$

   (ii) $\dfrac{8x - 10}{16x^2 - 25}$

   (iii) $\dfrac{a^3 - b^3}{6a - 6b}$

   (iv) $\dfrac{by + b - y - 1}{b^3 - 1}$

   (v) $\dfrac{x^2 - x}{x^2 - 4x + 3}$

   (c) Expand:

   (i) $(3x + 7)^2$

   (ii) $(2x - 1)^3$

   (iii) $(4x - 5)^3$

   (iv) $(4p + 3)^3(p - 2)$

   (v) $2a(3a + 4)^2(2a + 5)^3$

   (d) Simplify $\left(\dfrac{1}{x} - \dfrac{1}{x + h}\right) \div h$.

2. (a) Factorise the following:

   (i) $x^2 - 100$

   (ii) $4x^2 - 81$

   (iii) $25x^2 - 49y^2$

   (iv) $121a^2 - 144b^2$

   (v) $(5x + 6y)^2 - (x + y)^2$

   (b) Write as a single fraction in its simplest form:

   (i) $\dfrac{3}{x - 3} + \dfrac{5}{x + 4}$

   (ii) $\dfrac{7}{2y + 1} - \dfrac{6}{2y - 1}$

   (iii) $\dfrac{2}{x + 1} - \dfrac{x}{x - 1}$

   (c) Using Pascal's triangle, expand the following polynomials:

   (i) $(2a + 1)^5$

   (ii) $(4b - 7c)^4$

   (iii) $(6x - 5)^6$

   (d) Show that $\dfrac{2}{x - 4} + \dfrac{2(9 - 2x)}{4 - x}$ simplifies to a constant for all $x \in R$, $x \neq 4$.

3. (a) Factorise:

   (i) $x^3 + 27$

   (ii) $a^3 + 8$

   (iii) $b^3 + 1000$

   (iv) $8x^3 + 125$

   (v) $125x^3 + 27y^3$

(b) Simplify the following:

(i) $\dfrac{2x^2 + 9x + 4}{2x^2 + 11x + 5}$ (iv) $\dfrac{2x - 2y}{3y - 3x}$

(ii) $\dfrac{a^2 - b^2}{a^3 - b^3}$ (v) $\dfrac{x - 3}{9 - x^2}$

(iii) $\dfrac{a^2 - b^2}{a^4 - b^4}$

(c) Write as single fractions in their lowest terms:

(i) $\dfrac{5}{x - 2} + \dfrac{1}{2 - x}$ (iii) $\dfrac{2}{b - a} + \dfrac{2}{a - b}$

(ii) $\dfrac{7}{2y - 1} + \dfrac{5}{1 - 2y}$ (iv) $\dfrac{9}{2x - 1} - \dfrac{4}{1 - 2x}$

4. (a) Factorise:

(i) $y^3 - 1$ (iv) $x^3 - 216$

(ii) $8y^3 - 1$ (v) $1000a^3 - 343b^3$

(iii) $27a^3 - 8b^3$

(b) Express as single fractions in their lowest terms:

(i) $\dfrac{6x}{x^2 - 9} - \dfrac{1}{x + 3}$ (ii) $\dfrac{4}{3y - 2} - \dfrac{2y}{9y^2 - 4}$

(c) The sides of a triangle are $(m^2 + n^2)$, $(m^2 - n^2)$ and $2mn$ in length.

(i) Prove that the triangle is right-angled.

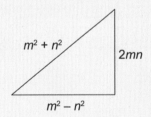

$m^2 + n^2$ $2mn$

$m^2 - n^2$

(ii) Deduce the three lengths of the sides if $m = 5$ and $n = 2$.

5. (a) Factorise fully:

(i) $3x^2 - 75$ (iv) $x^4 - 81$

(ii) $9x^3 - 25x$ (v) $ax^2 - bx^2 - ay^2 + by^2$

(iii) $x^4 - y^4$

(b) Simplify:

(i) $\dfrac{ax + ay - cx - cy}{ax + ay + cx + cy}$

(ii) $\dfrac{9y^3 - y}{3y^2 + 8y - 3}$

(iii) $\dfrac{(a + b)^2 - c^2}{a^2 - (b + c)^2}$

(c) Write $\dfrac{2x}{x + 3} + \dfrac{3x}{x - 3} - \dfrac{5x^2 + 9}{x^2 - 9}$

as a fraction in the form $\dfrac{k}{x + t}$

where $k \in Z$.

6. (a) Simplify each of the following:

(i) $(4x^3 - 5x^2 - 2x + 3) \div (x - 1)$

(ii) $(36x^3 - 18x^2 - 10x + 4) \div (3x - 1)$

(iii) $(24x^4 - 22x^3 - 7x^2 + 4x + 1) \div (3x + 1)$

(iv) $(2x^4 + 13x^3 + 19x^2 - 10x - 24)$
$\div (2x + 3)$

(iv) $(36x^5 + 117x^4 + 95x^3 + 5x^2 - 11x - 2)$
$\div (3x - 1)$

(b) (i) Show that $8x + 1$ is a factor of $48x^3 + 62x^2 - 33x - 5$ and find the other factors.

(ii) Show that $x - 2$ is not a factor of $8x^3 + 22x^2 - 7x - 3$.

(c) Write down the dividend, divisor and quotient when
$6x^5 - 40x^4 - 26x^3 + 356x^2 - 312x - 144$
is divided by $3x^2 + 10x + 3$.

7. (a) Rearrange the order of the terms in these expressions and then factorise them:

(i) $51 + x^2 + 20x$

(ii) $-x^2 + 169$

(iii) $ax + by + ay + bx$

(iv) $a^2 + b^2 - 2ab$

(v) $a^2 + b^2 - c^2 - 2ab$

(b) (i) Write $1 + \dfrac{x}{y}$ as a single fraction.

(ii) Hence, simplify $\left(1 + \dfrac{x}{y}\right)\left(\dfrac{y^2}{y^2 - x^2}\right)$.

(c) (i) Show that $x - 1$ is not a factor of $4x^4 - 20x^3 - 7x^2 + 32x + 15$. Give a reason for your answer.

(ii) Show that $4x^2 - 1$ is a factor of $12x^4 + 4x^3 - 59x^2 - x + 14$ and find the other factors.

(iii) Show that $x^3 - x^2$ is a factor of $4x^5 - 7x^3 + 3x^2$ and find the other factors.

8. (a) Factorise fully the following expressions:

 (i) $x^3 + y^3 + 3x + 3y$

 (ii) $x^2 - y^2 + 5x + 5y$

 (iii) $x^2 - 2xy + y^2 - 4z^2$

 (iv) $x^3 - y^3 + x^2 - y^2$

 (v) $a^2 - (b + c)^2$

 (b) Simplify the following:

 (i) $\dfrac{x^2 - 2xy + y^2 - z^2}{x^2 - y^2 - 2yz - z^2}$ (iii) $\dfrac{9}{4x^2 - 16} \times \dfrac{2x - 4}{27}$

 (ii) $\dfrac{x^2 - 25}{x^2 - 64} \times \dfrac{x^2 - 8x}{x - 5}$

 (c) Car A leaves a town and drives north at a speed of 40 km/hr. Car B leaves 3 hours later and travels north along the same route at a speed of 60 km/hr. After a certain distance, Car B catches up with Car A.

 Let x be the time in hours that Car A travels before Car B catches up with it. Express for each car, in terms of x, the distance travelled.

 (d) Write $\dfrac{8}{6x - 15} - \dfrac{5}{4x - 10}$
 in the form $\dfrac{a}{b(2x - 5)}$ where $a, b \in Z$.

9. (a) Factorise the following:

 (i) $\dfrac{x^2}{100} - \dfrac{y^2}{49}$ (iv) $a^2b^2 - 64$

 (ii) $x^3 + \dfrac{1}{x^3}$ (v) $x^2 - y^2 + 2x + 1$

 (iii) $x^4 - 16$

 (b) Simplify:

 (i) $\dfrac{15x^2}{8y^2} \div \dfrac{5x^3}{2}$ (ii) $\dfrac{\frac{1}{9}(2x^2 - 50)}{\frac{1}{45}(4x^2 - 20x)}$

 (c) The area of a rectangle can be expressed as $2x^2 + 3x - 20$. The length of the rectangle is $x + 4$.

 (i) Find the breadth of the rectangle in terms of x.

 This rectangle is used as a base for a rectangular box. The volume of this box can be expressed as $6x^3 + 7x^2 - 63x + 20$.

 (ii) Find the height of this rectangular box in terms of x.

(d) (i) Write as single fractions:

 $y - \dfrac{1}{y}$ and $2 + \dfrac{2}{y - 1}$

 (ii) Simplify $\left(y - \dfrac{1}{y}\right)\left(2 + \dfrac{2}{y - 1}\right)$.

10. (a) (i) Factorise $x^3 + y^3$.

 (ii) Hence, write $x^3 + y^3 + 3xy(x + y)$ as a perfect cube (i.e. as (expression)^3).

 (iii) Hence, factorise $x^3 + y^3 + z^3 + 3xy(x + y)$.

 (b) If $x = \dfrac{5b^2}{a^2 - ab}$ and $y = \dfrac{10ab}{b^2 - a^2}$, show that $\dfrac{x}{y} = \dfrac{-b(b + a)}{2a^2}$.

 (c) Simplify $\dfrac{\frac{z}{z - 1} + \frac{z}{z + 1}}{\frac{z}{z - 1} - \frac{z}{z + 1}}$.

11. (a) (i) Show that $\dfrac{3t - 10}{3t - 2} - \dfrac{8}{2 - 3t}$

 simplifies to a constant, $t \neq \dfrac{2}{3}$.

 (ii) Simplify $\dfrac{8x^3 + 27}{4x^2 - 9}$.

 (iii) Simplify $\dfrac{x^2 - x - 6}{x^2 - 4}$.

 (b) Factorise:

 (i) $a^2 + 2ab + b^2$

 (ii) $a^2 + b^2 - c^2 + 2ab$

 (c) Show that

 $\dfrac{x^2}{(x - y)(x - z)} + \dfrac{y^2}{(y - z)(y - x)} + \dfrac{yz}{(z - x)(z - y)}$

 simplifies to $\dfrac{x}{(x - z)}$.

12. (a) Write $\dfrac{1}{x + 2} - \dfrac{1}{2x - 1}$ as a single fraction and hence solve:

 $\dfrac{1}{x + 2} - \dfrac{1}{2x - 1} = \dfrac{1}{2x^2 + 3x - 2}$

 (b) Express in the form $\dfrac{k}{x + 3}$:

 $\dfrac{4}{x - 2} + \dfrac{5}{x + 3} - \dfrac{20}{x^2 + x - 6}$

 (c) Factorise $8x^3 - 27y^3 + 4x^2 - 9y^2$.

3 chapter

Algebra II

Learning Outcomes

In this chapter you will learn to:

- ➲ Solve linear equations
- ➲ Solve simultaneous linear equations in two unknowns
- ➲ Solve simultaneous linear equations in three unknowns
- ➲ Solve quadratic equations of the form $ax^2 + bx + c = 0$
- ➲ Solve simultaneous equations: one linear, one non-linear
- ➲ Use the factor theorem for polynomials

- ➲ Solve cubic equations
- ➲ Manipulate formulae
- ➲ Determine unknown coefficients
- ➲ Solve problems using:
  - ➲ Linear equations
  - ➲ Simultaneous equations
  - ➲ Quadratic equations
  - ➲ Cubic equations

3.1 SOLVING LINEAR EQUATIONS

When solving an equation, we are being asked to find the value(s) of the unknown(s) that satisfy the equation. There are many different methods that can be used to solve an equation.

A linear equation is of the form $ax + b = 0$, $a \neq 0$. There are numerous ways of solving a linear equation.

YOU SHOULD REMEMBER...

■ Algebra from the Junior Cycle

■ How to find the factors of quadratic expressions

■ How to plot and read graphs

Using Trial and Error

Trial and error involves the following steps:

■ Make an educated guess as to what the unknown may be.

■ Check to see if your guess is correct by substituting your guessed value into the equation.

■ Keep guessing until you arrive at the correct solution.

KEY WORDS

■ **Solve**

■ **Unknown**

■ **Variable**

■ **Linear equation**

■ **LCD**

■ **Simultaneous equation**

■ **Quadratic equation**

■ **Quadratic trinomials**

■ **Quadratic formula**

■ **Solution**

■ **Roots**

■ **Cubic equation**

x^2 Worked Example 3.1

Using trial and error, solve the following linear equation:

$3(x - 1) = 9$

Solution

x	$3(x - 1)$	$= 9$	
1	$3(1 - 1)$	$= 0$	Answer too small. Pick a number bigger than 1.
6	$3(6 - 1)$	$= 15$	Answer too big. Pick a number smaller than 6.
4	$3(4 - 1)$	$= 9$	✓

Answer: $x = 4$

> If the unknown is being multiplied by a negative number, then bigger guesses will lead to smaller answers.

Using Graphs

Linear equations can also be solved by using graphs.

x^2 Worked Example 3.2

(i) Graph the line $y = 2x + 4$ and hence solve $y = 0$.

(ii) Explain the significance of the x-intercept.

(iii) Using your graph, solve $2x + 4 = 3x + 3$.

Solution

(i) We graph the line $y = 2x + 4$.

This line has a slope of 2 and the y-intercept is 4.

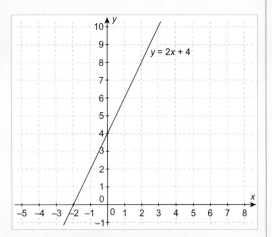

$y = 0$ anywhere on the x-axis.

The line crosses the x-axis at the point $(-2,0)$.

∴ The x-intercept $= -2$.

∴ $x = -2$ is the solution to $y = 0$.

(ii) The x-intercept is the solution or root of the equation $2x + 4 = 0$.

(iii) Using the same axes and scales, graph the line $y = 3x + 3$.

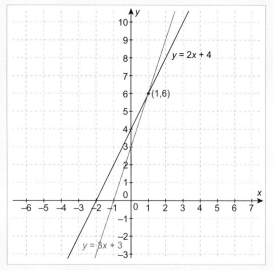

This line has a slope of 3 and the y-intercept is 3.

The point of intersection of the two lines gives the solution to $2x + 4 = 3x + 3$.

From our graph, the point of intersection of these two lines is $(1,6)$.

As the x co-ordinate here is 1,
⇒ $x = 1$ is the solution.

ACTIVITY 3.1

Using Algebra

Both of the previous methods have drawbacks.

▪ Trial and error can be tedious and difficult if the unknown is not an integer.

▪ Solving by graphing can be time-consuming and may only give us an estimate and not the exact answer we need.

A more accurate approach to solving an equation is to use algebra.

x^2 Worked Example 3.3

Solve the following equation and verify your answer.

$3(4a - 6) + 25(a + 2) = a - 4$

Solution

(i) Solve the equation.

$$3(4a - 6) + 25(a + 2) = a - 4$$
$$\Rightarrow 12a - 18 + 25a + 50 = a - 4 \quad \text{(Multiply through both brackets on the LHS.)}$$
$$37a + 32 = a - 4 \quad \text{(Simplify the LHS.)}$$
$$36a = -36 \quad \text{(Isolate the unknown on the LHS and constant terms on the RHS.)}$$
$$\therefore a = -1$$

(ii) Verify the answer.

We check to see if our answer is correct. We substitute the value we got for a into the original equation.

LHS: $3(4a - 6) + 25(a + 2)$

$\qquad = 3(4(-1) - 6) + 25((-1) + 2)$

$\qquad = 3(-4 - 6) + 25(-1 + 2)$

$\qquad = 3(-10) + 25(1)$

$\qquad = -30 + 25$

$\therefore$ LHS $= -5$

RHS: $a - 4$

$\qquad = (-1) - 4$

$\therefore$ RHS $= -5$

LHS $=$ RHS

$\therefore a = -1$ is the correct solution.

x^2 Worked Example 3.4

Solve: $\dfrac{y + 2}{3} - \dfrac{1}{6}(5y + 2) = 1$

Solution

The LCD of 3, 6 and 1 is 6.

We multiply every term in the equation by 6:

$$\frac{6(y + 2)}{3} - \frac{6(5y + 2)}{6} = 6(1)$$

$$2(y + 2) - 1(5y + 2) = 6(1)$$

$$2y + 4 - 5y - 2 = 6$$

$$-3y + 2 = 6$$

$$-3y = 4$$

$$\therefore y = -\frac{4}{3}$$

Exercise 3.1

Using trial and error, find the value of the unknown variable:

1. $2x + 4 = 2$
2. $x - 10 = 12$
3. $-3a + 2 = 17$
4. $4b + 11 = 9$
5. $2c - 8 = 5$
6. $3(2 - x) = -9$
7. $11 - 2x = 5$
8. $7p + 3 = 24$
9. $4(1 - a) = 16$
10. $2(x + 3) = 18$

Solve the following linear equations by graphing:

11. $x + 2 = 0$
12. $2x - 9 = 0$
13. $4x - 5 = 3$
14. $3x + 10 = 2x + 5$
15. $4x + 1 = x - 7$
16. $2x - 4 = x + 6$

Solve the following equations and verify your answer in each case:

17. $2x + 3 = 4(3x - 1)$
18. $4(2a - 1) = -3(2a - 1)$
19. $-(x - 3) - (x + 2) = 2(x - 1)$
20. $\dfrac{x - 1}{4} + \dfrac{2x}{3} = \dfrac{5}{2}$
21. $\dfrac{3x + 1}{4} - \dfrac{x - 5}{2} = 3$
22. $\dfrac{4x + 1}{5} - \dfrac{2x - 1}{2} = \dfrac{5x - 3}{10}$
23. $\dfrac{y + 3}{4} - \dfrac{1}{3}(y - 5) = 2\dfrac{3}{8}$
24. $\dfrac{2x - 5}{2} - \dfrac{x - 3}{7} = 3$

3.2 SOLVING SIMULTANEOUS LINEAR EQUATIONS IN TWO VARIABLES

Again, we can use various methods to solve simultaneous equations with two unknowns.

Using Trial and Error

x^2 Worked Example 3.5

Is $x = 1$ and $y = -2$ the correct solution for the equations:

$2x - y = 4$? $5x - 3y = 1$?

Solution

We substitute $x = 1$ and $y = -2$ into both equations.

$2x - y = 4$	$5x - 3y = 1$
$2(1) - (-2) = 4$	$5(1) - 3(-2) = 4$
$2 + 2 = 4$	$5 + 6 = 4$
$4 = 4$	$11 = 4$
True	False

$\therefore$ $x = 1$ and $y = -2$ is not the correct solution to both equations.

Using Graphs

x^2 Worked Example 3.6

Solve the following equations by graphing:

$2x - 4 = y$ $2x + y = 2$

Solution

We plot both lines using the same axes and scales:

$2x - 4 = y$	
This line has a slope of 2 and y-intercept of -4.	
$2x + y = 2$	
Let $x = 0$.	Let $y = 0$.
$2(0) + y = 2$	$2x + (0) = 2$
$y = 2$	$2x = 2$
	$x = 1$
If $x = 0$ then $y = 2$.	If $y = 0$ then $x = 1$.
Point (0,2)	Point (1,0)

ACTIVITY 3.2

Mark the point of intersection of both lines.

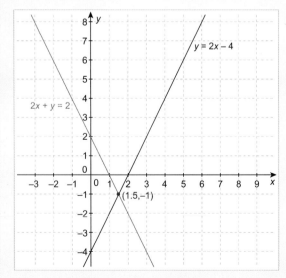

From our graph, we see that the point of intersection is (1.5,–1).

$\therefore$ $x = 1.5$ and $y = -1$

Using Elimination

x^2 Worked Example 3.7

Solve the equations:

$3x - 2y = 14 \qquad \dfrac{2x + 1}{3} - \dfrac{y + 1}{9} = 2$

Solution

First, ensure that both equations are in the same format:

$$\frac{2x + 1}{3} - \frac{y + 1}{9} = 2$$

$$\frac{9(2x + 1)}{3} - \frac{9(y + 1)}{9} = 9(2)$$

$$3(2x + 1) - 1(y + 1) = 9(2)$$

$$6x + 3 - y - 1 = 18$$

$$6x - y = 16$$

Now work with both equations simultaneously:

$$3x - 2y = 14$$

$$6x - y = 16$$

We make the y coefficients the same in each equation:

$3x - 2y = 14 \quad \times 1 \quad \rightarrow \quad 3x - 2y = 14$

$6x - y = 16 \quad \times 2 \quad \rightarrow \quad 12x - 2y = 32$

As the y coefficients are the same sign, we will subtract:

$$3x - 2y = 14$$
$$-(12x - 2y = 32)$$

$$\begin{aligned} 3x - 2y &= 14 \\ -12x + 2y &= -32 \\ \hline -9x &= -18 \end{aligned}$$

$$\therefore x = 2$$

Substitute $x = 2$ into one of the equations:

$$6x - y = 16$$
$$6(2) - y = 16$$
$$12 - y = 16$$
$$-4 = y$$

Answer: $x = 2$, $y = -4$

Exercise 3.2

Solve using trial and error:

1. $3x + 2y = 21$
$4x - 5y = 28$

2. $6x + 5y = 19$
$3x - 7y = 19$

Solve the following linear equations by graphing:

3. $x + y = 4$
$x - y = 10$

5. $x - y = 1$
$4x + 5y = 10$

4. $x + y = 6$
$2x - 4y = 12$

6. $5x - 2y = 9$
$3x + y = 1$

Solve the following equations by elimination:

7. $7x - 8y = -1$
$x - 4y = -23$

9. $9p - 4q + 16 = 0$
$-p + q = -1$

8. $4x + 5y = 0$
$x + y = 1$

10. $2x + 5y = -14$
$2x = 3y + 18$

11. $2x + 3y = 29$
$x - 7y = -28$

12. $-9x + 8y = 32$
$7x - 3y = -12$

13. $5x - 2y = 23$
$2x + 9y = -30$

14. $7r - 4s + 1 = 0$
$4r - 7s + 43 = 0$

15. $\dfrac{2}{3}x + \dfrac{3}{5}y = \dfrac{8}{5}$
$\dfrac{1}{2}x + \dfrac{2}{9}y = \dfrac{17}{18}$

16. $\dfrac{x - 3}{4} + \dfrac{5 - y}{2} = \dfrac{1}{4}$
$\dfrac{2x - 1}{3} - \dfrac{y + 3}{2} = -\dfrac{13}{6}$

17. $\dfrac{1}{2}x + \dfrac{1}{3}y = 3$
$\dfrac{3}{4}x - y = 0$

18. $7a + 5b = 5$
$22a - 20b = 5$

19. $5d + 3(e - 1) = 22$
$4d - 2e + 4 = 2$

20. $p + 2(q - 1) = -12$
$q + \dfrac{1}{3}p = -5$

ALGEBRA II

3.3 SOLVING SIMULTANEOUS EQUATIONS IN THREE VARIABLES

For three unknown quantities, we need three equations. Then one unknown at a time can be eliminated.

x^2 Worked Example 3.8

Solve the equations:

$x + y + z = 6$

$5x + 3y - 2z = 5$

$3x - 7y + z = -8$

> An equation of the form $Ax + By + Cz = D$ in three unknowns x, y, z (A, B, C, D constants) represents a plane (flat surface) in three dimensions. The three planes described by the system of equations in this example are shown in the diagram.

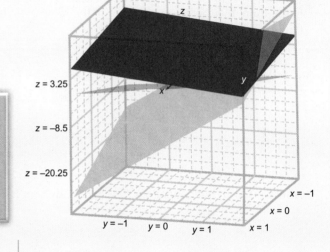

Solution

We will select one of the variables and eliminate it from a pair of equations.

The variable z looks to be the easiest to eliminate.

$x + y + z = 6$ $\times 2$ $\rightarrow 2x + 2y + 2z = 12$

$5x + 3y - 2z = 5$ $\times 1$ $\rightarrow 5x + 3y - 2z = 5$

As the coefficients of z have different signs, we will add the two equations.

$$2x + 2y + 2z = 12$$
$$\underline{5x + 3y - 2z = 5}$$
$$7x + 5y = 17 \qquad \text{(Equation 1)}$$

We now pick a different pair of equations and again eliminate the z variable.

$x + y + z = 6$

$3x - 7y + z = -8$

The z coefficients are the same sign, so we will subtract the two equations.

$$x + y + z = 6$$
$$\underline{-3x + 7y - z = +8}$$
$$-2x + 8y = 14 \qquad \text{(Equation 2)}$$

We now have two equations with two unknowns.

$7x + 5y = 17$ $\times 2$ $\rightarrow$ $14x + 10y = 34$

$-2x + 8y = 14$ $\times 7$ $\rightarrow -14x + 56y = 98$

The coefficients of x have different signs, so we add the two equations.

$$14x + 10y = 34$$
$$\underline{-14x + 56y = 98}$$
$$66y = 132$$
$$\therefore y = 2$$

Using Equation 1:

$$7x + 5y = 17$$
$$7x + 5(2) = 17$$
$$7x + 10 = 17$$
$$7x = 7$$
$$\therefore x = 1$$

We now have the values of x and y. We can substitute these values into any of the original equations to find the value of z.

$$x + y + z = 6$$
$$1 + 2 + z = 6$$
$$3 + z = 6$$
$$z = 3$$

$\therefore x = 1, y = 2$ and $z = 3$

Exercise 3.3

Solve the following systems of equations:

1. $2x + y + 4z = 23$
$5x + y + 2z = 19$
$3x - 2y + z = 13$

2. $x + y + z = 9$
$2x + 3y + z = 16$
$3x - 4y + 2z = 1$

3. $2a - 2b - 5c = -4$
$2a - 4b - c = -10$
$5a - 3b + 5c = -4$

4. $4x + y - 2z = 0$
$4x + 3y + 2z = 16$
$3x - y - 3z = -4$

5. $2x - 4y - 4z = -18$
$3x - 2y + 2z = 5$
$4x - 3y + z = 1$

6. $4x - 3y + z = -35$
$3x - y + z = -14$
$3x + 2y - 4z = -7$

7. $x - y - 3z = 0$
$3x + 3y + 2z = -16$
$x + 4y + 5z = -11$

8. $a - 4b + 3c = 14$
$3a + b - 4c = -10$
$2a + b + 3c = 22$

9. $3p + 4q - 2r = 8$
$9p + 8q + 2r = -13$
$6p - 12q + 14r = -59$

10. $x + y = z$
$2x + 3y = 2z$
$x + 2y = 10$

11. $x + 2y + 3z = 24$
$\dfrac{x}{2} + \dfrac{y}{3} + \dfrac{z}{6} = 4$
$x + 2y + 5z = 28$

12. $\dfrac{3}{4}x + \dfrac{2}{5}y - \dfrac{3}{10}z = 0$
$x + 2y + 3z = -1$
$\dfrac{3}{8}x + \dfrac{1}{2}y + \dfrac{1}{3}z = -\dfrac{5}{12}$

13. $x + y = z$
$3x + 2y - 4z = -1$
$x - 3y + 3z = 2$

14. Solve:
$x + y + z = 5$
$2x - y + 3z = 3$
$3x + 2y - 5z = 21$

Hence, solve:
$a^2 + b + (c + 1) = 5$
$2a^2 - b + 3(c + 1) = 3$
$3a^2 + 2b - 5(c + 1) = 21$

15. Solve:
$2x - 5y + 6z = 7$
$x - y - z = 3$
$3x + 2y + z = 4$

Hence, solve:
$\dfrac{2}{a} - \dfrac{5}{b} + \dfrac{6}{c} = 7$
$\dfrac{1}{a} - \dfrac{1}{b} - \dfrac{1}{c} = 3$
$\dfrac{3}{a} + \dfrac{2}{b} + \dfrac{1}{c} = 4$

3.4 SOLVING QUADRATIC EQUATIONS

Using Graphs

To estimate the roots of a quadratic equation of the form $ax^2 + bx + c = 0$, we read off the values of x where the graph of $y = ax^2 + bx + c$ intersects the x-axis.

x^2 Worked Example 3.9

Find the roots of $-x^2 + 7x - 12 = 0$ by graphing $f(x) = -x^2 + 7x - 12$ between $x = 1$ and $x = 6$.

Solution

We construct a table and substitute x-values to calculate y-values.

x	$-x^2 + 7x - 12$	y	Point
1	$-(1)^2 + 7(1) - 12$	-6	$(1, -6)$
2	$-(2)^2 + 7(2) - 12$	-2	$(2, -2)$
3	$-(3)^2 + 7(3) - 12$	0	$(3, 0)$
4	$-(4)^2 + 7(4) - 12$	0	$(4, 0)$
5	$-(5)^2 + 7(5) - 12$	-2	$(5, -2)$
6	$-(6)^2 + 7(6) - 12$	-6	$(6, -6)$

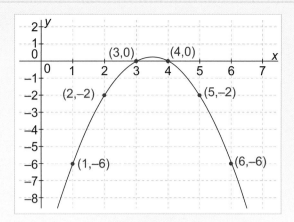

We now plot our points on an x and y co-ordinate diagram and then draw a curved graph.

The roots are the x-values where the graph crosses the x-axis.

∴ The roots of the equation are $x = 3$ or $x = 4$.

 **Worked Example 3.10**

The graph of the function $y = 2x^2 + 5x - 9$ is shown. Estimate the roots of this equation.

Solution

We can estimate the points of intersection between the graph and the x-axis.

∴ The roots of the equation are $x \approx -3.7$ or $x \approx 1.2$.

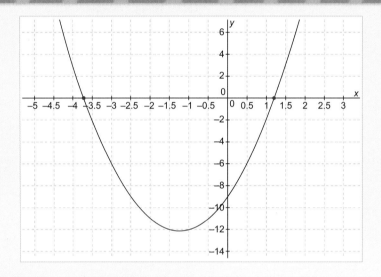

ACTIVITY 3.3

Using Algebra

x^2 **Worked Example 3.11**

(i) Solve $3x^2 + 5x - 12 = 0$.

(ii) Hence, solve $3(y - 1)^2 + 5(y - 1) - 12 = 0$.

Solution

(i) $3x^2 + 5x - 12 = 0$

Let both factors equal 0 and solve:

$(3x - 4)(x + 3) = 0$

$3x - 4 = 0$ **OR** $x + 3 = 0$

$3x = 4$ **OR** $x = -3$

$x = \dfrac{4}{3}$ **OR** $x = -3$

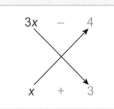

$3x \times x = 3x^2$ ✓

$-4 \times 3 = -12$ ✓

Using the arrows:

$3x \times 3 = 9x$

$\underline{x \times -4 = -4x}$

$5x$ ✓

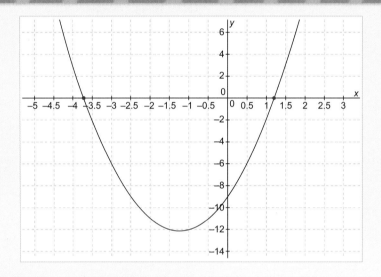

Alternatively, we can use the **Guide Number Method**.

Step 1: Multiply the coefficient of x^2 by the constant:

$3x^2 + 5x - 12$

$3 \times -12 = -36$

Step 2: Find two factors of -36 that will add up to give the middle term $5x$.

-4 and 9

Step 3: Use the answers from Step 2 to rewrite $3x^2 + 5x - 12$ as follows:

$3x^2 - 4x + 9x - 12$

$x(3x - 4) + 3(3x - 4)$ (Factorise by grouping)

$(x + 3)(3x - 4)$ (Distributive property)

$x + 3 = 0$ **OR** $3x - 4 = 0$

$x = -3$ **OR** $3x = 4$

$x = -3$ **OR** $x = \dfrac{4}{3}$

(ii) To solve $3(y - 1)^2 + 5(y - 1) - 12 = 0$, we note that this equation has the same structure as the original equation, except that each x has been replaced by $y - 1$.

$\therefore y - 1 = x$

$y - 1 = \dfrac{4}{3}$ **OR** $y - 1 = -3$

$\therefore y = \dfrac{7}{3}$ **OR** $y = -2$

x^2 Worked Example 3.12

Solve: $\dfrac{8}{y + 2} - \dfrac{2}{y + 3} = \dfrac{8}{5}$, $y \neq -2, -3$

Solution

The LCD is $(5)(y + 2)(y + 3)$.

$\dfrac{8(5)(y + 2)(y + 3)}{y + 2} - \dfrac{2(5)(y + 2)(y + 3)}{y + 3} = \dfrac{8(5)(y + 2)(y + 3)}{5}$

$\Rightarrow 8(5)(y + 3) - 2(5)(y + 2) = 8(y + 2)(y + 3)$

$40(y + 3) - 10(y + 2) = 8(y^2 + 5y + 6)$

$40y + 120 - 10y - 20 = 8y^2 + 40y + 48$

$30y + 100 = 8y^2 + 40y + 48$

$8y^2 + 10y - 52 = 0$

$4y^2 + 5y - 26 = 0$

$\therefore (4y + 13)(y - 2) = 0$

$(4y + 13)(y - 2) = 0$

$4y + 13 = 0$ **OR** $y - 2 = 0$

$4y = -13$ **OR** $y = 2$

$y = -\dfrac{13}{4}$ **OR** $y = 2$

Solving by Using the Quadratic Formula

There are alternative methods of solving quadratic equations.
One approach is to use the quadratic formula.

We can use this formula instead of factorising an equation and finding its roots.

Many quadratic equations cannot be solved by factorisation because they do not have simple factors. Using the quadratic formula will allow you to solve **any** quadratic equation.

When using the quadratic formula, it is important to note that in, for example, the equation $x^2 - 2x - 8 = 0$:

- $a = 1$; the coefficient of x^2
- $b = -2$; the coefficient of x
- $c = -8$; the constant

To use the quadratic formula, we should ensure that:

- The equation is written in the form $ax^2 + bx + c = 0$.
- The a value is positive (this is just to make calculations easier).

> The symbol $\pm$ requires two procedures:
> (i) Add $\sqrt{b^2 - 4ac}$ to $-b$ in the numerator.
> (ii) Subtract $\sqrt{b^2 - 4ac}$ from $-b$ in the numerator.

FORMULA

$$x = \frac{-b \pm \sqrt{b^2 - 4ac}}{2a}$$

a = coefficient of x^2
b = coefficient of x
c = constant term

This formula appears on page 20 of *Formulae and Tables*.

ACTIVITY 3.4

x^2 **Worked Example 3.13**

Solve $5x^2 - 2x = 25$ and give your answer:

   (i) In surd form

   (ii) Correct to three decimal places

Solution

We must first have the equation in the correct form:

$5x^2 - 2x - 25 = 0$

Using the quadratic formula:

$a = 5 \qquad b = -2 \qquad c = -25$

$$x = \frac{-(-2) \pm \sqrt{(-2)^2 - 4(5)(-25)}}{2(5)}$$

$$x = \frac{2 \pm \sqrt{4 + 500}}{10}$$

$$x = \frac{2 \pm \sqrt{504}}{10}$$

(i) Surd form

$$\sqrt{504} = \sqrt{36}\,\sqrt{14} = 6\sqrt{14}$$

$$\therefore x = \frac{2 \pm 6\sqrt{14}}{10}$$

This answer can be simplified further by dividing each term by the highest common factor of 2, 6 and 10 (which is 2).

$$\therefore x = \frac{1 \pm 3\sqrt{14}}{5}$$

(ii) $x = \dfrac{2 + \sqrt{504}}{10}$ **OR** $x = \dfrac{2 - \sqrt{504}}{10}$

$x = 2.444994432$ **OR** $x = -2.044994432$

Answer to three decimal places:

$x = 2.445$ **OR** $x = -2.045$

Roots of Quadratic Equations

If we are given the roots of a quadratic equation, it is possible to construct a quadratic equation with those roots. To form a quadratic equation when given the roots, we change the roots into factors and then use these factors to form the equation.

x^2 Worked Example 3.14

Form an equation from each of the following roots:

(i) $5, -\dfrac{2}{3}$ (ii) $\dfrac{1}{2}, -\dfrac{3}{4}$

Solution

(i) $5, -\dfrac{2}{3}$

Root	$x = 5$	$x = -\dfrac{2}{3}$
Factor	$x - 5 = 0$	$3x = -2$
		$3x + 2 = 0$
Equation	$(x - 5)(3x + 2) = 0$	
	$3x^2 - 13x - 10 = 0$	

 **ACTIVITY 3.5**

We can also use the formula:

FORMULA

Quadratic Equation $\Rightarrow x^2 - $ (sum of the roots)$x + $ (product of the roots) $= 0$

(ii) $\dfrac{1}{2}, -\dfrac{3}{4}$

Sum $= \dfrac{1}{2} + \left(-\dfrac{3}{4}\right)$	Product $= \left(\dfrac{1}{2}\right)\left(-\dfrac{3}{4}\right)$
Sum $= -\dfrac{1}{4}$	Product $= -\dfrac{3}{8}$

$$x^2 - \left(-\dfrac{1}{4}\right)x + \left(-\dfrac{3}{8}\right) = 0$$

$$x^2 + \dfrac{1}{4}x - \dfrac{3}{8} = 0$$

Multiply by LCD, 8:

$$8x^2 + 2x - 3 = 0$$

Exercise 3.4

1. Use trial and error to find one whole number root of each of the following equations:

   (i) $x^2 + 11x - 42 = 0$

   (ii) $2x^2 - 7x + 3 = 0$

   (iii) $x^2 + 2x - 63 = 0$

2. For each graph, estimate the roots of the equation shown.

(i)

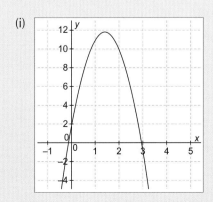

(ii)

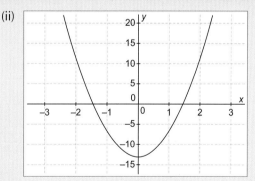

(iii)

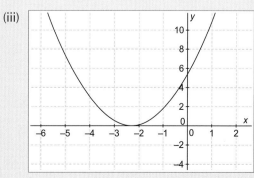

(iv)

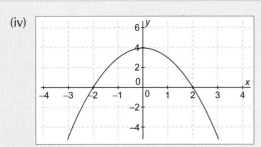

3. Solve $x^2 + x - 12 = 0$ by graphing the function between $x = -5$ and $x = 4$.

4. Solve $x^2 + 8x + 16 = 0$ by graphing the function between $x = -6$ and $x = -2$.

5. Solve $-x^2 + 4x - 4 = 0$ by graphing the equation between $x = -2$ and $x = 4$.

6. Graph the function $f(x) = 3x^2 - 6x - 5 = 0$ between $x = -2$ and $x = 5$.

   (i) Use your graph to find an estimate of the roots of the equation $3x^2 - 6x - 5 = 0$.

   (ii) Graph the line $g(x) = 4$. Mark the point of intersection of your two graphs.

   (iii) Explain what these points of intersection signify.

   (iv) Check your answer by solving $f(x) = g(x)$.

7. Solve the following equations:

   (i) $2x^2 - 13x + 18 = 0$

   (ii) $3x^2 + 5x - 42 = 0$

   (iii) $5x^2 - 17x + 6 = 0$

   (iv) $2x^2 + 5x + 2 = 0$

   (v) $25x^2 - 81 = 0$

   (vi) $7x^2 - 22x - 24 = 0$

8. Solve the following equations:

   (i) $3x^2 + x - 14 = 0$

   (ii) $4x^2 + 23x - 35 = 0$

   (iii) $4x^2 - 11x - 20 = 0$

   (iv) $10x^2 + 83x + 91 = 0$

   (v) $6x^2 - 25x + 26 = 0$

   (vi) $8x^2 - 11x - 10 = 0$

9. Solve $x^2 + 7x + 12 = 0$ and, hence, solve $(y^2 + 4y)^2 + 7(y^2 + 4y) + 12 = 0$.

10. Solve $x^2 + 8x + 15 = 0$ and, hence, solve $(2y^2 + 7y)^2 + 8(2y^2 + 7y) + 15 = 0$.

11. Solve $2x^2 - 17x + 35 = 0$ and, hence, solve $2\left(\frac{3}{2}t + 2t^2\right)^2 - 17\left(\frac{3}{2}t + 2t^2\right) + 35 = 0$.

12. Form a quadratic equation with each pair of roots, giving your answers in the form $ax^2 + bx + c = 0$ where $a, b, c \in Z$:

   (i) $3, 2$ (vi) $\dfrac{1}{2}, \dfrac{1}{5}$

   (ii) $5, 7$ (vii) $-\dfrac{3}{4}, \dfrac{3}{4}$

   (iii) $5, -2$ (viii) $4 + \sqrt{3}, 4 - \sqrt{3}$

   (iv) $6, 0$ (ix) $-1 - \sqrt{2}, -1 + \sqrt{2}$

   (v) $\dfrac{5}{2}, -3$ (x) $\dfrac{1 - \sqrt{3}}{2}, \dfrac{1 + \sqrt{3}}{2}$

13. A quadratic equation has roots p and $3p$. Form a quadratic equation with such roots.

14. Find the value of the constant c and the roots of the quadratic equation $x^2 - 10x + c = 0$, if one root is four times the other.

15. Find the value of the constant d and the roots of the quadratic equation $x^2 - 12x + d = 0$, if one root is two less than the other.

16. Use the quadratic formula to solve each of the following equations to two decimal places.

   (i) $2x^2 + 9x - 16 = 0$ (iv) $4x^2 + 9x - 5 = 0$

   (ii) $8x^2 + 5x - 9 = 0$ (v) $3x^2 - 2x - 23 = 0$

   (iii) $2x^2 - x - 17 = 0$ (vi) $7x^2 + 3x - 5 = 0$

17. Solve the following equations, leaving your answers in surd form.

   (i) $25x^2 - 125 = 0$ (iii) $6x^2 + 8x + 1 = 0$

   (ii) $x^2 + 6x + 7 = 0$ (iv) $3x^2 + 12x + 1 = 0$

18. Solve the following equations:

   (i) $2 - \dfrac{13}{x} + \dfrac{20}{x^2} = 0, x \neq 0$

   (ii) $\dfrac{3}{x^2} = \dfrac{11}{x} - 10, x \neq 0$

   (iii) $\dfrac{1}{x + 1} + \dfrac{1}{x} = \dfrac{5}{6}, x \neq -1, 0$

   (iv) $\dfrac{1}{x - 3} - \dfrac{1}{2x - 1} = \dfrac{1}{12}, x \neq -\dfrac{1}{2}, 3$

   (v) $\dfrac{2}{x - 5} + \dfrac{1}{4 + x} + \dfrac{3}{10} = 0, x \neq -4, 5$

   (vi) $\dfrac{5}{2x - 1} - \dfrac{4}{3x + 2} = -7, x \neq -\dfrac{2}{3}, \dfrac{1}{2}$

   (vii) $\dfrac{1}{x + 2} - \dfrac{2}{x} + \dfrac{1}{x - 6} = 0, x \neq 0, -2, 6$

   (viii) $\dfrac{1}{x + 1} + \dfrac{1}{x - 3} = 2, x \neq -1, 3$

   (ix) $\dfrac{4}{4x - 3} + 1 = \dfrac{2}{x - 1}, x \neq \dfrac{3}{4}, 1$

3.5 SIMULTANEOUS EQUATIONS: ONE LINEAR AND ONE NON-LINEAR

Another method to eliminate an unknown quantity from two equations is by substitution. From the linear equation, we can express one unknown in terms of the other and then substitute into the quadratic equation.

x^2 **Worked Example 3.15**

Solve for x and y:

$x + 4y = 1$ $\qquad$ $2x^2 + 3xy = 35$

> A non-linear equation contains terms of the form x^2 or xy or y^2, etc.

Solution

Step 1: Linear	We start with the linear equation. $x + 4y = 1$ $\Rightarrow x = 1 - 4y$
Step 2: Substitution *Always substitute from the linear into the non-linear.*	$2x^2 + 3xy = 35$ Substitute $x = 1 - 4y$ into this equation. $\quad 2(1 - 4y)^2 + 3(1 - 4y)(y) = 35$ $2(1 - 4y)(1 - 4y) + 3(1 - 4y)(y) = 35$ $2(1 - 8y + 16y^2) + (1 - 4y)(3y) = 35$ $\quad 2 - 16y + 32y^2 + 3y - 12y^2 = 35$ $\qquad\qquad 2 - 13y + 20y^2 = 35$ $\qquad\qquad 20y^2 - 13y - 33 = 0$
Step 3: Solving for one variable	$20y^2 - 13y - 33 = 0$ $(20y - 33)(y + 1) = 0$ $20y - 33 = 0$ **OR** $y + 1 = 0$ $20y = 33$ **OR** $y = -1$ $y = \dfrac{33}{20}$ **OR** $y = -1$
Step 4: Solving for the other variable *Always substitute back into the linear. This will avoid obtaining an incorrect solution.*	As we know the two values of y, we can now find the corresponding values of x. <table><tr><td colspan="2" align="center">x = 1 − 4y</td></tr><tr><td>If $y = \dfrac{33}{20}$ $x = 1 - 4\left(\dfrac{33}{20}\right)$ $x = 1 - \dfrac{33}{5}$ $x = -\dfrac{28}{5}$</td><td>If $y = -1$ $x = 1 - 4(-1)$ $x = 1 + 4$ $x = 5$</td></tr></table>
Step 5: Write answer	$x = -\dfrac{28}{5}, y = \dfrac{33}{20}$ **OR** $x = 5, y = -1$ $\left(-\dfrac{28}{5}, \dfrac{33}{20}\right)$ $\qquad\qquad (5, -1)$

Using Graphs

We used graphs to solve linear equations and quadratic equations. We can also use graphs to solve a system of one linear and one non-linear equation. The solution will be the co-ordinates of the point(s) of intersection between the linear and non-linear graphs. The concern with this method is that it may not be accurate.

x^2 Worked Example 3.16

Using the diagram/graphs, write down the points of intersection of $2x + 3y = 0$ and $2x^2 + y^2 = 22$.

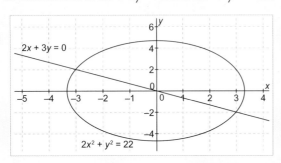

ACTIVITY 3.6

Solution

We find the points of intersection between the two equations by reading them off the graph:

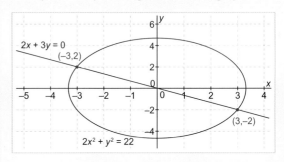

$\therefore \quad x = -3, y = 2 \qquad$ **OR** $\qquad x = 3, y = -2$

$\qquad (-3, 2) \qquad\qquad\qquad\qquad (3, -2)$

Exercise 3.5

1. Estimate the points of intersection between the linear and non-linear graphs shown. Interpret what these points of intersection mean in each case.

(i)

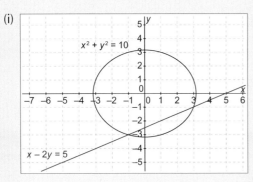

(ii)

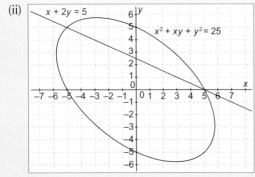

(iii)

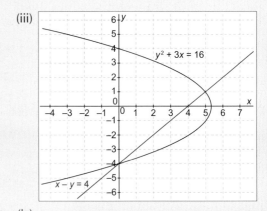

(iv)

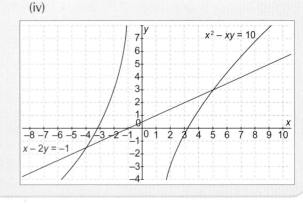

Solve the simultaneous equations:

2. $x + y = 5$
$x^2 + y^2 = 13$

3. $x + y = -3$
$x^2 + y^2 = 65$

4. $x - y = 2$
$2x^2 + y^2 = 36$

5. $2x + y = 9$
$xy = 10$

6. $2x - y = 3$
$3xy = 15$

7. $4x - y = -3$
$x^2 - y^2 = 0$

8. $3x - y - 3 = -4$
$xy - y = -1$

9. $5x - y = -13$
$x^2 + y^2 = 13$

10. $x = 2y$
$x^2 + y^2 - 2xy - 9 = 0$

11. $y = x - 4$
$2x^2 + xy = 20$

12. $x = y$
$x^2 + y^2 + 2x - 3y - 36 = 0$

13. $x - 4y = -13$
$x^2 + 2y^2 + 6xy = 29$

14. $4x = 3y$
$4x^2 - 6y^2 - 6xy - 2y + 5 = 0$

15. $\dfrac{2}{y} = \dfrac{x}{y} - 1$
$2x^2 + y^2 = 11$

16. $8x - 2y = 0$
$x^2 + y^2 = 17$

17. $x - 2y = 12$
$x^2 + y^2 - 10x - 4y + 4 = 0$

18. $3x + 5y = 15$
$x^2 + y^2 - 10x - 9 = 0$

19. $-\dfrac{1}{2}x + \dfrac{1}{4}y = -4$
$x^2 + y^2 - 4x - 6y = 52$

3.6 THE FACTOR THEOREM

A polynomial function of one variable x, $f(x)$, is of the form:

$$f(x) = a_n x^n + a_{n-1} x^{n-1} + \ldots + a_2 x^2 + a_1 x + a_0$$

where all powers are non-negative whole numbers and the a's are constants.

Examples: $f(x) = 3x^2 + 5x + 7$ $\qquad$ $g(x) = 1 + 2x^2 - 11x^3 + x^4$

The following are **not** polynomials, as they are not of the required form above:

$h(x) = x^2 - 7\sqrt{x} + 3$ $\qquad$ (Here, $\sqrt{x} = x^{\frac{1}{2}}$, so the power is **not** a non-negative integer.)

$k(x) = 2 + \sqrt{3}x^{\frac{2}{3}} - x^2 + x^3$ $\qquad$ (Here, the power $\frac{2}{3}$ is **not** a non-negative integer.)

The factor theorem can be used to find the roots of, or the factors of, a polynomial function.

> A polynomial $f(x)$ has a factor $(x - a)$ if and only if $f(a) = 0$.

This means that if $(x - a)$ is a factor of $f(x)$, then $f(a) = 0$. Also, if $f(a) = 0$, then $(x - a)$ is a factor of $f(x)$.

The factor theorem can be very useful when finding the roots or factors of cubic polynomials (polynomials where the highest power is 3). We can use the factor theorem to find one factor and then use long division to proceed further.

x^2 **Worked Example 3.17**

Solve the equation $2x^3 - 3x^2 - 17x + 30 = 0$.

Solution

$\frac{30}{2} = 15$. We investigate if one of the roots is a factor of 15.

The factors of 15 are ± 1, ± 3, ± 5 and ± 15.

We now use trial and error:

x	$2x^3 - 3x^2 - 17x + 30$	$= 0$	
1	$2(1)^3 - 3(1)^2 - 17(1) + 30$	$= 12$	Not a root
-1	$2(-1)^3 - 3(-1)^2 - 17(-1) + 30$	$= 42$	Not a root
3	$2(3)^3 - 3(3)^2 - 17(3) + 30$	$= 6$	Not a root
-3	$2(-3)^3 - 3(-3)^2 - 17(-3) + 30$	$= 0$	Root ✓

$x = -3$ is a root.

$\therefore x + 3$ is a factor.

We can now use long division to find the other factors and, hence, the other roots.

$$
\begin{array}{r}
2x^2 - 9x + 10 \\
x + 3 \overline{\smash{)}\, 2x^3 - 3x^2 - 17x + 30} \\
-(2x^3 + 6x^2) \\
\hline
-9x^2 - 17x \\
-(-9x^2 - 27x) \\
\hline
10x + 30 \\
-(10x + 30) \\
\hline
0
\end{array}
$$

$\therefore 2x^3 - 3x^2 - 17x + 30 = 0$

$\Rightarrow (x + 3)(2x^2 - 9x + 10) = 0$

$(x + 3)(2x - 5)(x - 2) = 0$

Put each factor $= 0$ and solve:

$x = -3$, $x = \frac{5}{2}$, $x = 2$

x^2 **Worked Example 3.18**

Let $f(x) = ax^3 + bx^2 - 9$, where a and b are constants.

Given that $(x + 3)$ and $(x - 1)$ are factors of $f(x)$, find the value of a and the value of b.

Solution

$x + 3$ is a factor.

$\therefore x = -3$ is a root.

$f(-3) = a(-3)^3 + b(-3)^2 - 9$

$\Rightarrow -27a + 9b - 9 = 0$

$-3a + b - 1 = 0$

$-3a + b = 1$

$x - 1$ is a factor.

$\therefore x = 1$ is a root.

$f(1) = a(1)^3 + b(1)^2 - 9$

$a + b - 9 = 0$

$a + b = 9$

We now solve the simultaneous equations.

$-3a + b = 1$

$a + b = 9$

As the b's are the same sign, we will subtract:

$-3a + b = 1$

$\underline{-a - b = -9}$

$-4a = -8$

$\therefore a = 2$

$a + b = 9$

$2 + b = 9$

$\therefore b = 7$

Using a Graph to Estimate a Polynomial

> A polynomial $f(x)$ has a factor $(x - a)$ if and only if its graph touches or crosses the x-axis at $x = a$ ($a \in R$).

For example, the polynomial
$y = x^4 + 6x^3 - 13x^2 - 66x + 72$ has the following factors and, hence, roots:

Factors: $x + 6$ $x + 4$ $x - 1$ $x - 3$

Roots: $x = -6$ $x = -4$ $x = 1$ $x = 3$

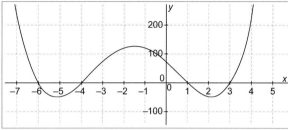

By graphing this polynomial, we notice that at a root (or zero), the graph will either cross or touch the x-axis.

- The values of x for which $f(x) = 0$ are called the **roots** or **zeros** of the function.
- The **degree** of a polynomial is the highest power within the polynomial.
- The maximum number of distinct roots a polynomial can have is the same as its **degree**.
- The **leading coefficient** of a polynomial is the coefficient of the term with the highest power.

Example: $f(x) = x^3 - 5x^2 + 7x - 11$ Degree is 3; leading coefficient is 1.

A polynomial may have a factor or root that occurs multiple times. This is called **multiplicity**.

For example, $(x - 2)^2$ is a factor of the polynomial
$y = x^5 - 2x^4 - 23x^3 + 64x^2 + 4x - 80$.

$\therefore x = 2$ is a root that has a multiplicity 2.

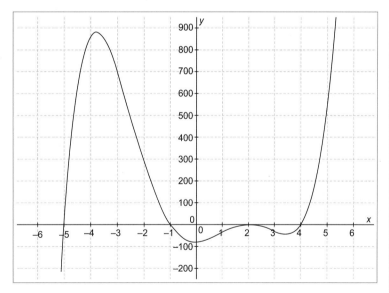

Consider a polynomial which has a factor of $(x - a)^n$ ($a \in R$, $n \in N$).

If n is an even number, the graph of the polynomial touches the x-axis at $x = a$ but does not cross the x-axis here.

The x-axis is a tangent to the graph at the point (a,0).

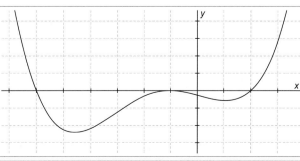

If *n* is an odd number, the graph of the polynomial crosses the *x*-axis at $x = a$.

If a polynomial has a factor with an odd multiplicity greater than 1, the graph appears to flatten out before and after $x = a$.

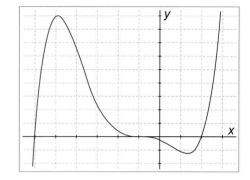

To determine the general shape of a polynomial, we consider the polynomial's **end behaviour**. The end behaviour is how the function's graph looks as we move further and further in either direction (left/right). The two 'end' pieces of the graph are known as the arms of the graph.

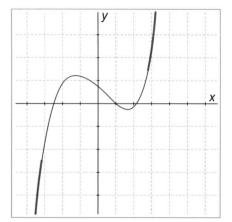

The end behaviour of a polynomial function will always follow these rules:

1. If the polynomial is of **even degree**, then the arms of the graph both point up or both point down.

2. If the polynomial is of **odd degree**, then one arm points up and one points down.

3. If the **leading coefficient is positive**, then the right arm points up.

4. If the **leading coefficient is negative**, then the right arm points down.

ACTIVITIES 3.7, 3.8

Example: $f(x) = x^3 - 6x^2 + 11x - 6$

Degree is 3, which is odd; leading coefficient is 1, which is positive.

∴ The left arm points down and the right arm points up.

x^2 Worked Example 3.19

Find a polynomial of degree 5 whose graph is shown below.

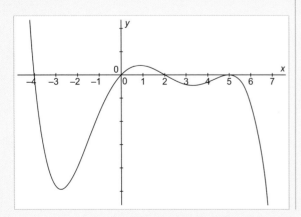

Solution

The polynomial is of degree 5, so it has a maximum of five distinct roots. From the graph, we see that the polynomial touches the *x*-axis at $x = -4, 0, 2$ and 5. Therefore, one root will be repeated.

At $x = 5$, it touches the *x*-axis but does not cross it. Therefore, $(x - 5)^2$ is a factor. $x = 5$ is the repeated root.

Both $x = 0$ and $-x = 0$ are possible roots of this polynomial. Two possible polynomials are:

$$x(x + 4)(x - 2)(x - 5)^2 \quad \textbf{OR} \quad (-x)(x + 4)(x - 2)(x - 5)^2$$

We now test which polynomial will correctly describe the end behaviour of the graph. In this example, we will pick $x = 6$. From our graph, we know that when $x > 5$, the graph (y-value) is negative.

x	Polynomial	$= y$	y-value (positive/negative)
6	$x(x + 4)(x - 2)(x - 5)^2$	$6(6 + 4)(6 - 2)(6 - 5)^2 = 240$	+
6	$(-x)(x + 4)(x - 2)(x - 5)^2$	$(-6)(6 + 4)(6 - 2)(6 - 5)^2 = -240$	−

$\therefore (-x)(x + 4)(x - 2)(x - 5)^2$ is a possible answer.

Alternatively, from inspection of the graph, we can see that the right arm points down. So the leading coefficient must be negative.

$\therefore (-x)(x + 4)(x - 2)(x - 5)^2$ is a possible answer.

x^2 Worked Example 3.20

Sketch a graph of a polynomial $y = x(x + 3)(x - 2)^2(x - 4)$.

Solution

Factors: x $x + 3$ $x - 2$ $x - 4$ } The roots or zeros of the equation are $x = -3, 0, 2$ and 4. However, a **multiple root** occurs at $x = 2$.

Roots: $x = 0$ $x = -3$ $x = 2$ $x = 4$

$\therefore$ The graph of the polynomial crosses the x-axis at $x = -3$, 0 and 4. It touches the x-axis at $x = 2$ but does not cross it. We can mark these points in on our sketch.

We next need to find the general shape of the graph.

The degree of the polynomial is 5, i.e. it has five factors – remember that $(x - 2)$ occurs twice. 5 is an odd number. This means one arm points up and one arm points down. The leading coefficient is 1 (a positive number), so the right arm points up.

Alternatively, we can substitute into the polynomial an x-value to determine the end behaviour of the graph. The smallest x-intercept occurs at $x = -3$; therefore, we test an x-value less than -3. Let us test for $x = -4$.

x	Polynomial	$= y$	y-value (positive/negative)
-4	$-4(-4 + 3)(-4 - 2)^2(-4 - 4)$	$-1{,}152$	Negative

As the y-value is negative, we start the graph on the left-hand side from below the y-axis.

Using either of the above approaches, we can then graph the polynomial.

Remember: when sketching, we are looking for the general shape of the graph and where the graph crosses or touches the x-axis.

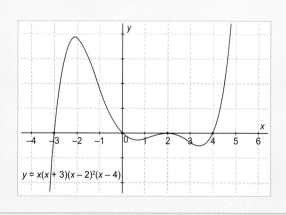

$y = x(x + 3)(x - 2)^2(x - 4)$

ALGEBRA II

Exercise 3.6

ALGEBRA II

1. Show that $x - 1$ is a factor of $x^3 - 2x^2 - 5x + 6$ and find the two other factors.

2. Show that $x + 3$ is a factor of $x^4 + 2x^3 - 25x^2 - 26x + 120$ and find the other factors.

3. Show that $x = 5$ is a root of the equation $4x^3 - 32x^2 + 68x - 40 = 0$ and, hence, find the other roots.

4. Show that $x = -4$ is a root of the equation $2x^3 - 7x^2 - 42x + 72 = 0$ and, hence, find the other roots.

5. Show that $x = 5$ is a root of the equation $6x^4 - 19x^3 - 56x^2 - x + 30 = 0$ and, hence, find the other roots.

6. Show that $x = \frac{1}{2}$ is a root of the equation $32x^4 - 8x^3 - 52x^2 + 42x - 9 = 0$ and, hence, find the other roots.

7. Show that $x = 3$ is a root of the equation $x^5 - 10x^4 + 35x^3 - 50x^2 + 24x = 0$ and, hence, find the other roots.

8. Write in the form $ax^3 + bx^2 + cx + d = 0$ an equation with the roots:

   (i) $-1, 2, 5$

   (ii) $3, \frac{1}{2}, -7$

   (iii) $1, -1, -\frac{1}{3}$

   (iv) $0, 5, -2$

   (v) $1, 1, 1$

9. Solve the following cubic equations:

   (i) $x^3 - 6x^2 + 11x - 6 = 0$

   (ii) $3x^3 - 19x^2 + 33x = 9$

   (iii) $x^3 - 9x^2 + 16x + 16 = 0$

   (iv) $2x^3 - 9x^2 + 2x + 21 = 0$

   (v) $x^3 - 19x - 30 = 0$

10. Solve the following equations:

    (i) $2x^4 + 12x^3 - 2x^2 - 108x - 144 = 0$

    (ii) $6x^5 - 17x^4 - 19x^3 + 27x^2 + 13x - 10 = 0$

    (iii) $x^4 - 8x^3 + 13x^2 + 10x - 12 = 0$

11. Write down a polynomial function for each of the given graphs.

    (i) Polynomial of degree 3

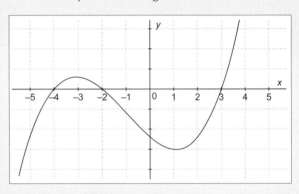

    (ii) Polynomial of degree 4

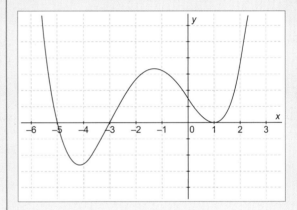

    (iii) Polynomial of degree 5

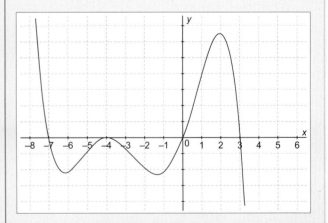

(iv) Polynomial of degree 7

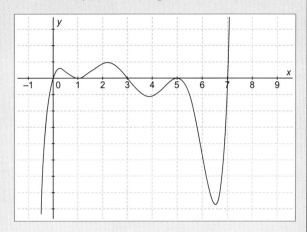

(v) Polynomial of degree 6

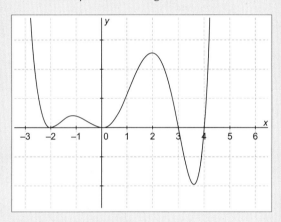

(vi) Polynomial of degree 7

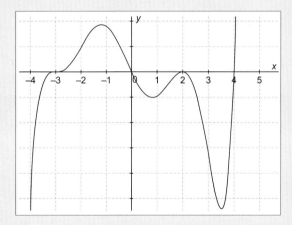

12. Sketch a graph of the following polynomials:

   (i) $(x + 3)(x + 1)(x - 2)(x - 5)(x - 6)$

   (ii) $(x + 2)(x - 1)^2(x - 4)$

   (iii) $-x(x + 4)(x - 2)(x - 3)^2$

   (iv) $x(x + 7)^2(x + 4)(x - 2)^2$

   (v) $x^2(x - 5)(x + 2)(x + 3)$

   (vi) $x^2(x - 2)^3$

   (vii) $-x(x + 3)(x + 4)^2$

13. The graph of the polynomial
$2x^4 - 6x^3 - 65x^2 + 120x + 225$ is shown.

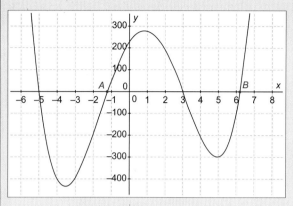

Find, correct to three decimal places, the non-integer roots of this polynomial.

14. Find all the roots of the polynomial
$x^5 - 12x^4 - 40x^3 + 120x^2 = 0$. Hence, draw a sketch of this polynomial.

15. If $(x - 4)$ is a factor of $x^3 - 2x^2 - 11x + k$, find the value of k.

16. Form an equation whose roots are
$(2 - \sqrt{3})$, $(2 + \sqrt{3})$ and 3.

17. $(x + 1)$ is a factor of $2x^3 + kx^2 - 10x - 3k$, $k \in R$. Find the value of k and the two other factors.

18. If $(x - 3)$ and $(x - 5)$ are factors of
$x^3 - 7x^2 + ax + b = 0$, find the value of a and the value of b.

19. If $(x + 2)$ and $(x - 1)$ are factors of
$x^3 - ax^2 - bx + 6 = 0$, find the value of a and the value of b.

20. If $f(x) = px^3 - qx^2 - 36x + 18 = 0$, $f(-3) = 0$ and $f\left(\frac{1}{2}\right) = 0$, find the value of p and the value of q.

21. $x^2 - 4x - 12$ is a factor of $rx^3 - sx^2 + 36$. Find the value of r and the value of s.

22. If $(x - 1)$, $(x + 3)$ and $(x - 2)$ are factors of
$x^4 + ax^3 - bx^2 + cx - 6 = 0$, find the values of a, b and c.

23. $f(x) = x^3 + ax^2 + bx + c$ is a cubic function such that $f(3) = 0$, $f(-2) = 0$ and $f(1) = -36$. Solve for a, b and c and, hence, solve $x^3 + ax^2 + bx + c = 0$.

3.7 MANIPULATION OF FORMULAE

The volume of a cylinder is given by the formula $V = \pi r^2 h$.

However, if we wish to find the radius of a cylinder using this formula, we must rearrange or manipulate the formula:

$r = \sqrt{\dfrac{V}{\pi h}}$ $\left(\text{as } r > 0, \text{ we ignore the } r = -\sqrt{\dfrac{V}{\pi h}}\right)$

x^2 Worked Example 3.21

Given that $a = \sqrt{\dfrac{p}{1-q}}$, write q in terms of p and a.

Solution

$a = \sqrt{\dfrac{p}{1-q}}$

Square both sides:

$a^2 = \dfrac{p}{1-q}$

Multiply both sides by $1 - q$:

$a^2(1-q) = p$

$a^2 - a^2 q = p$

$a^2 - p = a^2 q$

$\dfrac{a^2 - p}{a^2} = q$ $\left(\text{or } q = 1 - \dfrac{p}{a^2}\right)$

x^2 Worked Example 3.22

Express b in terms of a and c.

$\dfrac{1}{a} = \dfrac{2}{b^2} - \dfrac{3}{c}$

Solution

The LCD is $ab^2 c$.

$ab^2 c \left(\dfrac{1}{a}\right) = ab^2 c \left(\dfrac{2}{b^2}\right) - ab^2 c \left(\dfrac{3}{c}\right)$

$b^2 c = 2ac - 3ab^2$

$b^2 c + 3ab^2 = 2ac$

$b^2(c + 3a) = 2ac$

$b^2 = \dfrac{2ac}{c + 3a}$

$\therefore b = \pm \sqrt{\dfrac{2ac}{c + 3a}}$

Exercise 3.7

In each case, express the variable in the square brackets in terms of the other variables.

1. $a = 3bc - d$ [b]

2. $x = y + 3z$ [z]

3. $2p = \dfrac{q + r}{5}$ [r]

4. $s = \dfrac{a + b + c}{2}$ [c]

5. $a - bc = \dfrac{1}{2}b$ [b]

6. $s = ut + \dfrac{1}{2}at^2$ [u]

7. $\dfrac{1}{u} + \dfrac{1}{v} = \dfrac{1}{f}$ [f]

8. $\sqrt{\dfrac{x}{y}} = z$ [y]

9. $\sqrt{\dfrac{p}{r - q}} = p$ [r]

10. $h = \sqrt{a^2 + b^2}$ [a]

11. $a = b\sqrt{x} + c$ [x]

12. $S = 4\pi r^2$ [r]

13. $T = 2\pi\sqrt{\dfrac{l}{g}}$ [l]

14. $s = pq^2 - r$ [q]

15. $R = \sqrt[3]{ab}$ [a]

16. $v = \sqrt{u^2 + 2as}$ [u]

17. $a = \dfrac{1 - x}{1 + x}$ [x]

18. $p = \dfrac{1}{2}q + \sqrt{r}$ [r]

19. $a = \dfrac{p}{p + b}$ [p]

20. $V = \dfrac{1}{3}\pi r^2 h$ [r]

21. $a + b^3 = \dfrac{c}{d}$ [b]

3.8 UNKNOWN COEFFICIENTS

$x^2 = 9$ is an equation. There are only two values of x where x^2 will be equal to 9: $x = 3$ or $x = -3$.
$(x - 1)^2 = x^2 - 2x + 1$ is an identity. It is true for all values of $x \in R$. This is because the LHS will always be equal to the RHS. We can use this property of identities to find the value of unknown coefficients.

x^2 Worked Example 3.23

If $c(x - a)^2 + b = 3x^2 - 6x + 5$ for all values of x, find the values of $a, b, c \in R$.

Solution

$$c(x - a)^2 + b = 3x^2 - 6x + 5$$
$$c(x^2 - 2ax + a^2) + b = 3x^2 - 6x + 5$$
$$cx^2 - 2acx + a^2c + b = 3x^2 - 6x + 5$$

We can now equate like terms from each side:

x^2 terms	x terms	Constants
$cx^2 = 3x^2$	$-2acx = -6x$	$a^2c + b = 5$
$\therefore c = 3$	$-2ac = -6$	$(1)^2(3) + b = 5$
	$\Rightarrow -2a(3) = -6$	$3 + b = 5$
	$-6a = -6$	$\therefore b = 2$
	$\therefore a = 1$	

x^2 Worked Example 3.24

If $x^2 - ax + b$ is a factor of $x^3 + cx + d$, prove that:

   (i) $b = a^2 + c$ (ii) $d = a^3 + ac$

Solution

$$
\begin{array}{r}
x + a \\
x^2 - ax + b \overline{\big)\, x^3 + 0x^2 + cx + d} \\
-\underline{(x^3 - ax^2 + bx)} \\
ax^2 + (c - b)x + d \\
-\underline{(ax^2 - a^2x + ab)} \\
(c - b + a^2)x + d - ab = 0
\end{array}
$$

Since remainder $= 0$

$\Rightarrow c - b + a^2 = 0$ and $d - ab = 0$

(i) $c - b + a^2 = 0$
$$c + a^2 = b$$
$$\text{So } b = a^2 + c$$

(ii) $d - ab = 0$
$$\Rightarrow d = ab$$
$$d = a(a^2 + c) \quad \text{(from (i))}$$
$$\therefore d = a^3 + ac$$

x^2 Worked Example 3.25

If $x^2 + px + r$ is a factor of $x^3 + 2px^2 + 9x + 2r$, find the value of p and r.

Solution

Let $(x + k)$ be the other factor.

$$(x + k)(x^2 + px + r) = x^3 + 2px^2 + 9x + 2r$$
$$x^3 + px^2 + rx + kx^2 + kpx + kr = x^3 + 2px^2 + 9x + 2r$$
$$x^3 + px^2 + kx^2 + rx + kpx + kr = x^3 + 2px^2 + 9x + 2r$$

ALGEBRA II

We now group the like terms:

x^3 terms	x^2 terms	x terms	Constants
$x^3 = x^3$	$px^2 + kx^2 = 2px^2$	$rx + kpx = 9x$	$kr = 2r$
	$p + k = 2p$	$r + kp = 9$	$\therefore k = 2$
	$\therefore k = p$		

(i) $k = 2$
But $k = p$
$\therefore p = 2$

(ii) $r + kp = 9$
$r + (2)(2) = 9$
$r + 4 = 9$
$\therefore r = 5$

Exercise 3.8

1. If $(x + b)^2 = x^2 + 6x + q$ for all values of x, find the value of b and the value of q.

2. If $(x - 3)(x + 4) = ax^2 + bx + c$ for all values of x, solve for a, b and c.

3. $(y + a)^2 + b = y^2 + 4y + 8$ for all values of y, solve for a and b.

4. $a(x + 3) + b(2x - 5) = 11x - 11$ for all values of x, find the value of a and the value of b.

5. If $(ax - 2)(x - 3) + b = 4x^2 - 14x + 8$ for all values of x, find the value of a and the value of b.

6. If $(x - p)(qx - 4) = 3x^2 - 19x + 20$ for all values of x, solve for p and q.

7. $(x - a)^2 - (x - b)^2 = 12 - 4x$ for all values of x, find the value of a and the value of b.

8. If $a(2x^2 - 5) + b(x - 5) + c = 8x^2 + 2x - 13$ for all values of x, solve for a, b and c.

9. If $y^2 + 2y - 8 = y^2 + (a + b)y + ab$ for all values of y, find the value of a and the value of b.

10. If $a(p + 3) + b(p + 5) = 5p + 21$ for all values of p, find the value of a and the value of b.

11. If $(x + a)^3 = x^3 + px^2 + qx + 64$ for all values of x, solve for p and q.

12. If $a(3x^2 + 1) + (x - 3)(bx + c) = 8x^2 - 3x - 7$ for all values of x, find the values of a, b and c.

13. Given that $p(x + 2)(x + 1) + q(x - 3)(x - 1) + r(x - 2)(x - 6) = 2x^2 + 7x - 13$ for all values of x, find the values of p, q and r.

14. If $(2x - a)^3$ is a factor of $8x^3 - px^2 + qx - 27$ for all values of x, find the value of p and the value of q.

15. If $3x^2 - 11x + r$ is a factor of $3x^3 - 14x^2 + 17x - r$, find the value of r. Hence, solve $3x^3 - 14x^2 + 17x - r = 0$.

16. Find the values of p, q, r, s such that, for all values of x:
$(2x + 5)(px^3 + qx^2 - rx + s)$
$= 4x^4 + 20x^3 + 19x^2 - 13x + 5$

17. Given that
$(ax + b)(2x^2 - 5x + 1) = 6x^3 - 5x^2 - cx + 5$ for all values of x, find the values of a, b and c.

18. If $(x + p)^2 = x^2 + ax + b$ for all values of x, show that:

(i) $p = \dfrac{a}{2}$ (ii) $b = \dfrac{a^2}{4}$

19. If $a[(y + b)^2 - c] = 2y^2 + 4y - 5$ for all values of y, find the values of a, b and c.

20. $(x - 3)$ and $(x + 4)$ are factors of $x^3 + ax^2 + bx + c$.

(i) Express b in terms of a.

(ii) Express c in terms of b.

21. $x^2 - ax + 2$ is a factor of $x^3 - x^2 + 5ax - b$. Express a in terms of b.

22. Verify that $x = a$ is always a solution of the equation $3x^4 - 3ax^3 + 2ax^2 - 2a^2x = 0$. Hence, find the other roots of the equation in terms of a.

23. If $x^2 + ax - b$ is a factor of $x^3 - 2bx^2 + ax - 6$, show that $a = -2b - \dfrac{6}{b}$.

ALGEBRA II

24. One of the factors of $px^3 + qx^2 + rx + s = 0$ is $x - a$. Another factor is $x + a$. Show that:

(i) $a^2 = -\dfrac{s}{q}$ (ii) $ps = qr$ (iii) $p = -\dfrac{r}{a^2}$

25. Verify that $x = p$ is always a solution of the equation $x^4 - 2px^3 + (2p^2 - 1)x^2 - p(p^2 - 1)x = 0$. Hence, find the other roots of the equation in terms of p.

26. If $x^2 + 5x + c = x^2 + (a + b)x + ab$ for all values of x, show that $a = b$ or $a = 5 - b$.

27. Given that
$4x^2 - 16x + 15 = prx^2 + (ps + qr)x + qs$,
show that $p = -\dfrac{2}{3}q$ or $-\dfrac{2}{5}q$.

28. If $x^2 + px + q$ is a factor of $x^3 + ax^2 + b$, prove that:

(i) $b = q(a - p)$ (iii) $q^2 + bp = 0$

(ii) $q = p(p - a)$

29. Verify that $x = r$ is always a solution of the equation $x^4 - (4r - 1)x^3 - (3r - 3r^2)x^2 + 2r^2x = 0$. Hence, find the other roots of the equation in terms of r.

30. If $x^2 - px + 1$ is a factor of $ax^3 + bx + c$, prove that:

(i) $c = ap$ (iii) $c^2 = a(a - b)$

(ii) $b - a = -ap^2$

3.9 PROBLEM-SOLVING USING ALGEBRA

x^2 Worked Example 3.26

A manufacturer produces a calculator that sells for €12. It costs €x to manufacture each calculator.

(i) Write an expression to show the profit per calculator.

The manufacturer must sell $50 - x$ of these calculators per day to achieve a daily profit of €215.

(ii) Find the total cost of producing the required number of calculators.

Solution

(i) Profit per calculator = Selling price − cost price
$$= €(12 - x)$$

(ii) Daily profit of €215 = Profit per calculator × number of calculators sold
$$= (12 - x)(50 - x)$$
$$\therefore (12 - x)(50 - x) = 215$$
$$600 - 12x - 50x + x^2 = 215$$
$$x^2 - 62x + 385 = 0$$
$$(x - 7)(x - 55) = 0$$
$$x - 7 = 0 \ \textbf{OR} \ \ x - 55 = 0$$
$$x = 7 \ \textbf{OR} \qquad x = 55$$

> Double check your work in context questions, as you may need to reject an answer due to the nature of the question.

Check both solutions:

■ If $x = 55$, then $50 - x = -5$. It is not possible to sell −5 calculators. Therefore, reject $x = 55$.

■ $x = 7$ is acceptable, as $50 - x = 43$ and it is possible to sell 43 calculators.

$\therefore$ Cost per calculator = €7

The total cost of producing the required number of calculators

= Cost per calculator × number of calculators sold

= 7 × 43

= €301

x^2 Worked Example 3.27

Seán requires an alloy of metal that is 30% copper. He has 50 g of an alloy that is 20% copper. Let x be the amount of an alloy that is 70% copper which Seán will mix with all of the 20% alloy to produce the 30% copper alloy.

Find the value of x.

Solution

We can now write an equation for the amount of copper alloy:

$$0.2(50) + 0.7(x) = 0.3(50 + x)$$
$$10 + 0.7x = 15 + 0.3x$$
$$0.4x = 5$$
$$x = 12.5 \text{ g}$$

Copper (%)	Mass (g)	Amount of copper in alloy
0.2	50	0.2(50)
0.7	x	0.7(x)
0.3	50 + x	0.3(50 + x)

∴ 12.5 g of the 70% copper alloy must be added.

Exercise 3.9

ALGEBRA II

1. A small bag of cement weighs x kg. A large bag of cement is four times as heavy as the small bag. A medium bag of cement is 5 kg lighter than the large bag. Two small bags plus a heavy bag of cement weigh the same as two medium bags.

How much does each type of bag of cement weigh?

2. A company's formula for its production costs is: Cost (€) = 200 + 4x, where x is the number of units produced. Determine the cost if:

(i) No units are produced.

(ii) 3,000 units are produced.

If the company spends €5,000 on production, how many units are produced?

3. Karl's and Eddie's ages added together are equal to 65. Ten years ago, Karl was twice as old as Eddie. How old are they now?

4. Paul is offered two different sale contracts in a goods company. The first contract has a salary of €25,000 per year with an end-of-year commission of 2% of total sales. The other contract offers a salary of €20,000 with a 3% end-of-year commission.

(i) How much would Paul have to sell in order for him to earn him the same amount of money under each contract?

(ii) Paul expects to sell €700,000 worth of goods. Which contract should he take?

5. Two cars leave a town at the same time but travelling in opposite directions. Car A travels at a speed of 50 km/hr and car B travels at a speed of 70 km/hr. How long will it take for the cars to be 200 km apart?

6. Catherine has €3,000 to invest. She invests a sum of money at 9% per annum and the rest at 5% per annum. If the return on the higher interest rate is €95 more than the lower rate, how much did she invest at each rate?

7. A metal alloy is 30% nickel. Another metal alloy is 70% nickel. The two alloys are mixed to produce 20 kg of a metal alloy that is 48% nickel. How much of each metal alloy is used?

8. The relationship between degrees Fahrenheit (F) and degrees Celsius (C) is given by the formula $F = \frac{9}{5}C + 32$.

(i) At what temperature will degrees Fahrenheit and degrees Celsius be the same?

Find, to the nearest degree:

(ii) The temperature at which degrees Celsius will be twice degrees Fahrenheit

(iii) The temperature at which degrees Fahrenheit will be twice degrees Celsius

9. The first two sections of a bicycle race are x and y metres long. Annie cycles the first part of the race at 6 m/s and the second part at 12 m/s. Barry cycles the same sections at 10 m/s and 6 m/s. It takes Annie half a minute to cycle these two sections, whereas it takes Barry 46 seconds to cover the same distance.

   How long are these two sections of the race?

10. When the two digits of a two-digit number are added together, the answer is 12. The two-digit number obtained by swapping the digits around is 18 more than the original number. Find the two digits.

11. A cinema contains 315 seats. It has x numbers of rows with an equal number of seats in each row. Six rows of seats are removed to create a fire escape. To ensure the same capacity, the number of seats per row must be increased by six.

   How many rows of seats did the cinema originally have?

12. The longest side of a right-angled triangle is 31 m. Find the lengths of the other two sides, given that one of these sides is 5 m longer than the other side. Give your answers correct to the nearest centimetre.

13. The linear path of a ship is given by the equation $2x + y = 6$. The boundary of a reef is represented by the equation $x^2 + y^2 = 17$.

   At what two points will the ship cross the boundary of the reef?

14. Harry takes 2 hours less to travel 50 km than Cara takes to travel 35 km. Cara travels at a speed that is 5 km/hr slower than that of Harry. Find the time taken by Harry and Cara to complete their respective journeys and the speed at which they each travelled.

15. The sum of the digits of a three-digit number is 16. The second digit in the number is three times the third digit. The three-digit number obtained by reversing the order of the digits is 594 less than the original number. Find the three digits.

16. A shop sells 30 LCD televisions per month at €350 each. A computer model suggests that for every €25 drop in price, two more televisions would be sold per month.

Let x represent the number of €25 drops in price.

   (i) Write down an expression for the suggested price.

   (ii) Write down an expression for the number sold.

   (iii) Hence, what price should the televisions be sold at to ensure that the shop achieves a sales target of €9,000 per month?

17. Working together, Peter and Simon can build a wall in four hours. It would take Peter 15 hours more to build the wall than Simon. How long would it take Peter and Simon to build the wall if working alone?

18. The linear flight path of a plane is give by the equation $x + y = -3$. The airspace boundary of a certain city is given by the equation $x^2 + y^2 = 17$.

   (i) At which two points does the flight of this plane cross the boundary of the airspace of the city?

The airplane control tower is situated at the point (0,0). The point (–5,1) is 5 km west and 1 km north of the tower.

   (ii) Give the co-ordinates of each point of intersection as kilometres east/west and kilometres north/south.

   (iii) How far are these two points from the tower? Give your answer to three significant figures.

19. The price of gold is approximately €40/g. The price of silver is approximately €800/kg. A jeweller wishes to produce 20 g of a gold–silver alloy (mixture) worth €15/g.

   (i) Write an equation that represents this alloy.

   (ii) Find to two decimal places the number of grams of gold and silver used in the alloy.

20. Two taps running together take 6 minutes to fill a bath. The hot tap, working by itself, takes 100 seconds longer to fill the bath than the cold tap working by itself. To the nearest second, how long would it take each tap to fill the bath by itself?

21. A landlord rents out 30 apartments. The monthly rent of each apartment is €750. For each €75 increase in rent, the landlord expects to lose one tenant.

Let x represent each €75 increase in the rent.

Calculate the monthly rent needed to ensure that the landlord makes €30,000 in rent per month.

22. The minimum speed formula is used by police to calculate the minimum velocity at which a car is travelling by measuring the tyre marks formed by the car skidding to a stop. The formula assumes that the car stops at the end of the skid.

$V_0 = \sqrt{19.6\,\mu d}$, where V_0 = minimum velocity in m/s, μ = coefficient of friction and d = distance of the skid marks in metres.

(a) Calculate the minimum speed for the following tyre skid marks:

   (i) 30 m on a wet road ($\mu = 0.6$)

   (ii) 40 m on a dry road ($\mu = 0.8$)

(b) (i) Explain how doubling the distance of the skid marks affects the minimum velocity (assume that the coefficient of friction is constant).

   (ii) Derive a formula that will find the length of the tyre skid marks when given the velocity and coefficient of friction.

(c) A car on old tyres is travelling at a velocity of 90 km/hr on a wet road ($\mu = 0.4$). The driver slams on the brakes and skids to a halt. Find the approximate length of the tyre skid marks expected at this speed.

23. A company produces an algebraic model that accurately predicts the number of units sold per month of a seasonal item for a certain period in time.

$$y = -x^4 + 11x^3 - 39x^2 + 45x$$

where y is the number of units (in thousands) sold per month and x is the time in months.

(a) Calculate the number of units sold per month at:

   (i) 1 month   (ii) 4 months

(b) The company knows that this model is accurate for only a few months before it becomes unreliable. By sketching this equation, explain at what time this occurs and why.

24. The formula for the approximate velocity (V) of sound in metres per second in dry air at a temperature of $T\,°C$ is given by the following formula:

$$V = 331\sqrt{1 + \frac{T}{273}}$$

(i) Find the velocity of sound when the temperature is 30°C (answer to two decimal places).

(ii) Derive a formula which shows the temperature T when given the velocity V of the sound.

(iii) Use this formula to find the temperature to the nearest degree, if the velocity of sound is 1,200 km/hr.

(iv) The formula to convert degrees Celsius into degrees Fahrenheit is given by the formula $F = \frac{9}{5}C + 32$.

Find the velocity of sound at a temperature of 150° F (to the nearest metre per second).

Revision Exercises

1. (a) Solve the following equations:

   (i) $5x - 3y - 11 = 0$

      $3x + 10y + 17 = 0$

   (ii) $x + 3(y - 1) = 5$

      $5x + 13 - y = 5$

   (iii) $\dfrac{x + y}{5} + \dfrac{y - x}{2} = 5$

      $\dfrac{x + 2y}{9} = 2$

   (iv) $5x - 12y - 17 = 0$

      $\dfrac{1}{9}(x + 2) - (y + 1) + \dfrac{3}{2} = 0$

(b) Solve:

    (i) $4x^2 - 4x + 1 = 0$

    (ii) $4x^2 - 9 = 0$

    (iii) $\dfrac{1}{2}x^2 - \dfrac{5}{2}x - 12 = 0$

    (iv) $4x^2 - 3x - 1 = 0$

    (v) $\dfrac{1}{x-3} + \dfrac{1}{2x-1} = \dfrac{1}{2}$

(c) Solve:

    (i) $x + y + z = 1$

       $2x + 3y + z = 4$

       $4x + 9y + z = 16$

    (ii) $2x + y + z + 7 = 0$

       $x + 2y + z + 8 = 0$

       $x + y + 2z + 9 = 0$

    (iii) $x + y = z$

       $x + z = 11$

       $y + z = 7$

    (iv) $\dfrac{2x}{5} + \dfrac{y}{8} + z = \dfrac{5}{2}$

       $\dfrac{x+1}{3} - \dfrac{y}{2} - 4z = 0$

       $\dfrac{x+y+z}{2} = 1$

2. (a) Solve the following quadratic equations to two decimal places:

    (i) $2x^2 - 5x - 9 = 0$

    (ii) $5x^2 - 12x + 5 = 0$

    (iii) $\dfrac{1}{x} - \dfrac{1}{x-5} = \dfrac{2}{x-1}$

    (iv) $\dfrac{1}{x} = \dfrac{2}{2x-5} - \dfrac{1}{x+2}$

(b) (i) Solve $x^2 - 15x + 56 = 0$ and, hence, solve:

$$\left(y + \frac{10}{y}\right)^2 - 15\left(y + \frac{10}{y}\right) + 56 = 0$$

    (ii) Solve $4x^2 - 23x + 15 = 0$.

    Hence, solve:
    $4(y^2 + y)^2 - 23(y^2 + y) + 15 = 0$

    (iii) Solve $x^2 - 6x - 2 = 0$, giving your answer in the form $a \pm \sqrt{b}$, where $a, b \in N$. Hence, solve $(t + 3)^2 - 6(t + 3) - 2 = 0$.

(c) Solve for x and y:

    (i) $2x + y = 7$

       $xy = 3$

    (ii) $x - y = 1$

       $x^2 + y^2 = 5$

    (iii) $x - y = 0$

       $x^2 + y^2 - 3x + y - 12 = 0$

    (iv) $5x - 2y = 3$

       $x^2 + y^2 - 2xy = 0$

    (v) $\dfrac{1}{2}(x + y) = \dfrac{5}{2}$

       $xy + 6 = 3x + 2y$

3. (a) In each case, express the variable in the square brackets in terms of the other variables.

    (i) $a = b - \dfrac{1}{2}c$ $[c]$

    (ii) $a = b + c(d + 5)$ $[c]$

    (iii) $pq + pr = q$ $[p]$

    (iv) $A = \pi r l + 2\pi r h$ $[r]$

    (v) $y = \sqrt{\dfrac{ax^2}{1-r}}$ $[x]$

    (vi) $x = \dfrac{y^3 + 1}{y^3 - 3}$ $[y]$

(b) (i) If $(x + a)^2 + b = x^2 + 8x + 11$ for all values of x, find the values of $a, b \in R$.

    (ii) If $(x + p)^2 - q = x^2 - 4x - 10$, for all values of x, find p and q.

    (iii) If $2x^2 + 7x + 10 = p(x + q)^2 + r$ for all values of x, find the values of $p, q, r \in Q$.

(c) (i) If $(x - 3)$ is factor of $3x^3 - 2x^2 + kx - 6$, find the other two factors.

    (ii) $(x - 2)$ and $(x + 2)$ are factors of $x^3 + 7x^2 + ax + b$. Find the value of a and the value of b and, hence, find the third factor.

    (iii) $f(x)$ is a cubic function with roots 2, –1 and k. If $f(3) + 5 f(0) = 0$, find the value of k.

4. (a) Solve the following equations:

    (i) $x^3 - 3x^2 - 6x + 8 = 0$

    (ii) $2x^3 + 5x^2 - 4x - 12 = 0$

    (iii) $x^4 - x^3 - 15x^2 - 23x - 10 = 0$

    (iv) $6x^4 + 7x^3 - 59x^2 - 63x + 45 = 0$

    (v) $2x^5 - 5x^4 - 12x^3 + 30x^2 + 10x - 25 = 0$

(b) Sketch a graph of the following polynomials:

(i) $(x + 4)(x + 1)(x - 2)(x - 5)^2$

(ii) $x(x + 2)(x - 3)^2(x - 6)^2$

(iii) $-x(x + 1)^2(x + 4)^2(x - 3)$

(iv) $x(x + 8)^2(x + 3)(x - 2)^2$

(v) $-x^3(x - 3)(x - 5)^2$

(c) The graphs of a linear, a quadratic and a cubic function are shown.

(i) Write down the points of intersection marked.

(ii) Interpret the significance of each point (note that there may be more than one interpretation).

(iii) Find the equation of the line shown. Also, write down a functional form for both the quadratic and the cubic graphs shown.

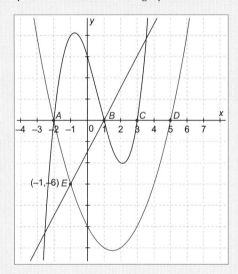

5. (a) Find a functional form for each of the following polynomials:

(i) Polynomial of degree 5

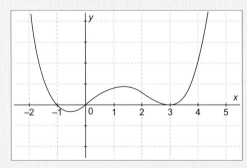

(ii) Polynomial of degree 5

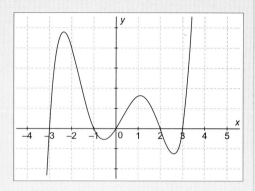

(iii) Polynomial of degree 6

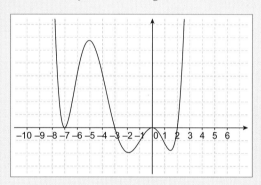

(iv) Polynomial of degree 7

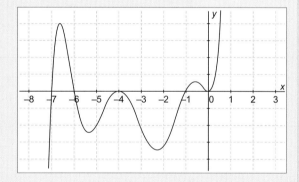

(v) Polynomial of degree 7

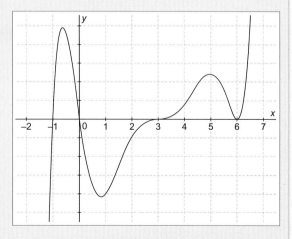

(b) Using the same axes and scales, graph $f(x) = x^3 + 7x^2 + 14x + 8$ and $g(x) = x^2 + 5x + 6$ between $x = -5$ and $x = 1$.

    (i) Mark the points of intersection of the two graphs.

    (ii) What do these points of intersection signify?

    (iii) Use another solving method to confirm your answer from part (i).

(c) If $x^2 + ax + b$ is a factor of $x^3 + 3ax^2 + c$, prove that $b + 2a^2 = 0$ and that $c + 4a^3 = 0$.

6. (a)   (i) The volume of a frustum of a cone is given by the following formula:

$$V = \frac{1}{3}\pi h\{R^2 + Rr + r^2\}$$

Find the height of the frustum if $V = 33 \text{ cm}^3$, $R = 2$ cm, $r = 1$ and $\pi = \frac{22}{7}$.

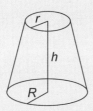

    (ii) The amount earned (F) after investing P for t years at a rate of interest (i) is given by the formula: $A = P(1+i)^t$.

Find the rate of interest if $P = €4,500$, $t = 3$ years and $A = €6,000$.

(b) Given that $(x + 2)$ is a factor of $x^3 + tx^2 + 3x - 10$, find the value of t and the solutions of the equation $x^3 + tx^2 + 3x - 10 = 0$.

(c) The diagram shows two squares. The sum of their areas is 58 m^2. The sum of the lengths of their sides is 10 m. Find the values of x and y, as shown. ($y > x$)

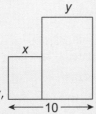

7. (a) One-third of a number is four more than one-half of another number. The first number is one more than twice the second. Find the two numbers.

(b) A quadratic equation has the roots p and $4p$. Form a quadratic equation with these roots.

(c) If $x^2 + px + q$ is a factor of $x^3 + ax^2 + bx + c$, prove that:

    (i) $b - q = p(a - p)$

    (ii) $c = q(a - p)$

8. (a) Write $\dfrac{1}{x + 2} - \dfrac{q}{2x - 1}$ as a single fraction and, hence, solve:

$$\frac{1}{x + 2} - \frac{1}{2x - 1} = \frac{1}{2x^2 + 3x - 2}$$

(b) If $(x + a)^3 + bx^2 + cx = x^3 - 8$ for all values of x, find the values of the real numbers a, b, c.

(c) $f(x) = x^3 + ax + b$ is a function such that $f(2) = 0$ and $f(3) = -20$. Solve for a and b and, hence, solve $f(x) = 0$.

9. (a) The perimeter of this right-angled triangle is 60 units.

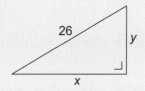

    (i) Write down two equations in x and y.

    (ii) Find the values of x and y, given that $x > y$.

(b) If $x^2 + ax + b$ is a factor of $x^3 + cx + d$, prove that:

    (i) $d + ab = 0$ (ii) $a^2 = b - c$

(c) (i) Show that, if $f(x) = ax^2 + bx + c$ and if $f(k) = 0$, then $(x - k)$ is a factor of $f(x)$.

    (ii) Find a quadratic function with roots $3 + \sqrt{7}$ and $3 - \sqrt{7}$.

    (iii) Find a cubic equation with roots $3 + \sqrt{7}$, $3 - \sqrt{7}$ and -1.

10. (a) If $x^2 - x - 2$ is a factor of $3x^3 + ax^2 - 10x + b$, find the value of a and the value of b.

(b) If $(x + a)^2$ is a factor of $x^3 + 6px + k$, show that:

    (i) $k + 2a^3 = 0$ (iii) $k^2 + 32p^3 = 0$

    (ii) $a^2 + 2p = 0$

(c) (i) Show that if f(x) = $ax^3 + bx^2 + cx + d$ and if $f(k) = 0$, then $(x - k)$ is a factor of f(x).

(ii) The roots of a cubic function g(x) are −1, 3 and k.
If $7g(0) + 3g(2) = 0$, find the value of k.

11. (a) 3n is an odd natural number. The product of this number and the next consecutive odd number is 483.
Find the two consecutive odd natural numbers.

(b) Fiona travels by train from town A to town B at a speed of 85 km/hr. At the same time, Gerry travels by train from town B to town A at a speed of 65 km/hr. If the two towns are 100 km apart:

(i) How long will it take before the trains meet?

(ii) How far will each train have travelled?

(c) The linear path of a comet is given by the equation $x - 2y = 4$. The orbit of a planet around a star is represented by the equation $x^2 + y^2 = 25$. This planet orbits the star at an average distance of 450 million km.

The star is situated at the point (0,0). A satellite orbits this star and is represented by the equation $3x^2 + 10y^2 = 150$.

If the comet, planet and satellite all orbit the sun in the same plane, at what distances from the star will the comet cross the orbits of the planet and the satellite?

12. (a) A pet shop has rabbits and guinea pigs for sale. They have 30 in total for sale. They sell four rabbits. Two guinea pigs are also sold. The shop now has twice as many guinea pigs as rabbits. How many of each type did the shop start with?

(b) A restaurant bill that comes to €200 is to be divided equally among a group of people. However, three people leave before the bill is settled and the remainder of the group have to pay an extra €15 each.

How many people were originally in the group?

(c) The formula $s = \frac{1}{2}gt^2$ represents the distance (s) in metres a free-falling object falls from rest in a given time (t) in seconds. The gravitational acceleration (g) is the acceleration of an object caused by gravity and is measured in m/s².

(i) Express g in terms of s and t.

(ii) A free-falling object takes 3.5 seconds to fall 60 m from rest on Earth. Find the value of g for Earth.

(iii) The gravitational acceleration (g) value for the moon is $\frac{1}{6}$ that of the Earth. Find how long it would take an object to fall 30 m from rest on the moon's surface.

13. Gold jewellery is made from a gold alloy – that is, a mixture of pure gold and other metals. The purity of the material is measured by its 'carat rating', given by the formula

$$c = \frac{24m_g}{m_t}$$

where c = carat rating, m_g = mass of gold in the material and m_t = total mass of the material.

A jeweller is recycling old gold jewellery. He has the following old jewellery in stock:

■ 147 g of 9-carat gold   ■ 85 g of 18-carat gold

He can melt down this old jewellery and mix it in various proportions to make new jewellery of different carat values. The value of the old jewellery is equal to the value of its gold content only. Gold is valued at €36 per gram.

(a) What is the total value of the jeweller's stock of old jewellery?

(b) The jeweller wants to make a 15-carat gold pendant weighing 21 g. He melts down some 9-carat gold and some 18-carat gold to do this. How many grams of each should he use in order to get the 21 g of 15-carat gold?

(c) The other metals in the gold alloy are copper and silver. The colour of the alloy depends on the ratio of copper to silver. In all of the old jewellery, the amount of silver is equal to the amount of copper. The jeweller has a stock of pure silver that he can add to any mixture. He wants to make an item that:

■ Weighs 48 g   ■   Is of 15-carat gold purity   ■   Has twice as much silver as copper

(i) How many grams of copper will this item contain?

(ii) How many grams of each type of stock (9-carat gold, 18-carat gold, and pure silver) should the jeweller use in order to make this item?

(d) A large jewellery business makes and sells 14-carat gold wedding rings, weighing an average of 5 g each. The cost of producing each ring is €135 plus the value of the gold. The manager has noted that the more they charge for the rings, the fewer they sell. In particular:

■ If they charge €200, they sell an average of 20 per month.

■ For each additional €20 charged, the number sold drops by one per month.

(i) Taking the price charged as €(200 + 20x), find an expression in x for the monthly profit from these rings.

(ii) Find the range of selling prices for which the monthly profit is at least €1,600.

SEC Project Maths Paper 1,
Leaving Certificate Higher Level, 2011

Algebra III

Learning Outcomes

In this chapter you will learn to:

- Solve equations containing surds
- Find solutions to inequalities of the following forms:
    - Linear
    - Quadratic
    - Rational
- Understand absolute value (modulus) and use its notation, $|x|$
- Find solutions to modulus inequalities
- Use discriminants to determine the nature of roots of quadratic equations
- Prove algebraic inequalities

4.1 SURD EQUATIONS

$\sqrt{a}$ is called a surd if it cannot be written as a rational number.

In this section we will deal with equations that contain surds. These are often referred to as irrational equations.

When solving irrational equations, it is important that we check our answer, as an incorrect solution can sometimes be generated as a result of squaring.

YOU SHOULD REMEMBER...

■ How to solve equations

■ How to solve inequalities

■ How to work with surds

KEY WORDS

■ Surd

■ Square

■ Inequality

■ Linear

■ Quadratic

■ Rational modulus

■ Discriminant

x^2 Worked Example 4.1

(i) Solve $\sqrt{x + 1} = 5$. (ii) Solve $\sqrt{x + 2} = x - 4$.

Solution

Square **both sides** to eliminate the square root.

$(\sqrt{x + 1})^2 = 5^2$

$\Rightarrow x + 1 = 25$

$\therefore x = 24$

Check:

$\sqrt{24 + 1} = \sqrt{25} = 5$ ✔

$(\sqrt{x + 2})^2 = (x - 4)^2$

$x + 2 = x^2 - 8x + 16$

$x^2 - 9x + 14 = 0$

$(x - 7)(x - 2) = 0$

$x = 7$ **OR** $x = 2$

Check: $\sqrt{7 + 2} = 7 - 4$ $\qquad$ $\sqrt{2 + 2} = 2 - 4$

$\qquad\qquad \sqrt{9} = 3$ ✔ $\qquad\qquad \sqrt{4} = -2$ ✖

Note: $\sqrt{}$ means 'the positive square root of'.

$\therefore x = 7$ is the only solution.

x^2 Worked Example 4.2

Solve $\sqrt{x + 12} - 2 = 2x - 6$.

Solution

We leave our surd term on one side of the equation and every other term on the other side.

$\sqrt{x + 12} = 2x - 4$

$(\sqrt{x + 12})^2 = (2x - 4)^2$ $\quad$ Square both sides.

$x + 12 = 4x^2 - 16x + 16$

$4x^2 - 17x + 4 = 0$

$(4x - 1)(x - 4) = 0$

$4x - 1 = 0$ **OR** $x - 4 = 0$

$x = \dfrac{1}{4}$ **OR** $\quad x = 4$

Check:

Always substitute into the original equation.

If $x = \dfrac{1}{4}$ $\quad$ LHS $= \sqrt{\dfrac{1}{4} + 12} - 2 = 3.5 - 2 = 1.5$

$\qquad\qquad$ RHS $= 2\left(\dfrac{1}{4}\right) - 6 = -5\dfrac{1}{2} \neq$ LHS

$\therefore x = \dfrac{1}{4}$ does **not** satisfy the equation.

If $x = 4$ $\qquad$ LHS $= \sqrt{4 + 12} - 2 = 4 - 2 = 2$

$\qquad\qquad$ RHS $= 2(4) - 6 = 2 =$ LHS

$\therefore x = 4$ does satisfy the equation.

Answer: $x = 4$

x^2 **Worked Example 4.3**

Solve $\sqrt{x + 7} + \sqrt{x + 2} = 5$.

Solution

| As we have more than one surd term, we leave one surd term on one side of the equation and every other term on the other side, to simplify the arithmetic. |

$\sqrt{x + 7} = 5 - \sqrt{x + 2}$

| Square both sides. |

$(\sqrt{x + 7})^2 = (5 - \sqrt{x + 2})^2$

$x + 7 = (5 - \sqrt{x + 2})(5 - \sqrt{x + 2})$

$x + 7 = 25 - 5\sqrt{x + 2} - 5\sqrt{x + 2} + (\sqrt{x + 2})^2$

$x + 7 = 25 - 10\sqrt{x + 2} + x + 2$

$10\sqrt{x + 2} = 25 + x + 2 - x - 7$

| Again, leave surd term on one side of the equation. |

$10\sqrt{x + 2} = 20$

$\sqrt{x + 2} = 2$

| Divide both sides by 10. |

$\therefore x + 2 = 4$

$\Rightarrow x = 2$

Check (in the original equation):

If $x = 2$ LHS $= \sqrt{2 + 7} + \sqrt{2 + 2} = 3 + 2 = 5$

RHS $= 5$

$\therefore x = 2$ does satisfy the equation.

Answer: $x = 2$

Exercise 4.1

Solve the following equations:

1. $\sqrt{x + 3} = 4$

2. $\sqrt{x - 5} = 2$

3. $\sqrt{7x - 3} = 4$

4. $\sqrt{4x - 4} = x$

5. $x + \sqrt{2x} = 4$

6. $x - \sqrt{5x - 1} = 5$

7. $\sqrt{4x - 3} = 2x - 1$

8. $5x - 4 = \sqrt{3x - 2}$

9. $\sqrt{x + 5} + 1 = x$

10. $\sqrt{6x + 4} - 1 = \sqrt{3x + 1}$

11. $\sqrt{5x + 1} + \sqrt{x + 1} = 6$

12. $\sqrt{x} + \sqrt{x + 7} = 7$

13. $\sqrt{x + 4} = \sqrt{x - 1} + 1$

14. $1 - \sqrt{2x - 1} = \sqrt{x - 1}$

15. $3\sqrt{x - 6} = -4 + x$

4.2 LINEAR INEQUALITIES

Sometimes, when solving for an unknown, we cannot find an exact value. Instead, we end up with a range of values.

| An **inequality** gives a range of values. |

| < means 'less than' |
| ⩽ means 'less than or equal to' |
| > means 'greater than' |
| ⩾ means 'greater than or equal to' |

Examples: $x < 3$ means 'x is less than 3'.

$x \geqslant 5$ means 'x is greater than or equal to 5'.

$x + 1 > 6$ means '$x + 1$ is greater than 6'.

We may be asked to graph a solution to an inequality. In such cases it is important that we distinguish between the different types of number we may be asked to graph.

Natural Numbers – N

A **natural number** is any positive whole number (i.e. any whole number greater than 0).

$N = \{1, 2, 3, 4, ...\}$

The set of naturals is denoted by the letter N.

> We are usually told when we are dealing with natural numbers – the question will say $x \in N$. This means that x is an element of N, i.e. from the set of natural numbers.

As natural numbers are whole numbers, in order to graph them on the numberline we use dots.

Integers – Z

An **integer** is any whole number; positive, negative or zero.

$Z = \{..., -3, -2, -1, 0, 1, 2, 3, ...\}$

The set of integers is denoted by the letter Z.

> If x is an integer, we can write $x \in Z$.

As integers are also whole numbers, in order to graph them on the numberline we use dots.

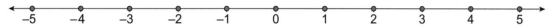

Real Numbers – R

A real number is any number that can be plotted on the numberline.

The set of reals is denoted by the letter R.

> If x is a real number, we can write $x \in R$.

As real numbers can be any number, in order to show them on the numberline we use a solid line.

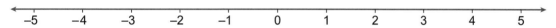

Multiplication/Division of an Inequality by a Negative Number

It is important to remember the following rule:

> When we multiply or divide both sides of an inequality by a negative number, we reverse the inequality sign, as well as changing the signs of all terms in the inequality.

Example: $-x < 5$

$\Rightarrow x > -5$

x^2 Worked Example 4.4

Solve the following inequality and show the solution on the numberline:

$x - 1 > 2(x - 3) - 1, \, x \in N$

> The smallest natural number is 1; there are no further values. Therefore, we don't put an arrow on the numberline.

Solution

$x - 1 > 2(x - 3) - 1$

$x - 1 > 2x - 6 - 1$

$x - 1 > 2x - 7$

$-x > -6$

$\therefore x < 6, \, x \in N$

> When we multiply or divide an inequality by a negative number, we reverse the inequality sign.

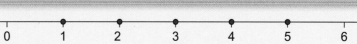

x^2 Worked Example 4.5

Solve the following inequality and show the solution set on the numberline: $-1 \leqslant \dfrac{2x + 4}{3} < 2, x \in R$

Solution

Method 1

Multiply every term by 3:

$\therefore -3 \leqslant 2x + 4 < 6$

$-3 - 4 \leqslant 2x + 4 - 4 < 6 - 4$

$-7 \leqslant 2x < 2$

$-3.5 \leqslant x < 1, x \in R$

Method 2

$-1 \leqslant \dfrac{2x + 4}{3}$ $\qquad$ $\dfrac{2x + 4}{3} < 2$

$-3 \leqslant 2x + 4$ $\qquad$ $2x + 4 < 6$

$-7 \leqslant 2x$ $\qquad$ $2x < 2$

$-3.5 \leqslant x$ $\qquad$ $x < 1$

$\therefore -3.5 \leqslant x < 1$

> ○ at $x = 1$ indicates that x is not equal to 1.
>
> ● at $x = -3.5$ indicates that x can be equal to -3.5.

numberline: -5 -4 -3.5 -3 -2 -1 0 1 2 3

x^2 Worked Example 4.6

(i) Find the solution set E of $-4 > \dfrac{x - 6}{2}, x \in Z$.

(ii) Find the solution set F of $x \geqslant \dfrac{2x + 1}{3}, x \in Z$.

(iii) Graph the solution sets of E and F on the same numberline.

(iv) Find the solution sets of $E \cap F$ and $E \cup F$.

Solution

(i) $\quad -4 > \dfrac{x - 6}{2}, x \in Z$

$\therefore -8 > x - 6$

$-x > -6 + 8$

$-x > 2$

$\therefore x < -2, x \in Z$

$\therefore E = \{x < -2, x \in Z\}$

(ii) $\quad x \geqslant \dfrac{2x + 1}{3}$

$\therefore 3x \geqslant 2x + 1$

$\Rightarrow x \geqslant 1, x \in Z$

$\therefore F = \{x \geqslant 1, x \in Z\}$

(iii) numberline: -5 -4 -3 -2 -1 0 1 2 3 4

(iv) In the graph, the solution sets of E and F do not intersect/overlap.

Hence, $E \cap F = \{ \ \}$ or $\emptyset$, the null set.

$E \cup F = \{x \leqslant -3, x \geqslant 1, x \in Z\}$

> The arrows on the numberline indicate that the solution set continues to infinity in that direction.

Exercise 4.2

Solve each of the following inequalities and show each solution on a numberline:

1. $2(x - 1) < 4x, x \in Z$

2. $5(2x - 1) > 2(x - 1) + 5, x \in N$

3. $3(x - 6) \leqslant 4(x - 1) - 15, x \in R$

4. $2(3 - 2x) > 2(3 - x) - 3 + x, x \in N$

5. $11 < 7(x + 1) - 2(3 - 8x) - 3x, x \in R$

6. $\dfrac{2x - 1}{3} > x - 1, x \in N$

7. $\dfrac{3x - 2}{8} - \dfrac{x - 1}{2} < 0, x \in Z$

8. $\dfrac{x + 2}{3} > \dfrac{x + 1}{4} + \dfrac{1}{3}, x \in R$

9. Solve the following inequalities and graph the solution to each on a numberline:

(i) $2 < x \leqslant 4, x \in N$

(ii) $-7 < -x < 2, x \in Z$

(iii) $3 \geqslant x - 2 > -5, x \in R$

(iv) $0 \leqslant 3 - 4x < 2, x \in R$

(v) $-4 < -\dfrac{x + 2}{3} \leqslant -3, x \in R$

10. The recommended daily intake of calories for a man is 2,500 calories. Maurice usually eats within 10% of his recommended daily intake.

    What range of caloric intake does Maurice usually eat each day?

11. If 5 is added to an integer, the result is less than 15. If 3 is subtracted from the integer, the result is greater than 5. What is the number?

12. (i) Graph the solution set A of :
    $$-3 < \frac{5x - 1}{2}, x \in R$$

    (ii) Graph the solution set B of:
    $$7 \geqslant \frac{15x - 2}{4}, x \in R$$

    (iii) Find the solution set of A ∩ B.

13. (i) Graph the solution set C of:
    $$15 - 4x > -1, x \in N$$

    (ii) Graph the solution set D of:
    $$\frac{2x + 1}{2} - \frac{x + 2}{3} \leqslant 1, x \in N$$

    (iii) Find the solution set of C ∩ D.

14. (i) Graph the solution set E of :
    $$2x + 3 \leqslant 5x - 12, x \in R$$

    (ii) Graph the solution set F of:
    $$\frac{9x - 1}{3} \leqslant \frac{2(2x - 4)}{5} + 2, x \in R$$

    (iii) Find the solution set of E ∪ F.

4.3 QUADRATIC AND RATIONAL INEQUALITIES

A quadratic inequality is of the form $ax^2 + bx + c \;\square\; 0$, where the box is filled by one of the four inequality signs. ($a, b, c \in R, a \neq 0$)

When trying to solve quadratic inequalities, we must be able to sketch quadratic functions. From the graph we can then determine the solution required.

> means 'above the x-axis'

⩾ means 'on or above the x-axis'

< means 'below the x-axis'

⩽ means 'on or below the x-axis'

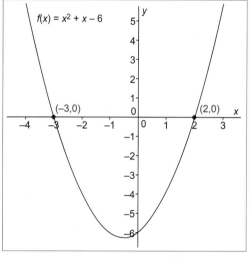

ACTIVITY 4.1

x^2 **Worked Example 4.7**

Solve the inequality $x^2 + 7x + 12 \leqslant 0, x \in R$.

Solution

Let $x^2 + 7x + 12 = 0$ and solve.

$x^2 + 7x + 12 = 0$

$(x + 3)(x + 4) = 0$

$x + 3 = 0$ **OR** $x + 4 = 0$

$x = -3$ **OR** $x = -4$

Sketch the quadratic function.

The coefficient of x^2 is **positive**. Therefore, the graph is U-shaped. The roots are $x = -3$ and $x = -4$.

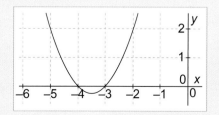

From our graph, we can now determine where $x^2 + 7x + 12 \leqslant 0$ (lies on or below the x-axis).

∴ The solution is $-4 \leqslant x \leqslant -3, x \in R$.

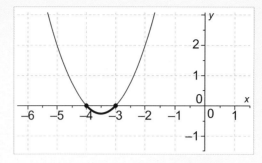

■ Use shaded dots at $x = -4$ and $x = -3$ since these two points lie **on** the x-axis.

■ Shade in the part of the graph that is **below** the x-axis.

x^2 Worked Example 4.8

Solve the inequality $-3x^2 - 8x < -16, x \in R$.

Solution

$-3x^2 - 8x + 16 < 0$

$3x^2 + 8x - 16 > 0$

Let $3x^2 + 8x - 16 = 0$.

$(3x - 4)(x + 4) = 0$

$3x - 4 = 0$ **OR** $x + 4 = 0$

$∴ x = \dfrac{4}{3}$ **OR** $x = -4$

Sketch the quadratic function. (Using the inequality $3x^2 + 8x - 16 > 0$, the quadratic function is $3x^2 + 8x - 16$.)

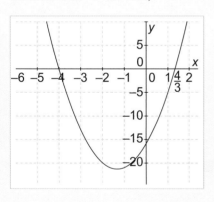

From our graph, we can now determine where $3x^2 + 8x - 16 > 0$ and, hence, solve the inequality $-3x^2 - 8x < -16$.

∴ The solution is $x < -4$ **OR** $x > \dfrac{4}{3}$.

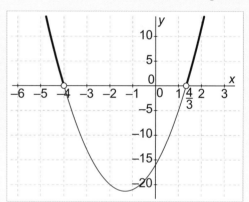

Rational Inequalities

A complication occurs when we try to solve an inequality whose numerator and denominator are both algebraic expressions. These are referred to as **rational inequalities**.

Example: $\dfrac{4x - 3}{2x - 5} > 4 \left(x \neq \dfrac{5}{2}\right)$

We cannot be sure whether the denominator $2x - 5$ is positive or negative. Therefore, if we multiply both sides by $(2x - 5)$, we do not know whether or not to reverse the inequality sign.

So, we multiply both sides of the inequality by $(2x - 5)^2$, which we know is positive.

x^2 Worked Example 4.9

Solve the inequality $\dfrac{2x + 4}{x + 1} < 3$, $x \in R$, $x \neq -1$.

Solution

> Multiply both sides by $(x + 1)^2$.

$\dfrac{(x + 1)^2(2x + 4)}{(x + 1)} < 3(x + 1)^2$

$(x + 1)(2x + 4) < 3(x + 1)^2$

$2x^2 + 6x + 4 < 3(x^2 + 2x + 1)$

$2x^2 + 6x + 4 < 3x^2 + 6x + 3$

$-x^2 + 1 < 0$

$x^2 - 1 > 0$

Let $x^2 - 1 = 0$ and solve.

$x^2 - 1 = 0$

$\Rightarrow x^2 = 1$

$\therefore x = \pm 1$

Sketch the quadratic function. (Using the inequality $x^2 - 1 > 0$, the quadratic function is $x^2 - 1$.)

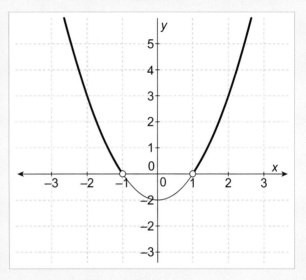

The solution is $x < -1$ **OR** $x > 1$.

Exercise 4.3

Solve each of the following inequalities for $x \in R$:

1. $x^2 + x - 12 > 0$

2. $2x^2 + 11x + 14 < 0$

3. $3x^2 - 26x + 16 \leqslant 0$

4. $2x^2 - x \geqslant 10$

5. $7x^2 + 21x < -14$

6. $-72 \geqslant -5x^2 + 54x$

7. $-5x^2 - 13x - 3 \geqslant 3$

8. $2x^2 + 3x < 0$

9. $121x^2 \leqslant 25$

10. $\dfrac{2x + 1}{x + 3} < 1$, $x \neq -3$

11. $\dfrac{3x - 7}{x - 4} < 2$, $x \neq 4$

12. $\dfrac{x + 2}{x - 3} \leqslant 5$, $x \neq 3$

13. $\dfrac{x + 5}{x - 2} > 4$, $x \neq 2$

14. $\dfrac{x + 1}{2x + 4} \geqslant 3$, $x \neq -2$

15. $\dfrac{2x - 6}{3x - 5} \geqslant 2$, $x \neq \dfrac{5}{3}$

16. (i) Use the quadratic formula to find the roots of $x^2 - 13x - 13 = 0$ correct to one decimal place.

(ii) Hence, find the least value of $n \in N$ such that $n^2 - 13n - 13 > 0$.

17. Find, in surd form, the range of values of x for which $x^2 + 6x + 4 \geqslant 0$, $x \in R$.

18. A delivery company is designing a new rectangular box to be used for packaging fragile items prior to transit. The box's dimensions must meet the following specifications:

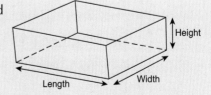

- The length must be 60% greater than the width.

- The surface area of the base must not exceed 300 cm².

- The height of the box must be at least 3 cm but should not exceed one-fifth of the length.

(i) Letting x be the width of the box in centimetres, write down an expression for the surface area of the base of the box in terms of x.

(ii) Write down an inequality for the surface area of the base.

(iii) Solve this inequality for x, answering correct to two decimal places.

(iv) If the width finally chosen is the largest whole number that satisfies the inequality in part (ii), find the range of values for the box's volume in cm^3.

19. A stuntman is about to jump off a 20 m building. Once in flight, his height in metres above the ground will be given by the function $h(t) = 20 - 5t^2$, where h is his height above the ground and t is the time elapsed in seconds. The film crew want to film him when he is between 15 m and 10 m above the ground.

(i) Form a quadratic inequality representing the above information.

(ii) Hence, write down the time at which the film crew should start filming and the time at which they should stop filming. Give your answers correct to one decimal place.

20. A Transition Year mini-company decide to produce and sell keyrings emblazoned with their school logo. They research an idea and discover that their projected monthly costs (C) and revenues (R) in hundreds of euro will be given by the equations:

$$R = 5p - p^2 \qquad C = 7 - p$$

where p is the price per keyring in euro.

(i) Find the range of prices for which the mini-company will make a profit (Profit = Revenues − Costs).

(ii) If the mini-company decide to charge €2 per keyring, what monthly percentage profit margin will they make? (Answer correct to the nearest percentage.)

4.4 ABSOLUTE VALUE (MODULUS)

> The **absolute value** or **modulus** of a real number x, written as $|x|$, is the magnitude of the number without regard to its sign (i.e. the non-negative value of the number.)

Examples: $|-7| = 7$ $\qquad |1.3| = 1.3$ $\qquad \left|-\frac{1}{2}\right| = \frac{1}{2}$ $\qquad |0| = 0$

Geometrically, the absolute value is how far away the number is from zero on the numberline.

So, $|-2| = |2| = 2$.

> If $|x| = a$, then $x = -a$ or $x = a$.

Note: if $|x| = 5$, then $x = -5$ **OR** $x = 5$.

x^2 Worked Example 4.10

Find two values of x if $|x + 1| = 3$.

Solution

$|x + 1| = 3$

$\Rightarrow x + 1 = 3$ **OR** $x + 1 = -3$

$\therefore x = 2$ **OR** $x = -4$

Alternative method

$(1x + 1)^2 = (3)^2$

$x^2 + 2x + 1 = 9$

$x^2 + 2x - 8 = 0$

$(x + 4)(x - 2) = 0$

$x + 4 = 0$ **OR** $x - 2 = 0$

$x = -4$ **OR** $x = 2$

Note: Squaring both sides removes the modulus notation.

x^2 **Worked Example 4.11**

Graph the functions $f(x) = |x + 2|$ in the domain $-8 \leqslant x \leqslant 3$ and $g(x) = 4$. Hence, solve $|x + 2| = 4$.

Solution

We plot $f(x) = |x + 2|$ and $g(x) = 4$:

x	$|x + 2|$	y
-8	$|-8 + 2|$	6
-7	$|-7 + 2|$	5
-6	$|-6 + 2|$	4
-5	$|-5 + 2|$	3
-4	$|-4 + 2|$	2
-3	$|-3 + 2|$	1
-2	$|-2 + 2|$	0
-1	$|-1 + 2|$	1
0	$|0 + 2|$	2
1	$|1 + 2|$	3
2	$|2 + 2|$	4
3	$|3 + 2|$	5

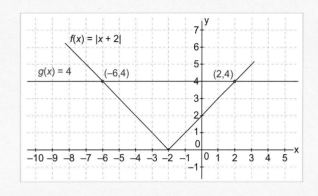

Hence, solve $|x + 2| = 4$.

The two graphs intersect at $(-6,4)$ and $(2,4)$.

$\therefore x = -6$ **OR** $x = 2$

We can also graph modulus equations by drawing half-lines. If $y = |x + 2|$, then $y \geqslant 0$.
We graph the parts of the lines $y = x + 2$ and $y = -x - 2$ which are on or above the x-axis.

x^2 **Worked Example 4.12**

(i) Solve for x if $3|x + 1| - |x + 5| = 0$.

(ii) Hence, check your answer by graphing the functions $f(x) = 3|x + 1|$ and $g(x) = |x + 5|$.

Solution

(i) Using algebra

> We leave one modulus term on one side of the equation and every other term on the other side.

$$3|x + 1| = |x + 5|$$

$$3^2(x + 1)^2 = (x + 5)^2 \quad \boxed{\text{Square both sides.}}$$

$$9(x + 1)^2 = (x + 5)^2$$

$$9(x^2 + 2x + 1) = x^2 + 10x + 25$$

$$9x^2 + 18x + 9 = x^2 + 10x + 25$$

$$8x^2 + 8x - 16 = 0$$

$$x^2 + x - 2 = 0$$

$$(x + 2)(x - 1) = 0$$

$$x + 2 = 0 \quad \textbf{OR} \quad x - 1 = 0$$

$$x = -2 \quad \textbf{OR} \quad x = 1$$

(ii) Using graphs

We plot $f(x) = 3|x + 1|$ and $g(x) = |x + 5|$.

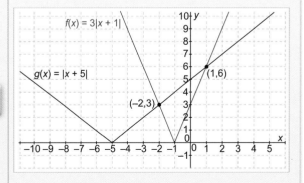

The two functions intersect at $(-2,3)$ and $(1,6)$.

$\therefore x = -2$ **OR** $x = 1$

Modulus Inequalities

If $|x| = 4$, then $x = -4$ **OR** $x = 4$.

If $|x| < 4$, then x must be less than 4 units away from 0 on the numberline.

$\therefore$ x must have a value between -4 and 4.

$\therefore$ $|x| < 4 \Rightarrow -4 < x < 4$

If $|x| > 4$, then x must be more than 4 units away from 0 on the numberline.

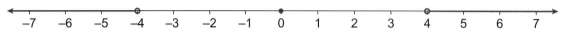

$\therefore$ x must have a value less than -4 **OR** greater than 4.

$\therefore$ $|x| > 4 \Rightarrow x < -4$ **OR** $x > 4$

> The method which works for either type of modulus inequality is to square both sides.

x^2 Worked Example 4.13

Graph the function $f(x) = |x + 2|$ and $g(x) = 4$ in the domain $-8 \leqslant x \leqslant 4$ and, hence, solve $|x + 2| \geqslant 4$, $x \in R$.

Solution

We graph the function $f(x) = |x + 2|$ and $g(x) = 4$.

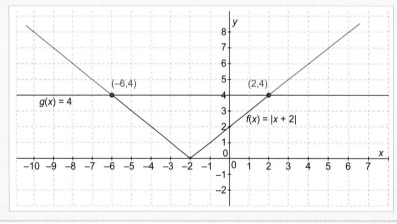

We are looking for the range of values for which $|x + 2| \geqslant 4$.

$\therefore x \leqslant -6$ **OR** $x \geqslant 2$

x^2 Worked Example 4.14

Solve the inequality $|x + 1| > 2|x + 3|$, $x \in R$.

Solution

$|x + 1|^2 > 2^2|x + 3|^2$

$x^2 + 2x + 1 > 4(x^2 + 6x + 9)$

$x^2 + 2x + 1 > 4x^2 + 24x + 36$

$-3x^2 - 22x - 35 > 0$

$\therefore 3x^2 + 22x + 35 < 0$

Let $3x^2 + 22x + 35 = 0$.

$(3x + 7)(x + 5) = 0$

$3x + 7 = 0$ **OR** $x + 5 = 0$

$\therefore x = -\dfrac{7}{3}$ **OR** $x = -5$

ACTIVE MATHS

Sketch the quadratic function. (Here, we use the inequality $3x^2 + 22x + 35 < 0$, so the quadratic function is $3x^2 + 22x + 35$.)

$\therefore -5 < x < -\dfrac{7}{3}$

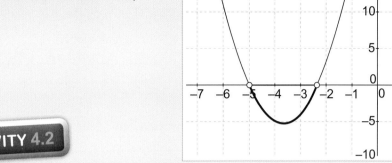

ACTIVITY 4.2

Exercise 4.4

1. Evaluate the following:

   (i) $|8|$ (iv) $|8 - 3|$

   (ii) $|-3|$ (v) $|-8| + |3|$

   (iii) $|-8 + 3|$ (vi) $|8| + |-3|$

2. If $p = 2$, $q = 5$ and $r = -4$, find the value of:

   (i) $|p + q|$ (iv) $5|rq|$

   (ii) $|r + q|$ (v) $2|pr| - 3|q|$

   (iii) $|pq|$ (vi) $|p||q| + 3|q - r|$

Solve questions 3–25 for $x \in R$:

3. $|x| = 5$ 7. $|x + 3| - 4 = 9$

4. $|x| = 10$ 8. $2|x + 2| - 2 = 0$

5. $|x + 1| = 8$ 9. $2 + |2x - 4| = 10$

6. $|x - 8| = 3$ 10. $3|x + 7| = 0$

11. $|x + 3| = |9|$

12. $2|4x + 1| = |x + 3|$

13. $|2x| - 3|x + 1| = 0$

14. $\dfrac{3}{4}|x + 3| - \dfrac{1}{2}|x - 1| = 0$

15. $|x + 1| < 5$

16. $|x - 4| > 3$

17. $|x - 3| > 3|x - 1|$

18. $2|x + 4| \leqslant |x + 5|$

19. $3|x - 6| \leqslant |x + 2|$

20. $2|3x - 2| < |-2x - 1|$

21. $|5x - 3| \leqslant \left| x - \dfrac{1}{5} \right|$

22. $2|x + 3| - |x - 2| < 0$

23. $\left| \dfrac{1}{x} + 3 \right| \leqslant 4$

24. $\left| \dfrac{x - 2}{5} \right| > 1$

25. $\left| \dfrac{x + 2}{x - 3} \right| < 4$

26. Using the same axes and scales, graph the functions $f(x) = |x - 4|$ and $g(x) = 2$. Using your graph, find the value of x for which $|x - 4| = 2$.

27. Using the same axes and scales, graph the functions $f(x) = 2|x + 1|$ and $g(x) = 3$. Using your graph, find the value of x for which $2|x + 1| \geqslant 3$, $x \in R$.

28. A speedometer has an accuracy of ±5% of a car's speed. If the car is moving at 120 km/hr, write a modulus inequality that expresses the range of speeds that the odometer may show.

29. Using the same axes and scales, graph the functions $f(x) = |3x + 5|$ and $h(x) = |x - 1|$. Using your graph, find the values of $x \in R$ for which:

   (i) $f(x) = h(x)$

   (ii) $f(x) < h(x)$

   (iii) $h(x) \geqslant f(x)$

30. Using the same axes and scales, graph the functions $g(x) = -|2x + 4|$ and $h(x) = -6$, $x \in R$. Using your graph, find the value(s) of x for which:

(i) $g(x) = h(x)$ (ii) $g(x) < h(x)$

Explain with the aid of your graph if $-|2x + 4| = 2$ has a real solution.

4.5 DISCRIMINANTS

The formula $x = \dfrac{-b \pm \sqrt{b^2 - 4ac}}{2a}$ can be used to solve equations of the form $ax^2 + bx + c = 0$, $a \neq 0$.

$b^2 - 4ac$ is called the **discriminant**.

The value of the discriminant, $b^2 - 4ac$, can be used to determine whether the graph of the function (the parabola) cuts, touches or does not cut the x-axis.

Discriminant			
	$b^2 - 4ac > 0$	$b^2 - 4ac = 0$	$b^2 - 4ac < 0$
Number of roots	Two distinct real roots	One repeated real root (2 equal roots)	No real roots
Intersection with the x-axis	Two distinct points	Curve touches x-axis	Curve and x-axis do not meet
Sketch for $a > 0$			
Sketch for $a < 0$			

Real roots $\Rightarrow b^2 - 4ac \geqslant 0$ Real and equal roots $\Rightarrow b^2 - 4ac = 0$

Real and distinct roots $\Rightarrow b^2 - 4ac > 0$ No real roots $\Rightarrow b^2 - 4ac < 0$

 **ACTIVITY 4.3**

x^2 Worked Example 4.15

Find the value of k if $x^2 + 6x + k$ has two equal roots.

Solution

Equal roots: $b^2 - 4ac = 0$ $36 - 4k = 0$

$a = 1, b = 6, c = k$ $36 = 4k$

$(6)^2 - 4(1)(k) = 0$ $\therefore 9 = k$

Worked Example 4.16

For what values of p does $2px^2 - px + 1 = x^2 + x$ have real roots?

Solution

$$2px^2 - px + 1 = x^2 + x$$

$$\Rightarrow 2px^2 - px + 1 - x^2 - x = 0$$

$$2px^2 - x^2 - px - x + 1 = 0$$

$$(2p - 1)x^2 + (-p - 1)x + 1 = 0$$

$$a = 2p - 1, b = -p - 1, c = 1$$

Real roots: $b^2 - 4ac \geqslant 0$

$$(-p - 1)^2 - 4(2p - 1)(1) \geqslant 0$$

$$p^2 + 2p + 1 - 8p + 4 \geqslant 0$$

$$p^2 - 6p + 5 \geqslant 0$$

Let $p^2 - 6p + 5 = 0$.

$$(p - 1)(p - 5) = 0$$

$$p - 1 = 0 \quad \textbf{OR} \quad p - 5 = 0$$

$$p = 1 \quad \textbf{OR} \qquad p = 5$$

We sketch the quadratic function. (Here the inequality we use is $p^2 - 6p + 5 \geqslant 0$, so we graph $p^2 - 6p + 5$.)

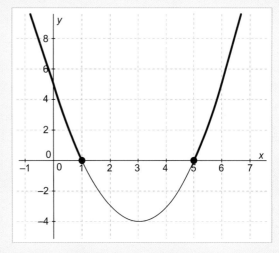

$\Rightarrow p \leqslant 1 \quad \textbf{OR} \quad p \geqslant 5$ for real roots

Exercise 4.5

1. The graphs of five quadratic functions are shown. In each case, comment on the nature of the roots and on whether the discriminant will be greater than, equal to or less than 0.

(i)

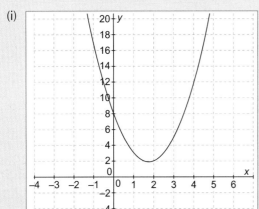

(ii)

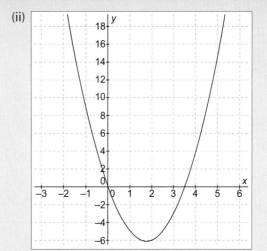

(iii)

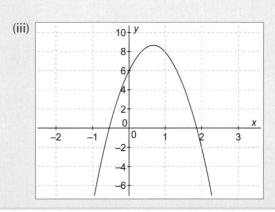

(iv)

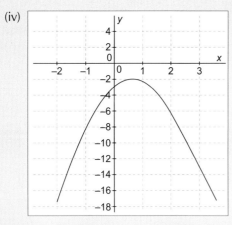

(v)

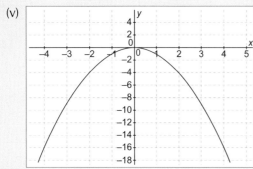

2. For each equation given below, calculate the discriminant and comment appropriately on the nature of the roots.

   (i) $x^2 + 6x + 5 = 0$

   (ii) $x^2 - 4x + 4 = 0$

   (iii) $x^2 - 2x + 5 = 0$

   (iv) $-x^2 + 6x + 9 = 0$

   (v) $5x^2 + 2x - 10 = 0$

   (vi) $x^2 - kx - a^2 = 0$

   (vii) $x^2 + 2ax + a^2 = 0$

   (viii) $3(4x - 2)^2 + 1 = 12$

   (ix) $x^2 + (a - 1)x - 9 = 0$

3. Find the values of $a \in R$ for which $x^2 + ax + 16 = 0$ has real roots.

4. Find the value of $b \in R$ if $x^2 + 6x - b = 0$ has two equal real roots.

5. Find the range of values of $c \in R$ if $cx^2 + 4x - 2 = 0$ has no real roots.

6. Graph that function $f(x) = 2x^2 - 3x + 5$ in the domain $-3 \leqslant x \leqslant 3$, $x \in R$.
   From your graph, determine the nature of the roots of $2x^2 - 3x + 5 = 0$.

7. If $x^2 - 14x + k = 0$ has no real roots, prove that $k > 49$.

8. For what values of $q \in R$ does the equation $x^2 + qx + q = 0$ have no real roots?

9. $(2p + 1)x^2 + (p + 2)x + 1 = 0$ has real roots. Find all possible values of p.

10. $(b + 1)x^2 + bx + b + 1 = 0$ has two equal real roots. Find the values of b.

11. If $x, y \in R$, prove that $x^2 \geqslant y(2x - y)$.

12. Prove that for all values of $a \in R$, $(a - 2)x^2 + 2x - a = 0$ has real roots.

13. Show that the equation $4ax^2 - 4ax + a + c^2 = 0$ has no real roots for $a \in N$, $c \in R$, $c \neq 0$.

14. Prove that the equation $kx^2 + (2k - 1)x - 2 = 0$ has real roots for all values of $k \in R$.

15. Prove that the equation $x^2 + (a - 2d)x + (ab - ad - b^2) = 0$ has real roots for all values of a, b and d.

4.6 INEQUALITIES: PROOFS

We may be asked to prove that certain inequalities are true or false. One of the more useful tools in answering such questions is the property that the square of any real number is non-negative.

$$(\text{real})^2 \geqslant 0$$

x^2 Worked Example 4.17

Prove that if a and b are real numbers, then $a^2 + b^2 \geqslant 2ab$.

Solution

Note: Always give a reason in your solution.

$$a^2 + b^2 \geqslant 2ab$$
$$\Rightarrow a^2 + b^2 - 2ab \geqslant 0$$
$$\Rightarrow (a - b)^2 \geqslant 0 \quad \text{True, as } (a - b) \in R$$
$$\text{and } (\text{real})^2 \geqslant 0$$
$$\therefore a^2 + b^2 \geqslant 2ab$$

x^2 Worked Example 4.18

If $a, b \in R$, prove that
$a^2 + 4b^2 - 10a + 25 \geqslant 0$.

Solution

$$a^2 - 10a + 25 + 4b^2 \geqslant 0$$
$$(a - 5)(a - 5) + (2b)^2 \geqslant 0$$
$$\Rightarrow (a - 5)^2 + (2b)^2 \geqslant 0$$

True, as $a, b \in R$, and $(\text{real})^2 + (\text{real})^2 \geqslant 0$.

Exercise 4.6

1. Prove that for all $p \in R$, $p^2 + 1 \geqslant 2p$.

2. Prove that for all $a, b \in R$, $a^2 + 2ab + b^2 \geqslant 0$.

3. Prove that if $b > 0$ then $b + \dfrac{1}{b} \geqslant 2$.

4. Prove that for all $x, y \in R$, $x^2 + y^2 \geqslant 2xy$.

5. If $x, y \in R$, prove that $(x + y)^2 \leqslant 2(x^2 + y^2)$.

6. If $x, y \in N$, prove that $(x + y)\left(\dfrac{1}{x} + \dfrac{1}{y}\right) \geqslant 4$.

7. Prove that $a^2 + b^2 - 8a + 16 \geqslant 0$, for all $a, b \in R$.

8. Prove that for all $p, q > 0$, $p + q \geqslant 2\sqrt{pq}$.

9. Prove that $x^2 + 2xy + 3y^2 \geqslant 0$, for all $x, y \in R$.

10. If $a > b > 0$, prove that $a^2 - b^2 > (a - b)^2$.

11. If $x, y \in R$, prove that $x^2 + y^2 - 6y + 9 \geqslant 0$.

12. Let $a, b, x, y \in R$.

    (a) Prove that $a^2 + b^2 \geqslant 2ab$.

    (b) Complete (without proof) the following inequalities:

    $x^2 + y^2 \geqslant$

    $a^2 + x^2 \geqslant$

    $b^2 + y^2 \geqslant$

    (c) Deduce that, if $x^2 + y^2 = 1$ and if $a^2 + b^2 = 1$, then:

    (i) $ab + xy \leqslant 1$

    (ii) $ax + by \leqslant 1$

13. (a) Prove that $x^2 + y^2 \geqslant 2xy$.

    (b) Deduce that $x^4 + y^4 \geqslant 2x^2y^2$.

    (c) Deduce that $x^4 + y^4 + z^4 + w^4 \geqslant 4xyzw$.

14. (i) Factorise $a^3 - a^2b - ab^2 + b^3$.

    (ii) If $a, b \in N$, show that $a^3 + b^3 \geqslant a^2b + ab^2$.

Revision Exercises

1. (a) Solve (and check your answer):

    (i) $\sqrt{x + 3} = x - 3$

    (ii) $\sqrt{2x + 1} = x - 1$

    (iii) $x - \sqrt{x - 3} = 5$

    (b) Solve the following inequalities and show the solution on a numberline.

    (i) $7(2x - 1) \geqslant 3(4 - x) - 2x$, $x \in N$

    (ii) $2x - 1 < \dfrac{x + 7}{3}$, $x \in Z$

    (iii) $\dfrac{6x + 1}{5} > \dfrac{2x - 3}{3}$ $x \in R$

(c) (i) Solve $x^2 - 7x + 10 = 0$.

(ii) Hence, solve $x^2 - 7x + 10 < 0$.

(iii) Solve $x^2 - 8x + 15 = 0$.

(iv) Hence, find the solution set of $x^2 - 8x + 15 \geqslant 0$.

2. (a) If $x = -2.4$ and $y = 1.8$, investigate if:

(i) $|x + y| = |x| + |y|$

(ii) $|xy| = |x||y|$

(iii) $|x - y| = |x| - |y|$

(iv) $|y - x| = |y| - |x|$

(v) $\left|\dfrac{y}{x}\right| = \dfrac{|y|}{|x|}$

(b) If $x, y \in R$, show that $x^2 + 2xy + y^2 \geqslant 0$.

(c) (i) Find the value of k if $x^2 + 16x + k = 0$ has equal roots.

(ii) Find the value of t if $x^2 - 12x + 9t = 0$ has equal roots.

3. (a) Here are four statments which are true for any $x, y \in R$:

(i) $|x| + |y| \geqslant |x + y|$

(ii) $|x| - |y| \leqslant |x - y|$

(iii) $|x||y| = |xy|$

(iv) $\left|\dfrac{x}{y}\right| = \dfrac{|x|}{|y|}$

Verify each by putting $x = 5$ and $y = -2$.

(b) (i) Graph the solution set A of $-4x - 1 < 2, x \in R$.

(ii) Graph the solution set B of $\dfrac{5x - 8}{6} \leqslant -\dfrac{x}{2}, x \in R$.

(iii) Find the solution set of $A \cap B$.

(c) Solve (and check your answers):

(i) $x + \sqrt{x} = 2$ (ii) $\sqrt{7x + 1} - x = 1$

4. (a) Solve for x in each case, and verify your answers.

(i) $|x| = 5$ (iv) $|1 - x| = 9$

(ii) $|x + 1| = 10$ (v) $|1 - 4x| = 9$

(iii) $|x - 1| = 10$

(b) If the equation $x^2 + 8x + p = 0$ has no real roots, show that $p > 16$.

(c) (i) Factorise $a^4 - a^3b - ab^3 + b^4$.

(ii) If $a, b \in R$, show that $a^4 + b^4 \geqslant a^3b + ab^3$.

5. (a) Solve for x in each case, and verify your answers.

(i) $2|x + 1| = 4$

(ii) $2|x + 1| = |x - 3|$

(iii) $4|x + 1| = 3|x + 1|$

(b) Find the values of $x \in R$ that satisfy each of the following inequalities:

(i) $x^2 - 2x - 8 < 0$

(ii) $x^2 + x - 20 \geqslant 0$

(iii) $x^2 - 3x - 10 \leqslant 0$

(iv) $x^2 - 4 > 0$

(c) If the equation $x^2 + kx + (k + 3) = 0$ has two equal roots, find two possible values of k. In each case, find the two roots.

(d) Using the same axes and scales, graph the functions $f(x) = |x - 5|$ and $g(x) = 3$. For what values of x is $|x - 5| > 3$?

6. (a) Solve for x in each case, and verify your answers.

(i) $\left|x + \dfrac{1}{2}\right| = 4$

(ii) $4\left|x - \dfrac{1}{3}\right| = 2$

(iii) $\dfrac{1}{2}|x - 3| = 2\left|x + \dfrac{5}{2}\right|$

(b) Solve for x in each case, and verify your answers.

(i) $\sqrt{x + 6} = x - 6$

(ii) $\sqrt{3x + 1} = \sqrt{x - 1} + 2$

(iii) $\sqrt{x} + \sqrt{x - 3} = \sqrt{x + 5}$

(c) Find the values of $x \in R$ that satisfy the following inequalities:

(i) $2x^2 + x - 10 \leqslant 0$

(ii) $6x^2 > x + 1$

(iii) $(x - 3)(1 - x) > -15$

(d) Using the same axes and scales, graph the functions $f(x) = |x|$ and $g(x) = |2x - 3|$. Use your graph to solve for $x \in R$:

(i) $|x| = |2x - 3|$

(ii) $|2x - 3| < |x|$

7. (a) Solve the following inequalities, $x \in R$:

    (i) $|x| < 4$

    (ii) $|x + 1| > 4$

    (iii) $2|x + 4| \geqslant |x - 1|$

    (iv) $6|x - 2| \leqslant |x|$

    (v) $|x - 5| < 3|x + 5|$

(b) Let $f(x) = (x^2 - 1)(x - 1)$.

    (i) Show why $f(x) \geqslant 0$ in each of the following cases:

        1. $x = 0$

        2. $x = 1$

        3. $x > 1$

        4. $0 < x < 1$

        5. $-1 < x < 0$

    (ii) Hence, deduce that $x^3 + 1 \geqslant x^2 + x$ for all $x > -1$.

(c) Show that, for all values of $k \in R$, $x^2 - 3kx + (k^2 - 6) = 0$ has real roots.

(d) Using the same axes and scales, graph the functions $f(x) = 2|x + 1|$ and $g(x) = |4x - 8|$. Using your graph, find the value(s) of $x \in R$ for which $2|x + 1| \geqslant |4x - 8|$. Check your answer using algebra.

8. (a) (i) Use the quadratic formula to find the roots of $2x^2 - 11x - 22 = 0$ correct to one decimal place.

    (ii) Hence, find the greatest value of $n \in Z$, such that $2n^2 < 11(n + 2)$.

(b) Solve the following inequalities, $x \in R$:

    (i) $\dfrac{x + 3}{x - 4} > 3$, $x \neq 4$

    (ii) $\dfrac{x - 3}{x + 7} < 2$, $x \neq -7$

    (iii) $\dfrac{2x - 1}{x - 3} \geqslant 3$, $x \neq 3$

    (iv) $\left|\dfrac{1 - x}{2}\right| \geqslant 5$

(c) (i) Factorise $q^3 - p^3$.

    (ii) If p and q are distinct positive real numbers, prove that:
$$\frac{q^3 - p^3}{pq^2 - qp^2} > 3$$

(d) Using the same axes and scales, graph the functions $f(x) = |x - 2|$ and $g(x) = 2|x|$. Using your graph, find the value(s) of $x \in R$ for which:

    (i) $f(x) = 0$ (iii) $f(x) = g(x)$

    (ii) $g(x) = 0$ (iv) $g(x) \geqslant f(x)$

Use algebra to check each of your answers.

Give one advantage and one disadvantage of using a graph to find roots.

9. (a) If $x^2 + 2kx + (k + 2) = 0$ has equal roots, find two possible values for k. Find the roots in both cases.

(b) Explain graphically why the equation $|2x - 5| = -3$ has no solution. Using your graph, find the range of values of $k \in R$ for which $|2x - 5| = k$ has two real and distinct roots.

(c) Let a, b, c be three distinct positive real numbers.

    (i) Prove that $a^3 + b^3 > a^2b + b^2a$.

    (ii) Write down similar inequalities for $(a^3 + c^3)$ and $(b^3 + c^3)$.

    (iii) Hence, or otherwise, prove that $3(a^3 + b^3 + c^3) > (a^2 + b^2 + c^2)(a + b + c)$.

(d) Mohamad has just celebrated his birthday. He knows that if he doubles the age he will be in three years' time, the answer that he gets will be less than five times his age three years ago. He also knows that if he tripled his age now, he would still be younger than his older brother Saif, who is 27. Given that today is Mohamad's birthday:

    (i) Write down two inequalities representing the above information.

    (ii) Solve each inequality.

    (iii) Write down what age Mohamad is today.

10. (a) Find the least value of $n \in N$, for which $\dfrac{5n + 3}{7 - n} < 1$, $n \neq 7$.

(b) If $p > 0$ and if $x^2 - 2(p - q)x + q^2 = 0$ has real roots, prove that $p \geqslant 2q$.

(c) A drug is administered to a patient by injection into their left arm. The concentration (C) of the drug in the patient's bloodstream is measured in mg/ml and is given by the formula:

$$C = \frac{0.12t}{t^2 + 2}$$

where t is the time since injection measured in hours.

When will the concentration of the drug in the patient's blood exceed 0.04 mg/ml?

11. (a) $f(x) = \dfrac{100}{x + 1}$ is a function, defined for all $x \in R$, $x \neq -1$. Find the values of x for which $f(x) > 5$.

(b) Prove that the roots of the equation $(p + q - r)x^2 + 2(p + q)x + (p + q + r) = 0$ are real for all $p, q, r \in R$.

(c) If a is the area of the rectangle and p is the perimeter, prove that $p^2 - 16a \geqslant 0$.

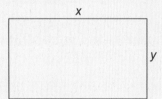

12. (a) Find the values of k for which $(2k + 1)x^2 - (k + 2)x + 1 = 0$ has two equal roots.

(b) Show that it is impossible for the equation $(x - 1)(x + 7) = k(x + 2)$ to have equal roots, where $k \in R$.

(c) In August 2010, Washington Redskins NFL footballer Albert Haynesworth was reportedly suffering from rhabdomyolysis, a rare medical condition that can result from extreme physical exertion. Rhabdomyolysis causes levels of creatine kinase to rise in the blood. The levels of creatine kinase in the blood for the first six days after onset of the condition are given by the formula:

$$(0.0004)L = 3 + 11t - 2t^2$$

where L is level in units/litre and t is time (since onset) in days.

A patient with rhabdomyolysis requires hospitalisation when levels of creatine kinase exceed 8,000 units/litre.

For how long would you expect Albert Haynesworth to have required hospitalisation? Answer to the nearest hour.

chapter 5

Arithmetic

Learning Outcomes

In this chapter you will learn how to:

- ⊃ Calculate percentage error and tolerance
- ⊃ Solve problems involving:
  - ⊃ Rates, income tax and PRSI
  - ⊃ Value added tax (VAT)
  - ⊃ Costing (materials, labour and wastage)

5.1 APPROXIMATION, PERCENTAGE ERROR AND TOLERANCE

Estimates and Approximations of Calculations

Sometimes it is necessary for us to make **estimates** and **approximations** of calculations. This can be to save time or money or simply for convenience. In performing rough calculations or estimates we sometimes round off numbers to make our calculations easier and quicker.

If a hardware store was doing a stocktake (i.e. a count of all stock in the shop), it would be far too time consuming and costly for staff to count every single screw. Equally if a shop owner had a pick-and-mix stand for sweets, they would rarely count every sweet. They would simply make estimates.

Rounding is often used when we are estimating or approximating calculations.

KEY WORDS

- **Percentage error**
- **Accumulated error**
- **Tolerance**
- **Gross income**
- **Net/take-home pay**
- **Statutory deductions**
- **Non-statutory deductions**
- **Income tax (PAYE)**
- **PRSI**
- **USC**
- **Standard rate cut-off point**
- **Tax credit**
- **Gross tax**
- **Tax payable**
- **VAT**

Error

Humans are bound to make errors from time to time. Using estimates and approximations also leads to errors. To improve our precision, it is good practice to have an idea of how much we have possibly erred. Also, small errors left unchecked can grow over time. That is why we calculate **percentage error**.

Calculating Percentage Error

Step 1 Get the **observed value** and the **accurate value**.

Step 2 Subtract the observed value from the accurate value and take the positive:

Error = |Accurate – Observed|

Step 3 Divide the error by the accurate value:

$$\text{Relative error} = \frac{\text{Error}}{\text{Accurate value}}$$

Step 4 Multiply by 100 to calculate the percentage error.

FORMULA

$$\text{Relative error} = \frac{\text{Error}}{\text{Accurate value}}$$

$$\text{Percentage error} = \text{Relative error} \times 100$$

Worked Example 5.1

Find the percentage error in taking 1 cm for 0.8 cm.

Solution

Step 1 Observed value = 1 cm

Accurate value = 0.8 cm

Step 2 Error = $|0.8 - 1|$

$= 0.2$

Step 3 Relative error $= \dfrac{0.2}{0.8} = \dfrac{1}{4}$

Step 4 Percentage error

$= \dfrac{1}{4} \times 100$

$= 25\%$

Tolerance

Any measurement made with a measuring device is approximate.

If two students were asked to measure an object, they may very well come back with two different measurements. The difference between the two measurements is called a **variation**.

Note that variations and errors due to approximations are not the same as 'mistakes'.

Tolerance is the greatest range of variation that can be allowed.

To determine the tolerance in a measurement, add and subtract one-half of the precision of the measuring instrument that is being used.

For example, a metric ruler is used to measure the length of an object. The result is 10.5 cm and the ruler has a precision of 0.1 cm (i.e. the ruler gives measurement to the nearest millimetre). The **tolerance interval** is 10.5 ± 0.05 cm. Any measurements within the tolerance interval are regarded as correct or acceptable.

Worked Example 5.2

Colin works as a quality control officer in a factory that manufactures 14-cm-long pencils. He uses a metric ruler to check the length of pencils he randomly samples. The ruler has a precision of 0.5 cm.

(i)   What is the tolerance interval for a pencil in this factory?

(ii) If Colin picks a pencil at random and it is 14.06 cm, will it be accepted or rejected?

Solution

(i)   Tolerance interval $= 14 \pm \dfrac{1}{2}(0.5)$

$= 14 \pm 0.25$ cm

(ii) The pencil will be accepted, as its length (14.06 cm) is inside the tolerance interval, i.e. $13.75 \leqslant 14.06 \leqslant 14.25$.

ARITHMETIC

Accumulated Error

> **Accumulated error** is the collected inaccuracy that can occur when multiple errors are combined.

If the solution of a problem requires many arithmetic operations, each of which is performed using rounded numbers, the accumulated error may significantly affect the result.

Worked Example 5.3

ABC Ltd has a policy of rounding its invoices to the nearest euro when billing clients.
If ABC had the following invoices in the last month, calculate the accumulated error:

Invoice 1   Amount before rounding = €1,560.46

Invoice 2   Amount before rounding = €950.32

Invoice 3   Amount before rounding = €144.52

Solution

Step 1   Calculate the actual amount billed.

Invoice 1   Rounded amount = €1,560

Invoice 2   Rounded amount = €950

Invoice 3   Rounded amount = €145

Amount billed = €2,655

Step 2   Calculate the amount that would be billed if rounding was not applied.

Total bill = 1,560.46 + 950.32 + 144.52

= €2,655.30

Step 3   Calculate the accumulated error.

Error = 2,655.30 − 2,655

= €0.30

Exercise 5.1

1. Copy and complete the following table:

	Accurate value	Observed value	Error	Relative error	% Error correct to 2 decimal places
(i)	150	149			
(ii)	36	36.9			
(iii)	180	183			
(iv)	4.8	5			
(v)	6.7	7			
(vi)	54.15	55			
(vii)	1.36	1.5			
(viii)	502	500			
(ix)	360	359			
(x)	58.6	60			

2. If 56 is taken as an approximation for 55.4, calculate to two decimal places the percentage error.

3. If 2.3 is taken as an approximation for 2.33, calculate to two decimal places the percentage error.

4. The mass of a bag of flour should be 1 kg. A quality control inspector misreads the weight of one bag and finds it to be 1,010 grams. What is the percentage error?

5. The depth of water in a reservoir is estimated to be 1.6 m. The true depth is 1.56 m. What is the percentage error, correct to one decimal place?

6. The value of $\dfrac{49.27 + 11.15}{15.24 - 3.06}$ was estimated to be 5. Calculate:

   (i) The error

   (ii) The percentage error, correct to one decimal place

7. The value of $\dfrac{40.354}{\sqrt{16.45}}$ was estimated to be 10. Calculate:

   (i) The error

   (ii) The percentage error, correct to one decimal place

8. A statement arrives at an office showing four invoices that need to be paid:

Invoice 1	€245.45
Invoice 2	€364.78
Invoice 3	€1,445.12
Invoice 4	€4,500.25

   The office manager checks the statement quickly to make sure the final figure is accurate. She ignores the cent amount on each invoice.

   (i) What is the total that she arrives at?

   (ii) What is the correct amount owed?

   (iii) What is the accumulated error?

9. A door is measured with a measuring tape of accuracy 0.1 cm. The observed measurement is 54 cm. What is the tolerance interval on this measurement?

10. A coffee producer sells coffee in 450 g bags. Packets of coffee are randomly picked and weighed with a precision of 5 g.

    (i) What is the tolerance interval for the weight of a bag of coffee?

    (ii) If a bag of coffee is picked at random and is found to be 453 g, should the packet be rejected?

5.2 COSTING: MATERIALS, LABOUR AND WASTAGE

Managers need to know the costs involved in getting their products to the market, for a number of reasons:

- **Planning** – Having an accurate cost of a product allows managers to set an accurate price.
- **Control** – By comparing the budgeted cost of a product with the actual cost of the product, managers can identify areas of the business that are underperforming or doing very well.

- **Stock valuation** – At the end of the financial year, all stocks need to be valued for accounting purposes. It is also important that businesses that manufacture their own products have a value for their goods for insurance purposes.

To get an accurate value, all the costs involved in getting the product to its finished state must be included in the valuation. The table below shows examples of both direct and indirect costs for a company manufacturing school desks.

Direct costs (costs directly linked to production)	Materials	Raw materials used in the manufacture of the product	Wood, metal frames
	Labour	Wages of those who work directly in the manufacture of the product	Saw operators who cut table tops, workers who assemble the desks, workers who spray the desk frames and varnish the table tops
	Direct expenses	Any expenses that may be attributed directly to the product	Hire of special equipment
Indirect costs (costs not directly linked to production)			Factory rent, rates, light and heat

Direct costs are costs linked directly to production.

Indirect costs are costs not linked directly to production, e.g. factory rent, rates, light and heat bills.

Variable costs are costs that vary directly with the level of output or activity, e.g. sales commission based on unit sales.

Fixed costs are costs that are not affected by the level of activity (within a given range of activity). For example, the rent for the factory is fixed regardless of the amount of product produced. If production exceeds the level the factory can cope with, additional space may need to be rented, causing the cost to rise.

Wastage

A manager will try to minimise wastage where possible in a business, as it reduces any profit that the company might make. However, there will inevitably be some wastage in almost all businesses because of human error and machine faults.

Worked Example 5.4

A company budgets to manufacture 5,000 units of its product.

The materials required are 50 kg per unit @ €0.50 per kg.

Each unit produced requires six hours of direct labour @ €7 per hour.

Indirect costs are €15,000.

Calculate:

(i) The cost of manufacture of the 5,000 units

(ii) The unit cost of manufacture

Solution

(i)

Cost of manufacture (5,000 units)		
Direct materials	5,000 units @ 50 kg	250,000 kg
Cost per kg		€0.50
Cost of materials	250,000 × 0.50	€125,000
Direct labour	5,000 units × 6 hours	30,000 hrs
Cost per labour hour		€7
Total labour cost	30,000 × 7	€210,000
Indirect costs		€15,000
Total cost of manufacture	125,000 + 210,000 + 15,000	€350,000

(ii) The unit cost of manufacture $= \dfrac{350,000}{5,000}$

$= €70$

Worked Example 5.5

A confectionary company receives an order for 250 custom-made products for Christmas hampers. The production team has given the following breakdown for the product:

Material requirements	
Material A	25 g per unit
Material B	100 g per unit
Labour hours	0.05 per unit
Variable costs	€0.75 per unit
Fixed costs allocated to the product	€500
Material A	€0.01 per g
Material B	€0.05 per g
Labour rate	€7 per hour

(i) Find the total cost of the order and the cost per unit.

(ii) Find the price the company should charge per unit to make a profit on cost of 25% on each unit produced.

(iii) If on average 5% of the finished goods are damaged in the warehouse, how many units should the company produce to ensure the order is covered?

Solution

(i)

Costs		Cost (€)
Material A	25 g × 250 × €0.01	62.50
Material B	100 g × 250 × €0.05	1,250.00
Labour	0.05 × 250 × €7	87.50
Variable costs	250 × €0.75	187.50
Fixed costs		500.00
Total cost		2,087.50

The total cost of the order is €2,087.50.

$$\text{Unit cost} = \frac{€2,087.50}{250} = €8.35$$

(ii) A profit on cost of 25%

Profit: €8.35 × 0.25 = €2.0875

Selling price: €8.35 + €2.0875 = €10.4375

$$\approx €10.44$$

∴ The company should charge approximately €10.44 per unit to make a profit on cost of 25% on each unit produced.

(iii) On average 5% of goods are damaged.

So the 250 units represent 95% of the required production.

95% = 250 units

$$1\% = \frac{250}{95}$$

$$100\% = \frac{250}{95} \times 100$$

$$= 263.1579 \text{ units}$$

∴ The company should produce 264 units to ensure that there will be enough stock to meet the order.

Exercise 5.2

1. Distinguish between:

   (i) Direct and indirect costs

   (ii) Fixed and variable costs

2. Jimmy Jeans received an order from a retail outlet for a batch of 10,000 pairs of jeans.

The following information relates to the production costs of the jeans:

	€
Direct materials	25,000
Factory rent	11,000
Wages of material cutters	4,000
Wages of machinists	€0.75 per unit produced
Factory overheads	20,000

(i) Calculate the total manufacturing costs of the batch.

(ii) Calculate the unit cost of a pair of jeans.

3. A deli recently received an order for 135 mini quiches.

(i) If wastage of the finished product is assumed to be 10%, how many quiches should the deli prepare?

The production costs of the quiches are as follows:

Direct materials	€250
Labour	€11 per hour
Labour hours required	4
Deli overheads allocated to this job	€100

(ii) Calculate the cost of the batch (based on the number of units calculated in (i)).

(iii) Calculate the cost per unit.

(iv) If the deli wishes to make a profit of 20%, what price should it charge per quiche?

4. Townsend Ltd manufactures two products X and Y. Both products use the same raw materials.

The production costs are as follows:

	Product *X*	Product *Y*
Units produced	6,000	5,000
Materials in each product	8 kg	9 kg
Production time per unit	6 hours	5 hours
Wages	€5 per hour	
Cost of materials per kg	€3	

(i) Calculate the materials required for the production of product X.

(ii) Calculate the materials required for the production of product Y.

(iii) Calculate the cost of materials for product X and product Y.

(iv) Calculate the total cost of labour for products X and Y.

5. Nolan Plc is a boat manufacturing company. Two materials are used in the manufacture of the boat. An order is placed for 60 units.

The following table gives the production costs for one unit:

Material *A*	36 metres
Material *B*	108 metres
Expected price per metre	€7
Labour hours required	60
Labour rate	€7 per hour

There is approximate wastage of 10% on all materials used.

(i) How many metres of material A should be purchased to meet the requirements of the order?

(ii) How many metres of material B should be purchased to meet the requirements of the order?

(iii) Calculate the cost price of this order.

(iv) Calculate the selling price per unit this company should charge if they wish to make a profit of 15%.

6. SIOAL Ltd manufactures two products, Primary and Superb.

It expects to sell Primary at €190 and Superb at €230.

Sales demand is expected to be 6,000 units of Primary and 4,500 units of Superb.

Both products use the same raw materials and skilled labour but in different quantities per unit as follows:

	Primary	**Superb**
Material W	6 kg	5 kg
Material X	4 kg	7 kg
Skilled labour	7 hours	8 hours

The expected prices for raw materials during 2011 are:

- Material W: €3 per kg
- Material X: €5 per kg

The skilled labour rate is expected to be €11.00 per hour.

The company's production overhead costs are expected to be:

- Variable: €4.50 per skilled labour hour
- Fixed: €116,000 per annum

If SIOAL produces all units required for sales, find:

(i) The amount of material W needed

(ii) The amount of material X needed

(iii) The total labour hours used in production

(iv) The total labour cost of production

(v) The total cost of production (including variable and fixed costs)

(vi) The profit made on each product if the company sells at the expected prices

(vii) The profit made if the prices are to be reduced by 10%

5.3 INCOME TAX

Income and Deductions

Employees expect to earn money for the work they carry out.

- If you are paid according to the number of hours worked or goods produced, this is called a **wage**.
- If you are paid the same amount regardless of the number of hours worked or goods produced, this is called a **salary**.

Most people cannot keep all the money they earn. Employees have several **deductions** made to their earnings before they receive their money.

Gross pay or **gross income** is money earned before deductions are made.

Net pay or **net income** is money received after all deductions have been made.

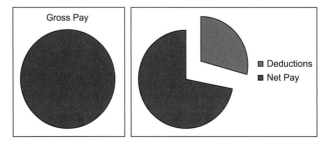

Statutory and Non-Statutory Deductions

Deductions can be **statutory** or **non-statutory**.

Statutory deduction	What is it used for?
Income tax (PAYE – Pay As You Earn)	Payment of public services, e.g. Gardaí, health care, education, etc.
Pay-Related Social Insurance (PRSI)	Old-age pensions, jobseeker's benefit, jobseeker's allowance, child benefit, etc.
Universal Social Charge (USC)	Income for the state

> **Statutory deductions** are payments that **must** be made to the government. They are taken from gross pay by the employer.

The rates for the universal social charge (USC) are as follows (figures accurate for 2011):

■ Zero, if total income is under €4,004

For people with an income of €4,004 or more, the rates will be:

Rate of USC	Charged on income from
2%	€0 to €10,036
4%	€10,036.01 to €16,016
7%	Above €16,016

> **Non-statutory deductions** are voluntary deductions. They are taken from gross pay by the employer at the request of the employee.

People over the age of 70 have a maximum USC rate of of 4% (even on incomes over €16,016).

Medical card holders also have a top USC rate of 4%.

Examples of voluntary deductions include healthcare payments, union fees, pension payments, etc.

Income Tax (PAYE)

There are two rates of income tax in Ireland.

■ The lower rate is called the **standard rate** of tax.

■ The higher rate is called the **higher rate** of tax.

> Note that these rates can vary from year to year.

For example, the first €32,800 that a single person earns is taxed at 20%, and any income above this amount is taxed at 41% (figures accurate for 2011).

For a married couple where both people are working, the first €65,600 is taxed at 20% and any additional income is taxed at 41%.

> The amount up to which an employee is taxed at the standard rate is called the **standard rate cut-off point**.

Every employee receives a **tax credit** certificate. This shows the employee's tax credit. This amount can change for individual employees.

Standard rate cut-off point → } Taxed at 41% } Taxed at 20%

> **Gross tax** is the amount of tax owed to the state before tax credits are deducted.

> **Tax payable** is gross tax less the tax credit.

> The **tax credit** is a sum deducted from the total amount (gross tax) a taxpayer owes to the state.

Worked Example 5.6

Albert earns €27,000 a year. He pays tax at a rate of 20%. He has instructed his employer to pay his annual health insurance premium of €550 directly from his salary. He has a tax credit of €1,950. Find Albert's:

(i) Tax payable   (iii) Net pay

(ii) Total deductions

Solution

(i) Gross tax = €27,000 × 20%

= €27,000 × 0.20 = €5,400

Tax payable = gross tax – tax credit

= €5,400 – €1,950 = €3,450

∴ The tax payable is €3,450.

(ii) Total deductions = tax payable + health insurance

= €3,450 + €550 = €4,000

∴ The total deductions are €4,000.

(iii) Net pay = gross pay – total deductions

= €27,000 – €4,000

= €23,000

∴ The net pay is €23,000.

 Worked Example 5.7

Sanabel earns €50,000 per annum.
Calculate the amount that will be deducted from her pay for the universal social charge.

Rate of USC	Charged on income from
2%	€0 to €10,036
4%	€10,036.01 to €16,016
7%	Above €16,016

Solution

Step 1

Break the salary down into the various threshold amounts.

€10,036 @ 2%

€16,016 – €10,036 = €5,980 @ 4%

€50,000 – €16,016 = €33,984 @ 7%

Step 2

Calculate the percentages.

First	Next	Remainder
€10,036	€5,980	€33,984
2%	4%	7%
€200.72	€239.2	€2,378.88

∴ The total USC = €200.72 + €239.20 + €2,378.88

= €2,818.80

Pay-Related Social Insurance (PRSI)

The amount of PRSI you pay depends on your earnings and the class under which you are insured.

For people in employment in Ireland, social insurance contributions are divided into different categories, known as classes or rates of contribution. The type of class and rate of contribution you pay is determined by the nature of your work.

ARITHMETIC

There are 11 different classes of social insurance in Ireland. The majority of people fall into Class A. The other classes are B, C, D, E, H, J, K, M, P and S. If you are insured under one of these classes, you are paying insurance at a lower rate than Class A contributors, which means that you are not entitled to the full range of social insurance payments. This is because you are paying less towards social insurance than a Class A contributor.

Class A applies to people in industrial, commercial and service employment who are employed under a contract of service with a **reckonable pay** of €38 or more per week. It also includes civil servants and public servants recruited from 6 April 1995.

> **Reckonable pay** is the employee's gross pay plus notional pay (or benefit in kind), if applicable.

The PRSI contribution is made up of a number of different components, which include:

- Social insurance at the appropriate percentage rate for employees and employers, which varies according to the pay and PRSI class of the employee and benefits for which he or she is insured
- A health contribution, paid by the employee where applicable, which goes towards funding the health service
- The 0.70% National Training Fund Levy, which is included in the employers' contribution in classes A and H

PRSI is calculated on the employee's weekly or reckonable pay.

PRSI contribution rates from 1 January 2011					
Non-cumulative weekly earnings bands	PRSI Subclass	How much of weekly earnings	Employee	Employer	Employee & Employer
			%	%	%
Private and some public sector employments					
Up to €37.99	JO*	All	0	0.50	0.50
€38–€352	AO	All	0	8.50	8.50
€352.01–€356	AX	First €127	0	8.50	8.50
		Balance	4.00	8.50	12.50
€356.01–€500	AL	First €127	0	10.75	10.75
		Balance	4.00	10.75	14.75
More than €500	A1	First €127	0	10.75	10.75
		Balance	4.00	10.75	14.75

Worked Example 5.8

Chloe earns €650 per week. She is in Class A1 for PRSI, which has the following rates:

	First €127	Balance
Employee %	0	4
Employer %	10.75	10.75

Calculate:

(i) Her PRSI payment this week

(ii) Her employer's PRSI payment this week

(iii) The total amount of PRSI that will be paid this week

Solution

(i) **Step 1**

Calculate the amount she must pay PRSI on.

€650 − €127 = €523

Step 2

Calculate the PRSI.

€523 × 4% = €20.92

∴ Chloe's PRSI payment is €20.92.

(ii) **Step 1**

Calculate the amount of PRSI paid on the first €127.

€127 × 0.1075 = €13.6525

Step 2

Calculate the PRSI paid on the balance of her earnings.

€650 – €127 = €523

€523 × 0.1075 = €56.2225

Step 3

Calculate the total PRSI paid by the employer.

€13.6525 + €56.2225 = €69.875

∴ The PRSI payment by Chloe's employer is approximately €69.88.

(iii) Total PRSI payment = €20.92 + €69.88

= €90.80

∴ Total PRSI payment is €90.80.

Calculating Income Tax and Net Income

Worked Example 5.9

Derek has a gross annual income of €50,000. His standard rate cut-off point is €32,000. The standard rate of tax is 20%. The higher rate is 40%. His tax credit is €3,500. Derek is in Class A1 for PRSI. Assuming a 52-week year, calculate Derek's:

(i) Gross tax   (iii) Net income (ignoring PRSI)   (v) Net income after PRSI has been paid

(ii) Tax payable   (iv) PRSI payment

Solution

(i) Gross tax = standard tax + higher tax

Standard tax = standard rate cut-off point × standard rate

= €32,000 × 0.20 = €6,400

Higher tax = income above standard cut-off point × higher rate

Income above standard rate cut-off point = €50,000 – €32,000 = €18,000

Higher tax = €18,000 × 0.40 = €7,200

Gross tax = standard tax + higher tax

= €6,400 + €7,200 = €13,600

∴ The gross tax is €13,600.

(ii) Tax payable = gross tax – tax credit

= €13,600 – €3,500 = €10,100

∴ The tax payable is €10,100.

(iii) Net income = gross income – tax payable

= €50,000 – €10,100 = €39,900

∴ Derek's net income is €39,900.

(iv) PRSI payment

The rate for the first €127 per week is 0% for the employee.

∴ Amount at 0% for one year = €127 × 52 = €6,604

PRSI is calculated based on €50,000 – €6,604 = €43,396.

€43,396 has a rate of 4%.

€43,396 × 0.04 = €1,735.84

∴ The PRSI payment is €1,735.84.

(v) Net income – PRSI

€39,900 – €1,735.84 = €38,164.16

∴ The net income after **all** deductions is €38,164.16.

 Exercise 5.3

Ignore USC and PRSI unless asked to calculate.

1. Robert earns €25,000 per annum. He pays tax at a standard rate of 20%. Calculate his tax payable (assume no tax credits).

2. Angela earns €46,000 per annum and pays tax at a rate of 22.5%. She has a tax credit of €2,600. Calculate her tax payable.

3. Shane earns €41,500 per annum. He pays tax at a rate of 22%. He has a tax credit of €2,340. Calculate his net income.

4. Jolene recently moved jobs. She is now earning €46,000 per annum. She has a standard rate cut-off point of €36,000. She pays standard tax at a rate of 20%. She pays 41% on the remainder of her earnings. She has no tax credits due to an underpayment of tax last year. Calculate her net income.

5. Sally earns €94,500 per annum. She has a standard rate cut-off point of €34,000. She pays tax at a standard rate of 21% and a higher rate of 42%. Her tax credit is €2,450.
Calculate:

   (i) Her tax payable   (ii) Her net pay

6. Ian earns €37,000 a year. His standard rate cut-off point is €37,400. The standard rate of tax is 21%. His tax credit is €2,100. His union fees are €450 and his annual health insurance is €350. What is Ian's annual take-home pay?

7. Abdul earns €33,000 a year. His tax bill for the year is €6,930. What percentage of his income is paid in tax?

8. Neasa's tax bill for last year was €6,300. Her tax credit was €1,300. Her gross income was €38,000. She paid tax at the standard rate only.

   (i) How much was her gross tax?

   (ii) What rate did she pay tax at?

9. A married couple earn €74,000 a year. They have a tax credit of €4,600. Last year they paid tax of €10,940. They pay tax at the standard rate. What is the standard rate in this case?

10. Lorraine and Ger had a net income of €60,400 last year. They paid tax at the standard rate which amounted to €14,700. They had a combined tax credit of €3,600. Their non-statutory deductions were €2,000.
How much was their combined gross pay?

11. Bryan has a gross income of €50,000. He pays tax at 20% on the first €32,000 he earns and 42% on the remainder. His tax credit is €3,500. What is his tax payable?

12. Nicky earns €35,000 a year.
What is her USC charge?

13. Conor has a gross income of €72,000. His standard rate cut-off point is €34,600. The standard rate of tax is 20% and the higher rate is 41%. He has a tax credit of €3,000. He is in the class A1 for PRSI. (Assume a 52-week year.)

   (i) What is his PRSI contribution per week (two d.p.)?

   (ii) What is his employer's PRSI contribution per week?

   (iii) Calculate his USC payment for the year.

   (iv) What is his weekly net income after all deductions?

14. Larry has a gross income of €60,000 a year. His standard rate cut-off point is €36,400. The standard rate of tax is 20% and the higher rate is 41%. He has a tax credit of €2,400. He is in class A1 for PRSI. (Assume a 52-week year.)

   (i) What is his PRSI contribution per week?

   (ii) What is his employer's PRSI contribution per week?

   (iii) Calculate his USC payment for the year.

   (iv) What is his weekly net income after all deductions?

15. Peter and Siobhán have a combined income of €150,000. They pay tax at 20% on the first €65,300 they earn and 41% on the remainder. They both pay PRSI at class A1 rates.

   (i) What is their total PRSI payment for the year? (Assume a 52-week year.)

   (ii) What is their combined net pay for the year? (Ignore USC and tax credits.)

16. Carol has a standard rate cut-off point of €36,400. The standard rate of tax is 20% and the higher rate is 41%. If Carol's gross tax is €10,396, what is her gross income?

17. (i) Sorcha has tax credits of €2,800 for the year and her standard rate cut-off point is €32,000. Her gross income is €45,000. The standard rate of income tax is 20% and the higher rate is 41%. Calculate her total tax payable.

   (ii) Eoin pays tax at the same rate as Sorcha. Eoin's tax credits are €2,900, and he has the same standard cut-off point as Sorcha. His total tax payable amounts to €13,680. Calculate Eoin's gross income.

   (iii) What is Eoin's and Sorcha's universal social charge, respectively?

5.4 VAT: VALUE-ADDED TAX

> **VAT** is a tax charged by the government on consumer spending.

For example, if you buy a computer game, you pay **VAT** on the game.

VAT is collected by the Revenue Commissioner. It is collected in stages, starting with the manufacturing stage and ending with the sale of the finished product to the consumer. VAT is collected at the following stages from the following people:

- ■ Manufacturer
- ■ Wholesaler
- ■ Distributor
- ■ Retailer
- ■ Consumer

A tax is placed on the value added to the product or service at each stage, and this is where the name 'value-added tax' comes from.

VAT Rates

There are several different rates of VAT (standard for 2011):

Standard rate	Applies to most goods and services	21%
Reduced rate	Applies to labour-intensive services, e.g. hairdressing	13.5%
Zero rate	Applies to many foods and medicines and to children's clothes	0%
Special rate	Applies to the sale of livestock	4.8%

VAT is a tax on consumer spending. It is collected by VAT-registered traders on their supplies of goods and services effected within the State for consideration to their customers. Each such trader in the chain of supply from manufacturer through to retailer charges VAT on his or her sales and is entitled to deduct from this amount the VAT paid on his or her purchases. The effect of offsetting VAT on purchases against VAT on sales is to impose the tax on the added value at each stage of production - hence Value-Added Tax. The final consumer, who is not registered for VAT, absorbs VAT as part of the purchase price. The following example illustrates how this works:

	Purchase Transactions					Sale Transactions			
	Price Paid (Ex. VAT) €	VAT €	Total Purchase Price €	Value Added €	Price Charged (Ex. VAT) €	VAT @ 21% €	Total Sale Price €	Credit for VAT Paid €	Net to Collector General €
Manufacturer	-	-	-	100	100	21	121	0	21
Wholesaler	100	21	121	100	200	42	242	21	21
Distributor	200	42	242	100	300	63	363	42	21
Retailer	300	63	363	200	500	105	605	63	42
Consumer	500	105	605	-	-	-	-	-	-
							500		105

As may be seen from the above example, the consumer pays a total of €605 for the finished product, of which €105 is VAT.

Source: VAT Guide 2008, www.revenue.ie

> Remember that these rates can change from year to year and country to country.

You can find which rate of VAT applies to different goods and services by checking the list available on the Revenue website at www.revenue.ie.

Rates of VAT vary depending on the product or service being purchased. For example, chocolate spread has a zero rate but chocolate biscuits have a 21% rate.

Worked Example 5.10

Claire sees a handbag in a shop window. The sign says '€250 + VAT @ 21%'.

How much will she pay for the bag?

€250 + VAT @ 21%

Solution

Step 1 Find 21% of €250.

$$VAT = €250 × 0.21$$

$$∴ VAT = €52.50$$

Step 2 Find the total price.

$$Total\ price = €250 + VAT$$

$$= €250 + €52.50$$

$$∴ Price\ paid = €302.50$$

Worked Example 5.11

Craig buys his boyfriend a birthday present that costs €215.65 including VAT @ 13.5%.

What was the original bill before VAT was added?

Solution

Original bill = 100%

Original bill + VAT = 113.5%

$$113.5\% = €215.65$$

$$∴ 1\% = \frac{€215.65}{113.5}$$

$$1\% = €1.90$$

$$100\% = €1.90 × 100$$

$$= €190$$

$$∴ Original\ bill = €190$$

Worked Example 5.12

Una bought a new TV for €484. When she looked at the receipt, she noticed the amount of VAT charged was €84. What rate of VAT was charged?

Step 2 Express the VAT as a percentage of the original cost.

$$Rate\ of\ VAT = \frac{VAT}{Cost\ before\ VAT} × \frac{100}{1}$$

> Note that VAT is charged on the **original** cost figure.

$$= \frac{84}{400} × \frac{100}{1}$$

$$∴ Rate\ of\ VAT = 21\%$$

Solution

Step 1 Find the cost before VAT.

$$Cost\ before\ VAT = Final\ cost - VAT$$

$$= €484 - €84$$

$$∴ Cost\ before\ VAT = €400$$

Exercise 5.4

> Give all answers correct to the nearest cent where necessary.

1. If VAT charged on hairdressing is 13.5%, find the VAT to be charged on each of the following haircuts if the cost before VAT is:

   (i) €20   (iii) €16

   (ii) €14   (iv) €12.50

2. The VAT charged on TVs is 21%. Find the **total price** of the following TVs if the price before VAT is:

   (i) €450   (iii) €800

   (ii) €190   (iv) €899

3. Find the total price of ordering a pizza if the price of the pizza is €15 + VAT @ 21%.

4. The school canteen bought 600 bottles of fruit juice from a wholesaler at €0.50 each + VAT @ 21%. Find the total cost of the fruit juice.

5. Conor buys two DVDs. The DVDs cost €18 and €12 excluding VAT. VAT is charged at 20%.

   What is the total cost of the DVDs?

6. Mohamed was shopping in a cash and carry. He didn't realise that all the prices stated were before VAT. When he got to the cash desk his bill came to €283.75.

   If VAT was charged at 13.5%, what was the cost of his bill before VAT?

7. The government of a particular country have decided to charge one standard rate of VAT @ 25%. If the price of a car (including VAT) is €9,000, how much of this price is VAT?

8. A laptop costs €990.99 and this includes VAT at 21%.
   How much of the selling price should be given to the Revenue Commissioner?

9. An auctioneer charges VAT at a rate of 21%. If the auctioneer is successful in selling a house, she charges a fee of 1.25% of the selling price.

   If she sells a house for €270,000, how much will her fee to the client be:

   (i) Before VAT   (ii) After VAT

10. In a particular year's budget, the VAT rate falls from 13% to 12.5%. The price of a phone drops by €3.50.

    (i) What was the price of the phone before the change in VAT rate?

    (ii) What is the new VAT amount on the phone?

    (iii) What is the total price of the phone now?

    (iv) If the VAT rate had increased to 17%, how much would the phone cost?

Rate of USC	Charged on income from
2%	€0 to €10,036
4%	€10,036.01 to €16,016
7%	Above €16,016

PRSI contribution rates from 1 January 2011					
Non-cumulative weekly earnings bands	PRSI Subclass	How much of weekly earnings	Employee	Employer	Employee & Employer
			%	%	%
Private and some public sector employments					
Up to €37.99	JO*	All	0	0.50	0.50
€38–€352	AO	All	0	8.50	8.50
€352.01–€356	AX	First €127	0	8.50	8.50
		Balance	4.00	8.50	12.50
€356.01–€500	AL	First €127	0	10.75	10.75
		Balance	4.00	10.75	14.75
More than €500	A1	First €127	0	10.75	10.75
		Balance	4.00	10.75	14.75

1. Shane has an annual gross income of €60,000. He pays tax at 20% on the first €32,000 he earns and 42% on the remainder. His tax credit is €3,100.
   What is his tax payable?

2. Harry earns €35,600 per annum. What is his USC?

3. The standard rate of income tax is 20% and the higher rate is 42%. Eoin has tax credits of €1,493 for the year and a standard rate cut-off point of €30,000.
   He has a gross income of €31,650 for the year.

   (i) After tax is paid, what is Eoin's income for the year?

   (ii) What would Eoin's gross income for the year need to be in order for him to have an after-tax income of €29,379?

4. (a) The standard rate of income tax is 20% and the higher rate is 42%. Liz has tax credits of €2,700 for the year and a standard rate cut-off point of €22,000. She has a gross income of €45,000 for the year.
   Caculate the total tax payable by Liz for the year.

   (b) Donal pays tax at the same rates as Liz. Donal has tax credits of €2,900 for the year and has the same standard rate cut-off point as Liz.
   His total tax payable amounts to €13,680 for the year.
   Calculate Donal's gross income for the year?

5. Cormac has a gross income of €50,000. His total income tax payable amounts to €10,460. The standard rate cut-off point is €32,000. The standard rate of tax is 20% and the higher rate is 42%.
   What are Cormac's tax credits for the year?

6. (a) The standard rate of income tax is 20% and the higher rate is 41%. The standard rate cut-off point is €36,500. Molly has a gross income of €47,500 and total tax credits of €1,830.
   Calculate Molly's net income.

   (b) The following year Molly's gross income increases. The tax rates, cut-off point and tax credits remain unchanged. Her net tax now amounts to €15,105.
   What is her new gross income?

7. Laura has a gross income of €45,000 a year. Her standard rate cut-off point is €33,000.
   The standard rate of tax is 20% and the higher rate is 41%. She has a tax credit of €2,400.
   She is in Class A1 for PRSI. (Assume a 52-week year.)

   (i) What is her PRSI contribution per week?

   (ii) What is her employer's PRSI contribution per week?

   (iii) Calculate her USC payment.

   (iv) What is her weekly net income after all deductions?

8. Calculate the VAT to be paid to the Revenue Commissioner on the following invoice:

   > 20 Chairs @ €25 each
   >
   > 12 Tables @ €235 each
   >
   > 16 Stools @ €12 each
   >
   > VAT is charged @ 13.5% on all items.

9. In a particular year's budget, the VAT rate falls from 13.5% to 12.5%. The price of a phone drops
   by €4.50.

   (i) What was the price of the phone before the change in VAT rate?

   (ii) What is the new VAT amount?

   (iii) What is the price of the phone now?

   (iv) If the VAT rate had increased to 15%, how much would the phone have cost?

10. SVC Ltd has recently completed its sales forecasts for the year to 31 December 2012.
    It expects to sell two products: Product 1 @ €125 and Product 2 @ €145.

    Its budgeted sales for Product 1 are 12,000 units and 5,000 units for Product 2.

    Both products use the same materials but in different quantities per unit as follows:

	Product 1	Product 2
Material X	10 kg	5 kg
Material Y	5 kg	7 kg
Skilled labour	5 hours	4 hours

    - Material X: €1.50 per kg
    - Material Y: €3.50 per kg
    - Skilled labour: paid at €7.50 per hour
    - Variable costs: €7 per unit
    - Fixed costs: €180,000

    Calculate:

    (i) The amount of material X needed

    (ii) The amount of material Y needed

    (iii) The total labour hours used
    in production

    (iv) The total labour cost of production

    (v) The total cost of production (including
    variable and fixed costs)

    (vi) The profit made if the company sells at
    the expected prices

    (vii) The profit made if the prices are
    increased by 10%

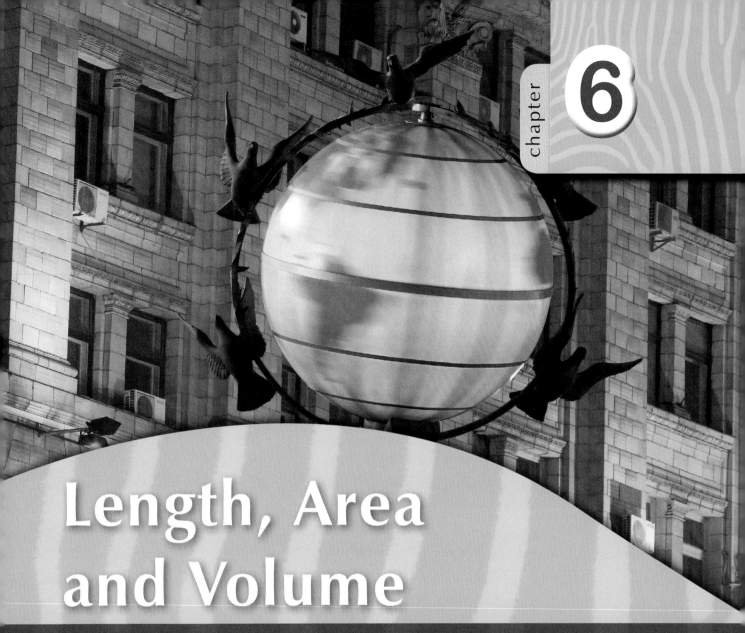

chapter 6

Length, Area and Volume

Learning Outcomes

In this chapter you will learn to:

- ➜ Find the area and perimeter of 2D shapes
- ➜ Find the area and circumference of circles and sectors of circles
- ➜ Solve problems involving area
- ➜ Investigate the nets of rectangular solids
- ➜ Find the surface area and volume of various 3D shapes
- ➜ Solve problems involving surface area and volume
- ➜ Use the trapezoidal rule to approximate area

6.1 TWO-DIMENSIONAL (2D) SHAPES

In everyday life there are many situations in which we need to know the area and perimeter of objects.

Area and Perimeter

Area is the amount of flat space that a shape occupies.

Perimeter is the sum of the length of all the sides of a shape.

Rectangle	**Square**
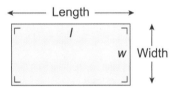 Area = (length × width) = $l \times w$ Perimeter = $2l + 2w$ **or** $2(l + w)$	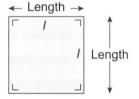 Area = (length)² = l^2 Perimeter = $4l$
Triangle	**Parallelogram**
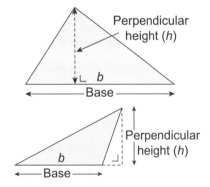 Area = $\frac{1}{2}$ × base × perpendicular height = $\frac{1}{2} bh$	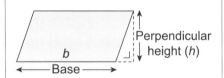 Area = base × perpendicular height = bh

Trapezium

A **trapezium** is a quadrilateral that has one pair of parallel sides.

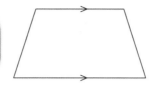

Trapezium	Area = Half the sum of the lengths of the parallel sides (a and b) × perpendicular height between them
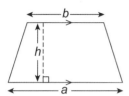	Area = $\frac{1}{2}(a + b)h$ **or** Area = $\left(\dfrac{a + b}{2}\right)h$ This formula appears on page 8 of *Formulae and Tables*.

Worked Example 6.1

The area of the shaded part of the trapezium shown is equal to 270 m². Calculate the value of h.

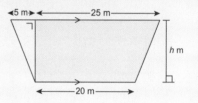

Solution

Area of shaded shape = total area – unshaded area.

Total area (trapezium):

$a = 20$, $b = 30$, $h = ?$

Area $= \frac{1}{2}(a + b)h = \frac{1}{2}(50)(h) = 25h$ m²

Unshaded area (triangle):

Area $= \frac{1}{2}bh = \frac{1}{2}(5)(h) = 2.5h$ m²

$\therefore 25h - 2.5h = 270$

$22.5h = 270$

$h = 12$

$\therefore$ Height $= 12$ m

Area and Circumference of a Circle and Sector of a Circle

The circumference of any circle divided by the length of its diameter is always the same.
This number is π (pronounced 'Pi'). We use π to calculate the area and circumference (length) of a circle or sector of a circle.

$$\pi = \frac{\text{Circumference of a circle}}{\text{Length of diameter}}$$

Circles

FORMULA

Area of a circle $= \pi \times r^2$, usually written as πr^2.

FORMULA

Circumference of a circle $= 2 \times \pi \times r$, usually written as $2\pi r$.

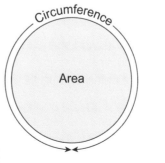

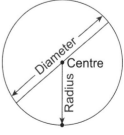

These formulae appear on page 8 of *Formulae and Tables*.

π is an irrational number. To eight decimal places, $\pi = 3.14159265$. As π is an infinite non-recurring decimal, we often use approximations of π in our calculations. In calculating the area or circumference of a circle, we may be told to use one of the following values for π:

■ $\pi = 3.14$ ■ The value of π from the calculator

■ $\pi = \frac{22}{7}$

We may also be asked to leave our answer in terms of π.

Sectors

A **sector** is a specific slice of a circle (a pie-shaped part).

> A **sector** of a circle is the portion of a circle bounded by two radii and the included arc.

FORMULA

Area of sector $= \pi r^2 \left(\dfrac{\theta}{360°} \right)$

FORMULA

Length of arc $l = 2\pi r \left(\dfrac{\theta}{360°} \right)$

These formulae appear on page 9 of *Formulae and Tables*.

Note: θ must be in degrees to use either of these two formulae.

Worked Example 6.2

The area of the sector shown is $1{,}414\frac{2}{7}$ cm^2.

Find the length of the radius r $\left(\pi = \frac{22}{7} \right)$.

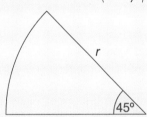

45°

Solution

Area of sector $= \pi r^2 \left(\dfrac{\theta}{360} \right)$

$\therefore \dfrac{22}{7} \times r^2 \times \dfrac{45}{360} = 1{,}414\frac{2}{7}$

$\dfrac{11}{28} r^2 = 1{,}414\frac{2}{7}$

$r^2 = \dfrac{1{,}414\frac{2}{7}}{\frac{11}{28}} = 3{,}600$

$\therefore r = 60$ cm

Worked Example 6.3

A rectangle's width is 3 cm less than its length.
The area of this rectangle is 810 cm^2.
Find both the length and width of this rectangle.

Solution

Let $x =$ length $\quad \therefore$ width $= x - 3$

$x(x - 3) = 810$

$x^2 - 3x = 810$

$x^2 - 3x - 810 = 0$

$(x - 30)(x + 27) = 0$

$x - 30 = 0 \quad$ or $\quad x + 27 = 0$

$x = 30 \quad$ or $\qquad x = -27$

Length $= 30$ cm

$\therefore$ Width $= 30 - 3$

Width $= 27$ cm

Solve the quadratic equation.

As we are dealing with length, we discard the negative answer.

Exercise 6.1

1. Find the area and perimeter (to two decimal places) of each of the following compound shapes (all units are in centimetres; $\pi = 3.14$):

(i)
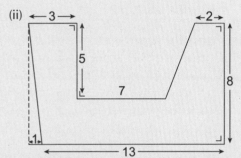

(ii)
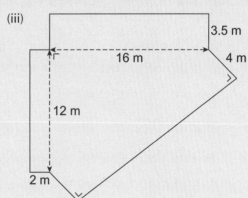

(iii)

![compound shape with 16 m, 3.5 m, 4 m, 12 m, 2 m]

2. Find the area and circumference of each of the following circles:

(i) Radius length = 5 cm
($\pi = 3.14$)

(ii) Radius length = 8 km
$\left(\pi = \frac{22}{7}\right)$

(iii) Radius length = 0.7 m
(in terms of π)

(iv) Diameter length = 2.5 mm
($\pi = 3.14$)

(v) Radius length = 4.5 cm
$\left(\pi = \frac{22}{7}\right)$

(vi) Diameter length = 126 mm
(in terms of π)

3. Find the area, arc length and perimeter of each of the following sectors:

(i) $\pi = 3.14$

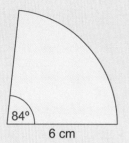

(ii) $\pi = \frac{22}{7}$

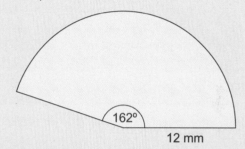

(iii) $\pi = 3.14$

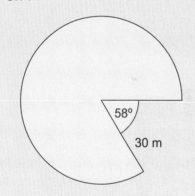

4. Fill in the table below by first finding the radius of each of the circles.

π	r	Area	Circumference
π			24π
3.14			4.71
$\frac{22}{7}$		1,386	
π		324	
3.14		254.34	
$\frac{22}{7}$		346.5	

5. Using the information given, find the measure of the unknown radius or angle of each of the following sectors:

(i) Length of arc = 7π cm

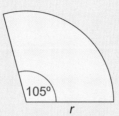

105°

r

(ii) Area = 439.6 cm² (π = 3.14)

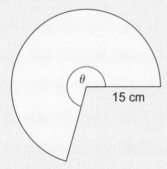

θ

15 cm

(iii) Area = 6.16 cm² (π = $\frac{22}{7}$)

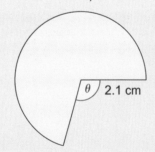

θ 2.1 cm

6. The area of a rectangular lawn is 204 m². The length of the lawn is 5 m more than its width. Calculate the perimeter of the lawn.

7. A part for a machine, pictured below, is cut from a sheet of metal of 1 m². Assuming 2% wastage during the manufacture of the part, how many complete parts can be made from this sheet (π = 3.14)?

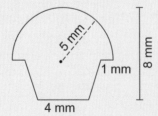

5 mm

1 mm

8 mm

4 mm

8. There is a path 5 metres wide around a small park as shown.

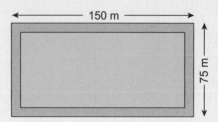

150 m

75 m

Find:

(i) The area of the park

(ii) The area of the path

(iii) The cost of replacing the path if each 2 m² of path costs €7.25

9. A square plastic cover for a drain is shown. Each cover has five circular holes, each with a diameter of 15 cm. If 1 cm² of plastic weighs 0.2 g, how much does the cover weigh, correct to the nearest gram?

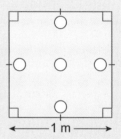

1 m

10. A circular cog has a circumference of 13.288 cm.

(i) Find the radius of the cog (π = $\frac{22}{7}$).

(ii) This cog must be replaced after 5,000 revolutions. How far is this in metres?

11. An office has 1,104 m² of floor space. An extension increases the length by 2 m, the width by 3 m and the floor space by 196 m².

Find the dimensions of the original office (two possible sets of dimensions).

12. The perimeter of a rectangular garden is 22.5 m. The area is 12.5 m². Find the dimensions of the garden.

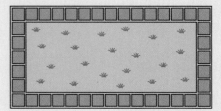

13. A design for a new metal medal is shown. Each medal costs €2 to make. The outer ring of the medal is then to be covered in gold leaf. Gold leaf costs €1 per 70 cm². Find the cost of producing 125 of these medals. (Assume that both sides are identical.)

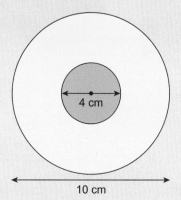

14. Find, to the nearest centimetre, the side length of a square that is inscribed in a circle of diameter 40 cm.

15. Find, in terms of π, the area of a circle which circumscribes a square of area 81 cm².

16. A square is to be constructed with a side length the same as the diagonal of a square of side length x cm. Find, in terms of x, the side length of the larger square.

17. The points P, Q, R, S are points on two circular arcs of centre O. If $|OP| = 13$ m and $|OR| = 6$ m, find to the nearest centimetre:

(i) The area of $PQSR$

(ii) The perimeter of $PQSR$

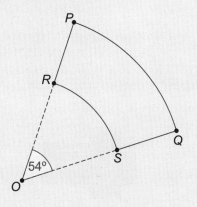

18. The range of radar at an airport is 12 km. An aeroplane flies parallel to the airport runway at a distance of 6 km from the runway and at a speed of 180 km/hr. For how long, to the nearest second, does the aeroplane show up on the radar?

19. Assuming the earth to be circular, its radius is approximately 6,378 km. The city of Tunis is situated at a latitude of 37° North of the equator and at a longitude of 10° East of the prime meridian. This can be written as 37°N 10°E. Oslo is located at 59°N 10°E.

(i) Find, to two significant figures, the distance in kilometres between Tunis and Oslo.

Two towns are located on the equator and are a distance of 10,850 km apart.

(ii) How far, to the nearest degree of longitude, are they apart?

20. The diagram below shows six circles with the same centre, each a distance x units apart. The diameter of the centre circle also measures x units. Which has the greater area: the inner shaded region (pink) or the outer shaded region (blue)?

21. A design for a garden is shown. The length of the rectangular part of the garden is 21 m, and the total area of the garden is 1,336.8 m². Find the radius of the circular part of the garden ($\pi = 3.14$).

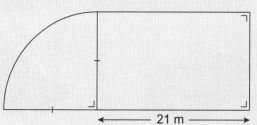

6.2 RECTANGULAR SOLIDS AND PRISMS

Rectangular Solids

One type of 3D object is the rectangular solid.
To find the volume of a rectangular solid (cuboid),
we multiply out the three dimensions given.

Cuboid

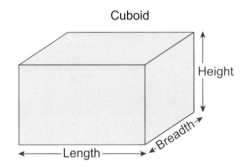

FORMULA

Volume of a cuboid = length × breadth × height

$\therefore$ Volume = lbh

If all sides of the rectangular solid are equal in length, then it can be
referred to as a **cube**.

Cube

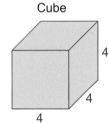

FORMULA

Volume of a cube = length × length × length

$\therefore$ Volume = l^3

Surface Area and Nets

A cube or cuboid has six flat sides or faces.

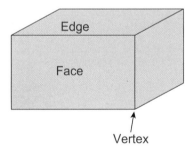

The line where two
faces meet is called
an **edge**.

The corner where
two edges meet is
called a **vertex**.

If we cut along the edges of a rectangular solid, we can create a **net** of that solid.

  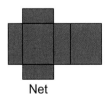

Net

A **net** is a 2D (flat) shape that folds up along its edges to make a 3D shape.

There can be many different nets for one rectangular solid.

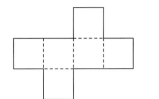 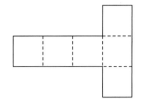

Nets can be used to help determine the **surface area** of a 3D shape.

> **Surface area of a cuboid** = the sum of the area of all six faces of its net.

Surface area = area of (top + base + front + back + side + side).

This can also be written as:

> **FORMULA**
>
> **Surface area of a cuboid** = 2*lb* + 2*lh* + 2*bh*

> **FORMULA**
>
> **Surface area of a cube** = 6(length)² or 6*l*²

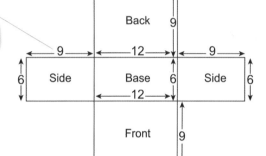

Worked Example 6.4

A cuboid has side length dimensions in the ratio 1 : 2 : 3. Find its dimensions if its volume is 2,058 cm³.

Solution

Let p = length of smallest side.

∴ Ratio of side lengths = $p : 2p : 3p$

$$\text{Volume} = 2{,}058 \text{ cm}^3$$

$$(p)(2p)(3p) = 2{,}058$$

$$6p^3 = 2{,}058$$

$$p^3 = 343$$

$$p = \sqrt[3]{343}$$

$$p = 7$$

∴ The dimensions are 7 cm, 14 cm and 21 cm.

Prisms

A **prism** is a 3D shape that has parallel congruent bases which are both polygons.

A **right prism** is a prism that has two bases, one directly above the other. Its side faces are rectangles.

The volume of a right prism is the area of its base multiplied by the prism's length.

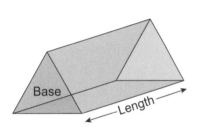
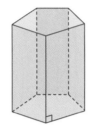

Base — Length

FORMULA

Volume of a prism = area of base × length

The surface area of a prism can be found by using nets.

Worked Example 6.5

Find the volume and surface area of the following right prism.

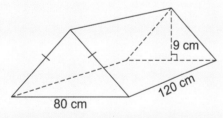

9 cm
120 cm
80 cm

Solution

Volume

Area of triangle $= \frac{1}{2}bh = \frac{1}{2}(80)(9) = 360$ cm^2

Volume = Area of base × Length
= (360)(120)
= 43,200 cm^3

Surface Area

$x^2 = (9)^2 + (40)^2$

$x^2 = 1,681$

$x = 41$

9   x
40

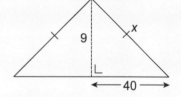

41 cm
120 cm
← 80 cm →
41 cm
9 cm

Work out the area of each face.

Surface area = 2(360) + 2(120)(41) + (80)(120)
= 20,160 cm^2

Exercise 6.2

1. Find the volume and surface area of the following right prisms:

(i)

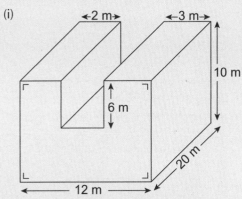

(ii)

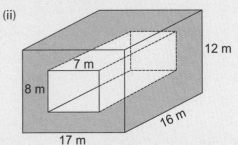

(iii)

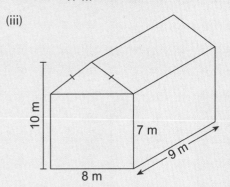

2. Draw a net for each of the following prisms and hence find their surface area (answer to two decimal places):

(i)

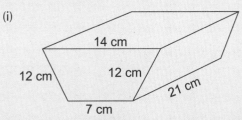

(ii)

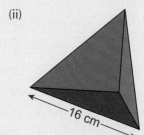

Note: The faces of a regular tetrahedron are equilateral triangles.

3. A box measuring 20 cm by 33 cm by 6 cm is gift-wrapped. What is the least amount of wrapping paper needed?

4. A rectangular tank with no lid has a surface area of 288 cm². If its length is three times its height and its width is half its height, find the volume of the tank.

5. A cuboid has a base of 30 cm by 20 cm. Water is poured into this cuboid to a depth of 12 cm. Another 2 litres of water is poured into the container. Calculate the rise in the height of the water in centimetres.

6. A podium for a medal ceremony is shown.

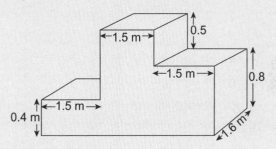

Find the volume and surface area of the podium

7. The volume of a cube is 32 times the volume of another cube. If the side length of the smaller cube is x cm, find in terms of x the surface area of the larger cube.

8. The diagram of a swimming pool is shown. The swimming pool is being re-tiled. Each square tile used has a side length of 50 cm.

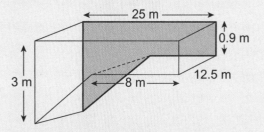

(i) Find the number of tiles needed to tile the pool.

(ii) Find the volume of water needed to fill the pool, if the water level is 10 cm below the top of the pool.

9. The diagonal length (d) of a cube is 48 cm. Find the volume and surface area of this cube.

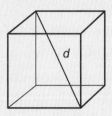

10. A cuboid with a length of x cm and a breadth of y cm is shown. ($x > y$)

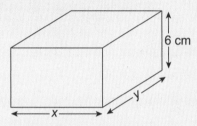

6 cm

(i) Draw a labelled net of this cuboid.

(ii) Write an expression for the volume and surface area of this cuboid in terms of x and y.

(iii) If the surface area of the cuboid is 568 cm² and the volume is 840 cm³, find the value of x and the value of y.

11. A rectangular sheet of metal is 18 cm long and 16 cm wide. A square of side length x cm is cut from each corner of this sheet. The sheet is then folded to form an open rectangular box with a volume of V cm³.

(i) Draw a labelled net of this box.

(ii) Show that $V = 4x^3 - 68x^2 + 288x$.

(iii) Find the possible values of x if the volume of the box is 320 cm³. (Give answers to decimal places where necessary.)

6.3 CYLINDERS, CONES, SPHERES AND HEMISPHERES

There are many other types of 3D shape.

Volume of a Cylinder

The volume of a cylinder is:

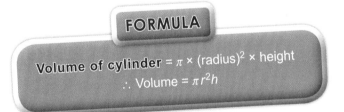

FORMULA

Volume of cylinder = $\pi \times$ (radius)² $\times$ height

$\therefore$ Volume = $\pi r^2 h$

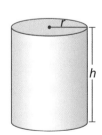

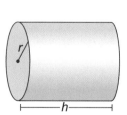

This formula appears on page 10 of *Formulae and Tables*.

Surface Area of a Cylinder

We can use a net to show how to calculate the two types of surface area of a cylinder.

Curved Surface Area (CSA) of a cylinder

This is the area of just the curved part of the cylinder.

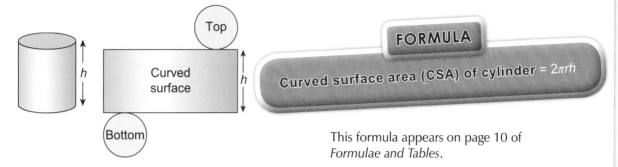

FORMULA

Curved surface area (CSA) of cylinder = $2\pi rh$

This formula appears on page 10 of *Formulae and Tables*.

Total Surface Area (TSA) of a solid cylinder

This is the area of the curved part of the cylinder **plus** the top and bottom circles.

(TSA = $2\pi rh + \pi r^2$ if either no top or no bottom)

FORMULA

Total surface area (TSA) of solid cylinder = $2\pi rh + 2\pi r^2$

∴ TSA = CSA + $2\pi r^2$ or $2\pi r(h + r)$

Right Circular Cones

A **right circular cone** has an apex (top) directly above the centre of a circular base.

Volume of a Cone

FORMULA

Volume of cone = $\frac{1}{3} \times \pi \times (\text{radius})^2 \times \text{height}$

∴ Volume = $\frac{1}{3}\pi r^2 h$

This formula appears on page 10 of *Formulae and Tables*.

Surface Area of a Cone

There are two types of surface area of a cone.

Curved Surface Area (CSA) of a Cone

This is the area of just the curved part of the cone.
To calculate the CSA, we must have the slant height (*l*) of the cone.

Using Pythagoras' theorem, we can state that $l^2 = h^2 + r^2$.

FORMULA

$l^2 = h^2 + r^2$

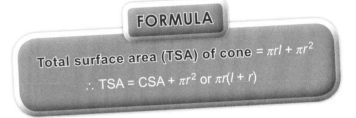

FORMULA

Curved surface area (CSA) of cone = $\pi r l$

This formula appears on page 10 of *Formulae and Tables*.

Total Surface Area (TSA) of a Cone

This is the area of the curved part of the cone **plus** the circular base.

FORMULA

Total surface area (TSA) of cone = $\pi r l + \pi r^2$

$\therefore$ TSA = CSA + πr^2 or $\pi r(l + r)$

Volume of a Sphere

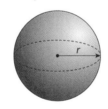

FORMULA

Volume of sphere = $\frac{4}{3} \times \pi \times$ (radius)^3

$\therefore$ Volume = $\frac{4}{3}\pi r^3$

This formula appears on page 10 of *Formulae and Tables*.

Surface Area of a Sphere

A sphere has no flat parts, so we can only have one type of surface area.

FORMULA

Surface area of sphere = $4\pi r^2$

This formula appears on page 10 of *Formulae and Tables*.

Volume of a Hemisphere

A hemisphere is **half** a sphere.

FORMULA

Volume of hemisphere = $\frac{2}{3}\pi r^3$

Surface Area of a Hemisphere

A hemisphere has a flat circular part, so two types of surface area can be found.

Curved Surface Area (CSA) of a Hemisphere

The area of the curved part of the sphere is **half** that of the surface area of a sphere.

FORMULA

Curved surface area (CSA)
of hemisphere = $2\pi r^2$

Total Surface Area (TSA) of a Hemisphere

This is the area of the curved part of the hemisphere **plus** the circular top.

FORMULA

Total surface area (TSA)
of hemisphere = $2\pi r^2 + \pi r^2$

∴ TSA = CSA + πr^2 = $3\pi r^2$

Worked Example 6.6

A cylinder of wax of volume $426\frac{2}{3}\pi$ cm³ is melted down into two candles, one in the shape of a sphere of radius 4 cm and the other in the shape of a cone with a radius half its height.
Assuming no wax is wasted in the melting process, calculate the dimensions of the cone.

Solution

Volume of sphere + volume of cone = $426\frac{2}{3}\pi$ cm³

$$\frac{4}{3}\pi r^3 + \frac{1}{3}\pi r^2 h = 426\frac{2}{3}\pi$$

$$\frac{4}{3}r^3 + \frac{1}{3}r^2 h = 426\frac{2}{3} \quad \text{(Divide both sides by } \pi)$$

Height of cone = $2r$

$$\frac{4}{3}(4)^3 + \frac{1}{3}r^2(2r) = 426\frac{2}{3}$$

$$85\frac{1}{3} + \frac{2}{3}r^3 = 426\frac{2}{3}$$

$$\frac{2}{3}r^3 = 341\frac{1}{3}$$

$$r^3 = 512$$

$$r = 8$$

∴ Radius of cone = 8 cm; height of cone = 16 cm

Worked Example 6.7

An experiment to measure the volume of a metal spherical ball is conducted.
The ball is dropped into a cylinder of water. The cylinder has a radius of 5 cm and a height of 9 cm and is half-full of water. When the ball is dropped into the cylinder, the water level rises by 4 cm.

Find the radius of the metal spherical ball correct to one decimal place.

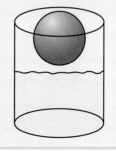

Solution

When the ball is dropped in, the water level rises by 4 cm.

The volume of the sphere is equal to the volume of the displaced water.

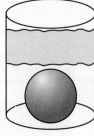

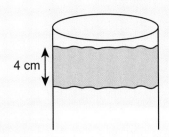 =

4 cm

Volume of displaced water $= \pi r^2 h = \pi \times (5)^2 \times 4$

$$= 100\pi \text{ cm}^3$$

$\therefore$ Volume of sphere $= 100\pi \text{ cm}^3$

$$\frac{4}{3}\pi r^3 = 100\pi$$

$$\frac{4}{3}r^3 = 100$$

$$r^3 = 75$$

$$\Rightarrow r = \sqrt[3]{75}$$

$$\Rightarrow r = 4.2172 \text{ cm}$$

$$\therefore r \approx 4.2 \text{ cm}$$

Exercise 6.3

1. Find the volume, curved surface area and total surface area of each of the following cylinders:

   (i) $r = 12$ cm, $h = 4$ cm ($\pi = 3.14$)

   (ii) $r = 7$ mm, $h = 2.8$ mm $\left(\pi = \frac{22}{7}\right)$

   (iii) $r = 4$ m, $h = 20$ m (in terms of π)

   (iv) $r = 6$ m, $h = 14$ m ($\pi = 3.14$)

2. Find the volume, curved surface area and total surface area of each of the following cones:

   (i) $r = 8$ cm, $h = 6$ cm ($\pi = 3.14$)

   (ii) $r = 40$ mm, $l = 4.1$ cm $\left(\pi = \frac{22}{7}\right)$

   (iii) $h = 36$ cm, $l = 600$ mm (in terms of π)

   (iv) $r = 240$ cm, $l = 5.1$ m $\left(\pi = \frac{22}{7}\right)$

3. Find the volume and surface area of each of the following spheres:

   (i) $r = 16$ m ($\pi = 3.14$)

   (ii) $r = 14$ mm $\left(\pi = \frac{22}{7}\right)$

   (iii) $r = 12$ cm (in terms of π)

4. Find the volume, curved surface area and total surface area of each of the following hemispheres:

   (i) $r = 25$ cm ($\pi = 3.14$)

   (ii) $r = 14.5$ mm $\left(\pi = \frac{22}{7}\right)$

   (iii) $r = 9$ m (in terms of π)

5. A cylindrical can with no top is made from metal. The cylinder has a height of 10 cm and a radius of 4 cm. Find in terms of π the amount of metal required to make the cylinder.

6. A cylindrical tank of radius 12 cm is partly filled with water. A sphere of radius 6 cm is immersed in the water. By how much will the water rise?

7. A cone of radius 10 cm has the same volume as a cylinder with height 8 cm and radius 4 cm. Find the height of the cone to the nearest millimetre.

8. Water flows through a cylindrical pipe at a speed of 10 cm per second. The pipe has diameter 4 cm. How long will it take to pour out 22 litres of water? $\left(\pi = \frac{22}{7}\right)$

9. A solid metal sphere of radius 6 cm is melted down and remoulded into a solid cone of diameter 18 cm.

   Find:

   (i) The volume of the sphere in terms of π

   (ii) The height of the cone

   (Assume no wastage in the manufacturing process.)

10. A fishing float consists of a solid hemisphere surmounted by a solid cone.

    The radius of the cone is of length 3 cm. The volume of the cone is half the volume of the hemisphere.
    Find:

    (i) The volume of the hemisphere in terms of π

    (ii) The height of the cone

    (iii) The overall height of the float

    (iv) The total surface of the float

11. The volume of a sphere of radius r is double the volume of a cone of radius r and height h.

    (i) Show that $h = 2r$.

    (ii) Find the ratio of the surface area of the cone to the surface area of the sphere.

12. Three cylinders (A, B and C) have radii in the ratio $10 : 3 : 4$ and heights in the ratio $4 : 5 : 2$. Which cylinder has the greatest volume?

13. An inflated spherical balloon has a diameter of 15 cm.

    (i) What is the volume of air in the balloon?

    (ii) While retaining its spherical shape, more air is pumped into the balloon until its volume reaches 2,500 cm³.
    Find, to two decimal places, the radius of the balloon.

    (iii) The balloon is then placed inside a rectangular box. What are the dimensions of this box, assuming that the inflated balloon fits exactly in the box?

    Take $\pi = 3.14$.

14. A cylindrical tin has a radius of 4 cm and a height of 12 cm. A rectangular label is glued to the outer surface of the tin as shown. There is a 15 mm gap between the label and the top and bottom of the tin and a 10 mm overlap. Find, to the nearest millimetre, the dimensions of this label.

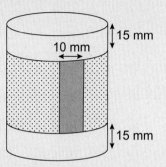

15. A cylindrical tank of radius 4 cm is partly filled with water. A cone of radius 2 cm and height 3 cm is immersed in the water. By how much will the water rise?

16. A solid metal spherical ball of radius 5 cm is coated with another metal. This metal forms a spherical shell around the original metal ball. If the total volume of the sphere increases by 516π cm³, find the thickness of the metal coat applied.

17. The radius of the base of a cylinder is x cm and its height is h cm. The radius of a sphere is $2x$ cm. The volume of the cylinder and the volume of the sphere are equal.
    Express h in terms of x.

18. A solid cone has a height of 20 cm and a radius of 10 cm. A small cone of height 1.5 cm is cut off the top. Calculate the volume (to two significant figures) of the remaining solid.

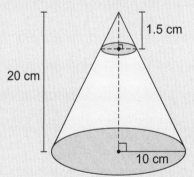

19. A sphere has a radius of x cm. Find, in terms of x, how much the radius of the sphere increases if the sphere's surface area is increased by 50%.

20. A cube is inscribed in a sphere. Find the ratio of their volumes.

21. An inverted plastic cone of radius 12 cm and height 25 cm is shown. A cone of the same radius and with a slant height of $3\sqrt{17}$ cm is cut from the top of this plastic cone. What is the volume and surface area of the plastic that remains?

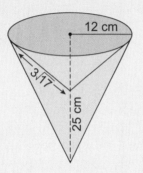

Take $\pi = 3.14$; answer to two decimal places.

22. A square-based pyramid is shown. Its sides are four identical isosceles triangles. The slant height is 20 cm and the base length is 16 cm.

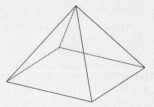

(i) Find the perpendicular height of the pyramid (to three significant figures).

(ii) Find the surface area of the pyramid.

(iii) A flat circular base circumscribes the base of the pyramid. Find the radius of this circular base.

6.4 TRAPEZOIDAL RULE

It is difficult to measure the exact area of an irregular shape and therefore we generally approximate the area.

The **trapezoidal rule** is used to estimate the area under a curve.

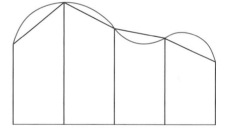

When we use this rule, the shape to be measured must be divided into **segments or strips of equal length**. We then need to measure the height at each interval.

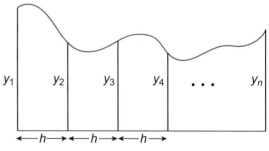

Area $\approx \dfrac{h}{2}$ [first height + last height + 2(the sum of the rest of the heights)]

When using the trapezoidal rule, the smaller the distance between each interval, the more accurate the approximation of the area will be.

FORMULA

$$\text{Area} \approx \frac{h}{2}[y_1 + y_n + 2(y_2 + y_3 + y_4 + \dots + y_{n-1})]$$

This formula appears on page 12 of *Formulae and Tables*.

Worked Example 6.8

Estimate the area of the piece of land shown below. (Units are in metres.)

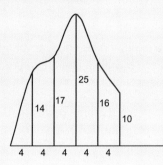

Solution

Fill in the following:

$h = 4$ m

First height $= 0$ m

Last height $= 10$ m

Area $\approx \frac{4}{2}[0 + 10 + 2(14 + 17 + 25 + 16)]$

$= 2[10 + 2(72)]$

$= 2[154]$

$\therefore$ Area ≈ 308 m²

Worked Example 6.9

The area of this irregular shape is approximately 40 square units. Find the value of x.

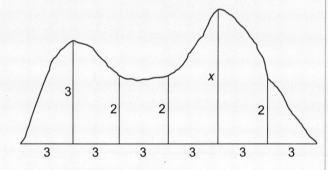

Solution

$h = 3$ First height $= 0$ Last height $= 0$

Area $= 40$ units²

$\therefore \frac{3}{2}[0 + 0 + 2(3 + 2 + 2 + x + 2)] = 40$

$\frac{3}{2}[2(x + 9)] = 40$

$\frac{3}{2}[2x + 18] = 40$

$6x + 54 = 80$

$6x = 26$

$x = 4\frac{1}{3}$ units

Exercise 6.4

Use the trapezoidal rule to estimate the area of each of the following:

1.

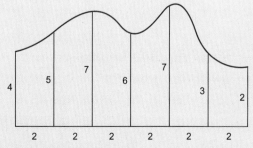

(Units are in metres.)

2.

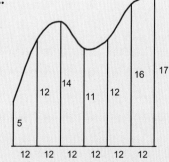

(Units are in centimetres.)

3.

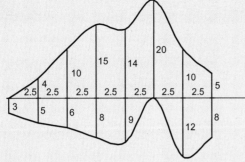

(Units are in metres.)

4. The diagram shows the plan of a lake. Use the trapezoidal rule to estimate the area of the lake, given that the offsets are a distance of 10 m apart, and all measurements are in metres.

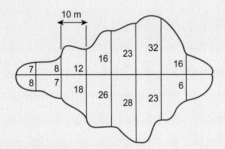

5. The diagram shows the curve $y = x^2 + 1$ in the domain $0 \leqslant x \leqslant 4$.

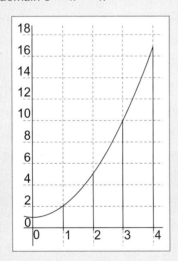

Use the equation of the curve to complete the following table.

x	0	1	2	3	4
y					

Hence, use the trapezoidal rule to estimate the area between the curve and the x-axis.

6. The speed of a runner in m/s was recorded every 10 seconds.

Time	0	10	20	30	40	50	60
Speed	1	2.5	4	3.2	2.8	3.1	2.4

The area under a time–speed graph represents the distance travelled. Use the trapezoidal rule to estimate the distance travelled by the runner.

7. An estimate for the area of this shape is 11,700 m². Find the value of h. Measurements are in metres.

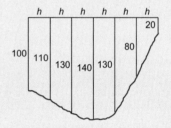

8. If $y = \sqrt{3x}$, complete the table below to three decimal places.

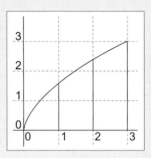

x	0	1	2	3
y				

(i) Hence, use the trapezoidal rule to estimate the area between the curve and the x-axis.

(ii) Explain how you could improve the accuracy of your answer.

(iii) Hence, using your method, estimate the area between the curve and the x-axis.

9. The area of the field below is approximately 6.775 hectares. Find the value of x. Measurements are in metres.

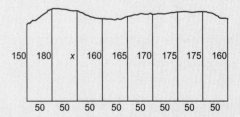

Revision Exercises

1. (a) Find the volume and surface area of the following right prisms:

(i)

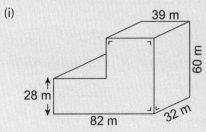

(ii)

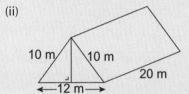

(iii)

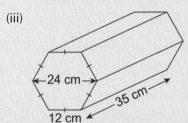

(b) Use the trapezoidal rule to estimate the area of each of the following (all measurements are in metres):

(i)

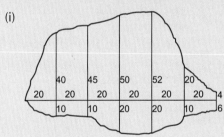

(ii)

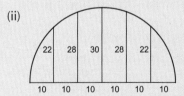

(iii)

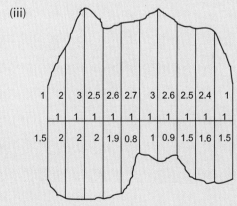

(iv)

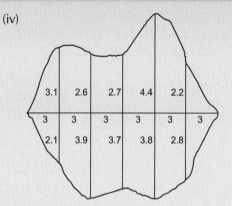

(c) (i) The area of this irregular shape is 690 square units. Find the value of x.

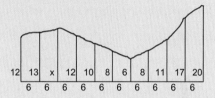

(ii) The area of this field is estimated as 583.15 m². Measurements are in metres. Find the value of h, the width of each strip.

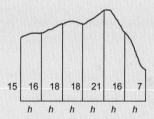

2. (a) A semicircular piece is cut from a piece of circular metal as shown. The circle has a diameter of 28 cm, and the area of the metal remaining is equal to 146 π cm². Find the radius of the semicircular piece cut.

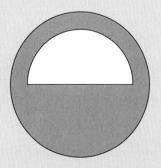

(b) The diagonal (d) of the cube shown is $5\sqrt{7}$ cm. Find the volume of this cube to the nearest cm³.

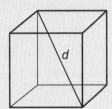

(c) The sides of a square are each of length 2r, as shown. Circles are drawn inside and outside the square.

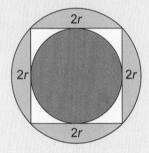

(i) Find the radius of each circle in terms of r.

(ii) Verify that the areas of the two circles are in the ratio 2 : 1.

3. (a) A machine part is formed by cutting a hemisphere from the circular top and a cone from the bottom of a cylinder as shown.

The cylinder has a radius of 12 cm and a height of 18 cm. Find the volume and surface area of this machine part.

(b) Water flows through a cylindrical pipe at a rate of 10 cm per second. The diameter of the pipe is 7 cm. The water is poured into an empty rectangular tank of length 55 cm and width 20 cm.

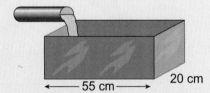

What is the depth of the water in the tank after one minute? ($\pi = 3.14$; Give your answer correct to nearest centimetre.)

(c) Water pours through a pipe of radius 3 cm at a rate of 15 cm per second. It flows into a conical tank of height 0.9 metres and radius 0.6 metres.

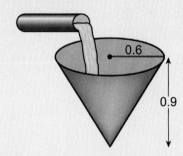

How long will it take to fill the tank?

4. (a) A sphere and a cone have equal volumes and equal radii. Find the ratio of the height of the cone to its radius.

(b) A beverage is sold in two different cylindrical jars. The height of the smaller jar is twice its radius. The larger jar has three times the radius and twice the height of the smaller jar. A small and large jar, if filled completely, can store 1.5 litres. Find the dimensions of each jar to two significant figures.

5. (a) A sheet of metal 2 m long, 75 cm wide and 10 mm thick is melted down to form spherical ball bearings. How many spherical ball bearings of radius 5 mm can be made from this sheet, assuming no wastage? ($\pi = 3.14$)

(b) The radius r of a cone is twice its height. Express the volume and total surface area of the cone in terms of r.

6. (a) A sphere fits exactly into an open cylindrical container. Show that both have the same curved surface area.

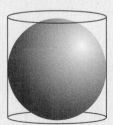

(b) A hollow container consists of a cylinder with a cone on top.

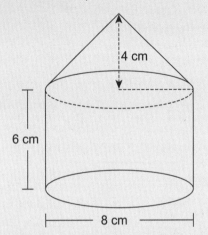

4 cm

6 cm

8 cm

The container contains oil up to the level of the top of the cylinder.
The container is then turned upside down. Find the depth of the oil.

7. (a) The perimeter of the shaded region consists of three semicircles. Find, in terms of x and π:

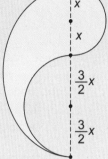

x

x

$\frac{3}{2}x$

$\frac{3}{2}x$

   (i) The perimeter of the region

   (ii) The area of the region

(b) The cross-section of a storage shed is shown. Beams that support the roof are marked as p and q.

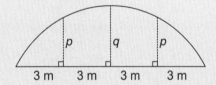

p q p

3 m   3 m   3 m   3 m

The longer beam (q) is 1.6 times the length of the smaller beam (p). An estimate of the cross-sectional area of the shed is 16.2 m². Find the value of p and the value of q.

8. (a) A solid sphere of radius r is melted down and recast into a cone that has a height five times the radius of the sphere. Find in terms of r:

   (i) The volume of the cone   (ii) The surface area of the cone

(b) The total surface area of a cylinder is P. If the height of the cylinder is twice the radius of the cylinder, express the volume of the cylinder in terms of P.

9. (a) A river is 21 m wide at a certain point. Students take a depth reading every 3 metres across a cross-section of the river at this point.

Distance from bank	0	3	6	9	12	15	18	21
Depth (m)	0.5	1.25	1.7	3	5	4	2.4	0.1

   (i) Estimate the cross-sectional area of the river.

   (ii) If the speed of the river is 0.7 m/s, find the number of cubic metres that flow down the river per minute, at this point of the river.

(b) The planet Mars orbits the Sun at an average distance of 227,940,000 km and at an average orbital speed of 24 km/s.

   (i) Assuming the orbit of Mars to be a circle, find the length of its orbit in kilometres to five significant figures.

   (ii) Calculate the time to the nearest day (Earth) that it takes Mars to complete one orbit.

The planet Neptune has an average orbital speed of 5.43 km/s and on average takes 165 years to complete one orbit.

   (iii) Find in kilometres, to three significant figures, the average distance Neptune is from the Sun.

   (iv) If light travels at a speed of 3×10^8 m/s, find to the nearest minute how long light from the Sun takes to reach Neptune.

10. (a) A solid made from a cone and hemisphere is shown.

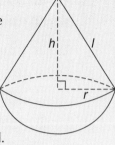

The curved surface area of the cone and the total surface area of the hemisphere are equal.

  (i) Express the slant height of the cone l in terms of r.

  (ii) Find h, the perpendicular height of the cone in terms of r.

  (iii) Find, in surd form, the ratio of the volume of the cone to the volume of the hemisphere.

(b) (i) A square-based pyramid with four congruent triangular sides has a base length

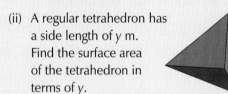

of x metres and a height of $3x$ metres. Find the surface area of the pyramid in terms of x.

  (ii) A regular tetrahedron has a side length of y m. Find the surface area of the tetrahedron in terms of y.

11. A regular tetrahedron has four faces, each of which is an equilateral triangle.

A wooden puzzle consists of several pieces that can be assembled to make a regular tetrahedron. The manufacturer wants to package the assembled tetrahedron in a clear cylindrical container, with one face flat against the bottom.

If the length of one edge of the tetrahedron is $2a$, show that the volume of the smallest possible cylindrical container is $\left(\frac{8\sqrt{6}}{9}\right)\pi a^3$.

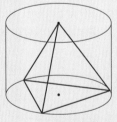

SEC Sample Paper 2, Leaving Certificate Higher Level, 2011

12. The Wonder Building is an arched building that does not need any support inside, due partly to the fact that its shape is an arc of a circle.

The photograph shows a Wonder Building being used in Antarctica.

The arc for a Wonder Building can be a full semicircle or less than a semicircle. It cannot be more than a semicircle. The 'span' of the building is the total width from one side of the arch to the other.

(a) A particular Wonder Building has a span of 30 metres and a height of 10 metres.

  Find the radius of the arc.

(b) A customer wants a building with a span of 18 metres and a height of 10 metres.

  (i) What arc radius would be required to give such a building?

  (ii) Explain why the Wonder Building that the customer wants is not possible.

(c) An air force needs a Wonder Building to house a Tornado military jet.

The dimensions of the aircraft are as follows:

  ■ Wingspan: 14 metres

  ■ Height: 6 metres

  ■ Height of wingtips above ground: 2 metres

The shelter must be at least 0.5 metres above the top of the tail, and at least 1 metre clear horizontally of the wingtips.

For the shelter to have minimum height, find the smallest possible radius of the arc.

NCCA Pre-Leaving Certificate Higher Level Paper 2, February 2010

13. A company has to design a rectangular box for a new range of jellybeans. The box is to be assembled from a single piece of cardboard, cut from a rectangular sheet measuring 31 cm by 22 cm. The box is to have a capacity (volume) of 500 cm³.

The net for the box is shown on the right. The company is going to use the full length and width of the rectangular piece of cardboard.

The shaded areas are flaps of width 1 cm which are needed for assembly.

The height of the box is *h* cm, as shown on the diagram.

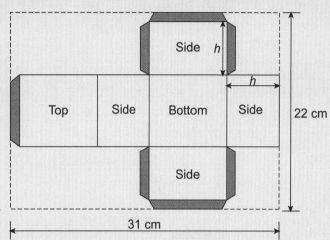

(a) Write the dimensions of the box, in centimetres, in terms of *h*.

(b) Write an expression for the capacity of the box in cubic centimetres, in terms of *h*.

(c) Show that the value of *h* that gives a box with a square bottom will give the correct capacity.

(d) Find, correct to one decimal place, the other value of *h* that gives a box of the correct capacity.

(e) The client is planning a special '10% extra free' promotion and needs to increase the capacity of the box by 10%. The company is checking whether they can make this new box from a piece of cardboard the same size as the original one (31 cm × 22 cm). A graph of the box's capacity as a function of *h* is shown.

Use the graph to explain why it is not possible to make the larger box from such a piece of cardboard.

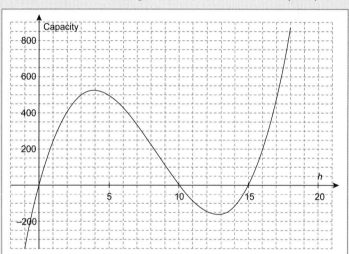

SEC Sample Paper 1, Leaving Certificate Higher Level, 2011

Indices and Logarithms

Learning Outcomes

In this chapter you will learn about:

- Exponents or indices
- The exponential function
- The natural exponential function
- The laws of indices
- The methods for solving equations of the form $a^x = b$, where a and b are constants and $x \in R$

- Surds
- Logarithms
- The laws of logarithms
- Using logs to solve real-life problems

7.1 INDICES (EXPONENTS)

Indices (sometimes called exponents) and logarithms are routinely applied to a wide range of 'real-life' problems. They are used to compare earthquakes of different strengths. Biologists use them to predict future sizes of human and animal populations. Archaeologists use them to determine the ages of artefacts. Medical technicians use them to monitor the decay of radioactive material in various diagnostic tests, such as bone scans.

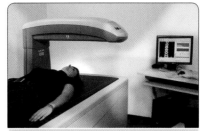

A bone-density scan is a low-dose x-ray which checks an area of the body such as the hip, hand or foot for signs of mineral loss and bone thinning.

KEY WORDS

■ **Exponent**

■ **Exponential function**

■ **Natural exponential function**

■ **Surd**

■ **Logarithm**

A number in index form is of the form b^n. We call b the **base** and n the **index**, **power** or **exponent**.

Index notation is useful for writing very large or very small numbers in a manageable form.

For example, the decimal number 10,000,000,000,000,000 can be written as 10^{16}.

Exponential Functions

A function of the form, $f(x) = a^x$, where a is a positive constant, is called an **exponential function**.

If $f(x) = a^x$, where $a > 0$, then $f(0) = a^0 = 1$

So all graphs of $f(x) = a^x$ will pass through the point (0,1).

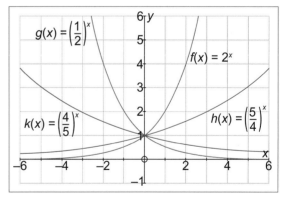

Here are the graphs of four exponential functions.

ACTIVITIES 7.1, 7.2

The Natural Exponential Function

Consider the infinite series:

$$1 + \frac{1}{1!} + \frac{1}{2!} + \frac{1}{3!} + \frac{1}{4!} + \dots$$

When you study calculus you will learn the reason why this infinite series converges to a limit. Mathematicians have chosen the letter e to represent this limit.

ACTIVITY 7.3

$$e = 1 + \frac{1}{1!} + \frac{1}{2!} + \frac{1}{3!} + \frac{1}{4!} + \dots$$

INDICES AND LOGARITHMS

Like π and $\sqrt{2}$, e is irrational, i.e. it cannot be written as a fraction.

To 20 decimal places, the value of e is 2.71828182845904523536.

This is the graph of the function $f(x) = e^x$. This function is also called the **natural exponential function**, because it arises naturally in maths and physical sciences (that is, in real-life situations).

The natural exponential function models many phenomena in nature, such as population growth and radioactive decay. It also appears in economic and finance models. In a later section we will solve some problems using the natural exponential function.

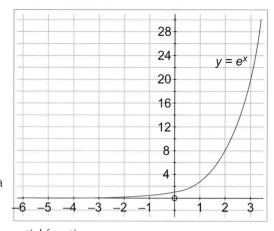

a^{pq} Worked Example 7.1

Graph the function $f(x) = e^{\frac{1}{2}x}$, $-4 \leqslant x \leqslant 5$, $x \in R$.

Step 2   Draw the graph.

Solution

Step 1   Draw a table of values. Use the calculator to evaluate the $f(x)$ row. (Write correct to one decimal place where necessary.)

x	−4	−3	−2	−1	0	1	2	3	4
$f(x)$	0.1	0.2	0.4	0.6	1	1.6	2.7	4.5	7.4

7.2 LAWS OF INDICES (EXPONENTS)

ACTIVITY 7.4

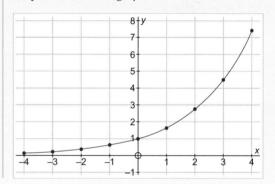

FORMULA

Law 1 $a^p \times a^q = a^{p+q}$ **Law 4** $a^0 = 1$ **Law 7** $a^{-p} = \dfrac{1}{a^p}$

Law 2 $\dfrac{a^p}{a^q} = a^{p-q}$ **Law 5** $a^{\frac{1}{q}} = \sqrt[q]{a}$ **Law 8** $(ab)^p = a^p b^p$

Law 3 $(a^p)^q = a^{pq}$ **Law 6** $a^{\frac{p}{q}} = \left(\sqrt[q]{a}\right)^p$ **Law 9** $\left(\dfrac{a}{b}\right)^p = \dfrac{a^p}{b^p}$

These laws appear on page 21 of *Formulae and Tables*.

$\sqrt[n]{a}$ is called the nth root of a.
If b is the nth root of a, then $b^n = a$.

In Activity 7.4 you derived the laws of indices for the case where a, the base, is a rational number. The laws also hold in the case where a is irrational. Therefore, the laws can be applied when the base is e.

Worked Example 7.2

(i) Write $64^{-\frac{4}{3}}$ in the form $\frac{1}{n}$, $n \in N$.   (ii) Use the law $\left(\frac{a}{b}\right)^p = \frac{a^p}{b^p}$ to show that $(0.75)^9 = \frac{3^9}{4^9}$.

Solution

(i) $64^{-\frac{4}{3}} = \dfrac{1}{64^{\frac{4}{3}}}$ **OR** $64^{-\frac{4}{3}} = \left(64^{\frac{1}{3}}\right)^{-4}$

$\qquad = \dfrac{1}{\left(\sqrt[3]{64}\right)^4}$ $\qquad\qquad\qquad = 4^{\frac{1}{4}}$

$\qquad = \dfrac{1}{4^4}$ $\qquad\qquad\qquad\qquad = \left(\dfrac{1}{4}\right)^4$

$\qquad \therefore 64^{-\frac{4}{3}} = \dfrac{1}{256}$ $\qquad\qquad \therefore 64^{-\frac{4}{3}} = \dfrac{1}{256}$

(ii) $0.75 = \dfrac{3}{4}$

$\qquad \therefore (0.75)^9 = \left(\dfrac{3}{4}\right)^9$

$\qquad\qquad = \dfrac{3^9}{4^9}$

Worked Example 7.3

(i) Simplify $\dfrac{e^5 + e^4}{e^3 + e^2}$.   (ii) Simplify the following, giving your answer in index form:

(a) $(-5)^{10}$ (b) $(-4)^3$

Solution

(i) $\dfrac{e^5 + e^4}{e^3 + e^2} = \dfrac{e^2\cancel{(e^3 + e^2)}^{1}}{\cancel{(e^3 + e^2)}^{1}}$

$\qquad = e^2$

(ii) (a) $(-5)^{10} = 5^{10}$ (A negative number raised to an even power is always positive.)

(b) $(-4)^3 = -4^3$ (A negative number raised to an odd power is always negative.)

Exercise 7.1

1. Graph the function:

   $f(x) = 10^x, -1 \leqslant x \leqslant 3, x \in R$

2. Graph the function:

   $f(x) = \left(\dfrac{1}{4}\right)^x, -3 \leqslant x \leqslant 1, x \in R$

3. Graph the function:

   $f(x) = 3^x, -1 \leqslant x \leqslant 3, x \in R$

   (i) Use your graph to find an approximation for $f(1.6)$. Give your answer to the nearest whole number.

   (ii) Use your graph to solve the equation $f(x) = 18$. Give your answer correct to 1 decimal place

4. Graph the function:

   $f(x) = \left(\dfrac{2}{3}\right)^x, -4 \leqslant x \leqslant 1, x \in R$

   (i) Use your graph to find $f(0)$.

   (ii) $f(-2)$ lies in the range $[1, a]$. If $a \in N$, then what is the minimum value of a?

5. Graph the following functions:

   (i) $f(x) = e^{2x}, -2 \leqslant x \leqslant 1.5, x \in R$

   (ii) $f(x) = e^{\frac{x}{3}}, -2 \leqslant x \leqslant 5, x \in R$

6. Using the same axes and scales, graph the following functions:

$$f(x) = \left(\frac{5}{2}\right)^x, \quad -3 \leqslant x \leqslant 3, x \in R$$

$$g(x) = \left(\frac{2}{5}\right)^x, \quad -3 \leqslant x \leqslant 3, x \in R$$

   (i) Using your graph, solve the equation $f(x) = g(x)$.

   (ii) What transformation maps $g(x)$ onto $f(x)$?

7. Without using a calculator, write the following in the form a^p.

   (i) $10^7 \times 10^2$

   (ii) $20^4 \times 20^2$

   (iii) $7^4 \times 7^4$

   (iv) $(e)^2 \times (e)^3$

   (v) $\dfrac{4^6}{4}$

   (vi) $\dfrac{1}{e^3}$

   (vii) $\dfrac{(-5)^{10}}{(-5)^3}$

   (viii) $(10^4)^9$

   (ix) $(e^2)^2$

   (x) $(e^5)^5$

8. Simplify the following, giving your answer in index notation:

   (i) $(-3)^3$

   (ii) $(-2)^{20}$

   (iii) $(-5)^{19}$

   (iv) $(3)^3$

   (v) $(-4)^{12}$

   (vi) $-(-1)^{100}$

   (vii) $-(6)^3$

   (viii) $-(-6)^3$

9. Write each of the following as fractions:

   (i) 2^{-3}

   (ii) 7^{-2}

   (iii) 4^{-2}

   (iv) 3^{-4}

   (v) $4(3^{-4})$

   (vi) $2(4^{-2})$

   (vii) $2(8^{-2})$

   (viii) $5(10^{-3})$

   (ix) $100^{-\frac{1}{2}}$

   (x) $36^{-\frac{1}{2}}$

   (xi) $16^{-\frac{1}{4}}$

   (xii) $81^{-\frac{3}{4}}$

   (xiii) $8^{-\frac{2}{3}}$

   (xiv) $9^{-\frac{5}{2}}$

10. Evaluate the following, without using a calculator:

   (i) $\sqrt{49}$

   (ii) $\sqrt[3]{27}$

   (iii) $\sqrt[4]{16}$

   (iv) $\sqrt[5]{32}$

   (v) $\sqrt[10]{1}$

   (vi) $\sqrt{36}$

   (vii) $\sqrt[4]{81}$

   (viii) $\sqrt[6]{64}$

   (ix) $\sqrt{121}$

11. Evaluate the following:

   (i) $8^{\frac{1}{3}}$

   (ii) $9^{\frac{1}{2}}$

   (iii) $1{,}000^{\frac{1}{3}}$

   (iv) $64^{\frac{1}{3}}$

   (v) $36^{\frac{1}{2}}$

   (vi) $256^{\frac{1}{4}}$

12. Evaluate the following:

   (i) $(-8)^{\frac{1}{3}}$

   (ii) $(-64)^{\frac{1}{3}}$

   (iii) $(-1{,}000)^{\frac{1}{3}}$

   (iv) $(32)^{\frac{1}{5}}$

   (v) $(128)^{\frac{1}{7}}$

   (vi) $(64)^{\frac{1}{6}}$

13. Using the law $a^{\frac{m}{n}} = (\sqrt[n]{a})^m$, evaluate each of the following:

   (i) $100^{\frac{3}{2}}$

   (ii) $125^{\frac{2}{3}}$

   (iii) $16^{\frac{5}{4}}$

   (iv) $81^{\frac{3}{4}}$

   (v) $9^{\frac{3}{2}}$

   (vi) $64^{\frac{4}{3}}$

   (vii) $\left(\dfrac{1}{25}\right)^{\frac{3}{2}}$

   (viii) $\left(\dfrac{4}{9}\right)^{\frac{5}{2}}$

   (ix) $\left(\dfrac{81}{25}\right)^{\frac{1}{2}}$

   (x) $\left(\dfrac{8}{27}\right)^{\frac{2}{3}}$

14. Write each of the following in the form a^p, where $p \in Q$:

   (i) $a^7 \div a^2$

   (ii) $a^7 \times a^2$

   (iii) $(a^7)^2$

   (iv) $\sqrt{a}$

   (v) $\sqrt{a^7}$

   (vi) $\dfrac{1}{a^3}$

   (vii) $\dfrac{1}{\sqrt{a}}$

15. Using the law $\left(\dfrac{a}{b}\right)^p = \left(\dfrac{a^p}{b^p}\right)$, verify that each of the following is true:

   (i) $\left(\dfrac{3}{4}\right)^8 = \dfrac{6^8}{8^8}$

   (ii) $\left(\dfrac{3}{5}\right)^9 = \dfrac{9^9}{15^9}$

   (iii) $\left(\dfrac{9}{16}\right)^{\frac{1}{2}} = \dfrac{18^{\frac{1}{2}}}{32^{\frac{1}{2}}}$

   (iv) $\left(\dfrac{25}{64}\right)^{-\frac{1}{2}} = \dfrac{75^{-\frac{1}{2}}}{192^{-\frac{1}{2}}}$

16. Find k, if:

$$\sqrt{\dfrac{(e^8 + e^4)(e^3 - 1)}{(e^8 - 1)(e^2 + e + 1)}} = \dfrac{e^k}{\sqrt{(e^k + 1)(e + 1)}}$$

17. The law $(ab)^p = a^p b^p$ can be used to find the prime factors of numbers of the form q^n, $q, n \in N$.

   (i) Write 15 as a product of prime numbers.

   (ii) Hence, find the prime factors of 15^9.

18. Write 36 as a product of prime factors and, hence, find the prime factors of $36^{2{,}011}$.

19. Write 100 as a product of prime factors and, hence, find the prime factors of $100^{1{,}601}$.

7.3 EQUATIONS WITH X AS AN INDEX

$2^x = 64$ is an example of an equation in which the unknown quantity x is an index or power. The laws of indices will help us to solve many equations where the unknown quantity is an index.

> If $a^x = a^y$, and $a \neq -1, 0, 1$, then $x = y$.

a^{pq} Worked Example 7.4

Solve $4^x = \dfrac{8}{\sqrt{2}}, x \in Q.$

Solution

All numbers in the equation can be written as powers of 2.

$2 = 2^1$

$4 = 2^2$

$8 = 2^3$

The equation can now be written as:

$(2^2)^x = \dfrac{2^3}{\sqrt{2}}$

$2^{2x} = \dfrac{2^3}{2^{\frac{1}{2}}}$

> Note that $\sqrt{2} = 2^{\frac{1}{2}}$.

$2^{2x} = 2^{2\frac{1}{2}}$

$2x = 2\dfrac{1}{2}$ (Drop the common base of 2.)

$x = \dfrac{2\frac{1}{2}}{2}$

$\therefore x = 1\dfrac{1}{4}$ $\left(\text{or } \dfrac{5}{4}\right)$

a^{pq} Worked Example 7.5

Solve the equation:

$$3^{2x + 1} - 28(3^x) + 9 = 0$$

Solution

Step 1   Transform the equation into a quadratic equation.

Let $y = 3^x$

Then:

$3^{2x + 1} = 3(3^{2x})$ (Law 1 of Indices)

$\quad\quad\;\; = 3(3^x)^2$ (Law 3 of Indices)

$\quad\quad\;\; = 3y^2$

Thus, the equation can be written as:

$$3y^2 - 28y + 9 = 0$$

Step 2   Solve the associated quadratic equation:

$$3y^2 - 28y + 9 = 0$$

$$(3y - 1)(y - 9) = 0$$

$\Rightarrow 3y - 1 = 0$ **OR** $y - 9 = 0$

$y = \dfrac{1}{3}$ **OR** $\quad y = 9$

Step 3   Solve for x:

$$y = 3^x$$

$\therefore 3^x = \dfrac{1}{3}$ **OR** $3^x = 9$

$3^x = 3^{-1}$ **OR** $3^x = 3^2$

$\Rightarrow x = -1$ **OR** $\quad x = 2$

Exercise 7.2

1. Solve the following equations:

   (i) $3^x = 81$

   (ii) $10^x = 10,000$

   (iii) $6^x = 216$

   (iv) $7^x = 49$

   (v) $3^x = 729$

   (vi) $2^x = \dfrac{1}{32}$

   (vii) $(0.2)^x = 125$

   (viii) $7^{-x} = 1$

2. Using the laws of indices, solve the following equations:

   (i) $2^x = 2^7\sqrt{2}$

   (ii) $5^x = \dfrac{125}{\sqrt{5}}$

   (iii) $10^{x-3} = \dfrac{\sqrt{10}}{100}$

   (iv) $7^x = \dfrac{49}{\sqrt[3]{7}}$

   (v) $49^x = \dfrac{49}{\sqrt{7}}$

   (vi) $8^{\frac{4}{3}} = \dfrac{2^{5x-2}}{\sqrt{2}}$

3. Write in the form 2^k, $k \in Q$:

   (i) 16

   (ii) 8

   (iii) $\sqrt{8}$

   (iv) $\dfrac{16}{\sqrt{8}}$

   Hence, solve the equation $2^{2x-1} = \left(\dfrac{16}{\sqrt{8}}\right)^3$.

4. Solve the following equations:

   (i) $3^{3x-1} = \left(\dfrac{27}{\sqrt{3}}\right)^5$

   (ii) $25^x = \left(\dfrac{\sqrt{125}}{\sqrt[3]{5}}\right)^{12}$

5. Copy and complete the table below. Answers in the second row must be in index form.

$2^2 - 2$	$2^3 - 2^2$	$2^4 - 2^3$	$2^5 - 2^4$	$2^6 - 2^5$	$2^7 - 2^6$
2	2^2				

   Hence, write $2^{p+1} - 2^p$ as a power of 2.

6. Solve for x:

   (i) $\left(\dfrac{2^{12}}{16}\right) = 2^{x+1} - 2^x$

   (ii) $\left(\dfrac{2^{16}}{8}\right) = 2^x - 2^{x-1}$

7. Solve for x:

   (i) $3^{2x} + 3^x = 90$

   (ii) $5^{2x} + 2(5^x) = 35$

   (iii) $2^{2x+1} - 15(2^x) - 8 = 0$

   (iv) $3^{2x+1} + 26(3^x) - 9 = 0$

   (v) $2^{2x} + 2^x - 6 = 0$

   (vi) $2^{2x} - 6(2^x) + 8 = 0$

8. Solve for x:

   (i) $2^x + 2^{2-x} = 5$

   (ii) $3^x + 3^{1-x} = 4$

   (iii) $2^x + 2^{-x} = \dfrac{17}{4}$

   (iv) $3^x - 3^{1-x} + 2 = 0$

   (v) $3^{2x+1} - 4(3^x) + 1 = 0$

9. Solve for x:

   (i) $5^{2x+1} - 124(5^x) - 25 = 0$

   (ii) $4^{2x+1} + 63(4^x) - 16 = 0$

10. (i) Show that $9^x = (3^x)^2$.

    (ii) Hence, solve $9^x - 4(3^{x+1}) + 27 = 0$.

7.4 SURDS

Roots that are irrational are called **surds**.

- $\sqrt{3}$ is a surd, as it cannot be written as a rational number.
- $\sqrt{4}$ is **not** a surd, as it can be written as a rational number.
- π is irrational but is **not** a surd, as it does not involve a root (or radical) sign.

In Activity 7.5 we derived two laws of surds.

ACTIVITY 7.5

FORMULA

Law 1 $\sqrt{a}\sqrt{b} = \sqrt{ab}$

Law 2 $\dfrac{\sqrt{a}}{\sqrt{b}} = \sqrt{\dfrac{a}{b}}$

Worked Example 7.6

What is $\sqrt{a^2}$?

Solution

$\sqrt{a^2} = (a^2)^{\frac{1}{2}}$

$\quad = a^1$ (Law 3 of Indices)

$\quad = a$

Worked Example 7.7

What is $\sqrt{a}\sqrt{a}$?

Solution

$\sqrt{a}\sqrt{a} = \sqrt{(a)(a)}$ (Law 1 of Surds)

$\quad = \sqrt{a^2}$

$\quad = a$

Reducing Surds

Surds can be reduced or simplified if the number under the radical sign (square root sign) has a square number as a factor.

Worked Example 7.8

Simplify $\sqrt{32}$.

Solution

Step 1 Find the largest square number that is a factor of 32. 16 is the largest square number that is a factor of 32.

Step 2 $\sqrt{32} = \sqrt{16}\sqrt{2}$ (Law 1 of Surds)

$\quad = 4\sqrt{2}$

Worked Example 7.9

Simplify $\sqrt{50} + \sqrt{8} + \sqrt{32}$.

Solution

$\sqrt{50} + \sqrt{8} + \sqrt{32} = \sqrt{25}\sqrt{2} + \sqrt{4}\sqrt{2} + \sqrt{16}\sqrt{2}$

$\quad = 5\sqrt{2} + 2\sqrt{2} + 4\sqrt{2}$

$\quad = 11\sqrt{2}$

Worked Example 7.10

Simplify $(\sqrt{5} + 2\sqrt{2})(\sqrt{5} - \sqrt{2})$.

Solution

$(\sqrt{5} + 2\sqrt{2})(\sqrt{5} - \sqrt{2}) = \sqrt{5}(\sqrt{5} - \sqrt{2}) + 2\sqrt{2}(\sqrt{5} - \sqrt{2})$

$\quad = \sqrt{5}\sqrt{5} - \sqrt{5}\sqrt{2} + 2\sqrt{2}\sqrt{5} - 2\sqrt{2}\sqrt{2}$

$\quad = 5 - \sqrt{10} + 2\sqrt{10} - 2(2)$

$\quad = 1 + \sqrt{10}$

a^{pq} **Worked Example 7.11**

Rationalise the denominator of: (i) $\dfrac{5}{\sqrt{5}}$ (ii) $\dfrac{4\sqrt{15}}{\sqrt{20}}$ (iii) $\dfrac{\sqrt{2} - \sqrt{3}}{\sqrt{2} + \sqrt{3}}$

Solution

(i) $\dfrac{5}{\sqrt{5}} = \dfrac{5\sqrt{5}}{\sqrt{5}\sqrt{5}}$ (Multiply numerator and denominator by $\sqrt{5}$)

$= \dfrac{5\sqrt{5}}{5}$

$= \sqrt{5}$

(ii) $\dfrac{4\sqrt{15}}{\sqrt{20}} = \dfrac{4\sqrt{15}}{\sqrt{4}\sqrt{5}}$

$= \dfrac{4\sqrt{15}}{2\sqrt{5}}$

$= 2\sqrt{3}$ (Laws of Surds)

(iii) $\dfrac{\sqrt{2} - \sqrt{3}}{\sqrt{2} + \sqrt{3}} = \dfrac{(\sqrt{2} - \sqrt{3})(\sqrt{2} - \sqrt{3})}{(\sqrt{2} + \sqrt{3})(\sqrt{2} - \sqrt{3})}$

$= \dfrac{\sqrt{2}\,(\sqrt{2} - \sqrt{3}) - \sqrt{3}\,(\sqrt{2} - \sqrt{3})}{\sqrt{2}\,(\sqrt{2} - \sqrt{3}) + \sqrt{3}\,(\sqrt{2} - \sqrt{3})}$

$= \dfrac{2 - \sqrt{6} - \sqrt{6} + 3}{2 - \sqrt{6} + \sqrt{6} - 3}$

$= \dfrac{5 - 2\sqrt{6}}{-1}$

$= -5 + 2\sqrt{6}$

Exercise 7.3

1. Evaluate each of the following:
(no calculators):

   (i) $(2\sqrt{7})^2$ (iv) $(10\sqrt{2})^2$

   (ii) $(5\sqrt{10})^2$ (v) $(3\sqrt{15})^2$

   (iii) $(2\sqrt{5})^2$ (vi) $(2\sqrt{5})^4$

2. Evaluate each of the following, without the use of a calculator:

   (i) $\sqrt{2}\sqrt{8}$ (iv) $\dfrac{\sqrt{27}}{\sqrt{3}}$

   (ii) $\sqrt{2}\sqrt{32}$ (v) $\dfrac{\sqrt{50}}{\sqrt{2}}$

   (iii) $\sqrt{50}\sqrt{2}$ (vi) $\dfrac{\sqrt{200}}{\sqrt{8}}$

3. Simplify these surds:

   (i) $\sqrt{8}$ (vi) $\sqrt{500}$

   (ii) $\sqrt{45}$ (vii) $\sqrt{27}$

   (iii) $\sqrt{300}$ (viii) $\sqrt{54}$

   (iv) $\sqrt{12}$ (ix) $\sqrt{75}$

   (v) $\sqrt{32}$ (x) $\sqrt{98}$

4. Write $\sqrt{50} + \sqrt{8}$ in the form $k\sqrt{2}$, $k \in Q$.

5. Write $\sqrt{27} + \sqrt{12}$ in the form $k\sqrt{3}$, $k \in Q$.

6. Write $\sqrt{125} + \sqrt{20}$ in the form $k\sqrt{5}$, $k \in Q$.

7. If $\sqrt{44} + \sqrt{11} = n\sqrt{11}$, then find n where $n \in N$.

8. For each of the following, rationalise the denominator:

   (i) $\dfrac{6}{\sqrt{2}}$ (iv) $\dfrac{3}{\sqrt{5}}$ (vii) $\dfrac{2\sqrt{3}}{\sqrt{6}}$

   (ii) $\dfrac{7}{\sqrt{7}}$ (v) $\dfrac{2}{\sqrt{11}}$ (viii) $\dfrac{-4\sqrt{5}}{\sqrt{12}}$

   (iii) $\dfrac{1}{\sqrt{2}}$ (vi) $\dfrac{3\sqrt{3}}{\sqrt{5}}$ (ix) $\dfrac{3}{\sqrt{45}}$

9. For each of the following, rationalise the denominator:

   (i) $\dfrac{1}{\sqrt{5} - 2}$ (iv) $\dfrac{2 - \sqrt{3}}{5 - \sqrt{3}}$ (vii) $\dfrac{1 + \sqrt{2}}{5\sqrt{2}}$

   (ii) $\dfrac{1}{3 + \sqrt{3}}$ (v) $\dfrac{\sqrt{3} - 7}{\sqrt{3} + 7}$ (viii) $\dfrac{\sqrt{3} - \sqrt{5}}{\sqrt{3} + \sqrt{5}}$

   (iii) $\dfrac{5\sqrt{2}}{\sqrt{2} - 1}$ (vi) $\dfrac{2 - \sqrt{11}}{3\sqrt{11} + 5}$ (ix) $\dfrac{2\sqrt{7} - 3\sqrt{3}}{5\sqrt{3} + 4\sqrt{7}}$

7.5 LOGARITHMS

John Napier (1550–1617) is credited with inventing logarithms. Napier was a Scottish landowner who devoted much of his spare time to the study of mathematics. He invented logarithms to allow for the easier calculation of products and quotients involving large quantities.

John Napier (1550–1617)

Consider the following information in index form:	**Index form** $2^3 = 8$ ('2 to the power of 3 is 8')
We can express the same information in logarithmic form:	**Log form** $\log_2 8 = 3$ ('log of 8 to base 2 is 3')

So, logarithms reverse the process of exponentiation.

As $a^m = n > 0$, for all $a > 0$, $m \in R$, we can write: $\log_a n = m$.

However, if $a \leqslant 0$, $m \in R$, $a^m = n$ is not always real. For example, $(-1)^{\frac{1}{2}} = i$ is not real. Also, $(0)^0$ is not defined. Therefore, we always use a **positive base** when using logarithms.

$a^m = n \Leftrightarrow \log_a n = m$, where a (the base) > 0, $m \in R$, $n > 0$.

ACTIVITY 7.6

Graphing a Logarithmic Function

A logarithmic function is a function of the form:

$$f(x) = \log_a x,$$

where $x \in R$, $x > 0$, and a is a positive constant.

We can study the behaviour of logarithms by looking at the graphs of logarithmic functions.

The graph of the logarithmic function

$$f(x) = \log_2 x, \; x \in R, \; x > 0$$

is shown on the right.

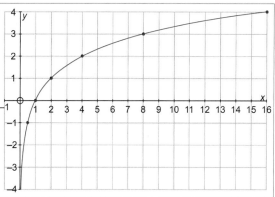

The graph of $y = \log_2 x$ is a reflection of the graph of $y = 2^x$ in the line $y = x$.

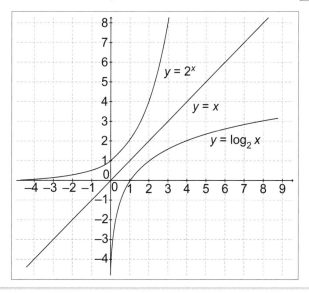

a^{pq} Worked Example 7.12

(i) Graph the function $f(x) = \log_3 x$, $x \in R$, $0 < x \leqslant 27$.

(ii) 'Logarithms expand small variations and compress large ones.' Explain this statement in the context of the graph of $f(x)$.

Solution

(i) Let $x = 1$ and all whole number powers of 3 within the given domain.

So, let $x = 1, 3, 9, 27$ in the table of values.

Then, let $x = 3^{-1}$ and 3^{-2} in the table of values.

This will give a sufficient number of points with which to construct a graph.

x	$\log_3 x$
$3^{-2} = \dfrac{1}{9}$	-2
$3^{-1} = \dfrac{1}{3}$	-1
1	0
3	1
9	2
27	3

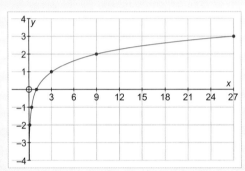

(ii) If we look at small variations in x, for $x < 1$ we see a comparitively large variation in $\log_3 x$.

For example, if $\dfrac{1}{9} \leqslant x \leqslant \dfrac{1}{3}$, we have $-2 \leqslant \log_3 x \leqslant -1$.

If we look at large variations in x, for $x > 1$ there is a comparitively small variation in $\log_3 x$.

For example, If $3 \leqslant x \leqslant 27$, we have $1 \leqslant \log_3 x \leqslant 3$.

The Laws of Logarithms

ACTIVITIES 7.7, 7.8, 7.9, 7.10, 7.11

FORMULA

Law 1 $\log_a (xy) = \log_a x + \log_a y$

Law 2 $\log_a \left(\dfrac{x}{y}\right) = \log_a x - \log_a y$

Law 3 $\log_a (x^q) = q \log_a x$

Law 4 $\log_a 1 = 0$

Law 5 $\log_a \left(\dfrac{1}{x}\right) = -\log_a x$

Law 6 $\log_a (a^x) = x$

Law 7 $a^{\log_a x} = x$

Law 8 $\log_b x = \dfrac{\log_a x}{\log_a b}$

Note: $\log_a a = 1$.

These laws appear on page 21 of *Formulae and Tables*.

In Activities 7.7–7.11 you derived the laws of logarithms in the case where the base a was rational. The laws also apply in the case where a is irrational, for example, $a = e$.

The **natural logarithm function**, $f(x) = \log_e x$, has the irrational number e as its base. It is also written as $f(x) = \ln x$.

a^{pq} Worked Example 7.13

Evaluate $\log_{16} 64$.

Solution

Let $\log_{16} 64 = x$.

$\Rightarrow 16^x = 64$

$(2^4)^x = 2^6$

$2^{4x} = 2^6$

$\Rightarrow 4x = 6$

$x = \dfrac{3}{2}$

Alternative Method

$\log_{16} 64 = \dfrac{\log_4 64}{\log_4 16}$ (Law 8 of Logarithms)

$= \dfrac{\log_4 4^3}{\log_4 4^2}$

$= \dfrac{3\log_4 4}{2\log_4 4}$

$= \dfrac{3}{2}$

a^{pq} Worked Example 7.14

(i) If $\log_{10} (3x + 1) = 2$, find x.   (ii) If $\log_2 (x + 3) = \log_2 (x - 9)^2$, find x.

Solution

(i) $\log_{10} (3x + 1) = 2$

$\Rightarrow 3x + 1 = 10^2$

$3x + 1 = 100$

$3x = 99$

$\therefore x = 33$

(ii) $\log_2 (x + 3) = \log_2 (x - 9)^2$ (Drop log notation, as base on LHS equals base on RHS.)

$\Rightarrow x + 3 = (x - 9)^2$

$x + 3 = x^2 - 18x + 81$

$x^2 - 19x + 78 = 0$

$(x - 6)(x - 13) = 0$

$x = 6$ **OR** $x = 13$

Both $x = 6$ and $x = 13$ satisfy the original equation.

a^{pq} Worked Example 7.15

Solve for x: $\log_2 (x + 1) - \log_2 (x - 1) = 1, x > 1, x \in R$

Solution

$\log_2 (x + 1) - \log_2 (x - 1) = 1$

$\log_2 \left[\dfrac{x + 1}{x - 1}\right] = 1$ (Law 2 of Logarithms)

$\dfrac{x + 1}{x - 1} = 2^1$

$x + 1 = 2x - 2$

$\therefore x = 3$

As $3 > 1$, $x = 3$ is solution.

a^{pq} Worked Example 7.16

Solve for x:

$$4\log_x 2 = \log_2 x + 3, \, x > 0, \, x \in R$$

Solution

Step 1 Ensure that all logs have the same base.

$$\log_x 2 = \frac{\log_2 2}{\log_2 x} \quad \text{(Law 8 of Logarithms)}$$

$$= \frac{1}{\log_2 x}$$

Step 2 $\quad 4\left[\dfrac{1}{\log_2 x}\right] = \log_2 x + 3$

Let $y = \log_2 x$

$$4\left[\frac{1}{y}\right] = y + 3$$

$$4 = y^2 + 3y$$

$$y^2 + 3y - 4 = 0$$

$$(y + 4)(y - 1) = 0$$

$$\Rightarrow y = -4 \quad \textbf{OR} \quad y = 1$$

$$\log_2 x = -4 \quad \textbf{OR} \quad \log_2 x = 1$$

$$x = 2^{-4} \qquad\qquad \therefore x = 2$$

$$\therefore \, x = \frac{1}{16}$$

As both $\dfrac{1}{16}$ and $2 > 0$, $x = \dfrac{1}{16}$ and $x = 2$ are solutions.

a^{pq} Worked Example 7.17

Solve the equation $2^{2x} - 8(2^x) + 15 = 0$.

Give your answer correct to two decimal places.

Solution

Step 1 Transform the equation into a quadratic equation.

Let $y = 2^x$.

Then:

$$2^{2x} = (2^x)^2 \quad \text{(Law 3 of Indices)}$$

$$= y^2$$

Thus, the equation can be written as:

$$y^2 - 8y + 15 = 0$$

Step 2 Solve the associated quadratic equation.

$$y^2 - 8y + 15 = 0$$

$$(y - 3)(y - 5) = 0$$

$$\Rightarrow y - 3 = 0 \quad \textbf{OR} \quad y - 5 = 0$$

$$y = 3 \quad \textbf{OR} \quad y = 5$$

Step 3 Solve for x.

$$y = 2^x$$

$$2^x = 3$$

$$\log 2^x = \log 3$$

$$x\log 2 = \log 3$$

$$\Rightarrow x = \frac{\log 3}{\log 2} \quad \text{(Any common base can be used.)}$$

$$\Rightarrow x = 1.58 \quad \text{(to two d.p.)}$$

OR

$$2^x = 5$$

$$\log 2^x = \log 5$$

$$x \log 2 = \log 5$$

$$\Rightarrow x = \frac{\log 5}{\log 2}$$

$$\Rightarrow x = 2.32 \quad \text{(to two d.p.)}$$

Calculator note:

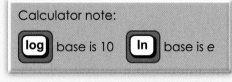 **log** base is 10 **ln** base is e

1. Express these statements in logarithmic notation:

   (i) $27 = 3^3$

   (ii) $125 = 5^3$

   (iii) $64 = 16^{\frac{3}{2}}$

   (iv) $\frac{1}{2} = 2^{-1}$

   (v) $e^0 = 1$

   (vi) $27 = 81^{\frac{3}{4}}$

   (vii) $4 = \left(\frac{1}{16}\right)^{-\frac{1}{2}}$

   (viii) $p^q = r$

2. Express these statements in index notation:

   (i) $\log_2 16 = 4$

   (ii) $7 = \log_2 128$

   (iii) $\log_{27} 3 = \frac{1}{3}$

   (iv) $\log_4 2 = \frac{1}{2}$

   (v) $\log_e 1 = 0$

   (vi) $y = \log_x z$

3. Evaluate:

   (i) $\log_9 3$

   (ii) $\log_{\frac{1}{2}} 4$

   (iii) $\log_{121} 11$

   (iv) $\log_5 1$

   (v) $\log_{27} 3$

   (vi) $\ln e$

   (vii) $\ln e^2$

   (viii) $\log_a a^3$

4. Evaluate each of the following:

   (i) $\log_2 16$

   (ii) $\log_3 81$

   (iii) $\log_5 125$

   (iv) $\log_4 64$

   (v) $\log_{10} 1{,}000$

   (vi) $\log_8 32$

   (vii) $\log_2 \frac{1}{128}$

   (viii) $\log_3 \frac{1}{81}$

5. Use a calculator to evaluate to three significant figures:

   (i) e^2

   (ii) $e^{1.5}$

   (iii) $e^{0.1}$

   (iv) $\ln 3$

   (v) $\ln 0.201$

   (vi) $\ln 15.3$

   (vii) $\log_{10} 6.4$

   (viii) $\log_{10} 250$

6. Graph the function:

   $$f(x) = \log_4 x, \, x \in R, \, 0 < x \leqslant 64$$

7. Graph the function:

   $$f(x) = \log_e x, \, x \in R, \, 0 < x \leqslant 30$$

8. Express as single logarithms:

   (i) $\log 2 + \log 5$

   (ii) $\log 20 - \log 4$

   (iii) $\log 4 + 2\log 3 - \log 6$

   (iv) $3\log 2 + 2\log 3 - 2\log 6$

   (v) $\log p - \frac{1}{3} \log q$

   (vi) $3\log a - \frac{1}{3} \log b + 1$

9. Solve for x:

   (i) $\log_2 (3x + 1) = 2$

   (ii) $\log_2 (x - 1) = 3$

   (iii) $\log_3 (5x + 2) = 3$

   (iv) $\log_5 (8x + 1) = 2$

10. Solve for x:

    (i) $\log_3 (2x + 5) - \log_3 (x - 8) = 1$

    (ii) $\log_3 (10x + 7) - \log_3 (x + 1) = 2$

    (iii) $\log_2 3 + \log_2 (x + 1) = \log_2 (x + 11)$

    (iv) $\log_5 (x + 1) = \log_5 (7x + 1) - 1$

11. Solve for x:

    (i) $\log_4 (3x - 2) = \dfrac{\log_2 (x - 1)}{2}, \, x \in R$

    (ii) $\log_5 (2x + 1) + \log_{125} (2x + 1) = 16, \, x \in R$

    (iii) $\log_{16} x - \log_4 x + 3 = 0, \, x \in R$

    (iv) $\log_{27} (x + 2) + \log_3 (x + 2) = 4, \, x \in R$

    (v) $\log_{27} (2x + 4) + \log_{81} (6x + 12) = \frac{5}{6}, \, x \in R$

12. Solve for x:

    (i) $\log_4 (3x + 1) = \log_2 (x - 1)$

    (ii) $\log_5 (x + 1) + \log_4 (x + 1) = 3$

    (iii) $\log_8 x - \log_9 x = 1$

    (iv) $\log_2 x + \log_3 x = 1$

13. Solve each of the following equations. Give your answers correct to two decimal places.

    (i) $2^{2x} - 8(2^x) + 15 = 0$

    (ii) $3^{2x} = 24 - 5(3^x)$

    (iii) $10^{2x} - 5(10^x) = 0$

    (iv) $(7^{x+1})^2 = 100$

    (v) $3^{2x+1} + 5(3^x) - 2 = 0$

14. Solve $9^x - 2(3^{x+1}) + 8 = 0$.

15. Solve each of the following equations. Give your answers correct to two significant figures.

(i) $3^{2x+1} - 13(3^x) + 14 = 0$

(ii) $9(5^{2x}) = 4(3(5^x) - 1)$

(iii) $2^{2x+1} = 12 - 5(2^x)$

(iv) $6^{2x} - 7(6^x) + 10 = 0$

(v) $2^{x+1}5^{x+1} - 9(2^x5^x) - 2 = 0$

16. Solve for x:

(i) $x = \log_e e$

(ii) $\log_e x = 2$

(iii) $\log_e \dfrac{1}{e} = x$

(iv) $\log_e \sqrt[3]{e} = x$

17. Solve for x:

(i) $e^{\log_e x} = 5$

(ii) $\log_e e^4 = x$

(iii) $e^{\log_e 2} = x$

(iv) $2\log_e x = 1 - \log_e 7$

18. Solve the following equations:

(i) $3 = e^{2x}$

(ii) $2 = \ln 3x$

(iii) $\ln x^{-\frac{1}{5}} = 1$

(iv) $7e^{7x} = 1$

19. Solve the following equations:

(i) $e^{\ln 5x} = 10$

(ii) $\ln e^{3x} + 4\ln e^{2x} = 7$

(iii) $e^x + e^{-x} = 2$

(iv) $5^{2x} = \dfrac{1}{3}$ (answer correct to two decimal places)

7.6 USING LOGARITHMS TO SOLVE PRACTICAL PROBLEMS

Many mathematical models that represent real life situations contain unknown powers or indices. Here are two examples:

■ $F = P(1 + i)^t$ (**Compound interest formula**)

■ $p = ae^{bt}$ (**Exponential model**: describes population growth, radioactive decay, etc. If $b > 0$, then p is growing. If $b < 0$, then p is decaying.)

When looking for the unknown exponent (power), logarithms are used to convert the exponential equation into a linear equation. The linear equation is then solved to find the unknown exponent.

There are other real-life models that use logarithmic scales. Here are two examples:

■ $M = \log_{10}\left[\dfrac{I}{S}\right]$ (**Richter scale**)

■ $D = 10\log_{10}\left[\dfrac{I}{I_0}\right]$ (**Decibel scale**: approximates loudness of sound as perceived by the human brain.)

The laws of logarithms are used to solve problems involving these models.

a^{pq} Worked Example 7.18

Scientists have shown that a particular population of insects grows exponentially according to the model $p = ae^{bt}$, where a and b are constants and t is time measured in weeks. A remote area of forest has a population of 500 of these insects. In one week the population increases to 560.

(i) Find the value of the constants a and b.

(ii) Find, to the nearest week, the time for the population to increase to 181,262, assuming the population remains unchecked (i.e. its increase is not interrupted by disease, etc.).

Solution

(i) $p = ae^{bt}$

We know that at time $t = 0$, $p = 500$.

$\therefore 500 = ae^0$

$\Rightarrow a = 500$

Substitute the value for a in the model.

$p = 500e^{bt}$

We also know that at time $t = 1$, $p = 560$.

$\therefore 560 = 500e^b$

$e^b = \dfrac{28}{25}$

$b = \log_e \dfrac{28}{25}$

$\Rightarrow b = 0.11332869$

Therefore the model is:

$p = 500e^{0.11332869t}$

(ii) $500e^{0.11332869t} = 181{,}262$

$e^{0.11332869t} = \dfrac{181{,}262}{500}$

$\Rightarrow 0.11332869t = \log_e \dfrac{181{,}262}{500}$

$\Rightarrow 0.11332869t = 5.893090679$

$\Rightarrow t = 51.999...$

$\Rightarrow t \approx 52$ weeks

a^{pq} Worked Example 7.19

The decibel scale is used to measure loudness. A sound is a vibration received by the ear and processed by the brain. The intensity of a sound is a measure of the strength of the vibration. If a sound has intensity I, then its decibel rating is

$$D = 10\log_{10}\left[\dfrac{I}{I_0}\right]$$

where I_0 is a standard intensity.
$I_0 = 10^{-16}$ W/cm^2.

(i) Find the decibel rating of a sound that has a measured intensity of 10^{-10} W/cm^2.

(ii) Find the increase in decibels when the sound intensity increases from 10^{-13} W/cm^2 to 10^{-9} W/cm^2.

Solution

(i) $D = 10\log_{10} \dfrac{10^{-10}}{10^{-16}}$

$= 10\log_{10} 10^6$

$= 60\log_{10} 10$

$= 60$ dB

(ii) $D = 10\log_{10} \dfrac{10^{-9}}{10^{-16}} - 10\log_{10} \dfrac{10^{-13}}{10^{-16}}$

$D = 70 - 30$

$\therefore$ Increase $= 40$ dB

Exercise 7.5

1. The radioactive substance Iodine-131 is used in medicine to measure liver and heart activity and in the treatment of certain cancers. It has a half-life of eight days, i.e. the quantity of Iodine-131 decays by a factor of 2 in eight days. A hospital purchases 30 g of the substance. In eight days 15 g remain. The decay can be modelled using the exponential model:

$$Q = ae^{bt}$$

where a and b are constants, t is time measured in days and Q is the quantity of the substance.

(i) Find the value of each of the constants a and b.

(ii) What quantity of the substance will remain after 20 days?

(iii) Find the time taken for the substance to decay to 1.49 g.

2. pH is a measure of the acidity or basicity of a solution. Solutions with a pH less than 7 are said to be acidic. Solutions with a pH greater than 7 are said to be basic or alkaline. A solution with a pH equal to 7 is said to be neutral. Chemists define pH by the formula $pH = -\log_{10}[H^+]$, where $[H^+]$ is the hydrogen ion concentration of the solution measured in moles per litre.

(i) A substance has a hydrogen ion concentration of 1.5×10^{-5} moles per litre. Determine the pH and classify the substance as an acid or a base.

(ii) A substance has a hydrogen ion concentration of 1.4×10^{-9} moles per litre. Determine the pH and classify the substance as an acid or a base.

(iii) If a solution has a pH of 8.2, find the hydrogen ion concentration of the solution. Give your answer in the form $a \times 10^n$, where $a \in N$ and $n \in Z$.

3. Normally, human blood has a hydrogen ion concentration of 1.3×10^{-8} moles per litre. pH is given by the formula $pH = -\log_{10}[H^+]$, where $[H^+]$ is the hydrogen in concentration of the solution measured in moles per litre.

(i) Determine the normal pH of human blood.

(ii) A condition known as acidosis sets in when the pH of a person's blood drops below 7.45. Acidosis can result in death if the pH reaches 7. What would the hydrogen ion concentration of a person's blood be at a pH value of 7?

4. The soil in a vegetable garden is tested and is found to have a hydrogen ion concentration of 7.2×10^{-7} moles per litre. If potatoes prefer soil that has a pH in the range 7.5 to 6, should potatoes be planted in the garden? pH is given by the formula $pH = -\log_{10}[H^+]$, where $[H^+]$ is the hydrogen in concentration of the solution measured in moles per litre.

5. The future value, F, of an investment is given by the formula $F = P(1 + i)^t$, where P is the present value of the investment, i is the annual rate of interest and t is the time in years. A sum of money, P, is invested in a post office account. Use logarithms to find the time taken for the investment to double in value if the annual rate of interest is:

(i) 5%   (ii) 7%   (iii) 10%

(Give your answers correct to the nearest month.)

6. Use logarithms to find the time taken for an investment of €15,000 to amount to €26,937 at a rate of 5% p.a. The interest is compounded annually.

7. Before the 1970s, the intensity of an earthquake was measured as the amplitude of a seismograph reading, taken 100 km from the epicentre of the quake. A standard earthquake had an amplitude of 10^{-3} mm on a seismogram.

In 1935 Charles Richter defined the magnitude, M, of an earthquake measured in this way to be $M = \log_{10}\frac{I}{S}$, where $I =$ the intensity of the earthquake in mm and $S =$ the intensity of a standard earthquake in mm.

This scale for measuring earthquakes became known as the Richter scale.

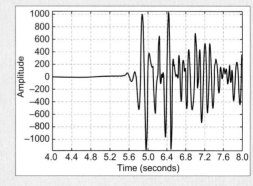

(i) What is the magnitude of a standard earthquake?

(ii) Calculate the magnitude of an earthquake with an intensity of 1,200 mm.

(iii) The earthquake that struck Salton City, California, on 19 March 1954 measured 6.4 on the Richter scale. What was the amplitude of this quake?

8. Nowadays, the moment magnitude scale is used to measure the magnitude of an earthquake. The formula used is $M = \frac{2}{3} \times \log_{10} m - 10.73$, where M is the reported magnitude of the quake and m is the size of the seismic moment measured in dyne centimetres.

   (i) What is the magnitude of an earthquake with a seismic moment of size 10^{25} dyne centimetres? (Answer correct to one decimal place.)

   (ii) The earthquake that struck Haiti on 12 January 2010 had a reported magnitude of 7.0. What was the size of this earthquake's seismic moment? Write your answer in the form 10^a (dyne centimetres), where $a \in R$.

   The seismic moment (m) is a measure of the total amount of energy that is released during an earthquake.

   (iii) In terms of released energy, how many times stronger was the earthquake of magnitude 8.9 that struck the coast of Japan on 11 March 2011 than the Haitian earthquake of January 2010? (Answer correct to the nearest whole number.)

   (iv) An increase in magnitude (M) of one unit corresponds to what increase in released energy? (Answer correct to the nearest whole number.)

Revision Exercises

1. Write the following in index notation:

   (i) $5^3 \times 5^8$

   (ii) $(3^2)^3$

   (iii) $\dfrac{16^9}{16^5}$

   (iv) $\dfrac{1}{7^5}$

   (v) $\sqrt[5]{17^3}$

   (vi) $\dfrac{5^3}{\sqrt{5^5}}$

2. Write these in the form a^n:

   (i) $a^4 \times a^6$

   (ii) $(a^4)^6$

   (iii) $\sqrt[4]{a^6}$

   (iv) $\sqrt[5]{a^3 \times a^7}$

3. Use the laws of surds to simplify each of the following:

   (i) $\sqrt{125} + \sqrt{98} + \sqrt{128}$

   (ii) $\sqrt{80} + \sqrt{245} + \sqrt{405}$

4. (i) Evaluate $64^{-\frac{1}{2}}$.

   (ii) Write (a) 128 and (b) $\sqrt{2}$ as a power of 2.

   (iii) Hence, solve the equation $2^{2x+1} = \dfrac{128}{\sqrt{2}}$.

5. (i) Simplify $a^4 + a^4 + a^4 + a^4$.

   Hence, write $2^4 + 2^4 + 2^4 + 2^4$ as a power of 2.

   (ii) Write $2^{\frac{1}{4}} + 2^{\frac{1}{4}} + 2^{\frac{1}{4}} + 2^{\frac{1}{4}}$ as a power of 2.

   (iii) Simplify $3a^5 + 6a^5$.

   Hence, write $3(3^5) + 6(3^5)$ as a power of 3.

   (iv) Write $20(3^8) + 7(3^8)$ as a power of 3.

6. Simplify the following by rationalising the denominator:

   (i) $\dfrac{5}{\sqrt{2}}$

   (ii) $\dfrac{6}{\sqrt{3}}$

   (iii) $\dfrac{12\sqrt{2}}{4\sqrt{3}}$

   (iv) $\dfrac{2\sqrt{2} + \sqrt{3}}{\sqrt{2} - \sqrt{3}}$

   (v) $\dfrac{\sqrt{5} - \sqrt{2}}{4\sqrt{5}}$

   (vi) $\dfrac{\sqrt{7} - \sqrt{2}}{2\sqrt{7} + 3\sqrt{2}}$

   (vii) $\dfrac{\sqrt{5}}{\sqrt{3} - 2}$

7. Solve for x, each of the following:

   (i) $\log 5 + \log x = \log 30,\ x > 0,\ x \in R$

   (ii) $\log 4 + 2\log x = \log 16,\ x > 0,\ x \in R$

   (iii) $2\log 2 + \log(x - 1) = \log 15,\ x > 1,\ x \in R$

   (iv) $\log_2(1 + x) - \log_2(1 - x) = 2,\ x > 1,\ x \in R$

   (v) $\log_7(x + 1) + \log_7(x - 5) = 1,\ x > 5,\ x \in R$

8. Solve for x:

   (i) $\log_x x - \log_9 x + 1 = 0$

   (ii) $\log_5(x + 100) - \log_5 x = 1$

   (iii) $\log_{25}(6x + 25) + \log_5(x + 25) = 5,\ x \in N$

   (iv) $\log_5 x = 1 + \log_5\left[\dfrac{3}{2x - 1}\right]$

9. (a) Use logarithms to find the least value of $n \in N$ for which $3^n > 1{,}000{,}000$.

   (b) Use logarithms to find the largest value of $n \in N$ for which $2^n < 500{,}000$.

10. Solve the following equations:

(i) $2^{2x} - 3(2^x) - 40 = 0$

(ii) $5^{2x} - 2(5^x) - 575 = 0$

(iii) $3^x - 3^{1-x} + 2 = 0$

(iv) $3e^x - 7 + 2e^{-x} = 0$

(v) $2^{x^2} = 8^{2x+9}$

11. Solve the following simultaneous equations:

(i) $\log_x (y + 1) = 2$

$\log_2 (y - 2x) = 1$

(ii) $\log_3 (3x - y) - \log_3 (y + 1) = 0$

$\log_3 2 + \log_3 (x + y) = 2$

(iii) $\log_2 x - \log_3 3 = \log_2 (1 - y)$

$\log_2 x + \log_2 (x + 2y) = 3$

12. (a) Show that $\log_b a = \dfrac{1}{\log_a b}$.

(b) Hence, show that:

$$\frac{1}{\log_2 x} + \frac{1}{\log_3 x} + \frac{1}{\log_5 x} = \frac{1}{\log_{30} x}$$

13. Two functions, $f(x) = \log_a x$ and $g(x)$, where a is a constant, are graphed below. $f(x)$ is defined for all $x > 0$, $x \in R$, while $g(x)$ is defined for all $x \in R$. The image of $f(x)$ by a reflection in the line $y = x$ is $g(x)$.

(i) Using the graph, find the value of a.

(ii) Hence, write the function $g(x)$ in the form $g(x) = b^x$, where b is a constant.

(iii) Show that the image of $(m, \log_a m)$ by a reflection in the line $y = x$ lies on the curve of $g(x)$.

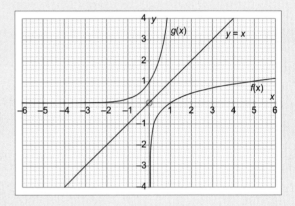

14. The decibel scale is used to measure loudness. A sound is a vibration received by the ear and processed by the brain. The intensity of a sound is a measure of the strength of the vibration. If a sound has intensity I, then its decibel rating is $D = 10\log_{10}\left[\dfrac{I}{I_0}\right]$, where I_0 is a standard intensity. $I_0 = 10^{-16}$ W/cm^2.

(i) The background noise of a quiet classroom has a measured intensity of 10^{-12} W/cm^2. Find the decibel rating of the sound.

(ii) The noise on a busy motorway varies from 80 dB to 90 dB. Find the corresponding variation in intensities.

(iii) If a single trumpet is playing at 78 dB, how many trumpets have joined in if the level increases to 88 dB and each trumpet is equally loud?

15. Many phenomena – from stock market prices and census data to heat capacities of chemicals – obey Benford's Law. This states that for a set of numerical data, the proportion of numbers starting with the digit D is approximately $\log_{10}\left(1 + \dfrac{1}{D}\right)$.

(i) Show that Benford's Law predicts that around 30.1% of numbers will start with a 1.

(ii) Copy and complete the following table using Benford's Law. Give your answers correct to one decimal place.

Starting digit (D)	1	2	3	4	5	6	7	8	9
Percentage (%)	30.1								

(iii) Make one observation on the pattern of percentages from part (ii).

(iv) Show $\displaystyle\sum_{D=1}^{9} \log_{10}\left(1 + \frac{1}{D}\right) = 1$.

16. Radioactive substances decay exponentially. The half-life of a radioactive substance is the amount of time that it takes for 50% of the quantity of the substance to decay (to become more stable).

Some radioactive substances decay very quickly, e.g. Lithium-8 has a half-life of only 0.84 seconds. Other substances decay very slowly, e.g. Uranium-238 has a half-life of 4.47 billion years!

Below is a diagram showing how a radioactive substance, Cobalt-60, decays over time.

(a) The equation for the curve is $Q = A.e^{-kt}$. The intial quantity of Cobalt-60 is 10 kg. Using this information, show algebraically that $A = 10$.

(b) Using the graph, estimate, to the nearest decimal place, the half-life (in years) of Cobalt-60.

(c) Using the fact that $A = 10$ and the value for the half-life that you calculated in part (b), find the value of the decay constant k in the equation of the curve, $Q = 10.e^{-kt}$.

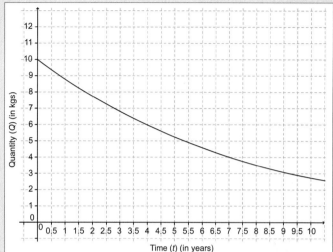

(d) Using your answer from part (c), calculate, to the nearest decimal place, how long (in years) it would take for 90% of a quantity of Cobalt-60 to decay.

17. $y = Ae^{-kt}$ represents the rate of decay of radium, where y is the amount present at a time t.

A is the initial quantity of radium present. If it takes 1,600 years for half the original amount to decay, find the percentage of the original amount that remains after 200 years.

18. According to Newton's Law of Cooling, the rate at which the temperature of a body falls is proportional to the amount by which its temperature exceeds that of its surroundings. For one such situation the temperature, $T°C$, of the body after t minutes is given by $T = 10 + 190\, e^{-kt}$, where $k = \frac{1}{40} \ln\left(\frac{19}{9}\right)$. Calculate the time it takes to reach 50°C.

19. The population of a village was 753 in 1980. If the population grows according to the equation $P = 753e^{0.03t}$, where P is the number of persons in the population at time t:

(a) Graph the population equation for $t = 0$ (in 1980) to $t = 30$ (in 2010).

(b) From the graph, estimate the population in (i) 1990 and (ii) 2000.

(c) Confirm your answers to part (b) algebraically.

(d) In what year will the population reach 1,750 persons?

Functions

Learning Outcomes

In this chapter you will learn to:

- Recognise that a function assigns a unique output to a given input
- Form composite functions
- Graph functions of the form:
  - $ax + b$, where $a, b \in Q, x \in R$
  - $ax^2 + bx + c$, where $a, b, c \in Q, x \in R$
  - $ax^3 + bx^2 + cx + d$, where $a, b, c, d \in Z, x \in R$
  - ab^x, where $a, b \in R$
- Graph logarithmic functions
- Interpret equations of the form $f(x) = g(x)$ as a comparison of the above functions
- Use graphical methods to find approximate solutions to:
  - $f(x) = 0$

- $f(x) = k$
- $f(x) = g(x)$

where $f(x)$ and $g(x)$ are of the stated form, or where graphs of $f(x)$ and $g(x)$ are provided

- Express quadratic functions in completed square form
- Use the completed square form to:
  - Find roots and turning points
  - Sketch the function
- Apply transformations to selected functions
- Recognise injective, surjective and bijective functions
- Find the inverse of a bijective function
- Sketch the inverse of a function given the function's graph

8.1 INTRODUCTION

What Is a Function?

> A **function** is a rule that maps an input to a unique output.

Functions can be described as 'number machines' that transform one number into another. If we think of functions as machines, then something is put into the machine, something happens in the machine, and then something comes out.

Lowercase letters are used to name functions. *f* and *g* are often used, but remember any letter may be used to name/denote a function.

Functions in Everyday Life

You meet functions several times throughout your normal day.

Television remote controls are an example of functions at work. If you have programmed your television so that channel 103 is assigned to TV3 (for example), then when you key in 103 on your remote, TV3 appears on the television screen. Of course, you could also have TV3 pre-programmed for channel 104 (say), but you could not pre-programme two or more television stations for the same channel number. In other words, each input (channel number) is mapped to a unique output (television station).

Important Terms

- An **input** is an object that is put into the function.
- The **domain** is the set of all inputs for which a function is defined.
- An **output** is the object that comes out of the function.
- The **range** is the set of **actual** output values of a function.
- The **codomain** is the set of all **possible** output values of a function.

> ### YOU SHOULD REMEMBER...
> - Substitution in algebra
> - Solving equations
> - Number patterns
> - Input–output tables
> - Domain, codomain, range
> - Linear, quadratic, cubic, exponential, logarithmic functions
> - Turning points

> ### KEY WORDS
> - **Relation**
> - **Function**
> - **Input**
> - **Output**
> - **Completing the square**
> - **Turning points**
> - **Transformation**
> - **Mapping diagram**
> - **Couples**
> - **Ordered pairs**
> - **Domain**
> - **Codomain**
> - **Range**
> - **Composite function**
> - **Injective ('one-to-one') function**
> - **Surjective ('onto') function**
> - **Bijective function**
> - **Inverse function**

FUNCTIONS

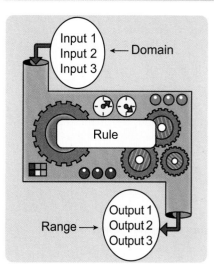

The following example illustrates the meanings of these terms.

Imagine a secondary school in which the Fifth Year classes are called 5.1, 5.2, 5.3 and 5.4. Each class is going on a class trip. They can choose from the following options:

cinema, ice-skating, go-karting, paint-balling or bowling

5.1 choose ice-skating, 5.2 choose go-karting, 5.3 choose ice-skating and 5.4 choose paint-balling. These choices can be represented by a function, as illustrated in the mapping diagram:

- 5.1 is an example of an input.
- Ice-skating is an example of an output.
- The domain is the set of all Fifth Year classes: {5.1, 5.2, 5.3, 5.4}.
- The range is the set of the three chosen activities: {ice-skating, go-karting, paint-balling}.
- The codomain is the set of all five trip options: {cinema, ice-skating, go-karting, paint-balling, bowling}.

Examples of Functions

Suppose you write $f(x) = x^2$. You have just defined a rule for a function f that transforms any number into its square.

Consider the following inputs to this function: {−1, 0, 1, 2}.

The resulting outputs can be computed using an input–output table:

Input	Application of function	Output
x	x^2	y
−1	$(-1)^2$	1
0	$(0)^2$	0
1	$(1)^2$	1
2	$(2)^2$	4

Here, y is the result of applying the rule (the function) to the input.

We can represent the rule for this function in a number of other ways.

Using function notation

$f(x) = x^2$

Pronounced 'f of x equals x-squared'.

OR

Using alternative function notation

$f: x \rightarrow x^2$

Pronounced 'f maps x to x^2'.

OR

As a set of couples/ordered pairs

Set of couples = {(−1,1), (0,0), (1,1), (2,4)}

For example, (2,4) tells us that if 2 is the input, then 4 is the output.

OR

Using a mapping diagram

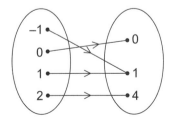

Points to Note: Inputs and Outputs

Look again at the function f defined as $f(x) = x^2$. You will note the following:

- An input can pass through the function and not change, i.e. the input 0 passes through the function and comes out as 0, giving the couple (0,0).
- Two inputs can result in the same output, i.e. the inputs −1 and 1 both result in the output 1.
- However, an input into a function will never result in two different outputs.

8.2 FUNCTIONS AS MAPPINGS FROM ONE SET TO ANOTHER

A function is a rule that maps an input from one set called the domain to a unique output in another set called the codomain. In dealing with functions, it is important to understand:

 (i) what set the inputs are coming from; and

 (ii) what set the outputs are to be found in.

An understanding of the notation used in functions is needed.

Notation

N = Natural numbers R^+ = Positive real numbers

Z = Integers Q = Rational numbers

Z^+ = Positive integers Q^+ = Positive rational numbers

R = Real numbers

The symbol | or : in mathematics means 'such that'.

Intervals

$[a, b] = \{x \in R \mid a \leqslant x \leqslant b\}$	This is a **closed interval**, which is denoted by square brackets.
	The a-value and b-value are included in this interval.
$(a, b) = \{x \in R \mid a < x < b\}$	This is an **open interval**, which is denoted by rounded brackets (also called parentheses).
	The a-value and b-value are not included.
$[a, b) = \{x \in R \mid a \leqslant x < b\}$	Here, the a-value is included but the b-value is not included.
$(a, b] = \{x \in R \mid a < x \leqslant b\}$	Here, the a-value is not included but the b-value is included.

Consider the functions below.

1. $f: N \rightarrow N: x \rightarrow 2x$	The domain is N. The codomain is N.
	For this particular function, the range consists of even natural numbers only. Odd natural numbers are not included in the range.
2. $f: R \rightarrow R: x \rightarrow x - x^2$	The domain is R. The codomain is R.
	For this particular function, the range is $(-\infty, 0.25]$.

3. $f: R \rightarrow R: x \rightarrow x^2$	The domain is R. The codomain is also R.
	For this particular function, the range is $[0, \infty)$.
	Zero is included, as $f(0) = 0$.
	Infinity is not included, as it is approached but never reached.
	Note that the codomain and the range can be different sets.
4. $f: R \rightarrow R^+: x \rightarrow e^x$	The domain is R. The codomain is R^+.
	For this particular function, the range is also R^+.
	For example: $f(-2) = e^{-2}$
	$\qquad\qquad\qquad = \dfrac{1}{e^2} > 0$
	For any x-value, $x \in R$, the output is a positive number.
	$\therefore$ The output is an element of R^+.

 Worked Example 8.1

$f: x \rightarrow 6x - n$ is a function.

(i) If $f(-2) = -23$, find the value of n. (ii) Find the value of x for which $f(x + 3) = -29$.

Solution

(i) $f(-2) = 6(-2) - n$

$\qquad = -12 - n$

$\therefore -12 - n = -23$

$\qquad -n = -23 + 12$

$\qquad -n = -11$

$\qquad \therefore n = 11$

(ii) From part (i): $n = 11$

$\qquad f(x) = 6x - 11$

$\therefore f(x + 3) = 6(x + 3) - 11$

$\qquad\qquad = 6x + 18 - 11$

$\qquad\qquad = 6x + 7$

$\therefore 6x + 7 = -29$

$\qquad 6x = -36$

$\qquad \therefore x = -6$

 Worked Example 8.2

The diagram shows part of the graph of the function g given by $g(x) = ax^2 + bx - 2, x \in R$.

Find the value of a and the value of b.

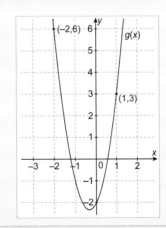

Solution

$(1,3) \in g(x)$

$\therefore a(1)^2 + b(1) - 2 = 3$

$\qquad a + b - 2 = 3$

$\qquad\qquad a + b = 5$ **Eq. 1**

$(-2,6) \in g(x)$

$\therefore a(-2)^2 + b(-2) - 2 = 6$

$\qquad 4a - 2b - 2 = 6$

$\qquad 4a - 2b = 8$

$\qquad\qquad 2a - b = 4$ **Eq. 2**

Now solve the simultaneous equations 1 and 2:

$$a + b = 5 \quad \textbf{Eq. 1}$$
$$\underline{2a - b = 4} \quad \textbf{Eq. 2}$$
$$3a = 9$$
$$\therefore a = 3$$

Substitute $a = 3$ into Equation 1:

$$3 + b = 5$$
$$\therefore b = 2$$

Answer: $a = 3$, $b = 2$

8.3 COMPOSITE FUNCTIONS

Let us say we have a function f given by $f(x) = x^2 + 1$, $x \in R$. You can replace x with any real number.

For example: $f(1) = (1)^2 + 1 = 2$ $\qquad f(-2) = (-2)^2 + 1 = 5$ $\qquad f(x + h) = (x + h)^2 + 1$

Now consider the function p given by $p(x) = 3x^2 + 5$.

If we take an input value of 4, let us describe what we do to find $p(4)$:

- Square the input, 4 in this case. $\qquad (4)^2 = 16$
- Multiply the square of the input by 3. $\qquad 3(16) = 48$
- Then add 5. $\qquad 48 + 5 = 53$

We could break the function p into two separate functions here:

- Function 1 tells us to square the input.
- Function 2 tells us to multiply the output of Function 1 by 3 and then add 5.

We can understand this type of function more easily if we break p into two separate functions, g and h.

- The function g is defined as $g(x) = x^2$, $x \in R$.
- The function h is defined as $h(x) = 3x + 5$, $x \in R$.

We want to find $g(x)$ first and then use $g(x)$ as the input for our function h.

It means that we perform the function g first and then perform the function h.

> This is read as 'the composition of h and g'.
>
> It is also read as 'h after g'.

If we perform function g first and then function h, we express this as:

$h \circ g(x)$ $\qquad$ **OR** $\qquad$ $(h \circ g)(x)$ $\qquad$ **OR** $\qquad$ $h(g(x))$ $\qquad$ **OR** $\qquad$ $hg(x)$

Note that the order in which we compose two functions is usually important.

For example, squaring 1 and adding 3 (= 4) is not the same as adding 3 to 1 and then squaring (= 16).

Worked Example 8.3

$f(x) = 6x + 2$ and $g(x) = x^3$, where both f and g are functions that map from R to R.

(i) Find the value of $f \circ g(2)$.

(ii) Find the value of $g \circ f(2)$.

(iii) Comment appropriately on your answers to parts (i) and (ii).

Solution

(i) $f \circ g(2)$

First find $g(2)$.

$g(2) = (2)^3$

$\quad = 8$

Now find $f(8)$.

$f(8) = 6(8) + 2$

$\quad\quad = 48 + 2 = 50$

$\therefore f \circ g(2) = 50$

(ii) $g \circ f(2)$

First find $f(2)$.

$f(2) = 6(2) + 2$

$\quad\quad = 12 + 2$

$\quad\quad = 14$

Now find $g(14)$.

$g(14) = (14)^3 = 2{,}744$

$\therefore g \circ f(2) = 2{,}744$

(iii) $\left.\begin{array}{l} f \circ g(2) = 50 \\ g \circ f(2) = 2{,}744 \end{array}\right\} \Rightarrow f \circ g(2) \neq g \circ f(2)$

> In general, composition of functions is not commutative, i.e. $f \circ g(x) \neq g \circ f(x)$.

Worked Example 8.4

Given the function h, where $h: R \mapsto R: t \mapsto (6t + 4)^3$:

(i) Decompose h into two separate functions.

(ii) Decompose h into three separate functions.

Solution

(i) Define the function a such that $a(t) = 6t + 4$.

Define the function b such that $b(t) = t^3$.

$\therefore h = b \circ a$

(ii) Define the function a such that $a(t) = 6t$.

Define the function b such that $b(t) = t + 4$.

Define the function c such that $c(t) = t^3$.

$\therefore h = c \circ b \circ a$

Worked Example 8.5

Write the following (a) as a single function and then (b) as a composition of functions.

(i) Square the input and add 6 to the answer (two functions).

(ii) Find the cubed root of the input, add 5 to this answer and then square it (three functions).

Solution

(i) (a) $f(x) = x^2 + 6$

(b) $g(x) = x^2$

$h(x) = x + 6$

$f(x) = h \circ g(x)$

(ii) (a) $f(x) = (\sqrt[3]{x} + 5)^2$

(b) $g(x) = \sqrt[3]{x}$

$h(x) = x + 5$

$j(x) = x^2$

$\therefore f(x) = j \circ h \circ g(x)$

Exercise 8.1

Note: $x \in R$ unless otherwise stated.

1. Which of the following mappings are functions?
   Give a reason for your answer.

   (a)
   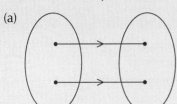

   (b)
   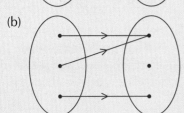

   (c)
   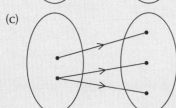

   (d)
   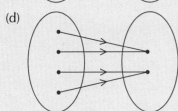

   (e)
   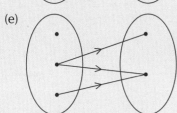

   (f)
   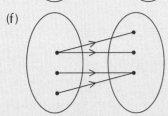

2. $f: x \mapsto 4x - 1$ defines a function.

   (a) Describe in words what the function f does.

   (b) (i) Find the value of $f(1)$.

   (ii) Find the value of $f\left(\frac{1}{2}\right)$.

   (iii) Find the value of k if $f(k) = 9$.

   (iv) Find the value of p if $f(p) = p$.

3. $f(x) = 2x + b$ defines a function.
   Find the value of b if $f(1) = 10$.

4. $g(x) = ax - 12$ defines a function.
   Find the value of a if $g(3) = 0$.

5. The following mapping is given:

   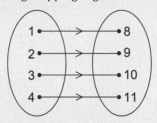

   (i) Is this mapping a function?
   Give a reason for your answer.

   (ii) Write out the domain and range of this mapping.

   (iii) Write an expression in terms of x for this mapping.

   (iv) Use this expression to find the input which would map to 77.

6. Write the following as functions, stating clearly what the letters you use stand for.

   (i) Square the input.

   (ii) The input is multiplied by 4 and 6 is then added.

   (iii) The temperature of the oil in a car engine on stopping is 98°C. Every five minutes that pass, the temperature decreases by 3°.

   (iv) The rate of change of the radius of a melting snowball is –2 cm/s. The radius is initially 10 cm.

7. A function f is defined by the rule:
   'Divide the input by 2 and add 3.'

   (i) Write an expression in x to represent this function.

   (ii) Using this expression, find the value of $f(4)$, $f(18)$ and $f(-6)$.

   (iii) For what value of x is $f(x) = 9$?

   (iv) What is $f(f(x))$ equal to?

   (v) What is $f(x - 5)$ equal to?

   (vi) What is $f(x + k)$ equal to?

   (vii) Show that $\frac{1}{k}[f(x + k) - f(x)] = \frac{1}{2}$.

8. If $g(x) = 2x$, show that $g(x + 3) - g(x - 1) = 8$.

9. The diagram shows part of the graph of a function given by $ax + by = 12$.

Find the value of a and the value of b.

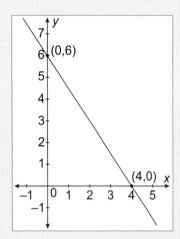

10. The diagram shows part of the graph of the function $y = mx + c$.

Find the value of m and the value of c.

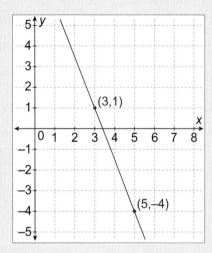

11. The diagram shows part of the graph of the function $f(x) = ax^2 + bx + 4$.

Find the value of a and the value of b.

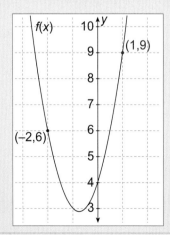

12. Water empties out of a leaking tank. The amount of water in the tank at any instant is given by the rule 'Two hundred minus the input squared', where the input is the number of minutes for which the tank has been leaking. (Volume is measured in litres.)

   (i) Define the function f such that $y = f(x)$, where y is the number of litres of water in the tank and x is the number of minutes passed.

   (ii) How long will it take the tank to empty?

   (iii) At what time will the tank be half empty?

13. A rectangular plot requires 200 metres of railings to enclose it. If one of the sides of the plot is x metres, express its area y as a function of x, and determine the domain of the function.

14. Express the length l of a chord of a circle of radius 5 as a function of its distance x from the centre of the circle, and determine the domain of the function.

15. A function is defined by $h(x) = 2x + 4$. A second function is defined by $g(x) = x^2 + 1$.

The function f is defined as $f = h \circ g$.

   (a) Find:

(i) $f(0)$	(v) $f(-1)$
(ii) $f(3)$	(vi) $f(-2)$
(iii) $f(4)$	(vii) $f(-3)$
(iv) $f(6)$	(viii) $f(-6)$

   (b) A function f is called an even function if $f(-x) = f(x)$ for all x.

   Show that the function $f = h \circ g$ is even.

16. A function is defined by $h(x) = x + 1$. A second function is defined by $g(x) = x^2$ and a third function is defined by $f(x) = x - 2$.

   (a) Find:

(i) $f \circ g(x)$	(v) $g \circ h \circ f(x)$
(ii) $g \circ f(x)$	(vi) $g \circ f \circ g(x)$
(iii) $g \circ h(x)$	(vii) $g \circ g \circ h(x)$
(iv) $h \circ g \circ f(x)$	(viii) $h \circ f \circ f(x)$

   (b) If a fourth function is defined by $p(x) = x^2 - 2x + 1$, express p as a composition of functions f, g and h.

17. (i) Given that $f(x) = 3x + 1$ and $g(x) = 5x + c$, find c if $fg(x) = gf(x)$.

    (ii) Test your answer to part (i) by showing that $fg(3) = gf(3)$.

18. (i) Given that $f(x) = 4x + 3$ and $g(x) = 6x - k$, find k if $fg(x) = gf(x)$.

    (ii) Test your answer to part (i) by showing that $fg(1) = gf(1)$.

19. Given that $g(x) = 3x + 4$ and $h(x) = ax - 2$, find a if $hg(x) = gh(x)$.

20. (a) Decompose the following functions into two simpler functions:

    (i) $h(x) = x^2 + 1$ (ii) $f(x) = 2x^2$

  (b) Decompose the following functions into three simpler functions:

    (i) $g(x) = 3x^2 - 5$

    (ii) $j(x) = (4x - 3)^2$

21. Write the following (a) as a single function and (b) as a composition of functions:

  (i) Square the input and then add 6 to the answer (two functions).

  (ii) Subtract 2 from the input, square the answer, and then multiply by 6 (three functions).

  (iii) Find the square root of the input, then add 4 to this answer, and then cube it (three functions).

  (iv) Find the sine of the input, square this answer, and then divide by 4 (three functions).

22. The functions f, g and h are defined by $f(x) = x^2 - 1$, $g(x) = 3x + 2$ and $h(x) = \frac{1}{x}$.

Solve:

  (i) $fg(x) = 0$ (ii) $gh(x) = -12$

23. Suppose $f: x \to 2x - 4$, $g: x \to 3x^2 + 2$, and $h: x \to ax + b$, where $a, b \in R$.

  (i) Show that $fg: x \to 6x^2$.

  (ii) Find a and b if $fgh(x) = 24x^2 + 72x + 5$.

24. The function f is defined as $f = h \circ g \circ j$. $j(x) = x + 2$, and $g(x) = x^2$.

Define a function h for each of the following situations:

  (i) $f(1) = 12$ (iii) $f(2) = 32$

  (ii) $f(1) = 3$ (iv) $f(-1) = -4$

25. Two functions are defined as $f(x) = 3x + 2$ and $g(x) = x^2 + 2$.

Evaluate:

  (i) $f \circ g(x)$ (ii) $g \circ f(x)$

Is the composition of these two functions commutative? Explain.

26. Consider the functions $f(x) = 3x$ and $g(x) = x^2$, both defined for $x \in R \setminus \{0\}$.

Which of the following composite functions would give you a higher output value for a given input value: $f \circ g$ or $g \circ f$? Explain.

Graphs of trigonometric functions are covered in detail in *Active Maths 4 Book 2*, Chapter 7.

8.4 LINEAR AND QUADRATIC FUNCTIONS

A linear function f in x is a function of the form $f(x) = ax + b$, where a and b are constants and x is a variable.

A constant is a value that does not vary.

A variable can change depending on the value we give it.

Variables are represented by letters.

Example: $f(x) = 2x + 1$. Here, x is the variable; 1 is the constant.

A graph is a pictorial representation of information showing how one quantity varies with another related quantity. The graph of a linear function is a straight line. The graph of $f(x) = 2x + 1$ is shown below.

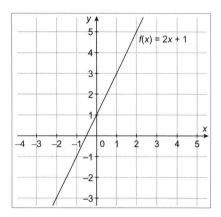

A **quadratic function** f in x involves an x^2 term and is of the form $f(x) = ax^2 + bx + c$, where a, b and c are constants ($a \neq 0$) and x is variable.

The graph of a quadratic function takes the form of a curve, known as a parabola. The graph of a quadratic function can be drawn by making a table of values for x and finding the corresponding values for y. Then plot the resultant couples.

The graph can be ∩-shaped or ∪-shaped, depending on the coefficient of the squared variable.

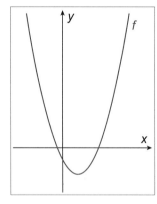

$f(x) = ax^2 + bx + c,\ x \in R$
Here, a is **positive**.

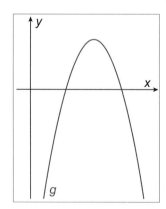

$g(x) = ax^2 + bx + c,\ x \in R$
Here, a is **negative**.

Worked Example 8.6

Using the same scales and axes, graph the functions $g(x) = -x^2 + 6x$ and $h(x) = \frac{2}{3}x + 1$ in the domain $0 \leqslant x \leqslant 6, x \in R$.

Use your graph to estimate the values of x for which:

(i) $g(x) = 5.5$ (ii) $h(x) = 3.5$ (iii) $g(x) = h(x)$ (iv) $\frac{2}{3}x - 1 = 0$

Solution

Set up a table for each function to find the couples that need to be graphed.

g(x)			
x	**$-x^2 + 6x$**	**y**	**(x,y)**
0	$-0 + 0$	0	(0,0)
1	$-1 + 6$	5	(1,5)
2	$-4 + 12$	8	(2,8)
3	$-9 + 18$	9	(3,9)
4	$-16 + 24$	8	(4,8)
5	$-25 + 30$	5	(5,5)
6	$-36 + 36$	0	(6,0)

$h(x) = \frac{2}{3}x + 1$ is a linear function, so three points will be sufficient to graph it.

Note: Always pick the first and end value of the domain (if given). Pick a third value as a checking device.

h(x)			
x	**$\frac{2}{3}x + 1$**	**y**	**(x,y)**
0	$0 + 1$	1	(0,1)
3	$2 + 1$	3	(3,3)
6	$4 + 1$	5	(6,5)

(i) Draw the line $y = 5.5$ (green line on graph).

Where this line cuts the graph of $g(x)$, drop perpendiculars to the x-axis and read off the x-values: $x = 1.2$ and $x = 4.8$.

(ii) Draw the line $y = 3.5$ (red line on graph).

Where this line cuts the graph of $h(x)$, drop a perpendicular to the x-axis and read off the x-value: $x = 3.7$.

(iii) Read off the two x-values where the graphs of the functions g and h intersect: $x = 0.2$ and $x = 5.2$.

(iv) $\frac{2}{3}x - 1 = 0$

$\Rightarrow \frac{2}{3}x + 1 - 2 = 0$

$\frac{2}{3}x + 1 = 2$

$\therefore h(x) = 2$

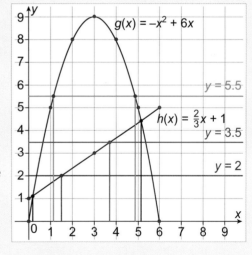

Draw the line $y = 2$ (blue line on graph). Where the line cuts the graph of $h(x)$, drop a perpendicular to the x-axis and read off the x-value: $x = 1.5$.

Exercise 8.2

1. Draw the graph of the linear function *f: x → 4x – 3* in the domain –3 ≤ *x* ≤ 4, *x* ∈ R.

   Use your graph to estimate:

   (i) The value of *f(x)* for which *x* = 2.5

   (iii) The value of *x* for which 4*x* – 3 = –7

   (ii) The value of *x* for which 4*x* – 3 = 6

   (iv) The range of values of *x* for which *f(x)* ≥ 1

2. The conversion formula for changing miles (*M*) into kilometres (*K*) is *K* = 1.6*M*.

   (i) Copy and complete the following table and hence, graph the function, putting miles on the horizontal axis:

Miles	10	20	30	40	50	60	70	80	90	100
Kilometres					80					

   (ii) Estimate from your graph the distance in kilometres if 75 miles has been travelled.

   (iii) Estimate from your graph the distance in miles if 140 km has been travelled.

   (iv) What is the range of distances in kilometres if a trip is said to be between 65 and 75 miles long?

3. Graph the function *f: x → x² – 2x – 5* in the domain –2 ≤ *x* ≤ 4, *x* ∈ R.

   Estimate from your graph:

   (i) The value of *f*(2.2)

   (iii) The values of *x* for which *x² – 2x – 5* ≤ 0

   (ii) The values of *x* for which *x² – 2x – 5* = 0

   (iv) The minimum value of *f(x)*

   Use an algebraic method to find the exact solutions to the equation given in part (ii).

4. Graph the function *f: x → ½x²* in the domain –2 ≤ *x* ≤ 2, *x* ∈ R.

5. Graph the function *g: x → ½x² + 2x + 4* in the domain –3 ≤ *x* ≤ 1, *x* ∈ R.

6. Graph the function *f: x → ½x² + ¾x + 2* in the domain –2 ≤ *x* ≤ 2, *x* ∈ R.

7. Graph the function *h*: [–3, 3] → R: *x → 4 – ¼x²*.

8. Graph the function *g*: [–4, 0] → R: *x → ¼ – 6x – 3/2 x²*.

9. A ball is thrown in the air so that *t* seconds after it is thrown, its height *h* (in metres) above the ground is given by *h(t)* = 25*t* – 5*t²*.

   Another ball is fired from a machine, and its height above the ground is given by *g(t)* = 5 + 3*t*, where *g* is height (in metres) and *t* is time (in seconds) after it is fired.

   The two balls start their flights at the same time.

   (i) Using the same axes and scales, graph the two functions.

   (ii) Use your graph to estimate the time(s) at which the two balls will be at the same height.

   (iii) What is the maximum height reached by each ball in the first 5 seconds?

   (iv) At what time does each ball reach its maximum height?

   (v) For how long is the first ball above the second ball?

   (vi) Which ball has the more realistic flight path? Explain your answer.

10. The functions $f(x) = 8x - x^2$ and $g(x) = 0.5x + 4$ are graphed below on the domain $0 \leqslant x \leqslant 8, x \in R$.

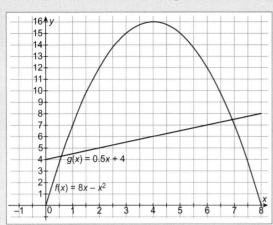

(i) What is the maximum value of $f(x)$?

(ii) Use the graph to estimate the values of x for which $f(x) = g(x)$.

(iii) Use the graph to estimate the values of x for which $f(x) \geqslant g(x)$.

(iv) Use the graph to estimate the values of x for which $f(x) < g(x)$.

11. Use the same scales and axes to draw the graphs of the two functions $f(x) = 2 + 2x + x^2$ and $g(x) = 5 - 2x - x^2$ in the domain $-3 \leqslant x \leqslant 2, x \in R$.

(i) Use your graph to estimate the values of x for which $f(x) = g(x)$.

(ii) Use your graph to estimate the values of x for which $f(x) \geqslant g(x)$.

12. A missile is launched into the air following the trajectory mapped out by the quadratic function $h(t) = 6t - t^2$, where h is the height in metres above the ground and t is the time in seconds.

(i) Graph the trajectory of the missile for 0–6 seconds.

(ii) At what times is the missile 8 metres above the ground?

A counter-attack missile is launched at the same time as the first missile from a height one metre above the ground. The trajectory of this missile is given by the function $j(t) = 1.2t + 1$, where j is the height in metres above the ground and t is the time in seconds.

(iii) Graph the trajectory of this counter-attack missile.

(iv) At what time will the two missiles collide?

(v) At what height will this collision take place?

13. The owner of a manufacturing company pays his workers on a piece rate basis. The owner uses a quadratic function to determine the pay each employee will receive each month. He has determined that above a certain level of production by each employee, he encounters a problem with wastage. To eliminate wastage, he has told his employees that above a given level of production, their pay will decline.

The quadratic function he uses for calculating pay is defined as $P = 10Q - Q^2$, where P is monthly pay in €100s and Q is quantity produced in 100s.

(i) Graph the function for pay, with quantity produced on the horizontal axis and monthly pay on the vertical axis. Use the domain $0 \leqslant Q \leqslant 10$.

(ii) What is the optimal amount for an employee to produce?

(iii) If the optimal amount is produced, what pay will the employee receive that month?

(iv) If a worker receives monthly pay of €2,400, what are the two possible levels of production she has reached?

(v) Is it more lucrative for an employee to produce 250 units or 725 units? Explain how you came to your decision.

(vi) Pay of €2,100 can be achieved at two different levels of production. Explain how P can still be considered a function of Q if this is the case.

14. Based on data from previous years, the profit earned by a company selling barbeques is modelled by the function

$$p(x) = -\frac{x^2}{2} + 300x - 18{,}000$$

where x is the number of units sold.

(i) Plot the function $p(x)$ for sales from 0 to 600 units.

(ii) How many barbeques should be sold to maximise profit?

(iii) What is the profit per barbeque when making maximum profit?

(iv) Do you think it makes sense to pursue this business interest? Explain.

8.5 EXPRESSING QUADRATIC FUNCTIONS IN COMPLETED SQUARE FORM (VERTEX FORM)

Consider the quadratic function $f(x) = x^2 - 4x + 7$.

A graph of f is presented on the right.

We can tell from the graph that the turning point of this function f is $(2,3)$.

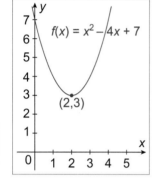

> The turning point of a quadratic function is called the **vertex** of the function.

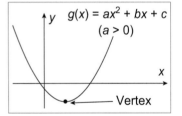

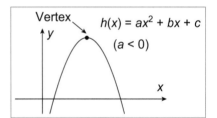

If we write the function f above in **completed square form** (**vertex form**), we can tell the co-ordinates of its vertex without having to graph the function.

To write $f(x) = x^2 - 4x + 7$ in completed square form, we need to 'complete the square'.

ACTIVITIES 8.1, 8.2, 8.3

Examine $f(x) = x^2 - 4x + 7$.

Half the x coefficient is -2. The square of -2 is 4.

So, $f(x) = x^2 - 4x + 7$

$\qquad = x^2 - 2x - 2x + \boxed{4} + 7 - \boxed{4}$

$\qquad = x^2 - 4x + 4 + 3$

$\qquad = (x - 2)^2 + 3 \quad \leftarrow$ Completed square form

> Completing the square is the method of converting from standard form ($ax^2 + bx + c$) to completed square form.

The co-ordinates of this vertex can be read directly as $(2,3)$.

To summarise:

> A quadratic function $f(x) = ax^2 + bx + c$ can be written in completed square form as $f(x) = a(x - h)^2 + k$ by 'completing the square'. (h, k) are the co-ordinates of the vertex of the function. The axis of symmetry is $x = h$.

$$y = a(x - h)^2 + k$$

- $a > 0 \Rightarrow$ U-shaped
  Vertex is a minimum point
- $a < 0 \Rightarrow$ ∩-shaped
  Vertex is a maximum point

Axis of symmetry
$x = h$

Vertex (h,k)

Worked Example 8.7

Express the quadratic function $y = x^2 + 8x + 7$ in completed square form.

Solution

Method 1: Geometrical

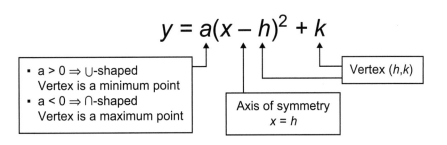

$$x^2 + 8x + 7 \quad = \quad x^2 + 4x + 4x + 7 \quad = \quad (x + 4)^2 - 4^2 + 7$$
$$= \quad (x + 4)^2 - 16 + 7$$
$$= \quad (x + 4)^2 - 9$$

Method 2: Algebraic

Step 1   Start with $x^2 + 8x + 7$.

Step 2   Complete the square: $x^2 + 8x + \left(\frac{8}{2}\right)^2 + 7 - \left(\frac{8}{2}\right)^2$

> To complete the square:
> (1) Take the coefficient of x (here = 8).
> (2) Halve it (here = 4).
> (3) Square it (here = 16).
> (4) Add and subtract this square.

Step 3   Tidy up the expression to the form $a(x - h)^2 + k$.

$$x^2 + 8x + (4)^2 + 7 - (4)^2$$
$$= x^2 + 8x + 16 + 7 - 16$$
$$= (x + 4)(x + 4) + 7 - 16$$
$$= (x + 4)^2 - 9$$

Worked Example 8.8

Express the quadratic function $y = 7 - 6x - x^2$ in completed square form.
State the turning point of this function.

Solution

$7 - 6x - x^2$

$= 7 - (x^2 + 6x)$

> Remember that 3^2 is the coefficient of the x-term halved and then squared.

$= 7 + \mathbf{3^2} - (x^2 + 6x + \mathbf{3^2})$

> Here, we are adding the 3^2.

> The $+3^2$ here is actually subtracting 3^2 in the expression due to the minus sign outside the bracket.

Tidy the expression to give the correct form.

$= 7 + 9 - (x^2 + 6x + 9)$

$= 16 - (x + 3)(x + 3)$

$= 16 - (x + 3)^2$

Given the general completed square form $a(x - h)^2 + k$, the turning point is (h,k).

$\therefore$ For $-(x + 3)^2 + 16$, the turning point is $(-3,16)$.

 Worked Example 8.9

(i) Express the quadratic function $y = 3x^2 - 12x + 10$ in completed square form.

(ii) State the turning point of this function.

(iii) By considering the completed square form, solve the equation $3x^2 - 12x + 10 = 0$, correct to four decimal places.

(iv) Sketch the function.

(v) Write down the equation of the axis of symmetry of the function.

Solution

(i) $3x^2 - 12x + 10$

$= 3\left(x^2 - 4x + \frac{10}{3}\right)$

$= 3\left[(x^2 - 4x) + \frac{10}{3}\right]$

$= 3\left[\left(x^2 - 4x + \left(\frac{4}{2}\right)^2\right) + \frac{10}{3} - \left(\frac{4}{2}\right)^2\right]$

$= 3\left[(x^2 - 4x + 4) + \frac{10}{3} - 4\right]$

$= 3\left[(x - 2)^2 - \frac{2}{3}\right]$

$\therefore y = 3(x - 2)^2 - 2$

(ii) $y = 3(x - 2)^2 - 2$

$\therefore$ The turning point is $(2,-2)$.

(iii) $3x^2 - 12x + 10 = 0$

$\Rightarrow 3(x - 2)^2 - 2 = 0$

$3(x - 2)^2 = 2$

$(x - 2)^2 = \frac{2}{3}$

$x - 2 = \pm\sqrt{\frac{2}{3}}$

$x = 2 \pm \sqrt{\frac{2}{3}}$

$x = 2.8165$ **OR** $x = 1.1835$

(iv)

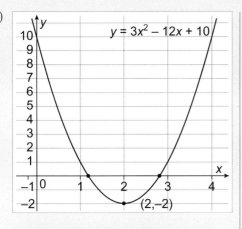

$y = 3x^2 - 12x + 10$

(2,−2)

Note: When sketching the graph, use the roots and the turning point to guide you as to where the function turns and where it cuts the x-axis.

(v) From the graph, the axis of symmetry is x = 2.

OR

From the completed square form

$$3(x - 2)^2 - 2,$$

x − 2 = 0 is the equation of the axis of symmetry.

$$\therefore x = 2$$

Exercise 8.3

For Questions 1–13 below:

(i) Write the function in completed square form.

(ii) Hence, find the roots of each function.

(iii) State the turning point for each function and write down the equation of the axis of symmetry.

(iv) Sketch the function.

1. $y = x^2 - 12x + 36$

2. $f(x) = x^2 + 2x - 6$

3. $g(x) = x^2 - 6x - 16$

4. $f(x) = 2x^2 + 4x - 7$

5. $f(x) = 3x^2 + 12x + 4$

6. $h(x) = 4x^2 + 9x + 5$

7. $f: x \rightarrow 5x^2 - 10x - 12$

8. $g: x \rightarrow (x - 3)^2 + 8x - 12$

9. $y = 3 - 4x - x^2$

10. $y = 9 + 4x - x^2$

11. $h(x) = 13 - 4x - 2x^2$

12. $g(x) = -2(1 - 2x) - x^2$

13. $g: x \rightarrow (x - 4)(2 - 3x) + 6$

14. $g(x) = (x - 1)^2 - 4$ is a quadratic function.

For the domain $-3 \leqslant x \leqslant 5, x \in R$, sketch the graphs of:

(i) $y = g(x)$ (ii) $y = |g(x)|$

For Questions 15–18, write the equation in completed square form before solving.

15. $\dfrac{x + 2}{6} = \dfrac{2x}{x - 2}$

16. $\dfrac{x - 2}{6} = \dfrac{2x}{-x - 2}$

17. $\dfrac{x + 3}{6 + x} = \dfrac{2x}{x - 3}$

18. $(x + 6)(2x - 3) = 4x^2 + 6x - 13$

8.6 CUBIC FUNCTIONS

> A cubic function f in x involves an x^3 term and is of the form:
> $f(x) = ax^3 + bx^2 + cx + d$, where a, b, c and d are constants $(a \neq 0)$ and x is a variable.

Examples of cubic functions:

$f(x) = x^3 - 6x^2 + 11x - 6$

$g(x) = 4x^3 + 5$

$h: x \rightarrow x^3 + 9x$

The graph of any function of this form is called a **cubic graph**. The shape of the graph depends on whether a, the coefficient of x^3, is negative or positive (among other factors):

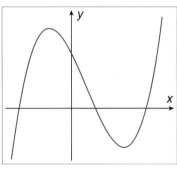 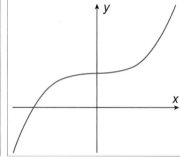

In these cases, a, the coefficient of x^3, is positive.

If the coefficient of x^3 is **positive**, the graph will **start low and end high**.

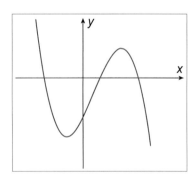 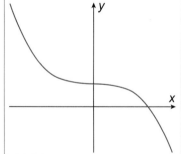

In these cases, a, the coefficient of x^3, is negative.

If the coefficient of x^3 is **negative**, the graph will **start high and end low**.

- A quadratic function may cross the x-axis at a maximum of two points. A cubic function may cross the x-axis at a maximum of three points.

- It is possible for the graph of a quadratic function not to touch or cross the x-axis, i.e. if the function has no real roots. However, this is **not** the case for a cubic function. There will always be at least one point where the graph of the cubic function will cross the x-axis.

- Not all cubic functions have two turning points. These will be explored further in a later chapter.

Worked Example 8.10

Graph the function g, where $g(x) = x^3 - 6x^2 + 11x - 6$, in the domain $0.5 \leqslant x \leqslant 3.5$, $x \in R$.

Solution

Set up the input–output table.

x	$x^3 - 6x^2 + 11x - 6$	y	(x,y)
0.5	$(0.5)^3 - 6(0.5)^2 + 11(0.5) - 6$	-1.875	$(0.5, -1.875)$
1	$(1)^3 - 6(1)^2 + 11(1) - 6$	0	$(1,0)$
1.5	$(1.5)^3 - 6(1.5)^2 + 11(1.5) - 6$	0.375	$(1.5, 0.375)$
2	$(2)^3 - 6(2)^2 + 11(2) - 6$	0	$(2,0)$
2.5	$(2.5)^3 - 6(2.5)^2 + 11(2.5) - 6$	-0.375	$(2.5, -0.375)$
3	$(3)^3 - 6(3)^2 + 11(3) - 6$	0	$(3,0)$
3.5	$(3.5)^3 - 6(3.5)^2 + 11(3.5) - 6$	1.875	$(3.5, 1.875)$

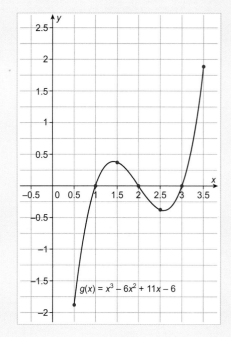

Graph the couples (x,y).

Points to note

- The graph starts low and finishes high.
  Reason: The coefficient of x^3 is positive ($=1$).

- The graph crosses the x-axis three times:
  At $x = 1$, $x = 2$ and $x = 3$.
  This indicates that the function has three real roots.

Worked Example 8.11

Graph the function $f: x \rightarrow x^3 - 5x^2 + 3x + 9$ in the domain $-1.5 \leqslant x \leqslant 4$, $x \in R$.

Use your graph to estimate:

    (i) The values of x for which $f(x) = 0$

    (ii) The value of $f(2.5)$

    (iii) The minimum value of $f(x)$, where $x > 0$

    (iv) The values of x for which $f(x)$ is decreasing

    (v) The solutions of $x^3 - 5x^2 + 3x + 9 = 2$

    (vi) The solutions of $x^3 - 5x^2 + 3x = -4$

Solution

Points to note

- This function could be factorised to $f(x) = (x + 1)(x - 3)^2$.

- See the table and graph on the next page.

  (i) Using the graph, establish where the graph of the function crosses or touches the x-axis. This gives the values of x for which $f(x) = 0$.

  $f(x) = 0$ at $x = -1$ or $x = 3$

x	x³ − 5x² + 3x + 9	y	(x,y)
−1.5	(−1.5)³ − 5(−1.5)² + 3(−1.5) + 9	−10.125	(−1.5,−10.125)
−1	(−1)³ − 5(−1)² + 3(−1) + 9	0	(−1,0)
−0.5	(−0.5)³ − 5(−0.5)² + 3(−0.5) + 9	6.125	(−0.5,6.125)
0	(0)³ − 5(0)² + 3(0) + 9	9	(0,9)
0.5	(0.5)³ − 5(0.5)² + 3(0.5) + 9	9.375	(0.5,9.375)
1	(1)³ − 5(1)² + 3(1) + 9	8	(1,8)
1.5	(1.5)³ − 5(1.5)² + 3(1.5) + 9	5.625	(1.5,5.625)
2	(2)³ − 5(2)² + 3(2) + 9	3	(2,3)
2.5	(2.5)³ − 5(2.5)² + 3(2.5) + 9	0.875	(2.5,0.875)
3	(3)³ − 5(3)² + 3(3) + 9	0	(3,0)
3.5	(3.5)³ − 5(3.5)² + 3(3.5) + 9	1.125	(3.5,1.125)
4	(4)³ − 5(4)² + 3(4) + 9	5	(4,5)

(ii) Draw the vertical line $x = 2.5$ and read off the y-value where it crosses the graph of f, i.e. $y = 0.9$.

∴ $f(2.5) = 0.9$

(iii) The minimum value of $f(x)$ where $x > 0$ is 0.

(iv) $f(x)$ is decreasing for $0.3 < x < 3, x \in R$.

(v) Draw the line $y = 2$ (green line). Where the line cuts the graph of f, drop perpendicular lines to the x-axis and read off the x-values. $x = −0.8, 2.2$ or 3.7

(vi) $x^3 − 5x^2 + 3x = −4$

$\Rightarrow x^3 − 5x^2 + 3x + 9 = −4 + 9$

∴ $f(x) = 5$
Draw the line $y = 5$.
This gives x-values of $x = −0.6, 1.6$ or 4.

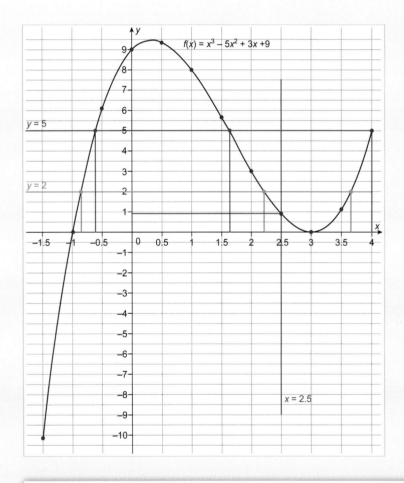

Note: Answers to parts (ii), (iii), (iv), (v), and (vi) are estimates and depend on the accuracy of the graph drawn.

FUNCTIONS

1. Graph the following functions in the given domains:

	Function	Domain
(i)	$b(x) = x^3 - x^2 - 2x + 2$	$-2 \leqslant x \leqslant 3, x \in R$
(ii)	$d(x) = 2x^3 - 3x^2 - 6x + 2$	$-2 \leqslant x \leqslant 3, x \in R$
(iii)	$f(x) = x^3 - 4x^2 + x + 6$	$-2 \leqslant x \leqslant 3, x \in R$
(iv)	$h(x) = -x^3 - 2x^2 + 4x + 2$	$-4 \leqslant x \leqslant 2, x \in R$
(v)	$j(x) = 8 - 12x + 6x^2 - x^3$	$0 \leqslant x \leqslant 4, x \in R$

2. Draw the graph of the function
   $f: x \to 2x^3 - x^2 - 5x - 3$ in the domain
   $-1.5 \leqslant x \leqslant 2.5, x \in R$.

   Estimate from your graph:

   (i) The value of x for which $f(x) = 0$

   (ii) The value of x for which $f(x) = 3$

3. Draw the graph of the function
   $f: x \to x^3 + 3x^2 - 5x + 3$ in the domain
   $-4 \leqslant x \leqslant 2, x \in R$.

   Estimate from your graph:

   (i) The values of x for which $f(x) = 3$

   (ii) The values of x for which $f(x) = 7$

4. Draw the graph of the function
   $g: x \to x^3 + 3x^2 - x - 2$ in the domain
   $-4 \leqslant x \leqslant 2, x \in R$.

   Estimate from your graph:

   (i) The values of x for which $g(x) = 0$

   (ii) The range of values of x for which $g(x)$ is
   negative and increasing

   (iii) The value of x for which
   $x^3 + 3x^2 - x - 2 = 6$

5. Using the same axes and scales, graph the
   functions:

   $f: x \to \frac{1}{4}x + 2$

   $g: x \to x^2 - 3x + 4$

   $j: x \to (x + 1)(x - 1)^2$

   in the domain $-2 \leqslant x \leqslant 3, x \in R$.

   Use your graph to:

   (i) Approximate the value of x for which
   $f(x) = j(x)$

   (ii) Approximate the value of x for which
   $g(x) = j(x)$

6. Using the same axes and scales, graph
   the functions $f: x \to x^3 - x^2 - 2x + 3$
   and $g: x \to 4 + x - x^2$ in the domain
   $-2 \leqslant x \leqslant 3, x \in R$.

   Use your graph to approximate the values
   of x for which $f(x) = g(x)$.

7. The growth model used for the weekly sales of
   a new product is given by the graph below.

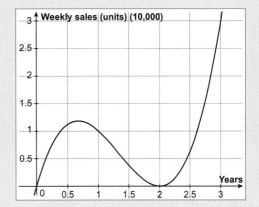

   (i) Estimate the maximum level of weekly
   sales reached in the first two years of the
   product's life cycle.

   (ii) At approximately what time is this
   maximum level reached?

   (iii) Two aggressive marketing campaigns
   are undertaken during the product's
   life cycle. Estimate from the graph when
   these two campaigns took place.
   Explain your answer.

   (iv) If the product has an expected life of
   three years, what is the maximum level
   of weekly sales that the product can
   achieve?

8. The graphs of $f(x) = -5x^3 + 11x^2 - 3$ and
   $g(x) = 3x + 0.5$ for $-1 \leqslant x \leqslant 2, x \in R$, are
   shown.

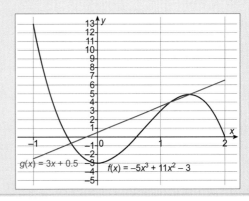

Use the graphs to find:

(i) The approximate value of $f(1.5)$

(ii) The approximate values of x for which $f(x) = 0$

(iii) The approximate values of x for which $f(x) = g(x)$

9. The graph below models the temperature in degrees Celsius of a computer server over a four-minute period.

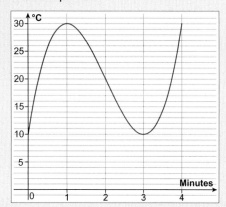

(i) What is the maximum temperature reached by the server?

(ii) After 2.5 minutes, what is the temperature of the server?

(iii) It is recommended that the temperature of the server should not exceed 28°C. Give the approximate time intervals for which the server is above the recommended temperature.

10. The graph below shows the sales cycle for a games console. The product will be removed from the market after 5.5 years.

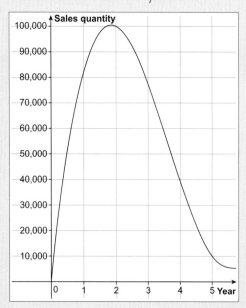

(i) At what time will sales quantity reach its peak?

(ii) At what two approximate times will sales quantity be 45,000 units?

(iii) The sales quantity can be represented by the cubic function $1{,}000(4x^3 - 44x^2 + 122x)$, where x is time in years. By substituting your answers to parts (i) and (ii) into this function, comment on the accuracy of your answer to these two parts.

11. The annual profits of a company (in thousands of euro) can be modelled by the function $P(x) = -x^3 + x^2 + 5x + 4$, where x is the amount of money (in thousands of euro) spent on product promotion.

(i) Draw a suitable graph to show the annual profit of the company.

(ii) From your graph, estimate the maximum annual profit of the company.

(iii) At approximately what level of spending on advertising is profit maximised?

(iv) The CEO of this company suggested that the company could generate a certain level of profit without any product promotion. Would you agree with this statement? Explain the reason for your answer.

12. The height (in 5 cm units) of a mosquito is modelled by the following function: $f(x) = x^3 - 7x^2 - 5x + 75$, where x is the time passed in seconds.

(i) Draw a suitable graph to show the height of the mosquito over the first 8 seconds.

(ii) What is the height of the mosquito after 8 seconds?

(iii) The mosquito is caught in the air at a height of 170 cm. At what two times can this happen? (Use your graph to answer.)

(iv) Verify your answer to part (iii) using algebra methods.

13. A company has to design a rectangular box for a new range of jellybeans. The box is to be assembled from a single piece of cardboard, cut from a rectangular sheet measuring 31 cm by 22 cm. The box is to have a capacity (volume) of 500 cm³.

The net for the box is shown below. The company is going to use the full length and width of the rectangular piece of cardboard. The shaded areas are flaps of width 1 cm that are needed for assembly. The height of the box is *h* cm, as shown on the diagram.

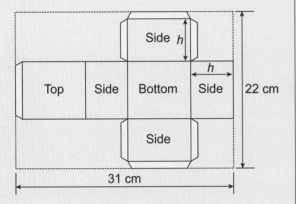

(a) Write the dimensions (length, width, height) of the box, in centimetres, in terms of *h*.

(b) Write an expression for the capacity of the box in cubic centimetres, in terms of *h*.

(c) Show that the value of *h* that gives a box with a square bottom will give the correct capacity.

(d) Find, correct to one decimal place, the other value of *h* that gives a box of the correct capacity.

(e) The client is planning a special '10% extra free' promotion and needs to increase the capacity of the box by 10 per cent. The company is checking whether they can make this new box from a piece of cardboard the same size as the original one (31 cm × 22 cm).

They draw the graph below to represent the box's capacity as a function of *h*. Use the graph to explain why it is **not** possible to make the larger box from such a piece of cardboard.

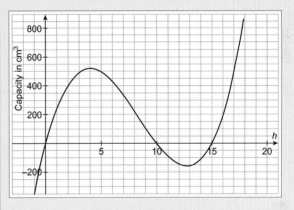

SEC Project Maths Sample Paper 1,
Leaving Certificate Higher Level, 2012

8.7 EXPONENTIAL FUNCTIONS

Exponential functions are functions of the form $y = b^x$, where *b* is constant and *x* is the variable exponent or power.

When dealing with exponential functions, we take a number called the base and raise it to a power called the exponent.

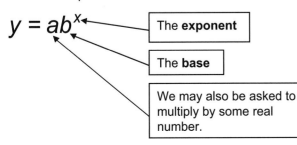

$y = ab^x$

The **exponent**

The **base**

We may also be asked to multiply by some real number.

The base and exponent make up the exponential function.

Before dealing with exponential functions, it is essential that you know the rules for working with indices. Some key laws of indices are shown below.

FORMULA

Law 1 $a^p \times a^q = a^{p+q}$ **Law 3** $(a^p)^q = a^{pq}$

Law 2 $\dfrac{a^p}{a^q} = a^{p-q}$ **Law 4** $a^0 = 1, a \neq 0$

These formulae appear on page 21 of *Formulae and Tables*.

Graphs of Exponential Functions

The graph of an exponential function has a very distinctive shape.

The graph of the function $f(x) = ab^x$ will pass through the point $(0,a)$.

Reason: At $x = 0$, $y = ab^0$
$$= a(1)$$
$$= a$$

The graph of an exponential function will never touch or cross the x-axis.

Worked Example 8.12

Graph the function $f(x) = 10^x$ in the domain $-2 \leqslant x \leqslant 1, x \in R$.

Solution

x	10ˣ	y	(x,y)
−2	10^{-2}	0.01	(−2,0.01)
−1	10^{-1}	0.1	(−1,0.1)
0	10^{0}	1	(0,1)
1	10^{1}	10	(1,10)

If the exponent is x and the base is greater than 1, the curve slopes upwards.

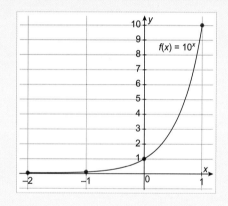

Worked Example 8.13

Graph the function $f(x) = 10^{-x}$ in the domain $-1 \leqslant x \leqslant 2, x \in R$.

Solution

x	10⁻ˣ	y	(x,y)
−1	$10^{-(-1)}$	10	(−1,10)
0	$10^{-(0)}$	1	(0,1)
1	10^{-1}	0.1	(1,0.1)
2	10^{-2}	0.01	(2,0.01)

Note: 10^{-x} can also be written as $\left(\dfrac{1}{10}\right)^x$ or 0.1^x.

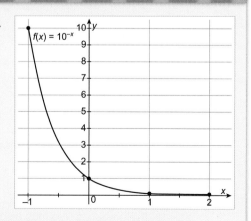

If the exponent is x and the base is positive and less than 1, the curve slopes downwards.

Worked Example 8.14

Graph the function $f(x) = 2(3^x)$ in the domain $-2 \leqslant x \leqslant 2, x \in R$.

Solution

x	$2(3^x)$	y	(x,y)
−2	$2(3^{-2})$	$\frac{2}{9}$	$\left(-2, \frac{2}{9}\right)$
−1	$2(3^{-1})$	$\frac{2}{3}$	$\left(-1, \frac{2}{3}\right)$
0	$2(3^0)$	2	(0,2)
1	$2(3^1)$	6	(1,6)
2	$2(3^2)$	18	(2,18)

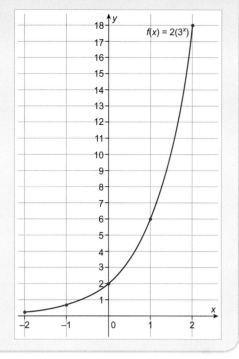

Worked Example 8.15

Find the value of a, given the graph of the function $f(x) = ab^x$, $b > 0$.

Solution

$f(0) = ab^0$

$= a(1)$

$= a$

From the graph, $f(0) = 3$.

$\therefore a = 3$

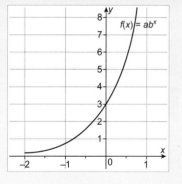

Worked Example 8.16

Bacterial growth can be modelled using exponential functions.

The population of a particular bacteria is given by the function $p(x) = 150{,}000(2^x)$, where x is time in hours.

(i) Graph this population function for the first four hours of growth.

(ii) Estimate the population size after 2.5 hours of growth by taking a suitable reading from your graph.

(iii) Find the exact population size after 2.5 hours of growth using algebra. Answer correct to the nearest whole number.

(iv) Calculate the percentage error in your estimate in part (ii) by using your answer from part (iii). Answer correct to one decimal place.

Solution

(i)

x	150,000(2ˣ)	y
0	150,000(1)	150,000
1	150,000(2)	300,000
2	150,000(4)	600,000
3	150,000(8)	1,200,000
4	150,000(16)	2,400,000

(ii) Draw the vertical line $x = 2.5$ and read off the y-value where it crosses the graph of the population function.

Answer: $\approx 850{,}000$

(iii) $p(2.5) = 150{,}000(2^{2.5}) = 848{,}528.1374 \approx 848{,}528.$

(iv) Percentage error $= \dfrac{850{,}000 - 848{,}528}{848{,}528} \times 100 \approx 0.2\%$

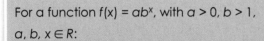

For a function $f(x) = ab^x$, with $a > 0$, $b > 1$, $a, b, x \in R$:

■ The graph of f passes through the point $(0, a)$.

■ The graph of f is upward-sloping.

For a function $f(x) = ab^{-x}$, with $a > 0$, $b > 1$, $a, b, x \in R$:

■ The graph of f passes through the point $(0, a)$.

■ The graph of f is downward-sloping.

Exercise 8.5

In Questions 1–5, graph each function in the domain $-2 \leqslant x \leqslant 3$, $x \in R$.

1. $y = 2^x$

2. $y = 4^x$

3. $y = \frac{1}{3^x}$

4. $y = 5^{-x}$

5. $y = 3^x$

In Questions 6–8, graph each function in the domain $-2 \leqslant x \leqslant 2$, $x \in R$.

6. $y = 3.5(3^x)$

7. $y = \frac{4}{3}(3^x)$

8. $y = 2^x(3^x)$

In Questions 9–13, identify the unknown values a and b.

9. $y = ab^x$

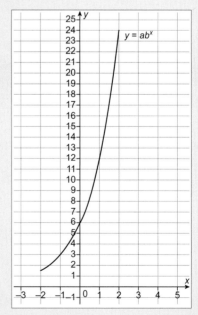

10. $y = ab^x$

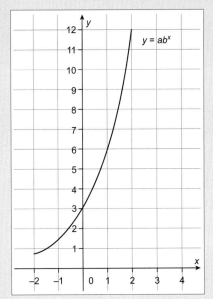

11. $y = ab^x$

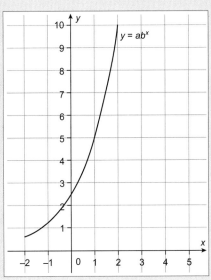

12. $y = ab^x$

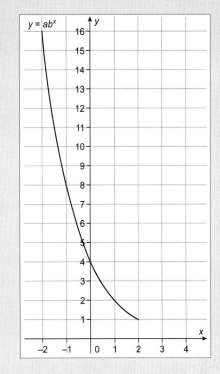

13. $y = ab^x$

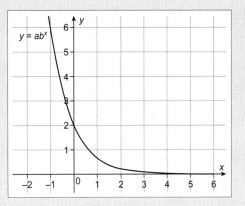

14. On 1 June, a type of algae was introduced to Lough Arrow. The algae grew and spread so that after t days the volume of water containing the algae was given by $A(t) = 2^t$, where A is the volume in m^3.

   (i) Draw a graph to show the volume of algae in the lake for the first six days.

   On the same date, a pollutant began to seep into the lake. The pollutant spread so that after t days the volume of water containing pollutant was given by $P(t) = 30 + 4t$, where P is the volume in m^3.

   (ii) Using the same axes and scales as for part (i) above, draw the graph of P.

   (iii) After how much time will the volume of water containing the algae equal the volume of water containing the pollutant? Answer correct to the nearest six hours.

15. While making pizza dough in Home Economics class, the teacher points out that ideally the yeast mixture should be made about one hour before use. She points out that the mixture doubles in volume every hour.

   Initially, Laura has 10 cm³ of the mixture.

   (i) Calculate the volume of the mixture each hour for the first four hours. (Use a table to display your results.)

   (ii) Draw a graph to display this data.

   (iii) Use your graph to estimate the volume of the mixture after 2.5 hours.

   (iv) Use your graph to estimate how long it takes for the volume of the mixture to reach 100 cm³ in size.

16. An economist estimates that the population of a country will increase by 25 per cent every 10 years. The population is 15 million in 2012.

   (i) Draw a graph to show the estimated population for the next 50 years.

   (ii) Use your graph to estimate when the population will reach 25 million.

   (iii) If x represents the number of years since 2012, define a function P in x that represents the population of the country.

17. Laser beams are very intense rays of light commonly used in medicine. The intensity of a laser beam decreases exponentially with the penetration of tissue. The intensity of a particular beam can be modelled as $I(x) = 800(0.6812^x)$, where x is depth of penetration in millimetres and I is intensity in watts per square metre (W/m²).

   (i) Graph the intensity of a laser beam over the domain $0 \leqslant x \leqslant 5$, $x \in R$.

   (ii) Using your graph, estimate the intensity at a depth of 4 mm.

   (iii) Use algebra to find the exact intensity at a depth of 4 mm. Answer correct to two decimal places.

   (iv) At what depth is the intensity equal to 500 W/m²?
   Estimate your answer using your graph and then use algebra to find the exact answer correct to two decimal places.

Note

Exponential and logarithmic functions are also covered in Chapter 7 of this book.

- For graphs of exponential functions, see Section 7.1 and Worked Example 7.1, pp 137–8.

- For graphs of logarithmic functions, see Section 7.5 and Worked Example 7.12, pp 145–6.

8.8 GRAPHING LOGARITHMIC FUNCTIONS

Each exponential function has an inverse function. We call these inverses **logarithmic functions**.

Consider the graphs below (the red line is the graph of the function $y = x$).

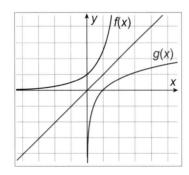

$f(x) = a^x$ (black curve)

$g(x) = \log_a x$ (blue curve)

$a > 1$

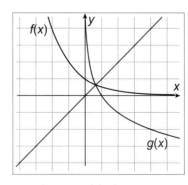

$f(x) = a^x$ (black curve)

$g(x) = \log_a x$ (blue curve)

$0 < a < 1$

In these graphs, the exponential and logarithm functions are symmetric to each other across the line $y = x$.

Later in this chapter, we will show in greater detail how to graph inverse functions.

 Worked Example 8.17

Graph the function $f(x) = \log_2 x$, $x \in R$, $0 < x \leqslant 16$.

Solution

As the base $= 2$, let $x = \frac{1}{2}$ and all the whole number powers of 2 within the given domain.

So, let $x = \frac{1}{2}, 1, 2, 4, 8, 16$.

x	y	(x, y)
$\frac{1}{2}$	-1	$\left(\frac{1}{2}, -1\right)$
1	0	$(1, 0)$
2	1	$(2, 1)$
4	2	$(4, 2)$
8	3	$(8, 3)$
16	4	$(16, 4)$

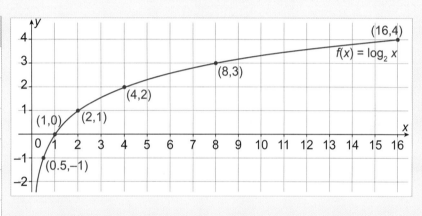

 Exercise 8.6

1. Graph the following functions:

    (i) $f(x) = \log_4 x$, $x \in R$, $0 < x \leqslant 64$

    (ii) $f(x) = \log_5 x$, $x \in R$, $0 < x \leqslant 125$

    (iii) $f(x) = \log_3 x$, $x \in R$, $0 < x \leqslant 27$

    (iv) $f(x) = \log_e x$, $x \in R$, $0 < x < 8$

2. Use graphical methods to solve $\log_3 x = \log_2 x$, $x \in R$.

3. Use graphical methods to solve $\log_3 x \leqslant \log_4 x$, $x \in R$.

> For practical problems involving logarithms, refer to Chapter 7, Exercise 7.5.

8.9 TRANSFORMATIONS OF LINEAR FUNCTIONS

This section will cover what happens to a graph of a function when one or more parts of the function change. This is called a **transformation** of the graph of the function. When we graph a function under a transformation, the graph changes shape and/or location.

Linear Functions

When we transform a linear function, the graph can shift up or down and/or change slope.

When we are transforming graphs of linear functions, it is best if the functions are in the form $y = mx + c$, where m is the slope and c is the y-intercept.

A change in the value of the slope m will result in the slope of the line increasing or decreasing.

A change in the value of the y-intercept c will result in the graph of the function moving vertically up or down the y-axis. This transformation will result in a line that is parallel to the original line.

For the function g, the y-intercept is 4.

For the function f, the y-intercept is 2.

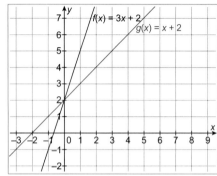

The slope of the graph of f is 3.

The slope of the graph of g is 1.

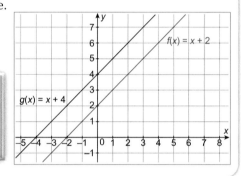

> There are two acceptable ways of writing the y-intercept:
>
> - Stating the y-value only
> - Giving the co-ordinates of the point where the graph crosses the y-axis

Worked Example 8.18

The graph of the function $y = 3x - 4$ is shown.

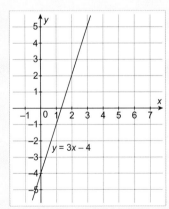

Sketch the graphs of the following functions:

    (i) $y = 3x + 2$

    (ii) $y = \frac{3}{4}x - 4$

Solution

(i) $y = 3x + 2$

The slope has not changed but the y-intercept is now (0,2).

The line will be parallel to the original line but will now be vertically higher so that it goes through the point (0,2).

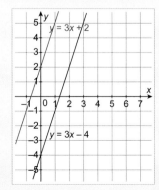

(ii) $y = \frac{3}{4}x - 4$

The y-intercept has not changed, but the slope has changed.

> Remember: Slope = $\dfrac{\text{Rise}}{\text{Run}}$

A slope of $\frac{3}{4}$ means that we move up three units for every four units we go to the right.

We draw a line which goes though the y-intercept (0,–4) with a slope of $\frac{3}{4}$.

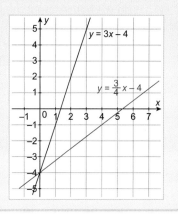

8.10 TRANSFORMATIONS OF QUADRATIC FUNCTIONS

Consider the function $y = x^2$ in the domain $-3 \leqslant x \leqslant 3$, $x \in R$.

x	x^2	y	(x,y)
–3	$(-3)^2$	9	(–3,9)
–2	$(-2)^2$	4	(–2,4)
–1	$(-1)^2$	1	(–1,1)
0	$(0)^2$	0	(0,0)
1	$(1)^2$	1	(1,1)
2	$(2)^2$	4	(2,4)
3	$(3)^2$	9	(3,9)

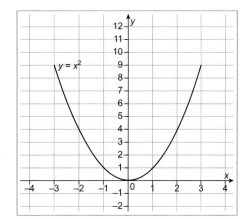

The graph of this function:

- Contains the point (0,0)
- Has (0,0) as its lowest point
- Is symmetrical about the y-axis

Graphs of Functions of the Form $y = ax^2$, $a > 0$

Consider the function $y = 2x^2$ in the domain $-3 \leqslant x \leqslant 3$, $x \in R$.

x	$2x^2$	y	(x,y)
–3	$2(-3)^2$	18	(–3,18)
–2	$2(-2)^2$	8	(–2,8)
–1	$2(-1)^2$	2	(–1,2)
0	$2(0)^2$	0	(0,0)
1	$2(1)^2$	2	(1,2)
2	$2(2)^2$	8	(2,8)
3	$2(3)^2$	18	(3,18)

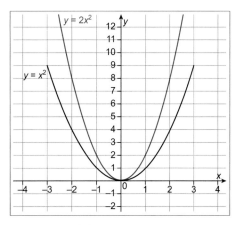

> Note: For a given x-value, the y-value has been multiplied by 2.

FUNCTIONS

What do we notice about the graph of $y = 2x^2$?

The graph of $y = 2x^2$:

- Still contains the point (0,0)
- Still has (0,0) as its lowest point
- Still is symmetrical about the y-axis
- Is **narrower** than the graph of $y = x^2$

Now, consider the function $y = 3x^2$ in the same domain.

x	$3x^2$	y	(x,y)
−3	$3(-3)^2$	27	(−3,27)
−2	$3(-2)^2$	12	(−2,12)
−1	$3(-1)^2$	3	(−1,3)
0	$3(0)^2$	0	(0,0)
1	$3(1)^2$	3	(1,3)
2	$3(2)^2$	12	(2,12)
3	$3(3)^2$	27	(3,27)

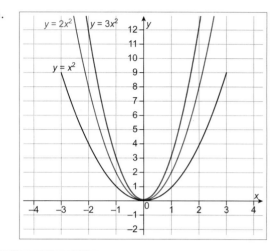

Note: For a given x-value, the y-value has been multiplied by 3.

We can see that the graph of $y = 3x^2$ is narrower than the graphs of the other two functions.

> For a quadratic function $f(x) = ax^2$, $a > 0$, as the value of a increases, the graph of $y = f(x)$ becomes narrower.

Graphs of Functions of the Form $y = x^2 + b$

Consider the function $y = x^2 + 3$ in the domain $-3 \leqslant x \leqslant 3$, $x \in R$.

x	$x^2 + 3$	y	(x,y)
−3	$(-3)^2 + 3$	12	(−3,12)
−2	$(-2)^2 + 3$	7	(−2,7)
−1	$(-1)^2 + 3$	4	(−1,4)
0	$(0)^2 + 3$	3	(0,3)
1	$(1)^2 + 3$	4	(1,4)
2	$(2)^2 + 3$	7	(2,7)
3	$(3)^2 + 3$	12	(3,12)

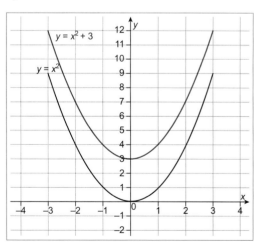

What do we notice about the graph of $y = x^2 + 3$?

The graph of $y = x^2 + 3$:

- Contains the point (0,3)
- Has (0,3) as its lowest point
- Is symmetrical about the y-axis

In other words, the graph of $y = x^2 + 3$ is the graph of $y = x^2$ shifted (translated) three units upwards.

If b is positive, the graph of $f(x) = x^2 + b$ is the graph of $y = x^2$ shifted b units upwards.

If b is negative, the graph of $f(x) = x^2 + b$ is the graph of $y = x^2$ shifted $-b$ units downwards.

Graphs of Functions of the Form $y = (x + b)^2$

Consider the function $y = (x + 1)^2$ in the domain $-3 \leqslant x \leqslant 3, x \in R$.

x	$(x + 1)^2$	y	(x,y)
−3	$(-3 + 1)^2$	4	(−3,4)
−2	$(-2 + 1)^2$	1	(−2,1)
−1	$(-1 + 1)^2$	0	(−1,0)
0	$(0 + 1)^2$	1	(0,1)
1	$(1 + 1)^2$	4	(1,4)
2	$(2 + 1)^2$	9	(2,9)
3	$(3 + 1)^2$	16	(3,16)

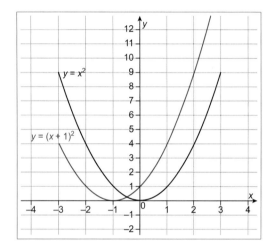

What do we notice about the graph of $y = (x + 1)^2$?

The graph of $y = (x + 1)^2$:

- Contains the point (−1,0)

- Has (−1,0) as its lowest point

- Is symmetrical about the line $x = -1$

In other words, the graph of $y = (x + 1)^2$ is the graph of $y = x^2$ shifted (translated) one unit to the left.

What do you think the graph of $y = (x - 2)^2$ would look like?

It would be the graph of $y = x^2$ shifted (translated) two units to the right.

If b is positive, the graph of $f(x) = (x + b)^2$ is the graph of $y = x^2$ shifted b units to the left.

If b is negative, the graph of $f(x) = (x + b)^2$ is the graph of $y = x^2$ shifted $-b$ units to the right.

The y-intercept of the function $f(x) = (x + b)^2$ is $(0, (b)^2)$.

Worked Example 8.19

Graph the function $f(x) = (x + 2)^2$ in the domain $-5 \leqslant x \leqslant 1, x \in R$.

Use your graph to sketch the graph of:

(i) $g(x) = (x - 1)^2$ (ii) $h(x) = (x + 2)^2 - 5$

Solution

We first draw the graph of the function $f(x) = (x + 2)^2$ in the domain $-5 \leqslant x \leqslant 1, x \in R$.

x	$(x + 2)^2$	y	(x,y)
−5	$(-3)^2$	9	(−5,9)
−4	$(-2)^2$	4	(−4,4)
−3	$(-1)^2$	1	(−3,1)
−2	$(0)^2$	0	(−2,0)
−1	$(1)^2$	1	(−1,1)
0	$(2)^2$	4	(0,4)
1	$(3)^2$	9	(1,9)

Couples: {(−5,9), (−4,4), (−3,1), (−2,0), (−1,1), (0,4), (1,9)}

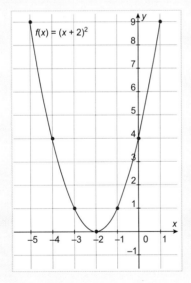

(i) $g(x) = (x - 1)^2$

The graph touches the x-axis at (1,0).

The y-intercept is $(0,(-1)^2) = (0,1)$

The graph of $g(x)$ is the graph of $f(x)$ shifted three units to the right.

Sketch the function through the point (1,0) and the point (0,1).

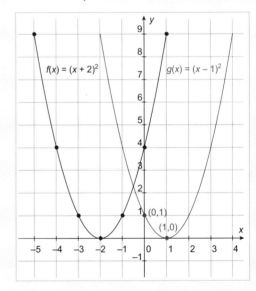

(ii) $h(x) = (x + 2)^2 - 5$

The graph of $h(x)$ is the graph of $f(x)$ shifted downwards by five units.

∴ The lowest point is (−2,−5) and the y-intercept is (0,−1).

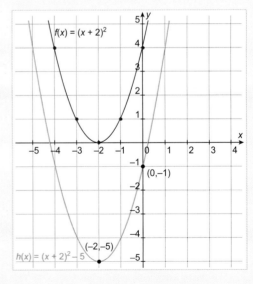

1. The graph of the linear function $f(x) = 2x + 5$ is shown. Use your graph to match the following functions with the functions shown below:

   (a) $g(x) = 2x - 1$ (b) $h(x) = 2x + 2$

   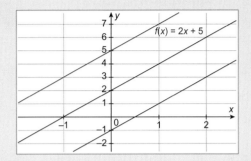

2. The graph of the linear function $f(x) = 4x - 1$ is shown. Use your graph to match the following functions with the functions shown below:

   (a) $g(x) = x - 1$ (b) $h(x) = x + 3$

   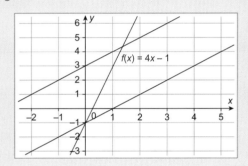

3. The graph of the function $y = 2x + 1$ is shown.

   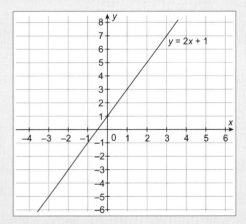

   Copy this diagram into your copybook and sketch the graphs of the following functions:

   (i) $y = 2x + 4$

   (ii) $y = 2x - 3$

   (iii) $y = 3x + 1$

4. Graph the function $y = -2x + 4$ in the domain $-3 \leqslant x \leqslant 3, x \in R$.

   Hence, sketch the graphs of the following functions:

   (i) $f(x) = -2x + 3$ (iii) $h(x) = x + 3$

   (ii) $g(x) = 2x + 4$

5. Graph the function $f: x \rightarrow 3x - 2$ in the domain $-5 \leqslant x \leqslant 2, x \in R$.

   Hence, sketch the graphs of the following functions:

   (i) $j(x) = 3x + 3$ (iii) $h(x) = x + 3$

   (ii) $g(x) = -3x + 3$

6. The graph of the function $y = x^2$ is shown. Use this graph to match the following functions with the functions shown below:

   (i) $y = 3x^2$ (ii) $y = 5x^2$

   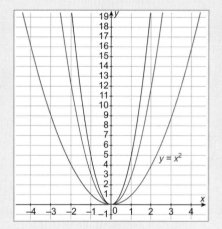

7. The graph of the function $y = x^2$ is shown. Use this graph to match the following functions with the functions shown below:

   (i) $y = x^2 - 3$ (ii) $y = x^2 + 4$

   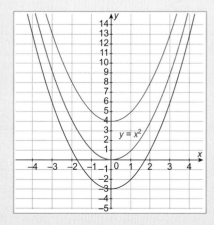

8. The graph of $f(x) = x^2 + x + 2$ is shown.
Use this graph to match the following functions
with the functions shown below:

(i) $g(x) = 3x^2 + 3x + 6$

(ii) $h(x) = x^2 + x + 4$

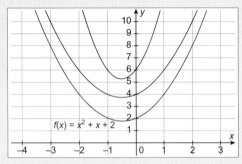

9. The graph of the function $y = x^2$ is shown.
Use this graph to match the following functions
with the functions shown below:

(i) $y = (x + 1)^2$ (ii) $y = (x - 5)^2$

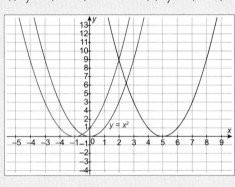

10. Graph the function $f(x) = 2x^2$ in the domain
$-3 \leqslant x \leqslant 3, x \in R$.

Hence, sketch the following functions:

(i) $g(x) = 4x^2$ (ii) $h(x) = 3x^2$

11. Graph the function $f(x) = 2x^2 + 4$ in the
domain $-4 \leqslant x \leqslant 3, x \in R$.

Hence, sketch the following functions:

(i) $g(x) = 2x^2 + 1$ (ii) $h(x) = 2x^2 - 2$

12. The graph of the function $f(x) = (x - 3)^2$ on the
domain $0 \leqslant x \leqslant 5, x \in R$, is shown.

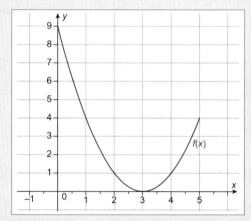

Copy this diagram into your copybook and
sketch the following functions:

(i) $g(x) = (x - 3)^2 + 3$ (iii) $i(x) = (x - 2)^2$

(ii) $h(x) = 2(x - 3)^2$

8.11 TRANSFORMATIONS OF CUBIC FUNCTIONS

Consider the function $y = x^3$ in the domain $-2 \leqslant x \leqslant 2, x \in R$.

x	x^3	y	(x,y)
−2	$(-2)^3$	−8	(−2,−8)
−1	$(-1)^3$	−1	(−1,−1)
0	$(0)^3$	0	(0,0)
1	$(1)^3$	1	(1,1)
2	$(2)^3$	8	(2,8)

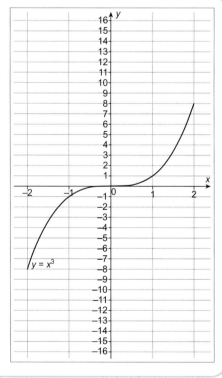

Note the shape of this graph. It has no turning points.

The graph also contains the point (0,0).

Graphs of Functions of the Form $y = ax^3$, $a > 0$

Consider the function $y = 2x^3$ in the same domain.

x	2x³	y	(x,y)
−2	$2(-2)^3$	−16	(−2,−16)
−1	$2(-1)^3$	−2	(−1,−2)
0	$2(0)^3$	0	(0,0)
1	$2(1)^3$	2	(1,2)
2	$2(2)^3$	16	(2,16)

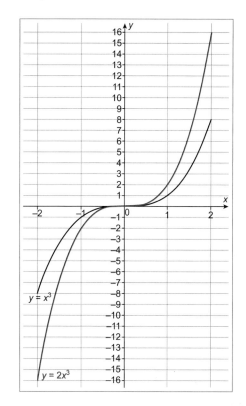

Note: For a given x-value, the y-value has been multiplied by 2.

We can see that, in comparison with the graph of $y = x^3$, the graph of $y = 2x^3$ is stretched vertically.

Now consider the function $y = 0.5x^3$ in the same domain.

x	0.5x³	y	(x,y)
−2	$0.5(-2)^3$	−4	(−2,−4)
−1	$0.5(-1)^3$	−0.5	(−1,−0.5)
0	$0.5(0)^3$	0	(0,0)
1	$0.5(1)^3$	0.5	(1,0.5)
2	$0.5(2)^3$	4	(2,4)

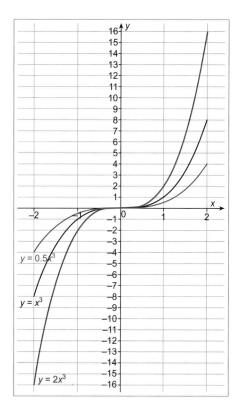

Note: For a given x-value, the y-value has been multiplied by 0.5.

We can see that, in comparison with the graph of $y = x^3$, the graph of $y = 0.5x^3$ is compressed vertically.

For a cubic function of the form $f(x) = ax^3$, $a > 0$, as a increases in value, the graph of $f(x)$ is stretched vertically. As a decreases in value, the graph of $f(x)$ is compressed vertically.

Graphs of Functions of the Form $y = x^3 + b$

Consider the function $y = x^3 + 1$ in the domain $-2 \leqslant x \leqslant 2$, $x \in R$.

x	x³ + 1	y	(x,y)
−2	$(−2)^3 + 1$	−7	(−2,−7)
−1	$(−1)^3 + 1$	0	(−1,0)
0	$(0)^3 + 1$	1	(0,1)
1	$(1)^3 + 1$	2	(1,2)
2	$(2)^3 + 1$	9	(2,9)

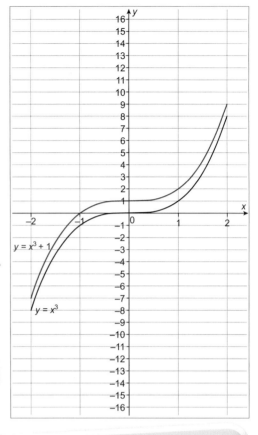

We can see that the graph of $y = x^3 + 1$ is the graph of $y = x^3$ shifted (translated) one unit upwards.

What would you expect the graph of $y = x^3 − 2$ to look like?

The graph of $y = x^3 − 2$ is the graph of $y = x^3$ shifted (translated) two units downwards.

If b is positive, the graph of $f(x) = x^3 + b$ is the graph of $y = x^3$ shifted b units upwards.

If b is negative, the graph of $f(x) = x^3 + b$ is the graph of $y = x^3$ shifted −b units downwards.

Graphs of Functions of the Form $y = (x + b)^3$

Consider the function $y = (x + 1)^3$ in the domain $-2 \leqslant x \leqslant 2$, $x \in R$.

x	(x + 1)³	y	(x,y)
−2	$(−1)^3$	−1	(−2,−1)
−1	$(0)^3$	0	(−1,0)
0	$(1)^3$	1	(0,1)
1	$(2)^3$	8	(1,8)
2	$(3)^3$	27	(2,27)

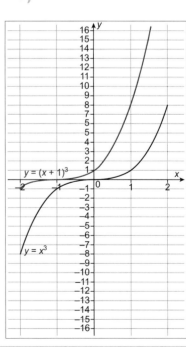

What do you notice about the graph of $y = (x + 1)^3$?

It is the graph of $y = x^3$ shifted (translated) one unit to the left.
The y-intercept is $(0, (1)^3) = (0,1)$.

What would you expect the graph of $y = (x - 2)^3$ to look like?

The graph of $y = (x - 2)^3$ is the graph of $y = x^3$ shifted (translated) two units to the right.
The y-intercept is $(0, (-2)^3) = (0, -8)$.

> If b is positive, the graph of $f(x) = (x + b)^3$ is the graph of $y = x^3$ shifted b units to the left.

> If b is negative, the graph of $f(x) = (x + b)^3$ is the graph of $y = x^3$ shifted $-b$ units to the right.

> The y-intercept of the function $f(x) = (x + b)^3$ is $(0, (b)^3)$.

Worked Example 8.20

Graph the function $f(x) = x^3 - 2x^2 - 5x + 6$ in the domain $-2 \leqslant x \leqslant 3, x \in R$.

Hence, sketch the following functions:

    (i) $g(x) = 0.5(x^3 - 2x^2 - 5x + 6)$

    (ii) $h(x) = x^3 - 2x^2 - 5x + 9$

Solution

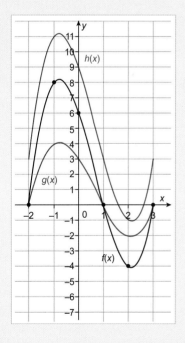

x	$x^3 - 2x^2 - 5x + 6$	y	(x,y)
–2	$(-2)^3 - 2(-2)^2 - 5(-2) + 6$	0	(–2,0)
–1	$(-1)^3 - 2(-1)^2 - 5(-1) + 6$	8	(–1,8)
0	$(0)^3 - 2(0)^2 - 5(0) + 6$	6	(0,6)
1	$(1)^3 - 2(1)^2 - 5(1) + 6$	0	(1,0)
2	$(2)^3 - 2(2)^2 - 5(2) + 6$	–4	(2,–4)
3	$(3)^3 - 2(3)^2 - 5(3) + 6$	0	(3,0)

    (i) Multiplying the function by 0.5 causes the graph of $f(x)$ to be compressed by a factor of 0.5. Each y-value is halved.

    (ii) $h(x) = x^3 - 2x^2 - 5x + 9$

          $= x^3 - 2x^2 - 5x + 6 + 3$

    $\therefore h(x) = f(x) + 3$

    Adding 3 to the function shifts the graph of $f(x)$ vertically upwards by three units.

Worked Example 8.21

Graph the function $y = (x - 3)^3$ in the domain $2 \leqslant x \leqslant 4, x \in R$.

Hence, sketch the following functions:

(i) $f(x) = (x - 2)^3$

(ii) $g(x) = (x - 3)^3 + 1$

Solution

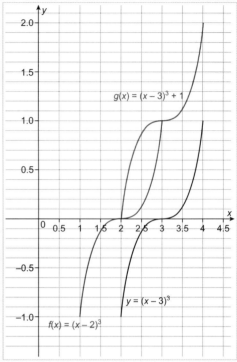

x	$(x - 3)^3$	y	(x, y)
2	$(2 - 3)^3$	-1	$(2, -1)$
2.5	$(2.5 - 3)^3$	-0.125	$(2.5, -0.125)$
3	$(3 - 3)^3$	0	$(3, 0)$
3.5	$(3.5 - 3)^3$	0.125	$(3.5, 0.125)$
4	$(4 - 3)^3$	1	$(4, 1)$

(i) All the points on the graph of $y = (x - 3)^3$ have been shifted to the left by one unit.

(ii) All the points on the graph of $y = (x - 3)^3$ have been shifted vertically upwards by one unit.

Exercise 8.8

1. Shown below is the graph of the function $f(x) = x^3 - 5x + 1$. Use the graph to match the following functions with those graphed below.

   (i) $g(x) = 2(x^3 - 5x + 1)$

   (ii) $h(x) = 2(x^3 - 5x + 1) - 2$

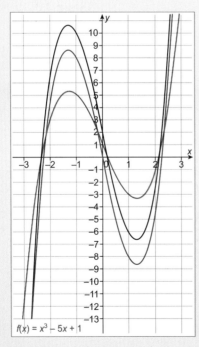

2. Shown below is the graph of the function $f(x) = (x - 4)^3$. Use the graph to match the following functions with those graphed below.

   (i) $g(x) = (x - 3)^3$ (ii) $h(x) = (x + 3)^3$

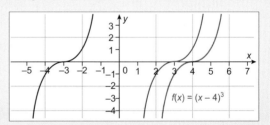

3. Graph the function $f(x) = x^3$ over the domain $-2 \leqslant x \leqslant 2, x \in R$.

   Hence, sketch the following functions:

   (i) $g(x) = x^3 + 2$ (iii) $k(x) = 2x^3 - 2$

   (ii) $h(x) = 2x^3$

4. Sketch the following functions using the same axes and scales (use a domain of $-2 \leqslant x \leqslant 2, x \in R$):

   (i) $f(x) = 2x^3$ (ii) $g(x) = -x^3$

   What do each of these graphs have in common? How are they different?

5. Graph the function $f(x) = -x^3$ over the domain $-2 \leqslant x \leqslant 2, x \in R$.
Hence, sketch the function $g(x) = -x^3 + 4$.

6. Sketch the function $f(x) = 2(x - 2)^3 + 4$.
Hint: Begin by graphing the function $y = x^3$, using a domain of $-2 \leqslant x \leqslant 2, x \in R$.

7. Sketch the function $h: x \rightarrow 3(x + 1)^3 + 4$.

8. The graph of $f(x) = 2x^3$ has been vertically compressed by a factor of 0.5.
What is the new functional form?

9. The graph of $f(x) = x^3 - 3$ has been shifted right by two units and down by three units.
What is the new functional form?

10. The graphs of $f(x)$ and $g(x)$ are given below.

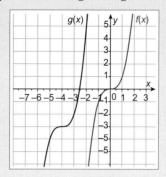

(i) Describe in your own words a transformation that would map the graph of $f(x)$ to the graph of $g(x)$.

(ii) Write the functional form of $g(x)$ in terms of x.

8.12 TRANSFORMATIONS OF EXPONENTIAL FUNCTIONS

Consider the function $y = 2^x$ in the domain $-2 \leqslant x \leqslant 2, x \in R$.

x	2^x	y	(x,y)
-2	$2^{-2} = \frac{1}{2^2}$	$\frac{1}{4}$	$\left(-2, \frac{1}{4}\right)$
-1	$2^{-1} = \frac{1}{2^1}$	$\frac{1}{2}$	$\left(-1, \frac{1}{2}\right)$
0	2^0	1	$(0,1)$
1	2^1	2	$(1,2)$
2	2^2	4	$(2,4)$

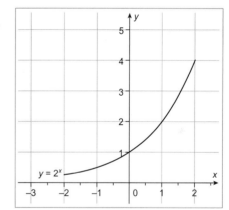

The graph of $y = 2^x$ is upward sloping and contains the point $(0,1)$.

Graphs of Functions of the Form $y = ak^x$, $a > 0$

Consider the function $y = 2(2^x)$ in the same domain.

x	$2(2^x)$	y	(x,y)
-2	$2(2^{-2}) = 2\left(\frac{1}{2^2}\right)$	$\frac{1}{2}$	$\left(-2, \frac{1}{2}\right)$
-1	$2(2^{-1}) = 2\left(\frac{1}{2^1}\right)$	1	$(-1,1)$
0	$2(2^0) = 2(1)$	2	$(0,2)$
1	$2(2^1) = 2(2)$	4	$(1,4)$
2	$2(2^2) = 2(4)$	8	$(2,8)$

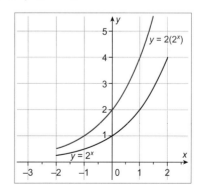

Note: For a given x-value, we multiply the y-value by 2.

What do you notice about the graph of $y = 2(2^x)$?

- The graph of $y = 2(2^x)$ is upward sloping.
- The graph contains the point $(0,2)$.
- The graph of $y = 2(2^x)$ lies above the graph of $y = 2^x$. This is because, compared with $y = 2^x$, for a given x-value, each y-value has been multiplied by 2.

Consider the function $y = \frac{1}{2}(2^x)$ in the same domain.

x	$\left(\frac{1}{2}\right)2^x$	y	(x,y)
-2	$\frac{1}{2}(2^{-2}) = \frac{1}{2}\left(\frac{1}{2^2}\right)$	$\frac{1}{8}$	$\left(-2,\frac{1}{8}\right)$
-1	$\frac{1}{2}(2^{-1}) = \frac{1}{2}\left(\frac{1}{2}\right)$	$\frac{1}{4}$	$\left(-1,\frac{1}{4}\right)$
0	$\frac{1}{2}(2^0) = \frac{1}{2}(1)$	$\frac{1}{2}$	$\left(0,\frac{1}{2}\right)$
1	$\frac{1}{2}(2^1) = \frac{1}{2}(2)$	1	$(1,1)$
2	$\frac{1}{2}(2^2) = \frac{1}{2}(4)$	2	$(2,2)$

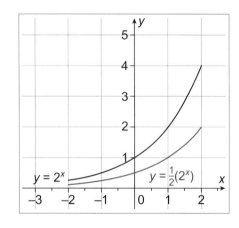

Note: For a given x-value, we multiply the y-value by $\frac{1}{2}$.

What do you notice about the graph of $y = \frac{1}{2}(2^x)$?

- The graph of $y = \frac{1}{2}(2^x)$ is upward sloping.
- The graph contains the point $\left(0,\frac{1}{2}\right)$.
- The graph of $y = \frac{1}{2}(2^x)$ lies below the graph of $y = 2^x$. This is because, compared with $y = 2^x$, for a given x-value, each y-value has been multiplied by $\frac{1}{2}$.

The graph of $f(x) = a.k^x$, $a > 0$, lies above the graph of $y = k^x$ if $a > 1$.

The graph of $f(x) = a.k^x$, $a > 0$, lies below the graph of $y = k^x$ if $a < 1$.

The graph of $f(x) = a.k^x$ contains the point $(0,a)$.

Graphs of Functions of the Form $y = k^x + b$

The graph of the function $f(x) = k^x + b$ is the graph of $y = k^x$ shifted b units upwards if $b > 0$ **or** shifted $-b$ units downwards if $b < 0$.

Consider the function $y = 2^x + 1$ in the domain $-2 \leqslant x \leqslant 2$, $x \in R$.

x	$2^x + 1$	y	(x,y)
−2	$2^{-2} + 1 = \frac{1}{2^2} + 1$	1.25	(−2,1.25)
−1	$2^{-1} + 1 = \frac{1}{2^1} + 1$	1.5	(−1,1.5)
0	$2^0 + 1 = 1 + 1$	2	(0,2)
1	$2^1 + 1 = 2 + 1$	3	(1,3)
2	$2^2 + 1 = 4 + 1$	5	(2,5)

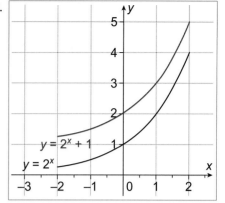

We can see that the graph of $y = 2^x + 1$ is the graph of $y = 2^x$ shifted (translated) one unit upwards.

Graphs of Functions of the Form $y = k^{x + h}$

Consider the function $y = 2^{x + 1}$ in the domain $-2 \leqslant x \leqslant 2$, $x \in R$.

x	2^{x+1}	y	(x,y)
−2	2^{-1}	$\frac{1}{2}$	$\left(-2,\frac{1}{2}\right)$
−1	2^0	1	(−1,1)
0	2^1	2	(0,2)
1	2^2	4	(1,4)
2	2^3	8	(2,8)

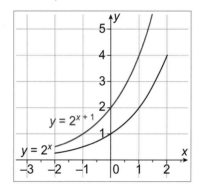

Note the position of the graph of $y = 2^{x + 1}$. There are two ways of thinking about this graph:

(1) The graph of $y = 2^{x + 1}$ ($= 2(2^x)$) lies above the graph of $y = 2^x$.

(2) The graph of $y = 2^{x + 1}$ is the graph of $y = 2^x$ shifted one unit to the left.

Consider the function $y = 2^{x - 1}$ in the same domain.

x	2^{x-1}	y	(x,y)
−2	$2^{-3} = \frac{1}{2^3}$	$\frac{1}{8}$	$\left(-2,\frac{1}{8}\right)$
−1	$2^{-2} = \frac{1}{2^2}$	$\frac{1}{4}$	$\left(-1,\frac{1}{4}\right)$
0	$2^{-1} = \frac{1}{2^1}$	$\frac{1}{2}$	$\left(0,\frac{1}{2}\right)$
1	$2^0 = 1$	1	(1,1)
2	$2^1 = 2$	2	(2,2)

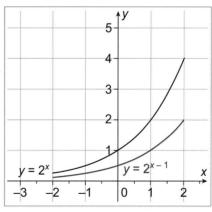

Note the position of the graph of $y = 2^{x - 1}$.

(1) The graph of $y = 2^{x - 1}$ ($= 2^{-1} . 2^x = \frac{1}{2}(2^x)$) lies below the graph of $y = 2^x$.

(2) The graph of $y = 2^{x - 1}$ is the graph of $y = 2^x$ shifted one unit to the right.

> The graph of $f(x) = k^{x + h}$ is the graph of $y = k^x$ shifted h units to the left if $h > 0$ **or** $-h$ units to the right if $h < 0$.

FUNCTIONS

Worked Example 8.22

Graph the function $y = 3(3^x)$ in the domain $-3 \leqslant x \leqslant 2, x \in R$.

Hence, sketch the functions:

(i) $f(x) = 3^x$　　(ii) $g(x) = 3^{x-1}$

Solution

x	$3(3^x)$	y	(x,y)
−3	$3(3^{-3})$	0.11	(−3,0.11)
−2	$3(3^{-2})$	0.33	(−2,0.33)
−1	$3(3^{-1})$	1	(−1,1)
0	$3(3^0)$	3	(0,3)
1	$3(3^1)$	9	(1,9)
2	$3(3^2)$	27	(2,27)

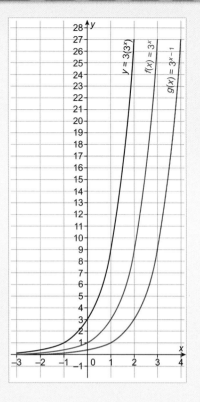

(i) $y = 3(3^x) \Rightarrow y = 3^{x+1}$

Therefore, the graph of $f(x) = 3^x$ is the graph of 3^{x+1} shifted one unit to the right.

(ii) $f(x) = 3^x$. Therefore, the graph of $g(x) = 3^{x-1}$ is the graph of 3^x shifted one unit to the right.

Exercise 8.9

1. Shown below is the graph of the function $f(x) = 3(2^x)$. Use the graph to match the following functions with those graphed below.

   (i) $g(x) = 2^x$　　(ii) $h(x) = 2^{x-1}$

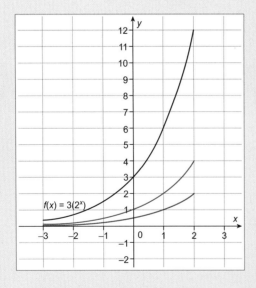

2. Shown below is the graph of the function $f(x) = 4^x$. Use the graph to match the following functions with those graphed below.

   (i) $g(x) = (0.5)4^x$　　(ii) $h(x) = 4^{x+1}$

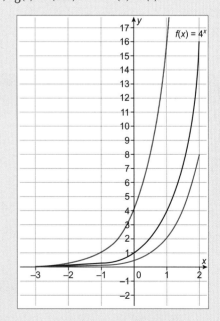

3. Shown below is the graph of the function $f(x) = 8^x$. Use the graph to match the following functions with those graphed below.

    (i) $g(x) = 0.5(8^x)$ (ii) $h(x) = 8^x - 2$

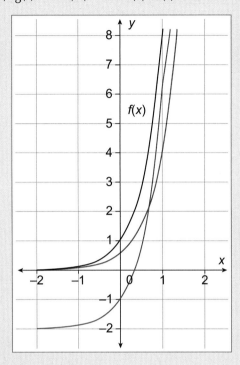

4. Graph the function $y = 2^x$ over the domain $-2 \leqslant x \leqslant 2, x \in R$.

    Hence, sketch the following functions:

    (i) $f(x) = 2^{x+1}$ (iii) $h(x) = 3(2^x)$

    (ii) $g(x) = 2^x + 2$

5. Graph the function $f(x) = \left(\frac{1}{2}\right)^x$ over the domain $-3 \leqslant x \leqslant 3, x \in R.$

    Hence, sketch the following functions:

    (i) $g(x) = 2\left(\frac{1}{2}\right)^x$ (ii) $h(x) = \left(\frac{1}{2}\right)^x + 1$

6. The graphs of the functions $f(x) = 2^x$ and $g(x)$ are given.

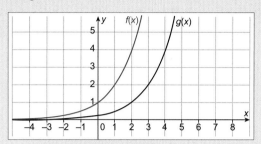

    (i) Describe in your own words a transformation that would map the graph of $f(x)$ to the graph of $g(x)$.

    (ii) What is the functional form of $g(x)$?

7. The graph of the function $y = 3^x$ is shifted three units to the right.
    What is the new functional form?

8. The graph of the function $y = 4^x$ is stretched vertically by a factor of 3 and is shifted to the right by three units.
    What is the new functional form?

9. The graph of the function $y = 2^x$ is shifted to the left by two units and is shifted upwards by three units.
    What is the new functional form?

8.13 TRANSFORMATIONS OF LOGARITHMIC FUNCTIONS

Consider the function $g(x) = \log_2 x, x \in R, 0 < x \leqslant 16$.

x	y	(x,y)
$\frac{1}{2}$	−1	$\left(\frac{1}{2},-1\right)$
1	0	(1,0)
2	1	(2,1)
4	2	(4,2)
8	3	(8,3)
16	4	(16,4)

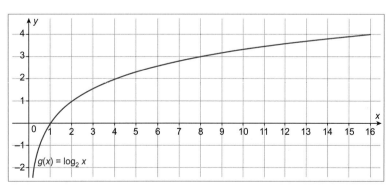

The graph of $y = \log_2 x$ is increasing and contains the point (1,0).

Graphs of Functions of the Form $y = a \log_c x$

Consider the function $h(x) = 2 \log_2 x$ in the same domain.

x	y	(x,y)
$\frac{1}{2}$	$2(-1) = -2$	$\left(\frac{1}{2}, -2\right)$
1	$2(0) = 0$	$(1,0)$
2	$2(1) = 2$	$(2,2)$
4	$2(2) = 4$	$(4,4)$
8	$2(3) = 6$	$(8,6)$
16	$2(4) = 8$	$(16,8)$

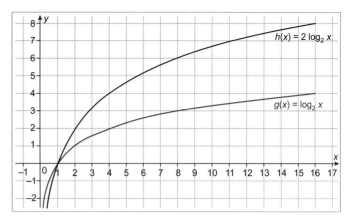

Note: For a given x-value, we multiply the y-value by 2.

What did you notice about the graph of $h(x) = 2 \log_2 x$?

- It is increasing.

- It contains the point $(1,0)$.

- It lies above the graph of $g(x) = \log_2 x$ for all $x > 1$ and below the graph of $g(x) = \log_2 x$ for all $x < 1$.

Consider the function $h(x) = \frac{1}{2} \log_2 x$ in the same domain.

x	y	(x,y)
$\frac{1}{2}$	$\frac{1}{2}(-1) = -\frac{1}{2}$	$\left(\frac{1}{2}, -\frac{1}{2}\right)$
1	$\frac{1}{2}(0) = 0$	$(1,0)$
2	$\frac{1}{2}(1) = \frac{1}{2}$	$\left(2, \frac{1}{2}\right)$
4	$\frac{1}{2}(2) = 1$	$(4,1)$
8	$\frac{1}{2}(3) = 1.5$	$(8,1.5)$
16	$\frac{1}{2}(4) = 2$	$(16,2)$

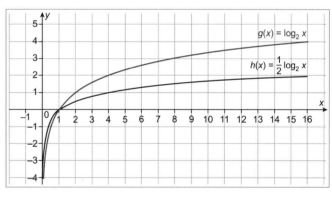

Note: For a given x-value, we multiply the y-value by $\frac{1}{2}$.

What did you notice about the graph of $h(x) = \frac{1}{2} \log_2 x$?

- It is increasing.

- It contains the point $(1,0)$.

- It lies below the graph of $g(x) = \log_2 x$ for all $x > 1$ and above the graph of $g(x) = \log_2 x$ for all $x < 1$.

Graphs of Functions of the Form $y = \log_c x + b$

The graph of the function $f(x) = \log_c x + b$ is the graph of the function of $y = \log_c x$ shifted b units upwards if $b > 0$ or shifted $-b$ units downwards if $b < 0$.

Consider the function $h(x) = \log_2 x + 3$ in the domain $0 < x \leqslant 16, x \in R$.

x	$\log_2 x + 3$	(x,y)
$\frac{1}{2}$	$-1 + 3$	$\left(\frac{1}{2}, 2\right)$
1	$0 + 3$	(1,3)
2	$1 + 3$	(2,4)
4	$2 + 3$	(4,5)
8	$3 + 3$	(8,6)
16	$4 + 3$	(16,7)

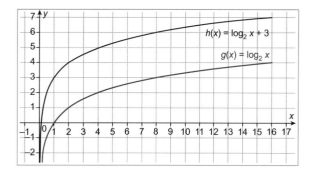

We can see that the graph of $h(x) = \log_2 x + 3$ is the graph of $g(x) = \log_2 x$ shifted three units upwards.

Graphs of Functions of the Form $y = \log_c (x + h)$

Consider the function $h(x) = \log_2 (x + 2), -2 < x \leqslant 16, x \in R$.

x	y	(x,y)
−1.5	−1	(−1.5,−1)
−1	0	(−1,0)
0	1	(0,1)
2	2	(2,2)
6	3	(6,3)
14	4	(14,4)
16	≈ 4.2	(16,4.2)

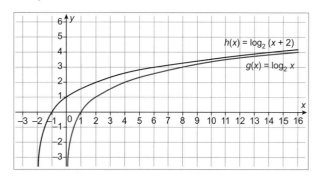

We can see that the graph of $h(x) = \log_2 (x + 2)$ is the graph of $g(x) = \log_2 x$ shifted two units to the left.

Consider the function $h(x) = \log_2 (x - 2), 2 < x \leqslant 16, x \in R$.

x	y	(x,y)
2.5	−1	(2.5,−1)
3	0	(3,0)
4	1	(4,1)
6	2	(6,2)
10	3	(10,3)
16	≈ 3.8	(16,3.8)

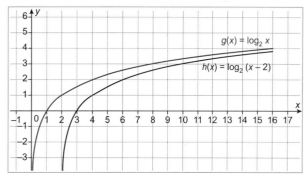

We can see that the graph of $h(x) = \log_2 (x - 2)$ is the graph of $g(x) = \log_2 x$ shifted two units to the right.

The graph of $f(x) = \log_c (x + h)$ is the graph of $y = \log_2 x$ shifted h units to the left if $h > 0$ and $-h$ units to the right if $h < 0$.

Exercise 8.10

1. Shown below is the graph of the function $g(x) = \log_2 x$. Use the graph to match the following functions with those graphed below:

   (i) $h(x) = 4\log_2 x$

   (ii) $f(x) = 3\log_2 x$

2. Shown below is the graph of the function $g(x) = \log_2 x$. Use the graph to match the following functions with those graphed below.

   (i) $h(x) = \log_2 (x + 1)$

   (ii) $f(x) = 0.5\log_2 x$

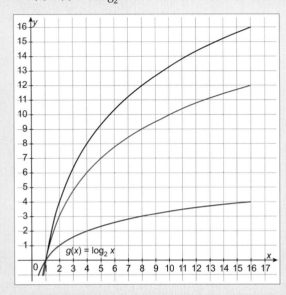

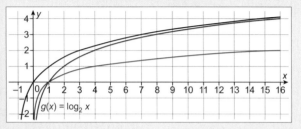

3. Graph the function $y = \log_3 x$ over the domain $0 < x \leqslant 27, x \in R$.

   Hence, sketch the following functions:

   (i) $f(x) = 2\log_3 x$

   (ii) $g(x) = \log_3 (x - 1)$

   (iii) $h(x) = \log_3 9x$

4. The graphs of $g(x) = \log_4 x$ and $f(x)$ are given.

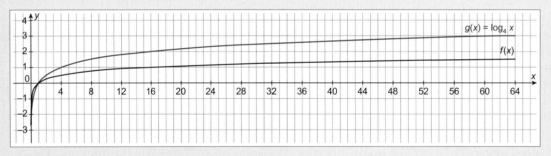

   (i) Describe in your own words a transformation that would map the graph of $g(x)$ to the graph of $f(x)$.

   (ii) What is the functional form of $f(x)$?

5. The graph of the function $y = \log_5 x$ is shifted five units to the right. What is the new functional form?

6. The graph of the function $y = 3\log_6 x$ is shifted three units downwards and three units to the right. What is its new functional form?

7. For each function below, identify the largest domain for which the function is defined and hence identify the corresponding range. Then sketch a graph of each function.

   (i) $y = \log_3 (x - 1) - 5$

   (ii) $y = \log_2 (x + 1) - 2$

   (iii) $y = \log_3 (3x) - 5$

   (iv) $y = \log_2 (3x - 1) + 2$

FUNCTIONS

8.14 INJECTIVE, SURJECTIVE AND BIJECTIVE FUNCTIONS

Consider the following functions that map elements from set *A* to elements in set *B*.

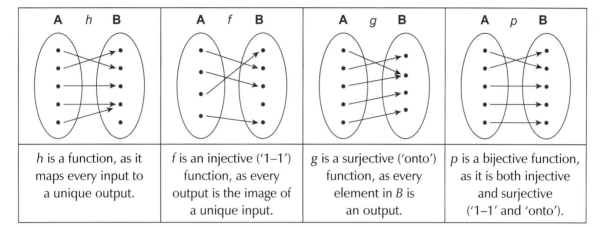

| h is a function, as it maps every input to a unique output. | f is an injective ('1–1') function, as every output is the image of a unique input. | g is a surjective ('onto') function, as every element in B is an output. | p is a bijective function, as it is both injective and surjective ('1–1' and 'onto'). |

The Vertical Line Test

Usually when we draw a graph of a mapping, the horizontal axis is the input axis and the vertical axis is the output axis. If this is the case, then we can use the 'vertical line test' to determine if the mapping is a function or not.

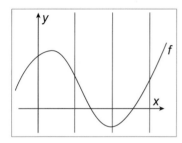

Within the domain of input values, any vertical line cuts the graph of *f* at one point only, so *f* is a function, as each input gets mapped to just one output.

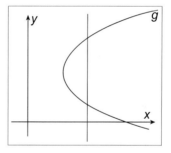

It is possible to draw a vertical line that cuts the curve at more than one point. So *g* cannot be a function, as some inputs get mapped to more than one output.

> **Vertical Line Test**
>
> If the horizontal axis is the input axis, then, if any vertical line cuts the graph of a mapping at more than one point, the mapping cannot be a function. Otherwise, it is a function.

Injective Functions ('One-to-One' or '1–1' Functions)

Let *f* be the function that maps the elements of a set *A* (domain) to the set *B* (codomain).

> The function *f* is **injective** if $\forall\, a, b \in A$, whenever $f(a) = f(b)$, then $a = b$.

> The symbol $\forall$ means 'for all' or 'for any'.

In other words, if a function is **injective** (also called a '**one-to-one**' or '**1–1**' function), and an input value *a* gives the same output as an input value *b*, then *a* = *b*. Therefore, an injective function never assigns the same output value to two different input values.

A function *f* maps from a domain to a codomain as shown:

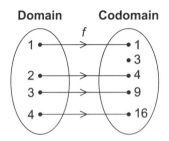

The function is injective, as no two domain values are assigned to the same output value. It does not matter that the element 3 in the codomain has no corresponding element in the domain; this is not necessary for the function to be injective.

Horizontal Line Test for Injectivity

Consider the function $g: R \to R: x \to x + 3$.

A graph of *g* is shown.

Any horizontal line drawn will never cut the graph of *g* at more than one point. This shows that the function *g* is injective.

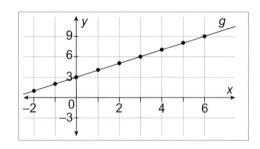

Horizontal line test for injectivity

If the horizontal axis is the input axis, then, if any horizontal line cuts the graph of a function at no more than one point, the function is injective.

Surjective Functions ('Onto' Functions)

Let *f* be the function that maps the elements of a set *A* (domain) to the set *B* (codomain).

The function *f* is **surjective** if $\forall \, b \in B$, $\exists \, a \in A$ such that $f(a) = b$.

The symbol $\exists$ means 'there exists'.

If a function is **surjective** or '**onto**', every value in the codomain is an output of the function. Every element in the codomain will have at least one matching element in the domain. Therefore, the codomain is also the range.

For example, if *E* is the set of all even natural numbers, then the function $h: N \to E$, where *N* is the set of naturals, defined by $h(x) = 2x$, is surjective.

Consider the set *E*. If the elements of the set *N* are substituted into the function *f*, every element in *E* will have a value in *N* assigned to it.

- $f(1) = 2$
- $f(2) = 4$
- $f(3) = 6$
- $f(n - 1) = 2(n - 1)$, which is an even number
- $f(n) = 2n$, which is an even number

Horizontal Line Test for Surjectivity

Consider the function $f: A \to B$.

If f is surjective, then every horizontal line $y = b$, where $b \in B$ intersects the graph of f at **at least one** point.

Worked Example 8.23

Consider the function $f: R \to [-1, 1]: x \to \sin x$.

Use the horizontal line test for surjectivity to determine whether the given function is surjective or not.

Solution

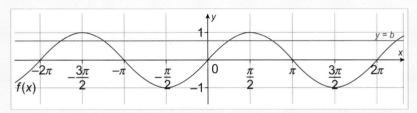

Draw a horizontal line $y = b$ on the graph where $b \in [-1, 1]$. As this line is moved up and down the y-axis, but within the codomain of $[-1, 1]$, b intersects the graph of f at least once. Therefore, the given function is surjective, as each element in the codomain has at least one matching element in the domain.

Bijective Functions

A function f is said to be **bijective** if it is both injective ('one-to-one') and surjective ('onto').

No two domain values are assigned to the same output value and every element in the codomain has at least one matching element in the domain.

Worked Example 8.24

Find the range of the function f where $f(x) = 1 - 3x$ on the domain $\{0, 1, 2, 3, 4\}$, and determine whether the function is injective or not.

Solution

x	1 – 3x	y
0	1 – 3(0)	1
1	1 – 3(1)	–2
2	1 – 3(2)	–5
3	1 – 3(3)	–8
4	1 – 3(4)	–11

Each x-value maps to a different y-value.

$\therefore f$ is an injective function.

Range = $\{1, -2, -5, -8, -11\}$

FUNCTIONS

Worked Example 8.25

Find the range of the function g where $g(x) = 3x^2 - 1$ on the domain $x \in R$, and determine if the function is one-to-one or not.

Solution

x	3x² – 1	y
–3	3(9) – 1	26
–2	3(4) – 1	11
–1	3(1) – 1	2
0	3(0) – 1	–1
1	3(1) – 1	2
2	3(4) – 1	11
3	3(9) – 1	26

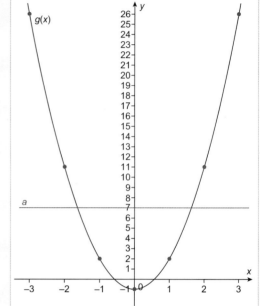

From the sketch, we can see that the minimum value of $g(x)$ is –1.

$\therefore$ Range = $\{y \mid y \geqslant -1, y \in R\}$ (or Range = $[-1, \infty)$)

Horizontal line test

The horizontal line a intersects the graph of $g(x)$ at two points.

$\therefore$ g is not an injective function.

Alternatively, we can see from the input–output table that, for example, –2 is mapped to 11, as is 2.

$\therefore$ g is not an injective function.

Worked Example 8.26

What is the range of the function $f: [0, 2\pi] \to R: x \to \sin x$?

State, giving a reason in each case, if the function is:

    (i) Injective   (ii) Surjective

Solution

From our knowledge of trigonometry, we know that the sine function is periodic, with a range of $[-1, 1]$.

  (i) Consider the graph of the sine function in the domain $0 \leqslant x \leqslant 2\pi$.

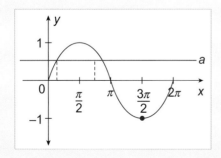

The function is not injective.
Reason: Using the horizontal line test, it is clear that the line a cuts the graph at more than one point, so some inputs get mapped to the same output.

  (ii) The function is not surjective.

      Reason: The codomain is R, but the range is only $[-1, 1]$.

Note: If the codomain had been defined as $[-1, 1]$, then the function would be surjective.

FUNCTIONS

Worked Example 8.27

Is the function $f: R \rightarrow R: x \rightarrow 4x + 2$, a bijection?

Solution

Method 1: Algebraically

Show injective

Take any two elements of R, a and b.

$$f(a) = 4(a) + 2 \qquad f(b) = 4(b) + 2$$

Let $f(a) = f(b)$.

$$4a + 2 = 4b + 2$$
$$4a = 4b$$
$$\therefore a = b$$

So no two domain values get mapped to the same output value.

$\therefore f(x)$ is injective.

Show surjective

Take any $c \in R$.

It can be written as $c = 4d + 2$, where d is some real number.

$\therefore f(x)$ is surjective.

As f is both injective and surjective, f is a bijection.

Method 2: Graphically

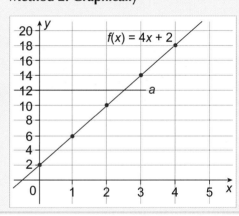

Any horizontal line intersects the graph at no more than one point.

$\therefore f$ is injective.

Any horizontal line intersects the graph of f once. Therefore, the function is surjective, as each element in the codomain has one matching element in the domain.

As f is both injective and surjective, f is a bijection.

Worked Example 8.28

Examine the following functions and state, giving reasons, whether each function is:

    (a) Injective only   (c) Bijective

    (b) Surjective only   (d) None of these

      (i) $f: R \rightarrow R^+$, $f(x) = e^x$ (ii) $g: R \rightarrow R$, $g(x) = x^2$

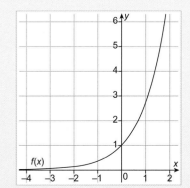

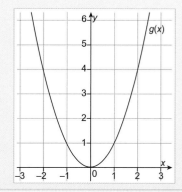

FUNCTIONS

Solution

(i) The function is injective. The horizontal line test shows that the function is injective (there is no more than one point of intersection between any horizontal line and the curve).

The function is surjective. The codomain of this function is defined as R^+. Every element of the codomain has a corresponding domain value.

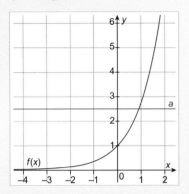

∴ As the function is injective and surjective, the function is bijective.

(ii) The function is not injective. The horizontal line test shows that the function is not injective (it is possible to draw a horizontal line with more than one point of intersection with the curve).

The function is not surjective. The codomain is R but the range is $[0, \infty)$.

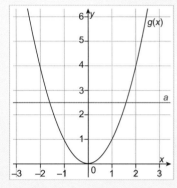

∴ The function is none of (a), (b) or (c).

Exercise 8.11

1. For each of the following functions from set A to B, state whether the function is:

   (a) Injective only

   (b) Surjective only

   (c) Bijective

   (d) None of the above

   (i)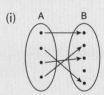

   (ii)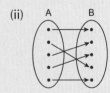

   (iii)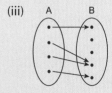

   (iv)

   (v)

   (vi)

2. Which of the following are **not** injective?

   In the case of a function that is not injective, explain why not.

   (i) $f: R \to R$, $f(x) = x^3 + 3$

   (ii) $f: N \to N$, $f(x) = x^3 + 3$

   (iii) $f: R \to R$, $f(x) = x^2 + 3$

   (iv) $f: N \to N$, $f(x) = x^2 + 3$

3. By sketching their graphs, or otherwise, (a) find the range of each of the functions described below and (b) state whether each function is one-to-one or not.

   (i) $f(x) = 2x$, for the domain $\{0, 2, 4, 8\}$

   (ii) $f(x) = x^2 + 2$, $x \in R$

   (iii) $f(x) = 3x - 1$ for the domain $-2 < x < 2$, $x \in R$

   (iv) $f(x) = \frac{1}{x}$, $x \in R$, $x \neq 0$

   (v) $f(x) = (x - 1)^2 + 2$, $x \in R$

   (vi) $f(x) = x^3$, $x \in R$

   (vii) $f(x) = \sin x$, for the domain $0 \leqslant x \leqslant 2\pi$

   (viii) $f(x) = \sqrt{x}$, $x \in R$, $x \geqslant 0$

4. State whether each of the functions graphed below is:

(a) Injective only

(b) Surjective only

(c) Bijective

(d) None of the above

(i)

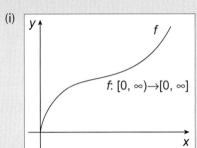

$f: [0, \infty) \rightarrow [0, \infty]$

(ii)

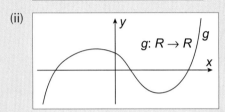

$g: R \rightarrow R$

(iii)

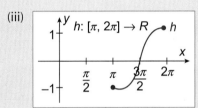

$h: [\pi, 2\pi] \rightarrow R$

5. State whether each mapping graphed below is a function or not.

(i)

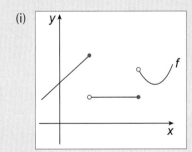

(ii)

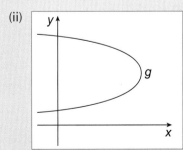

(iii)

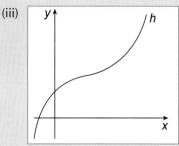

(iv)

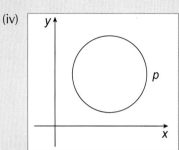

6. For each of the functions graphed below, state whether it is:

(a) Injective only

(b) Surjective only

(c) Bijective

(d) None of the above

(i)

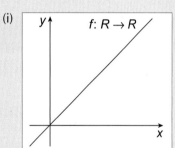

$f: R \rightarrow R$

(ii)

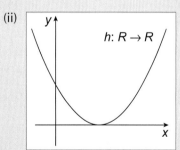

$h: R \rightarrow R$

(iii)

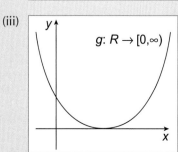

$g: R \rightarrow [0, \infty)$

(iv)

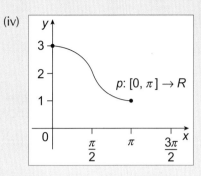

$p: [0, \pi] \rightarrow R$

7. Consider the function f graphed below.

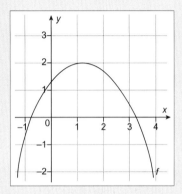

   (i) Is this function injective? Explain.

   (ii) Under what circumstances would this function be surjective?

> In Questions 8–10, investigate if the functions are injective using (a) algebraic methods and (b) graphical methods.

8. $f(x) = x^2 - 3x + 2$ in the domain $-1 \leqslant x \leqslant 4$, $x \in R$

9. $f(x) = x - 3x^2$, $x \in R$

10. $f(x) = 5x - 3$, $x \in R$

11. Define a 1–1 function from N to E, where E is the set of all positive even numbers.

12. Define a 1–1 function from N to O, where O is the set of all odd positive numbers.

13. Define a 1–1 function from N to M, where M is the set of all negative even numbers.

14. Given set $A = \{a, b, c\}$ and set $B = \{d, e, f, g\}$:

   (i) Is it possible to define a 1–1 function from A to B?

   (ii) Is it possible to define a 1–1 function from B to A?

   Explain your answers.

15. State whether the following functions are surjective or not. Explain your answers.

(i)   A   B

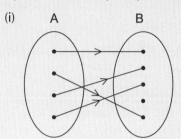

(ii)   A   B

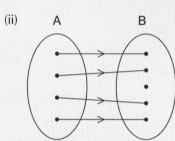

(iii)   A   B

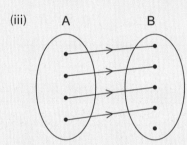

(iv)   A   B

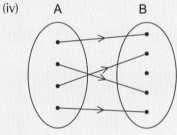

(v)   A   B

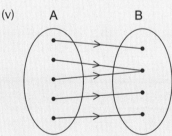

(vi)   A   B

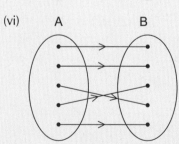

(vii) A   B

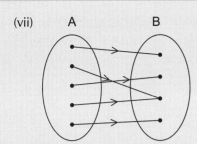

(iii) A   B

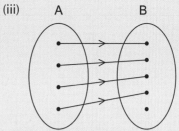

16. Show that the following functions are 'onto' functions:

   (i) $f: [-2, 2] \mapsto [-4, 0]: x \mapsto x^2 - 4$

   (ii) $g: [-6, 0] \mapsto [-5, 4]: x \mapsto x^2 + 6x + 4$

   (iii) $h: R \to [-1, 1]: x \to \sin x$

17. $f: N \to E$, $f(x) = 2x$. E is the set of even naturals. Is f onto? Explain.

18. $f: N \to E$, $f(x) = 4x$. E is the set of even naturals. Is f onto? Explain.

19. $f: R \to R$, $f(x) = 3x + 1$. Is f onto? Explain.

20. $f: R \to R$, $f(x) = |x|$. Is f onto? Explain.

21. $g: R \to R$, $g(x) = x^2$. Is g onto? Explain.

22. $h: R \to R$, $h(x) = \sin x$. Is h onto? Explain.

23. $p: R \to R$, $p(x) = e^x$. Is p onto? Explain.

24. $q: R \to R^+$, $q(x) = e^x$. Is q onto? Explain.

25. State whether the following functions are bijective or not.

   (i) A   B

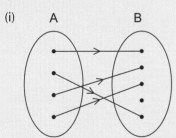

   (ii) A   B

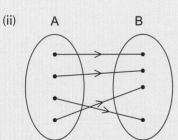

(iv) A   B

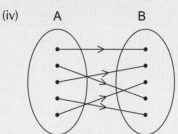

(v) A   B

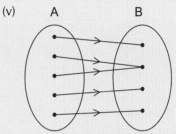

(vi) A   B

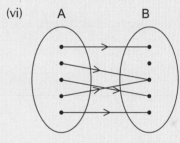

(vii) A   B

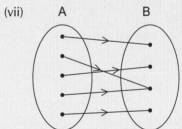

26. State whether the following functions are bijections or not.

   (i) $f: R \to R$, $f(x) = 3x + 1$

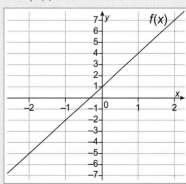

(ii) $g: R \rightarrow R, g(x) = x^2 + 1$

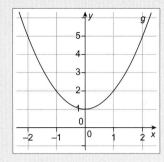

(iii) $h: N \rightarrow Z \setminus N, h(x) = 1 - x$

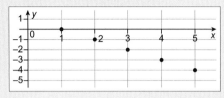

27. Consider the function $f: \left[-\dfrac{\pi}{2}, \dfrac{\pi}{2}\right] \rightarrow [-1, 1]$, $f(x) = \sin x$. Is f a bijection? Explain.

28. Is the function f where $f(x) = 2x$, which maps the natural numbers to the set of positive even numbers, a bijection? Explain.

29. $f: N \rightarrow Z, f(n) = \begin{cases} \dfrac{n-1}{2} & \text{if } n \text{ is odd} \\ -\dfrac{n}{2} & \text{if } n \text{ is even} \end{cases}$

  (i) Is this function 1–1?

  (ii) Is this function onto?

  (iii) Is this function bijective?

  Explain your answer in each case.

30. Consider the function $f: R \rightarrow R$.

  (i) If $f(x) = \sin x$, is the function a bijection? Explain your answer.

  (ii) If $f(x) = \cos x$, is the function a bijection? Explain your answer.

  (iii) If $f(x) = \tan x$, where $f: \left(-\dfrac{\pi}{2}, \dfrac{\pi}{2}\right) \rightarrow R$, is f a bijection? Explain your answer.

31. Find a bijection from $(-1, 1)$ to R.

32. Show that $f: R \rightarrow R: x \rightarrow 4x^3 - 7$ is a bijection.

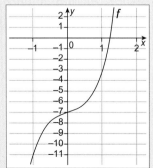

33. Show that $g: R \rightarrow R: x \rightarrow x^3 + 1$ is a bijection.

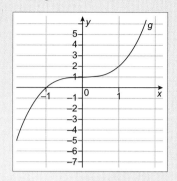

34. Consider the graph of $h(x) = 2^x$ below.

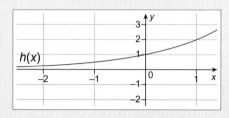

  (i) If $h: R \rightarrow R: x \rightarrow 2^x$, show that h is not a bijection.

  (ii) If $h: R \rightarrow R^+: x \rightarrow 2^x$, show that h is a bijection.

35. Show that the function f, where $f(x) = x^3 - 2x^2 - 5x + 6$, is not a bijection. (Assume a domain of R.)

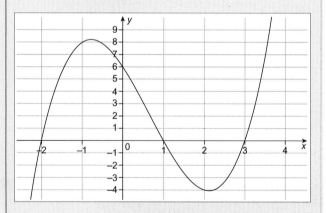

36. Give an example of a bijective function $f: Z \rightarrow N$. (*Hint:* See Question 29.)

8.15 INVERSE FUNCTIONS

Consider the functions f and g defined below:

$$f: R \to R: x \to 3x + 1$$
$$g: R \to R: x \to \frac{x-1}{3}$$

Look at what happens if we input the value 2 into f:

$$f(2) = 3(2) + 1 = 6 + 1 = 7$$

Now, if we input this value of 7 into g, we get:

$$g(7) = \frac{7-1}{3} = \frac{6}{3} = 2$$

Now, look at what happens if we input a value of, say, 5 into g:

$$g(5) = \frac{5-1}{3} = \frac{4}{3}$$

Now, if we input this value of $\frac{4}{3}$ into f, we get:

$$f\left(\frac{4}{3}\right) = 3\left(\frac{4}{3}\right) + 1 = 4 + 1 = 5$$

What appears to be happening here?

In the first example, g appears to undo the work of f. In the second example, f appears to undo the work of g.

The question is, was this coincidence due to the values that we picked, or do f and g undo each other's work, generally speaking?

To answer this question, let us take a closer look at both functions.

f is a bijection that maps from R to R, and g is a bijection that maps from R to R. So, the range of f ($= R$) is the domain of g ($= R$), and the range of g ($= R$) is the domain of f ($= R$).

Let us think about what each function does. f multiplies the input by 3 and then adds 1. How would you undo this work?

You would subtract 1 and then divide by 3. But this is exactly what g does.

Likewise, g subtracts 1 and then divides by 3. What does f do? It undoes this work by multiplying by 3 and then adding 1.

Two functions that have these characteristics are said to be **inverses** of each other.

> If two functions f and g are defined so that $f: A \to B$ and $g: B \to A$, then, if $(f \circ g)(x) = (g \circ f)(x) = x$, we say that f and g are inverse functions of each other.

Some functions do not have an inverse function. For example, consider the function $h: R \to R: x \to x^2$. h is not bijective. Therefore, h will not have an inverse.

To see this, consider input values of -2 and 2. $h(-2) = h(2) = 4$. So, undoing this work requires a mapping from 4 to two values, -2 and 2. However, such a mapping is not a function, since a function has to assign a unique value to a given input value.

Note

1. A function f has an inverse function f^{-1} if and only if f is bijective (that is 'one-to-one' and 'onto').

2. A function f that is bijective will have a unique inverse function f^{-1}. A function cannot have more than one inverse.

Finally, note how important the domain and codomain are in determining if a function is invertible (has an inverse) or not.

For example, if we define a function h such that $h: R \to R: x \to e^x$, then h is not bijective (it is injective but not surjective) and so it has no inverse.

However, if we define h to be $h: R \to R^+: x \to e^x$, then h is bijective (invertible), with h^{-1} defined as $h^{-1}: R^+ \to R: x \to \ln x$.

 ## Worked Example 8.29

Find the inverse of the function f where $f(x) = 2x + 3$, $x \in R$.

Solution

Consider what f does.

It multiplies the input by 2 and then adds 3.

f^{-1} must therefore subtract 3 from the input and then divide by 2.

So, f^{-1} is defined by $f^{-1}(x) = \dfrac{x-3}{2}$, $x \in R$.

(Note: f is bijective, so it is invertible, with domain R and range R.)

 ## Worked Example 8.30

Given a function g, where $g(x) = \dfrac{12 - 4x}{3}$, $x \in R$:

(i) Find the inverse function g^{-1}.

(ii) Test the result in part (i) using $x = 2$.

(iii) Show that $gg^{-1}(x) = g^{-1}g(x) = x$, $\forall\, x \in R$.

Solution

(i) $g(x) = \dfrac{12 - 4x}{3}$

Write as $y = \dfrac{12 - 4x}{3}$.

Write x in terms of y.

$3y = 12 - 4x$

$4x = 12 - 3y$

$x = \dfrac{12 - 3y}{4}$

So, to undo the work of g you need to:

- Multiply by -3.
- Add 12.
- Divide by 4.

$\therefore$ g^{-1} is defined by:

$g^{-1}(x) = \dfrac{12 - 3x}{4}$, $x \in R$

(ii) $g(2) = \dfrac{12 - 4(2)}{3}$

$= \dfrac{12 - 8}{3} = \dfrac{4}{3}$

$g^{-1}\left(\dfrac{4}{3}\right) = \dfrac{12 - 3\left(\dfrac{4}{3}\right)}{4}$

$= \dfrac{12 - 4}{4} = \dfrac{8}{4}$

$= 2$

So we see how g^{-1} undoes the work of g.

(iii) $gg^{-1}(x) = g\left(\dfrac{12 - 3x}{4}\right)$

$\qquad = \dfrac{12 - 4\left(\frac{12 - 3x}{4}\right)}{3}$

$\qquad = \dfrac{12 - 12 + 3x}{3}$

$\qquad = \dfrac{3x}{3}$

$\therefore gg^{-1}(x) = x$

$g^{-1}g(x) = \dfrac{12 - 3\left(\frac{12 - 4x}{3}\right)}{4}$

$\qquad = \dfrac{12 - 12 + 4x}{4}$

$\qquad = \dfrac{4x}{4}$

$\therefore g^{-1}g(x) = x$

$\therefore gg^{-1}(x) = g^{-1}g(x) = x, \ \forall \, x \in R$

Alternative method for part (i)

(i) g is invertible, as g is bijective.

g has domain R and range R.

We could decompose g as $c \circ b \circ a$

where $a(x) = -4x$

$\qquad b(x) = x + 12$

$\qquad c(x) = \dfrac{x}{3}$

So $a^{-1}(x) = -\dfrac{x}{4}$

$\qquad b^{-1}(x) = x - 12$

$\qquad c^{-1}(x) = 3x$

So $g^{-1} = a^{-1} \circ b^{-1} \circ c^{-1}$

$(b^{-1} \circ c^{-1})(x) = 3x - 12$

$a^{-1} \circ (b^{-1} \circ c^{-1})(x) = -\dfrac{3x - 12}{4}$

$\qquad = \dfrac{12 - 3x}{4}$

$\therefore g^{-1}$ is defined by:

$g^{-1}(x) = \dfrac{12 - 3x}{4}, \ x \in R$

Note: Since $g: R \to R$, $g^{-1}: R \to R$.

 Worked Example 8.31

Investigate if the function $f: R \to R: x^3 + 1$ has an inverse.

Solution

Consider the graph of the function.

The horizontal line test shows that the function is injective.

The function is also surjective, as every element in the codomain has a corresponding domain value.

$\therefore$ The function is a bijection and therefore has an inverse.

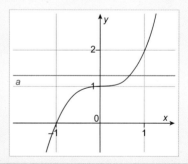

Exercise 8.12

In Questions 1–3, find the inverse of each function.

1. $f(x) = 2x, x \in R$

2. $g(x) = 3x + 1, x \in R$

3. $p(x) = 6x - 4, x \in R$

4. For each of Questions 1–3, show that $F^{-1}F(x) = FF^{-1}(x) = x$, where F is the original function in each question.

5. $h: R \to R^+: x \to 2^x$

(i) Find h^{-1}, the inverse of h.

(ii) Verify that $h^{-1}h(x) = hh^{-1}(x) = x$.

In Questions 6–10, investigate if the functions have inverses.

6. $f: R \to R: x \to x^3$

7. $g: R \to R: x \to x^2$

8. $h: [0, \infty) \to [0, \infty): x \to x^2$

9. $f: \left[-\dfrac{\pi}{2}, \dfrac{\pi}{2}\right] \to [-1, 1]: x \to \sin x$

10. $g: \left[-\dfrac{\pi}{2}, \dfrac{\pi}{2}\right] \to [0, 1]: x \to \cos x$

11. Find the inverse of the function g defined as $g: [3, \infty) \to [-5, \infty): x \to 2(x - 3)^2 - 5$.

12. Find the inverse of the function $f: [0, \infty) \to [0, 1): x \to \dfrac{x^2}{x^2 + 1}$.

13. Find the inverse of the function $h(x) = e^x$, where $h: R \to R^+$.

14. Find the inverse of the function $f: x \to 2^{3x - 1}$, where $f: [0, \infty) \to \left[\dfrac{1}{2}, \infty\right)$.

15. Find the inverse of the function f defined by $f(x) = \log_b(x + 1)$, where $f: (-1, \infty) \to R, b > 0$.

8.16 GRAPHS OF FUNCTIONS AND THEIR INVERSES

Consider the following functions and their graphs:

Function	**Inverse function**	**Graph**
f where $f(x) = 2x, x \in R$	f^{-1} where $f^{-1}(x) = \dfrac{x}{2}, x \in R$	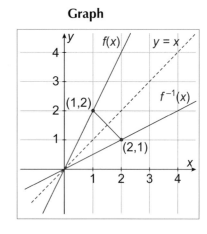

What do we notice about the graphs of f and f^{-1}?

The point $(1,2)$ lies on the graph of f, since $f(1) = 2$.

So, since $f^{-1}(2) = \dfrac{2}{2} = 1$, the point $(2,1)$ will lie on the graph of f^{-1}.

Consider a more general case:

The point $(a, 2a)$ lies on the graph of f, since $f(a) = 2a$. So, the point $(2a, a)$ lies on the graph of f^{-1}, since $f^{-1}(2a) = \dfrac{2a}{2} = a$.

Therefore, for any invertible function f and its inverse function f^{-1}, we get the following result:

If (c,d) is a point on the graph of f, then (d,c) is a point on the graph of f^{-1}.

Geometrically speaking, the graphs of f and f^{-1} are reflections of each other about the line $y = x$.

Below is the graph of the function f, where $f(x) = x + 2$, $x \in R$. Sketch the graph of the inverse of this function.

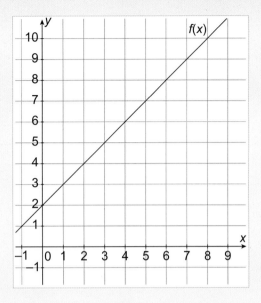

Solution

Method 1

Reverse the co-ordinates of the points that satisfy the given function, and plot the graph of the inverse.

From the graph, it can be seen that the points $(0,2)$, $(2,4)$ and $(4,6)$ satisfy the given function.

So $(2,0)$, $(4,2)$ and $(6,4)$ satisfy the inverse function.

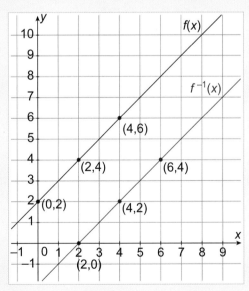

Method 2

Construct the line $y = x$ and find the image of the graph of f under axial symmetry in the line $y = x$.

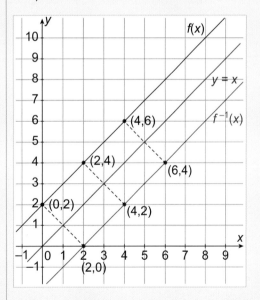

Worked Example 8.33

Sketch the inverse of the function $f: [0, \infty) \to \left[\frac{1}{2}, \infty\right): x \to x^2 + \frac{1}{2}$ on the graph below.

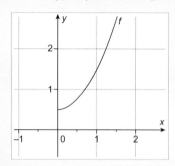

Solution

Step 1 Mark points A, B, C and D on the given curve.

Step 2 Draw the line $y = x$.

Step 3 Find the image of each point under axial symmetry in the line $y = x$.

Step 4 Sketch the resulting inverse function.

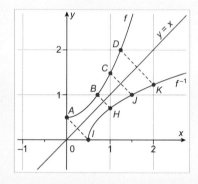

Exercise 8.13

Sketch the following functions and their inverse.

1. $f(x) = 2x$, $f: R \to R$

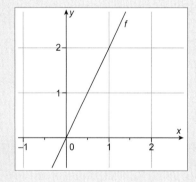

2. $g(x) = 3x + 1$, $g: R \to R$

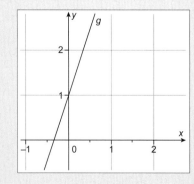

3. $h(x) = 6x - 4$, $h: R \to R$

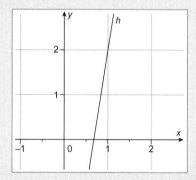

4. $f(x) = 2^x$, $f: [1, \infty) \to [2, \infty)$

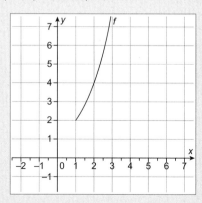

FUNCTIONS

5. $f(x) = 2(x - 3)^2 - 5, f: [3, \infty) \rightarrow [-5, \infty)$

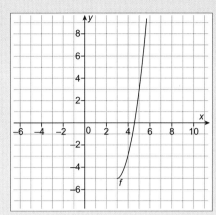

8. $h: [0, \infty) \rightarrow \left[\frac{1}{2}, \infty\right): x \rightarrow = 2^{3x - 1}$

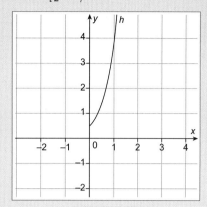

6. $f(x) = \dfrac{x^2}{x^2 + 1}, f: [0, \infty) \rightarrow [0, 1)$

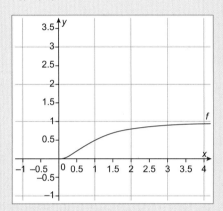

9. $p: R^+ \rightarrow R: x \rightarrow \ln x$

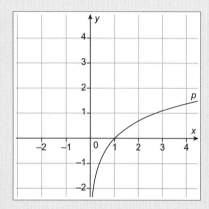

10. $f(x) = \ln(x + 1), f: (-1, \infty) \rightarrow R$

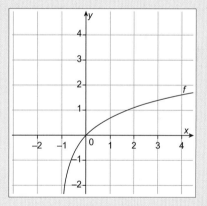

7. $g(x) = e^x, g: R \rightarrow R^+$

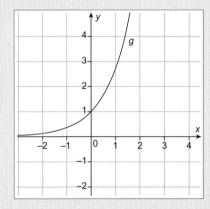

Revision Exercises

1. Given that the functions f and g are defined by $f(x) = 3x + 6$ and $g(x) = x^2 - 4x$, find:

    (i) $g(2)$ (ii) $fg(3)$ (iii) $gf(2)$ (iv) $fg(x)$

2. Given that the functions a, b and c are defined by

    $a: x \rightarrow x^2 - 3$, $b: x \rightarrow \dfrac{1}{x} - 4$ and $c: x \rightarrow x + 3$,

    define the following functions, writing your answer in the form FUNCTION NAME: $x \rightarrow ...$:

    (i) bb (ii) ba (iii) cc (iv) acb (v) bac (vi) cab

3. The functions f, g and h are defined by
   $f(x) = x^2 - 1$, $g(x) = 3x + 4$ and $h(x) = \frac{1}{x}$.

   Solve the following equations, giving your answers correct to two decimal places where necessary:

   (i) $fg(x) = 16$ (ii) $fh(x) = 5$

4. Graph the function $h: x \rightarrow x^3 + x^2 - x - 10$ in the domain $-2.5 \leqslant x \leqslant 2.5$, $x \in R$.
   From inspection of the graph, how many real roots does the function h have?

5. A function f is defined by the rule 'Divide the input by 4 and add 3.'

   (i) Write an expression in x to represent this function.

   (ii) Use this expression to find the value of $f(3)$, $f(-2)$ and $f(-8)$.

   (iii) For what value of x is $f(x) = 9$?

6. When the fire alarm is sounded in a school, the number of students left in the school at any time is given by the following rule:

   Seven hundred minus 20 times the input squared plus 40 times the input.

   (i) Define the function f such that $y = f(x)$, where y is the number of students in the building and x is the number of minutes passed.

   (ii) How long will it take for all students to exit the building?

   (iii) At what time will half of the students be outside the building?

7. For each of the following functions, state whether the function is one-to-one only, onto only or one-to-one and onto.

   (i)
   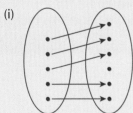

   (ii)
   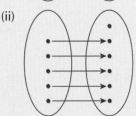

   (iii)
   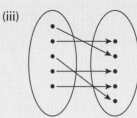

   (iv)
   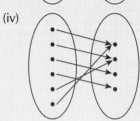

   (v)
   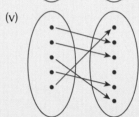

8. Consider the graphs below and identify the nature of the mapping in each case:

   ▦ Not a function

   ▦ 1–1 function

   ▦ Onto function

   ▦ 1–1 and onto function

   (i)
   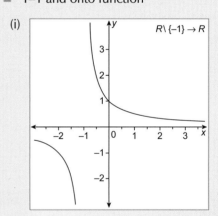
   $R \setminus \{-1\} \rightarrow R$

   (ii)
   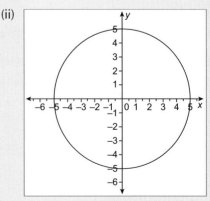

(iii)

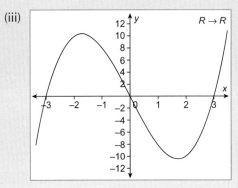

(iv)

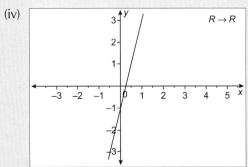

9. Identify which of the following functions are injective. In each case, the mapping is from R to R.

  (i) $f(x) = 2x + 5$ (iii) $h(x) = x(x - 1)$

  (ii) $g(x) = |x|$ (iv) $p(x) = x^3 + 5$

10. $f: R \rightarrow R, f(x) = 3x - 3$. Is $f(x)$ onto? Explain.

11. $f: R \rightarrow R, f(x) = |x + 1|$. Is $f(x)$ onto? Explain.

12. $g: R \rightarrow R, g(x) = (x + 2)^2$. Is $g(x)$ onto? Explain.

13. Are the following functions bijections?

  (i) $f: R \rightarrow R, f(x) = 3x + 4$

  (ii) $f: R \rightarrow R, f(x) = |x - 3|$

14. Show that $f: R \rightarrow R: x \rightarrow 4x^3$ is a bijection.

15. Show that $g: R \rightarrow R: x \rightarrow x^3 - 2$ is a bijection.

16. Show that $h: R \rightarrow R: x \rightarrow 3x^2$ is not a bijection.

17. Show that $f: R \rightarrow R, f(x) = x^3 + 3x^2 - x - 2$ is not a bijection.

18. A production manager is given the following blueprint for manufacturing a closed cylinder: The height of the cylinder is eight times the length of the radius.

  (i) Express the curved surface area of the cylinder as a function of r.

  (ii) Express the total surface area of the cylinder as a function of r.

  (iii) Express the volume of the cylinder as a function of r. Hence, find the volume of the cylinder when r is 4.5 cm.

19. A motor vehicle is depreciated at a rate of 12% per annum (reducing-balance method) from the date of purchase to the date of sale. The vehicle cost €40,000. Express the net book value of the vehicle as a function of t, where t is the number of years passed.

In Questions 20–24, find the inverse of each function.

20. $f(x) = 3x - 3, f: R \rightarrow R$

21. $g(x) = \dfrac{1}{3 - x}, g: R \setminus \{3\} \rightarrow R \setminus \{0\}$

22. $h(x) = \dfrac{12 - 3x}{8}, h: R \rightarrow R$

23. $h(x) = -\dfrac{4}{x}, h: R \setminus \{0\} \rightarrow R \setminus \{0\}$

24. $g(x) = \dfrac{4x}{7}, g: R \rightarrow R$

25. $g(x) = 3x$ and $h(x) = \dfrac{1}{x}, g: R \setminus \{0\} \rightarrow R \setminus \{0\}$ and $h: R \setminus \{0\} \rightarrow R \setminus \{0\}$

  (i) Find $g^{-1}(x)$, $h^{-1}(x)$ and $gh(x)$.

  (ii) Show that $(hg)^{-1}(x) = g^{-1}h^{-1}(x) = \dfrac{1}{3x}$.

26. The following functions are not invertible as is:

  (i) $f(x) = x^2, f: R \rightarrow R$

  (ii) $g(x) = (x + 3)^2, g: R \rightarrow R$

  (a) For each function, find the largest domain and codomain such that the function is invertible.

  (b) Then find the inverse of each function, using the restricted domain and codomain from part (a).

27. State which of the following functions are invertible, giving reasons in each case.

  (i) $f: x \rightarrow 4 - x^2$, $f: R \rightarrow R$

  (ii) $g: x \rightarrow \dfrac{1}{x - 3}$, $g: R \setminus \{3\} \rightarrow R$

  (iii) $h: x \rightarrow 3 - x^2$, $h: [0, \infty) \rightarrow (-\infty, 3]$

28. A colony of bacteria grows according to the law of uninhibited growth at a rate of 18% per hour. The initial number of bacteria is 125.

(i) Complete the following table:

x (number of hours passed)	P(x) (population size)
0	
1	
2	
3	
4	
5	
6	

(ii) Using suitable scales and axes, draw a graph for the population size for the first 10 hours of growth.

(iii) Estimate the population size after 3.5 hours.

(iv) By taking suitable readings, estimate the doubling time for the population.

(v) If a quantity A grows by 18% per hour, then in one hour the quantity has grown to $A(1.18)$. In terms of x, what has the quantity grown to after x hours?

(vi) Write down the population function for the colony of bacteria in terms of x. Answer in the form $P(x) = A.b^x$.

(vii) Hence, check the accuracy of your answer to part (iii).

> Sketch the inverse function of each function graphed below in Questions 29–33.

29.

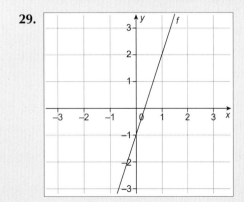

30.

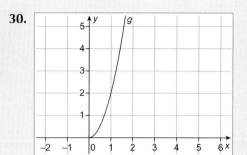

31.

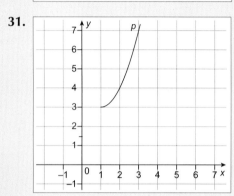

32.

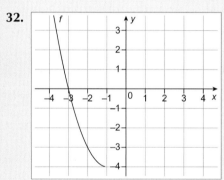

33.

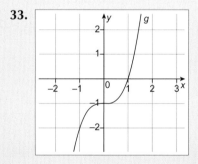

34. Sketch the inverse of $f(x) = e^x$, $f: R \rightarrow R^+$.

35. Use the same scales and axes to draw the graphs of the two functions $f(x) = 3 - 2x + x^2$ and $g(x) = 5 - 2x - x^2$ in the domain $-3 \leqslant x \leqslant 2$, $x \in R$.

(i) Use your graphs to estimate the values of x for which $f(x) = g(x)$.

(ii) Use your graphs to estimate the values of x for which $f(x) \geqslant g(x)$.

(iii) Use your graphs to estimate the values of x for which $f(x) < g(x)$.

36. The function graphed below is
$f(x) = ax^2 + bx + c, x \in R$.
Find the values of a, b and c.

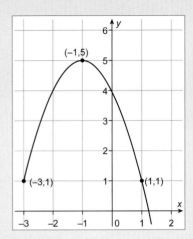

37. Draw the graph of the cubic function
$f: x \rightarrow x^3 + 3x^2 + 2x - 3$ in the domain
$-3 \leqslant x \leqslant 1, x \in R$.

Estimate from your graph:

(i) The value of x for which $f(x) = 0$

(ii) The values of x for which $f(x) = -3$

How many real roots does the function f have?

38. Sketch the following graphs, showing
relevant points:

(i) $y = (x - 4)^2$ (iii) $y = 5 - (x + 2)^2$

(ii) $y = x^3 - 8$ (iv) $y = 1 + 3(2^x)$

39. (a) Write the following quadratic functions in
completed square form.

(b) Hence, find the real roots of each
function.

(c) State the turning point for each function,
and write down the equation of the axis
of symmetry of the curve.

(d) Sketch each function.

    (i) $y = x^2 + 6x + 9$

    (ii) $y = x^2 + 2x - 8$

    (iii) $y = 2x^2 + 2x - 9$

    (iv) $y = (x - 3)^2 + 8x - 3$

    (v) $y = -(1 - 2x)^2 + x^2$

    (vi) $y = (x - 2)(2 + 3x) + 3$

40. Solve each of the following equations by first
writing in completed square form:

(i) $\dfrac{x + 3}{6} = \dfrac{2x}{x - 3}$

(ii) $\dfrac{x - 2}{5} = \dfrac{2x}{-x - 2}$

41. (a) Sketch the curve of $y = x^2 - 2x - 3$,
showing where the curve cuts the x-axis.

(b) The function f is defined as follows:
$f: [1, \infty) \rightarrow [-4, \infty): x \rightarrow x^2 - 2x - 3$.

    (i) State the codomain and range of f.

    (ii) Explain why f is invertible.

    (iii) State the domain and range of f^{-1}.

    (iv) Sketch the graph of f^{-1}, showing
where the graph meets the
co-ordinate axes.

42. The graph of $f(x) = x^2 + 2x + 3$ is shown.
Use this graph to match the following
functions with the functions
shown below:

(i) $g(x) = 2x^2 + 4x + 6$

(ii) $h(x) = x^2 + 2x + 4$

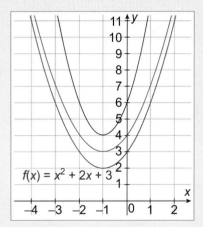

43. The graph of the function $y = 3^x$ is stretched
vertically by a factor of 2.
What is the new functional form?

44. Graph the following functions in the domain
$-3 \leqslant x \leqslant 2, x \in R$.

(i) $f(x) = 2.5(3^x)$

(ii) $g(x) = 2^{1 + x}(2^x)$

45. Identify the *a*-value in the function $y = ab^x$ shown below.

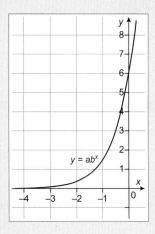

46. Identify the values of *a* and *b* in the function $y = ab^x$ graphed below.

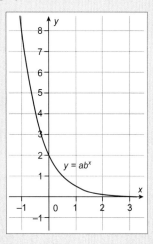

47. An old satellite is falling back to Earth and will strike a city block if it is not shot down. Two different scientists recommend firing missiles using two different models to hit the satellite when it is still over water at a height of 2,000 m.

Model A is given by the function *f*, where $f(x) = 3x - x^2$.

Model B is given by the function *g*, where $g(x) = 0.25x$.

In each case, the function gives the height (in 1,000s of metres) of the missile, where *x* is the time passed in minutes.

   (i) Using suitable axes and scales, graph the height of each missile against time.

   (ii) Which missile takes longer to hit the satellite?

   (iii) How could you sequence the firing of the two missiles so that they both hit the satellite at exactly the same moment?

48. Graph the following functions:

   (i) $f(x) = \log_2 x, \ x \in R, \ 0 < x \leqslant 64$

   (ii) $f(x) = \log_2 (x + 1), \ x \in R, \ 0 < x \leqslant 64$

49. An investment follows the following growth model: $F = P(1 + i)^t$, where *P* is the initial amount invested, *i* is the rate of interest as a decimal and *t* is the length of time in years.

Consider an initial investment of €400 invested at 12% per annum for five years.

   (i) Calculate the value of the investment at the end of each year for the first five years of the investment.

   (ii) Using the number of years as the *x*-variable and the final value as the *y*-variable, graph the growth of the investment over a five-year period.

   (iii) Clearly identify the base and the exponent in the formula $F = P(1 + i)^t$.

   (iv) Use your graph to estimate the value of the investment after three years and three months.

   (v) Use algebra to work out the percentage error made in answering part (iv).

50. The concentration of a drug, once injected into a patient's body, halves every 24 hours. A patient receives an injection of 120 mg of the drug.

   (i) Define a function in *x* that models the concentration of the drug, where *x* is the number of days from injection.

   (ii) Draw a graph to show the amount of the drug remaining in the patient's body over a period of seven days.

   (iii) After how long will 50 mg of the drug remain in the patient's body?

51. Statistics indicate that the world population has been growing at a rate of 1.9 per cent annually since the Second World War. The United States Census Bureau estimated the world population to be 7 billion in 2012.

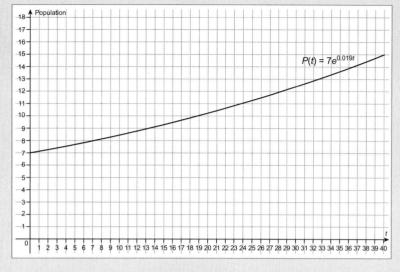

(i) Assuming exponential growth given by $P(t) = 7e^{0.019t}$, where t is years passed since 2012, use the graph shown to estimate what the world population will be in 2025.

(ii) When will the world population be 8 billion? Use your graph to estimate a solution.

(iii) Using the function $P(t) = 7e^{0.019t}$, investigate your answers to parts (i) and (ii) above.

In each case, calculate, to one decimal place, the percentage error made in estimation using the graph.

52. The rate at which a body cools is given by $\theta = 250e^{-0.05t}$, where the excess of temperature of a body above its surroundings at time t minutes is $\theta°C$.

Plot a graph showing the natural decay curve for the first hour of cooling.

Hence:

(i) Determine the temperature after 25 minutes.

(ii) Determine the time at which the temperature is 195°C.

(iii) Use algebra to calculate how long it takes for the temperature to drop to 50°C. Answer correct to the nearest minute.

53. The amount of Product X (in mol/cm³) found in a chemical reaction starting with 2.5 mol/cm³ of reactant is given by $x = 2.5(1 - e^{-4t})$, where t is the time, in minutes, to form Product X.

Plot a graph at 30-second intervals up to 2.5 minutes and estimate the amount of Product X after 45 seconds.

Over which 30-second interval would you be most likely to make the greatest percentage error in using your graph to estimate the quantity of Product X? Explain your answer clearly.

54. The crushing strength of mortar varies with the percentage of water used in its preparation, as shown below:

Crushing strength, F (tonnes)	1.64	1.36	1.08	0.8	0.52	0.24
Percentage of water used, w (%)	6	9	12	15	18	21

(i) Plot a graph of F (vertically) against w (horizontally).

(ii) Estimate the crushing strength when 10 per cent of water is used.

(iii) Assuming that the graph continues in the same manner, estimate the percentage of water used when the crushing strength is 0.15 tonnes.

(iv) What is the equation of the graph?

9 chapter

Number Patterns, Sequences and Series

Learning Outcomes

In this chapter you will learn about:

⊃ Using tables to represent patterns

⊃ Arithmetic (linear) patterns

⊃ Arithmetic series

⊃ Quadratic and cubic sequences

⊃ Exponential sequences

⊃ Geometric sequences

⊃ Geometric series

⊃ Limits

⊃ Infinite series

KEY WORDS

- **Pattern**
- **Linear pattern**
- **Arithmetic sequence**
- **Arithmetic series**
- **First difference (common difference)**
- **Second difference**
- **Third difference**
- **Quadratic sequence**
- **Cubic sequence**
- **Exponential sequence**
- **Geometric sequence**
- **Geometric series**
- **Limits**
- **Infinite series**

'Perhaps I could best describe my experience of doing mathematics in terms of entering a dark mansion. One goes into the first room, and it's dark, completely dark. One stumbles around bumping into the furniture, and gradually, you learn where each piece of furniture is, and finally, after six months or so, you find the light switch. You turn it on, and suddenly, it's all illuminated. You can see exactly where you were.'

Andrew Wiles, Professor of Mathematics, Princeton University and famous for discovering a proof of Fermat's Last Theorem

NUMBER PATTERNS, SEQUENCES AND SERIES

Mathematics is the study of **patterns**. Mathematicians seek out patterns and from these patterns they formulate new conjectures. They then try to establish the truth of these conjectures by rigorous deduction from axioms, definitions and theorems.

9.1 PATTERNS

Patterns appear all around us: a **recurring** theme or motif in a piece of music, a **repeating** decimal such as 0.232323..., or the passage of the seasons over time.

The word 'pattern' comes from the French word *patron*. In the 14th century, when the word 'pattern' first appeared, a patron was somebody who paid for work (like the construction of a sword or a piece of pottery) to be done, often by giving an example to the workman to **copy**.

This leads us to the following definition:

A **pattern** is a set of numbers, objects or diagrams that repeat in a particular manner.

Here are some examples of patterns:

(a)

(b)

(c) 1, 1, 2, 3, 5, 8, ... (the **Fibonnacci pattern**; the first two terms are 1 and each successive term is the sum of the two previous terms)

(d) 101, 1,001, 10,001, 100,001, 1,000,001, ...

> We call each distinct object, number or diagram in a pattern a **term** of the pattern.

The first term of a pattern is called T_1, the second term T_2, and so on. To predict what will come next in a pattern, we must find a rule that links one number, object or diagram in the pattern with the next.

ACTIVITY 9.1

A four-tile repeating pattern is made up of the shapes shown:

(i) Draw the next two shapes in the pattern.

(ii) What is the shape of T_{100}, the 100th tile?

(iii) What is the shape of T_{4n}, $n \in N$?

Solution

(i)

As the pattern repeats every four tiles, the 5th and 6th tiles will be the same as the 1st and 2nd tiles.

(ii) We can draw a table to help us:

Tile	Shape
1	Triangle
2	Square
3	Pentagon
4	Hexagon
5	Triangle
6	Square
7	Pentagon
8	Hexagon
9	Triangle

$\dfrac{100}{4} = 25$, with a remainder of 0.
(25 repeating blocks of four tiles)

∴ 100 is a multiple of 4.

If we consider our table we see that every multiple of 4 will be a hexagon.

∴ The 100th tile is a hexagon.

(iii) If $n \in N$, then T_{4n} is the set of tiles, $\{T_4, T_8, T_{12}, T_{16}, ...\}$. This set consists of every 4th tile. From part (ii), we know that every 4th tile is a hexagon. Therefore, the shape of T_{4n} is a hexagon.

Arithmetic Sequences

> A **sequence** is a set of terms, in a definite order, where the terms are obtained by some rule.
>
> A **number sequence** is an ordered set of numbers, with a rule to find every number in the sequence.

2, 6, 10, 14, 18, ... is an example of a number sequence. The first term is 2 ($T_1 = 2$).
The rule for finding a particular term is to add 4 to the previous term.

> In an **arithmetic (linear) sequence** the difference or change between one term and the next is always the same number. This means that the change in an arithmetic sequence is always constant.

2, 6, 10, 14, 18, ... is an example of an arithmetic sequence. The difference between consecutive terms is 4.

> The difference, $T_n - T_{n-1}$, between consecutive terms in any sequence is referred to as the **first difference**.
>
> The difference between consecutive terms in an arithmetic sequence can also be referred to as the **common difference**. The letter d is used to represent the common difference.

The two sequences shown below are arithmetic. The first sequence has first term, or start term, 11 and first difference 7. The second sequence has a first term, or start term, 2 and first difference −3.

	T_1	T_2	T_3	T_4
Term value:	11	18	25	32
First difference:	+7	+7	+7	

	T_1	T_2	T_3	T_4
Term value:	2	−1	−4	−7
First difference:	−3	−3	−3	

When we graph the terms of an arithmetic sequence against the term number, the result is a straight line, hence the name 'linear sequence'.

The first six terms of the arithmetic sequence: 2, 5, 8, 11, 14, 17, ... are graphed below.

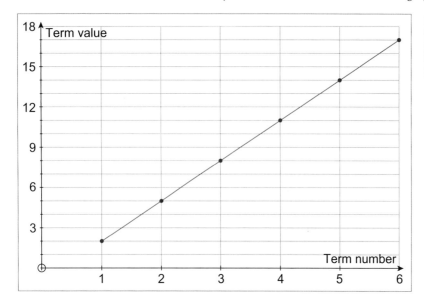

Note: **First difference** is also known as **first change**.

The General Term of an Arithmetic Sequence

Let a be the first term of an arithmetic sequence and d be the common difference.
The table shows the first five terms of the sequence.

T_1	T_2	T_3	T_4	T_5
a	$a + d$	$a + 2d$	$a + 3d$	$a + 4d$

What is T_n, the nth term of the sequence?
Continuing the pattern, $T_n = a + (n - 1)d$.

FORMULA

The **general term** for any arithmetic sequence is $T_n = a + (n - 1)d$, where a is the first term and d is the common difference.

This formula appears on page 22 of *Formulae and Tables*.

Worked Example 9.2

Show that for any arithmetic sequence, $T_n - T_{n-1}$ is a constant.

Solution

$$T_n = a + (n - 1)d$$

$$T_{n-1} = a + ([n - 1] - 1)d$$

$$= a + (n - 2)d$$

$$\therefore T_n - T_{n-1} = [a + (n - 1)d] - [a + (n - 2)d]$$

$$= a + nd - d - a - nd + 2d$$

$$= d \quad \text{(a constant)}$$

$\therefore T_n - T_{n-1}$ is a constant.

To prove a sequence is arithmetic, show that $T_n - T_{n-1}$ = a constant.

Worked Example 9.3

The first three terms of a pattern are shown.

$T_1 =$ • • $T_2 =$ • $T_3 =$ •

(i) Draw the next two terms of the pattern.

(ii) Count the number of dots in each of the first five terms and display the results in a table.

(iii) Describe the sequence of numbers generated by the pattern.

(iv) How many dots are there in T_7, the seventh term?

(v) How many dots are there in T_n, the nth term?

Solution

(i)

$T_4 =$ $T_5 =$

(ii)

T_1	T_2	T_3	T_4	T_5
6	8	10	12	14

(iii) The sequence is arithmetic, with first term 6 and common difference 2.

(iv)

T_1	T_2	T_3	T_4	T_5	T_6	T_7
6	8	10	12	14	16	18

+2   +2   +2   +2   +2   +2

From the diagram it is clear that $T_7 = 6 + (6)2 = 18$.

(v) Using the same reasoning as part (iv),

$$T_n = 6 + (n-1)2$$
$$= 6 + 2n - 2$$
$$\therefore T_n = 4 + 2n$$

 Worked Example 9.4

x, $2x + 1$ and $5x - 4$ are the first three terms of an arithmetic sequence. Find:

(i) The value of x

(ii) The fourth term of the sequence

Solution

(i) Since the sequence is arithmetic, the difference between any two consecutive terms is a constant.

$$T_2 - T_1 = T_3 - T_2$$
$$\therefore (2x + 1) - x = (5x - 4) - (2x + 1)$$

$$2x + 1 - x = 5x - 4 - 2x - 1$$
$$x + 1 = 3x - 5$$
$$-2x = -6$$
$$\Rightarrow x = 3$$

(ii) If $x = 3$, then the sequence is 3, 2(3) + 1, 5(3) - 4 ...
This gives the sequence 3, 7, 11, ...

The common difference is 4.

$$\therefore T_4 = 11 + 4 = 15$$

NUMBER PATTERNS, SEQUENCES AND SERIES

Worked Example 9.5

How many terms of the arithmetic sequence 45, 43, 41, ... are positive?

Solution

$a = 45$ and $d = -2$

We need to find the largest value of n, for which $T_n > 0$.

$T_n = a + (n - 1)d$

$T_n = 45 + (n - 1)(-2)$

$\quad = 45 - 2n + 2$

$\therefore T_n = 47 - 2n$

$T_n > 0$

$\Rightarrow 47 - 2n > 0$

$\quad -2n > -47$

$\quad 2n < 47$

$\quad n < 23.5$

$\Rightarrow n = 23 \quad (n \text{ must be a whole number})$

$\therefore 23$ terms of the sequence are positive.

Exercise 9.1

1. A 3-tile repeating pattern is shown.

   (i)   What is the shape of the 40th tile?

   (ii) What is the shape of the 30th tile?

   (iii) If T_1 is the shape of the first tile, T_2 the shape of the second and so on, then what shape will T_{3n}, $n \in N$, always be?
   Explain your answer.

2. A four-tile repeating pattern is shown below.

   (i)   What is the shape of the 15th tile?

   (ii) What is the shape of the 94th tile?

   (iii) What colour is the 100th tile?

   (iv) Copy and complete the following sentence:

   If n is even, then T_n will always be a _____-shaped tile, while if n is odd, T_n will always

   be a _____-shaped tile.

   (v)   Solve the equation $3(x + 2) = 5x + 2$.

   (vi) Taking your solution for x from (v), what colour will T_{xn}, $n \in \{1, 3, 5, 7, ...\}$ always be?
   Explain your answer.

NUMBER PATTERNS, SEQUENCES AND SERIES

3. To predict what will come next in a pattern, we must find a rule that will link one number or diagram with the next.

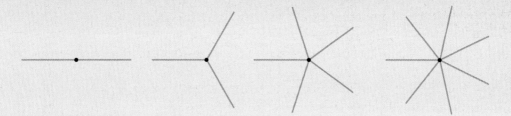

    (i) Identify two different rules for the above pattern.

    (ii) For each of the rules, draw the next two diagrams in the pattern.

4. The first three terms of a pattern are shown below.

    (i) Draw the next two terms of the pattern.

    (ii) Count the number of dots in each of the first five terms and display the results in a table.

    (iii) Describe the sequence of numbers generated by the pattern.

    (iv) How many dots are there in T_8, the eight term?

    (v) How many dots are there in T_n, the nth term?

5. The first three terms of a pattern are shown below.

    (i) Draw the next two terms of the pattern.

    (ii) Count the number of dots in each of the first five terms and display the results in a table.

    (iii) Describe the sequence of numbers generated by the pattern.

    (iv) How many dots are there in T_9, the ninth term?

    (v) How many dots are there in T_n, the nth term?

6. The first three terms of a pattern are shown.

    (i) Draw the next two terms of the pattern.

    (ii) Count the number of red squares in each of the first five terms and display the results in a table.

  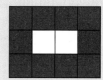

    (iii) Describe the sequence of numbers generated by the pattern.

    (iv) How many red squares are there in T_7, the seventh term?

    (v) How many red squares are there in T_n, the nth term?

    (vi) How many white squares are there in T_n, the nth term?

7. −11, −15, −19, ... is an arithmetic sequence.

   (i) Find the nth term of the sequence.

   (ii) Hence, write down the 55th term.

8. 0, 7, 14, 21, 28, ... is an arithmetic sequence.

   (i) Find the nth term of the sequence.

   (ii) Hence, write down the 85th term.

9. 3, 11, 19, ... is an arithmetic sequence.

   (i) Find the nth term of the sequence.

   (ii) Hence, write down the 96th term.

10. 31, 25, 19, ... is an arithmetic sequence.

   (i) Find the nth term of the sequence.

   (ii) Hence, write down the 21st term.

11. 116 is a term in the arithmetic sequence 14, 17, 20, ...

   Which term is 116?

12. The 51st term of an arithmetic sequence is 248. If d, the common difference, is 15, then find a, the first term.

13. A pattern consisting of isosceles triangles is drawn. The first triangle has a base length of 2 cm and a height of 1 cm. The base of the second triangle is 2 cm longer than the base of the first triangle and the height of the second triangle is 1 cm longer than the height of the first triangle. The same pattern of enlargement will continue with each triangle that follows.

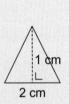 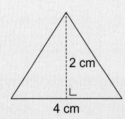 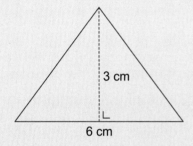

   (i)   What is the base length and height of the 100th triangle?

   (ii)   Derive a formula for finding the area of the nth triangle.

   (iii)   Which triangle has an area of 4.41 m²?

   (iv)   If the perimeter of the nth triangle is $an (1 + \sqrt{2})$ cm, $a \in R$, find the value of a.

   (v)   Which triangle has a perimeter of $4(1 + \sqrt{2})$ m?

14. By considering the difference $T_n - T_{n-1}$, state which of the following sequences are arithmetic:

   (i)   3, 5, 7, 9, ...

   (ii)   2, 4, 6, 8, 10, ...

   (iii)   1, 2, 4, 8, 16, ...

   (iv)   1, 1, 2, 3, 5, 8, ...

   (v)   5, 10, 15, 20, 25, ...

   (vi) $\dfrac{1}{2}, \dfrac{1}{3}, \dfrac{1}{4}, \dfrac{1}{5}, \dfrac{1}{6}, ...$

   (vii)   −5, −1, 3, 7, 11, ...

   (viii)   17, 14, 11, ...

   (ix)   3, −2, −8, −15, ...

   (x)   1.1, 1.35, 1.6, 1.85, ...

   (xi)   0.21, −0.43, −1.07, −1.71, ...

15. The nth term of some sequences are given below. By considering the difference $T_n - T_{n-1}$, state which of the following sequences are arithmetic:

   (i) $T_n = 2n + 1$

   (ii) $T_n = 3n - 1$

   (iii) $T_n = n^2 + 3$

   (iv) $T_n = 12 - 2n$

   (v) $T_n = \dfrac{1}{n}$

16. If the nth term of a sequence is of the form $xn + y$, where x and y are constants, prove that the sequence is arithmetic.

17. The graphs of three sequences are shown. Lines and curves are included for clarity.

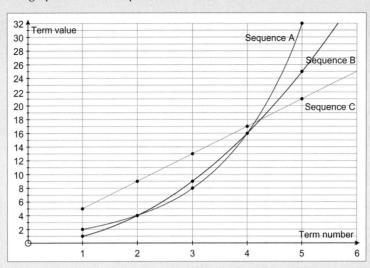

   (i) Identify the arithmetic sequence.

   (ii) Write down the first four terms of each sequence.

   (iii) Calculate the value of d, the common difference, in the arithmetic sequence.

18. The graphs of three sequences are shown. Lines are included for clarity.

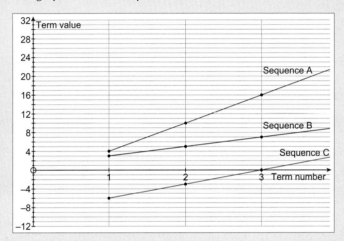

   (i) Find the common differences, d_A, d_B and d_C for each of the three sequences.

   (ii) Find m_A, m_B and m_C, the slopes of each of the lines associated with each sequence.

   (iii) What is the connection between each common difference and slope?

19. $3x + 2$, 20 and $2x + 3$ are the first three terms of an arithmetic sequence. Find:

   (i) The value of x

   (ii) The value of d, the common difference

   (iii) The fourth term, T_4

20. $3x - 2$, $2x + 1$ and $18 - x$ are the first three terms of an arithmetic sequence. Find:

   (i) The value of x

   (ii) The value of d, the common difference

   (iii) The fourth and fifth terms (T_4 and T_5)

21. A sequence has the following three consecutive terms:

$$7(x + 1) - 2,\ 3(x + 2) + 2(3 + 2x),\ 7(x + 3) - 2$$

Prove that the sequence is arithmetic.

22. A sequence has the following three consecutive terms:

$$5(x - 4) + 3,\ 3(x + 2) - 23,\ 5x - 17$$

Prove that the sequence is not arithmetic.

23. How many terms of the arithmetic sequence 91, 89, 87, ... are positive?

24. How many terms of the arithmetic sequence 17, 21, 25, ... are less than 100?

25. How many terms of the arithmetic sequence 100, 97, 94, ... are positive?

26. What is the greatest term in the following arithmetic sequence that is less than 69? 17, 21, 25, ...

27. The natural numbers greater than 1 are arranged as shown in the following chart:

	A	B	C	D	E
Row 1			2	3	4
Row 2	7	6	5		
Row 3			8	9	10
Row 4	13	12	11		
Row 5			14	15	16
Row 6					
Row 7					
Row 8					
Row 9					

(i) Copy and complete the pattern for rows 6 to 9.

(ii) What number will appear in row 100 of column A?

(iii) What number will appear in row 99 of column E?

(iv) Determine the position of the integer 2,011.

28. Show that the sequence, $T_n = \log ar^{n-1}$, where $a, r \in R$, $a > 0$ and $r > 0$, is arithmetic.

29. As part of a new tree-planting initiative, Seán has to plant 30 trees on his farm in 2011, 35 in 2012, 40 in 2013 and so on until the year 2030.

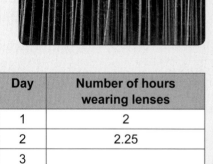

(i) How many trees will Seán plant in 2024?

(ii) In what year will Seán plant 75 trees?

(iii) Draw a graph showing the number of trees that will be planted in each of the years from 2025 to 2030.

30. A person just fitted for contact lenses is told to wear the lenses for two hours the first day and to gradually increase the amount of time they wear the lenses by 15 minutes per day.

(i) Complete the table.

(ii) On which day will the person be able to wear the contact lenses for 14 hours?

Day	Number of hours wearing lenses
1	2
2	2.25
3	
4	
5	

31. An architect is designing a skyscraper. He has been told that each floor must contain exactly 90 rooms. He has constructed a table showing the total number of rooms for each floor and all floors below it. Part of the table is shown below.

Floor number	Number of rooms on the floor and all floors below
1	90
2	180
3	270
4	360
5	450

(i) Construct the next five rows of the table.

(ii) All rooms on the first 20 floors will be equipped with a special security door. How many of these doors will be required?

(iii) The building must contain 9,090 rooms. How many floors will the skyscraper have?

32. Consider the sequence formed, by adding successive multiples of 10 to 7 and then squaring:

$$7^2, 17^2, 27^2, 37^2, \ldots$$

(i) Find a formula for T_n, the nth term of the sequence.

(ii) By considering the following pattern, find another formula for T_n:

$$7^2 = 100 - 6 \times 10 + 9$$
$$17^2 = 400 - 6 \times 20 + 9$$
$$27^2 = 900 - 6 \times 30 + 9$$

(iii) Prove that the formula in part (i) is identical to the formula in part (ii).

9.2 ARITHMETIC SERIES

> An **arithmetic series** is the sum of all the terms in an arithmetic sequence.

Carl Friedrich Gauss (1777–1855)

Carl Friedrich Gauss was a German mathematician who made significant contributions to many fields, including number theory, statistics, calculus, geometry and physics. He is often referred to as 'the greatest mathematician since antiquity'.

Gauss was a child prodigy. When he was in primary school, he was punished by his teacher for misbehaviour. His punishment was to add all the whole numbers from 1 to 100. To the amazement of his teacher, he calculated the sum in a matter of seconds. How did he do it?

FORMULA

The sum of the first n terms of an arithmetic series is given by the formula:

$$S_n = \frac{n}{2}\{2a + (n-1)d\}$$

This formula appears on page 22 of *Formulae and Tables*.

- a is the first term.
- d is the common difference.

Gauss's Method

It is most likely that the young Gauss used the following method to sum the first 100 natural numbers:

Step 1: Write the series in ascending order from 1 to 100.

$$1 + 2 + 3 + 4 + \ldots + 97 + 98 + 99 + 100$$

Step 2: Write the series in descending order from 100 to 1.

$$100 + 99 + 98 + 97 + \ldots + 4 + 3 + 2 + 1$$

Step 3: Add together both representations of the series.

$$1 + 2 + 3 + 4 + ... + 97 + 98 + 99 + 100$$

$$100 + 99 + 98 + 97 + ... + 4 + 3 + 2 + 1$$

$$\overline{101 + 101 + 101 + ... + 101 + 101 + 101}$$

This gives $100(101) = 10{,}100$.

This is the sum of two series; therefore, the sum of one series is $\frac{1}{2}(10{,}100) = 5{,}050$.

$$\therefore 1 + 2 + 3 + 4 + ... + 97 + 98 + 99 + 100 = 5{,}050$$

ACTIVITY 9.2

Worked Example 9.6

Find the sum of the first 100 terms of the arithmetic series $7 + 10 + 13 + ...$

Solution

$$S_n = \frac{n}{2}\{2a + (n-1)d\}$$

$$a = 7, \quad d = 3, \quad n = 100$$

$$S_{100} = \frac{100}{2}\{2(7) + (100-1)3\}$$

$$= 50\{14 + 99(3)\}$$

$$= 50\{311\}$$

$$\therefore S_{100} = 15{,}550$$

Worked Example 9.7

Find the sum of all the terms of the arithmetic series $11 + 13 + 15 + ... + 51$.

Solution

Step 1: We need to know how many terms there are in the series.

Let $n =$ the number of terms.
Therefore, $T_n = 51$.

$$a = 11, \quad d = 2$$

$$T_n = a + (n-1)d$$

$$\therefore T_n = 11 + (n-1)2$$

$$= 11 + 2n - 2$$

$$\Rightarrow T_n = 2n + 9$$

$$\therefore 2n + 9 = 51$$

$$2n = 51 - 9$$

$$2n = 42$$

$$\therefore n = 21$$

There are 21 terms.

Step 2: Next we must find the sum of these 21 terms.

$$S_n = \frac{n}{2}\{2a + (n-1)d\}$$

$$a = 11, \quad d = 2, \quad n = 21$$

$$S_{21} = \frac{21}{2}\{2(11) + (21-1)2\}$$

$$= 10.5\{22 + 20(2)\}$$

$$= 10.5\{62\}$$

$$\therefore S_{21} = 651$$

NUMBER PATTERNS, SEQUENCES AND SERIES

9

Worked Example 9.8

Show that, for any series, $T_n = S_n - S_{n-1}$.

Solution

$S_n = T_1 + T_2 + T_3 + T_4 + ... + T_{n-1} + T_n$

$S_{n-1} = T_1 + T_2 + T_3 + T_4 + ... + T_{n-1}$

$\therefore S_n - S_{n-1} = T_n$

Worked Example 9.9

An arithmetic sequence is defined by:

$$S_n = 4n^2 - 3n$$

where S_n is the sum of the first n terms of the sequence.

(i) Find T_n.

(ii) Hence, find T_{100}.

Solution

(i) $T_n = S_n - S_{n-1}$

$= [4n^2 - 3n] - [4(n-1)^2 - 3(n-1)]$

$= [4n^2 - 3n] - [4(n^2 - 2n + 1) - 3n + 3]$

$= 4n^2 - 3n - [4n^2 - 8n + 4 - 3n + 3]$

$= 4n^2 - 3n - 4n^2 + 8n - 4 + 3n - 3$

$\therefore T_n = 8n - 7$

(ii) $T_{100} = 8(100) - 7$

$\Rightarrow T_{100} = 793$

Exercise 9.2

1. Find the sum of the first 30 terms of each of the following arithmetic series:

   (i) $4 + 7 + 10 + ...$

   (ii) $3 + 8 + 13 + ...$

   (iii) $-5 + 2 + 9 + ...$

   (iv) $35 + 33 + 31 + ...$

   (v) $20 + 19 + 18 + ...$

2. $S_{80} = 1 + 2 + 3 + 4 + ... + 79 + 80$ is the sum of the first 80 natural numbers. Find S_{80}.

3. Find the sum of the first 30 odd natural numbers:

   $1 + 3 + 5 + ... + 59$

4. How many terms are there in the arithmetic series $2 + 4 + 6 + ... + 80$? Find their sum.

5. Given the arithmetic series:

   $2 + 10 + 18 + ...$

   (i) Find the sum of the first 20 terms.

   (ii) Find the sum of the first 40 terms.

   (iii) Hence, find the sum of the second 20 terms.

6. On 1 January 2010, John opened a bank account and deposited €100 in the account. On 1 February 2010, he deposited €105 in the account. He plans to make deposits on the first of every month, increasing the amount deposited by €5 each month.

   (i) How much will John deposit on 1 December 2014?

   (ii) In total, how much will John have deposited by the end of December 2014?

7. An athlete begins a training programme for a 10 km road race 50 weeks before the event. He plans to train each day for 49 weeks and rest on the week before the race. In the first week he runs 2 km each day, in the second week he runs 2.25 km, in the third 2.5 km, and so on, increasing his distance by 0.25 km each successive week.

(i) How many kilometres will he run each day in the 30th week?

(ii) During which week will he run the race distance?

(iii) How many kilometres in total will he run on the training programme, assuming he trains seven days a week?

8. A snail is crawling up a wall. The first hour it climbs 20 cm, the second hour it climbs 18 cm, the third hour 16 cm and so on.

(i) After how many hours will it have stopped climbing?

(ii) Assuming that the snail reaches the top of the wall just as it stops climbing, how high is the wall?

9. In an arithmetic sequence, the sixth term is half the fourth term and the third term is 15.

(i) Find the first term and the common difference.

(ii) How many terms are needed to give a sum that is less than 65?

10. A shop assistant is arranging a triangular display of tins so as to have one tin in the top row, two in the second, three in the third and so on.

If there are 100 tins altogether, how many rows can be completed and how many tins will be left over?

11. A lecture theatre has a trapezium-shaped floor plan, so that the number of chairs in successive rows are in arithmetic sequence. The back row of chairs contains eight chairs and the front row contains 30. There are 12 rows altogether.

(i) Find the number of seats in the theatre.

(ii) Find the percentage of seats that are in the rear half of the theatre.

12. A football stadium has a section of red seating in one of its stands (see the photograph below).

The first and second rows contain two red seats each. The third and fourth rows contain three red seats each. This pattern continues for all other rows in the section.

There are 100 rows in the section. The table below gives the pattern for the first nine rows.

Row number	1	2	3	4	5	6	7	8	9
Number of red seats	2	2	3	3	4	4	5	5	6

(i) How many red seats are in the 51st row?

(ii) How many red seats are in the 98th row?

(iii) How many red seats in total are in the section?

13. The sum to n terms of an arithmetic sequence is given by $S_n = 4n^2 - 5n$.

(i) Show that $T_n = 8n - 9$.

(ii) Show that the first difference $T_n - T_{n-1}$ is a constant.

14. The sum to n terms of an arithmetic sequence is given by $S_n = 3n^2 - 6n$.

(i) Show that $T_n = 6n - 9$.

(ii) Show that the first difference $T_n - T_{n-1}$ is a constant.

15. The sum to n terms of an arithmetic sequence is given by $S_n = 2n - 5n^2$.

    (i) Show that $T_n = 7 - 10n$.

    (ii) Show that the first difference $T_n - T_{n-1}$ is a constant.

16. (i) Show that:

$$\log a + \log ar + \log ar^2 + \ldots + \log ar^{n-1}$$

forms an arithmetic series.

    (ii) Hence, prove that:

$$\log a + \log ar + \log ar^2 + \ldots + \log ar^{n-1}$$
$$= \frac{1}{2}n\log(a^2 r^{n-1})$$

17. The sum of the first n terms of an arithmetic sequence is $S_n = n^2 - 3n$. Write down the fourth term and the nth term.

18. Given that, in an arithmetic sequence, T_n, the general term, is of the form $xn + y$, where x and y are constants, prove that S_n, the sum of the first n terms in the corresponding arithmetic series, is of the form $pn^2 + qn$, where p and q are constants.

19. Prove that S_n, the sum of the first n terms in an arithmetic series, is given by the formula $S_n = \frac{n}{2}[2a + (n-1)d]$, where a is the first term and d is the common difference.

9.3 NON-LINEAR SEQUENCES

In arithmetic (linear) sequences, the difference between consecutive terms, also called the first difference, is always constant. If the difference between consecutive terms is **not constant**, then we say that the sequence is **non-linear**.

> In **non-linear sequences**, the difference changes between each pair of consecutive terms.

The sequence 1, 8, 27, 64, … is non-linear.

Quadratic Sequences

Consider the non-linear sequence 2, 5, 10, 17…

We can see that the first difference between each term is **not** the same.

> A **quadratic sequence** is a sequence where the nth term is of the form $T_n = an^2 + bn + c$, $a, b, c \in R$, $a \neq 0$.
>
> The second difference is constant. It is also known as the second change.

When we look at the second difference, i.e. the difference between the differences, we may be able to spot a pattern.

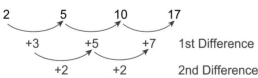

The second difference is the same value each time.

In this case, the pattern is referred to as a **quadratic pattern**.

The graph of a quadratic pattern will be a **curve** and **not** a straight line.

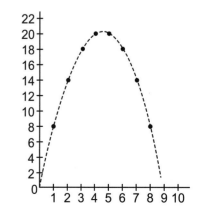

ACTIVITY 9.3

Worked Example 9.10

Show that the sequence 1, 6, 15, 28, 45, ... is quadratic.

Solution

Term	Sequence	First difference	Second difference
T_1	1		
T_2	6	5	
T_3	15	9	4
T_4	28	13	4
T_5	45	17	4

From the table we see that the second difference is a non-zero constant. Therefore, the sequence is quadratic.

The General Term of a Quadratic Sequence

It has been shown that for any quadratic sequence $T_n = an^2 + bn + c$, $a, b, c, \in R$, $a \neq 0$, the second difference is $2a$.

So, if the second difference is 2, then $a = 1$. If the second difference is 16, then $a = 8$. If the second difference is 6, then $a = 3$ and so on.

 Worked Example 9.11

Find the value of a, the coefficient of n^2, in the quadratic sequence $T_n = an^2$.
The first five terms of the sequence are 3, 12, 27, 48, 75, ...

Solution

Draw a table:

Term	Sequence	First difference	Second difference
T_1	3		
T_2	12	9	
T_3	27	15	6
T_4	48	21	6
T_5	75	27	6

$2a$ = second difference

$\therefore 2a = 6$

$\Rightarrow a = 3$

$\therefore T_n = 3n^2$ (substituting for a into T_n)

 Worked Example 9.12

$T_n = an^2 + bn + c$ is a quadratic sequence. The first five terms of the sequence are 12, 16, 23, 33, 46, ...

   (i) Find the values of a, b and c.

   (ii) Hence find T_{30}, the 30th term of the sequence.

Solution

(i) **Step 1:** Find the value of a:

Draw a table:

Term	Sequence	First difference	Second difference
T_1	12		
T_2	16	4	
T_3	23	7	3
T_4	33	10	3
T_5	46	13	3

$2a$ = second difference

$\therefore 2a = 3$

$\Rightarrow a = 1.5$

$T_n = 1.5n^2 + bn + c$ (substituting for a into T_n)

In Step 2, set up equations in b and c:

Step 2:

$T_1 \Rightarrow 1.5(1)^2 + b(1) + c = 12$

$\therefore b + c = 10.5$

$T_2 \Rightarrow 1.5(2)^2 + b(2) + c = 16$

$\therefore 2b + c = 10$

Step 3: Solve the simultaneous equations:

$b + c = 10.5$

$2b + c = 10$

Subtracting gives:

$b = -0.5$

$\therefore -0.5 + c = 10.5$

$\Rightarrow c = 11$

$\therefore T_n = 1.5n^2 - 0.5n + 11$

(ii) $T_n = 1.5n^2 - 0.5n + 11$

$\therefore T_{30} = 1.5(30)^2 - 0.5(30) + 11$

$T_{30} = 1,346$

Worked Example 9.13

The first three terms of a pattern are shown.

(i) Draw the next term of the pattern.

(ii) Count the number of squares in each of the first four terms and display the results in a table.

(iii) Describe the sequence of numbers generated by the pattern.

(iv) How many squares are there in T_7, the seventh term?

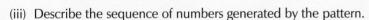

Solution

(i)

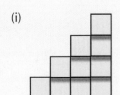

(ii)

Term	Number of squares
1	1
2	3
3	6
4	10

(iii)

Term	Number of squares	First difference	Second difference
1	1		
2	3	2	
3	6	3	1
4	10	4	1

The sequence is quadratic, as the second differences are all 1, a non-zero constant.

(iv) The second difference is a constant of 1.

Therefore, the first difference will increase by 1 each term.

Use a table to help find T_7.

T_1	=	1			
T_2	=	1	+	2	= 3
T_3	=	3	+	3	= 6
T_4	=	6	+	4	= 10
T_5	=	10	+	5	= 15
T_6	=	15	+	6	= 21
T_7	=	21	+	7	= 28

$\therefore$ T_7 has 28 squares.

Exponential Sequences

Another example of a non-linear pattern is 4, 8, 16, 32, ... In this sequence each term is double the previous term.

This type of sequence is called an **exponential sequence**.

> Sequences that involve doubling, tripling, halving, etc. are referred to as **exponential sequences**.

Worked Example 9.14

Orla is 8 m away from a wall. She moves towards the wall and, with each move, she halves the distance between herself and the wall.

(i) Construct a table showing Orla's distance from the wall after each of her first six moves.

(ii) Plot a graph of Orla's distance from the wall against move number towards the wall.

(iii) Find a formula for Orla's distance from the wall after n moves.

(iv) Hence, find Orla's distance from the wall after 10 moves.
Give your answer in centimetres, correct to the nearest centimetre.

Solution

(i)

Move	Distance from the wall (m)
0	8
1	4
2	2
3	1
4	$\frac{1}{2}$
5	$\frac{1}{4}$
6	$\frac{1}{8}$

(ii)

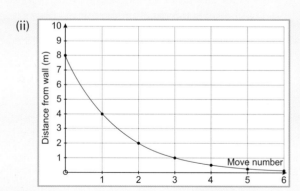

(iii)

Move	Distance from the wall
0	8
1	$8 \times \frac{1}{2}$
2	$8 \times \frac{1}{2} \times \frac{1}{2} = 8 \times \left(\frac{1}{2}\right)^2$
3	$8 \times \frac{1}{2} \times \frac{1}{2} \times \frac{1}{2} = 8 \times \left(\frac{1}{2}\right)^3$
4	$8 \times \frac{1}{2} \times \frac{1}{2} \times \frac{1}{2} \times \frac{1}{2} = 8 \times \left(\frac{1}{2}\right)^4$
5	$8 \times \frac{1}{2} \times \frac{1}{2} \times \frac{1}{2} \times \frac{1}{2} \times \frac{1}{2} = 8 \times \left(\frac{1}{2}\right)^5$
6	$8 \times \frac{1}{2} \times \frac{1}{2} \times \frac{1}{2} \times \frac{1}{2} \times \frac{1}{2} \times \frac{1}{2} = 8 \times \left(\frac{1}{2}\right)^6$

Following the pattern in the table, we can see that $T_n = 8 \times \left(\frac{1}{2}\right)^n$, where n represents the step number.

(iv) $T_{10} = 8\left(\frac{1}{2}\right)^{10}$

$= 0.0078125$ m

$= 0.78125$ cm

$= 1$ cm to the nearest centimetre.

Cubic Sequences

> A **cubic sequence** is a sequence of the form
> $T_n = an^3 + bn^2 + cn + d, \; a, b, c, d \in R, \; a \neq 0$.

ACTIVITY 9.4

For a cubic sequence the **third difference** is always a non-zero constant.

Worked Example 9.15

Show that the sequence 2, 10, 30, 68, 130, 222, ... is cubic.

Solution

Sequence	First difference	Second difference	Third difference
2			
10	8		
30	20	12	
68	38	18	6
130	62	24	6
222	92	30	6

The third difference is a non-zero constant. Therefore, the sequence is cubic.

Exercise 9.3

Remember: Linear sequence ⇒ 1st difference is a non-zero constant.
Quadratic sequence ⇒ 2nd difference is a non-zero constant.
Cubic sequence ⇒ 3rd difference is a non-zero constant.

1. The first four terms of a pattern are shown.

  (i) Draw the next two terms of the pattern.

  (ii) Count the number of dots in each of the first six terms and display the results in a table.

  (iii) Describe the sequence of numbers generated by the pattern.

  (iv) How many dots are there in T_7, the seventh term?

  (v) Find a formula for T_n, the nth term.

  (vi) The numbers generated by the pattern are called triangular numbers. By considering T_{n-1}, T_n and T_{n+1}, prove that the sum of any three consecutive triangular numbers is always 1 more than three times the middle of these triangular numbers.

2. The first four terms of a pattern are shown.

  (i) Draw the next two terms of the pattern.

  (ii) Count the number of dots in each of the first six terms and display the results in a table.

  (iii) Describe the sequence of numbers generated by the pattern.

  (iv) How many dots are there in T_8, the eighth term?

  (v) Derive a formula for T_n, the nth term.

3. The first three terms of a pattern are shown.

  (i) Draw the next two terms of the pattern.

  (ii) Count the number of red squares in each of the first five terms and display the results in a table.

  (iii) Describe the sequence of numbers generated by the pattern.

  (iv) How many red squares are there in T_7, the seventh term?

  (v) Derive the formula for T_n, the nth term.

4. Determine whether the following sequences are arithmetic, quadratic or exponential. In each case give a reason for your answer.

(i) −1, 2, 9, 20, ...
(ii) 2, 4, 8, 16, ...
(iii) 1, 5, 11, 19, ...
(iv) 5, 20, 45, 80, ...
(v) 5, 10, 15, 20, ...
(vi) 3, 9, 27, 81, ...
(vii) 3, 6, 13, 24, ...
(viii) 6, 8, 10, 12, ...
(ix) 5, 10, 20, 40, ...
(x) 4, 12, 36, 108, ...

(vi) 8, 12, 14, 14, 12, ...
(vii) 5, 7, 5, −1, −11, ...
(viii) 1, −2, −2, 1, ...
(ix) 10, 4, 1, 1, 4, ...

5. For each of the following quadratic sequences, find:

(a) a, the first term
(b) The first and second differences
(c) The next three terms

(i) 8, 14, 24, 38, ...
(ii) 1, 3, 6, 10, ...
(iii) 7, 16, 31, 52, ...
(iv) 3, 13, 27, 45, ...
(v) 15, 23, 39, 63, ...

6. Find T_n, the nth term for each of the following quadratic sequences:

(i) 3, 7, 13, 21, ...
(ii) 1, 3, 7, 13, ...
(iii) 6, 11, 18, 27, ...
(iv) 13, 15, 23, 37, ...
(v) 6, 11, 25, 48, ...

7. Find T_n, the nth term for each of the following quadratic sequences:

(i) 68, 44, 28, 20, ...
(ii) 11, 15, 17, 17, 15, ...
(iii) 8, 10, 8, 2, −8, ...
(iv) 6, 6, 4, 0, ...
(v) 13, 10, 10, 13, 19, ...

8. The patterns of dots shown represent the first three star numbers.

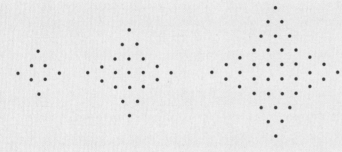

(i) What are the first three star numbers?

(ii) Find a formula for T_n, the nth star number.

(iii) Using your formula from (ii), find the 50th star number.

(iv) Are there any star numbers that are prime numbers? Explain.

9. $T_n = an^2 + bn + c$ is a quadratic sequence. The first five terms of the sequence are 12, 16, 23, 33, 46.

(i) The second differences are constant. Find the value of this constant.

(ii) Find the first three terms, T_1, T_2 and T_3 in terms of a, b, and c.

(iii) Form three simultaneous equations in a, b, and c.

(iv) Solve the equations to find a, b, and c and hence, find a formula for T_n.

(v) Find T_{30}, the 30th term of the sequence.

10. The first four terms of a pattern are shown.

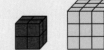

(i) How many cubes are there in each of the next three terms of the pattern?

(ii) Construct a table showing the first six terms of the sequence, the first difference, the second difference and the third difference.

(iii) Hence, explain why the sequence is cubic.

11. The first six terms of a pattern are shown.

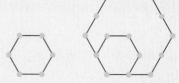

1 7 19 37 61 91

(i) Construct a table showing the first six terms of the corresponding number sequence, the first difference, the second difference and the third difference.

(ii) Hence, explain why the sequence is quadratic.

(iii) How many circles are there in the seventh term?

12. The first three terms of a pattern are shown.

(i) Draw the next shape in the pattern.

(ii) How many dots are there in terms 5 and 6?

(iii) Construct a table showing the first six terms of the corresponding number sequence, the first difference, the second difference and the third difference.

(iv) What type of sequence is this? Explain your answer.

13. Given that a quadratic sequence has a general term $T_n = an^2 + bn + c$, $a, b, c \in R$ and $a \neq 0$, show that the second difference for the sequence is $2a$.

9.4 GEOMETRIC SEQUENCES AND SERIES

A **geometric sequence**, also known as a **geometric progression**, is a set of numbers, where each term after the first is found by multiplying the previous term by a fixed non-zero real number called the **common ratio**.

For example, the sequence 2, 8, 32, 128, ... is a geometric sequence with first term 2 and common ratio 4.

Similarly 10, 5, 2.5, 1.25, ... is a geometric sequence with first term 10 and common ratio $\frac{1}{2}$.

The sum of the terms of a geometric sequence is known as a **geometric series**.

All exponential sequences are geometric.

General Term of a Geometric Sequence

Let a be the first term of a geometric sequence and r be the common ratio. The table below shows the first five terms of the sequence.

T_1	T_2	T_3	T_4	T_5
a	ar	ar^2	ar^3	ar^4

What is T_n, the nth term of the sequence? Continuing the pattern, $T_n = ar^{n-1}$.

FORMULA

The general term for any geometric sequence is $T_n = ar^{n-1}$, where a is the first term and r is the common ratio.

This formula appears on page 22 of *Formulae and Tables*.

Geometric Series

Step 1 Write out the series.

$$S_n = a + ar + ar^2 + ar^3 + ... + ar^{n-2} + ar^{n-1} \text{ (*)}$$

Step 2 Multiply both sides by the common ratio, r.

$$rS_n = ar + ar^2 + ar^3 + ar^4 + ... + ar^{n-1} + ar^n \text{ (**)}$$

Step 3 Subtract (**) from (*).

$$S_n = a + ar + ar^2 + ar^3 + ... + ar^{n-1}$$

$$rS_n = \quad ar + ar^2 + ar^3 + ar^4 + ... + ar^{n-1} + ar^n$$

$$\overline{S_n - rS_n = a \qquad\qquad\qquad\qquad\qquad - ar^n}$$

$$S_n(1 - r) = a(1 - r^n)$$

$$S_n = \frac{a(1 - r^n)}{1 - r}$$

ACTIVITY 9.5

FORMULA

$$S_n = \frac{a(1 - r^n)}{1 - r}$$

- Sum to n terms of a geometric series.
- a is the first term.
- r is the common ratio.

This formula appears on page 22 of *Formulae and Tables*.

Worked Example 9.16

The first three terms of a geometric series are 5, 10 and 20.

   (i) Find T_n, the nth term of the series.

   (ii) Find S_n, the sum to n terms of the series.

   (iii) Hence, evaluate
$5 + 10 + 20 + 40 + ... + 2,560$.

Solution

   (i) $a = 5$ and $r = \dfrac{10}{5} = 2$

$$T_n = ar^{n-1}$$

$$\therefore T_n = 5(2)^{n-1}$$

   (ii) $\quad S_n = \dfrac{a(1 - r^n)}{1 - r}$

$$S_n = \frac{5(1 - (2)^n)}{1 - 2}$$

$$= \frac{5 - 5(2)^n}{-1}$$

$$= 5(2^n) - 5$$

$$\therefore S_n = 5(2^n - 1)$$

   (iii) Firstly, we need to find which term is 2,560.

$$T_n = 2,560$$

$$\Rightarrow 5(2)^{n-1} = 2,560$$

$$(2)^{n-1} = 512$$

$$(2)^{n-1} = 2^9$$

$$\therefore n - 1 = 9$$

$$n = 10$$

Next we need to find S_{10}.

$$S_{10} = 5(2^{10} - 1)$$

$$\Rightarrow S_{10} = 5,115$$

Worked Example 9.17

An initial population of 600 turtles triples in size each year for six years.
Find:

   (i) The growth factor for the population

   (ii) The size of the population after six years

Solution

   (i) The sequence is geometric and the growth factor (common ratio) is 3.

   (ii) $T_n = ar^{n-1}$

      $a = 600$

      $r = 3$

      $T_6 = (600)3^{6-1}$

         $= (600)3^5$

         $= 145,800$

   $\therefore$ Size of population is 145,800

Worked Example 9.18

Show that the sequence $T_n = \left(\dfrac{1}{4}\right)^n$ is geometric.

Solution

A sequence is geometric if $\dfrac{T_n}{T_{n-1}}$ is constant.

$$\frac{T_n}{T_{n-1}} = \frac{\left(\frac{1}{4}\right)^n}{\left(\frac{1}{4}\right)^{n-1}}$$

$$= \left(\frac{1}{4}\right)^{n-(n-1)}$$

$$= \frac{1}{4} \quad \text{(a constant)}$$

$\therefore$ The sequence is geometric.

Exercise 9.4

1. In each of these geometric sequences, write down the value of r, the common ratio, and T_n, the nth term.

   (i) 1, 2, 4, 8, ...   (iv) $\dfrac{1}{2}, \dfrac{1}{4}, \dfrac{1}{8}, \dfrac{1}{16}, \ldots$

   (ii) 5, 10, 20, 40, ...   (v) 32, 16, 8, 4, ...

   (iii) 7, 21, 63, 189, ...   (vi) 3, –6, 12, ...

2. Write down the first four terms of these geometric sequences, given the following nth terms:

   (i) $T_n = 3^n$ (iv) $T_n = 5^{n-1}$

   (ii) $T_n = 3(2)^n$ (v) $T_n = 2(3)^{n-1}$

   (iii) $T_n = 2(10)^n$

3. The nth term of a geometric sequence is given by $T_n = 2^n$.

   (i) Write down the first five terms.

   (ii) Write down r, the common ratio.

   (iii) What is the difference between the 10th term and 1,000?

4. Which of the following sequences are geometric? Explain your reasoning.

   (i) $T_n = 5^n$ (iv) $T_n = 3(4)^n$

   (ii) $T_n = 2n$ (v) $T_n = n^2$

   (iii) $T_n = \left(\dfrac{1}{3}\right)^n$

5. Find the sum of the first eight terms of the following geometric series:

   (i) $3 + 6 + 12 + \ldots$

   (ii) $1 + 5 + 25 + \ldots$

   (iii) $5 + 10 + 20 + \ldots$

   (iv) $2 + 6 + 18 + \ldots$

   (v) $\dfrac{1}{2} + \dfrac{1}{4} + \dfrac{1}{8} + \ldots$

6. The nth term of a geometric sequence is given by $T_n = 12(4)^{n-8}$.

   (i) Find T_1, the first term, and r the common ratio.

   (ii) Find the sum of the first 13 terms.

7. The first two terms of a geometric series are $216 + 54$.

    (i) Find the common ratio.

    (ii) Find the sum of the first six terms correct to two decimal places.

    (iii) Find the sum of the second six terms correct to two decimal places.

8. Three terms, x, y and $x + y$, are in arithmetic sequence.

Three terms, x, y and xy, are in geometric sequence.

    (i) Find the value of x and the value of y.

    (ii) Find the difference between the sum of the first eight terms of the arithmetic sequence and the sum of the first eight terms of the geometric sequence.

9. Find the sum of the finite geometric series:

$$3 - 6 + 12 - \ldots + 49{,}152$$

10. The sixth term of a geometric sequence is 16 and the third term is 2. Find the first term and the common ratio.

11. Find the common ratio, given that it is negative, of a geometric progression whose first term is 8 and whose fifth term is $\frac{1}{2}$.

12. Evaluate $\displaystyle\sum_{r=1}^{15} (1.06)^r$.

13. Find the sum of the first n terms of the geometric series $2 + \frac{1}{2} + \frac{1}{8} + \ldots$ and find the least value of n for which this sum exceeds 2.65.

14. Evaluate $\displaystyle\sum_{r=1}^{10} 3\left(\frac{3}{4}\right)^r$.

15. The population of a town is presently 38,300. The town grows at an annual rate of 1.2%. Find the number of years it takes for the population to grow to 43,158.

16. A mortgage is taken out for €150,000 and is repaid by annual instalments of €20,000.

Interest is charged on the outstanding debt at 10%, calculated annually.

If the first repayment is made one year after the mortgage is taken out, find the number of years it takes for the mortgage to be repaid.

17. The third term of a geometric series is 10 and the fifth term is 18. Find two possible values of the common ratio and the second term in each case.

18. Estimates are produced for the number of babies born worldwide each year. The estimates for 2004 and for 2008, given in thousands of births to the nearest thousand, were 130,350 and 137,804 respectively. Assume that successive yearly estimates are in geometric progression.

    (i) Find the annual percentage increase in the number of births.

    (ii) Find the estimates for 2006 and 2011 (to the nearest thousand).

    (iii) Find the estimated total number of births between 2004 and 2012 inclusive (to the nearest thousand).

19. The value of a stock when purchased on 1 June was €10 a share. The stock grew daily at a rate of 3% during the month of June. On 1 July the stock fell by 2% and continued this pattern daily, until a recovery on 28 July.

    (i) Find the share value of the stock on 21 June.

    (ii) Find the share value of the stock on 15 July.

20. If a patient takes A milligrams of a drug at time $t = 0$, then $y = A(0.7)^t$ gives the concentration left in the blood after t hours.

    (i) If the initial dose is 125 mg, what is the concentration of the drug in the bloodstream after three hours?

    (ii) A patient has a concentration of 1.938 mg of the drug in their bloodstream. The patient was given 140 mg of the drug. How many hours ago was the drug administered?

    (iii) Another patient has a concentration of 0.0798 mg in their bloodstream. The drug was given 20 hours ago. How many milligrams of the drug were administered to the patient?

Limits of Sequences

> The **limit of a sequence** is the unique number, L, such that T_n, the nth term of the sequence, gets closer and closer to L for larger and larger values of n.

If the limit exists, then we say that the sequence is **convergent** and that the nth term converges to L. If the limit does not exist, then we say that the sequence is **divergent**.

The geometric sequence $1, \frac{1}{2}, \frac{1}{4}, \ldots$ converges to 0. As the number of terms increase, the value of the terms approach 0.

> ■ If $T_n \to L$ as $n \to \infty$, then $\lim\limits_{n \to \infty} T_n = L$ ($L \in R$).
>
> ■ $\lim\limits_{n \to \infty} \dfrac{1}{n^p} = 0$, for $p > 0$.

Properties of Limits

The following are some important properties of limits:

> (1) $\quad \lim\limits_{x \to a} [f(x) + g(x)] = \lim\limits_{x \to a} f(x) + \lim\limits_{x \to a} g(x)$ **(Sum property)**
>
> (2) $\quad \lim\limits_{x \to a} [f(x)] \times [g(x)] = \lim\limits_{x \to a} f(x) \times \lim\limits_{x \to a} g(x)$ **(Product property)**
>
> (3) $\quad \lim\limits_{x \to a} \left[\dfrac{f(x)}{g(x)} \right] = \dfrac{\lim\limits_{x \to a} f(x)}{\lim\limits_{x \to a} g(x)}$ **(Quotient property)**
>
> (4) $\quad \lim\limits_{x \to a} \sqrt{f(x)} = \sqrt{\lim\limits_{x \to a} f(x)}$ **(Root property)**

Worked Example 9.19

Evaluate $\lim\limits_{n \to \infty} \dfrac{2n^2 + 15n - 1}{3n^2 - 3n + 2}$.

Solution

Step 1   Divide above and below by the highest power of n:

$$\lim\limits_{n \to \infty} \frac{2n^2 + 15n - 1}{3n^2 - 3n + 2} = \lim\limits_{n \to \infty} \frac{\dfrac{2n^2}{n^2} + \dfrac{15n}{n^2} - \dfrac{1}{n^2}}{\dfrac{3n^2}{n^2} - \dfrac{3n}{n^2} + \dfrac{2}{n^2}}$$

$$= \lim\limits_{n \to \infty} \frac{2 + \dfrac{15}{n} - \dfrac{1}{n^2}}{3 - \dfrac{3}{n} + \dfrac{2}{n^2}}$$

Step 2   Apply the properties of limits:

$$= \frac{2 + 0 - 0}{3 - 0 + 0}$$

$$= \frac{2}{3}$$

Worked Example 9.20

Evaluate $\lim\limits_{n \to \infty} \dfrac{\sqrt{3n^4 - 5}}{n^2 + 2}$.

Solution

Here we use the root property of limits.

$$\lim\limits_{n \to \infty} \frac{\sqrt{3n^4 - 5}}{n^2 + 2} = \lim\limits_{n \to \infty} \frac{\sqrt{3n^4 - 5}}{\sqrt{(n^2 + 2)^2}}$$

$$= \lim\limits_{n \to \infty} \sqrt{\frac{3n^4 - 5}{n^4 + 4n^2 + 4}}$$

$$= \sqrt{\lim\limits_{n \to \infty} \frac{3n^4 - 5}{n^4 + 4n^2 + 4}}$$

$$= \sqrt{\lim\limits_{n \to \infty} \frac{3 - \dfrac{5}{n^4}}{1 + \dfrac{4}{n^2} + \dfrac{4}{n^4}}}$$

$$= \sqrt{\frac{3 - 0}{1 + 0 + 0}}$$

$$= \sqrt{3}$$

Exercise 9.5

1. Evaluate each of the following limits:

   (a) (i) $\lim\limits_{n\to\infty} \dfrac{3n-1}{n+2}$

   (ii) $\lim\limits_{n\to\infty} \dfrac{4n-3}{3n+2}$

   (iii) $\lim\limits_{n\to\infty} \dfrac{5n+1}{6n+2}$

   (iv) $\lim\limits_{n\to\infty} \dfrac{1-3n}{9n-5}$

   (v) $\lim\limits_{n\to\infty} \dfrac{13n+12}{15n-8}$

   (b) (i) $\lim\limits_{n\to\infty} \dfrac{3n^2-1}{n^2+2}$

   (ii) $\lim\limits_{n\to\infty} \dfrac{4n^2-1}{2n^2+2}$

   (iii) $\lim\limits_{n\to\infty} \dfrac{5n^3-1}{2n^3+2}$

   (iv) $\lim\limits_{n\to\infty} \dfrac{3n^4-1}{n^4+2}$

   (v) $\lim\limits_{n\to\infty} \dfrac{3n^8-1}{n^8+2}$

2. Evaluate each of the following limits:

   (i) $\lim\limits_{n\to\infty} \left(\dfrac{2n+4}{5n-3} + \dfrac{2}{2n+4} \right)$

   (ii) $\lim\limits_{n\to\infty} \left(\dfrac{3n+2}{2n+1} + \dfrac{5n-3}{2n-1} \right)$

   (iii) $\lim\limits_{n\to\infty} \left(\dfrac{2n-3}{6n+2} - \dfrac{6n^2+3n}{5n^2-7n} \right)$

   (iv) $\lim\limits_{n\to\infty} \left(\dfrac{n^2-2}{n^3-4} \right)\left(\dfrac{n+2}{5} \right)$

   (v) $\lim\limits_{n\to\infty} \left[\left(\dfrac{2n+3}{5n-3} \right)\left(\dfrac{3n^2+5}{7n^2-3} \right) + \left(\dfrac{2n-3}{5n+1} \right) \right]$

3. Evaluate each of the following limits:

   (i) $\lim\limits_{n\to\infty} \dfrac{6n-1}{3n^2+2}$

   (ii) $\lim\limits_{n\to\infty} \dfrac{5n^2-2n+1}{n^3+2}$

   (iii) $\lim\limits_{n\to\infty} \dfrac{6n^2-2n+3}{2n^2+3n-5}$

   (iv) $\lim\limits_{n\to\infty} \dfrac{3n-n^2}{n^2+2n}$

   (v) $\lim\limits_{n\to\infty} \dfrac{8n^3-2n^2+4}{5n^3+n+2}$

4. Evaluate each of the following limits:

   (i) $\lim\limits_{n\to\infty} \left[\dfrac{5}{3} - \dfrac{n-1}{2n+2} \right]$

   (ii) $\lim\limits_{n\to\infty} \left[\dfrac{17}{25} + \dfrac{7n^2-3n+1}{5n^3+2} \right]$

   (iii) $\lim\limits_{n\to\infty} \left[\dfrac{3}{4} - \dfrac{2n-1}{3n+2} \right]$

   (iv) $\lim\limits_{n\to\infty} \left[16 - \dfrac{12n^2+15n-1}{3n^2-3n+2} \right]$

   (v) $\lim\limits_{n\to\infty} \left[10 - \dfrac{5n^2-2n+1}{n^2+2} \right]$

5. Evaluate each of the following limits:

   (i) $\lim\limits_{n\to\infty} \sqrt{\dfrac{36n+2}{n+4}}$

   (ii) $\lim\limits_{n\to\infty} \sqrt{\dfrac{18n^2-3n}{2n^2+4}}$

   (iii) $\lim\limits_{n\to\infty} \dfrac{\sqrt{2n-3}}{\sqrt{72n+4}}$

   (iv) $\lim\limits_{n\to\infty} \dfrac{\sqrt{4n^2+5}}{n+1}$

   (v) $\lim\limits_{n\to\infty} \dfrac{\sqrt{3n^8-1}}{n^4+2}$

6. S_n is the sum to n terms of the arithmetic series $1 + 2 + 3 + \ldots + n$.

   (i) Find S_n.

   (ii) Evaluate $\lim\limits_{n\to\infty} \sqrt{\dfrac{S_n}{3n^2}}$.

9.5 INFINITE SERIES

Consider the infinite sequence $a_1, a_2, a_3, \ldots$ of real numbers. The addition of all the terms of this sequence:

$$\sum_{n=1}^{\infty} a_n = a_1 + a_2 + a_3 + \ldots$$

is called an **infinite series**.

For an infinite series there are infinitely many terms to add. If we add a_1 to a_2 and the result to a_3, then add this new result to a_4, etc., by hand or even by computer, then the operation will go on forever. The solution is to resort to limits.

We consider the sequence $S_1, S_2, S_3, \ldots, S_n, \ldots$ of **partial sums** of the infinite series, where

$$S_1 = a_1$$

$$S_2 = a_1 + a_2$$

$$S_3 = a_1 + a_2 + a_3$$

.

.

.

$$S_n = a_1 + a_2 + a_3 + \ldots + a_n$$

.

.

.

Thus, the sum of the series is now defined as the limit of the sequence: $S_1, S_2, S_3, \ldots, S_n$, as n approaches infinity.

Infinite Geometric Series

Consider the infinite geometric series
$a + ar + ar^2 + \ldots$

The sequence of partial sums for this series:

$$S_1 = a$$

$$S_2 = a + ar$$

$$S_3 = a + ar + ar^2$$

$$S_n = a + ar + ar^2 + \ldots + ar^{n-1}$$

The limit of S_n as n approaches infinity $= \displaystyle\lim_{n\to\infty} \frac{a(1 - r^n)}{1 - r}$

$$= \frac{a}{1 - r} \lim_{n\to\infty} (1 - r^n)$$

> A proper fraction has an absolute value less than 1.
>
> Examples:
>
> $\dfrac{1}{2}$ $\qquad$ $\dfrac{4}{7}$ $\qquad$ $-\dfrac{3}{10}$
>
> $\left|\dfrac{1}{2}\right| = \dfrac{1}{2} < 1$ $\quad$ $\left|\dfrac{4}{7}\right| = \dfrac{4}{7} < 1$ $\quad$ $\left|-\dfrac{3}{10}\right| = \dfrac{3}{10} < 1$
>
> If r is a proper fraction, then $\displaystyle\lim_{n\to\infty} r^n = 0$.

$\therefore$ If $-1 < r < 1$, then $\displaystyle\lim_{n\to\infty} r^n = 0$.

Therefore, if $-1 < r < 1$, then the limit of S_n as n approaches infinity $= \dfrac{a}{1 - r}$.

Hence, the limit of the sequence $S_1, S_2, S_3, \ldots, S_n$ is $\dfrac{a}{1 - r}$, $-1 < r < 1$.

The sum of the infinite series $a + ar + ar^2 + \ldots$ is $\dfrac{a}{1 - r}$, $-1 < r < 1$.

FORMULA

$$S_\infty = \frac{a}{1 - r}, \ |r| < 1$$

This formula appears on page 22 of *Formulae and Tables*.

> If the sequence of partial sums of an infinite series tends to a limit, we say that the series **converges**.

Worked Example 9.21

Find the sum to infinity of the geometric series $1 + \left[\dfrac{2}{5}\right] + \left[\dfrac{2}{5}\right]^2 + \ldots$

Solution

$$a = 1 \qquad r = \frac{2}{5}$$

As $|r| < 1$, the series converges.

$$\therefore S_\infty = \frac{a}{1 - r}$$

$$S_\infty = \frac{1}{1 - \dfrac{2}{5}}$$

$$\therefore S_\infty = \frac{5}{3}$$

Worked Example 9.22

Show that the infinite series

$$\sum_{n=0}^{\infty} \left[\frac{2x}{2x + 1}\right]^n, x > 0,$$

converges and find its sum.

Solution

$$\sum_{n=0}^{\infty} \left[\frac{2x}{2x + 1}\right]^n = 1 + \left[\frac{2x}{2x + 1}\right] + \left[\frac{2x}{2x + 1}\right]^2 + \ldots$$

This is an infinite geometric series with $a = 1$ and $r = \dfrac{2x}{2x + 1}$.

Because $x > 0$, $0 < r < 1$, therefore S_∞ exists, i.e. it converges.

$$S_\infty = \frac{a}{1 - r}$$

$$= \frac{1}{1 - \dfrac{2x}{2x + 1}}$$

$$= \frac{2x + 1}{2x + 1 - 2x}$$

$$\therefore S_\infty = 2x + 1$$

Worked Example 9.23

Express 1.2222... in the form $\frac{p}{q}$, $p, q \in Z$, $q \neq 0$.

Solution

$1.2222... = 1 + 0.2 + 0.02 + 0.002 + 0.0002 + ...$

$\qquad = 1 + (0.2 + 0.02 + 0.002 + 0.0002 + ...)$

The expression in brackets is an infinite geometric series.

$a = 0.2 \qquad r = \frac{1}{10}$

$S_\infty = \frac{a}{1 - r} \qquad \Rightarrow S_\infty = \frac{0.2}{1 - \frac{1}{10}}$

$\qquad\qquad\qquad\qquad = \frac{2}{9}$

$\Rightarrow 1.2222... = 1 + \frac{2}{9}$

$\qquad\qquad\qquad = \frac{11}{9}$

Exercise 9.6

1. Find the sum to infinity of each of the following geometric series:

   (i) $\frac{1}{2} + \frac{1}{4} + \frac{1}{8} + ...$

   (ii) $\frac{3}{7} + \frac{1}{7} + \frac{1}{21} + ...$

   (iii) $5 + 1 + \frac{1}{5} + ...$

   (iv) $4 + \frac{4}{3} + \frac{4}{9} + ...$

   (v) $\frac{2}{3} + \frac{1}{12} + \frac{1}{96} + ...$

2. Find the sum to infinity of each of the following geometric series:

   (i) $3 - \frac{3}{2} + \frac{3}{4} - ...$ (iv) $\frac{1}{2} - \frac{1}{4} + \frac{1}{8} - ...$

   (ii) $\frac{8}{5} - \frac{4}{5} + \frac{2}{5} - ...$ (v) $\frac{1}{2} - \frac{1}{8} + \frac{1}{32} - ...$

   (iii) $7 - \frac{7}{3} + \frac{7}{9} - ...$

3. Find the sum to infinity of each of the following geometric series:

   (i) $1 + (\sqrt{2} - 1) + (3 - 2\sqrt{2}) + ...$

   (ii) $(\sqrt{2} + 1) + 1 + (\sqrt{2} - 1) + ...$

   (iii) $\frac{1}{2} + \frac{1}{2^2} + \frac{1}{2^3} + ...$

   (iv) $\frac{1}{10} + \frac{1}{10^3} + \frac{1}{10^5} + ...$

   (v) $\frac{1}{5} - \frac{1}{5^4} + \frac{1}{5^7} - ...$

4. Evaluate each of the following:

   (i) $\sum_{n=0}^{\infty} (0.4)^n$ (iii) $\sum_{n=1}^{\infty} \left(\frac{1}{2}\right)^{n-1}$

   (ii) $\sum_{n=1}^{\infty} \left(-\frac{1}{2}\right)^{n-1}$

5. The sum to infinity of a geometric series is twice the first term.
   Find the common ratio.

6. The sum to infinity of a geometric progression is 16 and the sum of the first four terms is 15.
   Find the first four terms.

   Note: There are two possible series.

7. The second term of a geometric series is $\frac{1}{2}$ and the sum to infinity of the series is 4.
   Find the first term and the common ratio of the series.

8. Write the following recurring decimals in the form $\frac{p}{q}$, $p, q \in Z$, $q \neq 0$:

   (i) 0.999...   (iii) 1.777...   (v) 77.44...

   (ii) 0.333...   (iv) 3.111...   (vi) $1.00\dot{4}$

9. Write the following recurring decimals in the form $\frac{p}{q}$, $p, q \in Z$; $q \neq 0$:

   (i) 1.2333...   (iii) 8.1777...   (v) 3.4555...

   (ii) 4.6111...   (iv) 9.1888...   (vi) $0.7\dot{2}$

10. Write the following recurring decimals in the form $\frac{p}{q}$, $p, q \in Z$, $q \neq 0$:

   (i) 8.343434...   (iv) 3.454545...

   (ii) 0.121212...   (v) 0.656565...

   (iii) 6.181818...   (vi) $2.96\dot{0}$

11. Find the range of values of x for which the following series converge:

(i) $x + 1 + \dfrac{1}{x} + \dfrac{1}{x^2} + \ldots$

(ii) $1 + 2x + 4x^2 + 8x^3 + \ldots$

(iii) $(a + x) + 1 + \dfrac{1}{a + x} + \dfrac{1}{(a + x)^2} + \ldots$

12. Show that the series:

$$\sum_{n=1}^{\infty} \left[\frac{4x}{x^2 + 9} \right]^n$$

is convergent for all values of x and find the sum to infinity of the series.

13. $T_n = \left(\dfrac{2}{3} \right)^n$ defines a sequence.

(i) Write out the first six terms, T_1 to T_6, of this sequence.

(ii) What type of sequence is represented by T_n? Explain your answer.

(iii) From inspection of the first six terms in your answer to (i), does a limit exist for this sequence?

(iv) If so, what is this limit?

14. $\displaystyle \lim_{n \to \infty} r^n = 0$ if $-1 < r < 1$.

Solve for x ($x \in R$):

(i) $\displaystyle \lim_{n \to \infty} (2x - 1)^n = 0$

(ii) $\displaystyle \lim_{n \to \infty} (x^2 - 5)^n = 0$

 Revision Exercises

1. The diagram shows hexagon patterns made from matchsticks.

   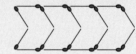

(i) Find an expression for the number of matchsticks needed to make n hexagons.

(ii) How many matchsticks are there in the 10th pattern?

(iii) Which pattern contains 90 matchsticks?

(iv) How many matchsticks are needed to make the first 30 patterns?

2. The first three terms of a pattern are shown.

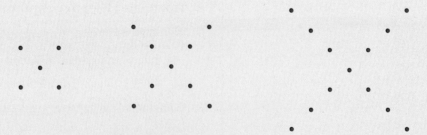

(i) Draw the next two terms of the pattern.

(ii) Count the number of dots in each of the first five terms and display the results in a table.

(iii) Describe the sequence of numbers generated by the pattern.

(iv) How many dots are there in T_n, the nth term?

(v) How many dots are there in T_8, the eighth term?

3. Consider the pattern consisting of equilateral triangles shown below. The first pattern is constructed by joining together the midpoints of the sides and shading the resulting triangle as shown. This creates a total of four triangles within the larger triangle. The second pattern is constructed by carrying out the same process on the remaining non-shaded triangles.

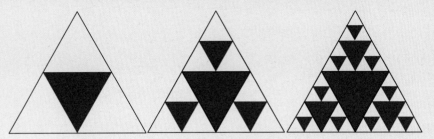

   (i) How many triangles will be shaded in the fourth pattern?

   (ii) What fraction of the area of the original triangle is shaded in the first pattern?

   (iii) What fraction of the area of the original triangle is shaded in the third pattern?

4. Copy the pattern shown.

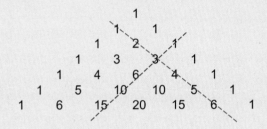

   (i) Write down the next two rows of the pattern.

   (ii) Identify the type of sequence along the diagonal marked with a broken red line and find its nth term.

   (iii) Identify the type of sequence along the diagonal marked with a broken blue line and find its nth term.

5. $T_n = 3n - 7$ is the nth term of an arithmetic sequence.

   (i) Write down the first four terms of the sequence.

   (ii) Find S_n, the sum to n terms of the sequence.

   (iii) Show that $T_n = S_n - S_{n-1}$.

6. The sum to n terms of an arithmetic sequence is given by $S_n = \frac{1}{2}[3n^2 + 11]$.

   (i) Show that $T_n = \frac{1}{2}(6n - 3)$.

   (ii) Show that $T_n - T_{n-1}$ is a constant.

7. For each of the following quadratic sequences, find:

   (a) The first term

   (b) The first and second differences

   (c) T_n, the nth term of the sequence

   (d) T_{100}, the 100th term of the sequence

      (i) 16, 17, 19, 22, ...

      (ii) 1, 3, 6, 10, ...

      (iii) 12, 14, 17, 21, ...

      (iv) 1, 6, 15, 28, 45, ...

      (v) 8, 9, 8, 5, ...

8. The nth term of a geometric sequence is given by $T_n = 5^{n-1}$.

   (i) Write down the first five terms of the sequence.

   (ii) Find r, the common ratio.

   (iii) Find S_n, the sum of the first n terms.

   (iv) Find in the form $4(5^P)$, the difference between the 1,000th term and the 999th term.

9. The sum of the first n terms of a series is given by $S_n = n^2 \log_e 3$

   (i) Find the nth term and prove that the series is arithmetic.

   (ii) How many terms of the series are less than $12 \log_e 27$?

10. Three numbers are in arithmetic sequence. Their sum is 27 and their product is 704. Find the three numbers, if the sequence is increasing.

11. Write the following recurring decimals in the form $\frac{p}{q}$, $p, q \in Z$, $q \neq 0$.

   (i) 5.262626...   (iii) 2.545454...

   (ii) 0.8888...   (iv) $3.\dot{1}\dot{2}$

12. $T_n = an^2 + bn + c$ is a quadratic sequence. The first five terms of the sequence are 1, 13, 30, 52, 79, ...

   (i) Graph the first five terms of the sequence.

   (ii) Find the values of a, b and c.

13. $P(n) = (U_1)(U_2)(U_3)(U_4)...(U_n)$ where $U_k = ar^{k-1}$ for $k = 1, 2, 3, ... n$ and $a, r, \in R$.

Write $P(n)$ in the form $a^n \, r^{f(n)}$, where $f(n)$ is a quadratic expression in n.

14. 3, 12, 29, 54, ... is a sequence of numbers.

   (i) Determine whether the sequence is arithmetic, quadratic or exponential.

   (ii) Find T_n, the nth term of the sequence.

   (iii) Hence, find T_{30}, the 30th term of the sequence.

15. $T_n = an^2 + bn + c$ is a quadratic sequence. The first five terms of the sequence are:

$$3, 7, 13, 21, 31$$

   (i) The second differences are constant. Find the value of this constant.

   (ii) Find the first three terms, T_1, T_2, T_3 in terms of a, b and c.

   (iii) Solve the equations to find a, b and c and hence find a formula for T_n.

   (iv) Using the fact that the second difference is 2a, find a formula for T_n.

   (v) Find T_{30}, the 30th term of the sequence.

16. Evaluate each of the following limits:

   (i) $\lim\limits_{n \to \infty} \dfrac{3n - 1}{n + 2}$ (iii) $\lim\limits_{n \to \infty} \dfrac{\sqrt{3n^2 + 6}}{n + 1}$

   (ii) $\lim\limits_{n \to \infty} \dfrac{4n^2 - 3n + 3}{7n^2 + 8n - 5}$

17. S_n is the sum to n terms of the arithmetic series $4 + 8 + 12 + ... + 4n$.

   (i) Find S_n.

   (ii) Evaluate $\lim\limits_{n \to \infty} \sqrt{\dfrac{S_n}{3n^2}}$.

18. Consider the geometric series:

$$1 + \frac{5}{6} + \left[\frac{5}{6}\right]^2 + ... + \left[\frac{5}{6}\right]^{n-1}$$

   (i) Find S_n, the sum to n terms of the series.

   (ii) Hence, find S_∞, the sum to infinity of the series.

19. S_n is the sum to n terms of the arithmetic series $5 + 10 + 15 + ... + 5n$.

   (i) Find S_n.

   (ii) Evaluate $\lim\limits_{n \to \infty} \sqrt{\dfrac{S_n}{5n^2}}$.

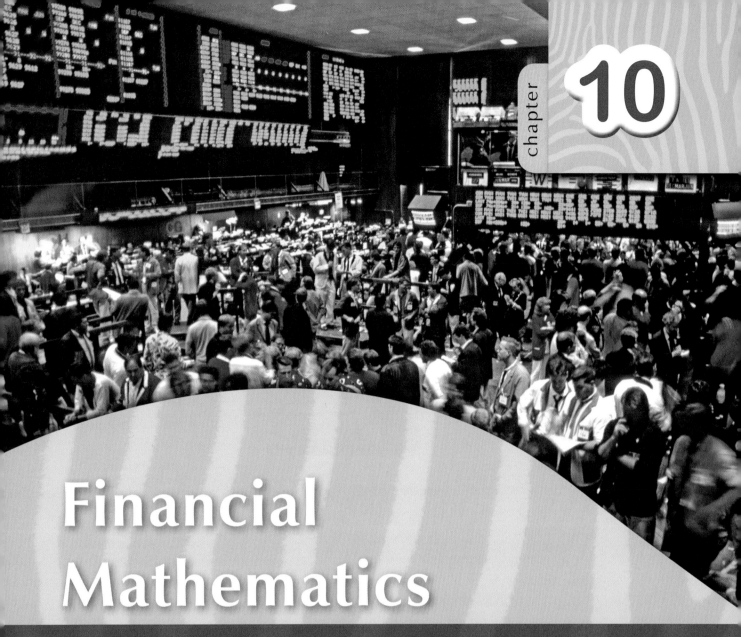

chapter 10

Financial Mathematics

Learning Outcomes

In this chapter you will learn how to:

○ Solve problems and perform calculations on compound interest and depreciation (reducing-balance method)

○ Use present value when addressing problems involving loan repayments and investments

○ Solve problems involving finite and infinite geometric series

○ Use financial applications such as deriving the formula for a mortgage repayment

10.1 PRESENT VALUE

The **time value of money** is the value of money when factoring in a given amount of interest earned over a given time period.

YOU SHOULD REMEMBER...

- How to calculate percentages
- How to find a given root of a number
- Logs
- Compound interest formula $F = P(1 + i)^t$
- Geometric series

For example, if you are given €100 today and invest it for one year at a rate of 5% per annum, it will be worth €105 one year from now. That is to say, €100 today has the same value as €105 one year from now, given an interest rate (also referred to as a growth rate) of 5%.

KEY WORDS

- **Present value**
- **Future value**
- **Net present value (NPV)**
- **Annual percentage rate (APR)**
- **Annual equivalent rate (AER)**
- **Equivalent annual rate (EAR)**
- **Compound annual rate (CAR)**

Present value, also known as **present discounted value**, is the value on a given date of a future payment or series of future payments, discounted to reflect the time value of money and other factors such as investment risk, etc.

Present value calculations are widely used in business and economics to provide a means to compare cash flows at different times on a meaningful like-to-like basis.

FORMULA

Formula: $P = \dfrac{F}{(1 + i)^t}$

F = Final value (amount borrowed/invested + interest)

P = Principal (amount borrowed/invested)

i = Rate of interest per annum (always use decimal form)

t = Time (length of time you had the loan or investment in years)

This formula can be found on page 30 of *Formulae and Tables*.

ACTIVITY 10.1

When future values are brought back to present values at a given rate of interest, the interest rate is referred to as the discount rate (also referred to as the interest or growth rate).

Worked Example 10.1

Compute the present value of a future payment of €58,564 in four years' time, given a discount rate of 10%.

Solution

$$P = \frac{F}{(1 + i)^t} \qquad F = 58{,}564 \quad t = 4 \quad i = 0.10$$

$$P = \frac{58{,}564}{(1 + 0.10)^4}$$

$$\Rightarrow P = €40{,}000$$

> i must be written in decimal form.

The present value is €40,000.

Worked Example 10.2

An investment opportunity arises for Andy. He will receive a payment of €10,000 for each of the next three years if he invests €25,000 now. Growth over this time period is estimated to be 5%.
Use present values to assess this investment.

Solution

To assess the investment, we need to compare like with like; therefore, it is necessary to calculate the present values of the future cash inflows.

Present values $\qquad P = \dfrac{F}{(1 + i)^t}$

Payment 1 $\qquad P1 = \dfrac{10{,}000}{(1.05)^1}$

$\qquad\qquad\qquad = €9{,}523.81$ [€9,523.81 would yield €10,000 in one year's time if invested at 5%]

Payment 2 $\qquad P2 = \dfrac{10{,}000}{(1.05)^2}$

$\qquad\qquad\qquad = €9{,}070.29$ [€9,070.29 would yield €10,000 in two year's time if invested at 5%]

Payment 3 $\qquad P3 = \dfrac{10{,}000}{(1.05)^3}$

$\qquad\qquad\qquad = €8{,}638.38$ [€8,638.38 would yield €10,000 in three year's time if invested at 5%]

The present value of all future cash inflows from this investment is:

$$€9{,}523.81 + €9{,}070.29 + €8{,}638.38 = €27{,}232.48$$

> The net present value (NPV) = present value of all cash inflows – present value of all cash outflows.

- If the NPV > 0 ⇒ Invest in the project.
- If the NPV ⩽ 0 ⇒ Do not invest in the project.

Net present value = €27,232.48 − €25,000 = €2,232.48

As the NPV is positive, Andy should invest in the project.

Worked Example 10.3

Conor is a young entrepreneur hoping to set up a new business. He approaches L. Jordan, a venture capitalist, with the following proposal, detailing cash outflows and inflows for the first five years of the investment.

Year	0	1	2	3	4
Cash flow €	−50,000	−10,000	15,000	20,000	35,000

If Jordan were to apply a discount rate of 5% to this project, would it be worthwhile for him to support Conor?

Solution

To assess the investment we need to compare like with like; it is necessary, therefore, to calculate the present values of the future cash outflows and inflows.

Year 0	$-50,000 = -€50,000$
Year 1	$\dfrac{-10,000}{(1.05)^1} = -€9,523.81$
Year 2	$\dfrac{15,000}{(1.05)^2} = €13,605.44$
Year 3	$\dfrac{20,000}{(1.05)^3} = €17,276.75$
Year 4	$\dfrac{35,000}{(1.05)^4} = \underline{€28,794.59}$
NPV	€152.97

> Initial outflow is not discounted.

> Outflows are discounted in the same way as inflows.

As the NPV > 0, it would be worthwhile for Jordan to support Conor.

 Exercise 10.1

1. Calculate the present value of each of the following cash flows:

	Cash flow (€)	Years from now	Discount rate (%)	Present value (€)
(i)	2,160.00	1	8.0	
(ii)	1,458.00	2	8.0	
(iii)	27,562.50	2	5.0	
(iv)	47,590.40	2	4.0	
(v)	635,548.16	3	4.0	
(vi)	13,676.31	3	11.0	
(vii)	375,334,031.87	7	14.0	
(viii)	341,907.75	3	11.0	
(ix)	488,410.00	2	10.5	
(x)	58,985,820.45	4	7.0	

2. Compute the present value of receiving €6,298.50 in three years' time when the discount rate is 8% (to the nearest cent).

3. Compute the present value of receiving €15,000 in three years' time when the discount rate is 7% (correct to the nearest cent).

4. Calculate the present value of €6,000 that is expected to be received in three years' time when the rate of interest for the period is 7.5% per annum compounded annually.

5. A project manager is presented with the following project as detailed in the table below.

Year	Cash flow
1	€20,000
2	€20,000
3	€20,000
Initial cash outflow (Year 0) €55,000	Discount rate = 6 %

(i) Calculate the present value for each cash flow.

(ii) Calculate the net present value for the project.

(iii) Should the manager take on this project?

6. An advertising executive brings a marketing proposal to his managing director. He proposes an initial spend on the campaign of €50,000. He projects that this advertising campaign will generate cash inflows of €15,000 each year for the next four years. Given a predicted growth rate of 5%, is this a good proposal? (Use present values in arriving at your conclusion.)

7. Sorcha is presented with the following investment projects. All amounts are in euro.

Year	0	1	2	3	4
Project A	−10,000	−3,000	4,000	6,000	8,000
Project B	−5,000	−2,000	1,000	3,000	7,000

Using present values, advise Sorcha as to which project is the more profitable, if a discount rate of 6% is used.

8. A new shopping centre is opening in a beach resort. The management company have to decide between building an area for restaurants or an area for amusements.

The following are the projections for both projects for the first five years. All amounts are in euro.

Year	0	1	2	3	4	5
Restaurant area	−420,000	−5,000	120,000	130,000	145,000	150,000
Amusements area	−95,000	−10,000	−120,000	200,000	110,000	−52,000

Use present values to advise the management company which project is more profitable if the discount rate used is:

(i) 6%   (ii) 9%

9. Shields and Larkin Enterprises is a start-up business developing a new Spanish verb book.
The company directors decide to approach a venture capitalist to look for funding. They present the following cash flows for consideration:

Initial cash outflow	Year 0	-€12,000
Cash inflow	Year 1	€5,000
Cash inflow	Year 2	€7,000
Cash inflow	Year 3	€5,000
Cash outflow	Year 4	-€5,000
Cash inflow	Year 5	€8,000

What advice would you give the venture capitalist, given a projected growth rate of 2% for the period?

10.2 COMPOUND INTEREST: LOANS AND INVESTMENTS

Individuals and businesses do not always have enough cash to buy what they want or to pay their bills. It is sometimes necessary for them to borrow money. Equally, there are individuals and businesses that have large amounts of cash and so they decide to invest some of it.

If you borrow money from a bank or any financial institution, they will expect you to pay back the money you borrowed, but they will also charge you for the use of the money they loaned you. This is called **interest payable**.

In the case of loans and other forms of credit, there is a legal obligation to display the **annual percentage rate (APR)** prominently. APR is the rate at which the loan interest is calculated.

Annual Percentage Rate (APR) and Annual Equivalent Rate (AER)

> The **annual percentage rate (APR)** is the annual interest rate (expressed as a percentage to at least one decimal place) that makes the present value of all future payments equal to the present value of the loan.

There are clear rules stated in legislation regarding how APR is to be calculated:

- All monies the customer will have to pay must be included in the calculation, i.e. loan repayments, set-up charges, etc.
- In calculating the present values, time is measured in years from the date the loan is drawn down (received).

When you invest money in an investment account or a financial institution, you are giving the people who run the account or institution the use of your money. So they must pay you for the use of this money. This is called **investment interest**.

> In the case of investments, the rate of interest that is used to calculate the amount that is to be paid to the investor is called the **annual equivalent rate (AER)**.

> In Ireland there are a number of different names for **annual equivalent rate (AER)**, all of which mean the same thing: equivalent annual rate (EAR), compound annual return/ compound annual rate (CAR).

- Rules governing AER are not as specific as those governing APR.
- Investments do not have a guaranteed return.
- Calculation of AER involves estimates of future interest/growth rates.

When a loan or an investment is paid back in full, the total amount is the sum borrowed or invested plus the interest that was paid.

> Despite the difference in name (APR and AER) the method of calculation of both is exactly the same.

When dealing with interest, we use the following symbols:

F = Final value (amount borrowed/invested + interest)

P = Principal (amount borrowed/invested)

i = Rate of interest per annum (always use decimal form)

t = Time (length of time you had the loan or investment in years)

FORMULA

$$F = P(1 + i)^t$$

> The rate of interest that is used here, i, is the annual equivalent rate (AER) in the case of investments or annual percentage rate (APR) in the case of loans, as this formula assumes that compounding takes place once every year.
>
> However, if compounding takes place more frequently, the respective AER/APR must be adjusted for this change in the compounding period.

 ## Worked Example 10.4

Noreen borrows €10,000 for three years at an APR of 5% compounded annually. How much will she owe at the end of the third year?

Solution

$F = P(1 + i)^t$ $\qquad$ $P = 10{,}000$ $\qquad$ $t = 3$ $\qquad$ $i = 0.05$

$F = 10{,}000(1 + 0.05)^3$

$\therefore F = €11{,}576.25$

Worked Example 10.5

€15,000 is invested at an AER of 3%. At the beginning of the second year, €1,000 is withdrawn from this amount. The AER rises to 3.5% in the second year and remains at this rate for three years.

Calculate:

   (i)   The value of the investment at the end of Year 1

   (ii) The value of the investment at the end of Year 4

Solution

(i) $F = P(1 + i)^t$

   $P_0 = €15,000$

   $i = 3\% = 0.03 \quad t = 1$

   $F = 15,000(1 + 0.03)^1$

   $= 15,000(1.03)^1$

   $= 15,000(1.03)$

   $\therefore F = €15,450$

(ii) Value at the end of Year 1 = €15,450

   At the beginning of Year 2, €1,000 is withdrawn.

   $P_1 = €15,450 - €1,000 = €14,450$

   $i = 3.5\% = 0.035 \quad t = 3$

   $F = €14,450(1 + 0.035)^3$

   $= €14,450(1.035)^3$

   $\therefore F = €16,020.97$

   The value at the end of Year 4 is €16,020.97.

Worked Example 10.6

Mark invested money in a 5.5 year **bond** when he started First Year. In the middle of Sixth Year the bond matures and he has earned 21% interest in total.
Calculate the AER for this bond.

> A **bond** is a cash payment made to the government or to a private company for an agreed number of years. In return, the investor is paid a fixed sum at the end of each year; in addition, the government or company repays the original value of the bond to the investor with the final payment.

Solution

Step 1: Write down the formula.

   $F = P(1 + i)^t$

Step 2: Identify the parts that we are given in the question.

F	Final value	= Original amount + interest
		= 100% + 21%
		= 121%
		= 1.21
P	Principal	= Original amount
		= 100%
		= 1.00
t	Time in years = 5.5	
i	Annual equivalent rate = [*This is what we are looking for*]	

FINANCIAL MATHEMATICS

Step 3: Solve for the unknown value i.

$$1.21 = 1.00(1 + i)^{5.5}$$
$$1.21 = (1 + i)^{5.5}$$
$$\sqrt[5.5]{1.21} = 1 + i$$
$$1.0353 = 1 + i$$
$$1.0353 - 1 = i$$
$$i = 0.0353$$
$$\Rightarrow i = 3.53\%$$

> It is good practice to quote such a rate of interest to two decimal places where appropriate.

∴ The annual equivalent rate is 3.53%.

 ## Worked Example 10.7

A loan advertisement quotes an APR of 14.9%. Find, correct to four significant figures, the equivalent rate of interest, if compounded monthly.

Solution

Take a simple case of borrowing €1.

If you were to borrow €1 today, a year from now you would expect to pay back €1.149.

Future value = €1.149

Present value = €1.00

Compounding periods = $t \times 12$

$= 1 \times 12$

> The formula in the tables gives t as time in years. If we compound more frequently than annually, simply multiply t by the number of compounding periods, in this case 12 (12 months in a year).

So:
$$F = P(1 + i)$$
$$1.149 = 1(1 + i)^{12}$$
$$1.149 = (1 + i)^{12}$$
$$\sqrt[12]{1.149} = 1 + i$$
$$1.01164 - 1 = i$$
$$i = 0.01164 \Rightarrow i = 1.164\%$$

If compounding is to take place monthly, the rate of interest used is 1.164%.

 ## Exercise 10.2

> In Questions 1–10, no repayments or withdrawals are made until the end of the loan/investment.

1. €23,500 was invested at 5% per annum for three years. Calculate the final value.

2. €16,000 was invested at 3% per annum for six years. Calculate the interest.

3. €100,200 was invested at 4% per annum for eight years. Calculate the final value.

4. €12,000 was borrowed at 8% per annum for four years. Calculate the final value.

5. €105,000 was borrowed at 6% per annum for five years. Calculate the interest.

6. €25,400 was borrowed at 3.5% per annum for 10 years. Calculate the interest.

7. €200,500 was invested at 4.25% per annum for 15 years. Calculate the interest.

8. €100,500 was borrowed at 4.5% per annum for six years. Calculate the final value.

9. €1,000,000 was invested at 10.5% per annum for 3.5 years. Calculate the final value.

10. €90,600 was borrowed at 2.35% per annum for four years. Calculate the interest.

11. Find the amount, to the nearest cent, that needs to be invested at a rate of 5% per annum to give €2,500 in five years' time?

12. Find the amount, to the nearest cent, that needs to be invested at a rate of 3.2% per annum to give €120,500 in six years' time?

13. How much would Sharon need to invest now at a rate of 3.5% per annum to have €15,000 two years from now?

14. Howard receives a tax bill from the Revenue Commissioners for €14,000. He has the option to repay the lump sum in three years' time.

    He shops around for investment accounts and finds one that offers a return of 6% compounded annually for the three years; however, all investments must be in multiples of €1,000.

    How much will Howard need to invest to have the €14,000 in three years' time?

15. A not-for-profit organisation is trying to secure funding for an overseas aid project. They need €150,000 in total for the project and are advised that a grant is available for half of the funds if they can secure the other half before the date of application (five years from today).

    How much needs to be invested now if the rate of interest being offered is:

    (i) 6% per annum compounded annually

    (ii) 5% per annum compounded annually

16. Mustafa borrowed €365,000 at 3.6% per annum. At the end of Year 1 he repaid €20,000. The rate of interest was then lowered to 3.2%.

    How much does he owe at the end of the second year?

17. A football club borrowed €15,000,000 to revamp its stadium. The rate for the first year was 3.5% and the rate for the second year was 4.2%. Calculate the amount owing at the end of the second year.

18. A business secures a three-year loan for €45,000 with the following conditions attached:

    ■ The loan must be repaid in full by the end of the third year.

    ■ The rate of interest is 3% for the first two years. Then it decreases by 0.5%.

    Calculate the total interest that will be paid on this loan (to the nearest euro).

19. A 10-year loan is drawn down for €350,000. The rate of interest is 5.2% per annum compound interest.

    (i) How much interest is charged in the first year?

    (ii) How much interest will have been charged after 10 years if no repayment is made in the 10 years? (Answer to the nearest cent.)

    (iii) If €60,000 euro is paid off at the end of Year 1, what will the interest charge be for Year 2?

20. Fagan & Hanlon Ltd secures a loan from a private bank at €50,000 for five years at a rate of 6% per annum. If the loan is repaid with interest in one lump sum at the end of five years, the lender will give a 15% discount. Alternatively, the business can repay €10,000 at the end of each of Years 1–4 and the balance at the end of Year 5.

    Which option will cost the business less?

21. A sum of €6,000 is invested in an eight-year government bond with an annual equivalent rate (AER) of 6%.
    Find the value of the investment when it matures in eight years' time.

22. A sum of €5,000 is invested in an eight-year government bond with an annual equivalent rate (AER) of 3%.
    Find the value of the investment when it matures in eight years' time.

23. A bond offers a return of 20% after six years. Calculate the AER for this bond.

24. The National Treasury Management Agency offers a three-year savings bond with a return of 10%. Calculate the AER for this bond.

25. There are two types of National Solidarity Bond on offer:

    (A) A 4-year bond offering a gross return of 13.5%.

    (B) A 10-year bond offering a gross return of 45%.

    Using the AER, compare the two bonds and state which bond offers the better return.

26. Calculate the AER offered on this bond.

27. Calculate the number of years that it will take for a sum of €5,000 to grow to €20,000 when invested at 5.5% interest compounded annually (answer to two decimal places). (Hint: Use logs.)

28. Calculate the number of years that it will take for a sum of €400,000 to grow to €539,693.05 when invested at an AER of 10.5%

29. After a number of years, a €45,000,000 loan had risen in value to €58,985,820.45.
    If the fixed rate of interest on this loan was 7%, how many years had passed?

30. Calculate the number of years it will take for an investment fund to mature to €15,000, if €10,000 is invested at a growth rate of 5.5% per annum (answer to two decimal places).

31. An investment bond quotes an annual equivalent rate of 12.5%. If interest on the investment fund is compounded bi-annually (twice a year), what is the rate of interest for each compounding period?

32. A loan advertisement quotes an APR of 14.5%. If the loan interest is compounded monthly, what is the rate of interest per month?

33. Joe recently retired and received a lump sum of €100,000. He wants to invest his money in an An Post savings scheme. He gets information on two different products that are on offer.

Investments	Description
National Solidarity Bond (10-year)	50% gross return over 10 years
National Solidarity Bond (4-year)	15% gross return over 4 years

Which bond offers the better AER?

34. A bank is offering a Thrifty Savers account to all recent graduates. The account offers an AER of 6%. If the interest is to be compounded on a quarterly basis, what will the rate per quarter be?

35. (i) Danny borrowed €15,000 at an APR of 6%. Several years later, he discovered that the amount he repaid was €17,865.24.

    How many years did Danny have this loan for?

    (ii) At the time of the initial loan, Danny was offered a loan for €16,000 at a rate of 4.5% for the same period of time. Which loan would have been cheaper?

    (iii) Danny is currently borrowing money to purchase a new car. He saw an advertisement which quotes an APR of 7.8%. If this loan is compounded monthly, what is the rate of interest per month?

    (iv) Will there be a difference in the amount to be repaid if the loan is compounded monthly or annually? Explain your answer.

10.3 DEPRECIATION (REDUCING-BALANCE METHOD)

> **Depreciation** is calculated in order to write off the value of an asset over its useful economic life.

Causes of Depreciation

Wear and tear	Assets that are used over a period of time eventually wear out.	Example: Vehicles
Obsolescence	An asset becomes out of date because of the development of a more efficient or less expensive alternative.	Example: Computers
Passage of time	Assets lose value as they near the end of their licence.	Example: Patents
Extraction	The value of an asset reduces as the asset is extracted.	Example: Mining

Types of Depreciation

There are two methods of calculating depreciation in practice:

- **Straight-line method:** The amount written off the asset is the same each year until the total value of the asset is written off or it is reduced to its residual value.

- **Reducing-balance method:** Rather than charging a fixed amount every year, a (fixed) percentage of the remaining value of the asset is charged every year. Compared to straight-line depreciation, this method is more heavily weighted towards the early years.

For our syllabus, we will study the reducing-balance method only.

FORMULA

$$F = P(1 - i)^t$$

This formula appears on page 30 of *Formulae and Tables*.

ACTIVITY 10.2

> F is called the **later value** in the *Formulae and Tables* (page 30).
> In accounting, this is known as the **net book value (NBV)** of the asset.

 Worked Example 10.8

A van was purchased for €45,000. It is company policy to depreciate all vans at a rate of 20% per annum using the reducing-balance method.

(i) What is the net book value (NBV) of the asset after three years?

(ii) How much depreciation is written off this van in the first three years?

Solution

(i) $F = P(1 - i)^t$

$F = 45{,}000(1 - 0.20)^3$

$\quad = 45{,}000(0.8)^3$

$F = €23{,}040$

After three years, NBV = €23,040.

(ii) Depreciation written off

$\quad$ = Cost − Net book value

$\quad$ = €45,000 − €23,040

$\quad$ = €21,960

∴ Depreciation = €21,960

Worked Example 10.9

ABC Ltd purchased a delivery van costing €60,000. It is the policy of the company to depreciate all delivery vans at a rate of 20% using the reducing-balance method.

(i) Complete the schedule of depreciation below for the first five years of the asset's useful economic life:

Year	Cost (€)/NBV	Rate of depreciation	Depreciation (€)	NBV (€)
1	60,000.00	0.2	12,000.00	48,000.00
2				
3				
4				
5				

(ii) Verify the NBV at the end of Year 5 by using the formula for depreciation.

Solution

Step 1: Calculate the depreciation for the first year.

Step 2: Calculate the NBV of the asset at the end of Year 1.

NBV = Cost – Depreciation

Step 3: Repeat for Years 2 to 5.

Year	Cost (€)/NBV	Rate of depreciation	Depreciation (€)	NBV (€)
1	60,000.00	0.2	12,000.00	48,000.00
2	48,000.00	0.2	9,600.00	38,400.00
3	38,400.00	0.2	7,680.00	30,720.00
4	30,720.00	0.2	6,144.00	24,576.00
5	24,576.00	0.2	4,915.20	19,660.80

The value of the asset at the end of five years will be €19,660.80.

(ii) $F = P(1 - i)^t$

$F = 60,000(1 - 0.20)^5$

$= 60,000(0.8)^5$

$= 19,660.80$

∴ NBV after five years = €19,660.80

Worked Example 10.10

An accountant is auditing a set of books and sees that the net book value of an asset eight years after the date of purchase is €154,624. The policy of the company is to depreciate this asset at a rate of 12.5% using the reducing-balance method.
What was the original cost of the asset to the nearest euro?

Solution

$F = P(1 - i)^t$

$154,624 = P(1 - 0.125)^8$

$154,624 = P(0.875)^8$

$\Rightarrow \dfrac{154,624}{(0.875)^8} = P$

$\therefore P = €449,999.9647$

The original cost was approximately €450,000.

Worked Example 10.11

An asset which cost €150,000 now has a net book value of €88,573.50. The asset had been depreciated at a rate of 10% per annum. How many years' depreciation have been written off on the asset?

Solution

$F = P(1 - i)^t$

$88,573.50 = 150,000(1 - 0.10)^t$

$\dfrac{88,573.50}{150,000} = (0.9)^t$

$0.59049 = (0.9)^t$

$\ln(0.59049) = \ln(0.9)^t$

$\ln(0.59049) = t \ln(0.9)$

$\dfrac{\ln(0.59049)}{\ln(0.9)} = t$

$5 = t \qquad \therefore t = 5 \text{ years}$

Exercise 10.3

1. Using the reducing-balance method for depreciation, calculate the missing values in the table below correct to the nearest euro where necessary:

	Asset cost (€)	Rate of depreciation (%)	Number of years	Net book value
(i)	200,000	10	1	
(ii)	1,500,000	15	4	
(iii)	60,600	3	8	
(iv)	21,000	3.5	2	
(v)	34,000	18	4	
(vi)	16,000	2	6	
(vii)	12,000	25	4	

2. Using the reducing-balance method, calculate the missing values in the table below correct to two decimal places where necessary:

	Asset cost (€)	Rate of depreciation (%)	Number of years	Net book value
(i)	200,000	17	1	208,802.50
(ii)	400,000		4	
(iii)	140,000	3	8	
(iv)	100,000		2	93,122.50
(v)	34,000,000	18	4	
(vi)	24,000	2	6	
(vii)	120,000		4	37,968.75

3. How much will a €30,000 car be worth at the end of five years, given a depreciation rate of 20% per annum (reducing-balance method)?

4. A coal mine is depleted at a rate of 15% per annum. If the initial volume of coal in the mine is 400,000 m³, what volume of coal would there be in the mine after six years?

5. A car has a net book value of €19,660.80 at the end of five years, having been depreciated at a rate of 20% per annum (reducing-balance method).

What was the initial cost of the car?

6. A building has an NBV of €800,000 at the end of 10 years, having been depreciated at a rate of 2% (reducing-balance method). What was the original cost of the building? Give your answer correct to the nearest €100.

7. An asset which cost €95,000 now has a net book value of €56,096.55, having been depreciated for a number of years at a rate of 10%. For how many years was the asset depreciated?

8. The NBV of an asset is €162,901.25 and the depreciation rate for this particular asset is 5%. If the original cost was €200,000, how many years' depreciation have been written off this asset?

9. An accountant recently secured a new client who had not been keeping complete accounting records. The only information in relation to motor vehicles the client could present was as follows:

She changed her fleet of vehicles a number of years ago. The cost of the new fleet was €350,000. Her accountant at the time advised that she depreciate the fleet at a rate of 10% per annum. She provided one account which stated the net book value of the fleet was €206,671.50 and the date on this account was 31/12/2007.

(i) What was the net book value of the assets on 31/12/2010?

(ii) How many years' depreciation had been written off the asset by 31/12/2007?

(iii) In what year were the assets purchased (assuming a full year's depreciation is charged in the year of acquisition)?

10. A company's policy is to change all of its vehicles after three years, as it helps to reduce maintenance costs. If a vehicle which originally cost €45,400 now has a net book value of €29,056, having been depreciated for a number of years, is it due for a change? The company uses a 20% rate of depreciation per annum.

11. A data analysis system, with a total cost of €346,000, was installed in a university. The policy of the university is to  depreciate all analysis equipment and systems at a reducing-balance rate of 12.5% per annum. Due to the rapid development of technology, it is felt that such a system will be due for renewal every two and a half years. If the net book value of the system is now €264,906.25, how much longer will it be before the system should be updated?

12. A computer was purchased at the start of 2010 for €2,500. It is expected that the computer will only be worth €1,378.42 at the end of 2012.

    What is the rate of depreciation (reducing-balance method)? (Give your answer as a percentage correct to two decimal places.)

13. A lorry was purchased for €150,000 at the end of 2006. At the start of 2011 the lorry was sold at its NBV of €49,152. What was the annual rate of depreciation charged (reducing-balance method) on the lorry? (Answer correct to four significant figures.)

14. A pharmaceutical company has a patent on its newest headache tablet. The patent office has granted the patent for a 10-year period. In line with company policy, the accountants for the firm decide to write off the patent using a reducing-balance method. The patent is estimated to be worth €15,000,000 now. What annual rate of depreciation should the firm's accountants use in order to write the patent off over a 10-year period? (Hint: Let the residual value be €0.01.)

15. A company has a policy to depreciate all computers at a reducing-balance rate of 20%. Computers owned by the firm are valued (net book value) at €150,000. An auditor recently pointed out that due to increases in technology, computers were losing value at a much quicker rate than in previous years. The auditor estimated that the value of the computers in two years' time would only be €95,000. Does the firm have an adequate depreciation policy? Explain your answer.

10.4 APPLICATIONS AND PROBLEMS INVOLVING GEOMETRIC SERIES

Savings schemes and **loans** often involve making regular payments at fixed intervals of time.

- A **Smart Save account** is an example of a product where banks encourage customers to save a set amount each week or each month.
- A **mortgage** holder must make a monthly repayment against their loan.

Calculations involving regular payments discounted back to present values or adjusted to future values will involve the **summation** of a geometric series.

An **annuity** is a regular stream of fixed payments over a specified period of time, taking into account the time value of money. It is sometimes used in relation to a regular pension payment that lasts as long as the person is alive.

A **perpetuity** is an annuity in which regular payments (coupons) begin on a particular date and continue indefinitely. The amount invested is never redeemed. The value of the perpetuity is simply the payment divided by the rate:

$$PV = \frac{A}{r}$$

Amortisation is the process of accounting for a sum of money by making it equivalent to a series of payments over time.

An **amortised loan** is a loan that involves paying back a fixed amount at regular intervals over a fixed period of time, e.g. term loans and mortgages.

A **bond** is a cash payment made to the government or to a private company for an agreed number of years. In return, the investor is paid a fixed sum at the end of each year; in addition, the government or company repays the original value of the bond to the investor with the final payment.

Annuities also have a more specific meaning than the general meaning above.

An annuity is a form of investment involving a series of fixed regular payments (sometimes called contributions) made by a person to an account for a specified time period.

Interest may be compounded at the beginning **or** end of each period.

Pension funds involve making contributions to an annuity before retirement and receiving payments from the annuity after retirement.

■ When receiving payments from an annuity, the present value of the annuity is the lump sum that would have to be invested **now** in order to provide those regular future payments.

■ The future value of an annuity is the total value of the investment at the end of the specified period of time – it includes all payments as well as the interest earned.

Amortisation: Mortgages and Loans

FORMULA

$$A = P\dfrac{i(1+i)^t}{(1+i)^t - 1}$$

This formula appears on page 31 of *Formulae and Tables*.

ACTIVITY 10.3

A = Annual repayment amount i = Interest rate (as decimal)

P = Principal t = Time (in years)

This formula is usually used for calculating loan repayments.

The formula assumes that payments are made at the end of each accounting period.

To use it for calculating the payment that must be made into an annuity or pension fund, the total value of the fund must be discounted back to present value.

 ## Worked Example 10.12

A building society offers a savings account with an AER of 4%. If a customer saves €1,000 per annum starting now, how much will the customer have in five years' time?

Solution

Method 1

Present value		Future value
€1,000 invested for 5 years	$1,000(1.04)^5$	€1,216.65
€1,000 invested for 4 years	$1,000(1.04)^4$	€1,169.86
€1,000 invested for 3 years	$1,000(1.04)^3$	€1,124.86
€1,000 invested for 2 years	$1,000(1.04)^2$	€1,081.60
€1,000 invested for 1 years	$1,000(1.04)^1$	€1,040.00
		Total future value = €5,632.97

Method 2

Write as a series:

Amount $(A) = 1,000(1.04)^5 + 1,000(1.04)^4 + 1,000(1.04)^3 + 1,000(1.04)^2 + 1,000(1.04)^1$

$= 1,000[(1.04)^5 + (1.04)^4 + (1.04)^3 + (1.04)^2 + (1.04)^1]$

This is a geometric series with:

$$a = (1.04)^5 \qquad r = \frac{1}{1.04} \qquad n = 5$$

FORMULA

$$S_n = \frac{a(1 - r^n)}{1 - r}$$

This formula appears on page 22 of *Formulae and Tables*.

- Using a geometric series is particularly useful if n is large.
- Calculations may be easier if the order of the geometric series is reversed, i.e. write as $(1.04)^1 + (1.04)^2 + (1.04)^3 + (1.04)^4 + (1.04)^5$.

$$\therefore A = 1,000 \left[\frac{(1.04)^5 \left[1 - \left(\frac{1}{1.04}\right)^5\right]}{1 - \frac{1}{1.04}} \right]$$

$$= 1,000 \left[\frac{(1.04)^6 \left[1 - \left(\frac{1}{1.04}\right)^5\right]}{0.04} \right] \qquad \text{(Multiplying above and below by 1.04)}$$

$$= 1,000(5.6329754)$$

$$\therefore A = €5,632.97$$

Worked Example 10.13

If a loan for €60,000 is taken out at an APR of 3%, how much should the annual repayments be if the loan is to be repaid in 10 equal instalments over a 10-year period? Assume the first instalment is paid one year after the loan is drawn down. Give your answer correct to the nearest euro.

Solution

Method 1 Using the formula:

$$A = P\frac{i(1 + i)^t}{(1 + i)^t - 1}$$

$$P = €60,000 \qquad i = 0.03 \qquad t = 10$$

$$A = 60,000\frac{0.03(1 + 0.03)^{10}}{(1 + 0.03)^{10} - 1}$$

$$A = 7,033.830396$$

$$\therefore A \approx €7,034, \text{ i.e. the annual repayments should be } €7,034.$$

Method 2 Using present values and geometric series:

Let the annual repayments $= A$

The sum of all the discounted payments equals the loan amount.

As the initial repayment is made at the end of the first year, all repayments will be discounted.

$$€60,000 = \frac{A}{1.03} + \frac{A}{1.03^2} + \frac{A}{1.03^3} + \ldots + \frac{A}{1.03^{10}}$$

The right-hand side is a geometric series.

$$\frac{A}{1.03} + \frac{A}{1.03^2} + \frac{A}{1.03^3} + \ldots + \frac{A}{1.03^{10}}$$

$$= A\left[\frac{1}{1.03} + \frac{1}{1.03^2} + \frac{1}{1.03^3} + \ldots + \frac{1}{1.03^{10}}\right]$$

$$a = \frac{1}{1.03} \qquad r = \frac{1}{1.03} \qquad n = 10$$

$$\therefore 60{,}000 = A\left[\frac{\frac{1}{1.03}\left[1-\left(\frac{1}{1.03}\right)^{10}\right]}{1 - \frac{1}{1.03}}\right]$$

$$\Rightarrow 60{,}000 = A\left[\frac{1-\left(\frac{1}{1.03}\right)^{10}}{0.03}\right] \qquad \text{(Multiplying above and below by 1.03)}$$

$$60{,}000 = A\,(8.530202837)$$

$$\frac{60{,}000}{8.530202837} = A$$

$$A = \text{€}7{,}033.83 \approx \text{€}7{,}034$$

Note: Both methods must be known, as a particular method may be specified in a question.

Regular Payments at Intervals Other than Annually

Calculations are the same as for annual payments, but the AER or APR must be treated properly.

Option 1

- Leave time in years.
- Do not change the APR/AER.
- Use fractional units of time.

Option 2

- Switch to a different time period.
- We must adjust the APR/AER.
- Use integer units of time.

Worked Example 10.14

Alan borrows €10,000 at an APR of 6%. The terms of the loan state that the loan must be repaid in equal monthly instalments over 10 years. The first repayment will be one month from the date the loan is taken out. How much should the monthly repayment be? Give your answer to the nearest cent.

Solution

Using Option 1: Leave time in years

$$10{,}000 = \frac{A}{1.06^{\frac{1}{12}}} + \frac{A}{1.06^{\frac{2}{12}}} + \frac{A}{1.06^{\frac{3}{12}}} + \ldots + \frac{A}{1.06^{\frac{120}{12}}}$$

$$a = \frac{A}{1.06} \qquad r = \frac{1}{1.06^{\frac{1}{12}}} \qquad n = 120$$

$$S_{120} = \frac{\dfrac{A}{1.06^{\frac{1}{12}}}\left(\left(\dfrac{1}{1.06^{\frac{1}{12}}}\right)^{120} - 1\right)}{\dfrac{1}{1.06^{\frac{1}{12}}} - 1}$$

$$10{,}000 = 90.7243(A)$$

$$A = \frac{10{,}000}{90.7243}$$

$$A = 110.22405$$

$$A \approx \text{€}110.22$$

Using Option 2: Change time to months

Adjust APR:

$$F = P(1 + i)^t$$

$$1.06 = 1(1 + i)^{12}$$

$$\sqrt[12]{1.06} = 1 + i$$

$$i = 0.004867$$

$$A = P\frac{i(1 + i)^t}{(1 + i)^t - 1}$$

$$P = €10,000$$

> **Note:** This formula should only be used for a LOAN.

$t = 120$, i.e. compounded every month for 10 years

$$i = 0.004867$$

$$A = 10,000\frac{0.004867(1 + 0.004867)^{120}}{(1 + 0.004867)^{120} - 1}$$

$$A = €110.22$$

Worked Example 10.15

Denise wants to have €10,000 in her savings account in five year's time. If the expected interest rate is 2%, how much would Denise need to invest at the end of each year to reach her target?

Solution

Method 1: Using a geometric series

> It is important to note that Denise is investing at the **end** of each year.

$$10,000 = A + A(1.02)^1 + A(1.02)^2 + A(1.02)^3 + A(1.02)^4$$

RHS is a geometric series:

$$a = A \qquad r = 1.02 \qquad n = 5$$

$$S_5 = \frac{A(1 - 1.02^5)}{1 - 1.02}$$

$$\therefore 10,000 = \frac{A(1 - 1.02^5)}{1 - 1.02}$$

$$10,000 = 5.20404016A$$

$$\Rightarrow A = \frac{10,000}{5.20404016}$$

$$\Rightarrow A \approx €1,921.58$$

Method 2: Using the formula for amortisation of a loan

The only way to use this formula for an investment is to find the present value of the sum required and establish how many payments would be required to generate this amount.

Payments must also be made **at the end** of each accounting period (year in this case) for this formula to work.

Step 1: Find the present value of €10,000.

$$P = \frac{F}{(1 + i)^t}$$

$$P = \frac{10,000}{(1.02)^5}$$

$$\therefore P = €9,057.31$$

Step 2: Using the amortisation formula:

$$A = P\frac{i(1 + i)^t}{(1 + i)^t - 1}$$

$$A = 9,057.31\frac{0.02(1 + 0.02)^5}{(1 + 0.02)^5 - 1}$$

$$\Rightarrow A \approx €1,921.58$$

1. A building society offers a savings account with an AER of 4%. If a customer saves €2,000 per annum starting now, how much will the customer have in five years' time?

2. A bank offers a savings account with an effective annual rate of 3%. If a customer saves €1,000 per annum starting now, how much will the customer have in six years' time?

3. A building society offers a savings account with an AER of 4.5%. If a customer saves €2,000 per annum starting now, how much will the customer have in four years' time?

4. A building society offers a savings account with an AER of 4% compounded monthly. If a customer saves €150 each month starting now, how much will the customer have in five years' time?

5. A bank offers a savings account with an AER of 10% compounded monthly. If a customer saves €110 per month starting now, how much will the customer have in five years' time?

6. If a loan for €50,000 is taken out at an APR of 3%, how much should annual repayments be if the loan is to be repaid in 10 equal instalments over a 10-year period? Assume the first instalment is paid one year after the loan is drawn down.

7. A loan for €450,000 is taken out at an APR of 5.2%. How much should annual repayments be if the loan is to be repaid in 15 equal instalments over a 15-year period? Assume the first instalment is paid one year after the loan is drawn down.

8. A loan for €450,000 is taken out at an APR of 5.2%. If the customer wishes to make monthly repayments, how much should the repayments be if the loan is to be repaid in equal instalments over a 15-year period? Assume the first instalment is paid one month after the loan is drawn down.

9. A loan for €360,000 is taken out at an APR of 6%. How much should monthly repayments be if the loan is to be repaid in equal instalments over a 10-year period? Assume the first instalment is paid one month after the loan is drawn down.

10. A student wishes to set up his own business. He borrows €5,000 to finance the initial set-up costs and charges. The terms of the loan are as follows: interest is compounded monthly at a rate of 1% and the duration of the loan is six months.

    (a) Calculate the monthly repayment amount.

    (b) Make a schedule showing the monthly payment, the monthly interest and the balance outstanding at the end of each month.

11. A company wishes to raise capital to expand. It offers a 10-year €2,000 bond that will pay €100 every year for 10 years. Given that the expected annual market interest rate over the lifetime of the bond is 5%, is €2,000 a fair price to pay for this bond? Be careful to state clearly any assumptions that have been made.

12. ABC Finance issues a bond offer as detailed below:

    - 10-year bond
    - Pays €30 at the end of every six months for 10 years
    - AER = 6% interest compounded bi-annually

    What is a fair price for this bond?

13. Nicki deposits €200 at the end of each quarter in her savings account. The money earns 5.5% (AER). How much will the investment be worth at the end of four years? State clearly any assumptions that you make.

14. Eoin wants to have €5,000 in three years' time to travel to the USA on a J1 visa. How much will he need to deposit at the end of each month into an account that pays 8% (EAR)? (Remember: EAR and AER are used interchangeably.)

15. Mercedes took part in a TV game show and won the top prize. She is given two options:

(a) Receive €1,000 at the end of every month for the next 20 years.

(b) Take a lump sum now.

If the AER is 8%, what is the minimum amount Mercedes should accept as a lump sum?

16. Suppose you expect to receive a payment of €200 at the end of each year for an indefinite period of time.
What is the present value of this annuity?

17. Jack and David borrow €200,000 over 25 years at 3% APR.

(i) How much will they repay annually on this mortgage?

(ii) If they decide to make monthly repayments, how much will these repayments be?

18. Carol and James bought a house in 1992. They obtained a 35-year mortgage at a fixed annual interest rate of 5.2%. They had monthly payments of €1,800. In 2012, they decided to repay the mortgage in full. How much did they need to pay?
(Assume they had been paying their mortgage for exactly 20 years.)

19. Chelsea's parents wish to set up a regular savings account from the day she is born so that on her 21st birthday she will have €21,000. How much should they plan to deposit each month if they choose a regular savings plan with an AER of 3.5%?

20. Pádraig is 25 years old and is planning for his pension. He intends to retire in forty years' time, when he is 65. First, he calculates how much he wants to have in his pension fund when he retires. Then he calculates how much he needs to invest in order to achieve this. He assumes that in the long run, money can be invested at an inflation-adjusted annual rate of 3%. Your answers throughout this question should therefore be based on a 3% annual growth rate.

(a) Write down the present value of a future payment of €20,000 in one year's time.

(b) Write down, in terms of t, the present value of a future payment of €20,000 in t years' time.

(c) Pádraig wants to have a fund that could, from the date of his retirement, give him a payment of €20,000 at the start of each year for 25 years. Show how to use the sum of a geometric series to calculate the value on the date of retirement of the fund required.

(d) Pádraig plans to invest a fixed amount of money every month in order to generate the fund calculated in part (c). His retirement is $40 \times 12 = 480$ months away.

(i) Find, correct to four significant figures, the rate of interest per month that would, if paid and compounded monthly, be equivalent to an effective annual rate of 3%.

(ii) Write down, in terms of n and P, the value on the retirement date of a payment of €P made n months before the retirement date.

(iii) If Pádraig makes 480 equal monthly payments of €P from now until his retirement, what value of P will provide him with the fund he wants?

(iv) If Pádraig waits for 10 years before starting his pension investments, how much will he then have to pay each month in order to generate the same pension fund?

SEC Leaving Certificate Sample Paper 1, 2011

21. Most lottery games in the USA allow winners of the jackpot prize to choose between two forms of the prize: an *annual-payments* option or a *cash-value* option. In the case of the New York Lotto, there are 26 annual payments in the *annual-payments* option, with the first payment immediately, and the last payment in 25 years' time. The payments increase by 4% each year. The amount advertised as the jackpot prize is the total amount of these 26 payments. The *cash-value* option pays a smaller amount than this.

(a) If the amount of the first annual payment is A, write down, in terms of A, the amount of the second, third, fourth and 26th payments.

(b) The 26 payments form a geometric series. Use this fact to express the advertised jackpot prize in terms of A.

(c) Find, correct to the nearest dollar, the value of A that corresponds to an advertised jackpot prize of $21.5 million.

(d) A winner who chooses the cash-value option receives, immediately, the total of the present values of the 26 annual payments. The interest rate used for the present-value calculations is 4.78%. We want to find the cash value of the prize referred to in part (c).

   (i) Complete the table below to show the actual amount and the present value of each of the first three annual payments.

Payment number	Time to payment (years)	Actual amount ($)	Present value ($)
1	0		
2	1		
3	2		

   (ii) Write down, in terms of n, an expression for the present value of the nth annual payment.

   (iii) Find the amount of prize money payable under the cash-value option. That is, find the total of the present values of the 26 annual payments. Give your answer in millions, correct to one decimal place.

(e) The jackpot described in parts (c) and (d) above was won by an Irish woman earlier this year. She chose the cash-value option. After tax, she received $7.9 million. What percentage of tax was charged on her winnings? Give your answer to one place of decimals.

SEC Leaving Certificate Paper 1, 2011

22. Julie contributed €200 at the end of each week for 20 years to a pension fund earning 4.5% AER.

(a) Find the rate of interest per week that, if compounded weekly, would be equivalent to an AER of 4.5% (assume a 52-week year).

(b) What was her lump sum payment when she retired?

(c) Julie used her lump sum to purchase an annuity at 3.8% AER, giving her a regular payment at the start of each month for the next 20 years. What was her monthly payment?

1. Calculate the present value of each of the following correct to the nearest cent:

	Cash flow (€)	Years from now	Discount rate (%)	Present value (€)
(i)	210,000.00	1	8.0	
(ii)	148,000.50	2	8.0	
(iii)	27,800.00	2	5.0	
(iv)	450,000.00	10	4.0	
(v)	635,548.00	15	4.0	

2. Calculate the present value of €16,000 that is expected to be received in three years' time when the rate of interest for the period is 7.5% per annum compounded annually.

3. A project manager is presented with the following project as detailed in the table below:

Year	Cash flow (€)
1	120,000
2	120,000
3	120,000
Initial cash outflow (year 0) €40,000	Discount rate = 6%

   (a) Calculate the present value for each cash flow.

   (b) Calculate the net present value for the project.

   (c) Should the manager take on this project? Justify your answer.

4. Greg is presented with the following investment projects (all amounts are in euro.)

Year	0	1	2	3	4
Project A	−50,000	−13,000	14,000	26,000	28,000
Project B	−5,000	−2,000	1,000	4,000	7,000

   Using present values, advise Greg as to which project is the more profitable, if a discount rate of 6% is used.

5. (a) €1,000,000 was invested at 11.5% for 4.5 years. Calculate the final value. (No withdrawal is made over the 4.5 years.)

   (b) €90,000 was borrowed at 2.35% for 15 years. Calculate the interest earned. (No repayments are made until the end of the term.)

6. Find the amount, to the nearest cent, that needs to be invested at a rate of 3.2% per annum to give €245,000 in eight years' time.

7. How much would Sarah need to invest now at a rate of 3.25% to have €105,000 two years from now?

8. An investment bond quotes an annual equivalent rate of 13.5%. If interest on the investment fund is compounded bi-annually, what is the rate of interest for each compounding period? Answer correct to four significant figures.

9. A loan advertisement quotes an APR of 17.5%. If the loan interest is compounded monthly, what is the rate of interest per month? Answer correct to four significant figures.

10. Verify that the figures given in this advertisement are accurate.

Investments	Description
Savings certificates	Interest 21% after 5.5 years, AER 3.53% tax free
Savings bonds	Interest 10% after 3 years, AER 3.23% tax free

11. Calculate the missing values in the table below:

	Principal	Discount/ interest rate (annual)	Time (years)	Final value (€)
(i)	€120,000	10%	1	
(ii)	€4,000,000		6	8,327,807.01
(iii)	€280,000	−3%	8	
(iv)	€100,000		2	106,090
(v)	€34,000,000		4	15,372,139.34

12. A car has a net book value of €22,185.27 at the end of five years, having been depreciated at a rate of 20% per annum (reducing-balance method).

What was the initial cost of the car?

13. A building has an NBV of €700,000 at the end of eight years, having been depreciated at a rate of 2% (reducing-balance method). What was the original cost of the building? (Give your answer correct to the nearest €100.)

14. An asset which cost €95,000 now has a net book value of €50,486.90, having been depreciated for a number of years at a rate of 10%. How many years was the asset depreciated for?

15. The NBV of an asset is €694,511.89. The depreciation rate for this particular asset is 2%. Having originally cost €850,000, how many years depreciation have been written off this asset?

16. A building society offers a savings account with an AER of 4%. If a customer saves €5,000 per annum starting now, how much will the customer have in five years' time?

17. A bank offers a savings account with an effective annual rate of 3%. If a customer saves €1,500 per annum starting now, how much will the customer have in 12 years' time?

18. If a loan for €150,000 is taken out at an APR of 3%, how much should the annual repayments be if the loan is to be repaid in 10 equal instalments over a 10-year period? Assume the first instalment is paid one year after the loan is drawn down.

19. The management company for a sports centre estimates that it will need €30,000 to replace the floors in the squash courts in five years' time. If regular payments are made to an investment fund earning 2.75% AER, calculate:

(a) The rate of interest per month that would be equivalent to an AER of 2.75%; answer correct to four significant figures

(b) The amount that must be deposited at the end of each month to meet this target

(c) How much interest will be earned in the five-year period

20. O'Reilly-Elwood Finance Company issues a bond offer as detailed below:

- 10-year bond
- Pays €100 at the end of every six months for 10 years
- AER = 5% interest compounded bi-annually

What is a fair price for this bond?

21. Ruadhán recently retired and was offered the following retirement package: a regular payments option valued at €110,000.

The annual payments option offered 21 payments over 20 years, with an initial payment on the date of retirement and an annual payment for the next 20 years. To reflect increases in the cost of living, all payments increase by 2.5% each year. The value of the regular payments option is the sum of the 21 payments.

  (i) If the annual payment is A, write down in terms of A the value of the second, third and last payment.

 (ii) Using a geometric series, express the value of the regular payments option in terms of A.

(iii) How much will the regular payment A amount to?

chapter 11

Proof by Induction

Learning Outcomes

In this chapter you will learn:

- ➲ The notation for summations
- ➲ Mathematical induction
- ➲ How to use induction to prove statements about series
- ➲ How to use induction to prove statements about divisibility
- ➲ How to use induction to prove statements about inequalities

11.1 INTRODUCTION

Proof is central to mathematics and is one of the reasons why the subject is regarded as having many 'truths'. In mathematics, theories must be proved to be accepted as being true. Proof is the process of reaching the conclusion that is believed to be true. We start with what we believe or accept is true and construct a logical argument to arrive at what we want to prove.

> Axioms are mathematical statements that we accept as true from the start. They do not need to be proved.

There are several methods that can be used to prove that a hypothesis or proposition is true or that it is false. These include:

■ Proof by deduction (e.g. the sum of the angles in a triangle is 180°)

■ Disproof by counter-example (e.g. the sum of two primes is prime)

■ Proof by contradiction – *reductio ad absurdum* (e.g. to prove that $\sqrt{2}$ is irrational)

■ Proof by induction

This chapter will focus on proof by induction.

> **Mathematical induction** is a method of proof. We use this method to prove certain propositions involving the natural numbers.

Francesco Maurolico

Andrew Wiles

The earliest example of **mathematical induction** can be found in Euclid's proof that there are an infinite number of prime numbers. The Greek mathematician Francesco Maurolico, in his *Arithmeticorum libri duo* (1575), used the technique to prove that the sum of the first n odd integers is n^2.

In more recent times, the British-born mathematician Andrew Wiles used mathematical induction to prove Fermat's Last Theorem. He spent 10 years working on the proof, which was published in 1994.

11.2 SUMMATIONS

In this section we introduce notation for summations. The following notation represents the sum of the linear or arithmetic sequence 3, 6, 9, 12, ... $3n$.

$$\sum_{r=1}^{n} 3r = 3(1) + 3(2) + 3(3) + \ldots + 3(n) = 3 + 6 + 9 + 12 + \ldots + 3n$$

The symbol on the left-hand side of the equation above is the Greek capital letter **sigma**. r runs through all the natural numbers from 1 to n, to give each term in the series.

Worked Example 11.1

Evaluate $\displaystyle\sum_{r=1}^{8} r^4$.

Solution

$$\sum_{r=1}^{8} r^4 = 1^4 + 2^4 + 3^4 + 4^4 + 5^4 + 6^4 + 7^4 + 8^4$$

$$= 8772$$

Worked Example 11.2

Show that:

$$\sum_{r=1}^{4} (r^4 + r^2) = \sum_{r=1}^{4} r^4 + \sum_{r=1}^{4} r^2$$

Solution

$$\sum_{r=1}^{4} (r^4 + r^2) = (1^4 + 1^2) + (2^4 + 2^2) + (3^4 + 3^2) + (4^4 + 4^2)$$

$$= 1^4 + 2^4 + 3^4 + 4^4 + 1^2 + 2^2 + 3^2 + 4^2$$

$$= \sum_{r=1}^{4} r^4 + \sum_{r=1}^{4} r^2$$

Worked Example 11.3

Evaluate $\displaystyle\sum_{r=1}^{5} 3$.

Solution

$$\sum_{r=1}^{5} 3 = \sum_{r=1}^{5} 3\, r^0$$

$$= 3(1^0) + 3(2^0) + 3(3^0) + 3(4^0) + 3(5^0)$$

$$= 3 + 3 + 3 + 3 + 3$$

$$= 5(3)$$

$$\therefore \sum_{r=1}^{5} 3 = 15$$

ACTIVITY 11.1

Exercise 11.1

1. Find the value of each of the following sums:

(i) $\displaystyle\sum_{r=1}^{10} r$

(ii) $\displaystyle\sum_{r=1}^{10} r^2$

(iii) $\displaystyle\sum_{r=1}^{10} 2^r$

(iv) $\displaystyle\sum_{r=1}^{10} 2$

2. Find the value of each of the following sums:

(i) $\displaystyle\sum_{r=4}^{8} (r-2)$

(ii) $\displaystyle\sum_{r=2}^{7} (r-2)^2$

(iii) $\displaystyle\sum_{r=1}^{6} r!$

(iv) $\displaystyle\sum_{r=3}^{9} r(r+1)$

3. Express each of the following using $\sum$ notation:

   (i) $1^3 + 2^3 + 3^3 + 4^3 + 5^3 + 6^3$

   (ii) $5 + 5 + 5 + 5 + 5 + 5$

   (iii) $3 + 3^2 + 3^3 + 3^4 + 3^5$

   (iv) $5 + 25 + 125 + 625 + 3125$

4. Express each of the following using $\sum$ notation:

   (i) $1 + 2 + 3 + 4 + 5 + \ldots (n-1) + n$

   (ii) $5^2 + 6^2 + 7^2 + \ldots + n^2$

   (iii) $3! + 4! + 5! + \ldots n!$

   (iv) $16 + 20 + 24 + \ldots + 4n$

5. Prove each of the following:

   (i) $\displaystyle\sum_{r=1}^{5} r^2 + \sum_{r=1}^{5} 2r + \sum_{r=1}^{5} 1 = \sum_{r=1}^{5} (r+1)^2$

   (ii) $\displaystyle\sum_{r=3}^{8} r^3 + \sum_{r=3}^{8} 1 = \sum_{r=3}^{8} (r+1)(r^2 - r + 1)$

   (iii) $\displaystyle\sum_{r=6}^{10} r^2 - \sum_{r=6}^{10} 1 = \sum_{r=6}^{10} (r-1)(r+1)$

   (iv) $\displaystyle\sum_{r=5}^{12} 6r^2 = 6\sum_{r=5}^{12} r^2$

6. Express each of the following in terms of x and y, where $x = \displaystyle\sum_{r=m}^{n} r$ and $y = \displaystyle\sum_{r=m}^{n} r^2$:

   (i) $\displaystyle\sum_{r=m}^{n} 7r$ (iii) $\displaystyle\sum_{r=m}^{n} r(r-1)$

   (ii) $\displaystyle\sum_{r=m}^{n} (r^2 + r)$ (iv) $\displaystyle\sum_{r=m}^{n} (3r^2 + 2r)$

11.3 PROOF BY INDUCTION

As stated earlier, the Greek mathematician Francesco Maurolico proved that the sum of the first n odd natural numbers is n^2. Before he embarked on this proof, he would have first **conjectured** that the sum was n^2.

> To conjecture is to make a guess based on the available evidence.

How would Maurolico have come up with the idea that the sum of the first n odd natural numbers is n^2? More than likely he would have studied patterns of numbers, as shown in the table below.

1	1	1^2
1 + 3	4	2^2
1 + 3 + 5	9	3^2
1 + 3 + 5 + 7	16	4^2
1 + 3 + 5 + 7 + 9	25	5^2

The table indicates that the sum of the first n odd natural numbers is n^2. To be more confident that the conjecture could be true, we should include more rows. However, no matter how many rows we include, we could not include every case as there is an infinite amount of natural numbers. What is needed is a proof for every natural number that exists and the correct method of proof in this case is mathematical induction.

Mathematical Induction

Mathematical induction is a method of mathematical proof used to establish that a given statement is true for natural numbers.

The first step in the proof is proving that the first statement in the infinite sequence of statements is true (i.e. verifying that $1 = 1^2$ in the example above).

The next step is proving that if any one statement in the infinite sequence of statements is true, then so is the next one.

Imagine an infinitely long hotel corridor containing an infinite number of rooms.

All rooms are locked and you need to open all of the doors. You have secured the key for room number 1.
Also, you have just discovered that the key for room number $k + 1$ is locked in room number k. For example, the key for room number 1000 is locked in room number 999. Will you be able to open all doors? The answer is yes. When you open room number 1, you will find the the key for room 2, room 2 will contain the key for room 3 and so on. This is an example of mathematical induction.

11.4 PROOFS INVOLVING SERIES

In this section we will use induction to prove statements involving series.

Worked Example 11.4

Prove by induction, for all $n \in N$: $\displaystyle\sum_{r=1}^{n} 4n = 2n(n + 1)$

Solution

To prove:

$$\sum_{r=1}^{n} 4n = 2n(n + 1), \text{ for all } n \in N \quad \textbf{OR} \quad 4 + 8 + 12 + \ldots + 4n = 2n(n + 1), \text{ for all } n \in N$$

Proof:

Step 1: Show that the proposition is true for $n = 1$.

LHS: 4

RHS: $2(1)(1 + 1) = 4$

Hence, the proposition is true for $n = 1$.

Step 2: Assume that the proposition is true for $n = k$.

$$4 + 8 + 12 + \ldots + 4k = 2k(k + 1)$$

Step 3: Prove that the proposition is true for $n = k + 1$, given that it is true for $n = k$.

To prove:

$$4 + 8 + 12 + \ldots + 4k + 4(k + 1) = 2(k + 1)(k + 2)$$

Proof:

$$4 + 8 + 12 \ldots + 4k = 2k(k + 1) \quad [\text{Assumption}]$$

$$4 + 8 + 12 \ldots + 4k + 4(k + 1) = 2k(k + 1) + 4(k + 1) \quad [\text{Add } 4(k + 1) \text{ to both sides}]$$

$$= 2k^2 + 2k + 4k + 4$$

$$= 2k^2 + 6k + 4$$

$$= 2(k^2 + 3k + 2)$$

$$= 2(k + 1)(k + 2)$$

$\therefore$ The proposition is true for $n = k + 1$, given that it is true for $n = k$.

Step 4: The proposition is true for $n = 1$. If the proposition is true for $n = k$, then it will be true for $n = k + 1$. Therefore, by induction it is true for all $n \in N$.

Prove by induction, for all $n \in N$: $\displaystyle\sum_{r=1}^{n} n^3 = \left[\frac{n}{2}(n+1)\right]^2$

Solution

To prove:

$$\sum_{r=1}^{n} n^3 = \left[\frac{n}{2}(n+1)\right]^2, \text{ for all } n \in N$$

OR

$$1^3 + 2^3 + 3^3 + \ldots + n^3 = \left[\frac{n}{2}(n+1)\right]^2, \text{ for all } n \in N$$

Proof:

Step 1: Show true for $n = 1$

LHS: $1^3 = 1$

RHS: $\left[\frac{1}{2}(1+1)\right]^2 = 1$

Hence, the proposition is true for $n = 1$.

Step 2: Assume that the proposition is true for $n = k$.

$$1^3 + 2^3 + 3^3 + \ldots + k^3 = \left[\frac{k}{2}(k+1)\right]^2$$

Step 3: Prove that the proposition is true for $n = k + 1$, given that it is true for $n = k$.

To prove:

$$1^3 + 2^3 + 3^3 + \ldots + k^3 + (k+1)^3 = \left[\frac{k+1}{2}(k+2)\right]^2$$

Proof:

$$1^3 + 2^3 + 3^3 + \ldots + k^3 = \left[\frac{k}{2}(k+1)\right]^2 \quad \text{[Assumption]}$$

$$1^3 + 2^3 + 3^3 + \ldots + k^3 + (k+1)^3 = \left[\frac{k}{2}(k+1)\right]^2 + (k+1)^3$$

$$= \frac{k^2}{4}(k+1)^2 + (k+1)^3$$

$$= (k+1)^2\left[\frac{k^2}{4} + k + 1\right]$$

$$= \frac{(k+1)^2}{4}[k^2 + 4k + 4]$$

$$= \frac{(k+1)^2}{2^2}[k+2]^2$$

$$= \left[\frac{k+1}{2}(k+2)\right]^2$$

$\therefore$ The proposition is true for $n = k + 1$, given that it is true for $n = k$.

Step 4: The proposition is true for $n = 1$. If the proposition is true for $n = k$, then it will be true for $n = k + 1$. Therefore by induction it is true for all $n \in N$.

Exercise 11.2

1. Prove by induction for all positive integers n:

   $$1 + 5 + 9 + 13 + ... + (4n - 3) = \frac{n}{2}(4n - 2)$$

2. Prove by induction for all $n \in N$:

   $$\sum_{r=1}^{n} 2r = n(n + 1)$$

3. Prove by induction for all $n \in N$:

   $$\sum_{r=1}^{n} 5r = \frac{5n}{2}(n + 1)$$

4. Prove by induction for all positive integers n:

   $$\sum_{r=1}^{n} 3r = \frac{3n}{2}(n + 1)$$

5. Prove by induction that:

   $$10 + 10^2 + 10^3 + ... + 10^n = \frac{10}{9}(10^n - 1)$$

   for all $n \in N$.

6. Prove by induction that:

   $$\sum_{r=1}^{n} x^{r-1} = \frac{1 - x^n}{1 - x} \text{ for all } n \in N, x \notin \{0, 1\}$$

7. Prove by induction that:

   $$\sum_{r=1}^{n} 2^{r-1} = 2^n - 1 \text{ for all } n \in N$$

8. Prove by induction for all positive integers n:

   $$1 + 2(2) + 3(2^2) + 4(2^3) + ... + n(2^{n-1})$$
   $$= (n - 1) \cdot 2^n + 1$$

9. Prove by induction that:

   $$\sum_{r=1}^{n} (r^2 + 1)(r!) = n[(n + 1)!] \text{ for all } n \in N$$

10. $f(x) = \frac{x}{6}(x + 1)(2x + 1)$

    (i) Evaluate $f(1)$ and $f(2)$.

    (ii) Given that $f(x + 1) = \frac{x + 1}{6}(ax + b)(x + a)$ and using your answers to (i), find the value of a and the value of b, where $a, b \in N$.

    (iii) Prove by induction that:

    $$\sum_{r=1}^{n} r^2 = \frac{n}{6}(n + 1)(2n + 1)$$

---

11. (i) Prove that:

    $$1 + 3 + 5 + ... + (2n - 1) = n^2, \text{ for all } n \in N$$

    (ii) Prove that:

    $$2 + 4 + 6 + ... + 2n = n(n + 1), \text{ for all } n \in N$$

    (iii) Using only your results from (i) and (ii), explain why:

    $$\sum_{r=1}^{2n} r = n(2n + 1), \text{ for all } n \in N$$

12. Prove that:

    $$\sum_{r=2}^{n} \frac{1}{r^2 - 1} = \frac{3}{4} - \frac{2n + 1}{2n(n + 1)}, n \geqslant 2, n \in N$$

ACTIVITIES 11.2, 11.3

11.5 DIVISIBILITY PROOFS

When an integer is divided by a second non-zero integer, the answer may or may not be an integer. For instance, $\frac{45}{9} = 5$ is an integer, whereas $\frac{12}{5} = 2.4$ is not an integer.

> If a and b are integers with $a \neq 0$, we say that b is divisible by a if there is an integer c such that $b = ac$.

Proposition: If $f(k)$ is divisible by some non–zero integer m, and $f(k + 1) \pm f(k)$ is divisible by m, then $f(k + 1)$ is divisible by m.

Proof: $f(k) = mn_1$, for some $n_1 \in N$

$f(k + 1) \pm f(k) = mn_2$, for some $n_2 \in N$

$\therefore f(k + 1) \pm mn_1 = mn_2$

$\therefore f(k + 1) = mn_2 \pm mn_1$

$= m(n_2 \pm n_1)$

Therefore, $f(k + 1)$ is divisible by m.

Σ Worked Example 11.6

Prove by induction that $10^n - 7^n$ is divisible by 3, for all $n \in N$.

Solution

First, write the expression using function notation:

$f(n) = 10^n - 7^n$

To prove:

$f(n) = 10^n - 7^n$ is divisible by 3, for all $n \in N$

Proof:

Step 1: Show that the proposition is true for $n = 1$.

$f(1) = 10^1 - 7^1$

$= 10 - 7$

$= 3$

3 is divisible by 3, therefore the proposition is true for $n = 1$.

Step 2: Assume the proposition is true for $n = k$.

$f(k) = 10^k - 7^k$ is divisible by 3.

Step 3: Prove the proposition is true for $n = k + 1$, given that it is true for $n = k$.

$f(k + 1) = 10^{k+1} - 7^{k+1}$

$= (10)10^k - (7)7^k$

$f(k + 1) - f(k) = (10)10^k - (7)7^k - 10^k + 7^k$

$= 10^k(10 - 1) + 7^k(-7 + 1)$

$= 10^k(9) + 7^k(-6)$

$= 3\left[10^k(3) + 7^k(-2)\right]$

Therefore, $f(k + 1) - f(k)$ is divisible by 3. As a result, we conclude that $f(k + 1)$ is divisible by 3, having assumed $f(k)$ is divisible by 3.

$\therefore$ The proposition is true for $n = k + 1$.

Step 4: The proposition is true for $n = 1$. If the proposition is true for $n = k$, then it will be true for $n = k + 1$. Therefore, by induction it is true for all $n \in N$.

Alternative method

Proposition: $P(n)$: $10^n - 7^n$ is divisible by 3, $n \in N$.

Step 1: Show that the proposition is true for $n = 1$.

$$P(1) = 10^1 - 7^1$$

$$= 10 - 7$$

$$= 3 \qquad \qquad \therefore P(1) \text{ is true.}$$

Step 2: Assume that the proposition is true for $n = k$,

i.e. $10^k - 7^k = 3A$, $A \in Z$.

$$\therefore 10^k = 3A + 7^k$$

Step 3: Prove that the proposition is true for $n = k + 1$, given that it is true for $n = k$.

$$P(k + 1) = 10^{k+1} - 7^{k+1}$$

$$= 10.10^k - 7.7^k$$

$$= 10[3A + 7^k] - 7.7^k$$

$$= 30A + 10.7^k - 7.7^k$$

$$= 30A + 3.7^k$$

$$\therefore P(k + 1) = 3[10A + 7^k]$$

$$\therefore P(k + 1) = 3B, \ B \in Z$$

$\therefore$ The proposition is true for $n = k + 1$, given that it is true for $n = k$.

Step 4: The proposition is true for $n = 1$.

If the proposition is true for $n = k$, then it will be true for $n = k + 1$.

Therefore, by induction it is true for all $n \in N$.

Σ Worked Example 11.7

Prove by induction that $n^2 + 3n$ is divisible by 2 for all $n \in N$.

Solution

First, write the expression using function notation:

$$f(n) = n^2 + 3n$$

To prove:

$$f(n) = n^2 + 3n \text{ is divisible by 2 for all } n \in N.$$

Proof:

Step 1: Show that the proposition is true for $n = 1$.

$$f(1) = 1^2 + 3(1)$$

$$= 4$$

4 is divisible by 2.

Hence, the proposition is true for $n = 1$.

Step 2: Assume that the proposition is true for $n = k$.

$$f(k) = k^2 + 3k \text{ is divisible by 2.}$$

Step 3: Prove that the proposition is true for $n = k + 1$, given that it is true for $n = k$.

$$f(k + 1) = (k + 1)^2 + 3(k + 1)$$
$$= k^2 + 2k + 1 + 3k + 3$$
$$= k^2 + 3k + 2(k + 2)$$
$$= f(k) + 2(k + 2)$$

$\therefore$ We conclude that $f(k + 1)$ is divisible by 2, having assumed that $f(k)$ is divisible by 2.

$\therefore$ The proposition is true for $n = k + 1$.

Step 4: The proposition is true for $n = 1$. If the proposition is true for $n = k$, then it will be true for $n = k + 1$. Therefore, by induction it is true for all $n \in N$.

Exercise 11.3

1. Prove that $P(n) = 7^n - 1$ is divisible by 6, for all $n \in N$.

2. Prove that $3^{2n} - 1$ is divisible by 8, for all $n \in N$.

3. $f(n) = 8^n + 6$, for all $n \in N$.

   (i) Evaluate $f(1)$.

   (ii) Show that $f(k + 1) = 8(8^k + 6) - 42$.

   (iii) Assuming that $f(k)$ is divisible by 7, explain why $f(k + 1)$ must also be divisible by 7.

   (iv) Hence prove by induction that:

   $8^n + 6$ is divisible by 7, for all $n \in N$.

4. $f(n) = 6^n - 1$, for all $n \in N$.

   (i) Evaluate $f(1)$.

   (ii) Show that $f(k + 1) = 6(6^k - 1) + 5$.

   (iii) Assuming that $f(k)$ is divisible by 5, explain why $f(k + 1)$ must also be divisible by 5.

   (iv) Hence, prove by induction that:

   $6^n - 1$ is divisible by 5, for all $n \in N$.

In Questions 5 to 9 below, use induction to prove the statements.

5. $7^{2n + 1} + 1$ is divisible by 8, for all $n \in N$.

6. 3 is a factor of $4^n - 1$, $n \in N$.

7. $2^{3n} - 1$ is divisible by 7, for all $n \in N$.

8. $7^n - 3^n$ is divisible by 4, for all $n \in N$.

9. $5^{2n} + 12^{n - 1}$ is divisible by 13, for all $n \in N$.

10. Prove by induction that $n^2 + 15n + 4$ is an even number for all $n \in N$.

11. Prove by induction that $n^3 - n$ is divisible by 3, for all $n \in N$.

12. Prove by induction that $n^2 + n$ is divisible by 2, for all $n \in N$.

13. Prove by induction that $n(n + 1)(2n + 1)$ is divisible by 3, for all $n \in N$.

11.6 INEQUALITIES

When dealing with **inequalities**, it is important to know the rules of inequalities.

1. If $a \neq b$, then either $a < b$ or $b < a$.

2. If $a < b$ and $b < c$, then $a < c$.

3. If $a < b$, then $a + c < b + c$.

4. If $a < b$ and $c > 0$, then $ac < bc$.

5. If $a < b$ and $c < 0$, then $ac > bc$.

6. $a^2 \geqslant 0$

$$a, b, c \in R$$

Worked Example 11.8

Prove by induction that $4^n > 4n + 1, n \geqslant 2, n \in N$.

Solution

To prove: $4^n > 4n + 1, n \geqslant 2, n \in N$

Proof:

Step 1: Show that the proposition is true for $n = 2$.

LHS: $(4)^2 = 16$

RHS: $4(2) + 1 = 9$

$16 > 9$

Hence, the proposition is true for $n = 2$.

> Be careful with the initial condition. It does not have to be $n = 1$.

Step 2: Assume the proposition is true for $n = k$.

$4^k > 4k + 1$

Step 3: Prove the proposition is true for $n = k + 1$, given that it is true for $n = k$.

To prove:

$$4^{k+1} > 4(k + 1) + 1$$
$$\Rightarrow 4^{k+1} > 4k + 5$$

Proof:

$4^{k+1} = 4(4^k)$

$\qquad > 4(4k + 1)$ [Assumption]

Now we need to show that $4(4k + 1) \geqslant 4k + 5$.

$4(4k + 1) \geqslant 4k + 5$

if $16k + 4 \geqslant 4k + 5$

if $12k - 1 \geqslant 0$ This inequality is true if $k \geqslant 2$.

$\therefore 4^{k+1} > 4k + 5$

$\therefore$ The proposition is true for $n = k + 1$, given that it is true for $n = k$.

Step 4: The proposition is true for $n = 2$. If the proposition is true for $n = k$, then it will be true for $n = k + 1$. Therefore, by induction it is true for $n \geqslant 2, n \in N$.

Worked Example 11.9

Prove by induction that $n! \leqslant n^n$ for $n \in N$.

Solution

To prove: $n! \leqslant n^n$ for $n \in N$.

Proof:

Step 1: Show true for $n = 1$

$1! \leqslant 1^1$

$1 \leqslant 1$

Hence, the proposition is true for $n = 1$.

Step 2: Assume the proposition is true for $n = k$.

$k! \leqslant k^k$

Step 3: Prove the proposition is true for $n = k + 1$, given that it is true for $n = k$.

To prove:

$(k + 1)! \leqslant (k + 1)^{k + 1}$

Proof:

$(k + 1)! = (k + 1)k!$

$\leqslant (k + 1)k^k$ [Assumption]

$< (k + 1)(k + 1)^k$ [since $k^k < (k + 1)^k$]

$\therefore (k + 1)! \leqslant (k + 1)^{k + 1}$

$\therefore$ The proposition is true for $n = k + 1$, given that it is true for $n = k$.

Step 4: The proposition is true for $n = 1$. If the proposition is true for $n = k$, then it will be true for $n = k + 1$. Therefore by induction, it is true for all $n \in N$.

Exercise 11.4

In Questions 1 to 5 below, prove each statement is true using induction:

1. $2^n \geqslant 1 + n$, for all $n \in N$.

2. $3^n > 2n$, for all $n \in N$.

3. $n! > 2^n, n \geqslant 4, n \in N$.

4. $n^2 > 4n + 3, n \geqslant 5, n \in N$.

5. $2^n \geqslant n^2, n \geqslant 4, n \in N$.

6. (i) Prove that $3^n > n^2, n \geqslant 2, n \in N$.

(ii) Prove that $3^n < (n + 1)!, n \geqslant 4, n \in N$.

(iii) Explain why $n^2 < 3^n < (n + 1)!, n \geqslant 4$, $n \in N$.

(iv) Arrange the following in order of increasing magnitude, giving a reason for your arrangement: 3^{700}, $701!$, 700^2.

7. (i) Prove that $4n + 2 < n^2, n \geqslant 5, n \in N$.

(ii) Prove that $n^2 < 2^n, n \geqslant 5, n \in N$.

(iii) Hence, show that $4n + 2 < n^2 < 2^n$, $n \geqslant 5, n \in N$.

8. Prove by induction that: $(1 + x)^n \geqslant 1 + nx$, $x > -1, n \in N$.

9. Prove that $(1 + 3x)^n \geqslant 1 + 3nx$ for $x > 0$ and $n \in N$.

10. There are n people in a room. All of the people in the room shake hands with one another. If H is the total number of handshakes, then prove using induction that:

$$H \leqslant \frac{n}{2}(n - 1)$$

11. Prove using induction that $(2n)! < 2^{2n}(n!)^2$, for every $n \in N$.

Revision Exercises

1. Find the value of each of the following sums:

(i) $\displaystyle\sum_{r=4}^{8} (r^2 - 2)$

(ii) $\displaystyle\sum_{r=2}^{7} (2r - 2)^3$

(iii) $\displaystyle\sum_{r=1}^{6} (r + 2)!$

(iv) $\displaystyle\sum_{r=3}^{9} r(r^2 + 1)$

2. (i) Evaluate $\displaystyle\sum_{r=1}^{6} 10r$.

(ii) Prove using induction that:

$$\sum_{r=1}^{n} 10r = 5n(n + 1), \text{ for all } n \in N.$$

(iii) Hence, evaluate $\displaystyle\sum_{r=1}^{40} 10r$.

3. A sum of €1,000 is invested at the beginning of each year for n years. The money earns 5.75% EAR.

   (i) Write in the form: $\sum_{r=1}^{n} P(1+i)^r$

   the value of the investment at the end of n years.

   (ii) Prove using induction that the value of the investment at the end of n years is:

   $I[1.0575^n - 1]$, where $I = \dfrac{423{,}000}{23}$.

   (iii) Find the value of the investment after 10 years.

4. A sum of €10,000 is invested at the beginning of each year for n years. The money earns 4.25% EAR.

   (i) Write in the form: $\sum_{r=1}^{n} P(1+i)^r$

   the value of the investment at the end of n years.

   (ii) Prove using induction that the value of the investment at the end of n years is:

   $I[1.0425^n - 1]$, where $I = \dfrac{4{,}170{,}000}{17}$.

   (iii) Find the value of the investment after 20 years.

5. (i) Prove that:

   $1^2 + 3^2 + 5^2 + \ldots + (2n-1)^2 = \dfrac{n}{3}(4n^2 - 1)$, for all $n \in N$.

   (ii) Prove that:

   $2^2 + 4^2 + 6^2 + \ldots + (2n)^2$

   $= \dfrac{2n}{3}(2n^2 + 3n + 1)$, for all $n \in N$.

   (iii) Using only your results from (i) and (ii), explain why:

   $\sum_{r=1}^{2n} r^2 = \dfrac{n}{3}(8n^2 + 6n + 1)$, for all $n \in N$.

6. Use induction to prove the following statements on divisibility:

   (i) $8^n - 3^n$ is divisible by 5, for all $n \in N$.

   (ii) $5^n - 4n + 3$ is divisible by 4, for all $n \in N$.

   (iii) $4n^3 - n$ is divisible by 3, for all $n \in N$.

   (iv) $2^{3n-1} + 3$ is divisible by 7, for all $n \in N$.

7. Use induction to prove the following inequalities:

   (i) $(1 + px)^n \geqslant 1 + pnx$ for $x > 0$, $p > 0$ and $n \in N$.

   (ii) $\dfrac{1}{(1+px)^n} \leqslant \dfrac{1}{1+pnx}$ for $x > 0$, $p > 0$ and $n \in N$.

8. A sum of €2,000 is invested at the beginning of each year for n years. The money earns 3.25% EAR.

   (i) Write in the form: $\sum_{r=1}^{n} p(1+i)^r$

   the value of the investment at the end of n years.

   (ii) Prove using induction that the value of the investment at the end of n years is:

   $I[1.0325^n - 1]$, where $I = \dfrac{826{,}000}{13}$.

9. $u_1 = 5$ and $u_{n+1} = \dfrac{n}{n+1}u_n$ for all $n \in N$.

   (i) Write down the value of each of u_2, u_3 and u_4.

   (ii) Hence, by inspection, write an expression for u_n in terms of n.

   (iii) Use induction to justify your answer for part (ii).

10. Use induction to prove that:

    $\sum_{r=1}^{n} (-1)^{r-1} r^2 = (-1)^{n-1} \dfrac{n}{2}(n+1)$, for all $n \in N$.

Complex Numbers

Learning Outcomes

In this chapter you will learn how to:

- Add, subtract, multiply and divide complex numbers

- Plot complex numbers on the Argand diagram

- Find the modulus of a complex number

- Use complex numbers to perform transformations

- Solve equations with complex roots

- Write complex numbers in polar form

- Prove the theorem of de Moivre

- Use the theorem of de Moivre to evaluate c^n, $n \in Z$, $c \in C$

- Use the theorem of de Moivre to find the roots of complex numbers

12.1 COMPLEX NUMBERS

The Italian mathematicians Gerolamo Cardano (1501–1576) and Niccolò Tartaglia (1500–1557) were the first to encounter complex numbers.

Gerolamo Cardano   *Niccolò Tartaglia*

While working on the solutions to cubic equations, they came upon some unusual solutions involving the square root of –1. Today we call such solutions **complex** solutions.

Complex numbers have many applications in the modern world in such diverse areas as electronic engineering, aircraft design, computer-generated imaging in the film industry and medicine.

Complex numbers have been introduced to allow for the solutions of certain equations that have no real solutions.

The equation $x^2 + 1 = 0$ has no real solution, since the square of a real number, x, is either 0 or positive. Therefore, $x^2 + 1$ cannot be zero.

To find a solution to such an equation we need to introduce a new number whose square is –1. We call this number i (the Greek letter iota).

$$i = \sqrt{-1}$$
$$\text{and } i^2 = -1$$

KEY WORDS

■ **Complex number**
■ **Argand diagram**
■ **Real part**
■ **Imaginary part**
■ **Translation**
■ **Dilation**
■ **Modulus**

■ **Conjugate**
■ **Polynomial**
■ **Degree of a polynomial**
■ **Polar form**
■ **Argument**
■ **De Moivre's theorem**
■ **General polar form**

Let us check that i is a solution to $x^2 + 1 = 0$.

Substitute i into the equation.

$(i)^2 + 1 = 0$

$-1 + 1 = 0$

$0 = 0$

∴ i is a solution.

This allows us to solve equations of the type $x^2 - 2x + 5 = 0$.

Using the quadratic formula $\Rightarrow x = \dfrac{2 \pm \sqrt{-16}}{2}$

$\qquad = \dfrac{2 \pm \sqrt{16}\sqrt{-1}}{2}$

$\qquad = \dfrac{2 \pm 4\sqrt{-1}}{2}$

$\qquad = 1 \pm 2\sqrt{-1}$

∴ $x = 1 \pm 2i$

If both $a < 0$ and $b < 0$, then $\sqrt{a}.\sqrt{b} \neq \sqrt{ab}$ ($a, b \in R$).

But if $a < 0$ and $b > 0$, or if $a > 0$ and $b < 0$, then $\sqrt{a}.\sqrt{b} = \sqrt{ab}$ ($a, b \in R$).

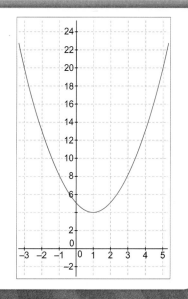

$\sqrt{-1}$ Worked Example 12.1

Simplify: (i) $\sqrt{-9}$ (ii) $\sqrt{-72}$

Solution

(i) $\sqrt{-9} = \sqrt{9}\,\sqrt{-1}$

    $= 3i$

(ii) $\sqrt{-72} = \sqrt{72}\,.\,\sqrt{-1}$

      $= 6\sqrt{2}\,i$

$\sqrt{-1}$ Worked Example 12.2

Simplify the following:

(i) i^3 (ii) i^4 (iii) i^{49}

Solution

(i) $i^3 = (i^2)(i)$

    $= (-1)(i)$

    $\therefore i^3 = -i$

(ii) $i^4 = (i^2)^2$

    $= (-1)^2$

    $\therefore i^4 = 1$

(iii) $i^{49} = (i^{48})(i)$

    $= (i^2)^{24}(i)$

    $= (-1)^{24}(i)$

    $= (1)i$

    $\therefore i^{49} = i$

$\sqrt{-1}$ Worked Example 12.3

Solve the equation $z^2 + 36 = 0$.

Solution

$$z^2 + 36 = 0$$
$$z^2 = -36$$
$$z = \pm\sqrt{-36}$$
$$z = \pm\sqrt{36}\,\sqrt{-1}$$
$$\therefore z = \pm 6i$$

Exercise 12.1

1. Write the following in the form ki, $k \in R$, $i^2 = -1$:

(i) $\sqrt{-100}$ (iv) $\sqrt{-36}$

(ii) $\sqrt{-81}$ (v) $\sqrt{-121}$

(iii) $\sqrt{-25}$ (vi) $\sqrt{-64}$

2. Write the following in the form $a\sqrt{b}\,i$, $a, b \in R$, b is square free and $i^2 = -1$:

(i) $\sqrt{-8}$ (iv) $\sqrt{-300}$

(ii) $\sqrt{-98}$ (v) $\sqrt{-12}$

(iii) $\sqrt{-45}$ (vi) $\sqrt{-125}$

3. Solve the following equations, giving your answers in the form $\pm pi$, $p \in R$, $i^2 = -1$:

(i) $z^2 + 9 = 0$

(ii) $z^2 + 4 = 0$

(iii) $z^2 + 25 = 0$

(iv) $z^2 + 49 = 0$

(v) $z^2 + 7 = 0$

(vi) $z^2 + 17 = 0$

(vii) $z^2 + 14 = 0$

4. Simplify each of the following:

(i) i^3 (iii) i^5 (v) i^{13}

(ii) i^6 (iv) i^{12} (vi) i^{59}

5. Match the numbers in Column A with those in Column B.

A	B
i^4	$1 - i$
$2i^3$	-3
$i^8 + i^3$	$-128i$
i^{98}	$i + 1$
$3(i)^2$	0
$i^4 - i^8$	$-64i$
$(2i)^7$	1
$i^4 - i^7$	$9i$
$(4i)^3$	$-2i$
$5i + 4i$	-1

6. The spinner has eight equal sectors and on each sector is a different power of i.

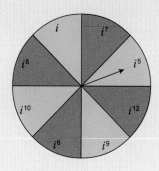

i	-1	$-i$	1
$-€5$	$€2$	$€10$	$€2$

The table gives possible winnings or losses for one spin of the spinner. By simplifying the powers of i on the spinner, find the probability of:

(i) Losing €5 on one spin

(ii) Winning €10 on one spin

12.2 COMPLEX NUMBERS AND THE ARGAND DIAGRAM

> The set of real numbers is a subset of the set of **complex numbers**.

> A **complex number**, z, is any number of the form $z = a + ib$, $a, b \in R$, $i^2 = -1$.
>
> a is called the **real part** of z, Re(z), and b is called the **imaginary part** of z, Im(z).

$2 + 3i$, $5 - 2i$, $\frac{1}{2} + \frac{3}{4}i$, and $\sqrt{2} - 3i$ are all examples of complex numbers.

> The complex numbers $z_1 = a + bi$ and $z_2 = c + di$ are equal if, and only if, $a = c$ and $b = d$.

The Argand Diagram

Just as a real number can be represented on a real numberline, a complex number can be represented on a diagram called the **Argand diagram**, also known as the **complex plane**. The Argand diagram is a two-dimensional plane with two perpendicular axes. The horizontal axis is the real axis and the vertical axis is the imaginary axis.

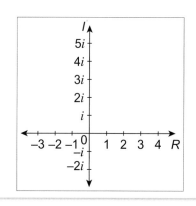

Here is the complex number $3 + 2i$ represented on an Argand diagram.

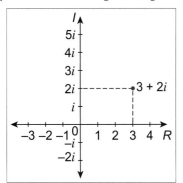

The Argand diagram was devised by the Swiss mathematician Jean-Robert Argand (1768–1822).

OR

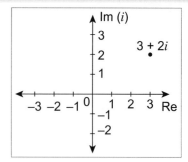

$\sqrt{-1}$ Worked Example 12.4

Represent the following numbers on an Argand diagram:

    (i) $-1 + 2i$

    (ii) $2 + 3i$

    (iii) $-3 - 2i$

    (iv) $3 - i$

Solution

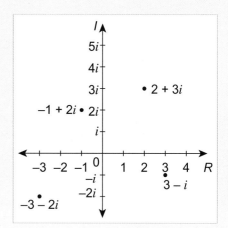

Modulus of a Complex Number

The **modulus** of a complex number, $a + bi$, is its distance from the origin on the Argand diagram.

ACTIVITY 12.1

In Activity 12.1, you found that the modulus of a complex number, $a + bi$, is $\sqrt{a^2 + b^2}$.

The modulus of $a + bi$ is written $|a + bi|$.

FORMULA

$$|a + bi| = \sqrt{a^2 + b^2}$$

$\sqrt{-1}$ Worked Example 12.5

$z_1 = 7 + 24i$ and $z_2 = -20 + 21i$.

Find: (i) $|z_1|$ (ii) $|z_2|$ (iii) $|z_1 + z_2|$

Hence, show that $|z_1 + z_2| < |z_1| + |z_2|$.

Solution

(i) $|z_1| = \sqrt{(7)^2 + (24)^2}$

$= \sqrt{49 + 576}$

$= \sqrt{625}$

$\therefore |z_1| = 25$

(ii) $|z_2| = \sqrt{(-20)^2 + (21)^2}$

$= \sqrt{400 + 441}$

$= \sqrt{881}$

$\therefore |z_2| = 29$

(iii) $|z_1 + z_2| = |(7 + 24i) + (-20 + 21i)|$

$= |-13 + 45i|$

$= \sqrt{(-13)^2 + (45)^2}$

$\therefore |z_1 + z_2| = \sqrt{2{,}194}$

$|z_1| + |z_2| = 25 + 29 = 54$

$|z_1 + z_2| = \sqrt{2{,}194} < 54$

$\therefore |z_1 + z_2| < |z_1| + |z_2|$

Exercise 12.2

1. Plot the following complex numbers on an Argand diagram:

(i) $3 + 2i$

(ii) $5 - 2i$

(iii) $-6 + 2i$

(iv) -2

(v) $3i$

(vi) 4

(vii) $-5i$

(viii) $2 + 0i$

2. Show the following numbers on the complex plane:

(i) $1 - \sqrt{-144}$

(ii) $-4 - \sqrt{-1}$

(iii) $7 - \sqrt{-81}$

(iv) $\frac{1}{2} + \sqrt{-\frac{1}{16}}$

(v) $\frac{3}{2} + \sqrt{\frac{1}{25}}$

(vi) $-\frac{1}{2} - \sqrt{-\frac{81}{4}}$

3. Study the Argand diagram below and complete the grid to spell the name of a famous composer.

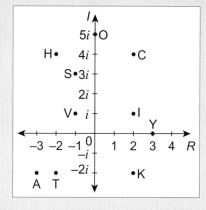

$-2 - 2i$	$2 + 4i$	$-2 + 4i$	$-3 - 2i$	$2 + i$	$2 - 2i$	$5i$	$-1 + i$	$-1 + 3i$	$2 - 2i$	$3 + 0i$

4. Using all the data in the box, form 12 different complex numbers in the form $a + bi$, where $a, b \in z$ and $a \neq b$.

$$0, \quad 3, \quad 4, \quad 5, \quad i,$$
$$+, \quad -$$

Plot the complex numbers on an Argand diagram.

5. Evaluate each of the following. Give your answer in surd form where necessary.

(i) $|1 + 2i|$

(ii) $|2 + 2i|$

(iii) $|3 - i|$

(iv) $|3 + \sqrt{2}i|$

(v) $|1 + \sqrt{8}i|$

(vi) $|3 + 2\sqrt{10}i|$

(vii) $|1 - i|$

(viii) $|3 - 10i|$

(ix) $|-3 - \sqrt{7}i|$

(x) $|2\sqrt{6} - i|$

6. If $\frac{1}{2}|6 - 8i| = |4 + ki|$, find two possible values of k, where $k \in R$.

7. If $|p + pi| = |7 - i|$, find two possible values of p, where $p \in R$.

8. Show that $|3 + 4i| = |0 + 5i|$.

9. If $z_1 = 2 + 3i$ and $z_2 = -2 + 5i$, verify that $|z_1 + z_2| < |z_1| + |z_2|$.

10. If $\omega = a + bi$, find two solutions to the equation, $\sqrt{5}\,|\omega| + i\omega = 3 + i$.

12.3 ADDITION AND SUBTRACTION OF COMPLEX NUMBERS; MULTIPLICATION BY A REAL NUMBER

Can we add, subtract, multiply and divide complex numbers, as we can real numbers? The answer is yes. In this section you will learn how to add and subtract complex numbers.

Addition of Complex Numbers

 **ACTIVITY 12.2**

In Activity 12.2, you discovered how to define addition and subtraction of complex numbers.

So, to add two complex numbers we add the real parts to the real parts and the imaginary parts to the imaginary parts.

> If z_1 and z_2 are two complex numbers, then $z_1 + z_2 = [\text{Re}(z_1 + z_2)] + [\text{Im}(z_1 + z_2)]i$.

$\sqrt{-1}$ Worked Example 12.6

$z_1 = 2 - 3i$ and $z_2 = 11 + 5i$. Evaluate $z_1 + z_2$.

Solution

$$z_1 + z_2 = (2 - 3i) + (11 + 5i)$$
$$= (2 + 11) + (-3 + 5)i$$
$$\therefore z_1 + z_2 = 13 + 2i$$

Subtraction of Complex Numbers

> If z_1 and z_2 are two complex numbers, then $z_1 - z_2 = [\text{Re}(z_1 - z_2)] + [\text{Im}(z_1 - z_2)]i$.

$\sqrt{-1}$ Worked Example 12.7

$z_1 = 18 + 16i$ and $z_2 = 14 - 2i$. Find $z_1 - z_2$.

Solution

$$z_1 - z_2 = (18 + 16i) - (14 - 2i)$$
$$= (18 - 14) + (16 - (-2))i$$
$$\therefore z_1 - z_2 = 4 + 18i$$

Multiplying a Complex Number by a Real Number

While this section focuses on addition and subtraction, we will also deal with multiplying a complex number by a real number now.

> If z is a complex number and a is a real number, then $az = a\,\text{Re}(z) + a\,\text{Im}(z)i$.

√−1 Worked Example 12.8

If $z = 10 - 2i$, find $5z$.

Solution

$$5z = 5(10 - 2i)$$
$$= 5(10) + 5(-2i)$$
$$\therefore 5z = 50 - 10i$$

Transformations I

In Activity 12.3, you learned that addition of complex numbers is the equivalent of a **translation** on the complex plane. Also, you discovered that multiplication by a real number is the equivalent of a **dilation** (stretching, contraction) on the complex plane.

ACTIVITY 12.3

√−1 Worked Example 12.9

$z_1 = 2 + 4i$, $z_2 = 2 + 3i$, $z_3 = -1 + 2i$ and $\omega = 1 + i$.

  (i) Plot z_1, z_2, and z_3 on an Argand diagram.

 (ii) Evaluate $z_1 + \omega$, $z_2 + \omega$, and $z_3 + \omega$.

(iii) Plot the answers to part (ii) on an Argand diagram.

(iv) Describe the transformation that is the addition of ω.

Solution

(i)

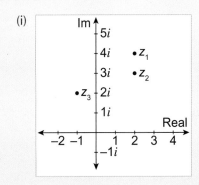

(ii) $z_1 + \omega = (2 + 4i) + (1 + i)$
$$= 3 + 5i$$
$$z_2 + \omega = (2 + 3i) + (1 + i)$$
$$= 3 + 4i$$
$$z_3 + \omega = (-1 + 2i) + (1 + i)$$
$$= 0 + 3i$$

(iii)

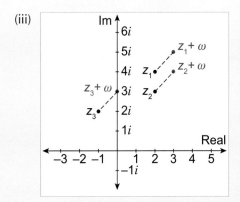

(iv) From the Argand diagram, the numbers z_1, z_2 and z_3 are moved a distance of $\sqrt{2}$ ($|\omega|$) in a north-east direction. We call such a transformation a **translation**.

Worked Example 12.10

$z_1 = 2 + 4i$, $z_2 = 2 + 3i$, $z_3 = -1 + 2i$ and $a = 2$.

   (i) Plot z_1, z_2 and z_3 on an Argand diagram.

  (ii) Evaluate az_1, az_2 and az_3.

 (iii) Plot the answers to part (ii) on an Argand diagram.

 (iv) Describe the transformation that is multiplication by a.

Solution

(i)

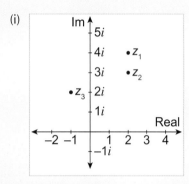

(ii) $az_1 = 2(2 + 4i)$

         $= 4 + 8i$

      $az_2 = 2(2 + 3i)$

         $= 4 + 6i$

      $az_3 = 2(-1 + 2i)$

         $= -2 + 4i$

(iii)

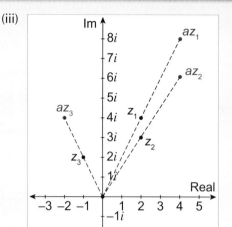

(iv) From the diagram we can see that all the points are moved further from the origin by a factor of 2.
We call such a transformation a dilation by a factor of 2.

- If F is the dilation factor and if $F > 1$ or $F < -1$, the dilation is sometimes referred to as a **stretching** on the complex plane.
- If $-1 < F < 1$, then the dilation is sometimes referred to as a **contracting** on the complex plane.

Exercise 12.3

1. Let $z = 2 + i$. Find:

   (i) $z + 3$ (iii) $z - 3z$ (v) $2z + 3 - 3i$

  (ii) $z + 3i$ (iv) $2z + 5z$ (vi) $-4z + i$

2. Let $z = 2 - 3i$. Show the following on an Argand diagram.

   (i) $z + 3$ (iii) $1 - z$

  (ii) $2z + 6i$ (iv) $\frac{1}{2}(z + i)$

3. Let $z = 1 + i$. Show the following on an Argand diagram:

   (i) z (iii) $3z$ (v) $5z$ (vii) $-z$

  (ii) $2z$ (iv) $4z$ (vi) $-3z$ (viii) $-5z$

Describe the transformation of z in parts (ii) to (viii) above.

4. Let $z = -24 + 48i$. Show the following on an Argand diagram:

   (i) z (iii) $\frac{1}{3}z$ (v) $\frac{1}{6}z$

  (ii) $\frac{1}{2}z$ (iv) $\frac{1}{4}z$

Describe the transformation of z in parts (ii) to (v) above.

5. $z_1 = 2 + 3i$, $z_2 = -2 + 5i$, $z_3 = -1 + 4i$ and $\omega = 1 + i$.

   (i) Plot z_1, z_2 and z_3 on an Argand diagram.

  (ii) Evaluate $z_1 + \omega$, $z_2 + \omega$ and $z_3 + \omega$.

 (iii) Plot the answers to part (ii) on an Argand diagram.

 (iv) Describe the transformation that is the addition of ω.

6. $z_1 = 3 + 2i$, $z_2 = -1 + 4i$, $z_3 = -3 + 5i$ and $\omega = 1 - i$.

   (i) Plot z_1, z_2 and z_3 on an Argand diagram.

   (ii) Evaluate $z_1 + \omega$, $z_2 + \omega$ and $z_3 + \omega$.

   (iii) Plot the answers to part (ii) on an Argand diagram.

   (iv) Describe the transformation that is the addition of ω.

7. Copy the Argand diagram and label the complex numbers z_1, z_2, z_3, z_4 and z_5, using the information given below.

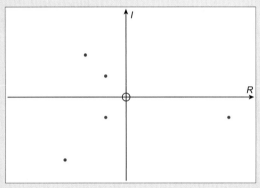

   (i) $z_1 = 2z_2$ (ii) $z_4 = \frac{1}{3}z_3$ (iii) $\mathrm{Re}(z_5) > 0$

8. Copy the Argand diagram and label the complex numbers z_1, z_2, z_3 and z_4, using the information given below.

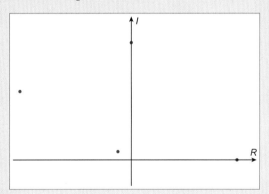

   (i) $\mathrm{Im}(z_1) > 0$ (iii) $\mathrm{Re}(z_3) = 0$

   (ii) $z_2 = 10z_1$ (iv) $\mathrm{Im}(z_4) = 0$

9. Copy the Argand diagram and label the complex numbers z_1, z_2, z_3, z_4 and z_5, using the information given below.

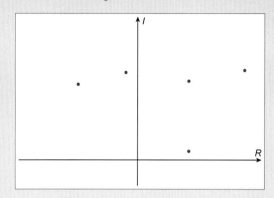

   (i) $\mathrm{Re}(z_1) = \mathrm{Re}(z_5)$

   (ii) $z_2 = z_1 + z_3$

   (iii) $z_4 = z_1 + z_5$

10. Copy the Argand diagram and label the complex numbers z_1, z_2, z_3 and z_4, using the information given below.

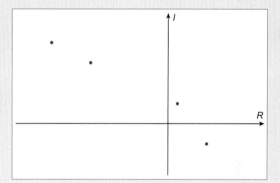

   (i) $z_4 = z_3 - z_2$

   (ii) $|z_2| = 2|z_1|$

12.4 MULTIPLICATION OF COMPLEX NUMBERS

Firstly, we will look at multiplication by a complex number whose real part is zero, i.e. a number of the form qi, $q \in R$. Such a number is called an imaginary number.

$\sqrt{-1}$ Worked Example 12.11

If $z = 4 + i$, find iz.

Solution

$$iz = i(4 + i)$$
$$= 4i + i^2$$
$$= 4i - 1$$
$$\therefore iz = -1 + 4i$$

Transformations II

In Activity 12.4, you discovered that multiplication of a complex number by i is the equivalent of rotating the complex number **anti-clockwise** through 90° about the origin. You also learned that multiplication by $-i$ is the equivalent of rotating the complex number **clockwise** through 90° about the origin.

ACTIVITY 12.4

$\sqrt{-1}$ Worked Example 12.12

$z_1 = 2 + i$

(i) Find z_2, if $z_2 = iz_1$.

(ii) Plot z_1 and z_2 on an Argand diagram.

(iii) Describe the transformation that maps z_1 onto z_2.

Solution

(i) $z_2 = i(2 + i)$
$$= 2i + i^2$$
$$\therefore z_2 = -1 + 2i$$

(ii)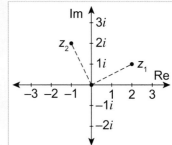

(iii) z_1 is mapped onto z_2 by an anti-clockwise rotation of 90° about the origin.

$\sqrt{-1}$ Worked Example 12.13

(i) $z_1 = 2 - 7i$ and $z_2 = 3 + 7i$. Find z_1z_2.

(ii) $z_1 = \frac{1}{2} - \frac{3}{2}i$ and $z_2 = 4 + 6i$. Find $z_1 z_2$.

Solution

(i) $z_1z_2 = (2 - 7i)(3 + 7i)$
$$= 2(3 + 7i) - 7i(3 + 7i)$$
$$= 6 + 14i - 21i - 49i^2$$
$$= 6 - 7i - 49(-1)$$
$$\therefore z_1z_2 = 55 - 7i$$

(ii) $z_1z_2 = \left(\frac{1}{2} - \frac{3}{2}i\right)(4 + 6i)$
$$= \frac{1}{2}(4 + 6i) - \frac{3}{2}i(4 + 6i)$$
$$= 2 + 3i - 6i - 9i^2$$
$$= 2 - 3i - 9(-1)$$
$$\therefore z_1z_2 = 11 - 3i$$

Closure is preserved under multiplication. The product of any two complex numbers is itself a complex number.

Exercise 12.4

1. Write these products in the form $a + bi$:

   (i) $(2 + 7i)(3 - 5i)$

   (ii) $(1 + 4i)(2 + 5i)$

   (iii) $(6 + i)(-2 + 3i)$

   (iv) $(2 + 3i)(2 - 3i)$

   (v) $(3 + 4i)(3 - 4i)$

   (vi) $3i(2 + 4i)$

   (vii) $(1 - i)(1 + i)$

   (viii) $5(6 - i)$

   (ix) $(-2 - 2i)(-2 + 2i)$

   (x) $(7 + 5i)(2 + i)$

2. Write these products in the form $a + bi$:

   (i) $\left(\frac{1}{2} + \frac{3}{2}i\right)\left(\frac{1}{2} - \frac{1}{4}i\right)$

   (ii) $\left(\frac{1}{5} + \frac{3}{5}i\right)\left(\frac{1}{5} - \frac{3}{5}i\right)$

   (iii) $\left(\frac{3}{8} - \frac{2}{11}i\right)\left(\frac{1}{4} - \frac{2}{5}i\right)$

   (iv) $\left(\frac{1}{2} + \frac{1}{2}i\right)\left(\frac{1}{2} - \frac{1}{2}i\right)$

   (v) $\left(\frac{2}{9} + \frac{3}{5}i\right)\left(\frac{3}{4} - \frac{1}{5}i\right)$

   (vi) $\left(\sqrt{3} + 2i\right)\left(\sqrt{3} - 2i\right)$

   (vii) $\left(3\sqrt{7} + 5i\right)\left(3\sqrt{7} - 5i\right)$

   (viii) $\left(\sqrt{2} + \sqrt{3}i\right)\left(\sqrt{8} - \sqrt{3}i\right)$

   (ix) $\left(3 - \sqrt{3}i\right)\left(2 + 3\sqrt{3}i\right)$

   (x) $\left(5 - \sqrt{2}i\right)\left(5 + \sqrt{2}i\right)$

3. $z_1 = 3 + i$

   (i) Find z_2, if $z_2 = iz_1$.

   (ii) Plot z_1 and z_2 on an Argand diagram.

   (iii) Describe the transformation that maps z_1 onto z_2.

4. $z_1 = -3 + 2i$

   (i) Find z_2, if $z_2 = iz_1$.

   (ii) Plot z_1 and z_2 on an Argand diagram.

   (iii) Describe the transformation that maps z_1 onto z_2.

5. $z_1 = -3 + 4i$

   (i) Find z_2, if $z_2 = -iz_1$.

   (ii) Plot z_1 and z_2 on an Argand diagram.

   (iii) Describe the transformation that maps z_1 onto z_2.

6. $z_1 = -2 - 3i$

   (i) Find z_2, if $z_2 = -iz_1$.

   (ii) Plot z_1 and z_2 on an Argand diagram.

   (iii) Describe the transformation that maps z_1 onto z_2.

7. Copy the diagram below.

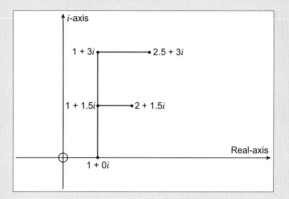

   (i) Multiply each complex number on the diagram by i.

   (ii) Plot your answers from part (i).

   (iii) Describe the transformation of the shape.

8. Copy the diagram below.

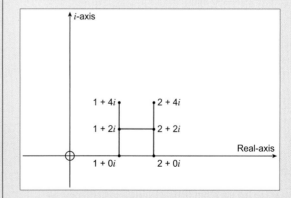

   (i) Multiply each complex number on the diagram by $-i$.

   (ii) Plot your answers from part (i).

   (iii) Describe the transformation of the shape.

9. Copy the diagram below.

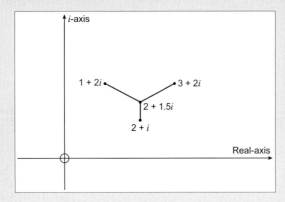

(i) Multiply each complex number on the diagram by $2i$.

(ii) Plot your answers from part (i).

(iii) Describe the transformation of the shape.

10. In the diagram, the red square has been translated and then rotated anti-clockwise through 90°. The translation was achieved by adding $5 - 2i$ to each vertex of the red square.

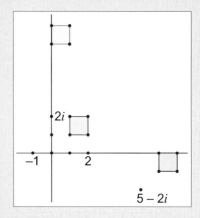

(i) Which square is the image of the red square under the translation?

(ii) Which square is the image of the red square under the composition of the translation and the rotation?

(iii) Write down the vertices of each square in the form $a + bi$.

12.5 DIVISION OF COMPLEX NUMBERS

In the real number system, if $a \div b = c$, then $a = b \times c$, where $a, b, c \in R$.

Similarly, in the complex number system, if $a \div b = c$, then $a = b \times c$, where $a, b, c \in C$.

However, in the complex number system, we need to follow certain well-defined steps to divide one complex number by another.

$\sqrt{-1}$ Worked Example 12.14

Calculate $\dfrac{15 + 10i}{5}$.

Solution

When we multiply a complex number z by a real number a, we multiply a by Re(z) and a by Im(z). Similarly, when we divide a complex number by a real number a, we divide Re(z) and Im(z) by a.

$$\frac{15 + 10i}{5} = \frac{15}{5} + \frac{10}{5}i$$
$$= 3 + 2i$$

Conjugate of a Complex Number

If $z = a + bi$, $a, b \in R$ and $i^2 = -1$, then the **conjugate** of z (writen as $\bar{z}$) $= a - bi$.

For example, if $z = -2 - 12i$, then $\bar{z} = -2 + 12i$.

Rule: Change the sign of the imaginary part.

√−1 Worked Example 12.15

$z = 2 - 2i$

(i) Find $\bar{z}$.
(ii) Plot z and $\bar{z}$ on the Argand diagram.

Solution

(i) $\bar{z} = 2 + 2i$

(ii)

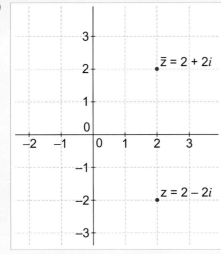

$\bar{z} = 2 + 2i$

$z = 2 - 2i$

> $\bar{z}$ is the image of z by an axial symmetry in the real axis.

√−1 Worked Example 12.16

Calculate $\dfrac{2 + 11i}{2 + i}$.

Solution

In this question, we are dividing a complex number by a complex number. If we could reduce the denominator to a real number, then our task would be much easier, as we know how to divide a complex number by a real number. Fortunately, if we multiply a complex number by its conjugate, the result is a real number.

Step 1

Write down the conjugate of the denominator:
$\overline{2 + i} = 2 - i$

Step 2

Multiply $2 + i$ by $2 - i$.

$$(2 + i)(2 - i) = 2(2 - i) + i(2 - i)$$
$$= 4 - 2i + 2i - i^2$$
$$= 4 + 1$$
$$= 5$$

Step 3

Multiply the numerator by $2 - i$.

$$(2 + 11i)(2 - i) = 2(2 - i) + 11i(2 - i)$$
$$= 4 - 2i + 22i - 11i^2$$
$$= 4 + 20i + 11$$
$$= 15 + 20i$$

Step 4

$$\frac{2 + 11i}{2 + i} = \frac{15 + 20i}{5}$$
$$= \frac{15}{5} + \frac{20}{5}i$$
$$= 3 + 4i$$

> When dealing with division by a complex number, multiply both the numerator and the denominator by the conjugate of the denominator.

Exercise 12.5

1. Write in the form $p + qi$, $p, q \in Q$:

(i) $\dfrac{16 - 8i}{8}$　　　　(iv) $\dfrac{-16 + 48i}{-4i}$

(ii) $\dfrac{5 + 12i}{7}$　　　　(v) $\dfrac{1 + i}{5i}$

(iii) $\dfrac{27 - 18i}{3i}$　　　　(vi) $\dfrac{33}{12i}$

2. Write in the form $p + qi$, $p, q \in R$:

(i) $\dfrac{5 + 5i}{1 + 2i}$　　　　(iv) $\dfrac{5}{1 + 2i}$

(ii) $\dfrac{1 - 5i}{1 - i}$　　　　(v) $\dfrac{1 + 3i}{1 + i}$

(iii) $\dfrac{10}{1 - 3i}$

3. Write in the form $p + qi$, $p, q \in R$:

(i) $\dfrac{5 - 5i}{2 + i}$　　　　(v) $\dfrac{1}{1 + i}$

(ii) $\dfrac{6}{1 - i}$　　　　(vi) $\dfrac{11 + 10i}{2(2 + 3i)}$

(iii) $\dfrac{1 + 5i}{i}$　　　　(vii) $\dfrac{1 - 9i}{2i}$

(iv) $\dfrac{6 + 8i}{2i}$

4. $z_1 = a + bi$ and $z_2 = c - di$.
Write, in terms of a, b, c, and d:

(i) $\overline{z_1}$

(ii) $\overline{z_2}$

(iii) $\overline{z_1} + \overline{z_2}$

(iv) $z_1 + z_2$

(v) $\overline{z_1 + z_2}$

(vi) Verify that $\overline{z_1 + z_2} = \overline{z_1} + \overline{z_2}$.

5. If $z = 1 - 3i$, write $\dfrac{\overline{z}}{z}$ in the form $a + bi$,
$a, b \in Q$.

6. Let $z_1 = -1 + 5i$ and let $z_2 = 2 + 3i$.
Investigate if $\overline{\left(\dfrac{z_1}{z_2}\right)} = \dfrac{\overline{z_1}}{\overline{z_2}}$.

7. Let $z_1 = 11 - 10i$ and let $z_2 = 4 + i$.

(i) Find $\dfrac{z_1}{z_2}$.

(ii) Calculate $|z_1|$ and $|z_2|$.

(iii) Investigate if $\left|\dfrac{z_1}{z_2}\right| = \dfrac{|z_1|}{|z_2|}$.

8. Identify z_1, z_2, z_3, z_4 and z_5 on the Argand diagram, given the information below.

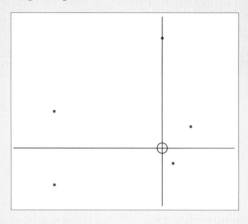

(i) $z_5 = \overline{z_2}$　　　　(iii) $\text{Re}(z_3) = 0$

(ii) $\text{Im}(z_5) > 0$　　　　(iv) $z_1 = 2iz_4$

9. Identify z_1, z_2, z_3, z_4 and z_5 on the Argand diagram, given the information below.

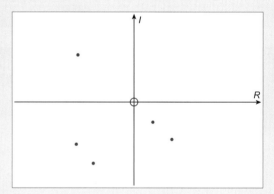

(i) $z_1 = 2z_2$　　　　(iii) $z_5 = \overline{z_3}$

(ii) $z_3 = -iz_4$

10. Identify z_1, z_2 and z_3, given the information below.

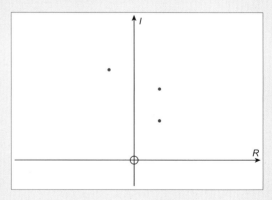

(i) $\text{Im}(z_2) < \text{Im}(z_3)$

(ii) $z_1 = z_2 z_3$

11. Identify z_1, z_2, z_3 and z_4, given the information below.

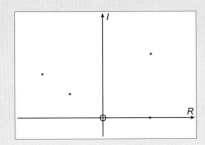

(i) $z_2 = 2z_1$

(ii) $z_3 = -iz_2$

(iii) $z_4 = \text{Re}(z_3)$

12.6 QUADRATIC EQUATIONS WITH COMPLEX ROOTS

From your knowledge of algebra, you know that the solution to a quadratic equation

$$ax^2 + bx + c = 0, \ a, b, c \in R, \ a \neq 0$$

is given by the formula:

FORMULA

$$x = \frac{-b \pm \sqrt{b^2 - 4ac}}{2a}$$

In this formula, we refer to $b^2 - 4ac$ as the **discriminant**.

If $b^2 - 4ac < 0$, then the solutions (roots) will be complex.

√−1 Worked Example 12.17

Solve the equation $z^2 - 6z + 13 = 0$ and show the roots on an Argand diagram.

Solution

$$z = \frac{6 \pm \sqrt{(-6)^2 - 4(1)(13)}}{2(1)}$$

$$= \frac{6 \pm \sqrt{-16}}{2}$$

$$= \frac{6 \pm \sqrt{16}\sqrt{-1}}{2}$$

$$= \frac{6 \pm 4i}{2}$$

$$= \frac{6}{2} \pm \frac{4i}{2}$$

$$\therefore z = 3 \pm 2i$$

Here are the roots on an Argand diagram.

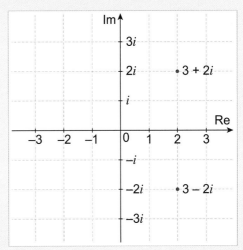

Exercise 12.6

1. Solve the equation $z^2 + 4z + 13 = 0$, giving your answer in the form $a + bi$, $a, b \in R$.

2. Evaluate the following:

(i) $(1 - 2i)^2$ (ii) $-2(1 - 2i)$

Hence, show that $1 - 2i$ is a root of the equation $z^2 - 2z + 5 = 0$.

3. Show that the roots of the equation $z^2 - 2z + 10 = 0$ are complex.

4. Solve the equation $z^2 - 8z + 17 = 0$, giving your answer in the form $a + bi$, $a, b \in R$.

5. Show that the roots of the equation $z^2 + 6z + 25 = 0$ are complex.

6. Evaluate the following:

   (i) $(-7 + i)^2$ (ii) $14(-7 + i)$

   Hence, show that $-7 + i$ is a root of the equation $z^2 + 14z + 50 = 0$.

7. Solve the equation $z^2 - 12z + 40 = 0$. Give your answer in the form $a + bi$, $a, b \in R$.

8. Find the complex roots of the equation $z^2 = -2(5z + 17)$.

9. Solve the following equations and show your solutions on an Argand diagram:

   (i) $z^2 - 4z + 5 = 0$ (iii) $z^2 + 2z + 17 = 0$

   (ii) $z^2 - 8z + 25 = 0$ (iv) $z^2 + 4z + 40 = 0$

10. Solve the following equations and show your solutions on an Argand diagram:

   (i) $z^2 + 16 = 0$

   (ii) $4z^2 - 12z + 25 = 0$

   (iii) $9z^2 - 6z + 5 = 0$

   (iv) $z^2 - 8z + 25 = 0$

11. (i) Write $\dfrac{14 + 5i}{4 - i}$ as $x + yi$.

   (ii) Hence, show that $\dfrac{14 + 5i}{4 - i}$ is a root of the equation $z^2 - 6z + 13 = 0$.

   (iii) Find the other root of $z^2 - 6z + 13 = 0$.

12.7 POLYNOMIALS WITH COMPLEX ROOTS

In this section we will find the complex roots of single variable polynomials with real coefficients.

A single variable polynomial with real coefficients is of the form:

$$f(x) = a_n x^n + a_{n-1}x^{n-1} + a_{n-2}x^{n-2} + ... + a_2 x^2 + a_1 x + a_0$$

where x is the single variable and each of $a_n, a_{n-1}, ..., a_2, a_1$ are real numbers.

For example, $f(x) = 4x^5 + 3x^3 - 2$ is a single variable polynomial with real coefficients.

In 1799, the German mathematician Carl Friedrich Gauss proved a very important theorem, known as the **Fundamental Theorem of Algebra**. A consequence of this theorem is that every single variable polynomial of degree n will have exactly n roots ($n \in N$).

The **degree** of a single variable polynomial or equation is the **highest power** of the variable in the polynomial or equation.

For example, the equation $z^5 + z - 5 = 0$ has exactly five solutions, as it is of **degree** 5.

√–1 Worked Example 12.18

The polynomial $f(z) = 3z^3 - 5z^2 + 18z + 12$ has n roots. What is the value of n?

Solution

The highest power of z in the polynomial is 3. By the Fundamental Theorem of Algebra, the polynomial will have three roots, therefore $n = 3$.

The Conjugate Root Theorem

If the complex number $z = a + bi$, where $a, b \in R$, is a root of the polynomial $f(z)$ with **real coefficients**, then $\bar{z} = a - bi$ (the conjugate of z) is also a root.

√−1 Worked Example 12.19

If $z = 4 + 3i$ is a root of the polynomial
$f(z) = z^2 - 8z + 25$,
then show that $\bar{z} = 4 - 3i$ is also a root.

Solution

$f(4 - 3i) = (4 - 3i)^2 - 8(4 - 3i) + 25$

$\qquad = 4(4 - 3i) - 3i(4 - 3i) - 8(4 - 3i) + 25$

$\qquad = 16 - 12i - 12i + 9i^2 - 32 + 24i + 25$

$\qquad = 16 - 32 + 25 + 9(-1)$

$\qquad = 41 - 41$

$\qquad = 0$

$\therefore \bar{z} = 4 - 3i$ is a root of $f(z)$.

√−1 Worked Example 12.20

Prove the following results for $z, z_1, z_2 \in C$ and $a, b, c \in R$:

(i) $\overline{az_1 + bz_2} = \overline{az_1} + \overline{bz_2}$

(ii) $\overline{az} = a\bar{z}$

(iii) $\overline{az^2} = a\overline{z^2}$

(iv) $\overline{z^2} = \bar{z}^2$

Hence, show that if z_1 is a root of the polynomial
$$f(z) = az^2 + bz + c,$$
then $\overline{z_1}$, the conjugate of z_1, is also a root.

Solution

(i) To prove: $\overline{az_1 + bz_2} = \overline{az_1} + \overline{bz_2}$

Let $z_1 = x_1 + y_1 i$ and $z_2 = x_2 + y_2 i, x, y \in R$.

LHS $\quad az_1 + bz_2 = a(x_1 + y_1 i) + b(x_2 + y_2 i)$

$\qquad\qquad = (ax_1 + bx_2) + (ay_1 + by_2)i$

$\therefore \overline{az_1 + bz_2} = (ax_1 + bx_2) - (ay_1 + by_2)i$

RHS $\quad \overline{az_1} + \overline{bz_2} = a(x_1 - y_1 i) + b(x_2 - y_2 i)$

$\qquad\qquad = (ax_1 + bx_2) - (ay_1 + by_2)i$

$\qquad\qquad = \overline{az_1 + bz_2}$

(ii) To prove: $\overline{az} = a\bar{z}$

Let $z = x + yi, x, y \in R$.

LHS $\quad az = ax + ayi$

$\qquad \overline{az} = ax - ayi$

RHS $\quad a\bar{z} = a(x - y)i$

$\qquad\qquad = ax - ayi$

$\qquad\qquad = \overline{az}$

(iii) To prove: $\overline{az^2} = a\overline{z^2}$

Let $z = x + yi, x, y \in R$.

$z^2 = (x + yi)(x + yi)$

$\qquad = x(x + yi) + yi(x + yi)$

$\therefore z^2 = x^2 - y^2 + 2xyi$

LHS $\quad az^2 = a(x^2 - y^2) + 2axyi$

$\qquad \overline{az^2} = a(x^2 - y^2) - 2axyi$

RHS $\quad \overline{z^2} = x^2 - y^2 - 2xyi$

$\qquad a\overline{z^2} = a(x^2 - y^2) - 2axyi$

$\qquad\qquad = \overline{az^2}$

(iv) To prove: $\overline{z^2} = \bar{z}^2$

$z^2 = x^2 - y^2 + 2xyi$

$\overline{z^2} = x^2 - y^2 - 2xyi$

$\bar{z} = x - yi$

$\bar{z}^2 = (x - yi)(x - yi)$

$\qquad = x(x - yi) - yi(x - yi)$

$\qquad = x^2 - y^2 - 2xyi$

$\qquad = \overline{z^2}$

$f(z) = az^2 + bz + c$

z_1 a root $\Rightarrow f(z_1) = az_1{}^2 + bz_1 + c = 0$

$\overline{az_1{}^2 + bz_1 + c} = \bar{0}$

$\overline{az_1{}^2} + \overline{bz_1} + \bar{c} = 0$ (part (i))

$a\overline{z_1{}^2} + b\overline{z_1} + c = 0$ (parts (ii) and (iii))

$a\overline{z_1}{}^2 + b\overline{z_1} + c = 0$ (part (iv))

$\therefore \overline{z_1}$, the conjugate of z_1, is a also a root of $f(z)$.

The polynomial $f(z) = 3z^3 - 5z^2 + 13z + 5$ has n roots.

   (i) What is the value of n?

  (ii) If $1 + 2i$ is a root of $f(z)$, write down another root of $f(z)$.

 (iii) Explain why $f(z)$ must have a real root.

 (iv) Find the real root of $f(z)$.

Solution

   (i) $f(z)$ is a polynomial of degree 3, therefore it has three roots.

      $n = 3$

  (ii) By the Conjugate Root Theorem, another root is $1 - 2i$.

 (iii) $f(z)$ has three roots. We have already identified two complex roots, and since complex roots come in pairs, the one remaining root has to be real.

(iv) Step 1: Form a quadratic polynomial $g(z)$, with roots $1 + 2i$ and $1 - 2i$.

          $g(z)$ divides $f(z)$.

          Sum of the roots $= 1 + 2i + 1 - 2i$
                            $= 2$

          Product of the roots $= (1 + 2i)(1 - 2i)$
                             $= 5$

          $\therefore g(z) = z^2 - 2z + 5$

Step 2: Divide $f(z)$ by $g(z)$.

$$
\require{enclose}
\begin{array}{r}
3z + 1 \\
z^2 - 2z + 5 \enclose{longdiv}{3z^3 - 5z^2 + 13z + 5} \\
\underline{3z^3 - 6z^2 + 15z} \\
z^2 - 2z + 5 \\
\underline{z^2 - 2z + 5} \\
0
\end{array}
$$

Step 3: $3z + 1$ is a linear factor of $f(z)$.

          Therefore, the solution to the equation $3z + 1 = 0$ gives the real root of $f(z)$.

          $3z + 1 = 0$

          $\Rightarrow z = -\frac{1}{3}$

Exercise 12.7

1. $f(z) = z^2 - 10z + 26$ is a quadratic polynomial.

   (i) Verify that $z = 5 + i$ is a root of the equation $z^2 - 10z + 26 = 0$.

  (ii) Write down the other root of $z^2 - 10z + 26 = 0$.

2. $f(z) = z^2 + 6z + 25$ is a quadratic polynomial.

   (i) Verify that $z = -3 - 4i$ is a root of $f(z)$.

  (ii) Write down the other root of the equation $z^2 + 6z + 25 = 0$.

3. $f(z) = z^3 - z^2 - 4z - 6$ is a cubic polynomial.

   (i) Show that $z = -1 + i$ is a solution to the equation $f(z) = 0$.

  (ii) Write down another solution to $f(z) = 0$.

4. Show that $z = -1$ is a root of the equation $z^3 - 5z^2 + 4z + 10 = 0$. Show that the other two roots are complex.

5. The polynomial $f(z) = 2z^3 - 3z^2 + 18z + 10$ has n roots.

   (i) What is the value of n?

  (ii) If $1 - 3i$ is a root of $f(z) = 0$, write down another root of $f(z) = 0$.

6. $2 + 3i$ is a root of the equation $z^4 + 40z + k = 0$.

   (i) Find the value of k.

  (ii) Write down another root of the equation.

7. The graph of $f(z) = z^3 + z - k$, over the domain $-2 < z < 2.4$, is shown.

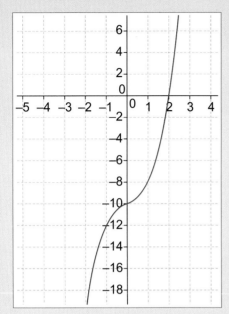

(i) The co-ordinates of the x- and y-intercepts are $(a,0)$ and $(0,b)$, $a, b \in Z$. Write down the value of each of a and b.

(ii) What is the value of the real root of $f(z)$?

(iii) What is the value of k?

(iv) $h(z) = z + c$ is a linear polynomial and $h(z)$ divides $f(z)$. Find $h(z)$.

(v) Find the non-real roots of $f(z)$.

8. Part of the graph of $f(z) = z^3 - 11z - k$ is shown.

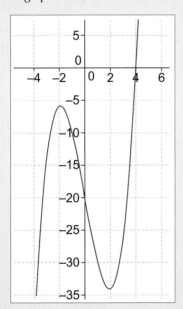

(i) If $k \in Z$, find the value of k.

(ii) Verify that the co-ordinates of the x-intercept are $(4,0)$.

(iii) $(z - 4)(Q(z)) = f(z)$, $Q(z)$ is a polynomial. Find $Q(z)$.

(iv) Solve $f(z) = 0$.

9. The equation $z^4 - 2z^3 - 2z^2 - 2z - 3 = 0$ has two integer roots.

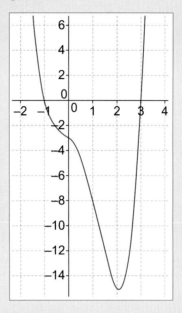

(i) Using the graph of $f(z) = z^4 - 2z^3 - 2z^2 - 2z - 3$, find the value of the real roots of $f(z) = 0$.

(ii) Show that $g(z) = z^2 - 2z - 3$ is a factor of $f(z)$.

(iii) Hence, find the two non-real roots of $f(z)$.

10. $f(z) = z^3 - 1$, $z \in C$

(i) Verify that $z = 1$ is a solution to the equation $z^3 - 1 = 0$.

(ii) Show that $z^3 - 1 = (z - 1)(z^2 + z + 1)$.

(iii) Show that the roots of $z^3 - 1 = 0$ are of the form 1, ω and ω^2.

(iv) Show that $1 + \omega + \omega^2 = 0$.

11. -2, z_1 and z_2 are the roots of the cubic equation $z^3 + 8 = 0$.

(i) Find z_1 and z_2 in the form $a + bi$, $a, b \in R$.

(ii) Show that $z_1 + z_2 = 2$ and find the value of $z_1 z_2$.

(iii) Write down a cubic equation whose roots are -2, $z_1 + z_2$ and $z_1 z_2$.

12. $f(z) = 2z^4 + 13z^3 + 19z^2 - 10z - 24$ is a polynomial of degree 4. Part of the graph of $f(z)$ is shown.

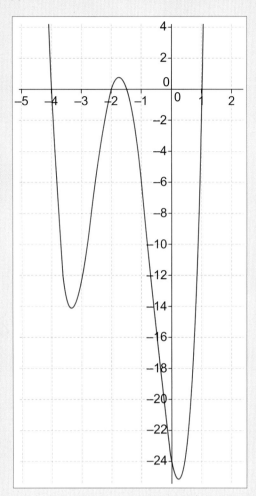

(i) How many roots does $f(z) = 0$ have?

(ii) Three of the roots, z_1, z_2 and z_3 are integers. Write down the value of each of z_1, z_2 and z_3.

(iii) Explain, with the aid of the graph, why there are no non-real roots.

(iv) Solve for the fourth root.

13. $z_1 = a + bi$, $a, b \in R$, $b \neq 0$ is a complex root of the equation $z^2 - 2z + 25 = 0$. Without evaluating the roots, answer the following questions:

(i) Show that $\overline{z_1}$, the conjugate of z_1, is also a root of $z^2 - 2z + 25 = 0$.

(ii) What is the value of $z_1 + \overline{z_1}$?

(iii) What is the value of $z_1 \overline{z_1}$?

(iv) Find the equation with roots $4z_1$ and $4\overline{z_1}$.

14. $z_1 = a + bi$, $a, b \in R$, $b \neq 0$ is a complex root of the equation $z^2 - 3z + 32 = 0$. Without evaluating the roots, answer the following questions:

(i) Is $\overline{z_1}$, the conjugate of z_1, also a root of $z^2 - 3z + 32 = 0$?

(ii) What is the value of $z_1 + \overline{z_1}$?

(iii) What is the value of $z_1 \overline{z_1}$?

(iv) Find an equation with roots $-z_1$ and $-\overline{z_1}$.

15. $z_1 = a + bi$, $a, b \in R$, $b \neq 0$ is a complex root of the equation $z^2 - 4z + 64 = 0$. Without evaluating the roots, answer the following questions:

(i) Is $\overline{z_1}$, the conjugate of z_1, also a root of $z^2 - 4z + 64 = 0$.

(ii) What is the value of $z_1 + \overline{z_1}$?

(iii) What is the value of $z_1 \overline{z_1}$?

(iv) Find an equation with roots $\frac{1}{4}z_1$ and $\frac{1}{4}\overline{z_1}$.

16. $f(z) = a_3 z^3 + a_2 z^2 + a_1 z + a_0$ is a cubic polynomial.

$g(z) = b_2 z^2 + b_1 z + b_0$ is a quadratic polynomial.

(i) If the roots of $g(z) = 0$ are $1 + i$ and $1 - i$, find a possible set of values for b_0, b_1 and b_2.

(ii) If the roots of $f(z) = 0$ are $1 + i$, $1 - i$ and 5, find a possible set of values for a_0, a_1, a_2 and a_3.

12.8 POLAR FORM OF A COMPLEX NUMBER

The complex number $z = x + yi$ is represented on the Argand diagram below.

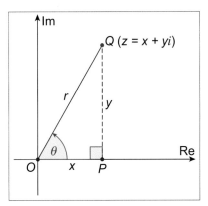

The line segment OQ makes an angle θ with the positive x-axis.

> The angle, θ, between the line segment joining a complex number, z, to the origin and the positive x-axis is called the **argument** of z or **arg(z)**. (The angle θ is anti-clockwise.)
>
> The length, r, of the line segment joining a complex number, z, to the origin is called the **modulus** of z.

In the triangle OPQ:

$$\sin \theta = \frac{y}{r}$$

$$\therefore \ y = r \sin \theta$$

$$\cos \theta = \frac{x}{r}$$

$$\therefore \ x = r \cos \theta$$

> The **polar form** of a complex number is $r(\cos \theta + i \sin \theta)$, where r is the modulus of the complex number and θ is its argument.
>
> Note: $-\pi < \theta \leqslant \pi$

$$\therefore \ z = x + yi \quad \text{(Cartesian form or rectangular form)}$$

$$= r \cos \theta + r \sin \theta i$$

$$\Rightarrow z = r(\cos \theta + i \sin \theta) \quad \text{(Polar form)}$$

$\sqrt{-1}$ Worked Example 12.22

Write the complex number $-\sqrt{3} + i$ in polar form.

Solution

Step 1: Show $-\sqrt{3} + i$ on an Argand diagram.

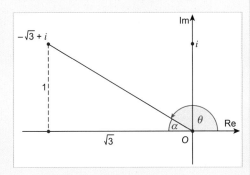

Step 2: Find the modulus of the complex number.

$$r = \sqrt{(-\sqrt{3})^2 + (1)^2}$$

$$r = \sqrt{4}$$

$$\therefore r = 2$$

Step 3: Find the argument of the complex number.

$$\tan \alpha = \frac{1}{\sqrt{3}}$$

$$\therefore \alpha = \frac{\pi}{6}$$

$$\therefore \theta = \pi - \frac{\pi}{6}$$

$$\Rightarrow \theta = \frac{5\pi}{6}$$

Step 4: Write the complex number in polar form, $r(\cos \theta + i \sin \theta)$.

$$-\sqrt{3} + i = 2\left(\cos \frac{5\pi}{6} + i \sin \frac{5\pi}{6}\right)$$

Multiplying and Dividing Numbers in Polar Form

In Activity 12.5, you derived a formula for multiplying and dividing complex numbers in polar form.

COMPLEX NUMBERS

FORMULA

If $z_1 = r_1(\cos \theta_1 + i \sin \theta_1)$ and $z_2 = r_2(\cos \theta_2 + i \sin \theta_2)$,
then $z_1 z_2 = r_1 r_2 (\cos (\theta_1 + \theta_2) + i \sin (\theta_1 + \theta_2))$.

If $z_1 = r_1(\cos \theta_1 + i \sin \theta_1)$ and $z_2 = r_2(\cos \theta_2 + i \sin \theta_2)$,
then $\dfrac{z_1}{z_2} = \dfrac{r_1}{r_2} [\cos (\theta_1 - \theta_2) + i \sin (\theta_1 - \theta_2)]$.

$\sqrt{-1}$ Worked Example 12.23

$z_1 = 3 \left(\cos \dfrac{\pi}{6} + i \sin \dfrac{\pi}{6}\right)$ and $z_2 = 4\left(\cos \dfrac{\pi}{3} + i \sin \dfrac{\pi}{3}\right)$. Find, in the form $x + yi$:

(i) $z_1 z_2$ (ii) $\dfrac{z_1}{z_2}$

Solution

(i) $z_1 z_2 = 3 \left(\cos \dfrac{\pi}{6} + i \sin \dfrac{\pi}{6}\right) 4 \left(\cos \dfrac{\pi}{3} + i \sin \dfrac{\pi}{3}\right)$

$= (3)(4) \left[\cos \left(\dfrac{\pi}{6} + \dfrac{\pi}{3}\right) + i \sin \left(\dfrac{\pi}{6} + \dfrac{\pi}{3}\right)\right]$

$= 12 \left[\cos \dfrac{\pi}{2} + i \sin \dfrac{\pi}{2}\right]$

$= 12[0 + i]$

$\Rightarrow z_1 z_2 = 0 + 12i$

(ii) $\dfrac{z_1}{z_2} = \dfrac{3 \left(\cos \dfrac{\pi}{6} + i \sin \dfrac{\pi}{6}\right)}{4 \left(\cos \dfrac{\pi}{3} + i \sin \dfrac{\pi}{3}\right)}$

$= \dfrac{3}{4} \left[\cos \left(\dfrac{\pi}{6} - \dfrac{\pi}{3}\right) + i \sin \left(\dfrac{\pi}{6} - \dfrac{\pi}{3}\right)\right]$

$= \dfrac{3}{4} \left[\cos \left(-\dfrac{\pi}{6}\right) + i \sin \left(-\dfrac{\pi}{6}\right)\right]$

$= \dfrac{3}{4} \left[\cos \dfrac{\pi}{6} - i \sin \dfrac{\pi}{6}\right]$

$= \dfrac{3}{4} \left[\dfrac{\sqrt{3}}{2} - \dfrac{1}{2}i\right]$

$\Rightarrow \dfrac{z_1}{z_2} = \dfrac{3\sqrt{3}}{8} - \dfrac{3}{8}i$

$\cos(-A) = \cos A$
$\sin(-A) = -\sin A$

Exercise 12.8

1. Write the following complex numbers in polar form, $r(\cos \theta + i \sin \theta)$:

   (i) $2 + 2i$

   (ii) $1 + \sqrt{3}i$

   (iii) $-1 + i$

   (iv) $2\sqrt{3} - 2i$

   (v) $5i$

   (vi) -2

   (vii) 3

   (viii) $-i$

   (ix) $-1 - i$

   (x) $-6 - 2\sqrt{3}i$

   (xi) $-2\sqrt{2} + 2\sqrt{2}i$

   (xii) $3 - \sqrt{3}i$

2. Write the following in the form $x + yi$, $x, y \in R$:

   (i) $\sqrt{32} \left(\cos \dfrac{\pi}{4} + i \sin \dfrac{\pi}{4}\right)$

   (ii) $3(\cos \pi + i \sin \pi)$

   (iii) $2\left(\cos \dfrac{\pi}{2} + i \sin \dfrac{\pi}{2}\right)$

   (iv) $2\left(\cos \dfrac{11\pi}{6} + i \sin \dfrac{11\pi}{6}\right)$

   (v) $100(\cos 25\pi + i \sin 25\pi)$

3. Given that $z = -2 + 2i$, evaluate:

   (i) $\arg(z)$ (ii) $-\arg(z)$ (iii) $-\arg\left(\dfrac{1}{z}\right)$

4. $z_1 = r_1(\cos \theta_1 + i \sin \theta_1)$ and
$z_2 = r_2(\cos \theta_2 + i \sin \theta_2)$.

Show that
$z_1 z_2 = r_1 r_2 (\cos (\theta_1 + \theta_2) + \sin (\theta_1 + \theta_2))$.

5. Write the following in polar form:

(i) $\left[2\left(\cos \frac{\pi}{8} + i \sin \frac{\pi}{8}\right)\right]\left[3\left(\cos \frac{\pi}{12} + i \sin \frac{\pi}{12}\right)\right]$

(ii) $\left[10\left(\cos \frac{\pi}{5} + i \sin \frac{\pi}{5}\right)\right]\left[5\left(\cos \frac{\pi}{10} + i \sin \frac{\pi}{10}\right)\right]$

(iii) $\dfrac{9\left(\cos \frac{\pi}{8} + i \sin \frac{\pi}{8}\right)}{3\left(\cos \frac{\pi}{16} + i \sin \frac{\pi}{16}\right)}$

(iv) $\dfrac{12\left(\cos \frac{\pi}{7} + i \sin \frac{\pi}{7}\right)}{4\left(\cos \frac{\pi}{14} + i \sin \frac{\pi}{14}\right)}$

6. $z_1 = \sqrt{3} + i$ and $z_2 = -1 + \sqrt{3}i$

(i) Plot z_1 and z_2 on an Argand diagram.

(ii) Write $z_1 z_2$ in the form $x + yi$.

(iii) Show that $\arg (z_1) + \arg(z_2) = \arg(z_1 z_2)$.

(iv) Show that $|z_1||z_2| = |z_1 z_2|$.

7. The complex numbers z and ω are such that:

$z = -\frac{1}{2} + \frac{\sqrt{3}}{2}i$ and $z\omega = 14 + 23i$

(i) Find ω in the form $a + bi$, where a and b are real.

(ii) Show z and ω on an Argand diagram.

(iii) Find $|z|$ and $\arg(z)$.

(iv) Write z in polar form.

(v) Multiplication by z rotates a complex number in an _____ direction, through ____°.

8. $z = \cos \theta + i \sin \theta$ is a complex number in polar form. Show that:

(i) $\cos \theta = \frac{1}{2}\left(z + \frac{1}{z}\right)$

(ii) $\sin \theta = -\frac{i}{2}\left(z - \frac{1}{z}\right)$

9. The set $\{z_1, z_2, z_3, z_4, z_5, z_6, z_7, z_8\}$ of complex numbers is shown on the Argand diagram. z_{n+1} is an anti-clockwise rotation of z_n through $\frac{\pi}{4}$ radians, $1 \leqslant n \leqslant 7, n \in N$.

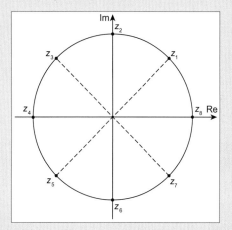

(i) Write z in the form $r(\cos \theta + i \sin \theta)$ given that $|z| = 1$.

(ii) Write z^3 in the form $r(\cos \theta + i \sin \theta)$.

(iii) $z^5 = a + bi$. Find the real numbers a and b.

12.9 DE MOIVRE'S THEOREM AND APPLICATIONS

Abraham de Moivre was a French mathematician. He was born in the Champagne region of France in 1667 and died in London in 1754. He is most famous for the theorem named after him, which links complex numbers and trigonometry. He also made contributions to probability and wrote a book, *The Doctrine of Chances*, on the subject.

Abraham de Moivre

De Moivre's Theorem

If $z = r(\cos \theta + i \sin \theta)$, then $z^n = r^n (\cos n\theta + \sin n\theta)$, for $n \in Z$,
i.e. $[r(\cos \theta + i \sin \theta)]^n = r^n (\cos n\theta + i \sin n\theta)$.

De Moivre's Theorem for $n \in N$

Proof by Induction

> This is a formal proof and may be asked in the exam.

Step 1: Is de Moivre's theorem true for $n = 1$?

LHS: $z^1 = [r(\cos \theta + i \sin \theta)]^1 = r(\cos \theta + i \sin \theta)$

RHS: $r^1(\cos (1)\theta + i \sin (1)\theta) = r(\cos \theta + i \sin \theta)$

$\therefore$ True for $n = 1$.

Step 2: Given that the theorem is true for $n = k$, prove that it is true for $n = k + 1$.

Given: $[r(\cos \theta + i \sin \theta)]^k = r^k(\cos k\theta + i \sin k\theta)$

To prove: $[r(\cos \theta + i \sin \theta)]^{k + 1} = r^{k + 1}(\cos (k + 1)\theta + i \sin (k + 1)\theta)$

Proof:

$$\begin{aligned}
\text{LHS} &= [r(\cos \theta + i \sin \theta)]^{k + 1} \\
&= [r(\cos \theta + i \sin \theta)]^k [r(\cos \theta + i \sin \theta)] \\
&= [r^k(\cos k\theta + i \sin k\theta)][r (\cos \theta + i \sin \theta)] \quad \text{(Given)} \\
&= r^{k + 1}[\cos k\theta \cos \theta + i \sin k\theta \cos \theta + i \cos k\theta \sin \theta - \sin k\theta \sin \theta] \\
&= r^{k + 1}[(\cos k\theta \cos \theta - \sin k\theta \sin \theta) + i(\sin k\theta \cos \theta + \cos k\theta \sin \theta)] \\
&= r^{k + 1}[\cos(k\theta + \theta) + i \sin (k\theta + \theta)] \\
&= r^{k + 1}(\cos (k + 1)\theta + i \sin (k + 1)\theta)
\end{aligned}$$

Step 3: By induction, de Moivre's theorem is true for all $n \in N$.

De Moivre's Theorem for $n \in Z$

To prove: $(r(\cos \theta + i \sin \theta))^n = r^n(\cos n\theta + i \sin n\theta), n \in Z$

Proof: The case of $n \in N$ has already been proved.

If we prove the theorem is true for the cases $n = 0$ and the negative integers, then we will have proved it true for all $n \in Z$.

Case 1: $n = 0$

LHS: $(r(\cos \theta + i \sin \theta))^0 = 1$

RHS: $r^0[\cos 0 (\theta) + i \sin 0 (\theta)] = r^0(\cos 0 + i \sin 0) = 1(1 + 0i) = 1$

$\therefore$ True for $n = 0$.

Case 2: n is a negative integer

Here we need to show that if p is a positive integer:

$(r(\cos \theta + i \sin \theta))^{-p} = r^{-p}(\cos (-p)\theta + i \sin (-p)\theta), p \in N$

$$\begin{aligned}
\text{LHS: } (r(\cos \theta + i \sin \theta))^{-p} &= \frac{1}{(r(\cos \theta + i \sin \theta))^p} \\
&= \frac{1}{r^p(\cos p\theta + i \sin p\theta)} \\
&= \frac{1}{r^p} \cdot \frac{1(\cos p\theta - i \sin p\theta)}{(\cos p\theta + i \sin p\theta)(\cos p\theta - i \sin p\theta)} \\
&= r^{-p} \cdot \frac{\cos p\theta - i \sin p\theta}{\cos^2 p\theta + \sin^2 p\theta} \\
&= r^{-p} \cdot \frac{\cos (-p\theta) + i \sin (-p\theta)}{1} \\
&= r^{-p}(\cos (-p)\theta + i \sin (-p)\theta)
\end{aligned}$$

(Multiplying above and below by complex conjugate)

> $\cos A = \cos(-A)$
> $\sin(-A) = -\sin A$

All cases are proved, therefore de Moivre's theorem holds for all integers.

De Moivre's Theorem, $n \in Q$

De Moivre's theorem is in fact true for all $n \in Q$. We prove the case only for integers, but we make use of the fact that it is true for all $n \in Q$.

√−1 Worked Example 12.24

Use de Moivre's theorem to write $(1 + i)^{10}$ in the form $x + yi$, $x, y \in R$.

Solution

Step 1: Write $1 + i$ in polar form, $r(\cos \theta + i \sin \theta)$.

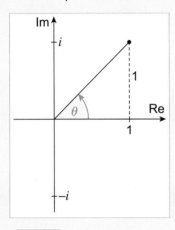

$r = \sqrt{1^2 + 1^2} = \sqrt{2}$

$\tan \theta = 1$

$\therefore \theta = \dfrac{\pi}{4}$

$1 + i = \sqrt{2}\left(\cos \dfrac{\pi}{4} + i \sin \dfrac{\pi}{4}\right)$

Step 2: Apply de Moivre's theorem.

$$(1 + i)^{10} = \left(\sqrt{2}\left(\cos \frac{\pi}{4} + i \sin \frac{\pi}{4}\right)\right)^{10}$$

$$= \sqrt{2}^{10}\left(\cos 10\left(\frac{\pi}{4}\right) + i \sin 10\left(\frac{\pi}{4}\right)\right)$$

$$= 32\left(\cos \frac{5\pi}{2} + i \sin \frac{5\pi}{2}\right)$$

$$= 32(0 + 1i)$$

$$\therefore (1 + i)^{10} = 0 + 32i$$

√−1 Worked Example 12.25

Use de Moivre's theorem to prove the identity $\sin 3\theta = 3 \sin \theta - 4 \sin^3 \theta$.

Solution

Binomial expansion:

$(\cos \theta + i \sin \theta)^3 = \dbinom{3}{0}\cos^3 \theta + \dbinom{3}{1}(\cos^2 \theta)(i \sin \theta) + \dbinom{3}{2}(\cos \theta)(i \sin \theta)^2 + \dbinom{3}{3}(i \sin \theta)^3$

$\qquad = \cos^3 \theta + (3\cos^2 \theta \sin \theta)i - 3\cos \theta \sin^2 \theta - (\sin^3 \theta)i$

$\qquad = \cos^3 \theta - 3\cos \theta \sin^2 \theta + (3\cos^2 \theta \sin \theta - \sin^3 \theta)i$

De Moivre's theorem: $(\cos \theta + i \sin \theta)^3 = \cos 3\theta + i \sin 3\theta$

Equate imaginary parts: $\sin 3\theta = 3\cos^2 \theta \sin \theta - \sin^3 \theta$

$\qquad\qquad = 3(1 - \sin^2 \theta)(\sin \theta) - \sin^3 \theta$

$\qquad\qquad = 3\sin \theta - 3\sin^3 \theta - \sin^3 \theta$

$\qquad\qquad = 3\sin \theta - 4\sin^3 \theta$

Exercise 12.9

1. Use de Moivre's theorem to write the following in the form $a + bi$:

   (i) $\left(\cos\frac{\pi}{32} + i\sin\frac{\pi}{32}\right)^8$

   (ii) $\left(\cos\frac{\pi}{36} + i\sin\frac{\pi}{36}\right)^9$

   (iii) $\left(\cos\frac{\pi}{6} + i\sin\frac{\pi}{6}\right)^2$

   (iv) $\left(\cos\frac{\pi}{3} + i\sin\frac{\pi}{3}\right)^6$

   (v) $\left[5\left(\cos\frac{\pi}{3} + i\sin\frac{\pi}{3}\right)\right]^6$

   (vi) $\left[\sqrt{2}\left(\cos\frac{\pi}{4} + i\sin\frac{\pi}{4}\right)\right]^4$

   (vii) $\left[\sqrt{3}\left(\cos\frac{\pi}{12} + i\sin\frac{\pi}{12}\right)\right]^8$

   (viii) $\left(\cos\frac{\pi}{3} + i\sin\frac{\pi}{3}\right)^5$

2. The complex number $z = \sqrt{3} + i$ is shown on the Argand diagram.

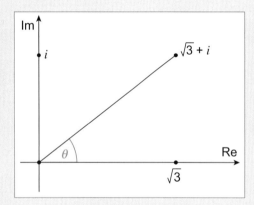

   (i) Find θ, the argument of z.

   (ii) Calculate r, the modulus of z.

   (iii) Write z in polar form.

   (iv) Use the theorem of de Moivre to write $(\sqrt{3} + i)^{10}$ in the form $a + bi$.

3. Let $z = 1 - i$.

   (i) Plot z on an Argand diagram.

   (ii) Find $\arg(z)$ and $|z|$.

   (iii) Hence write z in polar form.

   (iv) Use the theorem of de Moivre to evaluate z^9.

4. Let $z = -1 + i$.

   (i) Find θ, the argument of z.

   (ii) Calculate r, the modulus of z.

   (iii) Write z in polar form.

   (iv) Use the theorem of de Moivre to evaluate z^5 and z^9.

   (v) Show that $z^5 + z^9 = 12z$.

5. Use de Moivre's theorem to write the following in the form $a + bi$.

   (i) $(2 + 2i)^8$

   (ii) $(1 - i)^{16}$

   (iii) $\left(\frac{1}{2} + \frac{\sqrt{3}}{2}i\right)^{13}$

   (iv) $\left(\frac{1}{\sqrt{2}} + \frac{1}{\sqrt{2}}i\right)^{11}$

   (v) $\left(-\frac{1}{2} - \frac{\sqrt{3}}{2}i\right)^{60}$

   (vi) $\left(-\frac{\sqrt{3}}{2} + \frac{1}{2}i\right)^6$

   (vii) $(-2 - 2i)^9$

   (viii) $(-1 + i)^{13}$

6. Let $z = \frac{1}{\sqrt{2}} + \frac{1}{\sqrt{2}}i$.

   (i) Plot z on an Argand diagram.

   (ii) Find $\arg(z)$ and $|z|$.

   (iii) Write z in polar form.

   (iv) Use the theorem of de Moivre to evaluate z^6.

   (v) Find the least value of $n \in N$ for which $z^n = z$.

7. Let $\omega = \cos\theta + i\sin\theta$.

   (i) $\omega^3 = \cos\alpha + i\sin\alpha$. Use de Moivre's theorem to write α in terms of θ.

   (ii) $\omega^3 = \cos^3\theta + (a\cos^2\theta\sin\theta)i - a\cos\theta\sin^2\theta - (\sin^3\theta)i$.

   Expand $(\cos\theta + i\sin\theta)^3$ to find the value of a.

   (iii) Equate $\operatorname{Re}(\omega^3)$ from part (i) with $\operatorname{Re}(\omega^3)$ from part (ii) to prove the identity
   $$\cos 3\theta = 4\cos^3\theta - 3\cos\theta.$$

   (iv) Find the period and range of the function
   $$f(\theta) = 4\cos^3\theta - 3\cos\theta.$$

8. Let $z = \cos A + i \sin A$.

   (i) If $z^4 = \cos B + i \sin B$, then use de Moivre's theorem to write B in terms of A.

   (ii) $z^4 = \cos^m A - 6\cos^2 A \sin^2 A + \sin^m A + m(\cos^3 A \sin A - \cos A \sin^3 A)i$

     Expand $(\cos A + i \sin A)^4$ to find the value of m.

   (iii) Equate $\mathrm{Re}(z^4)$ from part (i) with $\mathrm{Re}(z^4)$ from part (ii) to prove the identity
$$\cos 4A = 8\cos^4 A - 8\cos^2 A + 1.$$

   (iv) Solve, for A, the equation $8\cos^4 A = 8\cos^2 A - 1$.

9. Let $z = \cos \theta + i \sin \theta$.
Use de Moivre's theorem to show that:

   (i) $z + \dfrac{1}{z} = 2\cos \theta$

   (ii) $z^n + \dfrac{1}{z^n} = 2\cos n\theta$

   (iii) $\cos^5 \theta = \dfrac{1}{16}[\cos 5\theta + 5\cos 3\theta + 10\cos \theta]$

10. Prove that, if $z = r(\cos \theta + i \sin \theta)$, then $z^n = r^n(\cos(n\theta) + i\sin(n\theta))$, for $n \in N$.

11. Let $\theta = \cos \theta + i \sin \theta$.
Use de Moivre's theorem to show that:

   (i) $z - \dfrac{1}{z} = 2i \sin \theta$

   (ii) $z^n - \dfrac{1}{z^n} = 2i \sin n\theta$

   (iii) $\sin^3 \theta = \dfrac{1}{4}[3\sin \theta - \sin 3\theta]$

12.10 DE MOIVRE'S THEOREM FOR $n \in Q$

De Moivre's theorem is also used to find the roots of equations. When de Moivre's theorem is applied to finding solutions to equations, then the **general polar form** of a complex number is used.

> The **general polar form** of a complex number is $r[(\cos(\theta + 2n\pi) + i\sin(\theta + 2n\pi)]$, where $n \in Z$.

ACTIVITY 12.6

In Activity 12.6, you learned why it is necessary to write complex numbers in general polar form to evaluate the roots of equations.

√–1 Worked Example 12.26

Let $\omega = -2 - 2\sqrt{3}i$.

   (i) Plot ω on an Argand diagram.

   (ii) Find $\arg(\omega)$ and $|\omega|$.

   (iii) Write ω in general polar form.

   (iv) What is the number of solutions to the equation $z^4 - \omega = 0$?

   (v) Solve the equation $z^4 - \omega = 0$. Plot your solutions on an Argand diagram.

Solution

   (i) Plot ω on an Argand diagram.

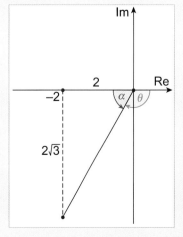

(ii) Find $\arg(\omega)$ and $|\omega|$.

$\arg(\omega)$ $\tan \alpha = \dfrac{2\sqrt{3}}{2} = \sqrt{3}$

$\therefore \alpha = \dfrac{\pi}{3}$

$\theta = \arg(\omega)$

$\therefore \theta = \left(-\pi + \dfrac{\pi}{3}\right)$

$\Rightarrow \arg(\omega) = -\dfrac{2\pi}{3}$

$|\omega| = \sqrt{(-2)^2 + (-2\sqrt{3})^2}$

$= \sqrt{4 + 12}$

$= \sqrt{16}$

$\therefore |\omega| = 4$

(iii) Write ω in general polar form.

$$\omega = 4\left[\cos\left(-\dfrac{2\pi}{3} + 2n\pi\right) + i\sin\left(-\dfrac{2\pi}{3} + 2n\pi\right)\right]$$

(iv) This is an equation of degree 4, therefore it has four solutions.

(v) Solve the equation $z^4 - \omega = 0$. Plot your solutions on an Argand diagram.

$z^4 - \omega = 0$

$\Rightarrow z = (\omega)^{\frac{1}{4}}$

$z = \left(-2 - 2\sqrt{3}i\right)^{\frac{1}{4}}$

Express in general polar form:

$$z = \left[4\left[\cos\left(-\dfrac{2\pi}{3} + 2n\pi\right) + i\sin\left(-\dfrac{2\pi}{3} + 2n\pi\right)\right]\right]^{\frac{1}{4}}$$

Apply the theorem of de Moivre:

$$= 4^{\frac{1}{4}}\left[\cos\dfrac{1}{4}\left(-\dfrac{2\pi}{3} + 2n\pi\right) + i\sin\dfrac{1}{4}\left(-\dfrac{2\pi}{3} + 2n\pi\right)\right]$$

$$= \sqrt{2}\left[\cos\left(\dfrac{n\pi}{2} - \dfrac{\pi}{6}\right) + i\sin\left(\dfrac{n\pi}{2} - \dfrac{\pi}{6}\right)\right]$$

Find the four solutions:

For $n = 0$	For $n = 1$
$z_1 = \sqrt{2}\left[\cos\left(-\dfrac{\pi}{6}\right) + i\sin\left(-\dfrac{\pi}{6}\right)\right]$	$z_2 = \sqrt{2}\left[\cos\left(\dfrac{\pi}{2} - \dfrac{\pi}{6}\right) + i\sin\left(\dfrac{\pi}{2} - \dfrac{\pi}{6}\right)\right]$
$= \sqrt{2}\left[\dfrac{\sqrt{3}}{2} - \dfrac{1}{2}i\right]$	$= \sqrt{2}\left[\cos\dfrac{\pi}{3} + i\sin\dfrac{\pi}{3}\right]$
$z_1 = \dfrac{\sqrt{6}}{2} - \dfrac{\sqrt{2}}{2}i$	$= \sqrt{2}\left[\dfrac{1}{2} + \dfrac{\sqrt{3}}{2}i\right]$
	$= \dfrac{\sqrt{2}}{2} + \dfrac{\sqrt{6}}{2}i$
For $n = 2$	**For $n = 3$**
$z_3 = \sqrt{2}\left[\cos\left(\pi - \dfrac{\pi}{6}\right) + i\sin\left(\pi - \dfrac{\pi}{6}\right)\right]$	$z_4 = \sqrt{2}\left[\cos\left(\dfrac{3\pi}{2} - \dfrac{\pi}{6}\right) + i\sin\left(\dfrac{3\pi}{2} - \dfrac{\pi}{6}\right)\right]$
$= \sqrt{2}\left[\cos\dfrac{5\pi}{6} + i\sin\dfrac{5\pi}{6}\right]$	$= \sqrt{2}\left[\cos\dfrac{4\pi}{3} + i\sin\dfrac{4\pi}{3}\right]$
$= \sqrt{2}\left[-\dfrac{\sqrt{3}}{2} + \dfrac{1}{2}i\right]$	$= \sqrt{2}\left[-\dfrac{1}{2} - \dfrac{\sqrt{3}}{2}i\right]$
$= -\dfrac{\sqrt{6}}{2} + \dfrac{\sqrt{2}}{2}i$	$= -\dfrac{\sqrt{2}}{2} - \dfrac{\sqrt{6}}{2}i$

By the Fundamental Theorem of Algebra, there are no more solutions. If we substitute $n = 4$, then we will get the same solution as for $n = 0$.

Also, note that each solution can be found by rotating the previous solution anti-clockwise through $\frac{1}{4}$ of 2π.

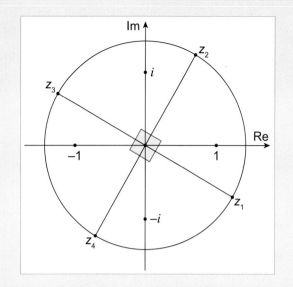

Worked Example 12.27

$f(z) = z^3 + 27$, $z \in C$ is a polynomial of degree 3.

(i) Show that $f(-3) = 0$.

(ii) The root $z_1 = -3$ is plotted on the Argand diagram.

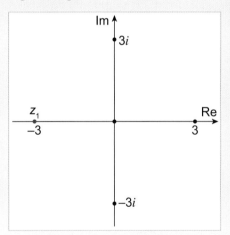

Locate the other roots on the diagram.

(iii) Find all three roots.

Solution

(i) $f(-3) = (-3)^3 + 27$

$\quad\quad = -27 + 27$

$\therefore f(-3) = 0$

(ii) By the Fundamental Theorem of Algebra, there are three solutions to the equation. We label these solutions z_1, z_2 and z_3. From de Moivre, we know that z_2 is an anti-clockwise rotation of z_1 through $\frac{1}{3}$ of 2π. Similarly, z_3 is an anti-clockwise rotation of z_2 through $\frac{1}{3}$ of 2π.

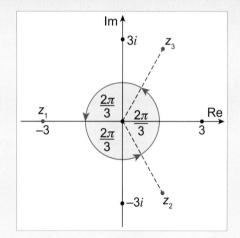

(iii) $\quad z_1 = 3(\cos \pi + i \sin \pi)$

$\quad\quad = 3(-1 + 0i)$

$\quad\quad = -3 + 0i$

$\quad z_2 = 3\left(\cos\left(\pi + \frac{2\pi}{3}\right) + i \sin\left(\pi + \frac{2\pi}{3}\right)\right)$

$\quad\quad = 3\left(\cos\left(\frac{5\pi}{3}\right) + i \sin\left(\frac{5\pi}{3}\right)\right)$

$\quad\quad = 3\left(\frac{1}{2} - i\left(\frac{\sqrt{3}}{2}\right)\right)$

$\therefore z_2 = \frac{3}{2} - \frac{3\sqrt{3}}{2}i$

$\quad z_3 = 3\left(\cos\left(\frac{5\pi}{3} + \frac{2\pi}{3}\right) + i \sin\left(\frac{5\pi}{3} + \frac{2\pi}{3}\right)\right)$

$\quad\quad = 3\left(\cos\left(\frac{7\pi}{3}\right) + i \sin\left(\frac{7\pi}{3}\right)\right)$

$\quad\quad = 3\left(\cos\frac{\pi}{3} + i \sin\frac{\pi}{3}\right)$

$\quad\quad = 3\left(\frac{1}{2} + i\left(\frac{\sqrt{3}}{2}\right)\right)$

$\therefore z_3 = \frac{3}{2} + \frac{3\sqrt{3}}{2}i$

1. Let $\omega = 1 - \sqrt{3}i$.

   (i) Plot ω on an Argand diagram.

   (ii) Find $\arg(\omega)$ and $|\omega|$.

   (iii) Write ω in general polar form.

   (iv) What is the number of solutions to the equation $z^2 - \omega = 0$?

   (v) Solve the equation $z^2 - \omega = 0$. Plot your solutions on an Argand diagram.

2. Use de Moivre's theorem to solve each of these equations. Plot your solutions on the complex plane.

   (i) $z^2 = 4i$ (v) $z^3 = 8$

   (ii) $z^2 + 1 + \sqrt{3}i = 0$ (vi) $z^3 + 1 = 0$

   (iii) $z^2 = 1 + \sqrt{3}i$ (vii) $z^4 + 2 + 2\sqrt{3}i = 0$

   (iv) $z^2 = \dfrac{1}{2} - \dfrac{\sqrt{3}}{2}i$ (viii) $z^3 = -64i$

3. Let $\alpha = -64i$.

   (i) Write α in general polar form.

   (ii) Find the solutions, z_1, z_2, z_3, z_4, z_5 and z_6 to the equation $z^6 = \alpha$.

   (iii) Plot the solutions on an Argand diagram.

   (iv) Write down the measure of $\angle z_2 O z_1$, where O is the origin.

   (v) Join $z_1 \to z_2 \to z_3 \to z_4 \to z_5 \to z_6 \to z_1$, with a straight edge. Name the shape thus formed.

4. Two roots, z_1 and z_2, of the equation $z^3 - 8 = 0$ are shown on the diagram.

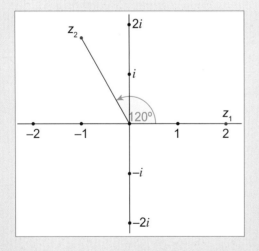

(i) Copy the diagram and plot z_3, the third root of the equation. Explain, using a geometric argument, how you located the third root.

(ii) Write z_2 and z_3 in the form $x + yi$, where x and y are real. (Note: you must use geometry and/or trigonometry to find z_2 and z_3.)

5. The solutions to the equation, $z^4 = 1 + \sqrt{3}i$ are plotted on the complex plane.

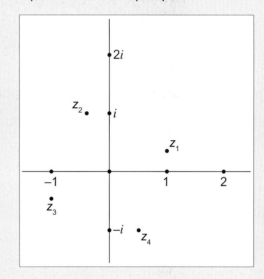

(i) $z_1 = 2^{\frac{1}{4}}\left(\cos \dfrac{\pi}{12} + i\sin \dfrac{\pi}{12}\right)$
What are $|z_1|, |z_2|, |z_3|$ and $|z_4|$?

(ii) Find, in the form $r(\cos \theta + i\sin \theta)$, z_2, z_3 and z_4. Explain, using a geometric argument, how you found the other three roots.

6. $f(z) = z^3 + 8$, $z \in C$ is a polynomial of degree 3.

   (i) Show that $f(-2) = 0$.

   (ii) The root $z_1 = -2$ is plotted on the Argand diagram.

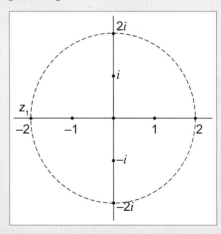

Locate the other roots on the diagram.

7. $f(z) = z^4 + 4$, $z \in C$ is a polynomial of degree 4.

    (i) Show that $f(z_1) = 0$, where $z_1 = 1 + i$.

    (ii) Plot z_1 on an Argand diagram.

    (iii) How many other roots does the equation, $f(z) = 0$ have?

    (iv) Locate these roots on the Argand diagram.

    (v) Explain why $f(i\omega) = 0$, where ω is any root of $f(z) = 0$.

8. Write $P(z) = z^5 - 1$ as a product of linear factors.

Revision Exercises

1. (a) Simplify:

    (i) $\sqrt{-144}$ (ii) i^{65} (iii) i^{-13}

  (b) Simplify and plot on an Argand diagram:

    (i) $(3 + i)(5 - 2i)$

    (ii) $(8 + 4i) + (2 - i)$

    (iii) $\dfrac{7 - i}{2 + i}$

2. $z_1 = 2 + i$, $z_2 = -3 + 2i$, $z_3 = -5 + 2i$, and $\theta = 1 + i$.

    (i) Plot z_1, z_2 and z_3 on an Argand diagram.

    (ii) Evaluate $z_1 + \theta$, $z_2 + \theta$ and $z_3 + \theta$.

    (iii) Plot the answers to part (ii) on an Argand diagram.

    (iv) Describe the transformation that is the addition of θ.

3. Let $z_1 = 2 - i$ and let $z_2 = 6 + i$.

    (i) Find $\dfrac{z_1}{z_2}$.

    (ii) Calculate $|z_1|$ and $|z_2|$.

    (iii) Investigate if $\left|\dfrac{z_1}{z_2}\right| = \dfrac{|z_1|}{|z_2|}$.

4. z is the complex number $1 + i$, where $i^2 = -1$.

  (a) (i) Find z^2 and z^3.

    (ii) Verify that $z^4 = -4$.

    (iii) Show z, z^2, z^3 and z^4 on an Argand diagram.

    (iv) Make one observation about the pattern of points on the diagram.

  (b) Using the value of z^4, or otherwise, find the values of z^8, z^{12} and z^{16}, and insert their values in the table below.

z^4	z^8	z^{12}	z^{16}
-4			

  (c) Based on the pattern of values in part (b), or otherwise, state whether z^{40} is positive or negative. Explain how you got your answer.

  (d) Write z^{40} as a power of 2.

  (e) Find z^{41}.

  (f) On an Argand diagram, how far from the origin is z^{41}?

SEC Leaving Certificate Project Maths Paper 1, 2011

5. The complex number z satisfies the equation $|z| = |z + 2|$.

    (i) Show that the real part of z is -1.

    (ii) The complex number z also satisfies $|z| = 2$. Find the two possible values of the imaginary part of z and show these on an Argand diagram.

    (iii) Write these two possible values of z in polar form.

NCCA Project Maths Pre-Leaving Certificate Sample Paper, February 2011

6. The equation $z^3 - 3z^2 - 23z - 35 = 0$ has one integer root.

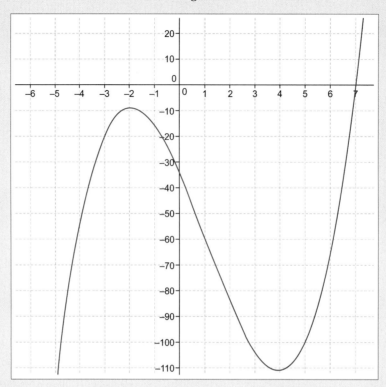

(i) Using the graph of $f(z) = z^3 - 3z^2 - 23z - 35$, find the value of the real root of $f(z) = 0$.

(ii) Hence, write down a linear factor of $f(z)$.

(iii) $f(z) = Q(z)(z - k)$, where $Q(z)$ is a quadratic polynomial and $k \in Z$.
Write $Q(z)$ in the form $Q(z) = az^2 + bz + c$.

(iv) Hence, find the two complex roots of $f(z)$.

7. $z_1 = -4 - 5i$

(i) Find z_2, if $z_2 = -iz_1$.

(ii) Plot z_1, and z_2 on an Argand diagram.

(iii) Describe the transformation that maps z_1 onto z_2.

8. $z = r(\cos \theta + i \sin \theta)$

Prove that $z^n = r^n (\cos n\theta + i \sin n\theta)$, for $n \in Z$.

9. $z_1 = a + bi$, $a, b \in R, b \neq 0$ is a complex root of the equation $z^2 - 2z + 44 = 0$.
Without evaluating the roots, answer the following questions:

(i) Is $\overline{z_1}$, the conjugate of z_1, also a root of $z^2 - 2z + 44 = 0$?

(ii) What is the value of $z_1 + \overline{z_1}$?

(iii) What is the value of $z_1 \overline{z_1}$?

Find the equation with roots $\frac{1}{2}z_1$ and $\frac{1}{2}\overline{z_1}$.

10. $z_1 = -2 + 3i$ and $z_2 = 3 + 2i$.

(i) Simplify $\frac{z_1}{z_2}$ and, hence, find the value of $\left|\frac{z_1}{z_2}\right|^9$.

(ii) Show that $\frac{|z_1|}{|z_2|} = \left|\frac{z_1}{z_2}\right|$.

11. $z_1 = -5 + 3i$

(i) Evaluate $z_1{}^2$ and $10z_1$.

(ii) Show that z_1 is a root of the quadratic equation $z^2 + 10z + 34 = 0$.

(iii) What is z_2, the other root of $z^2 + 10z + 34 = 0$?

(iv) Form the cubic equation with roots z_1, z_2 and z_3, where $z_3 = -2$.

12. $z = \dfrac{1}{\sqrt{3}} + i$

(i) Find θ, the argument of z.

(ii) Calculate r, the modulus of z.

(iii) Write z in polar form.

(iv) Use the theorem of de Moivre to write $\left(\dfrac{1}{\sqrt{3}} + i\right)^{20}$ in the form $a + bi$.

13. (i) Use de Moivre's theorem to find the three roots of the equation $z^3 + 64 = 0$.

(ii) ω is a complex number such that $\omega\overline{\omega} - 2i\omega = 7 - 4i$, where $\overline{\omega}$ is the complex conjugate of ω.
Find the two possible values of ω.
Express each in the form $p + qi$, $p, q \in R$.

14. Let $\beta = 16\sqrt{2} + 16\sqrt{2}i$.

(i) Write β in general polar form.

(ii) Find the solutions, z_1, z_2, z_3, z_4 and z_5 to the equation $z^5 = \beta$.

(iii) Plot the solutions on an Argand diagram.

(iv) Write down the measure of $\angle z_2 O z_1$ where O is the origin.

(v) Join $z_1 \to z_2 \to z_3 \to z_4 \to z_5 \to z_1$ with a straight edge. Name the shape thus formed.

15. (a) $w = -1 + \sqrt{3}i$ is a complex number, where $i^2 = -1$.

(i) Write w in polar form.

(ii) Use de Moivre's theorem to solve the equation $z^2 = -1 + \sqrt{3}i$, giving your answer(s) in rectangular form.

(b) Four complex numbers, z_1, z_2, z_3 and z_4, are shown on the Argand diagram.

They satisfy the following conditions:

$$z_2 = iz_1$$
$$z_3 = kz_1, \text{ where } k \in R$$
$$z_4 = z_2 + z_3$$

The same scale is used on both axes.

(i) Identify which number is which, by labelling the points on the diagram.

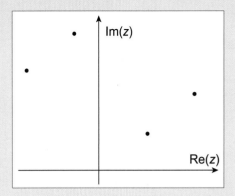

(ii) Write down the approximate value of k.

SEC Project Maths Paper 1 Sample Paper, Leaving Certificate Higher Level, 2011

16. (a) (i) Write the complex number $1 - i$ in polar form.

(ii) Use de Moivre's theorem to evaluate $(1 - i)^9$, giving your answer in rectangular form.

(b) A complex number z has modulus greater than 1.

The three numbers z, z^2 and z^3 are shown on the Argand diagram.

One of them lies on the imaginary axis, as shown.

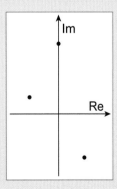

(i) Label the points on the diagram to show which point corresponds to which number.

(ii) Find θ, the argument of z.

SEC Project Maths Paper 1, Leaving Certificate Higher Level, 2011

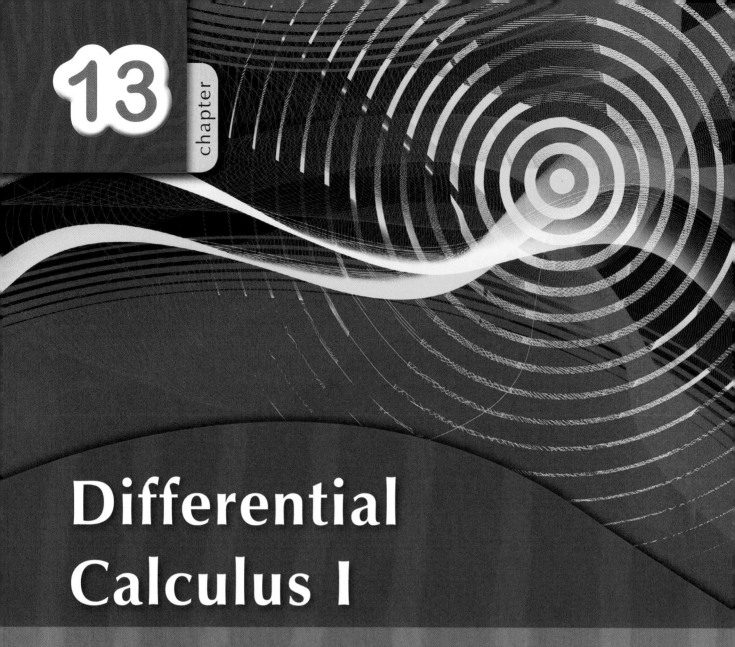

13 chapter

Differential Calculus I

Learning Outcomes

In this chapter you will learn:

- ➲ Limits and continuity
- ➲ Differentiation of linear and quadratic functions from first principles
- ➲ Differentiation of polynomials by rule
- ➲ Differentiation of functions with rational powers
- ➲ Differentiation of products and quotients
- ➲ The Chain Rule for differentiation of composite functions
- ➲ Differentiation of trigonometric functions
- ➲ To differentiate exponential functions
- ➲ To differentiate logarithmic functions
- ➲ To differentiate inverse trigonometric functions

13.1 CALCULUS

Over three hundred years ago, the branch of mathematics known as calculus was first developed.

Isaac Newton (1642–1727) was an English physicist and mathematician who, even during his own life, was considered to be one of the greatest and most influential scientists ever to have lived.

In his twenties, he started work on a new mathematics – the 'mathematics of moving things' or 'calculus'. He described this new mathematics to friends but did not publish any account of how he did it.

Isaac Newton (1642–1727)

KEY WORDS

- **Derivative**
- **First principles**
- **Slope**
- **Constant**
- **Product Rule**
- **Quotient Rule**
- **Chain Rule**
- **Polynomial**

Gottfried Leibniz (1646–1716)

At the same time, a young German mathematician called Gottfried Leibniz (1646–1716), working independently of Newton, came up with a different version of the same thing.

This was to have serious consequences years later when Newton accused Leibniz of plagiarism and was credited with inventing the new calculus, even though Leibniz had published his own work two decades before Newton.

Hundreds of years later, both men are now acknowledged as having invented this vital branch of mathematics, and while Newton may have enjoyed the initial credit, it is Leibniz who in some ways has had the last laugh, as it is his notation that is widely used today.

Why is calculus such a vital branch of modern mathematics, in areas as diverse as meteorology, fluid mechanics, engineering, economics and beyond?

Consider the following problem: if an apple falls from a tree, how can we measure its speed at a particular moment in time?

Since the apple is accelerating under gravity, its speed is constantly changing. So, to measure its speed at a particular point in time, we could measure the distance travelled in the next second of motion and divide by 1, since average speed is distance divided by time. However, this gives us the average speed over the next second of motion, which is not the precise speed at the particular moment of interest.

So, to get a more accurate estimate, we could measure the distance travelled in the next half-second and divide by one half, or in the next quarter-second and divide by one quarter.

Ultimately, to get the precise speed at a particular moment in time, we need to get the distance travelled over a time interval that is infinitesimally small. But this would leave us calculating zero divided by zero!

Calculus allows us to deal with such a seemingly impossible calculation, and therefore unlocks mankind's ability to use mathematics to model and predict all real-world behaviour involving moving things. No wonder Newton and Leibniz had such a squabble over who had invented it!

13.2 LIMITS AND CONTINUITY

Consider the function $f(x) = \frac{x^2}{x}$, $x \in R$. What value does $f(x)$ tend towards as x gets closer to zero? Let us complete an input–output table to investigate.

x	f(x)
−1	−1
−0.5	−0.5
−0.25	−0.25
−0.125	−0.125
−0.0625	−0.0625

} Approaching from the left

x	f(x)
1	1
0.5	0.5
0.25	0.25
0.125	0.125
0.0625	0.0625

} Approaching from the right

We can see that, as x gets closer and closer to zero (approaching from either side), $f(x)$ tends towards a value of zero.

In words, we say: 'The limit of the function $f(x) = \frac{x^2}{x}$ as x tends to 0 is equal to 0.'

In notation, we write: $\lim\limits_{x \to 0} f(x) = \lim\limits_{x \to 0} \frac{x^2}{x} = 0$

If $\lim\limits_{x \to a} f(x)$ exists, then $\lim\limits_{x \to a^+} f(x) = \lim\limits_{x \to a^-} f(x)$.

- The notation $\lim\limits_{x \to a^-} f(x)$ indicates that a is being approached from the left.

- The notation $\lim\limits_{x \to a^+} f(x)$ indicates that a is being approached from the right.

- The notation $\lim\limits_{x \to a} f(x)$ indicates that a is being approached from either side.

Continuity

What would a graph of the function $f(x) = \frac{x^2}{x}$, $x \in R$, look like?

It would have a 'break' in it at $x = 0$, since $f(x)$ is not defined at $x = 0$; that is, $\frac{(0)^2}{0} = 0$ is not defined.

We say that $f(x)$ is not continuous at $x = 0$, since there is a 'break' in the graph at $x = 0$. To draw a graph of this function, your pen would have to leave the page at $x = 0$. On the other hand:

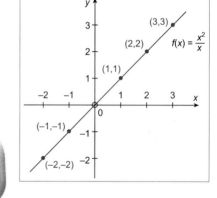

> If a function $g(x)$ is continuous at a particular input value, $x = c$, then $\lim\limits_{x \to c} g(x) = g(c)$. The converse is also true.

Note that with the previous function $f(x) = \frac{x^2}{x}$, although $\lim\limits_{x \to 0} f(x) = 0$, $f(0)$ was not defined. Therefore, $\lim\limits_{x \to 0} f(x) \neq f(0)$, so $f(x)$ was not continuous at $x = 0$.

Worked Example 13.1

Consider the function H given by:

$$H(x) = \begin{cases} 3x + 2, & \text{for } x < 1 \\ 3x - 3, & \text{for } x \geqslant 1 \end{cases}$$

Graph the function and find each of the following limits, if they exist.

(i) $\lim\limits_{x \to 3} H(x)$ (ii) $\lim\limits_{x \to 1} H(x)$

Solution

(i) We can check the limits from the left and the right both numerically (using a table) and graphically.

$x \to 3^-$ ($x < 3$)	$H(x)$	$x \to 3^+$ ($x > 3$)	$H(x)$
2	3	4	9
2.5	4.5	3.5	7.5
2.9	5.7	3.1	6.3
2.99	5.97	3.01	6.03
2.999	5.997	3.001	6.003

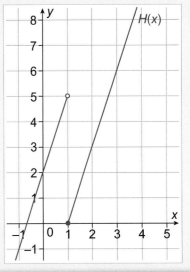

From the table, we can see that $\lim\limits_{x \to 3^+} H(x) = \lim\limits_{x \to 3^-} H(x) = 6$.

Therefore, $\lim\limits_{x \to 3} H(x) = 6$.

(ii)

$x \to 1^-$ ($x < 1$)	$H(x)$	$x \to 1^+$ ($x > 1$)	$H(x)$
0	2	2	3
0.5	3.5	1.5	1.5
0.9	4.7	1.1	0.3
0.99	4.97	1.01	0.03
0.999	4.997	1.001	0.003

From the table, we can see that $\lim\limits_{x \to 1^+} H(x) = 0$ and $\lim\limits_{x \to 1^-} H(x) = 5$.

Therefore, $\lim\limits_{x \to 1} H(x)$ does not exist.

> $H(x)$ is a **piecewise function.**
> This is a function whose definition changes depending on the value of the independent variable, x.
>
> $H(x)$ is defined differently for $x < 1$ than for $x \geqslant 1$, hence the split in the graph of $H(x)$.

Worked Example 13.2

The function $f(x) = \dfrac{1}{x - 2}$ is graphed in the domain

$-4 \leqslant x \leqslant 7, x \neq 2, x \in R$

Explain why the function is not continuous at $x = 2$.

Solution

$x = 2$ is not in the domain of this function. Therefore, $f(2)$ does not exist. This implies that $\lim\limits_{x \to 2} f(x) \neq f(2)$; hence, the function is not continuous at $x = 2$.

Alternatively: $f(2) = \dfrac{1}{2 - 2}$

$= \dfrac{1}{0}$, which is not defined

$\therefore f(2)$ is not continuous at $x = 2$.

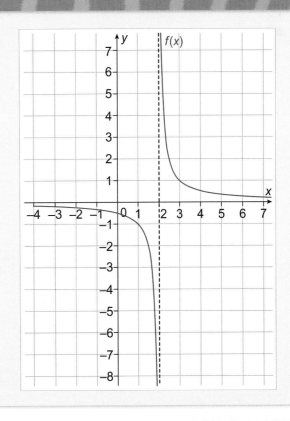

> Note: The line $x = 2$ shown on the graph is called an **asymptote.**
>
> An asymptote is a line whose distance to a given curve tends to zero.

Worked Example 13.3

Show that the function $f(x) = 2x + 3$, $x \in R$, is continuous at $x = 2$.

Solution

Looking at the algebraic form of $f(x) = 2x + 3$, we can see that the function is defined over all $x \in R$ and is a linear function.

So $f(x)$ is continuous at $x = 2$.

Alternatively, using an input–output table:

x	f(x)	x	f(x)
1.0	5	3.0	9
1.5	6	2.5	8
1.8	6.6	2.2	7.4
1.9	6.8	2.1	7.2
1.95	6.9	2.05	7.1
1.99	6.98	2.01	7.02
1.995	6.99	2.005	7.01
1.999	6.998	2.001	7.002

$$\left.\begin{array}{l} \lim_{x \to 2^-} f(x) = 7 \\ \lim_{x \to 2^+} f(x) = 7 \end{array}\right\} \therefore \lim_{x \to 2} f(x) \text{ exists and equals } 7.$$

But $f(2) = 2(2) + 3$
$$= 4 + 3$$
$$= 7$$

As $\lim_{x \to 2} f(x) = f(2)$, $f(x)$ is continuous at $x = 2$.

Worked Example 13.4

Evaluate the following limits. (Assume that the limits exist.)

(i) $\lim_{x \to 5} \dfrac{x^2 - 25}{x - 5}$ (ii) $\lim_{x \to 2} \dfrac{x^3 - 8}{x - 2}$

Solution

(i) We can check the limits from the left and the right numerically (using a table) and/or graphically.

Let $f(x) = \dfrac{x^2 - 25}{x - 5}$.

x→5⁻ (x < 5)	f(x)	x→5⁺ (x > 5)	f(x)
4	9	6	11
4.5	9.5	5.5	10.5
4.9	9.9	5.1	10.1
4.99	9.99	5.01	10.01
4.999	9.999	5.001	10.001

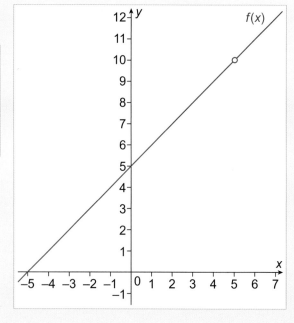

From the table and/or graph, it is clear that:

$$\lim_{x \to 5} \frac{x^2 - 25}{x - 5} = 10$$

Algebraic approach

We can shorten our work as follows:

$$\lim_{x \to 5} \frac{x^2 - 25}{x - 5} = \lim_{x \to 5} \frac{(x + 5)(x - 5)}{x - 5}$$

$$= \lim_{x \to 5} (x + 5)$$

$$= 5 + 5$$

$$= 10$$

(ii) Again, we can check the limits from the left and the right numerically (using a table) and/or graphically.

Let $f(x) = \dfrac{x^3 - 8}{x - 2}$.

$x \to 2^-$ (x < 2)	$f(x)$	$x \to 2^+$ (x > 2)	$f(x)$
1	7	3	19
1.5	9.25	2.5	15.25
1.9	11.41	2.1	12.61
1.99	11.9401	2.01	12.0601
1.999	11.994001	2.001	12.006001

From the table and/or graph, it is clear that:

$$\lim_{x \to 2} \frac{x^3 - 8}{x - 2} = 12$$

Algebraic approach

$$\lim_{x \to 2} \frac{x^3 - 8}{x - 2} = \lim_{x \to 2} \frac{(x - 2)(x^2 + 2x + 4)}{x - 2}$$

$$= \lim_{x \to 2} (x^2 + 2x + 4)$$

$$= (2)^2 + 2(2) + 4$$

$$= 12$$

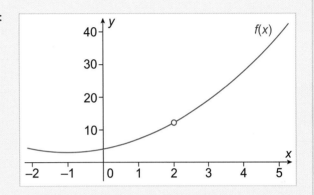

Exercise 13.1

1. Copy and complete the table to give values of the function $f(x) = 3x - 4$, $x \in R$, for x close to 2.

x	$f(x)$	x	$f(x)$
1.0		3.0	
1.5		2.5	
1.8		2.2	
1.9		2.1	
1.95		2.01	
1.99		2.01	
1.995		2.005	
1.999		2.001	

(i) Use the table to evaluate $\lim\limits_{x \to 2^+} f(x)$ and $\lim\limits_{x \to 2^-} f(x)$.

(ii) Hence, write down $\lim\limits_{x \to 2} f(x)$.

2. Consider the function H given by:

$$H(x) = \begin{cases} 2x + 2, & \text{for } x < 1 \\ 2x - 3, & \text{for } x \geqslant 1 \end{cases}$$

Graph the function and find each of the following limits, if they exist.

(i) $\lim\limits_{x \to 3} H(x)$ (ii) $\lim\limits_{x \to 1} H(x)$

3. Consider the function f given by

$$f(x) = \begin{cases} 2x + 2, & \text{for } x < 0 \\ x^2, & \text{for } x \geqslant 0 \end{cases}$$

Graph the function and find each of the following limits, if they exist.

(i) $\lim\limits_{x \to 2} f(x)$ (ii) $\lim\limits_{x \to 0} f(x)$

4. Find the following limits.
(You may assume the limit exists in each case.)

(i) $\lim\limits_{x \to 1} (3x + 4)$ (iv) $\lim\limits_{x \to 3} \dfrac{x^2 - 16}{x - 4}$

(ii) $\lim\limits_{x \to 3} (3x^2 - 2)$ (v) $\lim\limits_{x \to 2} \dfrac{x^3 - 8}{x - 2}$

(iii) $\lim\limits_{x \to 3} \dfrac{x^2 - 16}{x - 4}$

5. Find the following limits.
(You may assume the limit exists in each case.)

(i) $\lim_{x \to 2} \dfrac{x^2 - 4}{x^2 - x - 2}$

(ii) $\lim_{x \to 3} \dfrac{x^2 - 9}{x^2 + x - 12}$

(iii) $\lim_{x \to 5} \dfrac{x^2 - 25}{x^3 - 125}$

(iv) $\lim_{x \to 0} \dfrac{2x}{5x}$

(v) $\lim_{x \to 0} \dfrac{3x^2}{4x^2}$

6. Determine if the following functions are continuous at the given value of x.

(i) $f(x) = 3x - 4$, $x = 3$

(ii) $f(x) = \dfrac{3}{x - 4}$, $x = 3$

(iii) $f(x) = \dfrac{3}{x - 4}$, $x = 4$

(iv) $f(x) = \dfrac{x^2 - 16}{x - 4}$, $x = 4$

(v) $f(x) = \dfrac{x^2}{x - 3}$, $x = 3$

7. One of the most important limits in use today is the following:

$\lim_{x \to 0} \dfrac{\sin x}{x} = 1$, where x is measured in radians.

(i) Evaluate $\lim_{x \to 0^-} \dfrac{\sin x}{x}$ using a suitable input–output table.

(ii) Evaluate $\lim_{x \to 0^+} \dfrac{\sin x}{x}$ using a suitable input–output table.

(iii) Hence, explain why $\lim_{x \to 0} \dfrac{\sin x}{x}$ exists and is equal to 1.

13.3 DIFFERENTIATION FROM FIRST PRINCIPLES

Unlike the slope of a line, the slope of a curve is constantly changing. We define the slope of a curve at a point P on the curve to be the slope of the tangent to the curve at the point P.

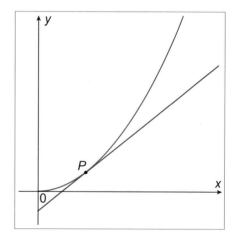

How do we calculate mathematically the slope of a tangent to a curve $y = f(x)$ at a certain point $(x, f(x))$?

We can approximate the slope by taking a nearby point on the curve and finding the slope of the line joining this point to the point of contact.

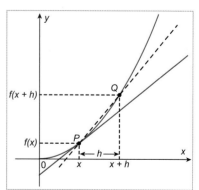

The slope of PQ is given by:

$m = \dfrac{f(x + h) - f(x)}{x + h - x}$, where h is a small change in the input variable x.

$\therefore m = \dfrac{f(x + h) - f(x)}{h}$

If we let h become smaller and smaller, the slope of PQ becomes closer and closer to the slope of the tangent.

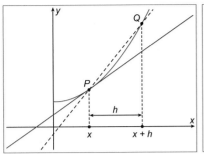 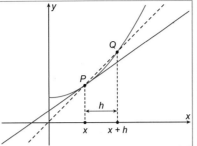 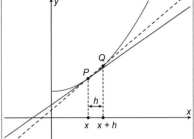

We say that the slope of the tangent is given by:

$\dfrac{f(x + h) - f(x)}{h}$ as h approaches zero,

or more formally as:

$\lim\limits_{h \to 0} \dfrac{f(x + h) - f(x)}{h}$

If $y = f(x)$, the slope of a tangent to the curve $y = f(x)$ at the point $(x, f(x))$ is:

$$\dfrac{dy}{dx} = f'(x) = \lim\limits_{h \to 0} \dfrac{f(x + h) - f(x)}{h}$$

Both $\dfrac{dy}{dx}$ and $f'(x)$ stand for the slope of the tangent to the curve, or the gradient of the curve, of $y = f(x)$.

$\dfrac{dy}{dx}$ is pronounced 'dee y dee x'.

$f'(x)$ is pronounced 'f prime of x'.

Differentiation is the process of finding this slope or gradient. Differentiation 'from first principles' involves calculating the difference between $f(x + h)$ and $f(x)$, dividing by h, and then taking the limit as h approaches zero.

$\dfrac{dy}{dx}$ or $f'(x)$ is called the **derivative** of the function $f(x)$ with respect to x.

 ## Worked Example 13.5

Differentiate $f(x) = 2x + 3$, with respect to x, from first principles.

Solution

$$f(x) = 2x + 3$$
$$f(x + h) = 2(x + h) + 3$$
$$= 2x + 2h + 3$$
$$f(x + h) - f(x) = 2x + 2h + 3 - 2x - 3$$
$$= 2h$$
$$\dfrac{f(x + h) - f(x)}{h} = \dfrac{2h}{h}$$
$$= 2$$
$$\lim\limits_{h \to 0} \dfrac{f(x + h) - f(x)}{h} = \lim\limits_{h \to 0} 2$$
$$= 2$$
$$\therefore \dfrac{dy}{dx} = f'(x) = 2$$

You can write $\dfrac{dy}{dx} = 2$ or $f'(x) = 2$.

Worked Example 13.6

Differentiate $f(x) = x^2$, with respect to x, from first principles.

Solution

$$f(x) = x^2$$
$$f(x + h) = (x + h)^2$$
$$= x^2 + 2hx + h^2$$
$$f(x + h) - f(x) = x^2 + 2hx + h^2 - x^2$$
$$= 2hx + h^2$$
$$\dfrac{f(x + h) - f(x)}{h} = \dfrac{2hx + h^2}{h}$$
$$= 2x + h$$
$$\lim\limits_{h \to 0} \dfrac{f(x + h) - f(x)}{h} = \lim\limits_{h \to 0} (2x + h)$$
$$= 2x + 0$$
$$= 2x$$
$$\therefore f'(x) = 2x$$

Worked Example 13.7

Differentiate $f(x) = 3 + 2x - x^2$, with respect to x, from first principles.

Solution

$$f(x) = 3 + 2x - x^2$$

$$f(x + h) = 3 + 2(x + h) - (x + h)^2$$

$$= 3 + 2x + 2h - (x^2 + 2hx + h^2)$$

$$= 3 + 2x + 2h - x^2 - 2hx - h^2$$

$$f(x + h) - f(x) = 3 + 2x + 2h - x^2 - 2hx - h^2 - (3 + 2x - x^2)$$

$$= 2h - 2hx - h^2$$

$$\frac{f(x + h) - f(x)}{h} = \frac{2h - 2hx - h^2}{h}$$

$$= 2 - 2x - h$$

$$\lim_{h \to 0} \frac{f(x + h) - f(x)}{h} = \lim_{h \to 0} (2 - 2x - h)$$

$$= 2 - 2x - 0$$

$$\therefore f'(x) = 2 - 2x$$

Worked Example 13.8

Show from first principles that the derivative of $f(x) = x^2$ at $x = 1$ is 2.

Solution

$$f(1) = 1^2 = 1$$

$$f(1 + h) = (1 + h)^2$$

$$= 1 + 2h + h^2$$

$$f(1 + h) - f(1) = 1 + 2h + h^2 - 1$$

$$= 2h + h^2$$

$$\frac{f(1 + h) - f(1)}{h} = \frac{2h + h^2}{h}$$

$$= 2 + h$$

$$\lim_{h \to 0} \frac{f(1 + h) - f(1)}{h} = \lim_{h \to 0} (2 + h)$$

$$= 2 + 0$$

$$\therefore f'(1) = 2$$

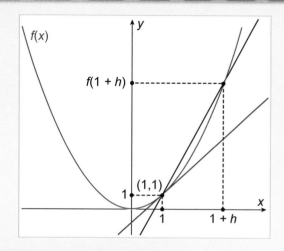

We could also have differentiated $f(x) = x^2$ from first principles and **then** substituted $x = 1$. See alternative solution.

Alternative solution:

$$f(x) = x^2$$

$$f(x + h) = (x + h)^2$$

$$= x^2 + 2hx + h^2$$

$$f(x + h) - f(x) = x^2 + 2hx + h^2 - x^2$$

$$= 2hx + h^2$$

$$\frac{f(x + h) - f(x)}{h} = \frac{2hx + h^2}{h}$$

$$= 2x + h$$

$$\lim_{h \to 0} \frac{f(x + h) - f(x)}{h} = \lim_{h \to 0} (2x + h)$$

$$= 2x + 0$$

$$\therefore f'(x) = 2x$$

$$f'(1) = 2(1)$$

$$= 2 \qquad \text{QED}$$

Exercise 13.2

1. $f(x) = 3x - 2, x \in R$

   (i) Graph $f(x)$ in the domain $-2 \leqslant x \leqslant 3$.

   (ii) Differentiate $f(x)$ with respect to x from first principles.

   (iii) Explain why the derivative of $f(x)$ is constant for all $x \in R$.

2. $f(x) = 5 - 6x, x \in R$

   (i) Graph $f(x)$ in the domain $-1 \leqslant x \leqslant 4$.

   (ii) Differentiate $f(x)$ with respect to x from first principles.

3. The function $g(x) = 3x^2$ is defined for all $x \in R$.

   (i) Differentiate $g(x)$ with respect to x from first principles.

   (ii) Hence, find the slope of the tangent to the curve $g(x) = 3x^2$ at the point $(1,3)$.

   (iii) Write in the form $y = mx + c$ the equation of the tangent to the graph of $g(x) = 3x^2$ at the point $(1,3)$.

4. The function $h(x) = x^2 + 2x$ is defined for all $x \in R$.

   (i) Differentiate $h(x)$ with respect to x from first principles.

   (ii) Hence, find the slope of the tangent to the curve $h(x) - x^2 + 2x$ at the point $(2,8)$.

   (iii) Write in the form $y = mx + c$ the equation of the tangent to the graph of $h(x) = x^2 + 2x$ at the point $(2,8)$.

5. The function $f(x) = 2 + 3x - x^2$ is defined for all $x \in R$.

   (i) Differentiate $f(x)$ with respect to x from first principles.

   (ii) Hence, find the slope of the tangent to the curve $f(x) = 2 + 3x - x^2$ at the point $(1,4)$.

   (iii) Write in the form $ax + by + c = 0$ the equation of the tangent to the graph of $f(x) = 2 + 3x - x^2$ at the point $(1,4)$.

6. Show from first principles that the derivative of $f(x) = 5x^2$ at $x = 1$ is 10.

7. Show from first principles that the derivative of $f(x) = 5x^2 - 2x + 5$ at $x = 2$ is 18.

8. The function $g(x) = 1 + 6x - 2x^2$ is defined for all $x \in R$.

   (i) Differentiate $g(x)$ with respect to x from first principles.

   (ii) Hence, find the co-ordinates of the point A on the graph of $g(x)$ where the tangent at A has a slope of 14.

9. The distance s of a car from a fixed point on a stretch of motorway is given by the formula $s = 7t^2 + 12t$, where t is time (in seconds) and s is measured in metres.

   (i) Use differentiation from first principles to show that the speed of the car at the fixed point on the motorway is 12 m/s.

   (ii) If acceleration is the change in speed per unit time, use differentiation from first principles to show that the car has a constant acceleration of 14 m/s² on this stretch of motorway.

13.4 DIFFERENTIATING POLYNOMIAL FUNCTIONS AND FUNCTIONS WITH RATIONAL POWERS

A polynomial function is a function of the form:

$$f(x) = a_nx^n + a_{n-1}x^{n-1} + \ldots + a_2x^2 + a_1x + a_0$$

ACTIVITY 13.1

where n is a non-negative integer and $a_0, a_1, \ldots, a_n$ are constant coefficients.

In the next Activity, you will prove that the derivative of any constant function is zero.

The Derivative of x^n

Rule 1
If $y = x^n$, then $\dfrac{dy}{dx} = nx^{n-1}$, $n \in N$.

Rule 2
If $y = a$, where a is any constant, then $\dfrac{dy}{dx} = 0$.

Rule 3
If $y = ax^n$, where a is any constant, then $\dfrac{dy}{dx} = anx^{n-1}$.

Rules for differentiating can be found on page 25 of the *Formulae and Tables*.

Differentiate the following with respect to x:

(i) $f(x) = x^2$

(ii) $f(x) = 2x$

(iii) $f(x) = 4$

Solution

(i) $f'(x) = 2x$

(ii) $f'(x) = 2$

(iii) $f'(x) = 0$

To differentiate a power of x, multiply by the power and reduce the power by 1.

Properties of Limits

The following are some important properties of limits:

(1) $\lim\limits_{x \to a} [f(x) + g(x)] = \lim\limits_{x \to a} f(x) + \lim\limits_{x \to a} g(x)$ (Sum property)

(2) $\lim\limits_{x \to a} [f(x) \times g(x)] = \lim\limits_{x \to a} f(x) \times \lim\limits_{x \to a} g(x)$ (Product property)

(3) $\lim\limits_{x \to a} \left[\dfrac{f(x)}{g(x)} \right] = \dfrac{\lim\limits_{x \to a} f(x)}{\lim\limits_{x \to a} g(x)}$ (Quotient property)

(4) $\lim\limits_{x \to a} \sqrt{f(x)} = \sqrt{\lim\limits_{x \to a} f(x)}$ (Root property)

The Sum Rule

Rule 4
If $y = f(x) + g(x)$, then $\dfrac{dy}{dx} = \dfrac{df}{dx} + \dfrac{dg}{dx}$.

 ACTIVITY 13.2

Differentiate the following with respect to x:

(i) $f(x) = x^2 - 2x + 5$

(ii) $g(x) = x^{10} + 4x^2$

Solution

(i) $f'(x) = 2x - 2$ (Differentiate term by term)

(ii) $g'(x) = 10x^9 + 8x$

Worked Example 13.11

If $y = x^2 - 3x + 8$, find $\dfrac{dy}{dx}$ when $x = -1$.

Solution

$y = x^2 - 3x + 8$ $\qquad$ At $x = -1$, $\dfrac{dy}{dx} = 2(-1) - 3$

$\Rightarrow \dfrac{dy}{dx} = 2x - 3$ $\qquad\qquad\qquad = -5$

Rational Powers

It can be shown that if $f(x) = x^p$, $p \in Q$ (i.e. p is any rational number), then $f'(x) = px^{p-1}$.

 Worked Example 13.12

If $f(x) = \sqrt{x} - \sqrt{x^3} - 8x$, find $f'(x)$.

Solution

Step 1 Write all terms of the expression in index form:

$f(x) = x^{\frac{1}{2}} - x^{\frac{3}{2}} - 8x$

Step 2 Differentiate the expression:

$f'(x) = \dfrac{1}{2}x^{-\frac{1}{2}} - \dfrac{3}{2}x^{\frac{1}{2}} - 8$

$f'(x) = \dfrac{1}{2\sqrt{x}} - \dfrac{3}{2}\sqrt{x} - 8$

 Worked Example 13.13

A graph of the cubic function $f(x) = 2x^3 + 5x^2 + x - 3$ is shown.
The tangent to $f(x)$ at the point $(0,-3)$ is also shown on the diagram.

(i) Write down $f'(x)$, the derivative of $f(x)$.

(ii) Hence, find the slope of the tangent to $f(x)$ at $(0,-3)$.

(iii) Find the equation of the tangent to the curve at $(0,-3)$.

(iv) Find the co-ordinates of the points where the tangent intersects the x-axis and the y-axis.

(v) Hence, calculate the area enclosed between the tangent, the x-axis and the y-axis.

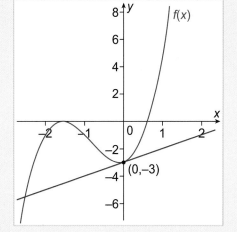

Solution

(i) $f(x) = 2x^3 + 5x^2 + x - 3$

$f'(x) = 6x^2 + 10x + 1$

(ii) To find the slope of the tangent to $f(x)$ at $(0,-3)$, we need to find $f'(0)$.

$f'(0) = 6(0)^2 + 10(0) + 1$

$\therefore f'(0) = 1$

Therefore, the slope of the tangent to the curve at $(0,-3)$ is 1.

(iii) $y - y_1 = m(x - x_1)$ $\qquad$ Point $(0,-3)$ $\qquad$ $m = 1$

$y + 3 = 1(x - 0)$

$\therefore y = x - 3$

(iv) $y = x - 3$

$x = 0$	$y = 0$
$y = -3$	$0 = x - 3$
	$3 = x$

∴ Intersects the x-axis at (3,0) and y-axis at (0,−3).

(v)

Area of shaded triangle $= \frac{1}{2}$ base × perpendicular height

$$= \frac{1}{2}(3) \times 3$$

$$= 4.5 \text{ units}^2$$

Exercise 13.3

1. Differentiate the following with respect to x:

(i) $y = 4x^2 + 2x + 6$

(ii) $y = x^{12} + 9x + 12$

(iii) $y = 3x^3 + 4x^2 - 3x + 8$

(iv) $y = 3x$

(v) $y = 5 - 2x$

(vi) $y = 2 - x$

(vii) $y = 4$

(viii) $y = \frac{1}{2}$

(ix) $y = -\sqrt{2}$

2. $f(x) = x^2 - 2x + 12$

(i) Find $f'(x)$.   (ii) Evaluate $f'(100)$.

3. $f(x) = x^3 - x^2 + 4$

(i) Find $f'(x)$.   (ii) Evaluate $f'(-5)$.

4. The function $f(x) = 5 + 2x - 2x^2$ is shown, together with the tangent to $f(x)$ at the point (2,1).

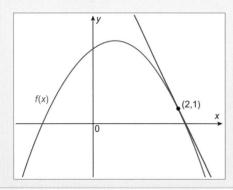

(i) Write down $f'(x)$, the derivative of $f(x)$.

(ii) Hence, find the slope of the tangent to $f(x)$ at (2,1).

(iii) Find the equation of the tangent to the curve at (2,1).

(iv) Find the co-ordinates of the point where this tangent intersects the y-axis.

5. A graph of the cubic function $f(x) = x^3 + 5x^2 + 5x + 1$ is shown. The tangent to $f(x)$ at the point (0,1) is also shown on the diagram.

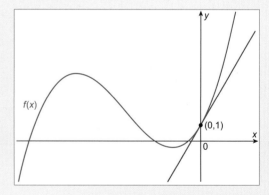

(i) Write down $f'(x)$, the derivative of $f(x)$.

(ii) Hence, find the slope of the tangent to $f(x)$ at (0,1).

(iii) Find the equation of the tangent to the curve at (0,1).

(iv) Find the co-ordinates of the points where the tangent intersects the x-axis and y-axis.

(v) Hence, calculate the area enclosed between the tangent, the x-axis and the y-axis.

6. A graph of the cubic function
$f(x) = 1 + 2x + 3x^2 - x^3$ is shown.
The tangent to $f(x)$ at the point $(0,1)$ is also
shown on the diagram.

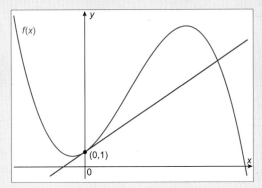

(i) Find $f'(x)$, the derivative of $f(x)$.

(ii) Hence, find the slope of the tangent to
$f(x)$ at $(0,1)$.

(iii) Find the equation of the tangent to the
curve at $(0,1)$.

(iv) Find the co-ordinates of the points
where the tangent intersects the x-axis
and the y-axis.

(v) Hence, calculate the area enclosed
between the tangent, the x-axis and the
y-axis.

(vi) Show that the tangent intersects the
graph of $f(x)$ at the point $(3,7)$.

7. Show that the tangent to the curve
$y = x^2 - 2x + 5$ at $(1,4)$ has a slope equal to 0.

8. Find the point on the curve $f(x) = x^2 - 6x + 11$
where the tangent is parallel to the x-axis.

9. Write the following as kx^n, $k \in R$, $n \in Q$, and,
hence, find their derivatives:

(i) $\sqrt[3]{x}$

(ii) $\dfrac{1}{x}$

(iii) $\dfrac{2}{\sqrt{x}}$

(iv) $\dfrac{5}{x^3}$

(v) $x\sqrt{x}$

(vi) $-\dfrac{3\sqrt{x}}{x^3}$

10. Differentiate the following with respect to x:

(i) $\dfrac{6x^2 + x^3 - 2x}{2x}$

(ii) $\dfrac{x^2 + x}{\sqrt{x}}$

(iii) $\dfrac{x^{\frac{1}{3}} + \sqrt{x} - x}{x}$

(iv) $\dfrac{x + 1}{\sqrt[3]{x}}$

11. Differentiate the following with respect to x:

(i) $\dfrac{x^2 - 16}{x - 4}$

(ii) $\dfrac{x^3 - 1}{x - 1}$

(iii) $\dfrac{x^3 + 1}{x + 1}$

(iv) $\dfrac{x^4 - 16}{x - 2}$

12. The curve $y = ax^2 + bx$ passes through the
point $(2,4)$ with gradient 8. Find a and b.

13. The curve $y = cx + \dfrac{d}{x}$ has gradient 6 at the
point $\left(\frac{1}{2},1\right)$. Find c and d.

14. Find the derivatives of each of the following:

(i) $3\sqrt{x} - \dfrac{1}{x^2}$

(ii) $\dfrac{1}{x^2} - \dfrac{1}{x^3} + \dfrac{1}{x^4}$

(iii) $\dfrac{2}{\sqrt{x}} - \dfrac{1}{\sqrt[3]{x}}$

(iv) $\dfrac{5}{x^3} + \sqrt{x}$

(v) $x\sqrt{x} + \sqrt{x^3}$

(vi) $\dfrac{2x + x^2\sqrt{x}}{\sqrt{x}}$

13.5 THE CHAIN RULE

Suppose you are asked to differentiate the following function:

$$F(x) = \sqrt[3]{x^2 + 4}$$

Note that $F(x)$ is a composite function.

If we let $f(u) = \sqrt[3]{u}$ and $u = h(x) = x^2 + 4$, then $F(x) = f(h(x))$.

It turns out that the derivative of the composite function $f(h(x))$ is the product of the derivatives of f and
h. To see why this is plausible, consider the following question:

> *If a car is going four times as fast as a bicycle and the bicycle is going three times as fast as
> a runner, how many times as fast as the runner is the car going?*

The car is going $4 \times 3 = 12$ times as fast as the runner.

If $\dfrac{dC}{dR}$ is the rate of change of the car with respect to the runner, $\dfrac{dC}{dB}$ the rate of change of the car with respect to the bicycle and $\dfrac{dB}{dR}$ the rate of change of the bicycle with respect to the runner, then we have the following formula:

$$\frac{dC}{dR} = \frac{dC}{dB} \times \frac{dB}{dR}$$

This is known as the **Chain Rule**.

The Chain Rule

f and g are both functions, and F is the composite function defined by $F(x) = f(g(x))$.

If $y = f(u)$ and $u = g(x)$, then $\dfrac{dy}{dx} = \dfrac{dy}{du} \times \dfrac{du}{dx}$

The Chain Rule is on page 25 of the *Formulae and Tables*.

Using the Chain Rule, it is now possible to differentiate:

$$F(x) = \sqrt[3]{x^2 + 4}$$

Worked Example 13.14

Use the Chain Rule to differentiate
$f(x) = \sqrt[3]{x^2 + 4}$, with respect to x.

Solution

This is the question posed in the introduction to this section.

Let $y = u^{\frac{1}{3}}$ and let $u = x^2 + 4$.

By the Chain Rule:

$$f'(x) = \frac{dy}{dx} = \frac{dy}{du} \times \frac{du}{dx}$$

$$y = u^{\frac{1}{3}} \qquad\qquad u = x^2 + 4$$

$$\frac{dy}{du} = \frac{1}{3}u^{-\frac{2}{3}} \qquad\qquad \frac{du}{dx} = 2x$$

$$\frac{dy}{dx} = \frac{dy}{du} \times \frac{du}{dx}$$

$$\frac{dy}{dx} = \frac{1}{3}u^{-\frac{2}{3}}(2x)$$

$$= \frac{1}{3}(x^2 + 4)^{-\frac{2}{3}}(2x)$$

$$\therefore f'(x) = \frac{2x}{3}(x^2 + 4)^{-\frac{2}{3}}$$

Worked Example 13.15

Differentiate $F(x) = (3x + 1)^3$, $x \in R$, with respect to x using the Chain Rule.

Solution

Let $y = u^3$ and let $u = 3x + 1$.

By the Chain Rule:

$$F'(x) = \frac{dy}{dx} = \frac{dy}{du} \times \frac{du}{dx}$$

$$y = u^3 \qquad\qquad u = 3x + 1$$

$$\frac{dy}{du} = 3u^2 \qquad\qquad \frac{du}{dx} = 3$$

$$\frac{dy}{dx} = \frac{dy}{du} \times \frac{du}{dx}$$

$$\therefore \frac{dy}{dx} = 3u^2(3)$$

$$= 9u^2$$

$$\therefore F'(x) = 9(3x + 1)^2$$

DIFFERENTIAL CALCULUS I

After much practice, the Chain Rule can be applied directly to questions of the form $f(x) = [g(x)]^{power}$.

Step 1 Bring down power.　　**Step 3** Reduce power by 1.

Step 2 Write down 'bracket'.　　**Step 4** Differentiate bracket.

 Worked Example 13.16

Differentiate $y = (x^2 + 3x)^3$ with respect to x.

Solution

$y = (x^2 + 3x)^3$

Using the Chain Rule:

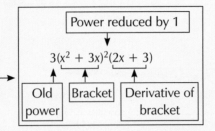

$$\frac{dy}{dx} = \boxed{3(x^2 + 3x)^2(2x + 3)}$$

| Old power | Bracket | Derivative of bracket |

Power reduced by 1

$3(x^2 + 3x)^2(2x + 3)$

$$= (6x + 9)(x^2 + 3x)^2$$

 Exercise 13.4

1. Differentiate, with respect to x, the following functions using the Chain Rule:

　(i)　$y = (3x + 1)^3$　　(iv)　$y = (8x + 3)^3$

　(ii)　$y = (x^2 + 7)^3$　　(v)　$y = (x^3 - 25)^2$

　(iii)　$y = (x^3 - 3x^2 + 2)^2$

2. Differentiate, with respect to x, the following functions using the Chain Rule:

　(i)　$(7x + 1)^2$　　(iv)　$(x^2 + 1)^3$

　(ii)　$(3 - x)^4$　　(v)　$(2 + 3x)^7$

　(iii)　$(4x - 5)^5$

3. Differentiate, with respect to x, the following functions using the Chain Rule:

　(i)　$(2 - 6x)^3$　　(iv)　$\sqrt{4x^3 - 5}$

　(ii)　$(2x^4 - 5)^{\frac{1}{2}}$　　(v)　$\dfrac{1}{\sqrt{x} + 7x}$

　(iii)　$(x^2 + 3)^{-1}$

4. Differentiate, with respect to x, the following functions using the Chain Rule:

　(i)　$\dfrac{6}{\sqrt{8 - x^2}}$　　(iv)　$(4 - x^2)^{-3}$

　(ii)　$\dfrac{-3}{(x^3 + 6x)^{\frac{1}{3}}}$　　(v)　$(x^7 - 6)^{-\frac{1}{2}}$

　(iii)　$(2 + x^2)^{\frac{3}{4}}$

5. Differentiate, with respect to x, the following functions using the Chain Rule:

　(i)　$\sqrt[4]{6 - \sqrt{x}}$　　(iv)　$\sqrt{\dfrac{x + 1}{x^2}}$

　(ii)　$\left(1 + \dfrac{1}{x}\right)^{\frac{1}{2}}$　　(v)　$\sqrt{\dfrac{8x^3 + 27}{2x + 3}}$

　(iii)　$\sqrt[3]{x^2 + \dfrac{1}{x^2}}$

6. A tangent is drawn to the curve $y = \sqrt{x^3 + 1}$, $x \geqslant -1$, $x \in R$, at the point $(2,3)$.

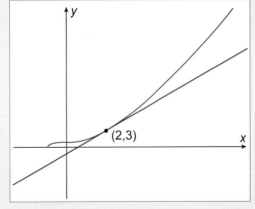

　(i)　Find the value of $\dfrac{dy}{dx}$ at $x = 2$.

　(ii)　Hence, find the equation of the tangent to the curve at $(2,3)$.

　(iii)　Find the area of the triangle bounded by the tangent, the x-axis and the y-axis.

7. The function $f(x) = (2 - x^2)^5$ is defined for all values of $x \in R$.

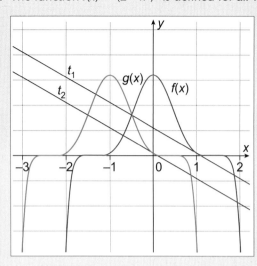

   (i) Find the equation of the tangent t_1 to the graph of $f(x)$ at the point $(1,1)$.

  (ii) $g(x) = (2 - (x + a)^2)^5$ for some constant a. Find the value of a.

 (iii) If t_2 is parallel to t_1, find the equation of t_2.

 (iv) Find the distance between t_1 and t_2.

  (v) Hence, find the area of the trapezoid bounded between the x-axis, the y-axis, t_1 and t_2.

8. The graph of the function, $f(x) = \sqrt{x^2 + 3x}$, $x \in R$ is shown.

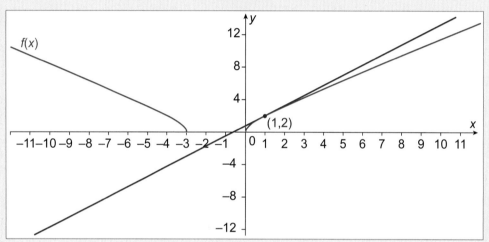

   (i) Explain why the function is not defined on the real numbers in the range $-3 < x < 0$.

  (ii) Write down the equation of the axis of symmetry of $f(x)$.

 (iii) Find $f'(x)$, the derivative of $f(x)$.

 (iv) Hence, find the equation of the tangent to $f(x)$ at the point $(1,2)$.

9. Let $y = [f(x)]^4$, where $f(x)$ is some function in x.

If $f(1) = 5$ and $\dfrac{dy}{dx} = -160$ at $x = 1$, find $f'(1)$.

10. Let $y = [g(x) + 3x^2]^3$, where $g(x)$ is a function in x.

What is the value of $g'(-1)$, given that $\dfrac{dy}{dx} = 3$ at $x = -1$ and $g(-1) = -5$?

13.6 THE PRODUCT RULE AND QUOTIENT RULE

We have already seen that the derivative of a sum is the sum of the derivatives.

 ACTIVITIES 13.3, 13.4

However, the derivative of a product is **not** the product of the derivatives.
Similarly, the derivative of a quotient is **not** the quotient of the derivatives.

The Product Rule

If $u(x)$ and $v(x)$ are two functions and $f(x) = u(x)v(x)$, then

$$f'(x) = u(x)v'(x) + v(x)u'(x)$$

OR

$$\frac{df}{dx} = u\frac{dv}{dx} + v\frac{du}{dx}$$

The Quotient Rule

If $u(x)$ and $v(x)$ are two functions and $f(x) = \dfrac{u(x)}{v(x)}$, then

$$f'(x) = \frac{v(x)u'(x) - u(x)v'(x)}{(v(x))^2}$$

OR

$$\frac{df}{dx} = \frac{v\frac{du}{dx} - u\frac{dv}{dx}}{v^2}$$

These rules can be found on page 25 of *Formulae and Tables*.

 Worked Example 13.17

Differentiate the following functions with respect to x:

(i) $f(x) = (x^2 - 4)(3x^3 - x^2 + 9)$ (ii) $g(x) = \dfrac{2x - 3}{x^2 - 4}$

Solution

(i) Let $u = x^2 - 4$ and $v = 3x^3 - x^2 + 9$.

$$\frac{du}{dx} = 2x \quad \text{and} \quad \frac{dv}{dx} = 9x^2 - 2x$$

$$f'(x) = u\frac{dv}{dx} + v\frac{du}{dx}$$

$$= (x^2 - 4)(9x^2 - 2x) + (3x^3 - x^2 + 9)(2x)$$

$$= 9x^4 - 2x^3 - 36x^2 + 8x + 6x^4 - 2x^3 + 18x$$

$$\therefore f'(x) = 15x^4 - 4x^3 - 36x^2 + 26x$$

(ii) Let $u = 2x - 3$ and $v = x^2 - 4$.

$$\frac{du}{dx} = 2 \quad \text{and} \quad \frac{dv}{dx} = 2x$$

$$g'(x) = \frac{v\frac{du}{dx} - u\frac{dv}{dx}}{v^2}$$

$$= \frac{(x^2 - 4)(2) - (2x - 3)(2x)}{(x^2 - 4)^2}$$

$$= \frac{2x^2 - 8 - 4x^2 + 6x}{(x^2 - 4)^2}$$

$$\therefore g'(x) = \frac{-2x^2 + 6x - 8}{(x^2 - 4)^2}$$

 ACTIVITY 13.5

DIFFERENTIAL CALCULUS I

1. Differentiate, with respect to x, the following functions in two ways:
   (a) using the Product Rule and (b) multiplying the expressions before differentiating. Compare your results as a check.

   (i) $y = (x^5)(x^{10})$

   (ii) $y = (x^9)(x^6)$

   (iii) $y = (3x + 2)(4x - 5)$

   (iv) $y = (x - 9)(x + 9)$

   (v) $y = x^2(x^3 + 5)$

2. Differentiate, with respect to x, the following functions in two ways:
   (a) using the Product Rule and (b) multiplying the expressions before differentiating. Compare your results as a check.

   (i) $f(x) = (4\sqrt{x} + 3)(x^2)$

   (ii) $g(x) = (5\sqrt{x} + 3)(x^3)$

   (iii) $h(x) = (2x - 3)(3x^2 + 2x + 5)$

   (iv) $y = (\sqrt{x} + 3)(3x - 2\sqrt{x} + 8)$

   (v) $f(x) = (2x + 3\sqrt{x} + 5)(\sqrt{x} + 4)$

3. Differentiate, with respect to x, the following functions in two ways:
   (a) using the Quotient Rule and (b) dividing the expressions before differentiating. Compare your results as a check.

   (i) $y = \dfrac{x^8}{x^2}$

   (ii) $y = \dfrac{x^2 - 9}{x + 3}$

   (iii) $f(x) = \dfrac{3x^5 + x^2}{x}$

   (iv) $g(x) = \dfrac{x^2 - 16}{x + 4}$

   (v) $h(x) = \dfrac{x^3 + 27}{x + 3}$

   (vi) $y = \dfrac{3x^7 - x^3}{x^2}$

4. Use the Product Rule to differentiate each of the following functions with respect to x:

   (i) $f(x) = (3x + 1)(5x + 2)$

   (ii) $g(x) = (x^2 - 1)(5x - 2)$

   (iii) $h(x) = (1 - x^2)(x^2 + 5x + 3)$

   (iv) $F(x) = \sqrt{x}(2x + 4)$

   (v) $G(x) = (3x^2 - 2x + 5)(4x^2 + 3x - 1)$

5. Use the Quotient Rule to differentiate each of the following functions with respect to x:

   (i) $f(x) = \dfrac{3x + 1}{7x + 2}$

   (ii) $g(x) = \dfrac{5x + 2}{9x + 1}$

   (iii) $h(x) = \dfrac{x}{x^2 + 1}$

   (iv) $F(x) = \dfrac{2x + 1}{x^2 - 5}$

   (v) $G(x) = \dfrac{1}{x + 2}$

6. Find the value of the derivative of
   $g(x) = \dfrac{3x + 4}{4x + 3}$ at $x = 0$.

7. The graph of
   $F(x) = (5x^2 + 4x - 3)(2x^2 - 3x + 1)$,
   $-1 \leqslant x \leqslant 1$, $x \in R$, is shown.

   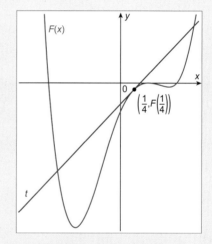

   (i) Find $F'(x)$, the derivative of $F(x)$.

   (ii) t is a tangent to the graph at $x = \frac{1}{4}$. Find the slope of t.

   (iii) Find the equation of t.

8. The graph of $F(x) = \dfrac{3x^2 - 5x}{x^2 - 1}$, $-3 \leqslant x \leqslant 3$, $x \in R$, is shown.

   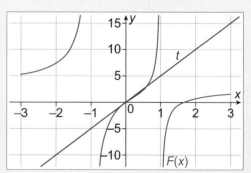

(i) *t* is a tangent to the graph at *x* = 0.
Use your graph to find the slope of *t*.

(ii) Use differentiation to find the slope of *t*.

(iii) Find, in the form *y* = *mx* + *c*, the
equation of *t*.

9. The function $F(x) = \dfrac{x^2 - 1}{\sqrt{x}(x + 3)}$ is defined for all

$x > 0$, $x \in R$, and the function $h(x) = \sqrt{x}(x + 3)$
is defined for all $x \geqslant 0$, $x \in R$.

(i) Find the derivative of $h(x)$.

(ii) Hence, find the derivative of $F(x)$.

(iii) What is the slope of the tangent to the
graph of $F(x)$ at $x = 1$?

10. The function $G(x) = \dfrac{(x^2 - 3x)(3x^3 - 8x^2 + 7x)}{x^2 - 9}$
is defined for $x \in R$, $x \neq \pm 3$.

(i) If $h(x) = (x^2 - 3x)(3x^3 - 8x^2 + 7x)$, find
$h'(x)$, the derivative of $h(x)$.

(ii) Hence, find $G'(1)$.

11. The function $H(x) = \dfrac{x^2 + 4}{(3x^3 - x^2)^{10}}$ is defined for

$x \in R$, $x \neq 0$, $x \neq \frac{1}{3}$.

(i) If $g(x) = (3x^3 - x^2)^{10}$, find $g'(x)$, the
derivative of $g(x)$.

(ii) Hence, find $H'(x)$, the derivative of $H(x)$.

12. Consider the function *H* given by

$$H(x) = \begin{cases} -x - 1, & \text{for } -3 \leqslant x < -1 \\ (x + 1)^2, & \text{for } -1 \leqslant x < 0 \\ (x^2 - 1)^4, & \text{for } 0 \leqslant x < 1.2 \end{cases}$$

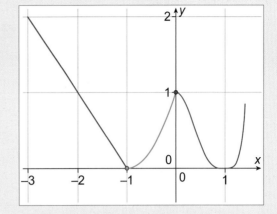

Evaluate the following derivatives:

(i) $H'(-2)$

(ii) $H'(-0.5)$

(iii) $H'(0.5)$

13.7 TRIGONOMETRIC FUNCTIONS

If we sketch the graph of $f(x) = \sin x$, $0 \leqslant x \leqslant 5\pi$, and use the interpretation of $f'(x)$ as the slope of the
tangent to the sine curve in order to sketch the graph $f'(x)$, then it looks as if the resulting graph may be
the same as the cosine curve.

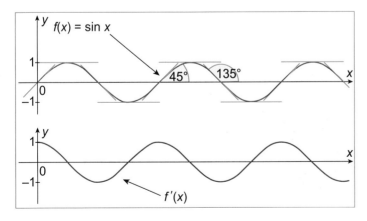

$f(x)$	$f'(x)$
$\sin x$	$\cos x$
$\cos x$	$-\sin x$
$\tan x$	$\sec^2 x$

▪ The derivative of $\sin x$ is $\cos x$.

▪ The derivative of $\cos x$ is $-\sin x$.

The derivatives of $\sin x$, $\cos x$ and $\tan x$ are given on page 25 of the *Formulae and Tables*.

Worked Example 13.18

Use the Chain Rule to differentiate each of the following functions with respect to x:

(i) $f(x) = \cos 4x$ (iii) $h(x) = \sqrt{\sin x}$

(ii) $g(x) = \tan^4 3x$

Solution

(i) $f(x) = \cos 4x$

$y = \cos u \qquad u = 4x$

$\dfrac{dy}{du} = -\sin u$ and $\dfrac{du}{dx} = 4$

By the Chain Rule:

$\dfrac{dy}{dx} = \dfrac{dy}{du} \times \dfrac{du}{dx}$

$\qquad = (-\sin u) \times 4$

$\therefore f'(x) = -4\sin 4x$ (Replacing u with $4x$)

(ii) $g(x) = \tan^4 3x = (\tan 3x)^4$

$y = u^4 \qquad u = \tan 3x$

$\dfrac{dy}{du} = 4u^3 \qquad \dfrac{du}{dx} = 3\sec^2 3x$

By the Chain Rule:

$\dfrac{dy}{dx} = \dfrac{dy}{du} \times \dfrac{du}{dx}$

$\therefore g'(x) = 4u^3 \times 3\sec^2 3x$

$\qquad = 12(\tan 3x)^3 \sec^2 3x$

$\qquad = 12\tan^3 3x \sec^2 3x$

(iii) $h(x) = \sqrt{\sin x}$

$\qquad = (\sin x)^{\frac{1}{2}}$

$y = u^{\frac{1}{2}} \qquad u = \sin x$

$\dfrac{dy}{du} = \dfrac{1}{2}u^{-\frac{1}{2}} \qquad \dfrac{du}{dx} = \cos x$

By the Chain Rule:

$\dfrac{dy}{dx} = \dfrac{dy}{du} \times \dfrac{du}{dx}$

$\therefore h'(x) = \dfrac{1}{2}u^{-\frac{1}{2}} \times \cos x$

$\qquad = \dfrac{1}{2}(\sin x)^{-\frac{1}{2}} \cos x$

$\qquad = \dfrac{\cos x}{2\sqrt{\sin x}}$

To differentiate functions of the form $f(x) = \sin^n(mx)$, it is often useful to use the following shortened version of the Chain Rule:

$$f'(x) = \underbrace{n\sin^{n-1}(mx)}_{\substack{\uparrow \\ \text{Differentiate} \\ \text{power}}} \quad \underbrace{(\cos mx)}_{\substack{\uparrow \\ \text{Differentiate} \\ \text{trigonometric} \\ \text{function}}} \quad \underbrace{(m)}_{\substack{\uparrow \\ \text{Differentiate} \\ \text{angle}}}$$

 Worked Example 13.19

Differentiate the function $g(x) = \cos^4 3x$ with respect to x.

Solution

$g'(x) = 4\cos^3 3x(-\sin 3x)3$ (using the shortened version)

$\qquad = -12\cos^3 3x \sin 3x$

Worked Example 13.20

Differentiate the function $f(x) = x \sin x$ with respect to x.

Hence, find the slope of the tangent to the curve $f(x) = x \sin x$ at the point $(\pi, 0)$.

Solution

$f(x)$ is a product of two other functions of x, namely $u(x) = x$ and $v(x) = \sin x$.
Therefore, the Product Rule can be used to differentiate $f(x)$.

Let $u = x$ and $v = \sin x$.

$$\frac{du}{dx} = 1 \text{ and } \frac{dv}{dx} = \cos x$$

$$\frac{df}{dx} = u\frac{dv}{dx} + v\frac{du}{dx}$$

$$\therefore f'(x) = (x)(\cos x) + (\sin x)(1)$$

$$= x \cos x + \sin x$$

$$f'(\pi) = (\pi)(\cos \pi) + \sin \pi$$

$$= (\pi)(-1) + 0$$

$$= -\pi$$

Hence, the slope of the tangent to the curve at the point $(\pi, 0)$ is $-\pi$.

Worked Example 13.21

Let $f(x) = \sin^4 x + \cos^4 x$.

Find the derivative of $f(x)$ and express it in the form $k \sin px$, where $k, p \in Z$.

Solution

$$f'(x) = 4 \sin^3 x \cos x - 4 \cos^3 x \sin x$$

$$= 4 \sin x \cos x(\sin^2 x - \cos^2 x)$$

$$= 2(2 \sin x \cos x)(\cos 2x) \quad \text{(Formulae and Tables, page 14)}$$

$$= 2 \sin 2x \cos 2x \quad \text{(Formulae and Tables, page 14)}$$

$$= \sin 4x \quad (\sin 2A = 2 \sin A \cos A \Rightarrow \sin 4x = 2 \sin 2x \cos 2x)$$

Exercise 13.6

1. Write down the derivative of each of the following expressions:

   (i) $\sin x + \cos x$

   (ii) $3 \cos \theta$

   (iii) $\sin \theta + 5$

   (iv) $4 \sin \theta - 8$

   (v) $2 \cos x - 3 \sin x$

2. Find the gradient of each curve at the point whose x co-ordinate is given.

   (i) $y = \sin x, x = \frac{\pi}{2}$

   (ii) $y = \sin x, x = 0$

   (iii) $y = \cos x, x = \pi$

   (iv) $y = -2 \sin x, x = \frac{\pi}{4}$

   (v) $y = x - \sin x, x = \frac{\pi}{2}$

3. Find the equation of the tangent to the curve $y = \cos \theta + 3 \sin \theta$, at the point where $\theta = \frac{\pi}{2}$.

4. Use the Product and Quotient Rules to differentiate the following functions with respect to x:

   (i) $F(x) = 2x \cos x$

   (ii) $G(x) = x^2 \sin x$

   (iii) $f(x) = x \tan x$

   (iv) $g(x) = \dfrac{x}{\sin x}$

   (v) $H(x) = \dfrac{4x}{\cos x}$

5. Find the derivative of each of the following functions:

    (i) $F(x) = \sin 5x$

    (ii) $G(x) = 3\cos 3x$

    (iii) $H(x) = 7\tan 5x$

    (iv) $f(x) = 2\sin 3x + 5\cos 2x$

    (v) $g(x) = \tan 2x + \tan 3x$

6. Find the derivative of each of the following functions:

    (i) $F(x) = \sin^2 x$

    (ii) $G(x) = \tan^2 x$

    (iii) $H(x) = \cos^3 5x$

    (iv) $f(x) = \sin^2 2x + \cos^2 3x$

    (v) $g(x) = \tan^4 3x + \tan^5 4x$

7. The function $f(x) = x\cos x$ is defined for all $x \in R$.

    (i) Find $f'(x)$, the derivative of $f(x)$.

    (ii) Hence, find the equation of the tangent to $f(x) = x\cos x$ at $x = \dfrac{3\pi}{2}$.

8. Given that $\dfrac{d(\sin x)}{dx} = \cos x$ and $\dfrac{d(\cos x)}{dx} = -\sin x$, find the derivatives of each of the following, using the Quotient Rule:

    (i) $\sec x$ (ii) $\tan x$ (iii) $\cot x$

9. The graph of the function $f(x) = \cos x \sin x$, $0 \leqslant x \leqslant 2\pi$ is shown.

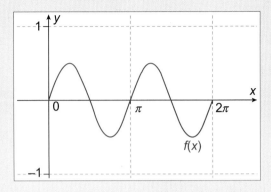

    (i) Show that $f'(x) = \cos 2x$.

    (ii) Hence, find the equation of the tangent to $f(x)$ at $x = \dfrac{11\pi}{8}$.

    (iii) $g(x) = x\,f(x)$ is defined for $0 \leqslant x \leqslant 2\pi$.

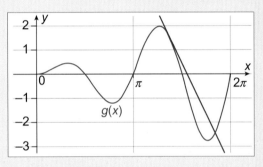

    Find the equation of the tangent to $g(x)$ at $x = \dfrac{11\pi}{8}$.

10. $H(x) = \dfrac{\sin x}{1 + \tan x}$ is defined for all $x \in R$, $x \neq n\pi - \dfrac{\pi}{4}$, $n \in Z$.

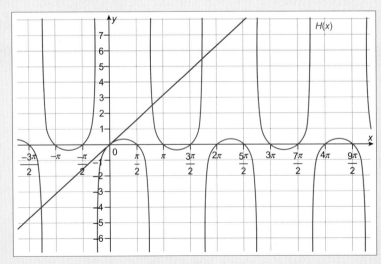

    (i) Find $H'(x)$, the derivative of $H(x)$.

    (ii) Hence, find the equation of the tangent to $H(x)$ at $(0,0)$.

11. Find the equation of the tangent to the curve $F(x) = \dfrac{1 + \sin x}{1 + x \sin x}$ at the point $(\pi, 1)$.

12. Find the derivative of
$H(x) = \dfrac{x \tan x}{\cos x}$ at $x = \dfrac{\pi}{4}$.

13. The function $f(\theta) = \dfrac{1}{3} \sin 3\theta + 3 \sin \theta$ is defined for all $\theta \in R$.

  (i) Find $f'(\theta)$, the derivative of $f(\theta)$.

  (ii) Hence, find positive integers a and b such that $f'(\theta) = a \cos^b \theta$.

14. The function $y = \dfrac{1 + \sin t}{1 - \sin t}$ is defined for $0 \leqslant t < \dfrac{\pi}{2}, t \in R$.

  (i) Find $\dfrac{dy}{dt}$.

  (ii) Show that $\dfrac{dy}{dt} = \dfrac{2\left(1 - \tan^4 \dfrac{t}{2}\right)}{\left(\tan \dfrac{t}{2} - 1\right)^4}$.

15. Given that $f(\theta) = \sin(\theta + \pi)\cos(\theta - \pi)$, find the derivative of $f(\theta)$ and express it in the form $\cos n\theta$, where $n \in Z$.

16. Let $y = \dfrac{1 - \cos x}{1 + \cos x}$.

  Show that $\dfrac{dy}{dx} = t + t^3$, where $t = \tan \dfrac{x}{2}$.

13.8 DIFFERENTIATION OF INVERSE TRIGONOMETRIC FUNCTIONS

The functions $\sin^{-1} x$, $\cos^{-1} x$ and $\tan^{-1} x$, can also be differentiated.

$f(x)$	$f'(x)$
$\cos^{-1} \dfrac{x}{a}$	$-\dfrac{1}{\sqrt{a^2 - x^2}}$
$\sin^{-1} \dfrac{x}{a}$	$\dfrac{1}{\sqrt{a^2 - x^2}}$
$\tan^{-1} \dfrac{x}{a}$	$\dfrac{a}{a^2 + x^2}$

These rules are on page 25 of *Formulae and Tables*.

Worked Example 13.22

Differentiate the function $y = \sin^{-1} \dfrac{x}{a}$ with respect to x, where $x \in R$ and a is a non-zero constant.

Solution

$y = \sin^{-1} \dfrac{x}{a}$

$\Rightarrow \sin y = \dfrac{x}{a}$

$\Rightarrow x = a \sin y$

So, $\dfrac{dx}{dy} = a \cos y$

$\Rightarrow \dfrac{dy}{dx} = \dfrac{1}{a \cos y}$

$\therefore \dfrac{dy}{dx} = \dfrac{1}{a\left[\dfrac{\sqrt{a^2 - x^2}}{a}\right]}$ (see work on right side)

$\dfrac{dy}{dx} = \dfrac{1}{\sqrt{a^2 - x^2}}$

When using the $\sin^{-1}$ function, we limit ourselves to the principal value.

So, for $y = \sin^{-1} \dfrac{x}{a}$, $y \in \left[-\dfrac{\pi}{2}, \dfrac{\pi}{2}\right]$.

If $0 < y < \dfrac{\pi}{2}$, we can construct a right-angled triangle containing y.

Let us assume that $x, a > 0$.

$\sin y = \dfrac{x}{a}$

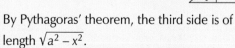

By Pythagoras' theorem, the third side is of length $\sqrt{a^2 - x^2}$.

$\therefore \cos y = \dfrac{\sqrt{a^2 - x^2}}{a}$

Worked Example 13.23

Differentiate the function $y = \sin^{-1}\left(\dfrac{1}{x^2}\right)$, $x \geqslant 1$ $x \in R$, with respect to x.

Solution

$y = \sin^{-1}\left(\dfrac{1}{x^2}\right)$

$y = \sin^{-1} u \qquad u = \dfrac{1}{x^2} = x^{-2}$

$\dfrac{dy}{du} = \dfrac{1}{\sqrt{1 - u^2}} \qquad \dfrac{du}{dx} = -2x^{-3} = -\dfrac{2}{x^3}$

By the Chain Rule:

$\dfrac{dy}{dx} = \dfrac{dy}{du} \times \dfrac{du}{dx}$

$\therefore \dfrac{dy}{dx} = \dfrac{1}{\sqrt{1 - u^2}} \times -\dfrac{2}{x^3}$

$= -\dfrac{2}{x^3 \sqrt{1 - \left(\dfrac{1}{x^2}\right)^2}}$

$= -\dfrac{2}{x^3 \sqrt{1 - \dfrac{1}{x^4}}}$

$= -\dfrac{2}{x^3 \sqrt{\dfrac{x^4 - 1}{x^4}}}$

$= -\dfrac{2}{x \sqrt{x^4 - 1}}$

Exercise 13.7

1. Differentiate each of the following with respect to x:

  (i) $f(x) = \sin^{-1} \dfrac{x}{3}$

  (ii) $g(x) = \cos^{-1} \dfrac{x}{4}$

  (iii) $h(x) = \tan^{-1} \dfrac{x}{5}$

  (iv) $F(x) = \sin^{-1} \dfrac{x}{7} + \sin^{-1} \dfrac{x}{9}$

  (v) $H(x) = \sin^{-1} \dfrac{x}{8} + \cos^{-1} \dfrac{x}{11}$

2. Differentiate each of the following with respect to x:

  (i) $y = x \sin^{-1} x$

  (ii) $y = (x + 4) \cos^{-1} \dfrac{x}{3}$

  (iii) $y = \left(x^2 + \dfrac{1}{x}\right) \tan^{-1} \dfrac{x}{4}$

  (iv) $y = \dfrac{1}{x} \sin^{-1} \dfrac{x}{2}$

3. Differentiate each of the following with respect to x:

  (i) $F(x) = \dfrac{\sin^{-1} x}{x^2}$

  (ii) $G(x) = \dfrac{\cos^{-1} \dfrac{x}{2}}{x - 1}$

  (iii) $H(x) = \dfrac{\tan^{-1} x}{x^4 - 1}$

  (iv) $f(x) = \dfrac{\cos^{-1} \dfrac{x}{3}}{x^2 + 1}$

4. Differentiate, with respect to x, each of the following:

  (i) $f(x) = \sin^{-1} 2x$

  (ii) $g(x) = \sin^{-1} x^2$

  (iii) $h(x) = \tan^{-1} (2x - \pi)$

  (iv) $F(x) = \cos^{-1}\left(5x + \dfrac{\pi}{2}\right)$

5. Find the derivative of each of these functions at the given value of x:

  (i) $\sin^{-1} x^3$ at $x = \dfrac{1}{4}$ \quad (iii) $\cos^{-1} 2x$ at $x = \dfrac{3}{8}$

  (ii) $\tan^{-1} 3x$ at $x = \dfrac{1}{5}$ \quad (iv) $\cos^{-1} x^2$ at $x = \dfrac{1}{3}$

6. A graph of the function $f(x) = 2 \tan^{-1} \sqrt{x}$, $x \in R$, $x \geqslant 0$, is shown.

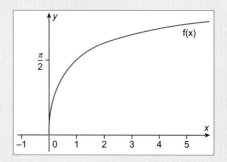

  (i) Find $f'(x)$, the derivative of $f(x)$.

  (ii) Hence find the equation of the tangent to $f(x)$ at $\left(1, \dfrac{\pi}{2}\right)$.

7. Find the equation of the tangent to the curve $y = \tan^{-1}(2x + 1)$ at $x = 0$.

8. If $y = \sin^{-1}(\cos x)$, show that $\dfrac{dy}{dx} = -1$ for all x, $x \in R$, where $\cos x \neq \pm 1$.

9. $g(x) = \dfrac{1 + x}{1 - x}$, $x \in R$, $x \neq 1$, and $f(x) = \tan^{-1} x$, $x \in R$.

   (i) Write in terms of x the composite function $F(x) = f(g(x))$.

   (ii) Find $g'(x)$, the derivative of $g(x)$.

   (iii) Hence, using the Chain Rule, find $F'(x)$, the derivative of $F(x)$ in its simplest form.

10. The graph of the function $f(x) = \dfrac{1}{x} \sin^{-1} \dfrac{1}{x}$, $x \in R$, $x \leq -1$ or $x \geq 1$, and the tangent to the graph at $x = \sqrt{2}$ are shown.

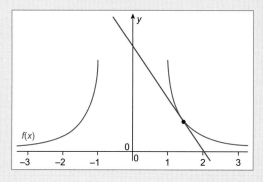

(i) Explain why the domain of $f(x)$ cannot include values in the range $-1 < x < 1$.

(ii) Using the Chain Rule, differentiate the following function:

$$h(x) = \sin^{-1} \dfrac{1}{x}, \ x \in R, \ x \leq -1 \text{ or } x \geq 1$$

(iii) Hence, find $f'(x)$, the derivative of $f(x)$.

(iv) Show that $f'(\sqrt{2}) = -\dfrac{1}{2} - \dfrac{\pi}{8}$.

11. $g(x) = \dfrac{x}{1 + x}$, $x \in R$, $x \neq -1$, and $f(x) = \tan^{-1} x$, $x \in R$.

(i) Write in terms of x the composite function $F(x) = f(g(x))$.

(ii) Find $g'(x)$, the derivative of $g(x)$.

(iii) Hence, using the Chain Rule, show that $F'(x) = \dfrac{1}{2x^2 + 2x + 1}$.

12. Let $f(x) = \tan^{-1} \dfrac{x}{2}$ and $g(x) = \tan^{-1} \dfrac{2}{x}$, $x \in R$, $x > 0$.

(i) Find $f'(x)$ and $g'(x)$.

(ii) Hence, show that $f(x) + g(x)$ is constant.

(iii) Find the value of $f(x) + g(x)$.

13.9 THE EXPONENTIAL FUNCTION AND THE NATURAL LOGARITHM FUNCTION

The Exponential Function

The irrational number e has a special property: if you draw the graph of e^x, you will find that the slope of the tangent to the graph at any point is equal to the y co-ordinate at that point.

So, if $f(x) = e^x$, then $f'(x) = e^x$.

Consider the graph of $f(x) = e^x$ shown on the right and the tangent to this graph at the point $(2, e^2)$.

The slope of this tangent is e^2.

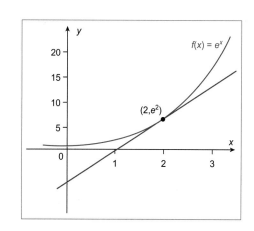

The Natural Logarithm Function

The function $f(x) = \log_e x = \ln x$ is the **natural logarithm function** in x. The natural logarithm function is the inverse of the exponential function.

If $f(x) = \ln x$, how would we find $f'(x)$?

If $y = \ln x$

$\Rightarrow x = e^y$

$\Rightarrow \dfrac{dx}{dy} = e^y$

$\Rightarrow \dfrac{dy}{dx} = \dfrac{1}{e^y}$

So, $\dfrac{dy}{dx} = \dfrac{1}{x}$ (as $e^y = x$)

The rules for differentiating e^x and $\ln x$ with respect to x are shown on page 25 of *Formulae and Tables*.

$f(x)$	$f'(x)$
$\ln x$	$\dfrac{1}{x}$
e^x	e^x
e^{ax}	ae^{ax}
a^x	$a^x \ln a$

Worked Example 13.24

Differentiate the following with respect to x:

(i) e^{3x} (ii) e^{-7x}

Solution

(i) $f(x) = e^{3x}$

$y = e^u$ $u = 3x$

$\dfrac{dy}{du} = e^u$ $\dfrac{du}{dx} = 3$

By the Chain Rule:

$\dfrac{dy}{dx} = \dfrac{dy}{du} \cdot \dfrac{du}{dx}$

$\therefore f'(x) = e^u \cdot 3$

$= 3e^{3x}$

> On page 25 of *Formulae and Tables*, a formula for derivative of e^{ax} is given:
> $$\dfrac{d(e^{ax})}{dx} = ae^{ax}, \text{ where } a \text{ is some constant.}$$

(ii) $f(x) = e^{-7x}$

$\therefore f'(x) = -7e^{-7x}$ (Using formula)

Worked Example 13.25

Differentiate the following with respect to x:

(i) $\log_e ax$, where $x > 0$ and a is a positive real number

(ii) $\log_e 3x$, where $x > 0, x \in R$

(iii) $\log_e(x^2 + 1)$

Solution

(i) $f(x) = \log_e ax$

$y = \log_e u$ $u = ax$

$\dfrac{dy}{du} = \dfrac{1}{u}$ $\dfrac{du}{dx} = a$

By the Chain Rule:

$\dfrac{dy}{dx} = \dfrac{dy}{du} \times \dfrac{du}{dx}$

$\therefore f'(x) = \left(\dfrac{1}{u}\right)a = \dfrac{a}{ax}$

$f'(x) = \dfrac{1}{x}$

(ii) $f(x) = \log_e 3x$

$\therefore f'(x) = \dfrac{1}{x}$ (from part (i))

(iii) $f(x) = \log_e(x^2 + 1)$

$y = \log_e u$ $u = x^2 + 1$

$\dfrac{dy}{du} = \dfrac{1}{u}$ $\dfrac{du}{dx} = 2x$

$\dfrac{dy}{dx} = \dfrac{dy}{du} \cdot \dfrac{du}{dx}$

$\therefore f'(x) = \dfrac{1}{u}2x$

$f'(x) = \dfrac{2x}{x^2 + 1}$

> It should now be clear that if $f(x) = \log_e g(x)$,
> then $f'(x) = \dfrac{g'(x)}{g(x)}$.

Sometimes, it is better to apply one or more laws of logarithms before differentiating.

These laws are on page 21 of *Formulae and Tables*.

> **Remember**
>
> **Law 1** $\ln xy = \ln x + \ln y$
>
> **Law 2** $\ln \dfrac{x}{y} = \ln x - \ln y$
>
> **Law 3** $\ln x^q = q \ln x$

Worked Example 13.26

Differentiate the function $f(x) = \log_e \sqrt{\dfrac{x^2}{x^2 + 1}}$ with respect to x.

Give your answer in the form $\dfrac{1}{ax^3 + ax}$, $a \in N$.

Solution

$f(x) = \log_e \sqrt{\dfrac{x^2}{x^2 + 1}}$

$= \log_e \left(\dfrac{x^2}{x^2 + 1}\right)^{\frac{1}{2}}$

$= \dfrac{1}{2} \log_e \dfrac{x^2}{x^2 + 1}$

$= \dfrac{1}{2}[\log_e x^2 - \log_e (x^2 + 1)]$

$= \dfrac{1}{2}[2 \log_e x - \log_e(x^2 + 1)]$

$f(x) = \log_e x - \dfrac{1}{2} \log_e (x^2 + 1)$

$\therefore f'(x) = \dfrac{1}{x} - \dfrac{1}{2} \cdot \dfrac{2x}{x^2 + 1}$

$= \dfrac{1}{x} - \dfrac{x}{x^2 + 1}$

$= \dfrac{x^2 + 1 - x^2}{x(x^2 + 1)}$

$= \dfrac{1}{x^3 + x}$

Worked Example 13.27

$y = a^x$, where $a > 0$ and $x \in R$.

(i) Find $\dfrac{dy}{dx}$.

(ii) Hence, find the derivative of 2^x with respect to x.

Solution

(i) $y = a^x$

$\log_e y = \log_e a^x$ (Find log to the base e of both sides)

$\log_e y = x \log_e a$ (Law 3 of Logarithms)

$\therefore x = \dfrac{1}{\log_e a} \log_e y$

$\dfrac{dx}{dy} = \left(\dfrac{1}{\log_e a}\right)\left(\dfrac{1}{y}\right)$

$= \dfrac{1}{(\log_e a)y}$

$\therefore \dfrac{dy}{dx} = (\log_e a)y$

$= a^x \log_e a$

(ii) $y = 2^x$

$\dfrac{dy}{dx} = 2^x(\log_e 2)$ (From part (i))

> $f(x) = a^x$
>
> $\therefore f'(x) = a^x \ln a$

Formulae and Tables, page 25

DIFFERENTIAL CALCULUS I

Exercise 13.8

1. Differentiate each of the following with respect to x:

   (i) e^{2x}

   (ii) e^{5x}

   (iii) e^{4x}

   (iv) e^{-2x}

   (v) $e^{\cos x}$

   (vi) e^{5x-4}

   (vii) e^{x^2+2x+1}

   (viii) $e^{\tan x}$

2. Differentiate each of the following with respect to x:

   (i) $\ln(3x+2)$

   (ii) $\ln(x^2-8)$

   (iii) $\ln(4x-5)$

   (iv) $\ln(\sin x)$

   (v) $\ln(x^4-5)$

   (vi) $\ln(x^2-2x+1)$

   (vii) $\ln(\tan x)$

   (viii) $\ln(1-4x)$

   (ix) $\ln(3-x^3)$

   (x) $\ln 3x$

3. Differentiate each of the following with respect to x:

   (i) $x \ln x$

   (ii) $x e^{2x}$

   (iii) $x^3 \ln x$

   (iv) $x^2 e^x$

   (v) $x^4 e^{3x}$

   (iii) $x^2 \ln e^x$

4. Differentiate each of the following with respect to x:

   (i) $\dfrac{e^{2x}}{x}$

   (ii) $\dfrac{\ln x^2}{e^x}$

   (iii) $\dfrac{e^{-2x}-1}{e^x+1}$

   (iv) $\ln \dfrac{2x}{x}$

   (v) $\dfrac{e^{x^2}}{x^3}$

   (vi) $\dfrac{x}{e^x}$

5. Differentiate each of the following with respect to x:

   (i) $\ln \dfrac{3}{x}$

   (ii) $\ln \sqrt[5]{x}$

   (iii) $\ln(3x+9)^3$

   (iv) $\ln \dfrac{3x+2}{2x-3}$

   (v) $\ln\sqrt{5x+2}$

   (vi) $\ln e^{5x}$

6. Differentiate each of the following with respect to x:

   (i) 3^x

   (ii) $3(2^x)$

   (iii) 2^{2x-3}

   (iv) $\dfrac{5^x}{2}$

   (v) $\dfrac{7^x}{8^x}$

   (vi) $3^x 5^x$

7. Find the value of the derivative of these functions at the given value of x:

   (i) $\ln(x^3+2)$ at $x = \dfrac{3}{4}$

   (ii) $e^{2\sin x-1}$ at $x = \dfrac{\pi}{2}$

   (iii) $\dfrac{\ln x}{x}$ at $x = e$

   (iv) $3x\, e^{5x}$ at $x = 0$

   (v) $\dfrac{1}{\ln x}$ at $x = e$

   (vi) e^x at $x = \ln 2$

8. Differentiate $\log_e \dfrac{x^2}{x^2+1}$, giving your answer in the form $\dfrac{k}{f(x)}$, where $k \in R$ and $f(x)$ is a function of x.

9. Show that the equation of the tangent to the curve $y = e^{\left(\frac{x}{x+1}\right)}$ at the point where $x = 0$ is $y = x + 1$.

10. Show that the derivative of $\log_e \dfrac{\sin x}{1+\sin x}$ is $2 - \sqrt{2}$ when $x = \dfrac{\pi}{4}$.

 Revision Exercises

1. Consider the function G given by

   $$G(x) = \begin{cases} x+4, & \text{for } x < 2 \\ 3x-6, & \text{for } x \geqslant 2 \end{cases}$$

   Graph the function and find each of the following limits, if they exist:

   (i) $\displaystyle\lim_{x\to 4} G(x)$

   (ii) $\displaystyle\lim_{x\to 0} G(x)$

   (iii) $\displaystyle\lim_{x\to 2} G(x)$

2. Evaluate the following limits (you may assume the limits exist):

   (i) $\displaystyle\lim_{x\to 10} 5x - 8$

   (ii) $\displaystyle\lim_{x\to 2} \dfrac{x-2}{x^2+x-6}$

   (iii) $\displaystyle\lim_{x\to 9} \dfrac{x-9}{\sqrt{x}-3}$

   (iv) $\displaystyle\lim_{x\to -2} \dfrac{x^3+8}{x^2-4}$

ACTIVE MATHS

3. The function $g(x) = x^2 - 3x$ is defined for all $x \in R$.

  (i) Differentiate $g(x)$ with respect to x from first principles.

  (ii) Hence, find the slope of the tangent to the curve $g(x) = x^2 - 3x$ at the point $(2,-2)$.

  (iii) Write in the form $y = mx + c$ the equation of the tangent to the graph of $g(x)$ at the point $(2,-2)$.

4. The function $h(x) = 1 - x^2$ is defined for all $x \in R$.

  (i) Differentiate $h(x)$ with respect to x from first principles.

  (ii) Find the equation of the tangent to the graph of $h(x)$ at the point $(2,-3)$.

5. Differentiate the following functions with respect to x from first principles:

  (i) $f(x) = 2x + 4$ (iii) $g(x) = x^2 + 4$

  (ii) $h(x) = 2 - 3x^2$ (iv) $k(x) = 2x - x^2$

6. Differentiate the following with respect to x:

  (i) $y = 2x^2 + 12x + 16$

  (ii) $y = 15x^2 + 10x - 12$

  (iii) $f(x) = x^4 - 19x + 120$

  (iv) $g(x) = 3x^7 - 12x^2 - 4x + 12$

  (v) $h(x) = 4x^3 + 4$

7. A graph of the cubic function $f(x) = x^3 - 3x + 2$ is shown. The tangent to $f(x)$ at the point $(1.5, 0.875)$ is also shown on the diagram.

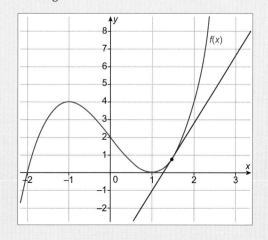

  (i) Write down $f'(x)$, the derivative of $f(x)$.

  (ii) Hence, find the slope of the tangent to $f(x)$ at $(1.5, 0.875)$.

  (iii) Find the equation of the tangent to the curve at this point.

  (iv) Find the co-ordinates of the points where the tangent intersects the x-axis and the y-axis.

  (v) Hence, calculate the area enclosed between the tangent, the x-axis and the y-axis.

8. A graph of the cubic function $g(x) = x^3 - 3x^2 - 10x + 24$ is shown. The tangent to $g(x)$ at the point $(3.5, -4.875)$ is also shown on the diagram.

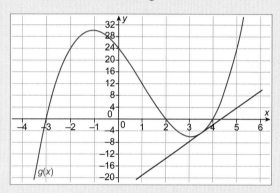

Find the equation of the tangent to $g(x)$ at $x = 3.5$.

9. Differentiate each of the following functions with respect to x:

  (i) $f(x) = (2x + 4)(6x - 3)$

  (ii) $f(x) = \dfrac{2x - 1}{5x + 2}$

  (iii) $f(x) = \left[\dfrac{x - 4}{x + 3}\right]^3$

  (iv) $g(x) = (x^2 - 5)(3x - 2)$

10. Differentiate each of the following functions with respect to x:

  (i) $h(x) = \dfrac{5x}{8x + 1}$

  (ii) $h(x) = (1 - 2x^2)(3x^2 - 6x - 13)$

  (iii) $k(x) = \dfrac{2x}{x^2 - 1}$

  (iv) $f(x) = \left[\dfrac{x + 5}{x^2 + 3}\right]^{12}$

  (v) $F(x) = \dfrac{3x - 1}{x^2 + 5}$

11. Differentiate the following functions with respect to x:

   (i) $F(x) = 2x^2 \cos x$

   (ii) $G(x) = (x^2 + 1)\sin x$

   (iii) $f(x) = x \sec x$

   (iv) $g(x) = 2 \sin x \cos x$

12. Evaluate the derivatives of each of the following functions at $x = \dfrac{\pi}{2}$.

   (i) $\sin 5x$ (iii) $\tan^2 6x$

   (ii) $\cos^2 2x$ (iv) $\sin^3 4x$

13. Differentiate each of the following with respect to the letter indicated:

   (i) $F(x) = \sqrt{x}(3x - 11)$ $[x]$

   (ii) $G(x) = \dfrac{1}{2x - 3}$ $[x]$

   (iii) $s(t) = \sqrt[5]{\dfrac{t^3 + 1}{t + 1}}$ $[t]$

   (iv) $f(x) = \dfrac{2x}{\sqrt{x^2 + 1}}$ $[x]$

14. Find the value of the derivative of these functions at the given value of x (answers to four decimal places where necessary):

   (i) $f(x) = \ln(x^4 - 8)$ at $x = 2$

   (ii) $g(x) = e^{5\cos x - 1}$ at $x = \dfrac{\pi}{2}$

   (iii) $f(x) = \sin^{-1} x^4$, $x = \dfrac{1}{3}$

   (iv) $g(x) = \left(\dfrac{1 + x}{1 - x}\right)$, $x = \dfrac{1}{2}$

   (v) $h(x) = \dfrac{\ln x}{x^2}$ at $x = e$

15. f is the function $f: R \rightarrow R: x \rightarrow e^{mx} + n$, where $m, n \in N$.

The graphs of f and its derivative f' are shown.

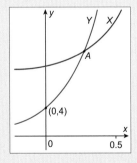

(i) Which graph is of f and which graph is of f'? Explain.

(ii) What is $f'(x)$?

(iii) The co-ordinates of A are $(\log_e \sqrt[4]{3}, 12)$. Find the function f.

16. $f(x) = \ln \dfrac{3x + 1}{2x - 5}$, $x \in R$, $x > \dfrac{5}{2}$

   (i) Find $f'(x)$, the derivative of $f(x)$.

   (ii) Hence, find the slope of the tangent to the curve $y = \ln \dfrac{3x + 1}{2x - 5}$ at $x = 1$.

17. Find the derivative of each of these functions at the given value of x (answers to four decimal places where necessary):

   (i) $F(x) = 4x\, e^{-4x}$ at $x = 0$

   (ii) $h(x) = \cos^{-1} 3x^2$, $x = \dfrac{1}{4}$

   (iii) $G(x) = \dfrac{x}{\ln x}$ at $x = e$

   (iv) $k(x) = \sin^{-1} \dfrac{1 + x}{1 + 2x}$, $x = 2$

18. (i) Write $\dfrac{2x^2 - x^{\frac{3}{2}}}{\sqrt{x}}$ in the form $2x^m - x^n$.

   (ii) Hence, find the derivative of the function $g(x) = 3x^5 - 2x^2 + \dfrac{2x^2 - x^{\frac{3}{2}}}{\sqrt{x}}$.

19. (i) Find the derivative of the function $f(\theta) = \dfrac{\sin 2\theta}{1 + \cos 2\theta}$.

   (ii) Show that $f'(\theta)$, the derivative of $f(\theta)$, can be written in the form $f'(\theta) = \sec^a b\theta$, where a and b are positive integers.

20. $\cos \alpha = \dfrac{2}{\sqrt{13}}$ and $\sin \alpha = \dfrac{3}{\sqrt{13}}$, $0 < \alpha < 2\pi$

   (i) Show that $2 \cos 3x - 3 \sin 3x = \sqrt{13}(\cos \alpha \cos 3x - \sin \alpha \sin 3x)$.

   (ii) Express $2 \cos 3x - 3 \sin 3x$ in the form $R \cos(3x + \alpha)$, where R and α are constants.

   (iii) If $f(x) = e^{2x} \cos 3x$, show that $f'(x)$ can be written in the form $f'(x) = Re^{2x} \cos(3x + \alpha)$.

   (iv) Hence, solve the equation $f'(x) = 0$.

DIFFERENTIAL CALCULUS I

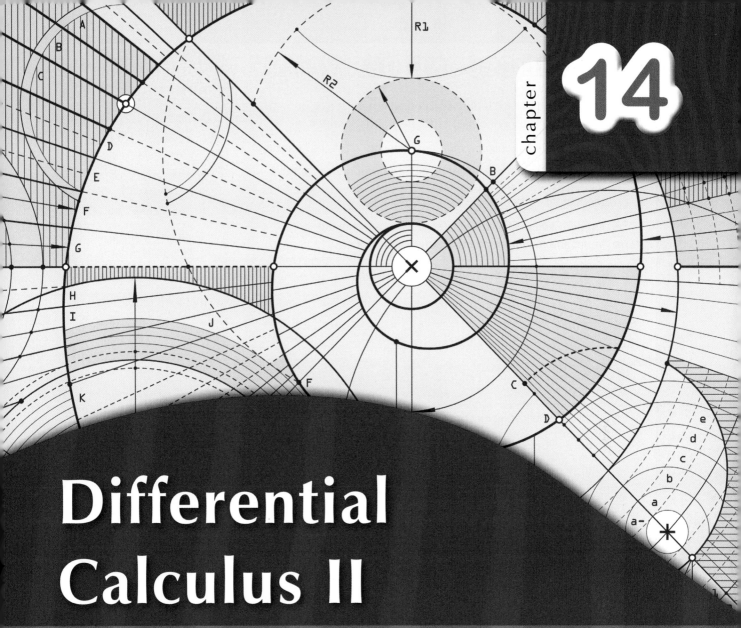

chapter 14

Differential Calculus II

Learning Outcomes

In this chapter you will learn about:

➲ Second derivatives

➲ Increasing and decreasing functions

➲ Stationary points

➲ Applying the differentiation of functions to solve problems

14.1 THE SECOND DERIVATIVE

YOU SHOULD REMEMBER...

- How to differentiate polynomials and rational functions
- The Sum Rule, the Product Rule, the Quotient Rule and the Chain Rule
- How to differentiate trigonometric functions
- How to differentiate inverse trigonometric functions
- How to differentiate exponential functions and logarithmic functions

When a function $y = f(x)$ is differentiated with respect to x, the differential coefficient or first-order derivative is written as $\frac{dy}{dx}$ or $f'(x)$. If the expression is differentiated with respect to x again, the second differential coefficient or second-order derivative is obtained and is written $\frac{d^2y}{dx^2}$ OR $f''(x)$.

Second derivatives will be used later to help us locate the maximum and minimum points of various functions.

- $\frac{d^2y}{dx^2}$ is read as 'dee squared y dee x squared'.

- $f''(x)$ is read as 'f double prime of x'.

Worked Example 14.1

For each of the following functions, find $\frac{d^2y}{dx^2}$.

   (i) $y = 5x^2 + 2x - 6$

   (ii) $y = \cos x$

Solution

(i) $y = 5x^2 + 2x - 6$

$\frac{dy}{dx} = 10x + 2$

$\frac{d^2y}{dx^2} = 10$

(ii) $y = \cos x$

$\frac{dy}{dx} = -\sin x$

$\frac{d^2y}{dx^2} = -\cos x$

KEY WORDS

- **Chain Rule**
- **Second derivative**
- **Differential equation**
- **Increasing function**
- **Decreasing function**
- **Stationary point**
- **Local maximum**
- **Local minimum**
- **Point of inflexion**

Differential Equations

A differential equation is an equation containing derivatives. If the highest-order derivative in the differential equation is a first-order derivative, then the equation is called a **first-order differential equation**.

> **First-order differential equation**
>
> Example: $x\dfrac{dy}{dx} = 10$

If the highest-order derivative in the differential equation is a second-order derivative, then the equation is called a **second-order differential equation**.

> **Second-order differential equation**
>
> Example: $\dfrac{d^2y}{dx^2} - 6\dfrac{dy}{dx} + 9y = 0$

In our course, we need to know how to verify solutions to differential equations.

Worked Example 14.2

Show that $y = xe^{-2x}$ is a solution to the differential equation

$$\frac{d^2y}{dx^2} + 4\frac{dy}{dx} + 4y = 0.$$

Solution

Step 1 $y = xe^{-2x}$

$$\frac{dy}{dx} = x(-2e^{-2x}) + e^{-2x}(1) \quad \text{(Product Rule)}$$

$$\frac{dy}{dx} = e^{-2x}(1 - 2x)$$

$$\boxed{\begin{array}{ll} u = x & v = e^{-2x} \\ \dfrac{du}{dx} = 1 & \dfrac{dv}{dx} = -2e^{-2x} \end{array}}$$

Step 2 $\dfrac{d^2y}{dx^2} = e^{-2x}(-2) + (1 - 2x)(-2e^{-2x})$

$$\boxed{\begin{array}{ll} u = e^{-2x} & v = 1 - 2x \\ \dfrac{du}{dx} = -2e^{-2x} & \dfrac{dv}{dx} = -2 \end{array}}$$

$$= -2e^{-2x}(1 + 1 - 2x)$$

$$= -2e^{-2x}(2 - 2x)$$

$$\therefore \frac{d^2y}{dx^2} = -4e^{-2x}(1 - x)$$

Step 3 $\dfrac{d^2y}{dx^2} + 4\dfrac{dy}{dx} + 4y = -4e^{-2x}(1 - x) + 4[e^{-2x}(1 - 2x)] + 4xe^{-2x}$

$$= 4e^{-2x}(-1 + x + 1 - 2x + x)$$

$$= 4e^{-2x}(0)$$

$$= 0$$

This verifies that $y = xe^{-2x}$ is a solution to the given differential equation.

 Exercise 14.1

1. For each of the following functions, find $\dfrac{d^2y}{dx^2}$:

   (i) $y = 2x^2 - x - 6$

   (ii) $y = 3x^4 - 10x + 2$

   (iii) $y = (9x^7 + x)(x^3 - 2)$

   (iv) $y = (23x^3 + 2x^2)(x - 8)$

   (v) $y = \dfrac{1}{3x^2 + 4}$

2. Find the second derivative of each of the following functions:

   (i) $f(t) = \sin t$ (iv) $F(t) = \ln t$

   (ii) $g(x) = \tan^{-1}\dfrac{x}{2}$ (v) $h(x) = e^x \sin x$

   (iii) $A(r) = \dfrac{2}{3}\pi r^2$

3. Show that $y = \cos 3x$ is a solution to the differential equation $\dfrac{d^2y}{dx^2} + 9y = 0$.

4. Show that $f(t) = e^{3t}$ is a solution to the differential equation $f''(t) - 6f'(t) + 9f(t) = 0$.

5. If $y = xe^{-x}$, show that $\dfrac{d^2y}{dx^2} + 2\dfrac{dy}{dx} + y = 0$.

6. If $f(t) = (\sin^{-1} t)^2$, show that $(1 - t^2) f''(t) - tf'(t) = 2$.

7. If $y = Axe^{-3x}$, where A is any constant, show that y is a solution to the differential equation $\dfrac{d^2y}{dx^2} + 6\dfrac{dy}{dx} + 9y = 0$.

   If $y = Be^{mx}$ is also a solution to this equation, where B and m are non-zero real numbers, find the value of m.

8. The rate of growth of a population of bacteria, if left unchecked, is modelled by the differential equation $\dfrac{dP}{dt} = kP$, where k is a constant, i.e. $\dfrac{dP}{dt}$ is the rate of change of the population at time t and P is the population size at time t. t is measured in minutes.

   (i) Show that $P = Ce^{kt}$ is a solution to the differential equation $\dfrac{dP}{dt} = kP$.

(ii) Show that C is the population size at the initial time, $t = 0$.

(iii) If the initial size of the population is 1,000 and the population has grown to a size of 32,000 in 60 minutes, find the value of the constant k.

9. x is the displacement of a particle, measured in metres, from a fixed point O. The particle has a mass of m kilograms.

   (i) Explain why the velocity of the particle is given by the differential coefficient $\dfrac{dx}{dt}$.

  (ii) Hence, say why its acceleration is $\dfrac{d^2x}{dt^2}$.

 (iii) The particle's motion can be modelled by the differential equation $\dfrac{d^2x}{dt^2} = -\left[\dfrac{k}{m}\right]x$,

      where m is the mass of the particle and k is a positive constant. Show that $x = \sin\left(\sqrt{\dfrac{k}{m}}\,t\right)$ is a solution to the differential equation.

 (iv) If $k = \pi^2$ and $m = 9$ kg, find the distance of the particle from O after 1 second.

14.2 INCREASING AND DECREASING FUNCTIONS

A function f is described as **increasing** on the interval $a < x < b$, if $f(x_2) > f(x_1)$, when $x_2 > x_1$ for all x on the interval $a < x < b$.

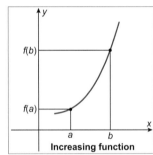

Increasing function

A function f is described as **decreasing** on the interval $a < x < b$, if $f(x_2) < f(x_1)$, when $x_2 > x_1$ for all x on the interval $a < x < b$.

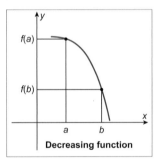

Decreasing function

Worked Example 14.3

A is the closed interval $[1, 5]$. The function f is defined on A by $f: A \to R: x \to (x - 4)^2$.

The graph of f is shown.

Explain why f is increasing on the interval $(4, 5]$.

Note: $(4, 5]$ means 4 is not included but 5 is.

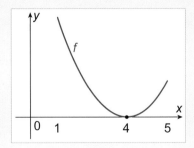

Solution

For every x_1, x_2 in the interval $(4, 5]$, where $x_2 > x_1$, $f(x_2) > f(x_1)$.

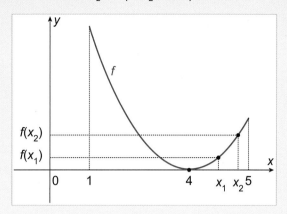

Therefore, f is increasing on the interval $(4, 5]$.

Tangents

In Chapter 13, we learned that the derivative of a function f gives us the slope of all tangents to the curve f.

The tangents to the curve of an increasing function will all have positive slope. Therefore, if a function $f(x)$ is increasing on an interval I, then $f'(x) > 0$ for all $x \in I$.

> If $f'(x) > 0$ for all x in an interval I, then f is **increasing** on that interval.

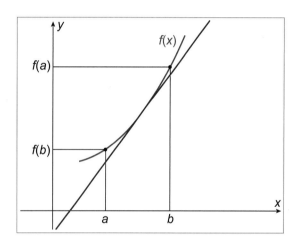

The tangents to the curve of a decreasing function will all have negative slope. Therefore, if a function $f(x)$ is decreasing on an interval I, then $f'(x) < 0$ for all $x \in I$.

> If $f'(x) < 0$ for all x in an interval I, then f is **decreasing** on that interval.

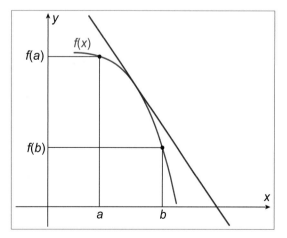

Worked Example 14.4

Investigate the values of x for which the function $f: R \to R: x \to x^3 - 4x^2$ is decreasing.

Solution

We need to find the values of x for which $f'(x) < 0$.

Step 1 Find the derivative of $f(x)$.

$$f'(x) = 3x^2 - 8x$$

Step 2 Solve $f'(x) < 0$, i.e. solve $3x^2 - 8x < 0$.

Let $3x^2 - 8x = 0$.

$$x(3x - 8) = 0$$

$$x = 0 \quad \textbf{OR} \quad x = \frac{8}{3}$$

Step 3

Sketch the graph.

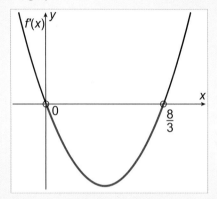

From the sketch, we can see that $f'(x) < 0$ when $0 < x < \frac{8}{3}$.

Therefore, f is decreasing on the interval $0 < x < \frac{8}{3}$, $x \in R$.

Worked Example 14.5

The function f is defined on $R \backslash \{2\}$ by $f: R \backslash \{2\} \to R: x \to \dfrac{x}{x-2}$.

Show that f is a decreasing function over $R \backslash \{2\}$.

Solution

Find the derivative of $f(x)$.

$$f'(x) = \frac{(x-2)(1) - x(1)}{(x-2)^2}$$

$$\therefore f'(x) = -\frac{2}{(x-2)^2}$$

$(x-2)^2 > 0$ for all values of $x \in R \backslash \{2\}$

$\therefore -\dfrac{2}{(x-2)^2} < 0$ for all values of $x \in R \backslash \{2\}$

Therefore, f is a decreasing function on the interval $R \backslash \{2\}$.

Exercise 14.2

1. For each of the following functions, state:

   (a) The range of values of x for which the function is defined

   (b) The range of values of x for which the function increases

   (c) The range of values of x for which the function decreases

(i)

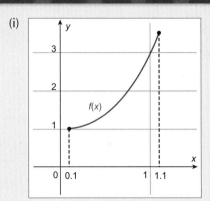

(ii)

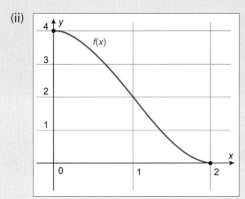

(iii)

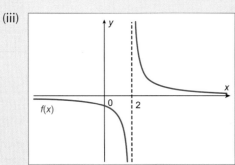

(iv)

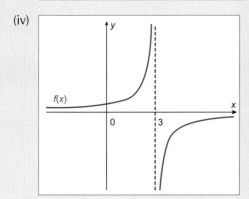

(ii)

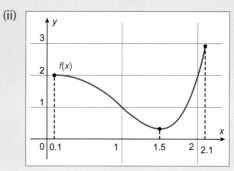

(iii)

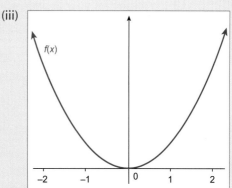

(iv)

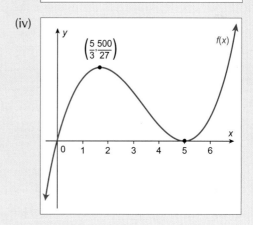

2. For each of the following functions, state:

(a) The range of values of x for which the function is defined

(b) The range of values of x for which the function is decreasing

(c) The range of values of x for which the function is increasing

(i)

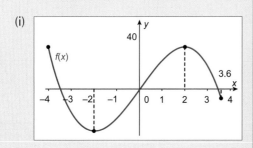

3. A is the closed interval $[1, 16]$.
The function f is defined on A by
$f: A \to R: x \to 2x^3 - 45x^2 + 216x + 128$.

The graphs of f and f', the derivative of f, are shown.

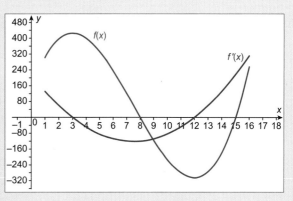

(i) Find, in the form
$f': A \rightarrow R: x \rightarrow ax^2 + bx + c$, the
derivative of f.

(ii) Using the graph, find the range of values
of x for which the function is increasing.

(iii) For which values of x is the function
decreasing?

(iv) State whether f is injective or not.
Give a reason for your answer.

4. B is the closed interval $[0, 5]$. The function
f is defined on B by
$f: B \rightarrow R: x \rightarrow x^3 - 5x^2 + 3x + 5$.

(i) Find, in the form
$f': B \rightarrow R: x \rightarrow ax^2 + bx + c$,
the derivative of f.

(ii) Hence, find the range of values of x for
which the function is decreasing.

(iii) For what range of values of x is the
function increasing?

(iv) State whether f is surjective or not.
Give a reason for your answer.

5. Let f be any function defined for some or all
real values. The graph of the derivative of
some functions of this kind is shown.
In each case, find:

(a) The range of values of x for which the
function is increasing

(b) The range of values of x for which the
function is decreasing

(i)
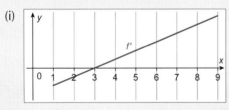

(ii)
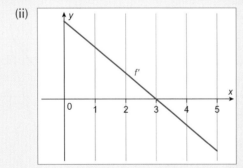

(iii)
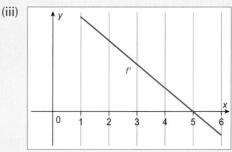

(iv)
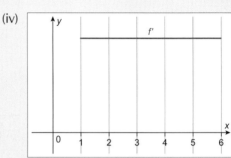

6. Let f be any function defined for some or all
real values. The graph of the derivative of
some functions of this kind is shown.
In each case, find:

(a) The range of values of x for which the
function is increasing

(b) The range of values of x for which the
function is decreasing

(i)
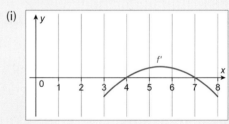

(ii)
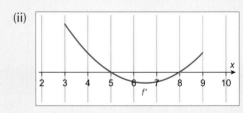

(iii)
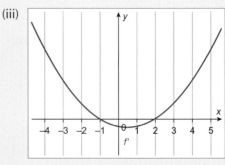

(iv)

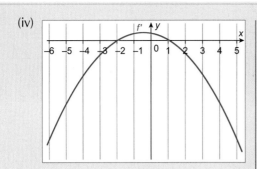

7. The function f is defined on $R\backslash\{1\}$ by
$f: R\backslash\{1\} \rightarrow R: x \rightarrow \dfrac{x}{x-1}$.

  (i) Explain the meaning of the following statement:

    'The function $f: R\backslash\{1\} \rightarrow R: x \rightarrow \dfrac{x}{x-1}$ decreases for all values of x on $R\backslash\{1\}$.'

  (ii) Show that f is a decreasing function on $R\backslash\{1\}$.

8. The function f is defined on $R\backslash\{1\}$ by
$f: R\backslash\{1\} \rightarrow R: x \rightarrow \dfrac{x}{x-1}$.

  (i) Explain the meaning of the following statement:

    'The function $f: R\backslash\{1\} \rightarrow R: x \rightarrow \dfrac{x}{1-x}$ increases for all values of x on $R\backslash\{1\}$.'

  (ii) Show that f is an increasing function on $R\backslash\{1\}$.

9. The function f is defined for all $x \in R$.

    $f: R \rightarrow R: x \rightarrow x^3 + 6x^2 + 15x + 36$

  (i) Find, in the form
$f': R \rightarrow R: x \rightarrow ax^2 + bx + c$, the derivative of f.

    Write f' in the form
$f': R \rightarrow R: x \rightarrow 3[(x + a)^2 + b]$.

  (ii) Hence, say why f is an increasing function for all $x \in R$.

14.3 STATIONARY POINTS

At a stationary point on a curve, the gradient is zero. There are three types of stationary point: maxima, minima and points of inflexion.

Local Maximum and Local Minimum Points

At a **turning point** on a curve, the gradient is zero. The derivative immediately to one side of a turning point has a different sign to the derivative immediately to the other side. Maximum and minimum points are called turning points because the graph turns at these points.

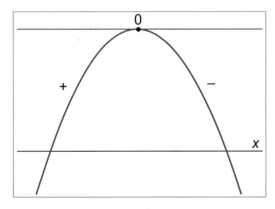

Maximum points – 'humps'

As x increases, the gradient goes from positive → zero → negative.

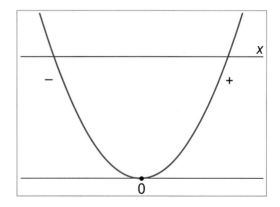

Minimum points – 'troughs'

As x increases, the gradient goes from negative → zero → positive.

The Second Derivative Test

The second derivative test can be useful for determining whether a given stationary point is a local maximum or a local minimum.

If $f'(x) = 0$ at $x = c$, then:

- If $f''(c) < 0$, then f has a local maximum at $x = c$.

- If $f''(c) > 0$, then f has a local minimum at $x = c$.

- If $f''(c) = 0$, then the second derivative test fails.

The diagram shows graphs of $f(x)$, $f'(x)$ and $f''(x)$.

$f(x)$ has a local maximum at $(a, f(a))$ and a local minimum at $(b, f(b))$.

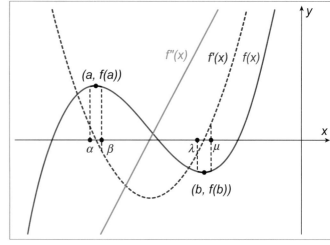

- In the interval (α, β), $f'(x)$ is decreasing. Therefore, for any $c \in (\alpha, \beta)$, $f''(c) < 0$. Hence, $f''(a) < 0$, as $a \in (\alpha, \beta)$.

- In the interval (λ, μ), $f'(x)$ is increasing. Therefore, for any $d \in (\lambda, \mu)$, $f''(d) > 0$. Hence, $f''(b) > 0$, as $b \in (\lambda, \mu)$.

Worked Example 14.6

Find the co-ordinates of the turning points of the function $f: R \to R: x \to 8x^2 - 4x^3$ and determine their nature.

Solution

$f(x) = 8x^2 - 4x^3$

$\Rightarrow f'(x) = 16x - 12x^2$ and $f''(x) = 16 - 24x$

Solve $f'(x) = 0$:

$16x - 12x^2 = 0$

$4x - 3x^2 = 0$

$x(4 - 3x) = 0$

$\therefore x = 0 \quad OR \quad 4 - 3x = 0$

$\therefore x = \frac{4}{3}$

Find the corresponding y-values:

When $x = 0$, $y = 8(0)^2 - 4(0)^3 = 0$

When $x = \frac{4}{3}$, $y = 8\left(\frac{4}{3}\right)^2 - 4\left(\frac{4}{3}\right)^3 = 4\frac{20}{27}$

Therefore, the co-ordinates of the turning points are $(0,0)$ and $\left(\frac{4}{3}, 4\frac{20}{27}\right)$.

Second derivative test to investigate the nature of points $(0,0)$ and $\left(\frac{4}{3}, 4\frac{20}{27}\right)$

$f''(x) = 16 - 24x$

Test $x = 0$:

$f''(0) = 16 - 24(0)$

$= 16$

$16 > 0$

At $x = 0$ there is a local minimum, as $f''(0) > 0$. Therefore, $(0,0)$ are the co-ordinates of the local minimum.

Test $x = \frac{4}{3}$:

$f''\left(\frac{4}{3}\right) = 16 - 24\left(\frac{4}{3}\right)$

$= -16$

$-16 < 0$

At $x = \frac{4}{3}$ there is a local maximum, as $f''\left(\frac{4}{3}\right) < 0$. Therefore, $\left(\frac{4}{3}, 4\frac{20}{27}\right)$ are the co-ordinates of the local maximum.

An alternative to the second derivative test (or to be used when second derivative test fails)

Work out the sign of the gradient on either side of the turning point.

Left of point	At point	Right of point	
+ (slope up)	0 (flat)	− (slope down)	⇒ Local maximum
− (slope down)	0 (flat)	+ (slope up)	⇒ Local minimum

When using this test, it is important to choose points in the neighbourhood of the turning points. If you choose points that are too far away, you may jump over another turning point.

Test $x = 0$

Left of point	At point	Right of point
$x = -0.1$	$x = 0$	$x = 0.1$
$\dfrac{dy}{dx} = 16(-0.1) - 12(-0.1)^2$ $= -1.72$ $< 0, \quad \text{i.e. } -$	$\dfrac{dy}{dx} = 0$	$\dfrac{dy}{dx} = 16(0.1) - 12(0.1)^2$ $= 1.48$ $> 0, \quad \text{i.e. } +$
(slope down)	(flat)	(slope up)

Therefore, (0,0) is a local minimum.

Test $x = \dfrac{4}{3}$

Left of point	At point	Right of point
$x = 1$	$x = \dfrac{4}{3}$	$x = 1.6$
$\dfrac{dy}{dx} = 16(1) - 12(1)^2$ $= 4$ $> 0, \quad \text{i.e. } +$	$\dfrac{dy}{dx} = 0$	$\dfrac{dy}{dx} = 16(1.6) - 12(1.6)^2$ $= -5.12$ $< 0, \quad \text{i.e. } -$
(slope up)	(flat)	(slope down)

Therefore, $\left(\dfrac{4}{3}, 4\dfrac{20}{27}\right)$ is a local maximum.

Points of Inflexion

The graphs of two functions are shown.

In Graph A, the slopes of the tangent lines increase as you move from left to right. In this case we say that the curve is **concave up** on the interval. Notice also that the tangent lines are below the curve.

Graph A

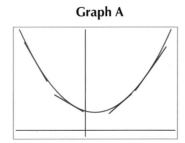

Graph B

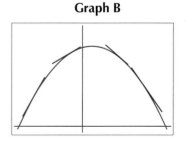

In Graph B, the slopes of the tangent lines decrease as you move from left to right. In this case, we say that the curve is **concave down** on the interval. If a curve is concave down on an interval, then the tangent lines are above the curve.

The point where the concavity of a curve changes from concave up to concave down or from concave down to concave up is called a **point of inflexion**.

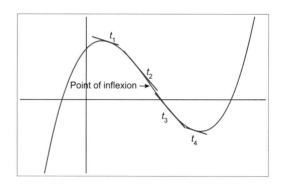

(a) If $f'(c) = 0$ and $f''(c) > 0$, then f has a **local minimum** at c.

(b) If $f'(c) = 0$ and $f''(c) < 0$, then f has a **local maximum** at c.

(c) If f has a **point of inflexion** at $x = c$, then $f''(c) = 0$.

If a point of inflexion occurs at $x = c$ and $f'(c) = 0$, then $(c, f(c))$ is called a horizontal point of inflexion or a saddle point.

Turning points and horizontal points of inflexion are collectively known as **stationary points**.

For a function $f(x)$, $f'(x) = 0$ at each stationary point of the function.

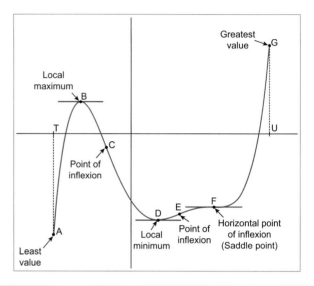

Worked Example 14.7

The function f is defined on R by $f: R \rightarrow R: x \rightarrow x^4 - 4x^3$.

  (i)   Find $f'(x)$, the derivative of $f(x)$.

  (ii) Find the co-ordinates of the stationary points of $f(x)$.

  (iii) Determine the nature of the stationary points.

  (iv) Find the x- and y-intercepts of the graph of $f(x)$.

  (v)   Hence, draw a graph of $f(x)$ in the domain $-1 \leqslant x \leqslant 4, x \in R$

Solution

(i) $f(x) = x^4 - 4x^3$

$\Rightarrow f'(x) = 4x^3 - 12x^2$

(ii) $f'(x) = 0$

$4x^3 - 12x^2 = 0$

$x^3 - 3x^2 = 0$

$x^2(x - 3) = 0$

$x^2 = 0$ **OR** $x - 3 = 0$

$\therefore x = 0$ **OR** $x = 3$

$f(0) = 0$ and $f(3) = -27$

Therefore, $(0,0)$ and $(3, -27)$ are two stationary points.

(iii) $f'(x) = 4x^3 - 12x^2$

$\Rightarrow f''(x) = 12x^2 - 24x$

$f''(0) = 12(0) - 24(0)$

$\qquad = 0 \dots$ Test fails.

We need to test nature of point at $x = 0$:

$f'(-0.1) = 4(-0.1)^3 - 12(-0.1)^2 = -0.124$

$f'(0) = 0$

$f'(0.1) = 4(0.1)^3 - 12(0.1)^2 = -0.116$

$\Rightarrow$ At $x = 0$, there is a horizontal point of inflexion.

$f''(3) = 12(3)^2 - 24(3)$

$\qquad = 108 - 72$

$\qquad = 36 > 0$

$\Rightarrow$ At $x = 3$, there is a local minimum.

(iv) *x*-intercepts

Let $f(x) = 0$.

$x^4 - 4x^3 = 0$

$x^3(x - 4) = 0$

$x^3 = 0 \quad$ **OR** $\quad x - 4 = 0$

$\therefore x = 0 \quad$ **OR** $\qquad x = 4$

(0,0) and (4,0) are the *x*-intercepts.

y-intercepts

Let $x = 0$.

$\therefore f(0) = (0)^4 - 4(0)^3$

$\qquad = 0$

(0,0) is the *y*-intercept.

(v) $\qquad f(-1) = (-1)^4 - 4(-1)^3$

$\therefore f(-1) = 5$

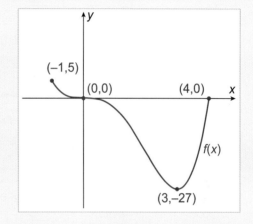

Worked Example 14.8

The graph of a cubic function *f* is shown.

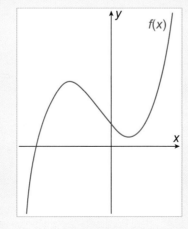

DIFFERENTIAL CALCULUS II

One of the four diagrams A, B, C and D below shows the graph of the derivative of f. State which one it is and justify your answer.

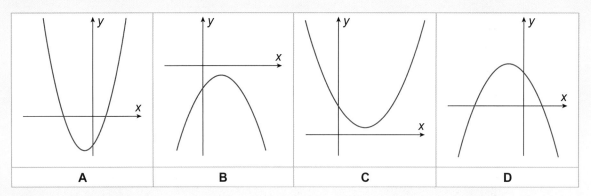

| A | B | C | D |

Solution

Graphs B and C can be eliminated for the following reasons:

■ Graph B lies entirely below the x-axis, which implies that the derivative is negative for all values of x. If the derivative is always negative, then the function is a decreasing function. f is not a decreasing function.

■ Graph C lies entirely above the x-axis, which implies that the derivative is positive for all values of x. If the derivative is always positive, then the function is an increasing function. f is not an increasing function.

Graph D can also be eliminated for the following reason:

■ Graph D begins below the x-axis, i.e. the function is decreasing initially. However, the function f shown is increasing initially.

Graph A is the correct solution.

■ The graph begins above the x-axis. Therefore, the function is increasing initially. The graph of the derivative then crosses the x-axis. The x-value of this intercept corresponds to the value of x for which f has a local maximum point. The derivative then becomes negative, showing that f is decreasing here. The graph then cuts the x-axis once more; this corresponds to the x-value of f for which the function has a local minimum. The derivative becomes positive once more, so f is increasing here.

 Exercise 14.3

1. Find the co-ordinates of the points on these curves where the gradient is zero.

   (i) $y = x^2 + 2x - 8$ (iii) $y = 9 + 27x - x^3$

   (ii) $y = x^2 + 8x + 12$ (iv) $y = \sqrt{x} + \dfrac{1}{\sqrt{x}}$

2. $y = x^2 - 5x - 2$

   (i) Show that $\dfrac{dy}{dx} = 0$ when $x = \dfrac{5}{2}$.

   (ii) By considering the sign of $\dfrac{dy}{dx}$ for two values of x, one less than $\dfrac{5}{2}$ and one

   greater than $\dfrac{5}{2}$, show that $x = \dfrac{5}{2}$ gives a minimum value of y.

   (iii) Find the co-ordinates of the minimum point on the curve $y = x^2 - 5x - 2$.

3. $y = x^3 - 75x$

   (i) Show that $\dfrac{dy}{dx} = 0$ when $x = \pm 5$.

   (ii) By considering the sign of $\dfrac{dy}{dx}$ for two values of x, one less than −5 and one greater than −5, show that $x = -5$ gives a local maximum value of y.

(iii) Similarly, show that $x = 5$ gives a local minimum value of y.

(iv) Find the co-ordinates of the local maximum and the local minimum point on the curve $y = x^3 - 75x$.

4. The diagram shows the graph of the function $f(x) = x^2 - 6x + 17$.

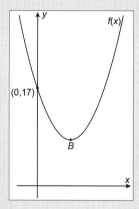

(i) Find a, the value of x for which $f'(x) = 0$.

(ii) Show that $f''(a) > 0$.

(iii) Hence, find the co-ordinates of the point B, the minimum point on the curve.

5. The function f is defined on R by
$f: R \to R: x \to 3 + 10x - x^2$.

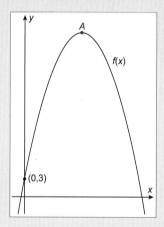

(i) Find a, the value of x for which $f'(x) = 0$.

(ii) Show that $f''(a) < 0$.

(iii) Hence, find the co-ordinates of the point A, the maximum point on the curve.

6. Let $f(x) = x^3 - 12x$, $x \in R$. The graph of $f(x)$ is shown. x_1 and x_2 are the x-values of the turning points of the curve of $f(x)$.

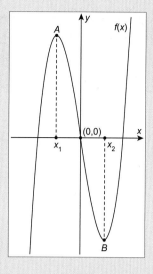

(i) Solve the quadratic equation $f'(x) = 0$.

(ii) Explain why the solutions to $f'(x) = 0$ are x_1 and x_2.

(iii) Find the co-ordinates of A and B.

(iv) Show that $f''(x_1) < 0$ and $f''(x_2) > 0$.

7. Find the co-ordinates of the local maximum point and the local minimum point on the curve $y = 2x^3 - 3x^2 - 36x + 10$.

8. The function f is defined on R by
$f: R \to R: x \to (x + 1)^2(2 - x)$.

(i) Find the co-ordinates of the local maximum point and the local minimum point on the curve of $f(x)$.

(ii) Find the co-ordinates of the points where the curve intersects the x-axis and the y-axis.

(iii) Draw a rough sketch of the curve.

(iv) Hence, write down the range of values of x for which $f(x)$ is increasing.

9. A is the closed interval $[0, 3\pi]$. The function f is defined on A by $f: A \to R: x \to x - 2\sin x$.

A graph of f is shown.

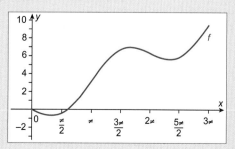

   (i) Find all stationary points and determine their nature.

   (ii) Use the graph to find the maximum value of f on the interval.

   (iii) Use algebra to find the actual maximum value of f on the given interval.

10. The function f is defined on R^+ by
$f: R^+ \rightarrow R: x \rightarrow x \ln x$.

   (i) Show that f has no points of inflexion.

   (ii) Find the minimum value of $f(x)$.

11. The graph of a quadratic function h is shown.

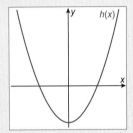

One of the two diagrams A and B below shows the graph of the derivative of h. State which one it is and justify your answer.

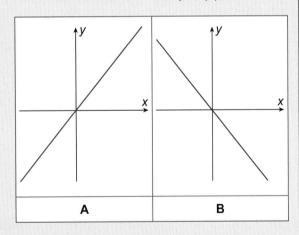

| A | B |

12. The graph of a quadratic function g is shown.

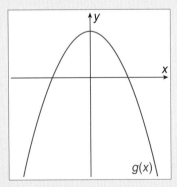

One of the two diagrams A and B below shows the graph of the derivative of g. State which one it is and justify your answer.

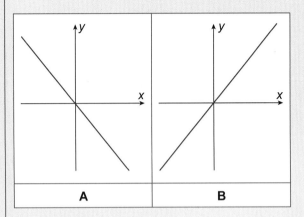

| A | B |

13. The graph of a cubic function f is shown.

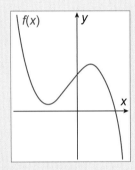

One of the four diagrams A, B, C and D below shows the graph of the derivative of f. State which one it is and justify your answer.

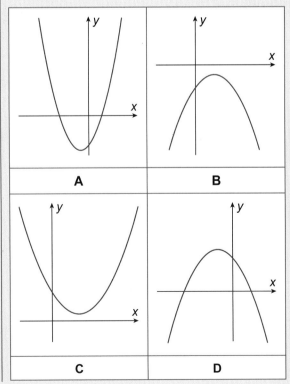

| A | B |
| C | D |

14. The function $f: x \rightarrow ax^3 - bx^2$ is defined for all $x \in R$. Graphs of $f'(x)$ and $f''(x)$, the first and second derivatives of $f(x)$, are shown.

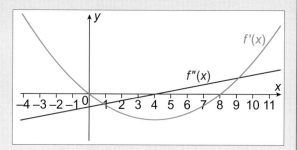

(i) Use the diagram to explain why the function does not have a horizontal point of inflexion.

(ii) Write down the x-values of the local maximum, local minimum and point of inflexion of the function, given that all exist.

(iii) Write, in terms of a and b, the x-value of the local minimum and the point of inflexion of $f(x)$.

(iv) If $(8, -256)$ is a point on the graph of f, find the value of a and the value of b.

(v) Find the co-ordinates of the local maximum, local minimum and point of inflexion of the function.

(vi) Draw a sketch of the function.

15. The function $f(x) = (1 + x)\log_e(1 + x)$ is defined for $x > -1$.

(i) Show that the curve $y = f(x)$ has a turning point at $\left(\dfrac{1-e}{e}, -\dfrac{1}{e}\right)$.

(ii) Determine whether the turning point is a local maximum or a local minimum.

16. $f(x) = \log_e(3x) - 3x$, $x > 0$

(i) Show that $\left(\dfrac{1}{3}, -1\right)$ is a local maximum point of $f(x)$.

(ii) Explain why $f(x)$ is continuous for all $x > 0$.

(iii) Hence, deduce that the graph of $f(x)$ does not intersect the x-axis.

17. The function $f: x \rightarrow e^{x^2}$ is defined for all $x \in R$.

(i) Find $f'(x)$ and $f''(x)$.

(ii) Find the turning point of the curve $y = e^{x^2}$.

(iii) Determine whether the turning point is a local maximum or a local minimum.

18. $f(x) = \dfrac{\ln x}{x}$, $x > 0$

(i) Show that the maximum of $f(x)$ occurs at the point $\left(e, \dfrac{1}{e}\right)$.

(ii) Hence, show that $x^e \leqslant e^x$ for all $x > 0$.

(iii) Which is bigger, π^e or e^π? Explain.

14.4 MAXIMUM AND MINIMUM PROBLEMS

Calculus is an important tool in solving maximum–minimum problems. We can use an analysis of stationary points to solve real-life problems from economics, engineering, physics, meteorology – in fact, from any area of life in which there is movement or change.

 Worked Example 14.9

From a 30 cm × 30 cm sheet of cardboard, square corners are cut out so that the sides are folded up to make a box.

(i) What dimensions will yield a box of maximum volume?

(ii) What is the maximum volume of the box?

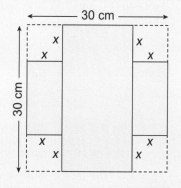

Solution

(i)

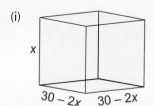

Side length in base = $30 - 2x$, height = x.

$\therefore$ Volume $(V) = (30 - 2x)(30 - 2x)(x)$

$\qquad = (900 - 120x + 4x^2)(x)$

$\therefore V = 900x - 120x^2 + 4x^3$

$\dfrac{dV}{dx} = 900 - 240x + 12x^2$

Let $\dfrac{dV}{dx} = 0$ and solve to find the stationary points:

$900 - 240x + 12x^2 = 0$

$4x^2 - 80x + 300 = 0$

$x^2 - 20x + 75 = 0$

$(x - 15)(x - 5) = 0$

$x = 15 \quad \textbf{OR} \quad x = 5$

$\dfrac{d^2V}{dx^2} = -240 + 24x$

At $x = 15$, $\dfrac{d^2V}{dx^2} = -240 + 24(15)$

$\qquad\qquad = -240 + 360$

$\qquad\qquad = 120 > 0$

Therefore, there is a local minimum at $x = 15$.

At $x = 5$, $\dfrac{d^2V}{dx^2} = -240 + 24(5)$

$\qquad\qquad = -240 + 120$

$\qquad\qquad = -120 < 0$

Therefore, there is a local maximum at $x = 5$.

Required dimensions for maximum volume (using $x = 5$):

Length = $30 - 2(5) = 20$ cm

Width = $30 - 2(5) = 20$ cm

Height = 5 cm

(ii) Maximum volume of box = $20 \times 20 \times 5$

$\qquad\qquad\qquad\qquad = 2{,}000$ cm³

OR

Volume $= 900x - 120x^2 + 4x^3$

So, maximum volume

$\qquad = 900(5) - 120(5)^2 + 4(5)^3$

$\qquad = 2{,}000$ cm³

To find the absolute maximum and absolute minimum values of a continuous function f on a closed interval $[a, b]$:

1. Find the values of f at the endpoints of the interval, i.e. find $f(a)$ and $f(b)$.

2. Find the local maximum and local minimum values of f in (a, b).

3. The largest of the values from Steps 1 and 2 is the absolute maximum, and the smallest of these values is the absolute minimum.

Worked Example 14.10

Between 0°C and 30°C (i.e. in the interval $[0, 30]$), the volume V (in cubic centimetres) of 1 kg of water at a temperature T is given approximately by the formula:

$$V = 999.87 - 0.06426T + 0.0085043T^2 - 0.0000679T^3$$

Find:

(i) The rate at which V is changing with respect to T in the interval $[0, 30]$

(ii) $V(0)$ and $V(30)$, the volumes at 0°C and 30°C, respectively

(iii) The temperature at which the water has its minimum volume in the interval $[0, 30]$

(iv) The temperature at which the water has its maximum volume in the interval $[0, 30]$

Solution

(i) $\dfrac{dV}{dT} = -0.06426 + 0.0170086T - 0.0002037T^2$

(ii) $V(0) = 999.87 \text{ cm}^3$

$V(30) = 999.87 - 0.06426(30) + 0.0085043(30)^2 - 0.0000679(30)^3$

$\qquad = 1{,}003.76277 \text{ cm}^3$

(iii) Investigate if the local minimum of V is in the range $[0, 30]$:

$\dfrac{dV}{dT} = 0$

$-0.06426 + 0.0170086T - 0.0002037T^2 = 0$

$T = \dfrac{-0.0170086 \pm \sqrt{(0.0170086)^2 - 4(-0.0002037)(-0.06426)}}{2(-0.0002037)}$

$T \approx 3.967 \quad \textbf{OR} \quad T \approx 79.532$

We accept $T = 3.967$ only, as $79.532 \notin [0, 30]$.

How do we know we have a minimum at $T = 3.967$?

$\left.\dfrac{dV}{dt}\right|_{T = 3.8} \approx -0.003 \qquad \left.\dfrac{dV}{dt}\right|_{T = 4.1} \approx 0.002$

$\therefore$ We have a local minimum at $T = 3.967$.

$V(3.967) = 999.74$

Minimum volume in $[0, 30] = \min\,[999.87, 999.74, 1003.76]$

$\qquad\qquad\qquad\qquad = 999.74 \text{ cm}^3$

Therefore, the temperature at which the water has its minimum volume in the interval $[0, 30]$ is 3.967°C.

(iv) $V(0) = 999.87$

$V(30) = 1{,}003.76$

Therefore, the temperature at which the water has its maximum value in the interval $[0, 30]$ is 30°C.

 ## Exercise 14.4

1. A farmer wishes to enclose a rectangular section of a field for grazing. She has purchased 200 m of electric fence to construct the enclosure. She designs the rectangular enclosure so that all 200 m of electric fence is just enough to enclose the grazing area.

(i) If one side of the enclosure is x metres long, explain why the adjacent side is $(100 - x)$ m long.

(ii) Find, in terms of x, the area of the enclosure.

(iii) Find the value of x that maximises the area of the enclosure.

(iv) If the farmer decides to use a circular enclosure, find the radius length of such an enclosure. Assume all 200 m of fencing is needed to form this enclosure. Answer correct to two decimal places.

(v) Find the area of the circular enclosure, correct to the nearest square metre.

(vi) If the farmer wants to have a maximum grazing area, which design should she use – rectangular or circular?

2. A farmer wants to enclose two rectangular paddocks, which are equal in area. A river runs along the side of both paddocks. The farmer has 300 m of fencing.

   (i) If x represents the length (from the river bank) of each paddock and y represents the width, show that $y = 150 - \frac{3}{2}x$.

   (ii) Find, in terms of x, the area of one of the paddocks.

   (iii) Find the value of x that maximises the area of each paddock.

   (iv) What is the maximum area of the enclosure?

3. A Norman window is shaped like a rectangle with a semicircle on top. Suppose that the perimeter of a Norman window is to be 8 m.

 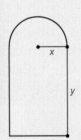

   (i) Assume that 2x represents the base length of the rectangular part of the window and that y represents the height of the rectangular part. Taking $\pi = 3.14$, show that $y = 4 - 2.57x$.

   (ii) Find, in terms of x, the area of the window.

   (iii) What dimensions should the window have to allow the maximum amount of light to enter through the window?

4. Of all the numbers whose sum is 80, find the two that have the maximum product; that is, maximise $P = xy$, where $x + y = 80$.

5. Of all the numbers whose sum is 100, find the two that have the maximum product; that is, maximise $P = xy$, where $x + y = 100$.

6. Liffey Appliances is marketing a new washing machine. It determines that in order to sell x machines, the price per machine (in euros) must be $440 - 0.3x$.

It also determines that the cost of producing x washing machines is given by $C(x) = 6{,}000 + 0.5x^2$.

   (i) If x machines are sold, find R(x), the total revenue received. Your answer will be a quadratic expression in x.

   (ii) Find P(x), the profit function, if x machines are sold. $[P(x) = R(x) - C(x)]$

   (iii) How many machines must be produced to maximise profit?

   (iv) What is the maximum profit?

7. A cylindrical can is manufactured to hold 1 litre of oil.

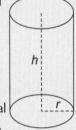

   (i) Find the height of the can in terms of the radius, r.

   (ii) Find the dimensions that will minimise the cost of the metal used to manufacture the can.

8. (i) Show that a rectangle with area 25 m² will have a minimum perimeter of length 20 m.

   (ii) Show that of all the rectangles with a given area, the one with the smallest perimeter is a square.

9. A sector of a circle has area 100 cm².

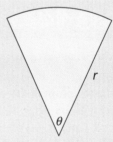

   (i) Show that $\theta = \frac{200}{r^2}$ (θ is measured in radians).

   (ii) Explain why $r > \sqrt{\frac{100}{\pi}}$. (Hint: $\theta < 2\pi$.)

   (iii) Show that the perimeter of the sector is given by $P = 2r + \frac{200}{r}$.

   (iv) Find the value of r that minimises the perimeter.

10. An equilateral triangle of length 4 cm has a rectangle inscribed in it.

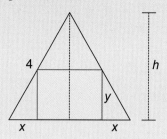

(i) Find h, the height of the triangle.

(ii) Use similar triangles to show that $y = \sqrt{3}x$.

(iii) Find, in terms of x, the area of the rectangle.

(iv) Hence, find the maximum possible area of this rectangle.

(v) What percentage of the triangle is occupied by this rectangle?

11. An open rectangular box is to be made with an external area of 1,620 cm². The ratio of the side lengths of the base of the box is 3 : 5.

Let the length of the shorter side of the base be $3x$ cm, let the height of the box be h cm and let its volume be V cm³.

(i) Sketch a net of the box and write in terms of x an expression for the longer side of the base of the box.

(ii) Show that $V = 15hx^2$.

(iii) Find the maximum volume of the box.

12. Let v_1 be the velocity of light in air and v_2 the velocity of light in water. A ray of light will travel from a point L in the air to a point M in the water by a path LKM that minimises the time taken.

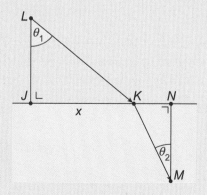

(i) The distances $|LJ| = d$, $|JN| = a$ and $|NM| = c$ are all constant. Let $|JK| = x$, $0 < x < a$.

Show that T, the total time taken for the ray to travel along the path LKM, is given by:

$$T = \frac{\sqrt{x^2 + d^2}}{v_1} + \frac{\sqrt{(a - x)^2 + c^2}}{v_2}$$

(ii) Find $\dfrac{dT}{dx}$.

(iii) Show that T has a stationary point when:

$$\frac{x}{v_1\sqrt{x^2 + d^2}} = \frac{a - x}{v_2\sqrt{(a - x)^2 + c^2}}$$

(iv) Assuming this stationary point to be a minimum, deduce that:

$$\frac{\sin \theta_1}{\sin \theta_2} = \frac{v_1}{v_2}$$

13. (i) Show that a rectangle with perimeter 20 m will have maximum area when it is a square with side lengths of 5 m.

(ii) Show that of all the rectangles with a given perimeter, the one with the greatest area is a square.

14. The probability of getting a head on flipping a biased coin is P.

The coin is flipped n times, producing a sequence containing m heads and $(n - m)$ tails.

(i) What is the probability of obtaining this sequence from n flips?

(ii) What value of P maximises the probability of obtaining this sequence?

15. The Hubble telescope was deployed in April 1990 by the space shuttle *Discovery*. A model for the velocity (in m/s) of the shuttle from lift-off at $t = 0$ seconds until the rocket boosters were jettisoned at $t = 126$ seconds is given by:

$$v(t) = 0.000396849t^3 - 0.027520392t^2 + 7.1963t + 0.939698$$

(i) Find, in terms of t, the acceleration of the shuttle in the interval $[0, 126]$.

(ii) Find the velocity and acceleration of the shuttle after 10 seconds.

(iii) Find the absolute maximum and absolute minimum values of the acceleration between lift-off and the jettisoning of the boosters.

16. A computer manufacturer determines that in order to sell x units of a new computer, the price per unit, in euros, must be $p(x) = 1{,}200 - x$.

The manufacturer also determines that the total cost of producing x units is given by $C(x) = 3{,}500 + 20x$.

  (i)   Find $R(x)$, the total revenue generated by the sale of x computers.

  (ii) Find the total profit, $P(x)$, generated by the sale of x computers.

  (iii) How many units must the company produce and sell in order to maximise profit?

  (iv) What is the maximum profit?

  (v)   What price per unit must be charged to make this maximum profit?

14.5 RATES OF CHANGE

Let $y = f(x)$, where x is a function of another variable t.

So, y can be considered to be a function of t.

The Chain Rule gives:

We can use the Chain Rule to deal with several real-life problems.

FORMULA

$$\frac{dy}{dt} = \frac{dy}{dx} \cdot \frac{dx}{dt}$$

ACTIVITY 14.2

Worked Example 14.11

The cost of extracting T tonnes of ore from a copper mine is $C = f(T)$ euros; in other words, the cost of extraction is a function of the amount of ore mined.

  (i)   Explain the meaning of $f'(T)$, the derivative of f with respect to T.

  (ii) What are the units of measurement for $f'(T)$?

Solution

  (i) $f'(T)$ is the rate of change of C (cost) with respect to the amount of ore mined. For example, if $f'(3{,}000) = 500$, this means that when 3,000 tonnes has been mined, the cost of mining the next tonne of ore will be €500.

  (ii) Euros per tonne

Worked Example 14.12

According to Boyle's Law, for a given mass of gas at a fixed temperature, $PV = C$, where P is the pressure exerted by the gas and V is the volume of the contained gas. C is a constant that depends on the type of gas. Initially, $V = 100 \text{ cm}^3$ and $P = 2$ atm (atm is an international standard unit of pressure).

  (i)   Find the value of the constant C.

  (ii) If the pressure is decreasing at a rate of 0.01 atm s^{-1}, find the rate at which the gas is expanding when the volume is 125 cm^3.

Solution

(i) $PV = C$

$C = 100(2) = 200$

(ii) Pressure is decreasing at a rate of 0.01 atm s^{-1}.

This is written as $\dfrac{dP}{dt} = -0.01$ (derivative is negative as pressure is decreasing).

We are looking to find $\dfrac{dV}{dt}$ at $V = 125$.

The Chain Rule gives:

$$\frac{dV}{dt} = \frac{dV}{dP} \cdot \frac{dP}{dt}$$

We now need to find $\dfrac{dV}{dP}$.

$$PV = 200$$

$$\Rightarrow V = \frac{200}{P} = 200P^{-1}$$

$$\frac{dV}{dP} = -200P^{-2} = -\frac{200}{P^2}$$

$$\therefore \frac{dV}{dt} = -\frac{200}{P^2} \times -0.01 = \frac{2}{P^2}$$

$$PV = 200$$

$$\therefore P = \frac{200}{V},$$

At $V = 125$, $P = \dfrac{200}{125}$

$$\therefore P = 1.6$$

$$\left.\frac{dV}{dt}\right|_{P = 1.6} = \frac{2}{(1.6)^2}$$

$$= \frac{25}{32}$$

$$= 0.78125 \text{ cm}^3 \text{ s}^{-1}$$

Worked Example 14.13

The area of a healing wound is given by $A = \pi r^2$, where r is the radius length of the wound.

If the radius length is decreasing at a rate of 0.5 mm per day, how fast is the area decreasing at the instant when the radius length is 10 mm?

Solution

$A = \pi r^2$

$\therefore \dfrac{dA}{dr} = 2\pi r$ (The rate at which the area of the wound is changing with respect to its radius length)

$\dfrac{dr}{dt} = -0.5$ mm/day

We require $\dfrac{dA}{dt}$, the rate of decrease of the area.

$\dfrac{dA}{dt} = \dfrac{dA}{dr} \cdot \dfrac{dr}{dt}$ (Chain Rule)

$= (2\pi r)(-0.5)$

$= -\pi r$

When $r = 10$, $\dfrac{dA}{dt} = -10\pi$ mm^2/day.

Exercise 14.5

1. The average weight W (in kilograms) of an ash tree is given by the function $W = f(x)$, where x is the height of the tree in metres.

   (i) Explain the meaning of $f'(x)$, the derivative of $f(x)$.

   (ii) Will $f'(x)$ be positive or negative? Explain.

   (iii) What are the units of measurement for $f'(x)$?

2. A rock is dropped from the top of the Spire on Dublin's O'Connell Street. After it falls x metres, its speed V is $V = h(x)$; that is, V is a function of x. What is the meaning of:

   (i) $h(5)$

   (ii) $h'(5)$

3. A loaf of bread has just been taken out of the oven and is cooling off before being eaten. The temperature T of the bread (measured in degrees Celsius) is a function of t (measured in minutes), the length of time the bread has been out of the oven. Therefore, we have $T = f(t)$.

(i) What is the meaning of $f(5)$?

(ii) Is $f'(t)$ positive or negative? Explain.

(iii) What are the units for $f'(t)$?

4. The weight W of an infant in kilograms is a function of its age, m (measured in months), so $W = f(m)$.

(i) Would you expect $f'(m)$ to be positive or negative? Explain.

(ii) What does $f(7) = 7.65$ tell you?

(iii) What are the units of $f'(m)$?

5. A car accelerates in a straight line so that its distance s (in metres) from its starting point p after t seconds is given by the function $s(t) = t^2$. Find:

(i) The distance of the car from p after 4 seconds

(ii) The distance of the car from p after 5 seconds

(iii) The speed of the car in terms of t

(iv) The speed of the car after 4 seconds

6. A ball is thrown straight up into the air. The height h (measured in metres) of the ball after t seconds is given by the function $h(t) = 40t - 5t^2$.

(i) Find the height of the ball after 1 second.

(ii) Explain why $h'(t)$ represents the speed of the ball after t seconds.

(iii) Find the speed of the ball after t seconds.

(iv) What is the speed of the ball when it reaches its maximum height?

(v) Find the time at which the ball reaches its maximum height.

(vi) Find the maximum height reached.

7. The temperature T of a patient during an illness is given by $T(t) = -0.6t^2 + 0.67t + 37$, where T is the temperature (in degrees Celsius) at time t (in days).

(Time is measured from the onset of the illness.)

(i) Find $T'(t)$, the rate at which the temperature is changing with respect to time.

(ii) Find the rate at which the temperature is changing at $t = 3$ days.

(iii) When will the patient's temperature begin to fall? Answer correct to the nearest hour.

8. The length of the edge of a cube is decreasing at a rate of 4 cm per minute.

(i) What is the value of n if V, the volume of the cube, is given by $V(x) = x^n$, where x is the length of an edge of the cube?

(ii) What is the value of m and n if S, the surface area of the cube, is given by $S(x) = mx^n$, where x is the length of an edge of the cube?

(iii) Explain why $x'(t)$ or $\dfrac{dx}{dt}$ is negative.

(iv) Find the rate at which the volume of the cube is decreasing when $x = 10$ cm.

(v) Find the rate at which the surface area of the cube is decreasing when $x = 10$ cm.

9. The length of the radius of a spherical balloon is increasing at a rate of 1 cm per second.

(i) Write down an expression for V, the volume of the balloon, in terms of r, the radius of the balloon.

(ii) Write down an expression for S, the surface area of the balloon, in terms of r, the radius of the balloon.

(iii) Explain why $r'(t)$ or $\dfrac{dr}{dt}$ is positive.

(iv) Find the rate at which the volume of the balloon is increasing when $r = 12$ cm.

(v) Find the rate at which the surface area of the balloon is increasing when $r = 12$ cm.

10. The surface area S of a sphere of radius r is given by the formula $S = 4\pi r^2$. The radius of the sphere is increasing at a rate of 2 cm s^{-1}.

   (i) Find $\dfrac{dS}{dr}$.

   (ii) Find $\dfrac{dS}{dt}$, the rate of increase of the surface area, when $r = 4$ cm.

11. The area of a circle is increasing at a rate of 6 cm^2 s^{-1}.

   (i) Find, in terms of r, $\dfrac{dC}{dr}$, the rate of change of the circumference with respect to the radius.

   (ii) Find, in terms of r, $\dfrac{dA}{dr}$, the rate of change of the area with respect to the radius.

   (iii) Hence, find $\dfrac{dC}{dA}$ in terms of r.

   (iv) Find $\dfrac{dC}{dt}$, the rate of increase of the circumference, when the radius is 3 cm.

12. The area and perimeter of the rectangle shown are denoted by A and P, respectively.

$\dfrac{dA}{dt}$, the rate at which the area of the rectangle is increasing, is 16 cm^2 s^{-1}.

   (i) Find $\dfrac{dP}{dx}$ and $\dfrac{dA}{dx}$.

   (ii) Hence, find $\dfrac{dP}{dA}$ in terms of x.

   (iii) Find $\dfrac{dP}{dt}$ at the instant when $x = 2$ cm.

13. The volume of oil, V m^3, in a tank changes with time t hours ($1 \leqslant t \leqslant T$) according to the formula $V = 32 - 10 \ln t$, where T represents the time when the tank is empty of oil.

   (i) What is the volume of oil in the tank when $t = 1$?

   (ii) Find the rate of change, in m^3 per hour, of the volume of oil in the tank when $t = 1$.

   (iii) Determine the value of T.

14. One end of a ladder is sliding down a vertical wall while the other end is sliding away from the wall along the horizontal ground.

   (i) Explain why $\dfrac{dy}{dt}$ and $\dfrac{dx}{dt}$ have opposite signs.

   (ii) Find the ratio $y : x$ when the top of the ladder is moving three times faster than the bottom.

15. A vessel in the shape of a right circular cone is placed so that it is standing on its apex. Water is flowing into the cone at a steady rate of 1 m^3 per minute. The vessel has a height of 2 m and a diameter of 2 m.

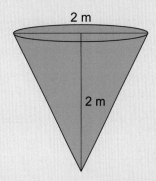

When the vessel is one-eighth full, find:

   (i) The rate at which the water is rising

   (ii) The rate at which the free surface of the water is increasing

16. An astronaut is at a height x km above the earth as shown.

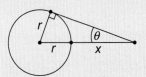

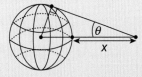

He moves vertically away from the earth's surface at a velocity $\dfrac{dx}{dt}$ of $\dfrac{r}{5}$ km/h, where r is the length of the earth's radius. He observes the angle θ as shown.

   (i) Express x in terms of r and θ.

   (ii) Hence, find $\dfrac{d\theta}{dt}$ when $x = r$.

17. A woman starts walking northwards from a point P at a rate of 1.5 m s^{-1}. Five minutes later, a man starts walking eastwards at 2 m s^{-1} from a point 500 m due east of P. Let t represent the time elapsed since the man started walking, where t is measured in seconds.

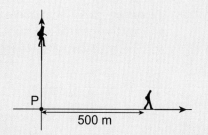

(i) Find Q, the distance the woman has travelled before the man sets out.

(ii) If x represents the distance travelled by the man and y represents the distance travelled by the woman, in t seconds, explain why $y = \frac{3}{4}x$.

(iii) What is $\frac{dx}{dt}$?

(iv) Find, in terms of x, the distance between the man and woman after t seconds. Let this distance be P.

(v) Find $\frac{dP}{dx}$.

(vi) At what rate are the people moving apart 15 minutes after the woman starts walking?

Revision Exercises

1. Differentiate each of the following functions with respect to x:

(i) $f(x) = x^3 + 3x^2 + 4x + 5$

(ii) $g(x) = (x^2 + 4)(x - 2)$

(iii) $F(x) = \dfrac{x^2 + 2x}{x - 4}$

(iv) $h(x) = \dfrac{(x^2 - 8x)(x + 2)}{x - 4}$

2. Evaluate the derivatives of each of the following functions at $x = \dfrac{\pi}{2}$:

(i) $\sin 5x$ (iii) $\tan^2 6x$

(ii) $\cos^2 2x$ (iv) $\sin^3 4x$

3. Differentiate each of the following:

(i) $f(x) = \left[\dfrac{x - 4}{x + 3}\right]^3$ (iii) $s(t) = \sqrt[5]{\dfrac{t^3 + 1}{t + 1}}$

(ii) $f(y) = \left[\dfrac{y + 5}{y^2 + 3}\right]^{12}$ (iv) $f(x) = \dfrac{2x}{\sqrt{x^2 + 1}}$

4. Find the derivative with respect to x of each of the following functions:

(i) $f(x) = \sin^{-1}\left(\dfrac{x}{4}\right)$

(ii) $g(x) = \tan^{-1}\left(\dfrac{x}{2}\right)$

(iii) $h(x) = \sin^{-1}\left(\dfrac{x + 1}{x - 1}\right)$

(iv) $F(x) = \cos^{-1}\left(\dfrac{3x + 4}{x - 2}\right)$

5. Differentiate with respect to x:

(i) $y = e^{x^2}$ (iv) $y = x \ln x$

(ii) $y = xe^2$ (v) $y = \ln\left(\dfrac{x + 4}{x - 2}\right)$

(iii) $y = \ln x^3$ (vi) $y = e^x \ln x^2$

6. For each of the following functions, find $f''(x)$ and, hence, $f''(-3)$:

(i) $f(x) = 3x^3 + 2x^2 + x$

(ii) $f(x) = 5x^3 - 12x$

(iii) $f(x) = -3x^3 + 5x$

7. The function f is defined on R by $f: R \to R: x \to x^3 - 108x$.

(i) Show that $\dfrac{dy}{dx} = 0$ when $x = \pm 6$.

(ii) By considering the sign of $\dfrac{dy}{dx}$ for two values of x, one less than -6 and one greater than -6, show that $x = -6$ gives a local maximum value of f.

(iii) Similarly, show that $x = 6$ gives a local minimum value of the function.

8. The function g is defined on R^+ by $f: R^+ \to R: x \to x^2 - 8x\sqrt{x} + 16x + 1$.

(i) Find $f'(x)$, the derivative of $f(x)$.

(ii) By putting $z = \sqrt{x}$, show that the equation $\dfrac{dy}{dx} = 0$ leads to $z^2 - 6z + 8 = 0$.

(iii) Hence, find the stationary points of the function.

(iv) Find $f''(x)$ and use this to determine the nature of the stationary points.

9. Below is a graph of the distance travelled by Carl Lewis (USA) in the first second of his victory in the final of the men's 100 metres at the 1988 Olympic Games in Seoul, Korea.

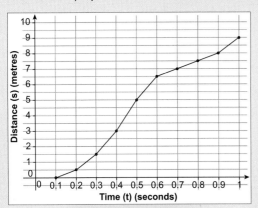

Showing all necessary work, calculate:

(i) His average speed over the first second of the race

(ii) His average speed over the first 0.8 seconds of the race

(iii) His average speed over the interval [0.3, 0.7] (seconds)

(iv) His average speed over the interval [0.3, 0.6] (seconds)

(v) His average speed over the interval [0.3, 0.5] (seconds)

Now, answer the following:

(vi) Over what interval is his average speed greatest? (Consider only each 0.1 second interval.)

(vii) If you could construct a function $s(t)$, where s was distance travelled in metres and t was time taken in seconds, then what would his average speed be over the interval $[t, t + h]$?

(viii) Using your knowledge of limits, what is his speed at t seconds?

10. A cough is a contraction of the trachea in order to increase the velocity of the air being expelled. The velocity of the outgoing air for a person can be modelled by a function $f(x) = c(a - x)x^2$, where a is the normal radius of the person's trachea (in centimetres), x is the radius while coughing and c is a positive constant.

(i) What is the unit of measurement for the velocity of outgoing air?

(ii) What is the radius of the trachea in a person who is not coughing? Answer in terms of a.

(iii) By what percentage does the radius of the trachea need to contract in order to expel air with maximum volume?

(iv) What is the maximum velocity with which air can be expelled while coughing, in terms of a and c?

11. A 30 cm piece of wire is cut in two pieces. One piece is used to form a circle and the other to form a square.

How should the wire be cut so that the sum of the areas is:

(i) A minimum   (ii) A maximum

12. The weight W of a young calf (in kilograms) is a function of its age m (measured in months), so $W = f(m)$.

(i) What are the units of $f'(m)$?

(ii) Interpret the meaning of $f'(3) = 4$.

13. A pebble is dropped into still water, and circular ripples spread out from the point of entry. The radius of the circles increase at a rate of 10 cm/s.

(i) If r is the radius of one of the circles, write down the area of the circle.

(ii) What is $\dfrac{dA}{dr}$ in terms of r?

(iii) Write down $\dfrac{dr}{dt}$.

(iv) Explain why $\dfrac{dA}{dt} = \dfrac{dA}{dr} \cdot \dfrac{dr}{dt}$.

(v) Find the rate at which the area of the circles is increasing when the radius length is 25 cm.

14. The force of attraction F (measured in Newtons) between two bodies is a function of the distance r between the two bodies (measured in metres), i.e. $F = f(r)$.

For two given bodies, A and B:
$$F = f(r) = \frac{1{,}000}{r^2}$$

(i) Show that $f'(r) = -\dfrac{2{,}000}{r^3}$.

(ii) What are the units of $f'(r)$?

(iii) Find the force of attraction F between the two bodies when $r = 10$ m.

(iv) Find the rate of change of F with respect to r when $r = 10$ m.

15. A runner sprints around a circular track of radius 100 m at a constant speed of 7 m s^{-1}. The runner's friend is standing at a distance of 200 m from the centre of the track.

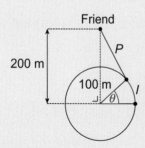

(i) If l is the distance travelled by the runner in a given interval of time, then write θ in terms of l, where θ is measured in radians.

(ii) Show that $\dfrac{d\theta}{dt} = 0.07$ rad s^{-1}.

(iii) If P is the distance between the runner and his friend, then show that $P = 100 \sqrt{5 - 4 \sin \theta}$ metres.

(iv) Find $\dfrac{dP}{d\theta}$ in terms of θ.

(v) How fast is the distance between the friends changing when the distance between them is 200 m?

16. An object of weight W is dragged along a horizontal plane by a force acting along a rope attached to the object.

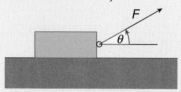

If the rope makes an angle θ with the plane, then the magnitude of the force F is given by the following equation:

$$F = \frac{\mu W}{\mu \sin \theta + \cos \theta}$$

where μ is a positive constant called the coefficient of friction and $0 \leqslant \theta < \dfrac{\pi}{2}$.

(i) Identify the variables and constants in the equation above.

(ii) Find $\dfrac{dF}{d\theta}$ in terms of θ.

(iii) Find $\dfrac{d^2F}{d\theta^2}$.

(iv) Show that F is minimised when $\tan \theta = \mu$.

17. An open cylindrical tank of water has a hole near the bottom. The radius of the tank is 52 cm. The hole is a circle of radius 1 cm. The water level gradually drops as water escapes through the hole.

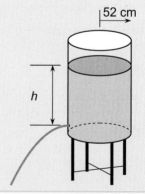

Over a certain 20-minute period, the height of the surface of the water is given by the formula

$$h = \left(10 - \frac{t}{200}\right)^2$$

where h is the height of the surface of the water, in centimetres, as measured from the centre of the hole, and t is the time in seconds from a particular instant $t = 0$.

(a) What is the height of the surface at time $t = 0$?

(b) After how many seconds will the height of the surface be 64 cm?

(c) Find the rate at which the volume of water in the tank is decreasing at the instant when the height is 64 cm.

Give your answer correct to the nearest cm³ per second.

(d) The rate at which the volume of water in the tank is decreasing is equal to the speed of the water coming out of the hole, multiplied by the area of the hole. Find the speed at which the water is coming out of the hole at the instant when the height is 64 cm.

(e) Show that, as t varies, the speed of the water coming out of the hole is a constant multiple of $\sqrt{h}$.

(f) The speed, in centimetres per second, of water coming out of a hole like this is known to be given by the formula

$$v = c\sqrt{1962h}$$

where c is a constant that depends on certain features of the hole.

Find, correct to one decimal place, the value of c for this hole.

SEC Project Maths Paper 1,
Leaving Certificate Higher Level, 2012

18. A company uses waterproof paper to make disposable conical drinking cups. To make each cup, a sector AOB is cut from a circular piece of paper of radius 9 cm. The edges AO and OB are then joined to form the cup, as shown.

The radius of the rim of the cup is r, and the height of the cup is h.

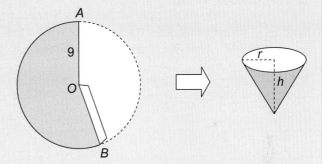

(a) By expressing r^2 in terms of h, show that the capacity of the cup, in cm³, is given by the formula

$$V = \frac{\pi}{3}h(81 - h^2)$$

(b) There are two positive values of h for which the capacity of the cup is $\frac{154\pi}{3}$.

One of these values is an integer.

Find the two values. Give the non-integer value correct to two decimal places.

(c) Find the maximum possible volume of the cup, correct to the nearest cm³.

(d) Complete the table below to show the radius, height and capacity of each of the cups involved in parts (b) and (c) above.

In each case, give the radius and height correct to two decimal places.

	Cups in part (b)		Cups in part (c)
Radius (r)			
Height (h)			
Capacity (V)	$\frac{154\pi}{3}$ = 161 cm³	$\frac{154\pi}{3}$ = 161 cm³	

(e) In practice, which one of the three cups above is the most reasonable shape for a conical cup? Give a reason for your answer.

(f) For the cup you have chosen in part (e), find the measure of the angle *AOB* that must be cut from the circular disc in order to make the cup.

Give your answer in degrees, correct to the nearest degree.

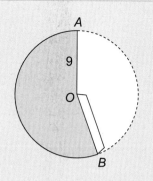

SEC Project Maths Paper 1,
Leaving Certificate Higher Level, 2012

19. Darragh and Sinéad are investigating the area of rectangles that can circumscribe a given rectangle of length 12 cm and width 5 cm.

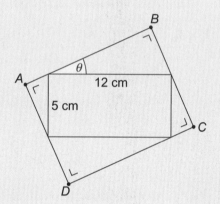

(i) Find the area of *ABCD* if $\theta = 30°$. Leave your answer in surd form.

(ii) Find, in terms of θ, the length and width of *ABCD*.

(iii) Find, in terms of θ, the area of the rectangle *ABCD*. Express your answer in the form $a \sin 2\theta + b$, where $a, b \in Q$.

(iv) What value of θ maximises the area of a rectangle that circumscribes a given rectangle of length 12 cm and width 5 cm? Hence, find the area of this rectangle.

(v) Sinéad says that the value of θ that maximises the area of the circumscribed rectangle depends on the dimensions of the given rectangle. Is she correct? Justify your answer.

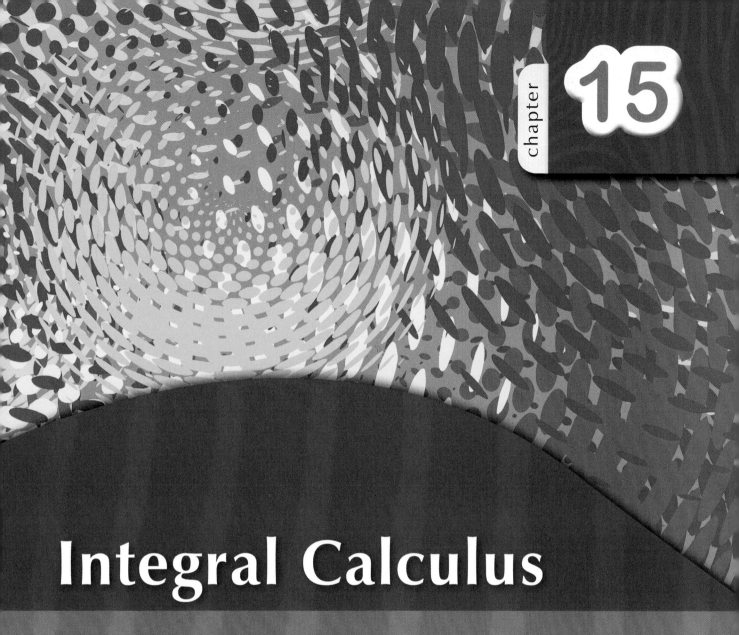

chapter 15

Integral Calculus

Learning Outcomes

In this chapter you will learn about:

- ➲ Antiderivatives
- ➲ Integrating polynomial functions
- ➲ Integrating exponential functions
- ➲ Finding the area under a curve
- ➲ The Trapezoidal Rule
- ➲ The average value of a function

Numerous real-world processes involve rates of change that may be constantly changing – the velocity of a projectile, the rate of temperature change of an object, the growth of money in a bank account.

Knowing these rates of change can be very important. Using a process called **integration** or **antidifferentiation**, we can use a rate of change to gain valuable information about the example at hand.

For example, microbiologists know that, for many species of bacterium, the rate of growth of the bacterial population is proportional to the size of the population at that time. That is:

$$P'(t) \qquad \propto \qquad P(t)$$

(Rate of change in population with respect to time) (population size at time t)

When boiling water cools to room temperature, the temperature of the water drops rapidly at first, but the rate of change slows as the water approaches room temperature.

So, $P'(t) = kP(t)$
(where k is a constant of proportionality)

Suitable measurements at different times of the rate of change in population and of the population size will allow for a calculation of k to be made. The process of antidifferentiation/integration does the rest, as follows:

$$\frac{dP(t)}{dt} = kP(t)$$

$$dP(t) = kP(t)\, dt$$

$$\frac{dP(t)}{P(t)} = k\, dt$$

$\ln P(t) = kt + c$ (c is a constant of integration)

$P(t) = A\, e^{kt}$ (A is population size at $t = 0$)

This process of antidifferentiation/integration, which undoes the process of differentiation, has thus allowed for the underlying population function to be identified. It is now possible to predict accurately what the population size will be at any time t.

15.1 ANTIDERIVATIVES AND THE INDEFINITE INTEGRAL

Suppose that the function $f(x)$ is such that $f'(x) = 5$. Can we find $f(x)$? One such $f(x)$ would be $f(x) = 5x$, since the derivative of $5x$, wrt x is 5. There are many other functions whose derivative is 5. Here are some examples:

$$f(x) = 5x + 2 \qquad f(x) = 5x - \frac{1}{2}$$
$$f(x) = 5x + 2.4 \qquad f(x) = 5x - \sqrt{3}$$

We say that any function of the form $5x + c$ is an antiderivative of 5, where c is any constant.

If two functions in x, f and g, have the same derivative, then $f(x) = g(x) + c$. c is called the constant of integration.

Worked Example 15.1

(i) Differentiate the function $f: R \rightarrow R: x \rightarrow \frac{1}{3}x^3$.

(ii) Hence, find three antiderivatives of x^2.

Solution

(i) $f(x) = \frac{1}{3}x^3$

$f'(x) = x^2$

(ii) If the derivative of $\frac{1}{3}x^3$ is x^2, then an antiderivative of x^2 is of the form $\frac{1}{3}x^3 + c$, where c is any constant.

So: $\frac{1}{3}x^3 + 5$, $\frac{1}{3}x^3 - 2\pi$ and $\frac{1}{3}x^3$ are three antiderivatives of x^2.

Indefinite Integrals

The general form of an antiderivative is called the **indefinite integral**. To indicate that an antiderivative of x^2 is of the form $\frac{x^3}{3} + c$, we write:

$$\int x^2 \, dx = \frac{x^3}{3} + c$$

This an indefinite integral. It involves an arbitrary constant of integration, c.
(Arbitrary means 'can take any value'.)

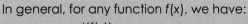

In general, for any function $f(x)$, we have:

$$\int \frac{d(f(x))}{dx} \, dx = f(x) + c$$

> **Note**
>
> Integration was initially intended for use, not as an antiderivative, but as a process of summation (adding). The notation for integration evolved from the summation approach.
>
> The sign for integration, the integral sign $\int$, is an elongated S.

Exercise 15.1

1. Write down the derivatives of each of the following functions with respect to the letter in the bracket:

(i) $f(x) = \sin x$ $[x]$

(ii) $g(x) = \cos x$ $[x]$

(iii) $f(t) = \tan t$ $[t]$

(iv) $h(t) = \ln t$ $[t]$

(v) $F(x) = e^x$ $[x]$

2. Using your results from Question 1, find an antiderivative of each of the following functions:

(i) $f'(x) = \cos x$

(ii) $g'(x) = -\sin x$

(iii) $f'(t) = \sec^2 t$

(iv) $h'(t) = \frac{1}{t}$

(v) $F'(x) = e^x$

3. Differentiate each of the following wrt x:

(i) $y = \cos 2x$

(ii) $y = 3 \sin 3x$

(iii) $y = e^{x2}$

(iv) $y = 2 \ln x$

(v) $y = 2^x$

4. Using your results from Question 3, find **two** antiderivatives of each of the following functions:

(i) $f'(x) = -2 \sin 2x$

(ii) $f'(x) = 9 \cos 3x$

(iii) $f'(x) = 2\,xe^{x^2}$

(iv) $f'(x) = \frac{2}{x}$

(v) $f'(x) = (\ln 2)2^x$

5. Find the derivatives of each of the following functions wrt x:

(i) $f(x) = \cos^{-1}\dfrac{x}{4}$

(ii) $g(x) = \sin^{-1}\dfrac{x}{5}$

(iii) $f(x) = \tan^{-1}\dfrac{x}{6}$

(iv) $p(x) = \cos^{-1} 3x$

(v) $h(x) = \tan^{-1} 4x$

6. Using your results from Question 5, find an antiderivative of each of the following functions:

(i) $f'(t) = -\dfrac{1}{\sqrt{16 - t^2}}$

(ii) $g'(t) = \dfrac{1}{\sqrt{25 - t^2}}$

(iii) $h'(t) = \dfrac{6}{36 + t^2}$

(iv) $f'(t) = -\dfrac{3}{\sqrt{1 - 9t^2}}$

(v) $q'(t) = \dfrac{4}{1 + 16t^2}$

7. A function f is defined as follows:

$f: R \to R: x^r \to \dfrac{1}{r+1}x^{r+1} + c, r \neq -1, r \in Q;$
c is any real valued constant.

(i) Find $f'(x)$, the derivative of $f(x)$.

(ii) Hence, find an antiderivative of $f'(x) = x^r$.

8. Using your results from Question 7, find each of the following indefinite integrals:

(i) $\int x^2\, dx$

(ii) $\int x^3\, dx$

(iii) $\int x\, dx$

(iv) $\int x^{\frac{1}{2}}\, dx$

(v) $\int x^{\frac{3}{2}}\, dx$

15.2 INTEGRATING POLYNOMIALS

A single variable polynomial in x of degree n is a function of the following form:

$$f(x) = a_n x^n + a_{n-1}x^{n-1} + \dots + a_2 x^2 + a_1 x + a_0, n \in N$$

 **ACTIVITY 15.1**

On our course, we need to know how to integrate single variable polynomial functions.

In Activity 15.1 you derived the following rules:

Rule 1 $\int x^r\, dx = \dfrac{x^{r+1}}{r+1} + c, r \neq -1$, where c is the constant of integration.

Rule 2 $\int kf(x)\, dx = k\int f(x)\, dx$, where k is a constant.

Rule 3 $\int (f(x) \pm g(x))\, dx = \int f(x)\, dx \pm \int g(x)\, dx$

 **FORMULA**

$$\int x^n\, dx = \dfrac{x^{n+1}}{n+1} + c, n \neq -1$$

Formulae and Tables, page 26.

Division by zero is not defined, so $n = -1$ is excluded.

Rule in words

To integrate a term in a polynomial, add one to the power and divide by the new power.

Worked Example 15.2

Find: (i) $\int (2x^2 + 5x^3)\,dx$ (ii) $\int (x + 2)^3\,dx$

Solution

(i) $\int (2x^2 + 5x^3)\,dx = \int 2x^2\,dx + \int 5x^3\,dx$

$= 2\int x^2\,dx + 5\int x^3\,dx$

$= \dfrac{2x^3}{3} + \dfrac{5x^4}{4} + c$

(ii) $(x + 2)^3 = x^3 + 6x^2 + 12x + 8$

$\therefore \int (x + 2)^3\,dx = \int (x^3 + 6x^2 + 12x + 8)\,dx$

$= \dfrac{x^4}{4} + 2x^3 + 6x^2 + 8x + c$

> The arbitrary constants from each integral can be combined into one constant.

 Worked Example 15.3

A particle moves in a straight line and has acceleration given by $a(t) = 6t + 40$.
Its initial velocity is $v(0) = -60$ cm s^{-1}, and its initial displacement from a fixed point O is $s(O) = 3$ cm.

(i) Find its velocity function $v(t)$ and hence, its speed after 10 seconds.

(ii) Find its displacement function $s(t)$ and hence, its distance from O after 10 seconds.

> Velocity is the rate of change of displacement with respect to time:
>
> $$s'(t) = v(t) \quad \textbf{OR} \quad \frac{ds}{dt} = v$$
>
> Velocity is measured in m/s or m s^{-1} (or in cm/s or cm s^{-1}, etc.).
>
> Acceleration is the rate of change of velocity with respect to time:
>
> $$v'(t) = a(t) \quad \textbf{OR} \quad \frac{dv}{dt} = a$$
>
> Acceleration is measured in m/s^2 or m s^{-2} (or in cm/s^2 or cm s^{-2}, etc.).

Solution

(i) $v'(t) = a(t) = 6t + 40$

$v(t) = \int v'(t)\,dt$

$= \int (6t + 40)\,dt$

$= \dfrac{6t^2}{2} + 40t + c$

$v(t) = 3t^2 + 40t + c$

We can now evaluate c, the constant of integration.

$v(0) = 3(0)^2 + 40(0) + c = c$

But we are given that $v(0) = -60$ cm s^{-1}, so $c = -60$.

$v(t) = 3t^2 + 40t - 60$

$v(10) = 3(10)^2 + 40(10) - 60$

$= 300 + 400 - 60$

$= 640$ cm s^{-1}

(ii) $s'(t) = v(t) = 3t^2 + 40t - 60$

$s(t) = \int (3t^2 + 40t - 60)\,dt$

$= \dfrac{3t^3}{3} + \dfrac{40t^2}{2} - 60t + c$

$s(t) = t^3 + 20t^2 - 60t + c$

$s(0) = (0)^3 + 20(0)^2 - 60(0) + c$

$\therefore s(0) = c$

But $s(0) = 3$ cm, so $c = 3$.

$s(t) = t^3 + 20t^2 - 60t + 3$

$s(10) = 10^3 + 20(10)^2 - 60(10) + 3$

$= 1{,}000 + 2{,}000 - 600 + 3$

$= 2{,}403$ cm

Exercise 15.2

1. Find each of the following indefinite integrals:

(i) $\int x^2 \, dx$ (iii) $\int x \, dx$

(ii) $\int x^3 \, dx$ (iv) $\int 4 \, dx$

2. Find each of the following indefinite integrals:

(i) $\int x^4 \, dx$ (iii) $\int x^8 \, dx$

(ii) $\int x^5 \, dx$ (iv) $\int x^n \, dx \, (n \in Q)$

3. Find each of the following indefinite integrals:

(i) $\int 5x^2 \, dx$ (iii) $\int 2 \, dx$

(ii) $\int 3x \, dx$ (iv) $\int ax^3 \, dx$ (a is a constant)

4. Find each of the following indefinite integrals:

(i) $\int (x^2 + 2x + 1) \, dx$

(ii) $\int (x^4 - 6) \, dx$

(iii) $\int (x^3 + 1) \, dx$

(iv) $\int (x^3 + 3x^2 - x + 2) \, dx$

5. Find $\int y \, dx$ if:

(i) $y = \dfrac{x^5 + x^6}{x^4}$ (iii) $y = \dfrac{8x^5 - 9x^3}{2x^2}$

(ii) $y = \dfrac{(x^2 + 4x)^2}{x}$ (iv) $y = \dfrac{(x^2 + x)(x^3 - x)}{x}$

6. Find each of the following indefinite integrals:

(i) $\int (5t + 3)^2 t^3 \, dt$

(ii) $\int (y + 1)^3 \, dy$

(iii) $\int (2x - 3)(x + 1)^2 \, dx$

(iv) $\int \dfrac{x^2 - 1}{x + 1} \, dx$

7. A particle moves in a straight line and has acceleration given by $a(t) = 5 + 4t - 2t^2$.

Its initial velocity $v(0) = 3 \text{ m s}^{-1}$, and its initial displacement from a fixed point is $s(0) = 10$ m.

(i) Find its velocity function $v(t)$ and hence, its speed after 10 seconds.

(ii) Find its displacement function $s(t)$ and hence, its distance from the fixed point after 20 seconds.

---

8. A ball is thrown upwards with a speed of 16 m s^{-1} from the edge of a cliff 144 m above sea level.

> An object dropped from a point above, but close to, the earth's surface is subject to a gravitational force that produces a downward acceleration of about 9.8 m s^{-2}.

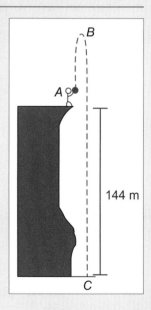

144 m

(i) Explain why the acceleration of the ball is $a = -9.8$ m s^{-2}.

(ii) Find $v(t)$, the velocity of the ball t seconds after it is thrown upwards.

(iii) What is the speed of the ball at the instant it reaches its maximum height?

(iv) How long does it take for the ball to reach its maximum height?

(v) Find $s(t)$, the displacement of the ball from the cliff top t seconds after it is thrown upwards.

(vi) How many seconds after it is thrown upwards does the ball hit the sea?
(*Hint:* The displacement of the sea from the top of the cliff is −144 m.)

9. The gradient of a curve is given by $\dfrac{dy}{dx} = 8x - 3x^2$. Given that the curve passes through the origin, find:

(i) The equation of the curve

(ii) Where the curve intersects the x-axis

10. In a memory experiment, the rate at which students memorise French vocabulary is found to be given by $M'(t) = 0.2t - 0.004t^2$, where $M(t)$ is the number of words memorised in t minutes from the start of the experiment.

   (i) Find $M(t)$ if it is known that $M(0) = 0$.

   (ii) How many words are memorised in the first eight minutes?

11. Raindrops grow as they fall, their surface area increases, and therefore the resistance to their falling increases. A raindrop has an initial downward velocity of 10 m s⁻¹ and its downward acceleration is given by

$$a(t) = \begin{cases} 9 - 0.9t & \text{if } 0 \leqslant t \leqslant 10 \\ 0 & \text{for } t > 10 \end{cases}$$

The raindrop is initially 500 m above the ground.

   (i) Find the velocity function $v(t)$ of the raindrop after t seconds, $0 \leqslant t \leqslant 10$.

   (ii) Find $v(10)$ and hence, write down the speed at which the raindrop hits the ground.

   (iii) Find $s(t)$, the distance travelled by the raindrop in t seconds, $0 \leqslant t \leqslant 10$.

   (iv) How long does it take the raindrop to fall?

12. The gradient function of a curve is $\dfrac{dy}{dx} = ax + b$, where a and b are constants.

   The curve passes through the points $(0,-1)$ and $(2,-5)$.

   At the point $(2,-5)$, the gradient of the curve is 1.

   Find the equation of the curve.

13. Express s as a function of t, given that $\dfrac{d^2s}{dt^2} = a$ (where a is a constant) and that when $t = 0$, $s = 0$ and $\dfrac{ds}{dt} = u$. (Note: s = displacement, v = velocity, t = time)

15.3 INTEGRATING EXPONENTIAL FUNCTIONS

An exponential function is any function of the form $f(x) = a^x$, where a is any positive constant.

The natural exponential function is the function $f(x) = e^x$.

The natural exponential function has the special property of being its own derivative, i.e. $f(x) = f'(x)$ for every $x \in R$. Therefore, $\int e^x \, dx = e^x + c$.

The derivative of a^x is $a^x \ln a$. Therefore:

$$\int a^x \ln a \, dx = a^x + \text{Constant}$$

$$\ln a \int a^x \, dx = a^x + \text{Constant}$$

$$\therefore \int a^x \, dx = \frac{a^x}{\ln a} + \text{Constant}$$

Note: $e^{\ln x} = x$ and $\ln e^x = x$

FORMULA

$$\int e^x \, dx = e^x + c$$

$$\int e^{ax} \, dx = \frac{1}{a} e^{ax} + c$$

$$\int a^x \, dx = \frac{a^x}{\ln a} + c$$

Formulae and Tables, page 26.

Worked Example 15.4

Find the following indefinite integral: $\int 2^x \, dx$.

Solution

$$\int 2^x \, dx = \frac{2^x}{\ln 2} + c$$

 Worked Example 15.5

f is the function $f: R \to R: t \to t^2 e^t$.

    (i) Find $f'(t)$, the derivative of $f(t)$.

    (ii) Hence, find $\int (t^2 + 2t)e^t \, dt$.

Solution

    (i) $f(t) = t^2 e^t$

        $f'(t) = t^2 e^t + e^t(2t)$

            $= (t^2 + 2t)e^t$

    (ii) The derivative of $f(t) = t^2 e^t$ is $f'(t) = (t^2 + 2t)e^t$.

        Therefore, $\int (t^2 + 2t)e^t \, dt = t^2 e^t + c$.

 Worked Example 15.6

Find the indefinite integral $\int \dfrac{e^{2t} - e^{-t}}{e^{-t} - 1} \, dt$.

Solution

$\dfrac{e^{2t} - e^{-t}}{e^{-t} - 1} = \dfrac{e^{3t} - e^0}{e^0 - e^t}$ (Multiply numerator and denominator by e^t)

$\qquad\qquad = \dfrac{e^{3t} - 1}{1 - e^t}$

$\qquad\qquad = \dfrac{(e^t)^3 - 1}{1 - e^t}$

$\qquad\qquad = \dfrac{(e^t - 1)(e^{2t} + e^t + 1)}{1 - e^t}$

$\qquad\qquad = \dfrac{-(1 - e^t)(e^{2t} + e^t + 1)}{1 - e^t}$

$\qquad\qquad = -(e^{2t} + e^t + 1)$

$\int \dfrac{e^{2t} - e^{-t}}{e^{-t} - 1} \, dt = \int -(e^{2t} + e^t + 1) \, dt$

$\qquad\qquad = -\int (e^{2t} + e^t + 1) \, dt$

$\qquad\qquad = -\left(\dfrac{e^{2t}}{2} + e^t + t \right) + c$

1. f is the function $f: R \to R: x \to e^{3x}$.

   (i) Find $f'(x)$, the derivative of $f(x)$.

   (ii) Hence, find an antiderivative of $h'(x) = e^{3x}$.

2. f is the function $f: R \to R: x \to e^{ax}$, where a is some constant.

   (i) Find $f'(x)$, the derivative of $f(x)$.

   (ii) Hence, find an antiderivative of $g'(x) = e^{2ax}$.

3. Using your result from Question 2, find the following indefinite integrals:

   (i) $\int (e^x - e^{-x})\, dx$

   (ii) $\int (e^x - e^{3x})(e^x + e^{3x})\, dx$

   (iii) $\int (e^x + 1)(e^{2x} - e^x + 1)\, dx$

   (iv) $\int \dfrac{e^x - e^{-x}}{e^{-x} + 1}\, dx$

4. Consider the function $y = a^x$, where a is some constant.

   (i) Show that $x = \dfrac{\ln y}{\ln a}$.

   (ii) Hence, find $\dfrac{dx}{dy}$.

   (iii) Given that $\dfrac{dy}{dx} = \dfrac{1}{\left(\dfrac{dx}{dy}\right)}$, show that $\dfrac{dy}{dx} = (\ln a)a^x$.

   (iv) Hence, find the indefinite integral $\int a^x\, dx$.

5. Find each of the following integrals:

   (i) $\int 2^x\, dx$ (iv) $\int 7^x\, dx$

   (ii) $\int 3^x\, dx$ (v) $\int 10e^{2x}\, dx$

   (iii) $\int 5^x\, dx$ (vi) $\int (x^2 + 4^x)\, dx$

6. f is the function $f: R \to R: t \to te^t - e^t$, and g is the function, $g: R \to R: t \to e^t$.

   (i) Find $g'(t)$, the derivative of $g(t)$.

   (ii) Find $f'(t)$, the derivative of $f(t)$.

   (iii) Hence, find $\int te^t\, dt$.

7. f is the function $f: R \to R: t \to ae^{-t}(t + 1)$, where a is constant.

   (i) Find $f'(t)$, the derivative of $f(t)$.

   (ii) Hence, find $\int ate^{-t}\, dt$.

8. The gradient function of a curve is $\dfrac{dy}{dx} = x^2 + e^{-x}$.

The curve passes through the point $(0,0)$. Find the equation of the curve.

9. (i) If $g(x) = \ln x$, find $g'(x)$, the derivative of $g(x)$ wrt x.

   (ii) Hence, or otherwise, find the integral $\int_x^1 \dfrac{1}{x}\, dx$.

   (iii) Radioactive substances decay at a rate that is proportional to the amount of the substance present. That is, if $Q(t)$ is the amount of the substance at time t, then $\dfrac{d(Q(t))}{dt} = k(Q(t))$, where k is a negative constant of proportionality. This result leads to the equation:

$$\int \frac{d(Q(t))}{Q(t)} = \int k\, dt$$

   By integrating on both sides of this equation, write $Q(t)$ in the form $Q(t) = Ae^{kt}$.

   (iv) If a radioactive substance has a half-life of 421 years, and there currently exists 2.8×10^8 kg of the substance on Earth, then define the quantity function $Q(t)$ for this substance, where t is in years.

   (v) The rate of change of another radioactive substance is calculated to be $Q'(t) = -1.5e^{-0.025t}$, where t is measured in years (from now) and $Q(t)$ is the quantity at time t, in kilograms.

   If the current quantity on Earth is 60 kg, what will be the quantity in 10 years?

15.4 DEFINITE INTEGRALS AND AREA

Definite Integrals

The indefinite integral $\int f(x)\,dx = F(x)$ is the general form of an antiderivative for a function in x, $f(x)$.

For example:

$$\text{If } f(x) = (x-5)^2 = x^2 - 10x + 25,$$

$$\text{then } \int f(x)\,dx = F(x) = \frac{x^3}{3} - 5x^2 + 25x + c, \text{ where } c \text{ is an arbitrary constant.}$$

The corresponding **definite integral** is defined as $\int_a^b f(x)\,dx = F(b) - F(a)$.

a and b are called the limits of integration. The significance of the definite integral will be examined later in this chapter in the context of area under a graph.

> If f is a continuous function defined on a closed interval $[a, b]$, then once an antiderivative F of f is known, the definite integral of f over that interval is given by:
>
> $$\int_a^b f(x)\,dx = F(b) - F(a)$$

Worked Example 15.7

Evaluate the following definite integral:

$$\int_1^3 \frac{x^3 - 64}{x - 4}\,dx$$

Solution

$$x^3 - 64 = (x)^3 - (4)^3 = (x - 4)(x^2 + 4x + 16)$$

$$\Rightarrow \frac{x^3 - 64}{x - 4} = x^2 + 4x + 16$$

$$\int_1^3 (x^2 + 4x + 16)\,dx = \frac{x^3}{3} + 2x^2 + 16x \Big|_1^3$$

$$= \left(\frac{(3)^3}{3} + 2(3)^2 + 16(3)\right) - \left(\frac{(1)^3}{3} + 2(1)^2 + 16(1)\right)$$

$$= 75 - 18\frac{1}{3}$$

$$= 56\frac{2}{3}$$

> Note: The arbitrary constant subtracts with itself when we evaluate a definite integral.

Worked Example 15.8

(i)   Find the derivative $F'(x)$ of the function $F(x) = \sin^2 x$.

(ii) Hence, find an antiderivative G of the function $g(x) = \sin 2x$.

(iii) Evaluate the definite integral $\int_{\frac{\pi}{4}}^{\frac{3\pi}{4}} \sin 2x\,dx$.

Solution

(i) $F(x) = \sin^2 x$

$\quad\quad = (\sin x)^2$

Let $u = \sin x \quad \therefore y = u^2$

$\dfrac{du}{dx} = \cos x \quad\quad \dfrac{dy}{du} = 2u$

By the Chain Rule:

$F'(x) = \dfrac{dy}{du} \times \dfrac{du}{dx}$

$\quad\quad = 2u(\cos x)$

$\quad\quad = 2\sin x \cos x$

$\therefore F'(x) = \sin 2x$ *(Formulae and Tables, page 14)*

(ii) The derivative of $\sin^2 x$ is $\sin 2x$. Therefore, an antiderivative G of the function $g(x) = \sin 2x$ would be $G(x) = \sin^2 x + c$, where c is any constant.

(iii) $\displaystyle\int_{\frac{\pi}{4}}^{\frac{3\pi}{4}} \sin 2x \, dx = G\left(\dfrac{3\pi}{4}\right) - G\left(\dfrac{\pi}{4}\right)$

$\quad\quad = \sin^2 \dfrac{3\pi}{4} - \sin^2 \dfrac{\pi}{4}$

$\quad\quad = \left(\dfrac{1}{\sqrt{2}}\right)^2 - \left(\dfrac{1}{\sqrt{2}}\right)^2$

$\quad\quad = 0$

Area Under a Graph

There are many real-life problems that can be solved by finding the area under a graph.

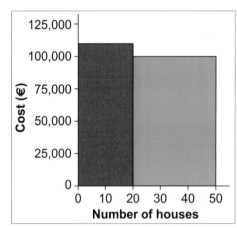

ABC Construction determines that the first 20 houses built on a site will cost €110,000 per house to build. The total cost for the 20 houses is €2,200,000 and is represented by the area shaded red in the graph. The company then estimates that the next 30 houses built will cost €100,000 to build. The total cost for these 30 houses is €3,000,000 and is represented by the area shaded blue in the graph.

The total cost of building the 50 houses is represented by the total area under the graph, i.e. €5,200,000.

Calculating the area under a graph is easy if the area can be divided into rectangles. If the graph is a curve, then it is not possible to get a precise value for the area by dividing the area up into rectangles. However, it is possible to get good approximations for the area under a curve by fitting rectangles under the curve and summing the areas of the rectangles.

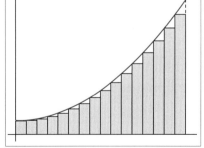

The accuracy of the approximations improves as the number of rectangles used increases while the width of each rectangle decreases.

ACTIVITY 15.2

Worked Example 15.9

(i) Approximate the area under the graph of $f(x) = x^2 + 1$ and the x-axis over the interval [0, 3] by fitting four rectangles of equal area under the graph and then adding.

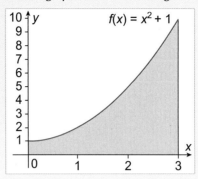

(ii) Approximate the area under the graph of $f(x) = x^2 + 1$ and the x-axis over the interval [0, 3] by fitting eight rectangles of equal area under the graph and then adding. Explain why this approximation is better than that obtained in part (i).

Solution

(i)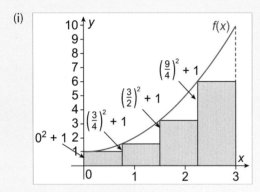

Step 1 Find the base length of the rectangles.

$$\text{Base length} = \frac{3 - 0}{4} = \frac{3}{4} = 0.75$$

Step 2 Find the height of each rectangle.

Rectangle	Height = $x^2 + 1$	Height
1	$0^2 + 1$	1
2	$\left(\frac{3}{4}\right)^2 + 1$	1.5625
3	$\left(\frac{3}{2}\right)^2 + 1$	3.25
4	$\left(\frac{9}{4}\right)^2 + 1$	6.0625

Step 3 Find the total area of the rectangles.

$$\text{Area} = 0.75(1) + 0.75(1.5625)$$
$$+ 0.75(3.25) + 0.75(6.0625)$$

Area of four rectangles
$= 8.90625$ units^2

∴ Area under graph ≈ 8.90625 units^2

(ii)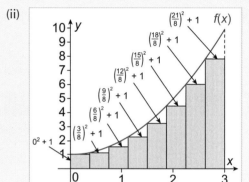

Step 1 Find the base length of the rectangles.

$$\text{Base length} = \frac{3 - 0}{8} = \frac{3}{8} = 0.375$$

Step 2 Find the height of each rectangle.

Rectangle	Height = $x^2 + 1$	Height
1	$0^2 + 1$	1
2	$\left(\frac{3}{8}\right)^2 + 1$	1.140625
3	$\left(\frac{6}{8}\right)^2 + 1$	1.5625
4	$\left(\frac{9}{8}\right)^2 + 1$	2.265625
5	$\left(\frac{12}{8}\right)^2 + 1$	3.25
6	$\left(\frac{15}{8}\right)^2 + 1$	4.515625
7	$\left(\frac{18}{8}\right)^2 + 1$	6.0625
8	$\left(\frac{21}{8}\right)^2 + 1$	7.890625

Step 3 Find the total area of the rectangles.

$$Area = 0.375(1 + 1.140625 + 1.5625 + 2.265625 + 3.25 + 4.515625 + 6.0625 + 7.890625)$$

$$= 0.375(27.6875)$$

$$Area = 10.3828125 \text{ units}^2$$

$$\therefore \text{ Area under graph} \approx 10.3828125 \text{ units}^2$$

This is a better approximation than that used in part (i) because by increasing the number of rectangles, we have reduced the area that was not calculated.

Theorem of Area

A curve $y = f(x)$ lies completely above the x-axis for x between a and b, as shown in the diagram.

The area between the curve, the x-axis and the lines $x = a$ and $x = b$ is given by:

$$\int_a^b f(x)\ dx$$

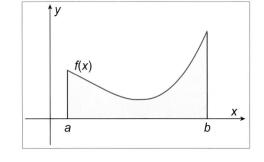

Proof

Consider the function $A(x)$, which we define to be the area under the curve from $x = a$ to $x = x$, $x \leqslant b$.

$A(x + h)$ is the area under the curve from $x = a$ to $x = x + h$.

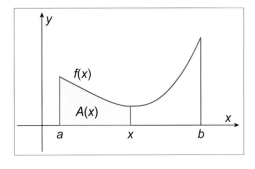

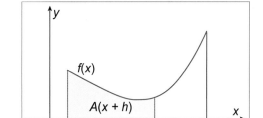

Consider the narrow strip between these two areas.

The area of this narrow strip may be written as $A(x + h) - A(x)$. However, the strip is approximately rectangular and hence, its area is approximately $f(x) \times h$ (base × height).

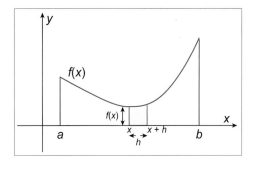

$$A(x + h) - A(x) \approx f(x) \times h$$

$$\frac{A(x + h) - A(x)}{h} \approx f(x)$$

As h becomes smaller, this approximation becomes more accurate:

$$\lim_{h \to 0} \frac{A(x + h) - A(x)}{h} = \lim_{h \to 0} f(x)$$

$$A'(x) = f(x)$$

$$\therefore A(x) + c = \int f(x)\ dx \quad (c \text{ is constant of integration})$$

$$\therefore A(b) - A(a) = \int_a^b f(x)\ dx \quad \text{(Definition of definite integral)}$$

$$\therefore \int_a^b f(x)\ dx \text{ is the area between the curve, the } x\text{-axis and the lines } x = a \text{ and } x = b.$$

Similarly, it can be proved that the area between $y = f(x)$ and the y-axis from $y = P$ to $y = Q$ is given by: $\int_P^Q x \, dy$, where $x = g(y)$, i.e. where x is some function of y.

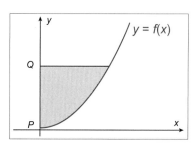

If a region lies completely below the x-axis and we calculate the area of the region using the definite integral, we will obtain a negative answer. Therefore:

$$\text{Area} = \left| \int_a^b f(x) \, dx \right|$$

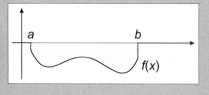

If a region lies partially above and partially below the x-axis, we must use separate integrals when calculating the area of the region. In the case shown on the right, the area is given by:

$$\text{Area} = \left| \int_a^c f(x) \, dx \right| + \int_c^b f(x) \, dx$$

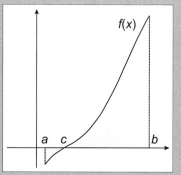

Worked Example 15.10

Find the area bounded by the curve $y = x^2 - 9$, the x-axis and the lines $x = 0$ and $x = 5$.

Solution

Method 1

Step 1 Draw a sketch of the curve $y = x^2 - 9$.

x-intercepts

Let $y = 0$.

$$x^2 - 9 = 0$$
$$(x - 3)(x + 3) = 0$$
$$x = \pm 3$$

The x-intercepts are $(-3,0)$ and $(3,0)$.

y-intercept

Let $x = 0$.

$$y = -9$$

The y-intercept is $(0,-9)$.

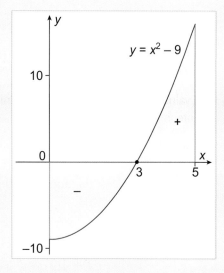

The curve is quadratic and the coefficient of x^2 is positive. Therefore, the curve is U-shaped.

Step 2 Area $= \left| \int_0^3 (x^2 - 9)\,dx \right| + \int_3^5 (x^2 - 9)\,dx$

$$= \left| \left[\tfrac{1}{3}x^3 - 9x \right]_0^3 \right| + \left[\tfrac{1}{3}x^3 - 9x \right]_3^5$$

$$= \left| \left[\tfrac{1}{3}(27) - 9(3) \right] - \left[\tfrac{1}{3}(0) - 9(0) \right] \right| + \left[\tfrac{1}{3}(125) - 9(5) \right] - \left[\tfrac{1}{3}(27) - 9(3) \right]$$

$$= |-18| + \left(-3\tfrac{1}{3} \right) - (-18)$$

$$= 18 - 3\tfrac{1}{3} + 18$$

$$= 32\tfrac{2}{3}\ \text{units}^2$$

Method 2

Area $= \int_3^5 (x^2 - 9)\,dx - \int_0^3 (x^2 - 9)\,dx$

$$= \left[\tfrac{1}{3}x^3 - 9x \right]_3^5 - \left[\tfrac{1}{3}x^3 - 9x \right]_0^3$$

$$= \left[\tfrac{1}{3}(125) - 9(5) \right] - \left[\tfrac{1}{3}(27) - 9(3) \right] - \left[\left(\tfrac{1}{3}(27) - 9(3) \right) - \left(\tfrac{1}{3}(0) - 9(0) \right) \right]$$

$$= -3\tfrac{1}{3} - (-18) - (-18)$$

$$= 36 - 3\tfrac{1}{3}$$

$$= 32\tfrac{2}{3}\ \text{units}^2$$

Exercise 15.4

1. Evaluate each of the following definite integrals:

   (i) $\int_0^1 (x^3 + x^2 - x - 2)\,dx$

   (ii) $\int_1^4 (x^4 + 8x + 2)\,dx$

   (iii) $\int_{-2}^3 (x^5 - x^4 + x^3 - x^2 + x)\,dx$

   (iv) $\int_{-5}^{-3} (x^6 - 32)\,dx$

2. Evaluate each of the following definite integrals:

   (i) $\int_2^3 x\,dx$

   (ii) $\int_1^8 x^2\,dx$

   (iii) $\int_{-1}^4 x^5\,dx$

   (iv) $\int_0^1 x^{10}\,dx$

3. (i) Find the derivative $f'(x)$ of the function $f(x) = e^{2x}$.

   (ii) Hence, or otherwise, evaluate the definite integral $\int_0^1 e^{2x}\,dx$.

4. Evaluate each of the following definite integrals:

   (i) $\int_1^2 e^x\,dx$

   (ii) $\int_{-1}^4 e^{3x}\,dx$

   (iii) $\int_0^5 e^{-2x}\,dx$

   (iv) $\int_1^5 \dfrac{1}{e^{5x}}\,dx$

5. Using page 25 of the *Formulae and Tables* and your knowledge of antiderivatives, evaluate each of the following definite integrals:

   (i) $\int_0^{\frac{\pi}{2}} \sin x\,dx$

   (ii) $\int_{\frac{\pi}{2}}^{2\pi} \cos x\,dx$

   (iii) $\int_0^{\frac{\pi}{3}} \sec^2 x\,dx$

   (iv) $\int_0^{\frac{\pi}{3}} \cos x\,dx$

6. Using page 25 of the *Formulae and Tables* and your knowledge of antiderivatives, evaluate each of the following definite integrals:

   (i) $\int_0^3 \dfrac{dx}{\sqrt{9 - x^2}}$

   (ii) $\int_0^4 \dfrac{dx}{\sqrt{16 - x^2}}$

   (iii) $\int_0^{5\sqrt{3}} \dfrac{5\,dx}{25 + x^2}$

   (iv) $6\int_0^6 \dfrac{dx}{36 + x^2}$

15

INTEGRAL CALCULUS

409

ACTIVE MATHS

7. (a) Approximate the area under the graph of $f(x) = \dfrac{1}{x^2}$ over the interval [1, 6] by computing the area of each rectangle and then adding.

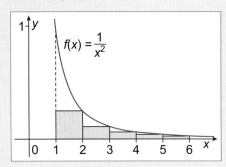

(b) Approximate the area under the graph of $f(x) = \dfrac{1}{x^2}$ over the interval [1, 6] by computing the area of each rectangle to four decimal places and then adding. Compare your answer to that for part (a).

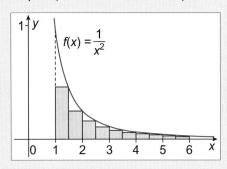

8. (a) Approximate the area under the graph of $f(x) = x^2$ over the interval [1, 6] by computing the area of each rectangle and then adding.

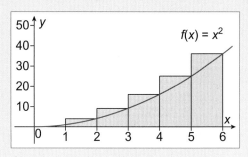

(b) Approximate the area under the graph of $f(x) = x^2$ over the interval [1, 6] by computing the area of each rectangle to three decimal places and then adding. Compare your answer to that for part (a).

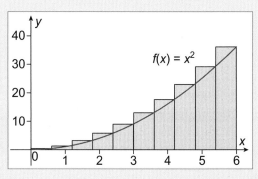

9. n rectangles of equal width are drawn under the graph of $f(x) = x^2 + 2$, $x \in R$ over the interval [0, 1].

(i) Explain why the width of each rectangle is $\dfrac{1}{n}$.

(ii) Show that the area of the rth rectangle is given by:
$$A_r = \frac{1}{n}\left(\left(\frac{r-1}{n}\right)^2 + 2\right)$$

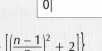

(iii) Hence, show that the sum of the areas of the n rectangles can be written as:
$$S_n = \frac{1}{n}\left\{[0^2 + 2] + \left[\left(\frac{1}{n}\right)^2 + 2\right] + \left[\left(\frac{2}{n}\right)^2 + 2\right] \dots + \left[\left(\frac{n-1}{n}\right)^2 + 2\right]\right\}$$

(iv) Show that the expression in part (iii) can be written as:
$$S_n = \frac{1}{n^3}[1^2 + 2^2 + 3^2 + \dots + (n-1)^2 + 2n^3]$$

(v) Given that $\displaystyle\sum_{r=1}^{n} r^2 = \frac{n}{6}(2n+1)(n+1)$, find another expression for S_n.

(vi) Explain why $\displaystyle\lim_{n\to\infty} S_n$ is the area under the graph of $f(x)$.

(vii) Show that $\displaystyle\lim_{n\to\infty} S_n = \int_0^1 (x^2 + 2)\, dx$.

10. n rectangles are drawn under the graph of $f(x) = x^3 + 4$, $x \in R$ over the interval $[0, 1]$.

    (i) Explain why the width of each rectangle is $\frac{1}{n}$.

    (ii) Show that the area of the rth rectangle is given by:

$$A_r = \frac{1}{n}\left(\left(\frac{r-1}{n}\right)^3 + 4\right)$$

    (iii) Hence, show that the sum of the areas of the n rectangles can be written as:

$$S_n = \frac{1}{n}\left\{[0^3 + 4] + \left[\left(\frac{1}{n}\right)^3 + 4\right] + \left[\left(\frac{2}{n}\right)^3 + 4\right] \dots + \left[\left(\frac{n-1}{n}\right)^3 + 4\right]\right\}$$

    (iv) Show that the expression above can be written as:

$$S_n = \frac{1}{n^4}[1^3 + 2^3 + 3^3 + \dots + (n-1)^3 + 4n^4]$$

    (v) Given that $\sum_{r=1}^{n} r^3 = \left[\frac{n}{2}(n+1)\right]^2$, find another expression for S_n.

    (vi) Show that $\lim_{n\to\infty} S_n = \int_0^1 (x^3 + 4)\, dx$.

> In Questions 11–20, use definite integrals to find the indicated areas.

11. Find the area between the curve $y = x^2 + 2$ and the lines $x = 2$ and $x = 4$.

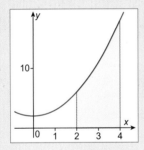

12. Find the area between the curve $y = x^2 - 1$ from $x = 1$ to $x = 4$.

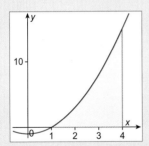

13. Find the area enclosed between the curve $y = \cos x$, the x-axis, the y-axis and the line $x = \frac{\pi}{3}$.

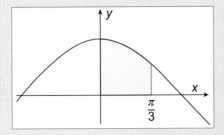

14. Find the area enclosed between the curve $y = e^x$, the x-axis, the y-axis and the line $x = \ln 5$.

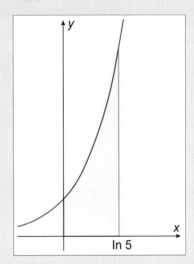

15. Find the area in the first quadrant between the curve $y = x^2$ and the y-axis, between the lines $y = 1$ and $y = 9$.

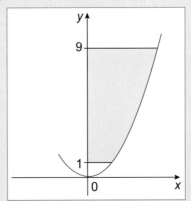

16. The diagram shows part of the graph of $y = x^3$.

Find:

(i) The values of p and q

(ii) The area A_1, by integrating with respect to x

(iii) The area A_2

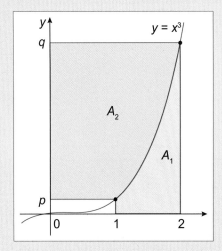

17. (i) Find the area, as shown below, between the curve $y = \cos x$ and the x-axis, $0 \leqslant x \leqslant \dfrac{\pi}{2}$.

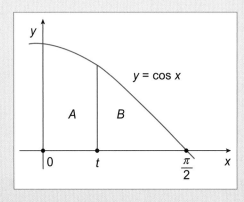

(ii) Find the value of t, if area of A = area of B.

18. The diagram shows the local maximum point, P, and the local minimum point Q of the curve $y = x^3 - 3x^2 - 9x$.

If O is the origin, show that the area of the shaded region is $50\frac{1}{2}$ square units.

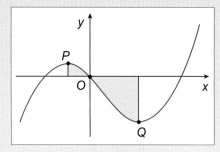

19. The sketch shows part of the graph of $y = (3x - 4)(3x + 4)$.

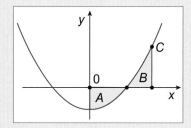

Find the co-ordinates of the point C such that the shaded regions A and B are equal in area.

20. The diagram shows the curve $y = e^{-x}$.

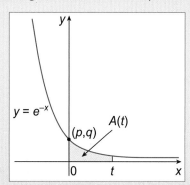

(i) Find the co-ordinates of the point (p,q) where this curve cuts the y-axis.

(ii) $A(t)$ is the area between this curve and the x-axis, $0 \leqslant x \leqslant t$.

Show that $A(t) = 1 - \dfrac{1}{e^t}$.

(iii) Find $\lim\limits_{t \to \infty} A(t)$.

15.5 INTERSECTING CURVES AND THE TRAPEZOIDAL RULE

Worked Example 15.11

Find the area enclosed between the curve $y = x^2 - 2x + 2$ and the line $y = x$.

Solution

Step 1 Find where the line and the curve intersect.

$y = x^2 - 2x + 2$

$y = x$

Solve the pair of simultaneous equations.

$x^2 - 2x + 2 = x$

$x^2 - 3x + 2 = 0$

$(x - 2)(x - 1) = 0$

The line cuts the curve at $x = 1$ and $x = 2$.

Step 2 Draw a rough sketch of the line and the curve, and shade the required area.

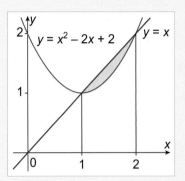

The area required =
(Area under $y = x$) – (Area under $y = x^2 - 2x + 2$)

$$\text{Area} = \int_1^2 x \, dx - \int_1^2 (x^2 - 2x + 2) \, dx$$

$$= \left[\frac{x^2}{2}\right]_1^2 - \left[\frac{x^3}{3} - x^2 + 2x\right]_1^2$$

$$= \left(2 - \frac{1}{2}\right) - \left[\frac{8}{3} - 4 + 4 - \left(\frac{1}{3} - 1 + 2\right)\right]$$

$$= \frac{1}{6}$$

Worked Example 15.12

(i) Use the Trapezoidal Rule with three trapezoids to approximate the area under the curve $y = e^{2x}$ between $x = 1$ and $x = 4$. Give your answer correct to to two decimal places.

(ii) Use a definite integral to find the true area and hence calculate the percentage error in using the Trapezoidal Rule to estimate the area.

(iii) Does the Trapezoidal Rule overestimate the true area? Explain.

Solution

(i) $A = \dfrac{h}{2}\left[y_l + y_n + 2\left(y_2 + y_3 + y_4 + \dots y_{n-1}\right)\right]$

$h = \dfrac{2 - 1}{3} = \dfrac{1}{3}$

$y_l = e^2, \quad y_2 = e^{\frac{8}{3}}, \quad y_3 = e^{\frac{10}{3}}, \quad y_4 = e^4$

$A = \dfrac{1}{6}\left[e^2 + e^4 + 2\left(e^{\frac{8}{3}} + e^{\frac{10}{3}}\right)\right]$

$= 24.47 \text{ units}^2$

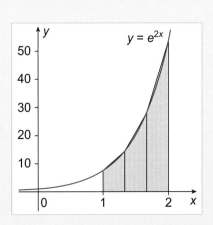

(ii) Area $= \int_1^2 e^{2x}\,dx$

$= \left[\dfrac{e^{2x}}{2}\right]_1^2$

$= \dfrac{1}{2}[e^4 - e^2]$

$= 23.60 \quad$ (2 d.p.)

Error $= 24.47 - 23.60$

$= 0.87$

% Error $= \dfrac{0.87}{23.60} \times 100$

$= 3.69\%$

(iii) The Trapezoidal Rule overestimates the true area, as $y = e^{2x}$ is an increasing function on $[1, 2]$ with $\dfrac{d^2y}{dx^2} > 0$.

> The Trapezoidal Rule is found on page 12 of *Formulae and Tables*.

Worked Example 15.13

Find the area enclosed between the curve $f(x) = x^2 + 5$ and the curve $g(x) = \dfrac{21}{16}x^2$.

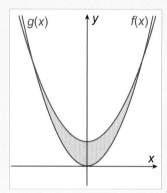

Solution

Step 1 Find the points of intersection of the two curves.

$$x^2 + 5 = \frac{21}{16}x^2$$
$$16x^2 + 80 = 21x^2$$
$$5x^2 = 80$$
$$x^2 = 16$$
$$x = \pm 4$$

The curves intersect at $x = -4$ and at $x = 4$.

Step 2 Shaded area = Area under $f(x)$ − Area under $g(x)$ from $x = 4$ to $x = -4$

$$\int_{-4}^{4}(x^2 + 5)\,dx - \int_{-4}^{4}\frac{21}{16}x^2\,dx$$

$$= \left[\frac{x^3}{3} + 5x\right]_{-4}^{4} - \left[\frac{7}{16}x^3\right]_{-4}^{4}$$

$$= \left[\left(\frac{64}{3} + 20\right) - \left(-\frac{64}{3} - 20\right)\right] - [(28) - (-28)]$$

$$= 26\frac{2}{3} \text{ units}^2$$

Exercise 15.5

1. Find the area enclosed between the curve $y = x - x^2$ and the line $y = \frac{x}{2}$.

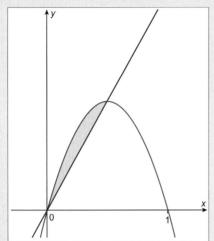

2. Find the area enclosed between the curve $y = 4x - x^2$ and the line $y = x$.

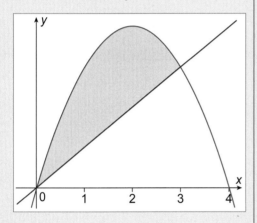

3. The diagram shows the curve $y = x(5 - x)$ and the line $y = 2x$.

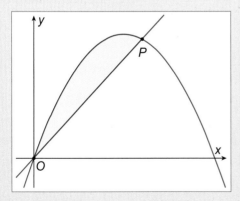

   (i) Find the co-ordinates of P, the point where the curve and line intersect.

   (ii) Find the area of the shaded region.

4. The diagram shows the curve $y = x^3$ and the line $y = 4x$.

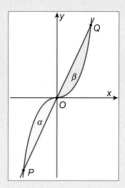

   (i) Find the co-ordinates of P and Q.

   (ii) Explain why the area labelled α is equal to the area labelled β.

   (iii) Explain why the curve and the line intersect only at P, O and Q.

   (iv) Find the total area bounded between the line and the curve.

5. The curves $y = x^2 - 4$ and $y = 8 - 2x^2$ are shown.

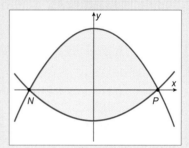

   (i) Find the co-ordinates of the points N and P.

   (ii) Hence, find the area bounded by the two curves.

6. The curves $y = x^3 - 9x^2 + 26x - 20$ and $y = x^2 - 5x + 10$ are shown.

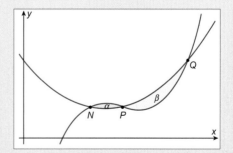

   (i) Show that the co-ordinates of N, P and Q are $(2,4)$, $(3,4)$ and $(5,10)$, respectively.

   (ii) Find the two finite areas, α and β, bounded by the two curves.

7. (i) Find the equation of the tangent to the curve $y = x^2$ at the point $(4,16)$.

(ii) Draw a sketch of the curve $y = x^2$ and the tangent found in part (i).

(iii) Find the area enclosed between the curve, the tangent and the x-axis.

(iv) Hence, or otherwise, find the finite area enclosed between the curve, the tangent and the y-axis.

8. A trapezoid of height h and parallel sides of lengths a and b is shown.

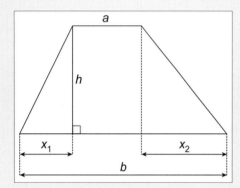

(i) Write $x_1 + x_2$ in terms of a and b.

(ii) Hence, show that the area of the trapezoid is given by $A = \dfrac{h}{2}(a + b)$.

(iii) $n - 1$ trapezoids of height h are placed on the graph of an increasing function f.

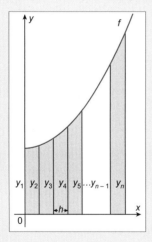

Show that the sum of the areas of the trapezoids is given by:

$$A = \frac{h}{2}[y_1 + y_n + 2(y_2 + y_3 + \ldots + y_{n-1})]$$

(iv) Use the Trapezoidal Rule derived in part (iii) with five trapezoids to approximate the area under the curve $y = x^2 + 1$ in the interval $[2, 3]$.

(v) Does the Trapezoidal Rule overestimate or underestimate the area under the curve $y = x^2 + 1$? Explain your answer.

(vi) Use integration to find the area under the curve $y = x^2 + 1$ over the interval $[2, 3]$.

(vii) What is the percentage error in using the Trapezoidal Rule to find this area?

9. Find an approximate value for the area under the curve $y = 16 - x^2$ between $x = 0$ and $x = 3$ by dividing the area into three trapezoids of equal width.

Explain why use of the Trapezoidal Rule underestimates the true area in this case.

10. (i) Use the Trapezoidal Rule to find an approximation for the area under the curve $y = 1 + 6x - x^2$ between $x = 0$ and $x = 6$. Divide the area into six trapezoids.

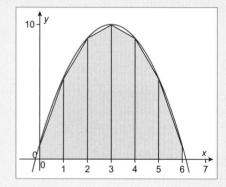

(ii) Approximate the area under the curve $y = 1 + 6x - x^2$ between $x = 0$ and $x = 6$ by summing the areas of the six rectangles constructed using the curve.

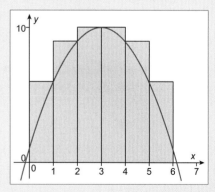

(iii) Find the exact area under the curve $y = 1 + 6x - x^2$ between $x = 0$ and $x = 6$ by evaluating the definite integral

$$\int_0^6 (1 + 6x - x^2)\, dx.$$

15.6 AVERAGE VALUE OF A FUNCTION

The graph shown gives the temperature readings at a certain location over a 24-hour period.

How can we compute the average temperature reading during a day when infinitely many temperature readings are possible?

One approach is to take readings at, say, six-hour intervals and compute the mean of these.

So, $T_0 = 6$, $T_6 = 6$, $T_{12} = 3$, $T_{18} = 2$ and $T_{24} = 4$.

Mean $= \dfrac{6 + 6 + 3 + 2 + 4}{5} = 4.2°C$

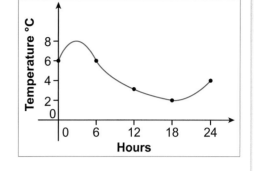

Taking readings over narrower intervals will improve the accuracy of our approximation of the average temperature during the day.

A different approach is to use integration to find what is known as 'the average value of a function'.

Consider the graph of a function $y = f(x)$ on an interval $a \leqslant x \leqslant b$. We divide the interval $[a, b]$ into n equal subintervals.

If we call the width of each subinterval Δx, then $\Delta x = \dfrac{b - a}{n}$.

So, $n = \dfrac{b - a}{\Delta x}$.

The average value of the numbers $f(x_0)$, $f(x_1)$, ..., $f(x_{n-1})$ is:

$$\frac{f(x_0) + f(x_1) + ... + f(x_{n-1})}{n}$$

$$= \frac{f(x_0) + f(x_1) + ... + f(x_{n-1})}{\left(\dfrac{b-a}{\Delta x}\right)}$$

$$= \frac{f(x_0)\Delta x + f(x_1)\Delta x + ... + f(x_{n-1})\Delta x}{b - a}$$

$$= \frac{1}{b - a}\left[f(x_0)\Delta x + f(x_1)\Delta x + ... + f(x_{n-1})\Delta x\right]$$

As $n \to \infty$, $f(x_0)\Delta x + f(x_1)\Delta x + ... + f(x_{n-1})\Delta x = \displaystyle\int_a^b f(x)\, dx.$

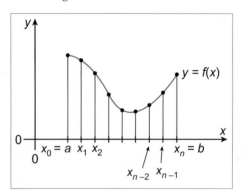

The **average value of a** function over the interval $[a, b]$ is:

$$\frac{1}{b - a}\int_a^b f(x)\, dx$$

Worked Example 15.14

(i) Find the average value of the function
$f: R \mapsto R: x \mapsto 2x^2 + x + 1$ on the interval $[1, 4]$.

(ii) Investigate the link between the area of region A and region B.

Solution

(i) Average value $= \dfrac{1}{4 - 1}\displaystyle\int_1^4 (2x^2 + x + 1)\, dx$

$= \frac{1}{3}\left[\frac{2}{3}x^3 + \frac{1}{2}x^2 + x\right]_1^4$

$= \frac{1}{3}\left(\left[\frac{2}{3}(4)^3 + \frac{1}{2}(4)^2 + 4\right] - \left[\frac{2}{3}(1)^3 + \frac{1}{2}(1)^2 + 1\right]\right)$

$= \frac{1}{3}\left(54\frac{2}{3} - 2\frac{1}{6}\right)$

$= 17\frac{1}{2}$

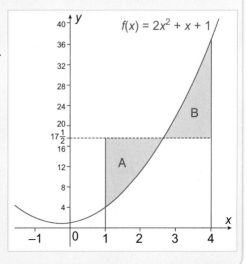

INTEGRAL CALCULUS

(ii) Area of rectangle $XYZW = 3\left(17\frac{1}{2}\right) = 52\frac{1}{2}$ units²

Area under $f(x)$ on $[1, 4] = \displaystyle\int_1^4 (2x^2 + x + 1)\, dx$

$$= \left[\frac{2x^3}{3} + \frac{x^2}{2} + x\right]_1^4$$

$$= 52\frac{1}{2} \text{ units}^2$$

As these two values are the same,
area of region A = area of region B.

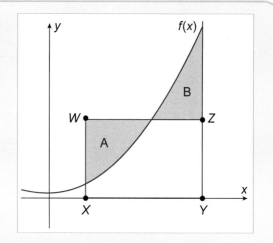

Worked Example 15.15

John's score on a test is given by $s(t) = t^2$, $0 \leqslant t \leqslant 10$, where $s(t)$ is his score after t hours of studying.

Marie's score on the same test is given by $q(t) = 10t$, $0 \leqslant t \leqslant 10$, where $q(t)$ is her score after t hours of studying.

(i) Find the average value of $s(t)$ over the interval $[7, 10]$, and explain what it represents.

(ii) Find the average value of $q(t)$ over the interval $[6, 10]$.

(iii) Assume that the students have the same study habits and are equally likely to study for any number of hours in the range $[0, 10]$. On average, how far apart will their test scores be?

Solution

(i) Average value $= \dfrac{1}{10-7}\displaystyle\int_7^{10} t^2\, dt$

$$= \frac{1}{3}\left[\frac{t^3}{3}\right]_7^{10}$$

$$= \frac{1}{3}\left[\frac{1{,}000}{3} - \frac{343}{3}\right]$$

$$= 73$$

This represents the average mark John would get if he spent between 7 and 10 hours studying.

(ii) Average value $= \dfrac{1}{10-6}\displaystyle\int_6^{10} 10t\, dt$

$$= \frac{1}{4}\left[5t^2\right]_6^{10}$$

$$= \frac{1}{4}[500 - 180]$$

$$= 80$$

This represents the average mark Marie would get if she spent between 6 and 10 hours studying.

(iii) Difference $= \left|\dfrac{1}{10}\displaystyle\int_0^{10} 10t\, dt - \dfrac{1}{10}\displaystyle\int_0^{10} t^2\, dt\right|$

$$= \left|\frac{1}{10}\int_0^{10} (10t - t^2)\, dt\right|$$

$$= \left|\frac{1}{10}\left[5t^2 - \frac{t^3}{3}\right]_0^{10}\right|$$

$$= \left|\frac{1}{10}\left(500 - \frac{1{,}000}{3}\right)\right|$$

$$= 16\frac{2}{3}$$

OR

Difference $= \dfrac{1}{10}\displaystyle\int_0^{10} (t^2 - 10t)\, dt$

$$= \frac{1}{10}\left(\frac{t^3}{3} - 5t^2\right)\Big|_0^{10}$$

$$= \frac{1}{10}\left(-166\frac{2}{3}\right)$$

$$= -16\frac{2}{3}$$

$\therefore$ Difference $= \left|-16\frac{2}{3}\right|$

$$= 16\frac{2}{3}$$

Exercise 15.6

1. The function f is defined by $f: R \mapsto R: x \mapsto x^2 + 1$.

   (i) Use the graph to estimate the average value of f on the interval $[1, 3]$.

   (ii) Complete the table and hence find another estimate for the average value of f on the interval $[1, 3]$.

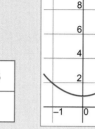

x	1	1.25	1.5	1.75	2	2.25	2.5	2.75	3
$f(x)$									

   (iii) Use integration to find the average value of f on the interval $[1, 3]$.

2. The function f is defined by $f: R \mapsto R: x \mapsto x^3$.

   (i) Use the graph to estimate the average value of f on the interval $[2, 4]$.

   (ii) Complete the table and hence find another estimate for the average value of f on the interval $[2, 4]$.

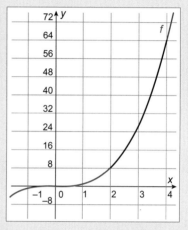

x	2	2.25	2.5	2.75	3	3.25	3.5	3.75	4
$f(x)$									

   (iii) Use integration to find the average value of f on the interval $[2, 4]$.

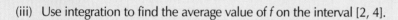

3. Find the average value of the function on the given interval.

   (i) $f(x) = 8 - x^2$ $[0, 2]$

   (ii) $g(t) = t^3 + t^2 - 8$ $[0, 1]$

   (iii) $h(x) = x^4 + 2x^2$ $[0, 3]$

   (iv) $s(t) = 2t^3 - 3t^2 + 4t$ $[1, 4]$

4. Find the average value of the function on the given interval.

   (i) $g(x) = \sin x$ $\left[\pi, \dfrac{3\pi}{2}\right]$

   (ii) $h(t) = \sqrt{t}$ $[4, 9]$

   (iii) $f(t) = e^t$ $[0, 4]$

   (iv) $g(x) = \sec^2 x$ $\left[0, \dfrac{\pi}{4}\right]$

5. Find the values of k such that the average value of $f(x) = 2 + 6x - 3x^2$ on the interval $[0, k]$ is equal to 3.

6. In a certain town, the temperature in degrees Celsius t hours after 8 a.m. is modelled by the following function:

   $$T(t) = 10 - 10 \sin \frac{\pi t}{12}$$

   Find the average value of the function during the period from 8 a.m. to 8 p.m.

7. Find the average value of the following functions over the given interval:

   (i) $f(x) = mx + 3$ $[0, 3]$

   (ii) $p(x) = 3x^2 + 2$ $[0, a]$

   (iii) $g(x) = x^n, n \neq -1$ $[0, 2]$

   (iv) $h(x) = e^x + 5x$ $[1, 4]$

8. The population of a certain region can be approximated by $P(t) = 145e^{0.01t}$, where P is in thousands and t is the number of years since 2006.

Find the average size of the population from 2007 to 2011.

9. Eddie's speed in kilometres per hour, t minutes after entering a motorway, is given by:

$$v(t) = -\frac{1}{250}t^3 + \frac{1}{10}t^2 - \frac{5}{8}t + 50, t \leqslant 30$$

(i) Find Eddie's average speed on the time interval [6, 25].

(ii) Find the distance travelled by Eddie over the time interval [6, 25].

10. A keyboarder's speed over a five-minute interval is given by
$W(t) = -5t^2 + 11t + 70, [0, 5]$.

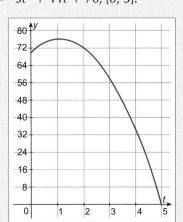

(i) Find the keyboarder's speed at the beginning of the interval.

(ii) Find his maximum speed and when it occurs.

(iii) What was his average speed over the five-minute interval?

11. The acceleration of a race car in m/s² during the first 25 seconds of a road test is modelled by $a(t) = 0.02t^2 - 1.8t + 25, 0 \leqslant t \leqslant 25$.

(i) Calculate the average acceleration during the first 25 seconds of the road test.

(ii) Find, in terms of t, the velocity of the car, $0 \leqslant t \leqslant 25$. Assume that the car starts from rest.

(iii) Calculate the average velocity during the first 25 seconds of the road test.

(iv) Find, in terms of t, the distance travelled, $0 \leqslant t \leqslant 25$.

(v) What distance did the car travel in 25 seconds?

(vi) If the car had travelled at its average velocity during the first 25 seconds, how far would it have travelled in that time?

 Revision Exercises

1. (a) Find the derivative of each of the following functions:

   (i) $f(x) = \sin 2x$

   (ii) $f(x) = \cos 2x$

   (b) Using your answers to part (a), find the following indefinite integrals:

   (i) $\int -2 \sin 2x \, dx$

   (ii) $\int 2 \cos 2x \, dx$

   (iii) $\int (\cos 2x - \sin 2x) \, dx$

   (iv) $\int (3 \cos 2x + \sin 2x) \, dx$

   (c) Using your answers to part (a), evaluate the following definite integrals:

   (i) $\int_0^\pi (5 \sin 2x - 3 \cos 2x) \, dx$

   (ii) $\int_0^{\frac{\pi}{4}} (2 \sin x \cos x) \, dx$

   (iii) $\int_0^\pi (\cos^2 x - \sin^2 x) \, dx$

2. A function f is defined as follows:
   $f: R \rightarrow R: x \rightarrow \sin^{-1} \frac{x}{a}$.

   (i) Find $f'(x)$, the derivative of $f(x)$.

   (ii) Hence, evaluate the definite integral
   $\int_0^4 \frac{dx}{\sqrt{16 - x^2}}$.

3. Evaluate each of the following definite integrals:

(i) $\int_2^3 (x^2 - 2x + 3)\,dx$

(ii) $\int_1^8 (x^2 - 5x + 5)\,dx$

(iii) $\int_{-1}^4 (x^5 + 4x^3 - 8x)\,dx$

(iv) $\int_0^1 (x^{10} - x^5 + 1)\,dx$

4. Evaluate each of the following definite integrals:

(i) $\int_1^2 e^x\,dx$

(ii) $\int_{-1}^4 e^{5x}\,dx$

(iii) $\int_0^5 e^{-3x}\,dx$

(iv) $\int_1^5 \frac{1}{e^{2x}}\,dx$

5. (a) Find the derivatives of sin ax, cos ax and tan ax.

(b) Hence, evaluate each of the following definite integrals:

(i) $\int_0^{\frac{\pi}{2}} \sin 5x\,dx$

(ii) $\int_{\frac{\pi}{2}}^{2\pi} \cos 3x\,dx$

(iii) $\int_0^{\frac{\pi}{4}} \sec^2 x\,dx$

(iv) $\int_0^{\frac{\pi}{3}} \cos 9x\,dx$

6. Using page 25 of the *Formulae and Tables* and your knowledge of antiderivatives, evaluate each of the following definite integrals:

(i) $\int_0^7 \frac{dx}{\sqrt{49 - x^2}}$

(ii) $\int_0^3 \frac{dx}{\sqrt{36 - x^2}}$

(iii) $\int_0^{5\sqrt{3}} \frac{15\,dx}{225 + x^2}$

(iv) $6\int_0^8 \frac{dx}{64 + x^2}$

7. Find the average value of each function on the given interval.

(i) $g(x) = \sin 5x$ $\quad \left[\pi, \frac{3\pi}{2}\right]$

(ii) $h(t) = \sqrt{2t}$ $\quad [9, 16]$

(iii) $f(t) = e^t$ $\quad [1, 4]$

(iv) $g(x) = \sec^2 x$ $\quad \left[0, \frac{\pi}{4}\right]$

8. The temperature T (in °C) recorded during a day was modelled by the following function: $T = 0.001t^4 - 0.28t^2 + 20$, where t is the number of hours from noon.

What was the average temperature during the day?

9. n rectangles of equal width are drawn on the interval $[0, 1]$ using the graph of $f(x) = x^2 + x + 1$, $x \in R$.

(i) Explain why the width of each rectangle is $\frac{1}{n}$.

(ii) Show that the area of the rth rectangle is given by:

$$A_r = \left[\frac{1}{n}\right]\left(\left[\frac{r}{n}\right]^2 + \frac{r}{n} + 1\right)$$

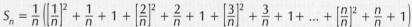

(iii) Hence, show that the sum of the areas of the n rectangles can be written as follows:

$$S_n = \frac{1}{n}\left(\left[\frac{1}{n}\right]^2 + \frac{1}{n} + 1 + \left[\frac{2}{n}\right]^2 + \frac{2}{n} + 1 + \left[\frac{3}{n}\right]^2 + \frac{3}{n} + 1 + \dots + \left[\frac{n}{n}\right]^2 + \frac{n}{n} + 1\right)$$

(iv) Show that the expression above can be written as follows:

$$S_n = \frac{1}{n^3}[1^2 + 2^2 + \dots + n^2] + \frac{1}{n^2}[1 + 2 + \dots + n] + 1$$

(v) Given that $\sum_{r=1}^n r = \frac{n}{2}(n+1)$ and $\sum_{r=1}^n r^2 = \frac{n}{6}(2n+1)(n+1)$, find another expression for S_n.

(vi) Show that $\lim_{n\to\infty} S_n = \int_0^1 (x^2 + x + 1)\,dx$.

10. The gradient of a curve $y = f(x)$ is given by $\frac{dy}{dx} = Ax(1 - x)$, where A is a constant. The gradient of the curve at the point $(2,-3)$ is -12.

(i) Find the value of A.

(ii) Find the equation of the curve.

11. Let $f(x) = x^2 - 2x - 8$, $x \in R$.

   (i) Show that the function has a local minimum at $x = 1$.

   (ii) Show that the function is increasing on the interval $[1, 5]$ and has an x-intercept at $x = 4$.

   (iii) Hence, sketch a graph of the function over the interval $[1, 5]$.

   (iv) Find the area bounded between the curve $y = x^2 - 2x - 8$, the x-axis and the lines $x = 1$ and $x = 5$.

12. $f(x) = 4 - x^2$, $0 \leqslant x \leqslant 2$, and $g(x) = \dfrac{4 - x^2}{2}$, $0 \leqslant x \leqslant 2$, are two real valued functions.

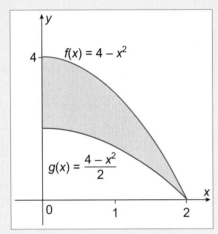

Find the area of the region bounded between f, g and the y-axis.

13. The rate of electrical energy used by a brewing company in kilowatt-hours (kWh) during a day is given by $f(t) = 8te^{-t}$, where t is time in hours, i.e. $t \in [0, 24]$, where $t = 0$ is midnight.

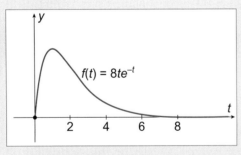

   (i) At what time is the rate of electrical energy usage at its highest?

   (ii) How many kilowatt-hours of electricity does the company use during the first T hours of the day?

   (*Hint*: Consider $\dfrac{d(te^{-t} + e^{-t})}{dt}$.)

   (iii) How many kilowatt-hours are used up during the first five hours of the day?

   (iv) What is the average rate of electrical energy usage between 5 a.m. and 8 a.m.?

14. (a) Differentiate $x \ln x - x$ with respect to x.

   (b) Find the area enclosed between the y-axis, the line $y = 10$ and the given exponential curve in the diagram below by evaluating a suitable definite integral along the x-axis.

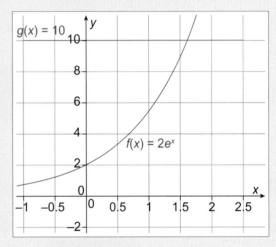

   (c) Now, by considering your answer to part (a) above, confirm your answer to part (b) above by evaluating a suitable definite integral along the y-axis.

15.

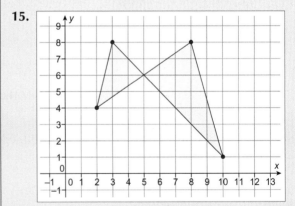

   (i) Find the area of the shaded region in the diagram above.

   (ii) Use integration methods to find the area of the same shaded area.

   (*Hint*: Define four functions, one for each side, and integrate using suitable differences and limits of integration.)

16.

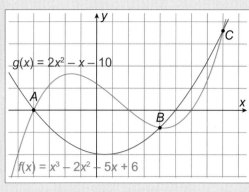

$g(x) = 2x^2 - x - 10$

A

B

C

x

y

$f(x) = x^3 - 2x^2 - 5x + 6$

(i) Find the co-ordinates of the points A, B and C, the points of intersection of the functions f and g.

(ii) Hence, or otherwise, find the total area enclosed by the graphs of f and g.

17. (a) (i) Write down three distinct antiderivatives of the function $g: x \rightarrow x^3 - 3x^2 + 3$, $x \in R$.

(ii) Explain what is meant by the indefinite integral of a function f.

(iii) Write down the indefinite integral of g, the function in part (i).

(b) (i) Let $h(x) = x \ln x$, for $x \in R$, $x > 0$.
Find $h'(x)$.

(ii) Hence, find $\int \ln x \, dx$.

SEC Project Maths Sample Paper 1, Leaving Certificate Higher Level, 2012

18. The stations of Liceu and Drassanes are consecutive stations on Line 3 of the Barcelona metro.

The metro trains on this line have been automated so that, under normal operating conditions, the velocity for a train travelling from Liceu to Drassanes is given by the piecewise function below:

$v(t) = 0$ on $[0, 0.5)$

$v(t) = (t - 0.5)^3$ on $[0.5, 2)$

$v(t) = 1.875t - 0.375$ on $[2, 5)$

$v(t) = 9$ on $[5, 11)$

$v(t) = 9 - (t - 11)^2$ on $[11, 14]$

where v is velocity (in metres/second) and t is time (in seconds).

(i) Graph the velocity of the train against time over the 14-second journey from Liceu to Drassanes.

(ii) What is the average velocity of a metro train between Liceu and Drassanes?

(iii) How far apart are the two stations?

(iv) What is the rate of deceleration of the train 2 seconds before arriving at Drassanes station?

19. (a) Let $f(x) = -0.5x^2 + 5x - 0.98$, where $x \in R$.

(i) Find the value of $f(0.2)$.

(ii) Show that f has a local maximum point at $(5, 11.52)$.

(b) A sprinter's velocity over the course of a particular 100-metre race is approximated by the following model, where v is the velocity in metres per second and t is the time in seconds from the starting signal:

$$v(t) = \begin{cases} 0, & \text{for } 0 \leqslant t < 0.2 \\ -0.5t^2 + 5t - 0.98, & \text{for } 0.2 \leqslant t < 5 \\ 11.52, & \text{for } t \geqslant 5 \end{cases}$$

Note that the function in part (a) is relevant to $v(t)$ above.

(i) Sketch the graph of v as a function of t for the first 7 seconds of the race.

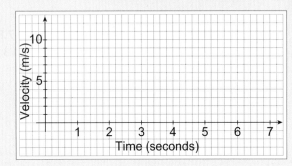

(ii) Find the distance travelled by the sprinter in the first 5 seconds of the race.

(iii) Find the sprinter's finishing time for the race. Give your answer correct to two decimal places.

(c) A spherical snowball is melting at a rate proportional to its surface area. That is, the rate at which its volume is decreasing at any instant is proportional to its surface area at that instant.

(i) Prove that the radius of the snowball is decreasing at a constant rate.

(ii) If the snowball loses half of its volume in an hour, how long more will it take for it to melt completely? Give your answer correct to the nearest minute.

SEC Project Maths Sample Paper 1, Leaving Certificate Higher Level, 2012

20. The functions f and g are defined for $x \in R$ as $f: x \mapsto 2x^2 - 3x + 2$ and $g: x \mapsto x^2 + x + 7$.

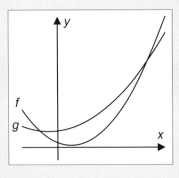

(a) Find the co-ordinates of the two points where the curves $y = f(x)$ and $y = g(x)$ intersect.

(b) Find the area of the region enclosed between the two curves.

SEC Project Maths Paper 1, Leaving Certificate Higher Level, 2012

Answers

Chapter 1

Exercise 1.1

1. (i) $2^5 \times 5$ (ii) $3 \times 7 \times 13$ (iii) 2^7 (iv) $2^4 \times 23$
(v) $3 \times 5 \times 7 \times 11$ (vi) $2 \times 5 \times 11 \times 17$
(vii) $2^2 \times 3 \times 5^3 \times 7$ (viii) $2 \times 3 \times 17$ (ix) $2^3 \times 3^2 \times 17$
(x) $2^7 \times 3^3 \times 11$ **2.** (a)(i) $102 = 2 \times 3 \times 17$;
$170 = 2 \times 5 \times 17$ (ii) $117 = 3^2 \times 13$; $130 = 2 \times 5 \times 13$
(iii) $368 = 2^4 \times 23$; $621 = 3^3 \times 23$ (iv) $58 = 2 \times 29$;
$174 = 2 \times 3 \times 29$ (v) $60 = 2^2 \times 3 \times 5$; $765 = 3^2 \times 5 \times 17$
(vi) $123 = 3 \times 41$; $615 = 3 \times 5 \times 41$ (vii) $69 = 3 \times 23$;
$123 = 3 \times 41$ (viii) $20 = 2^2 \times 5$; $30 = 2 \times 3 \times 5$;
$60 = 2^2 \times 3 \times 5$ (ix) $8 = 2^3$; $10 = 2 \times 5$; $20 = 2^2 \times 5$
(x) $294 = 2 \times 3 \times 7^2$; $252 = 2^2 \times 3^2 \times 7$;
$210 = 2 \times 3 \times 5 \times 7$ (b)(i) LCM = 510; HCF = 34
(ii) LCM = 1,170; HCF = 13 (iii) LCM = 9,936;
HCF = 23 (iv) LCM = 174; HCF = 58 (v) LCM = 3,060;
HCF = 15 (vi) LCM = 615; HCF = 123
(vii) LCM = 2,829; HCF = 3 (viii) LCM = 60; HCF = 10
(ix) LCM = 40; HCF = 2 (x) LCM = 8,820; HCF = 42
3. (i) n (ii) n **6.** (ii) 1 **7.** (i) 2 (ii) 1 **8.** 18 cm
9. July 16 **10.** 10 **11.** 1 cm width **12.** 700
13. (iii) 1, 2, 3, 4, 6, 8, 11, 13, 16, 18 **14.** (i) F(1) = 2;
F(2) = 1 **15.** (i) Nine

Exercise 1.2

1. (i) 0 (ii) –6 (iii) 40 (iv) 0 (v) $16\frac{2}{3}$ **2.** (i) $\frac{7}{20}$
(ii) $12\frac{1}{2}$ (iii) $2\frac{11}{12}$ (iv) $\frac{3}{8}$ (v) $1\frac{1}{2}$ (vi) $\frac{125}{126}$ (vii) $\frac{57,498}{1,331}$
(viii) $-\frac{2}{25}$ (ix) $5\frac{7}{100}$ **6.** $\frac{12}{17}$ **7.** 11 : 9 **8.** 36
9. $\frac{5}{9}$ units **10.** G **11.** 21 **12.** (ii) 21 units
13. 2,301 **14.** (i) 90 (ii) 9,000 (iii) 3,124,213

Exercise 1.3

4. (i) 3.0387 (ii) 3.1416 (iii) 3.28% **6.** (i) $r = \frac{1 + \sqrt{5}}{2}$
(ii) 1.6180

Exercise 1.4

1. (a)(i) 5.146 (ii) 7.298 (iii) 17.894 (iv) 62.124
(v) 23.765 (vi) 0.079 (b)(i) 1.26 (ii) 5.99 (iii) 21.46
(iv) 21.30 (v) 22.00 (vi) 0.00 **2.** (a)(i) 0.0099
(ii) 0.0023 (iii) 0.013 (iv) 0.00000079 (v) 1.0
(vi) 0.00085 (vii) 0.24 (viii) 52 (ix) 52 (x) 970,000
(b)(i) 30 (ii) 4 (iii) 20,000 (iv) 2,000 (v) 6,000
(vi) 1,000 **3.** (i) 3.4×10^7 (ii) 2.5×10^{-1}
(iii) 4.57×10^3 (iv) 1.258×10^{-4} (v) 7.206×10^3
(vi) 3.2×10^{-5} (vii) 5×10^6 (viii) 6.464×10^{-1}

(ix) 5.326×10^5 (x) 5×10^3 **4.** (i) 265 (ii) 0.00453
(iii) 7,200,000 (iv) 0.000017 (v) 300 (vi) 0.04
(vii) 26,400,000 (viii) 7,612 (ix) 276,000,000
(x) 0.00000000302 **5.** (i) 6,200 (ii) 8,700,000,000
6. (i) 2,000,000 (ii) 16,900 (iii) 2,480 (iv) 647,000
(v) 61.2 (vi) 943,000 **7.** (i) 3.6×10^{-5} (ii) 5.613×10^{-4}
(iii) 3.45×10^{-2} (iv) 6.3×10^{-4} (v) 7.8×10^{-3}
(vi) 1.1×10^{-3} **8.** (i) 6.8×10^{-4} (ii) 3.28×10^{-5}
(iii) 6.57×10^{-2} (iv) 9.7×10^{-9} (v) 5.6×10^{-7}
(vi) 3.0307×10^{-3} **9.** (i) 0.0015 (ii) 0.000254
(iii) 0.000035 (iv) 0.00000667 **10.** (i) Four (ii) Five
(iii) Five (iv) Five (v) Two

Revision Exercises

1. (i) 3 + 3 + 5 (ii) 7 + 13 + 13 (iii) 7 + 7 + 83
(iv) 5 + 97 + 97 (v) 3 + 7 + 7 **2.** 36 min
5. (i) 24, 25, 26, 27, 28
(ii) 10,001! + 2, 10,001! + 3, …, 10,001! + 10,001
6. (i) LCM: 204; HCF: 34 (ii) LCM: 2,829; HCF: 3
(iii) LCM: 2,808; HCF: 13 (iv) LCM: 615; HCF: 123
7. (a) $\frac{1}{12}$ (b) (i) 3 (ii) 17, 19, 23 **8.** (i) $2,332 = 2^2 \times 11 \times 53$;
$6,776 = 2^3 \times 7 \times 11^2$ (ii) HCF: 44; LCM: 359,128
9. (i) 850,000 (ii) 0.13 (iii) 2.0 (iv) 0.000054
(v) 650,000 (vi) 0.00081 **12.** (a) (i) $p = 2, q = 17$
(ii) $m = 19, n = 7$ (iii) HCF: 8; LCM: 705,432
(b) $4 \times 10{-}4$ **13.** (i) 0.0025 (ii) €99 (iii) 14.2
15. (i) 1×10^{-4} m (ii) 40 **16.** 15 **17.** 24,153;
42,153; 24,351; 42,351; 12,354; 21,354 **18.** 3.14

Chapter 2

Exercise 2.1

1. (i) –24 (ii) 27 (iii) $-\frac{1}{14}$ (iv) –100 (v) 6
2. (i) $3x^2 + 27x - 10$ (ii) $3a^2 - a$ (iii) $36x^3 + 34x^2 - 8x$
(iv) $-2y^2 - xy^2$ (v) $b^3 + 4b^2 - 4a^2c - 3bc$ **3.** (i) (a) 2
(b) –6 (c) 3 (d) –1 (ii) (a) 2 (b) –20 (c) 3 (d) –7
(iii) (a) 5 (b) None (c) 3 (d) –9 (iv) (a) 5 (b) –12
(c) 6 (d) 32 (v) (a) 5 (b) –7 (c) 6 (d) 25
4. (i) $35x^2 + 12x + 1$ (ii) $4x^2 + 9x - 9$
(iii) $30st - 15s - 10t^2 + 5t$ (iv) $6x^3 + 9x^2y - 15xy^2$
(v) $7xy^3 - 6x^2y^3 - y^3$ **5.** (i) $9p^2 + 24p + 16$
(ii) $16y^2 - 8xy + x^2$ (iii) $18a^2 - 12a + 2$
(iv) $ax^2 + 10ax + 25a + bx^2 + 10bx + 25b$
(v) $-7x^3y + 3xy^3 - 3x^2y^2 - 3x^4 + 2y^4$ (vi) $3p^3 - 3pq^2$
6. (i) $3b^2p + 12bp - 4b^2 + 3cp - 16b - 4c$
(ii) $4b^2y - xb^2 + 16by - 4bx + 4cy - cx$

(iii) $6a^3 + 21a^2b + 9ab^2 - 2a^2 - 7ab - 3b^2$
(iv) $5x^3 + 30x^2y + 45xy^2 + 20y^3$ (v) $z^4 - 2x^2z^2 + x^4$
7. (i) $p^2 + 2pq + q^2$ (ii) $p^2 - 2pq + q^2$ (iii) $p^2 - q^2$
(iv) $x^2 - 9$ (v) $32x^3 + 48x^2 + 18x$ (vi) $y^3 - 9y^2 + 27y - 27$
(vii) $x^3 + 12x^2 + 48x + 64$
(viii) $8a^3 + 60a^2b + 150ab^2 + 125b^3$
(ix) $p^3 - 24p^2q + 192pq^2 - 512q^3$ (x) $x^2y^2 - y^4$
8. (i) $4ps + 8pr - 2qs - 4qr$ (ii) $a^2 - 9b^2$
(iii) $64m^3 + 336m^2n + 588mn^2 + 343n^3$
(iv) $729x^3 - 486yx^2 + 108xy^2 - 8y^3$
(v) $40a^3 + 540a^2b + 2{,}430ab^2 + 3{,}645b^3$
(vi) $x^3 - x^2y - xy^2 + y^3$ (vii) $(ab)^3 - 3a^2b^4 + 3ab^5 - b^6$
9. (i) $a^4 + 4a^3 + 6a^2 + 4a + 1$ (ii) $b^3 - 9b^2 + 27b - 27$
(iii) $1x^5 + 5x^4y + 10x^3y^2 + 10x^2y^3 + 5xy^4 + 1y^5$
(iv) $8a^3 + 36a^2b + 54ab^2 + 27b^3$
(v) $81y^4 - 432xy^3 + 864x^2y^2 - 768x^3y + 256x^4$
(vi) $243x^5 - 810x^4y + 1{,}080x^3y^2 - 720x^2y^3 + 240xy^4 - 32y^5$
10. $11x - 4y + 20$ 11. $5y + 3$ 12. (i) Area: $x^2 + 4x + 4$;
Perimeter: $4x + 8$ (ii) Area: $2x^2 - xy - 3y^2$;
Perimeter: $6x - 4y$ 13. Volume: $x^3 + 16x^2 + 83x + 140$;
Surface area: $5x^2 + 53x + 138$ 14. 35
15. $2{,}867{,}200a^6b^2$ 16. $n = 6, a = 3$

Exercise 2.2

1. (i) $4ab^2(1 - 3b)$ 2. $(7x + 2)(x + 1)$ 3. $(3y - 7)(y + 1)$
4. $(5x + 2)(x + 2)$ 5. $(x + 3)(x - 6)$ 6. $(3x - 2)(x + 4)$
7. $(2y - 7)(y + 9)$ 8. $(7x - 19)(x + 3)$ 9. $(5a - 1)(5a + 1)$
10. $(2x - 1)(x - 4)$ 11. $(5x + 12)(x + 8)$
12. $(8a - 9b)(8a + 9b)$ 13. $(2x + 1)(x - 12)$
14. $(4x + 3)(x + 1)$ 15. $(10y + 17)(y + 1)$
16. $(3x + 2)(3x - 1)$ 17. $(3x - 2)(3x - 5)$
18. $(4y + 19)(y + 1)$ 19. $(3x + 5)(2x + 9)$
20. $4(3p - 5q)(3p + 5q)$ 21. $(4x - 7)(3x + 8)$
22. $(2x - 3)(4x - 5)$ 23. $2(5x + 3)(x - 1)$
24. $6(2x + 1)(x - 2)$ 25. $12y(2y + 1)(2y + 1)$
26. $4(2x - 5)(2x + 5)$ 27. $2x(x - 2)(x + 2)$
28. $p(3q + 4)(2q + 1)$ 29. $x^2(x - 6)(x + 6)$
30. $(x - 3)(x^2 + 3x + 9)$ 31. $(p + 2)(p^2 - 2p + 4)$
32. $(x - y)(x^2 + xy + y^2)$ 33. $(4a - 1)(16a^2 + 4a + 1)$
34. $(2a + 3b)(4a^2 - 6ab + 9b^2)$
35. $(5p + 8q)(25p^2 - 40pq + 64q^2)$
36. $(10x - 9)(100x^2 + 90x + 81)$
37. $(7c + d)(49c^2 - 7cd + d^2)$ 38. $3(x - 6)(x^2 + 6x + 36)$
39. $16(2 + x)(4 - 2x + x^2)$ 40. $54a(a + 2b)(a^2 - 2ab + 4b^2)$
41. $-2x - 5$ 42. $(x + p)(x + p)$ 43. $(ac - b)(ac + b)$
44. $(x^2 - 5)(x^2 + 5)$ 45. $(ab - 1)(ab - 1)$
46. $(x^2 + y^2)(x - y)(x + y)$ 47. $(x - y + 3)(x - y - 3)$
48. $(4x - 3y)(2x - 3y)$ 49. $a(a + 1)(a^2 - a + 1)$
50. $[a - (b + c)][a + (b + c)]$ 51. $ab^2(b - 1)(b^2 + b + 1)$
52. $(x^2 + 2)(x - 3)(x + 3)$

Exercise 2.3

1. $\frac{8x - 11}{4}$ 2. $\frac{-6x + 1}{6}$ 3. $\frac{13x - 23}{15}$ 4. $\frac{-3 + 8x}{4x - 5}$ 5. $-\frac{3}{35x}$
6. $\frac{8 + x^2 + x}{x + 1}$ 7. $\frac{2x - 5}{x^2 + 5x}$ 8. $\frac{17x - 9}{3x^2 - 7x + 2}$ 9. $\frac{11x + 14}{6x^2 + 7x - 5}$

10. $\frac{1}{3}$ 11. $\frac{b^2}{a}$ 12. $\frac{1}{x - y}$ 13. $\frac{b}{a - b}$ 14. -1 15. x
16. $\frac{x}{x + 1}$ 17. $x - 2$ 18. $\frac{x^2 + 5x + 25}{2}$ 19. $\frac{x^2 - xy + y^2}{x - y}$
20. $x^2 + y^2$ 21. $\frac{p^2 - 2pq + q^2}{p + q}$ 22. $\frac{x + 4}{x - 4}$ 23. $\frac{3x}{x - 1}$
24. $\frac{2x + 1}{x^2 + x - 20}$ 25. $\frac{-2x - 5}{(x + 2)(x - 3)}$ 26. $\frac{x - 1}{x^2 + 3x + 2}$ 27. $\frac{a^2 + 3}{a^2 - 1}$
28. $\frac{2a^2}{a^2 - b^2}$ 29. $\frac{2a^2 + 12}{(a - 2)(a + 3)}$ 30. $\frac{2p^2 - 4}{(p - 1)(p - 2)}$
31. $\frac{3n^6 + 6n + 2}{n(n + 1)(n + 2)}$ 32. $\frac{2a}{a^2 - b^2}$ 33. $\frac{2b}{(a - b)(a + b)}$
34. (i) $\frac{4}{x^2 - 1}$ (ii) $\frac{3}{x - 3}$

Exercise 2.4

1. $25ab$ 2. $\frac{y}{x^2}$ 3. $\frac{2x + 1}{2}$ 4. $\frac{x + 2}{2x - 2}$ 5. $\frac{4x^2}{x + 1}$ 6. $\frac{y^2 + 8y}{y + 4}$
7. $\frac{(2x + 1)^2}{(x + 1)^2}$ 8. $\frac{3x}{2x + 9}$ 9. $\frac{x + 3}{3x + 4}$ 10. $\frac{1}{(x + 7)(4x - 3)}$
11. $\frac{x - y}{5}$ 12. $(x - 5)^2$ 13. $\frac{2x + 1}{3}$ 14. $\frac{x}{2(x + 1)}$
15. $-\frac{x}{5}$ 16. $\frac{ab - 1}{b - 1}$ 17. pq 18. $-\frac{x + y}{x}$ 19. $\frac{x - y}{x(x + y)}$

Exercise 2.5

7. $(x - 4)(x + 3)$ 8. $2x^3 - 3x^2 - 8x - 3$
9. $(x - 3)(x + 2)(x - 2)(x^2 + 2x + 4)$
11. $(2x - 5)(3x - 4)(2x + 5)(3x + 4)$
13. $(3x + 2), (2x - 1), (4x - 1), (3x + 1)$
14. $3x + 4$ is a factor; $5x + 4$ is not a factor.

Revision Exercises

1. (a) (i) $(x + 9)(x - 10)$ (ii) $(2x + 1)(2x + 1)$
(iii) $(5x + 2)(2x - 1)$ (iv) $(3x - 2y)(3x - 2y)$
(v) $(7x - 4)(2x - 1)$ (b) (i) $\frac{1}{2}$ (ii) $\frac{2}{4x + 5}$ (iii) $\frac{(a^2 + ab + b^2)}{b}$
(iv) $\frac{y + 1}{b^2 + b + 1}$ (v) $\frac{x}{x - 3}$ (c) (i) $9x^2 + 42x + 49$
(ii) $8x^3 - 12x^2 + 6x - 1$ (iii) $64x^3 - 240x^2 + 300x - 125$
(iv) $64p^4 + 16p^3 - 180p^2 - 189p - 54$
(v) $144a^6 + 1464a^5 + 5836a^4 + 11370a^3 + 10800a^2$
$+ 4000a$ (d) $\frac{1}{x(x + h)}$ 2. (a) (i) $(x - 10)(x + 10)$
(ii) $(2x - 9)(2x + 9)$ (iii) $(5x - 7y)(5x + 7y)$
(iv) $(11a - 12b)(11a + 12b)$ (v) $(6x + 7y)(4x + 5y)$
(b) (i) $\frac{8x - 3}{(x - 3)(x + 4)}$ (ii) $\frac{2y - 13}{4y^2 - 1}$ (iii) $\frac{x - 2 - x^2}{x^2 - 1}$
(c) (i) $32a^5 + 80a^4 + 80a^3 + 40a^2 + 10a + 1$
(ii) $256b^4 - 1{,}792cb^3 + 4{,}704b^2c^2 - 5{,}488bc^3 + 2{,}401c^4$
(iii) $46{,}656x^6 - 233{,}280x^5 + 486{,}000x^4 - 540{,}000x^3 +$
$337{,}500x^2 - 112{,}500x + 15{,}625$ (d) 4
3. (a) (i) $(x + 3)(x^2 - 3x + 9)$ (ii) $(a + 2)(a^2 - 2a + 4)$
(iii) $(b + 10)(b^2 - 10b + 100)$ (iv) $(2x + 5)(4x^2 - 10x + 25)$
(v) $(5x + 3y)(25x^2 - 15xy + 9y^2)$ (b) (i) $\frac{x + 4}{x + 5}$
(ii) $\frac{a + b}{a^2 + ab + b^2}$ (iii) $\frac{1}{a^2 + b^2}$ (iv) $-\frac{2}{3}$ (v) $\frac{-1}{(x + 3)}$
(c) (i) $\frac{4}{x - 2}$ (ii) $\frac{2}{2y - 1}$ (iii) 0 (iv) $\frac{13}{2x - 1}$
4. (a) (i) $(y - 1)(y^2 + y + 1)$ (ii) $(2y - 1)(4y^2 + 2y + 1)$
(iii) $(3a - 2b)(9a^2 + 6ab + 4b^2)$ (iv) $(x - 6)(x^2 + 6x + 36)$
(v) $(10a - 7b)(100a^2 + 70ab + 49b^2)$ (b) (i) $\frac{5x + 3}{(x - 3)(x + 3)}$
(ii) $\frac{10y + 8}{9y^2 - 4}$ (c) (ii) 20, 21, 29 5. (a) (i) $3(x - 5)(x + 5)$
(ii) $x(3x - 5)(3x + 5)$ (iii) $(x^2 + y^2)(x - y)(x + y)$

(iv) $(x^2 + 9)(x - 3)(x + 3)$ (v) $(a - b)(x - y)(x + y)$

(b) (i) $\frac{(a - c)}{(a + c)}$ (ii) $\frac{y(3y + 1)}{y + 3}$ (iii) $\frac{a + b - c}{a - b - c}$ (c) (i) $\frac{3}{x + 3}$

6. (a) (i) $4x^2 - x - 3$ (ii) $12x^2 - 2x - 4$

(iii) $8x^3 - 10x^2 + x + 1$ (iv) $x^3 + 5x^2 + 2x - 8$

(v) $12x^4 + 43x^3 + 46x^2 + 17x + 2$ (b) (ii) Other factors:
$(3x + 5)(2x - 1)$ (c) Divisor: $3x^2 + 10x + 3$;
Dividend: $6x^5 - 40x^4 - 26x^3 + 356x^2 - 312x - 144$;
Quotient: $2x^3 - 20x^2 + 56x - 48$ **7.** (a) (i) $(x + 3)(x + 17)$

(ii) $-1(x - 13)(x + 13)$ (iii) $(a + b)(x + y)$ (iv) $(a - b)(a - b)$

(v) $(a - b - c)(a - b + c)$ (b) (i) $\frac{y + x}{y}$ (ii) $\frac{y}{y - x}$

(c) (ii) $(3x + 7)(x - 2)$ (iii) $(2x + 3)(2x - 1)$

8. (a) (i) $(x + y)(x^2 - xy + y^2 + 3)$ (ii) $x + y[x - y + 5]$

(iii) $(x - y - 2z)(x - y + 2z)$ (iv) $x - y(x^2 + xy + y^2 + x + y)$

(v) $(a - b - c)(a + b + c)$ (b) (i) $\frac{x - y + z}{x + y + z}$ (ii) $\frac{x(x + 5)}{x + 8}$

(iii) $\frac{1}{6x + 12}$ (c) Car A: $40x$ km; Car B: $(60x - 180)$ km

(d) $\frac{1}{6(2x - 5)}$ **9.** (a) (i) $\left(\frac{x}{10} - \frac{y}{7}\right)\left(\frac{x}{10} + \frac{y}{7}\right)$

(ii) $\left(x + \frac{1}{x}\right)\left(x^2 - 1 + \frac{1}{x^2}\right)$ (iii) $(x - 2)(x + 2)(x^2 + 4)$

(iv) $(ab - 8)(ab + 8)$ (v) $(x + 1 - y)(x + 1 + y)$

(b) (i) $\frac{3}{4y^2 x}$ (ii) $\frac{5(x + 5)}{2x}$ (c) (i) $2x - 5$ (ii) $3x - 1$

(d) (i) 1. $\frac{y^2 - 1}{y}$;   2. $\frac{2y}{y - 1}$ (ii) $2y + 2$

10. (a) (i) $(x + y)(x^2 - xy + y^2)$ (ii) $(x + y)^3$

(iii) $(x + y + z)(x^2 + y^2 + z^2 + 2xy - xz - yz)$ (c) z

11. (a) (i) 1   (ii) $\frac{4x^2 - 6x + 9}{2x - 3}$ (iii) $\frac{x - 3}{x - 2}$ (b) (i) $(a + b)^2$

(ii) $(a + b - c)(a + b + c)$ **12.** (a) (1) $\frac{x - 3}{2x^2 + 3x - 2}$

(2) $x = 4$ (b) $\frac{9}{x + 3}$

(c) $(2x - 3y)(4x^2 + 6xy + 9y^2 + 2x + 3y)$

Chapter 3

Exercise 3.1

1. $x = -1$ **2.** $x = 22$ **3.** $a = -5$ **4.** $b = -\frac{1}{2}$

5. $c = 6\frac{1}{2}$ **6.** $x = 5$ **7.** $x = 3$ **8.** $p = 3$ **9.** $a = -3$

10. $x = 6$ **11.** $x = -2$ **12.** $x = 4.5$ **13.** $x = 2$

14. $x = -5$ **15.** $x = -2\frac{2}{3}$ **16.** $x = 10$ **17.** $x = \frac{7}{10}$

18. $a = \frac{1}{2}$ **19.** $x = \frac{3}{4}$ **20.** $x = 3$ **21.** $x = 1$ **22.** $x = 1\frac{3}{7}$

23. $y = \frac{1}{2}$ **24.** $x = 5\frac{11}{12}$

Exercise 3.2

1. $x = 7, y = 0$ **2.** $x = -1, y = -1$ **3.** $x = 7, y = -3$

4. $x = 6, y = 0$ **5.** $x = 1\frac{2}{3}, y = \frac{2}{3}$ **6.** $x = 1, y = -2$

7. $x = 9, y = 8$ **8.** $x = 5, y = -4$ **9.** $p = -4, q = -5$

10. $x = 3, y = -4$ **11.** $x = 7, y = 5$ **12.** $x = 0, y = 4$

13. $x = 3, y = -4$ **14.** $r = 5, s = 9$ **15.** $x = \frac{57}{41}, y = \frac{46}{41}$

16. $x = \frac{14}{5}, y = \frac{22}{5}$ **17.** $x = 4, y = 3$ **18.** $a = \frac{1}{2}, b = \frac{3}{10}$

19. $d = 2, e = 5$ **20.** $p = 0, q = -5$

Exercise 3.3

1. $x = 2, y = -1, z = 5$ **2.** $x = 1, y = 3, z = 5$

3. $a = 1, b = 3, c = 0$ **4.** $x = 3, y = -2, z = 5$

5. $x = 1, y = 2, z = 3$ **6.** $x = -3, y = 9, z = 4$

7. $x = -5, y = 1, z = -2$ **8.** $a = 3, b = 1, c = 5$

9. $p = \frac{1}{3}, q = -\frac{3}{4}, r = -5$ **10.** $x = 10, y = 0, z = 10$

11. $x = 2, y = 8, z = 2$ **12.** $x = 2, y = -3, z = 1$

13. $x = \frac{1}{2}, y = \frac{1}{4}, z = \frac{3}{4}$ **14.** $x = 4, y = 2, z = -1$;
$a = 2, b = 2, c = -2; a = -2, b = 2, c = -2$

15. $x = \frac{51}{26}, y = -\frac{11}{13}, z = -\frac{5}{26}; a = \frac{26}{51}, b = -\frac{13}{11}, c = -\frac{26}{5}$

Exercise 3.4

1. (i) $x = 3$ or -14 (ii) $x = 3$ (iii) $x = -9$ or 7

2. (i) $x = -0.2, 0.9$ (ii) $x = -1.5, 1.5$ (iii) $x = -2.3$

(iv) $x = -2.2$ **3.** $x = -4$ or 3   **4.** $x = -4$ **5.** $x = 2$

6. (i) $x = -0.63, 2.63$ (iv) $x = -1$ or 3   **7.** (i) $x = 2$ or $\frac{9}{2}$

(ii) $x = 3$ or $-\frac{14}{3}$ (iii) $x = 3$ or $\frac{2}{5}$ (iv) $x = -\frac{1}{2}$ or -2

(v) $x = \frac{9}{5}$ or $-\frac{9}{5}$ (vi) $x = 4$ or $-\frac{6}{5}$ **8.** (i) $x = 2$ or $-\frac{7}{3}$

(ii) $x = -7$ or $\frac{5}{4}$ (iii) $x = 4$ or $-\frac{5}{4}$ (iv) $x = -7$ or $-\frac{13}{10}$

(v) $x = 2$ or $\frac{13}{6}$ (vi) $x = 2$ or $-\frac{5}{8}$ **9.** $x = -3$ or -4;

solution set $= \{-1, -2, -3\}$ **10.** $x = -3$ or -5;

solution set $= \left\{-\frac{1}{2}, -1, -\frac{5}{2}, -3\right\}$ **11.** $x = 5$ or $x = \frac{7}{2}$;

solution set $= \left\{-2, \frac{5}{4}, 1, -\frac{7}{4}\right\}$ **12.** (i) $x^2 - 5x + 6 = 0$

(ii) $x^2 - 12x + 35 = 0$ (iii) $x^2 - 3x - 10 = 0$ (iv) $x^2 - 6x = 0$

(v) $2x^2 + x - 15 = 0$ (vi) $10x^2 - 7x + 1 = 0$

(vii) $16x^2 - 9 = 0$ (viii) $x^2 - 8x + 13 = 0$

(ix) $x^2 + 2x - 1 = 0$ (x) $2x^2 - 2x - 1 = 0$

13. $x^2 - 4px + 3p^2 = 0$ **14.** Roots: 2, 8; $c = 16$

15. Roots: 7, 5; $d = 35$ **16.** (i) $x = 1.36$ or -5.86

(ii) $x = 0.79$ or $x = -1.42$ (iii) $x = 3.18$ or -2.68

(iv) $x = 0.46$ or $x = -2.71$ (v) $x = 3.12$ or $x = -2.46$

(vi) $x = 0.66$ or $x = -1.09$ **17.** (i) $x = \pm\sqrt{5}$

(ii) $x = -3 \pm \sqrt{2}$ (iii) $-\frac{4 \pm \sqrt{10}}{6}$ (iv) $-\frac{6 \pm \sqrt{33}}{3}$

18. (i) $x = \frac{5}{2}$ or 4   (ii) $x = \frac{3}{5}$ or $\frac{1}{2}$ (iii) $x = -\frac{3}{5}$ or 2

(iv) $x = 10\frac{1}{2}$ or -1 (v) $x = -10$ or 1   (vi) $x = 0$ or $-\frac{1}{3}$

(vii) $x = -6$ (viii) $x = 3.56$ or -0.56 (ix) $x = 2.18$ or 0.57

Exercise 3.5

1. (i) $(x = -1, y = -3), (x = 3, y = -1)$ (ii) $(x = -5, y = 5)$,
$(x = 5, y = 0)$ (iii) $(x = 0, y = -4), (x = 5, y = 1)$

(iv) $(x = -4, y = -1.5), (x = 5, y = 3)$ **2.** $(x = 2, y = 3)$;
$(x = 3, y = 2)$ **3.** $(x = 4, y = -7); (x = -7, y = 4)$

4. $\left(x = -\frac{8}{3}, y = -\frac{14}{3}\right); (x = 4, y = 2)$ **5.** $\left(x = \frac{5}{2}, y = 4\right)$;
$(x = 2, y = 5)$ **6.** $\left(x = \frac{5}{2}, y = 2\right); (x = -1, y = -5)$

7. $\left(x = -\frac{3}{5}, y = \frac{3}{5}\right); (x = -1, y = -1)$ **8.** $(x = 0, y = 1)$;
$\left(x = \frac{2}{3}, y = 3\right)$ **9.** $(x = -3, y = -2); (x = -2, y = 3)$

10. $(x = -6, y = -3); (x = 6, y = 3)$ **11.** $\left(x = \frac{10}{3}, y = -\frac{2}{3}\right)$;
$(x = -2, y = -6)$ **12.** $\left(x = \frac{9}{2}, y = \frac{9}{2}\right); (x = -4, y = -4)$

13. $\left(x = \frac{1}{3}, y = \frac{10}{3}\right); (x = -9, y = 1)$ **14.** $\left(x = \frac{1}{2}, y = \frac{2}{3}\right)$;
$x = -\frac{15}{22}, y = -\frac{10}{11}$ **15.** $\left(x = \frac{7}{3}, y = \frac{1}{3}\right); (x = -1, y = -3)$

16. $(x = 1, y = 4); (x = -1, y = -4)$ **17.** $(x = 6.4, y = -2.8)$;
$(x = 8, y = -2)$ **18.** $(x = 0, y = 3); (x = 10, y = -3)$

19. $(x = 10, y = 4); (x = 6, y = -4)$

Exercise 3.6

1. $(x - 1)(x - 3)(x + 2)$ **2.** $(x + 3)(x - 2)(x + 5)(x - 4)$

3. $x = \{2, 1, 5\}$ **4.** $x = \left(-4, \frac{3}{2}, 6\right)$

5. Factors: $(2x + 3)(3x - 2)(x + 1)(x - 5)$;
$x = \left\{-\frac{3}{2}, \frac{2}{3}, -1, 5\right\}$ **6.** $x = \left\{-\frac{3}{2}, \frac{3}{4}, \frac{1}{2}\right\}$

7. $x = \{3, 0, 1, 4, 2\}$ **8.** (i) $x^3 - 6x^2 + 3x + 10 = 0$
(ii) $2x^3 + 7x^2 - 46x + 21 = 0$ (iii) $3x^3 + x^2 - 3x - 1 = 0$
(iv) $x^3 - 3x^2 - 10x = 0$ (v) $x^3 - 3x^2 + 3x - 1 = 0$

9. (i) $x = \{1, 2, 3\}$ (ii) $x = \left\{3, \frac{1}{3}\right\}$ (iii) $x = \left\{4, \frac{5 \pm \sqrt{41}}{2}\right\}$
(iv) $x = \left\{3, \frac{3 \pm \sqrt{65}}{4}\right\}$ (v) $x = \{-2, -3, 5\}$

10. (i) $x = \{3, -2, -4, -3\}$ (ii) $x = \left\{1, -1, \frac{10}{3}, \frac{1}{2}\right\}$
(iii) $x = \{-1, 3, 3 + \sqrt{5}, 3 - \sqrt{5}\}$

11. (i) $f(x) = (x + 4)(x + 2)(x - 3)$
(ii) $f(x) = (x + 5)(x + 3)(x - 1)^2$
(iii) $f(x) = -x(x + 7)(x + 4)^2(x - 3)$
(iv) $f(x) = x(x - 1)^2(x - 3)(x - 5)^2(x - 7)$
(v) $f(x) = x(x + 2)(x - 3)(x - 4)$
(vi) $f(x) = x(x - 2)^2(x - 4)(x + 3)^3$ **13.** $x = 6.208$ or -1.208

14. $x = 0$ (repeated root), $2, 14.22, -4.22$ **15.** $k = 12$

16. $x^3 - 7x^2 + 13x - 3 = 0$ **17.** $x = \{-1, -3, 2\}$

18. $a = 7, b = 15$ **19.** $a = 2, b = 5$ **20.** $p = 4, q = 2$

21. $r = 1, s = 7$ **22.** $a = -1, b = 7, c = 13$

23. $a = 4, b = -11, c = -30$; $x = \{3, -2, 5\}$

Exercise 3.7

1. $b = \frac{a + d}{3c}$ **2.** $z = \frac{x - y}{3}$ **3.** $r = 10p - q$

4. $c = 2s - a - b$ **5.** $b = \frac{2a}{1 + 2c}$ **6.** $u = \frac{s - \frac{1}{2}at^2}{t}$

7. $f = \frac{uv}{v + u}$ **8.** $y = \frac{x}{z^2}$ **9.** $r = \frac{(1 + pq)}{p}$

10. $a = \pm\sqrt{h^2 - b^2}$ **11.** $x = \frac{(a - c)^2}{b^2}$ **12.** $r = \pm\sqrt{\frac{s}{4\pi}}$

13. $l = \frac{gT^2}{4\pi^2}$ **14.** $q = \pm\sqrt{\frac{s + r}{p}}$ **15.** $a = \frac{R^3}{b}$

16. $u = \pm\sqrt{v^2 - 2as}$ **17.** $x = \frac{1 - a}{1 + a}$

18. $r = p^2 - pq + \frac{1}{4}q^2$ **19.** $p = \frac{ab}{1 - a}$ **20.** $r = \pm\sqrt{\frac{3v}{\pi h}}$

21. $b = \sqrt[3]{\frac{c}{d} - a}$

Exercise 3.8

1. $b = 3, q = 9$ **2.** $a = 1, b = 1, c = -12$

3. $a = 2, b = 4$ **4.** $a = 3, b = 4$ **5.** $a = 4, b = 2$

6. $p = 5, q = 3$ **7.** $a = 4, b = 2$ **8.** $a = 4, b = 2, c = 17$

9. $a = 4, b = -2$ or $a = -2, b = 4$ **10.** $a = 2, b = 3$

11. $a = 4, p = 12, q = 48$ **12.** $a = 2, b = 2, c = 3$

13. $p = 1, q = 3, r = -2$ **14.** $p = 36, q = 54$

15. $r = 6; x = \left\{1, \frac{2}{3}, 3\right\}$ **16.** $p = 2, q = 5, r = 3, s = 1$

17. $a = 3, b = 5, c = 22$ **19.** $a = 2, b = 1, c = \frac{7}{2}$

20. (i) $b = a - 13$ (ii) $c = -12(b + 14)$ **21.** $a = 1 - \frac{1}{2}b$

22. $x = 0$ or $x = \pm\sqrt{-\frac{2a}{3}}$ **25.** $x = 0$ or $x = p \pm \frac{\sqrt{4 - 3p^2}}{2}$

26. $a = b$ or $a = 5 - b$ **29.** $x = 0(r), \frac{(3r - 1) \pm \sqrt{9r^2 + 2r + 1}}{2}$

Exercise 3.9

1. Small 5 kg, medium 15 kg, large 20 kg   **2.** (i) €200
(ii) €12,200; 1,200 units   **3.** Karl is 40, Eddie is 25

4. (i) €500,000   (ii) 2nd contract   **5.** $t = 1$ hr 40 mins

6. €1,750 at high rate (9%); €1,250 at lower rate (5%)

7. 9 kg of 70% nickel alloy; 11 kg of 30% nickel alloy

8. (i) $-40°$ (ii) $-24\frac{8}{13}°C$ (iii) $320°F$ **9.** 60 m, 240 m

10. 5, 7   **11.** 21 rows   **12.** 1,928 cm, 2,428 cm

13. $(3.8, -1.6)$ and $(1, 4)$ **14.** Harry's speed/time: 10 km/h,
5 hours; Cara's speed/time: 5 km/h, 7 hours

15. 862   **16.** (i) $350 - 25x$ (ii) $30 + 2x$ (iii) €225

17. Simon: 5 hours, Peter: 20 hours   **18.** (i) $(1, -4), (-4, 1)$
(ii) $(1, -4)$ is 4 km south and 1 km east; $(-4, 1)$ is 4 km west
and 1 km north   (iii) 4.12 km

19. (i) $40x + (20 - x)(0.8) = 300$ (ii) Gold: 7.24 g,
silver: 12.76 g   **20.** Hot: 773 seconds, cold: 673 seconds

21. €1,500   **22.** (a) (i) 18.78 m/s   (ii) 25.04 m/s
(b) (i) Minimum velocity increases by $\sqrt{2}$ (ii) $d = \frac{V_0^2}{19.6\mu}$
(c) 79.7 m   **23.** (a) (i) 16,000 units   (ii) 4,000 units
(b) It occurs at 5 months, as the graph becames negative
after 5   **24.** (i) 348.71 m/s   (ii) $T = \frac{273}{109561}V^2 - 273$
(iii) $\approx 4°$ (iv) 369 m/s

Revision Exercises

1. (a) (i) $x = 1, y = -2$ (ii) $x = -1, y = 3$ (iii) $x = 2, y = 8$
(iv) $x = 7, y = \frac{3}{2}$ (b) (i) $x = \frac{1}{2}$ (ii) $x = \frac{3}{2}$ or $-\frac{3}{2}$

(iii) $x = 8$ or -3 (iv) $x = -\frac{1}{4}$ or 1   (v) $x = \frac{11}{12}$ or 1
(c) (i) $x = -3, y = 3, z = 1$ (ii) $x = -1, y = -2, z = -3$
(iii) $x = 5, y = 1, z = 6$ (iv) $x = 5, y = -4, z = 1$

2. (a) (i) $x = 3.71$ or -1.21 (ii) $x = 1.86$ or 0.54
(iii) $x = 3.27$ or $x = -0.77$ (iv) $x = 5.85$ or -0.85
(b) (i) $x = 7$ or 8; $y = 5$ or 2   OR $y = 4 \pm \sqrt{6}$
(ii) $x = \frac{3}{4}$ or 5; $y = \frac{1}{2}$ or $-\frac{3}{2}$ OR $y = 1.79$ or -2.79
(iii) $x = 3 \pm \sqrt{11}$, $t = \sqrt{11}$ or $-\sqrt{11}$ (c) (i) $\left(\frac{1}{2}, 6\right)$, $(3, 1)$
(ii) $(-1, -2), (2, 1)$ (iii) $(3, 3)$ $(-2, -2)$ (iv) $x = 1, y = 1$
(v) $x = 2, y = 3$ **3.** (a) (i) $c = 2(b - a)$ (ii) $c = \frac{a - b}{d + 5}$

(iii) $p = \frac{q}{q + r}$ (iv) $r = \frac{A}{\pi l + 2\pi h}$ (v) $x = \pm\sqrt{\frac{y^2(1 - r)}{a}}$

(vi) $y = \sqrt[3]{\frac{3x + 1}{x - 1}}$ (b) (i) $a = 4, b = -5$ (ii) $p = -2$,
$q = 14$ (iii) $p = 2, q = \frac{7}{4}, r = \frac{31}{8}$ (c) (i) other factors:
$(3x + 1)(x + 2)$ (ii) $a = -4, b = -28$, 3rd factor is $(x + 7)$

(iii) $k = -2$ **4.** (a) (i) $x = \{1, 4, -2\}$ (ii) $x = \left\{-2, \frac{3}{2}\right\}$

(iii) $x = \{-1, -2, 5\}$ (iv) $x = \left\{3, -3, -\frac{5}{3}, \frac{1}{2}\right\}$

(v) $x = \left\{1, -1, \frac{5}{2}, \sqrt{5}, -\sqrt{5}\right\}$
(c) (i) $A(-2, 0), B(1, 0), C(3, 0), D(5, 0), E(-1, -6)$
(iii) $3x - y - 3 = 0$; quadratic: $f(x) = (x + 2)(x - 5)$;
cubic: $f(x) = (x + 2)(x - 1)(x - 3)$

5. (a) (i) $f(x) = x(x + 1)(x - 3)^2$
(ii) $f(x) = x(x + 3)(x + 1)(x - 2)(x - 3)$
(iii) $f(x) = x^2(x + 7)^2(x + 3)(x - 2)$
(iv) $f(x) = x^2(x + 7)(x + 6)(x + 4)^2(x + 1)$
(v) $f(x) = x(x + 1)(x - 3)^3(x - 6)^2$ (b) (i) $(-3.73, 1.27)$,

(−2,0), (−0.27,4.73)   (ii) The values for x for which
$x^3 + 7x^2 + 14x + 8 = x^2 + 5x + 6$ **6.** (a) (i) $h = \frac{9}{2}$
(ii) 10%   (b) $t = 6$; $x = \{-2, 1, -5\}$ (c) $x = 3$, $y = 7$
7. (a) $x = 45$, $y = 22$ (b) $x^2 - 5px + 4p^2 = 0$
8. (a) $x = 4$ (b) $a = -2$, $b = 6$, $c = -12$ (c) $a = -39$,
$b = 70$; $x = \{2, 5, -7\}$ **9.** (a) (i) $x + y + 26 = 60$,
$x^2 + y^2 = 26^2$ (ii) $x = 24$, $y = 10$ (c) (ii) $x^2 - 6x + 2 = 0$
(ii) $x^3 - 5x^2 - 4x + 2 = 0$ **10.** (a) $a = 1$, $b = -8$
(c) (ii) $k = \frac{3}{5}$ **11.** (a) 21, 23   (b) (i) 40 mins
(ii) Fiona: $56\frac{2}{3}$ km; Gerry: $43\frac{1}{3}$ km
(c) Planet: 450.36 million km; satellite: 609.29 million
km or 414.87 million km   **12.** (a) $x = 12$ rabbits, $y = 18$
guinea pigs   (b) 8 people   (c) (i) $g = \frac{2s}{t^2}$ (ii) 9.796 m/s^2
(iii) 6.06 seconds   **13.** (a) €4,279.50   (b) 7 g of 9-carat
gold and 14 g of 18-carat gold   (c) (i) 6 g of copper
(ii) 4 g of 9-carat gold, 38 g of 18-carat gold and
6 g of silver   (d) (i) €$(20x − 40)(20 − x)$
(ii) €400 $\leqslant$ selling price $\leqslant$ €440

Chapter 4

Exercise 4.1

1. $x = 13$ **2.** $x = 9$ **3.** $\frac{25}{7}$ **4.** $x = 2$ **5.** $x = 2$
6. $x = 13$ **7.** $x = 1$ **8.** $x = 1$ **9.** $x = 4$ **10.** $x = 0$
11. $x = 3$ **12.** $x = 9$ **13.** $x = 5$ **14.** $x = 1$
15. $x = 7$ or 10

Exercise 4.2

1. $x > -1$ **2.** $x > 1$ **3.** $x \geqslant -1$ **4.** $x < 1$ **5.** $x > \frac{1}{2}$
6. $x < 2$ **7.** $x > 2$ **8.** $x > -1$ **9.** (i) $x > 2$, $x \leqslant 4$
(ii) $x < 7$, $x > -2$ (iii) $x \leqslant 5$, $x > -3$ (iv) $x \leqslant \frac{3}{4}$, $x > \frac{1}{4}$
(v) $x < 10$, $x \geqslant 7$ **10.** 2,250 $\leqslant$ Calorie intake $\leqslant$ 2,750
11. $x = 9$ **12.** (i) $-1 < x$ (ii) $2 \geqslant x$ (iii) $-1 < x \leqslant 2$
13. (i) $x < 4$ (ii) $x \leqslant \frac{13}{4}$ (iii) $x \leqslant 1\frac{3}{4}$, $x < 4$
14. (i) $5 \leqslant x$ (ii) $x \leqslant \frac{1}{3}$

Exercise 4.3

1. $x < -4$ or $x > 3$ **2.** $-\frac{7}{2} < x < -2$ **3.** $\frac{2}{3} \leqslant x \leqslant 8$
4. $x \leqslant -2$ or $x \geqslant \frac{5}{2}$ **5.** $-2 < x < -1$ **6.** $x \leqslant -\frac{6}{5}$
or $x \geqslant 12$ **7.** $-2 \leqslant x \leqslant -\frac{3}{5}$ **8.** $-\frac{3}{2} < x < 0$
9. $-\frac{5}{11} \leqslant x \leqslant \frac{5}{11}$ **10.** $-3 < x < 2$ **11.** $-1 < x < 4$
12. $x \leqslant 3$ or $x \geqslant 4\frac{1}{4}$ **13.** $2 < x < 4\frac{1}{3}$
14. $-2\frac{1}{5} \leqslant x \leqslant -2$ **15.** $1 \leqslant x \leqslant 1\frac{2}{3}$ **16.** (i) $x = 13.9$
or -0.9 (ii) $n = 14$ **17.** $x \leqslant -3 - \sqrt{5}$ or $x \geqslant -3 + \sqrt{5}$
18. (i) $1.6x^2$ (ii) $1.6x^2 \leqslant 300$ (iii) $x \leqslant 13.69$
(iv) 811.2 cm$^3 \leqslant$ Volume $\leqslant$ 1124.864 cm^3
19. (i) $15 \geqslant 20 - 5t^2 \geqslant 10$, $t \in R$ (ii) Start filming at
$t = 1.0$ seconds; stop filming at $t = 1.4$ seconds
20. (i) €1.59 $<$ Price $<$ €4.41   (ii) $\approx$17%

Exercise 4.4

1. (i) 8   (ii) 3   (iii) 5   (iv) 5   (v) 11   (vi) 11   **2.** (i) 7
(ii) 1   (iii) 10   (iv) 100   (v) 1   (vi) 37   **3.** $x = -5$ or 5
4. $x = -10$ or 10   **5.** $x = -9$ or 7   **6.** $x = 11$ or 5

7. $x = -16$ or 10   **8.** $x = -3$ or -1 **9.** $x = -2$ or 6
10. $x = -7$ **11.** $x = 6$ or -12 **12.** $x = -\frac{5}{9}$ or $\frac{1}{7}$
13. $x = -3$ or $-\frac{3}{5}$ **14.** $x = -\frac{7}{5}$ or -11 **15.** $-6 < x < 4$
16. $x < 1$ or $x > 7$ **17.** $0 < x < \frac{3}{2}$ **18.** $-4\frac{1}{3} \leqslant x \leqslant -3$
19. $4 \leqslant x \leqslant 10$ **20.** $\frac{3}{8} < x < \frac{5}{4}$ **21.** $\frac{8}{15} \leqslant x \leqslant \frac{7}{10}$
22. $-8 < x < -1\frac{1}{3}$ **23.** $x < -\frac{1}{7}$ or $x > 1$
24. $x < -3$ or $x > 7$ **25.** $x < 2$ or $x > \frac{14}{3}$
26. $x = 2$ or 6   **27.** $x \leqslant -2.5$ or $x \geqslant 0.5$
28. $|x - 120| \leqslant 6$ **29.** (i) $x = -3$ or -1
(ii) $-3 < x < -1$ (iii) $-3 \leqslant x \leqslant 1$ **30.** (i) $x = -5$ or 1
(ii) $x < -5$ or $x > 1$

Exercise 4.5

1. (i) No real roots, discriminant < 0 (ii) Real distinct
roots, discriminant > 0 (iii) Real distinct roots,
discriminant > 0 (iv) No real roots, discriminant < 0
(v) Real equal roots, discriminant $= 0$
2. (i) 16, real distinct roots   (ii) 0, real equal roots
(iii) -16, no real roots   (iv) 72, real distinct roots
(v) 204, real distinct roots   (vi) $k^2 + 4a^2$;
real distinct roots if k, $a > 0$; real equal roots if k and $a = 0$
(vii) 0, real equal roots   (viii) 2112, real distinct roots
(ix) $(a - 1)^2 + 36$, real distinct roots   **3.** $a = 8$ or -8
4. $b = -9$ **5.** $c < -2$ **6.** No real roots   **8.** $0 < q < 4$
9. $p \leqslant 0$ or $p \geqslant 4$ **10.** $b = -\frac{2}{3}$ or -2

Exercise 4.6

12. (b) $x^2 + y^2 \geqslant 2xy$; $a^2 + x^2 \geqslant 2ax$; $b^2 + y^2 \geqslant 2by$

Revision Exercises

1. (a) (i) $x = 6$ (ii) $x = 4$ (iii) $x = 7$ (b) (i) $x \geqslant 1$
(ii) $x < 2$ (iii) $x > -2\frac{1}{4}$ (c) (i) $x = 5$ or 2   (ii) $2 < x < 5$
(iii) $x = 3$ or 5   (iv) $x < 3$ or $x > 5$ **2.** (a) (i) False
(ii) True   (iii) False   (iv) False   (v) True   (b) True
(c) (i) $k = 9$ (ii) $t = 4$ **3.** (a) (i) True   (ii) True
(iii) True   (iv) True   (b) (i) $x > -\frac{3}{4}$ (ii) $x \leqslant 1$
(c) (i) $x = 4$ or 1   (ii) $x = 0$ or 5
4. (a) (i) $x = 5$ or -5 (ii) $x = 9$ or -11
(iii) $x = 11$ or -9 (iv) $x = -8$ or 10
(v) $x = -2$ or $2\frac{1}{2}$ (c) (i) $(a - b)^2(a^2 + ab + b^2)$
5. (a) (i) $x = 1$ or -3 (ii) $x = \frac{1}{3}$ or -5 (iii) $x = -1$
(b) (i) $-2 < x < 4$ (ii) $x \leqslant -5$ or $x \geqslant 4$
(iii) $-2 \leqslant x \leqslant 5$ (iv) $x < -2$ or $x > 2$
(c) $k = -2$ or 6; for $k = -2$, $x = 1$; for $k = 6$, $x = 3$
(d) $x < 2$ or $x > 8$ **6.** (a) (i) $x = 3\frac{1}{2}$ or $-4\frac{1}{2}$
(ii) $x = \frac{5}{6}$ or $-\frac{1}{6}$ (iii) $x = -\frac{13}{3}$ or $-\frac{7}{5}$ (b) (i) $x = 10$
(ii) $x = 5$ or 1   (iii) $x = 4$ (c) (i) $-\frac{5}{2} \leqslant x \leqslant 2$
(ii) $x < -\frac{1}{3}$ or $x > \frac{1}{2}$ (iii) $-2 < x < 6$
(d) (i) $x = 1$ or $x = 3$ (ii) $1 < x < 3$
7. (a) (i) $-4 < x < 4$ (ii) $x < -5$ or $x > 3$
(iii) $x < -9$ or $x > -2\frac{1}{3}$ (iv) $\frac{12}{7} \leqslant x \leqslant \frac{12}{5}$
(v) $x < -10$ or $x > -\frac{5}{12}$ (d) $1 < x < 5$
8. (a) (i) $x = 7.1$ or -1.6 (ii) $n = 7$ (b) (i) $4 < x < \frac{15}{2}$

(ii) $x < -17$ or $x > -7$ (iii) $3 < x \leqslant 8$
(iv) $x \leqslant -9$ or $x \geqslant 11$ (c) (i) $(q - p)(q^2 + pq + p^2)$
(d) (i) $x = 2$ (ii) $x = 0$ (iii) $x = -2$ or $x \approx 0.7$
(iv) $x \leqslant -2$ or $x \geqslant 0.7$ 9. (a) $k = -1$ or 2;
for $k = -1$, $x = 1$; for $k = 2$, $x = -2$
(b) $2 > x > 8$; $k > 0$ (c) (ii) $a^3 + c^3 > a^2c + c^2a$;
$b^3 + c^3 > b^2c + c^2b$ (d) (i) $2(x + 3) < 5 (x - 3)$, $x \in N$,
and $3x - 27$, $x \in N$ (ii) $x > 7$, $x < 9$ (iii) 8 years old
10. (a) Least value of $n = 8$ (c) After one hour
11. (a) $-1 < x < 19$ 12. (a) $k = 0$ or 4
(c) 131 hours

Chapter 5

Exercise 5.1

1. (i) Error: 1; Rel. error: $\frac{1}{150}$; % error: 0.67%
(ii) Error: 0.9; Rel. error: $\frac{1}{40}$; % error: 2.5%   (iii) Error: 3;
Rel. error $\frac{1}{60}$; % error 1.67%   (iv) Error: 0.2;
Rel. error: $\frac{1}{24}$; % error: 4.17%   (v) Error: 0.3;
Rel. error: $\frac{3}{67}$; % error: 4.48%   (vi) Error: 0.85;
Rel. error: $\frac{17}{1,083}$; % error: 1.57%   (vii) Error: 0.14;
Rel. error: $\frac{7}{68}$; % error 10.29%   (viii) Error: 2;
Rel. error: $\frac{1}{251}$; % error: 0.40%   (ix) Error: 1;
Rel. error: $\frac{1}{360}$; % error 0.28%   (x) Error: 1.4;
Rel. error: $\frac{7}{293}$; % error: 2.93%   2. 1.08%   3. 1.29%
4. 1%   5. 2.6%   6. (i) 0.0394   (ii) $\approx 0.8\%$
7. (i) 0.05   (ii) $\approx 0.5\%$ 8. (i) €6,554   (ii) €6,555.60
(iii) €1.60   9. 54 ± 0.05 cm   10. (i) 450 ± 2.5 g
(ii) Yes, since 453 g > 452.5 g, the upper limit.

Exercise 5.2

2. (i) €67,500   (ii) €6.75   3. (i) 150 quiches   (ii) €349
(iii) €2.60   (iv) €3.50   4. (i) 48,000 kg   (ii) 45,000 kg
(iii) €279,000   (iv) €305,000   5. (i) 40 m   (ii) 120 m
(iii) €1,540   (iv) €29.52   6. (i) 58,500 kg   (ii) 55,500 kg
(iii) 78,000 hours   (iv) €858,000   (v) €1,778,000
(vi) €397,000   (vii) €179.500

Exercise 5.3

1. €5,000   2. €7,750   3. €34,710   4. €34,700
5. (i) €30,100   (ii) €64,400   6. €30,530   7. 21%
8. (i) €7,600   (ii) 20%   9. 21%   10. €73,500
11. €10,460   12. €1,768.80   13. (i) €50.30
(ii) €148.85   (iii) €4,358.80   (iv) €880.23
14. (i) €41.07   (ii) €124.04   (iii) €3,518.80
(iv) €765.19   15. (i) €5,471.68   (ii) €79,801.32
16. €44,000   17. (i) €8,930   (ii) €56,829.27
(iii) Eoin: €3,296.85; Sorcha: €2,468.80

Exercise 5.4

1. (i) €2.70   (ii) €1.89   (iii) €2.16   (iv) €1.69
2. (i) €544.50   (ii) €229.90   (iii) €968   (iv) €1,087.79

3. €18.15   4. €363   5. €36   6. €250   7. €1,800
8. €171.99   9. (i) €3,375   (ii) €4,083.75   10. (i) €791
(ii) €87.50   (iii) €787.50   (iv) €819

Revision Exercises

1. €15,060   2. €1,810.80   3. (i) €26,450
(ii) €36,700   4. (a) €11,360   (b) €51,000   5. €3,500
6. (a) €37,520   (b) €60,000   7. (i) €29.54   (ii) €93.03
(iii) €2,468.80   (iv) €612.99   8. €3,986.12
9. (i) €510.75   (ii) €60.75   (iii) €506.25   (iv) €517.50
10. (i) 145,000 kg   (ii) 95,000 kg   (iii) 80,000 hours
(iv) €600,000   (v) €1,449.000   (vi) €776,000
(vii) €553,500

Chapter 6

Exercise 6.1

1. (i) Area: 20.77 cm^2; perimeter: 21.49 m (ii) Area: 68 cm^2;
perimeter: ≈ 51.48 cm   (iii) Area: 256 m^2; perimeter: 67 m
2. (i) Area: 78.5 cm^2; perimeter: 31.4 cm
(ii) Area: 201.14 km^2; perimeter: 50.29 km
(iii) Area: 0.49π m^2; perimeter: 1.4π m
(iv) Area: 4.91 mm^2; perimeter: 7.85 mm
(v) Area: 63.64 cm^2; perimeter: 28.29 cm
(vi) Area: $3,969\pi$ mm^2 ; 126π mm
3. (i) Area: 36.376 units^2; length of arc: 8.79;
perimeter: 20.79   (ii) Area: 203.66 units^2;
length of arc: 33.94; perimeter: 57.94
(iii) Area: 2370.70 units^2; length of arc: 158.05;
perimeter: 218.05   5. (i) $r = 12$ (ii) $\theta = 224°$
(iii) $\theta = 160°$ 6. 58 m   7. 14,152 complete parts
8. (i) 9,100 m^2 (ii) 2,150 m^2 (iii) €7,793.75   9. 1,832 g
10. (i) $r = 2.114$ cm   (ii) 664.40 m   11. $y = 15.33$ m,
$x = 72$ m; $y = 48$ m, $x = 23$ m   12. Length: 10 m;
width: 1.25 m   13. €485   14. ≈ 28 cm   15. 40.5π cm^2
16. The side length of the larger square side = $x\sqrt{2}$
17. (i) ≈ 63 cm^2 (ii) ≈ 32 cm   18. 6 minutes 56 seconds
19. (i) 2,449 km   (ii) $\theta \approx 97°$ 20. The area of the inner
shaded region (pink) is greatest.   21. $r \approx 30$ m

Exercise 6.2

1. (i) Volume: 1,560 m^3; surface area: 1,276 m^2
(ii) Volume: 2,368 m^3; surface area: 1,704 m^2 (iii) Volume:
612 m^3; surface area: 424 m^2 2. (i) $\approx 1,065.06$ cm^2
(ii) ≈ 55.43 cm^2 3. 1,956 cm^2 4. 295.84 cm^3
5. Rise in height of water = $3\frac{1}{3}$ cm   6. Volume: 6 m^3;
surface area: 26.06 m^2 7. Surface area = $6\left(\sqrt[3]{32}\ x\right)^2$
or $6.32^{\frac{2}{3}} . x^2$ 8. (i) $\approx 1,774$ tiles needed   (ii) 473,125 litres
9. Volume: 21,283.44 cm^3; surface area: 4,608 cm^2
10. (ii) Volume: $6xy$ cm^3; surface area: $12y + 2xy + 12x$ cm^2
(iii) $x = 14$ cm, $y = 10$ cm   11. (iii) 4 cm or 1.78 cm

Exercise 6.3

1. V: 1,808.64 cm^3; CSA: 301.44 cm^2; TSA: 1,205.76 cm^2
(ii) V: 431.2 mm^3; CSA: 123.2 mm^2; 431.2 cm^2

(iii) V: 320π m³; CSA: 160π m²; 192π m²
(iv) V: 1,582.56 m³; CSA: 527.52 m²;
TSA: 753.6 m² **2.** (i) V: 401.92 cm³; CSA: 251.20 cm²;
TSA: 452.16 cm² (ii) V: 15,085.71 mm³;
CSA: 5,154.29 mm²; TSA: 10,182.86 mm²
(iii) V: 20,736,000.00π mm³; CSA: 216,000π mm²;
TSA: 345,600.00π mm² (iv) V: 27,154,285.71 cm³;
CSA: 384,685.71 cm²; TSA: 565,714.29 cm²
3. (i) V: 17,148.59 m³; SA: 3,215.36 m²
(ii) V: 11,498.67 mm³; SA: 2,464.00 mm²
(iii) V: 2,304.00π cm³; SA: 576.00π cm²
4. (i) V: 32,708.33 cm³; CSA: 3,925.00 cm²;
TSA: 5,887.50 cm² (ii) V: 6,387.60 mm³;
CSA: 1,321.57 mm²; TSA: 1,982.36 mm²
(iii) V: 486.00π m³; CSA: 162.00π m²; TSA: 243.00π m²
5. 96π cm² **6.** 2 cm **7.** ≈38 mm **8.** 175 seconds
9. (i) 288π cm³ (ii) $10\frac{2}{3}$ cm **10.** (i) 18π cm³ (ii) 3 cm
(iii) 6 cm (iv) $(18 + 9\sqrt{2})\pi$ cm² **11.** (ii) $\sqrt{5}$: 4
12. Cylinder A has the greatest volume.
13. (i) 1,766.25 cm³ (ii) $r \approx 8.42$ cm
(iii) Box = 16.84 cm × 16.84 cm × 16.84 cm
14. 261 mm × 90 mm **15.** 0.25 cm **16.** 3 cm
17. $h = \frac{32}{3}x$ **18.** ≈2,100 cm³ **19.** $\left(\sqrt{\frac{3}{2}} - 1\right)x$
20. $\pi\sqrt{3}$: 2 **21.** V = 3,315.84 cm³; TSA ≈ 1,510.97 cm²
22. (i) ≈16.5 cm (ii) 842.57 cm² (iii) $r = 8\sqrt{2}$

Exercise 6.4

1. 62 m² **2.** 912 cm² **3.** $302\frac{1}{2}$ m² **4.** 2,300 m²
5. 26 units² **6.** 173 m² **7.** $h = 18$ **8.** (i) 5.68 units²
9. $x = 175$ m

Revision Exercises

1. (a) (i) Volume: 113,408 m³; surface area: 15,152 m²
(ii) Volume: 480 m³; surface area: 688 cm²
(iii) Volume: 8,452.34 cm³; surface area: 3,002.99 cm²
(b) (i) 5,640 m² (ii) 1,300 m² (iii) 39.50 m²
(iv) 93.90 m² (c) (i) $x = 14$ (ii) $h = 5.8315$ m²
2. (a) $r = 10$ cm (b) ≈446 cm³ (c) (i) $\sqrt{2}r$ (ii) 2 : 1
3. (a) Volume: 1,440π cm³; surface area: 880.9969π cm²
(b) 21 cm (c) 800 seconds **4.** (a) 4 : 1
(b) Small jar: Radius: 2.3 cm; height: 4.6 cm.
Large jar: Radius: 6.9 cm; height: 9.2 cm **5.** (a) 2,866
(b) $\pi\left(r^2 = r^2\sqrt{\frac{5}{4}}\right)$ **6.** (b) ≈4.66 cm **7.** (a) (i) π(5x)
(ii) π5x² (b) $p = 1.5$ m, $q = 2.4$ m **8.** (a) (i) $\frac{4}{3}\pi r^3$
(ii) $\pi\left(\frac{4}{5}r^2 + 2\sqrt{\frac{129}{5}}\right)$ (b) $\frac{Pr}{3}$ **9.** (a) (i) 52.95 m²
(ii) 22,239 m³/min (b) (i) 1,432,189,259 km
(ii) ≈691 days (iii) 4,500,000,000 km (v) 0.25 minutes
10. (a) (i) $l = 3r$ (ii) $h = \sqrt{8}r^2$ (iii) $\sqrt{2}$: 1
(b) (i) $\sqrt{37}x^2 + x^2$ (ii) $\sqrt{3}y^2$ **12.** (a) $r = 16.25$ m
(b) (i) $r = 9.05$ m (c) $r = 9.3611...$ m **13.** (a) $(15 - h)$ cm
(b) Volume = $2h^3 - 50h^2 + 300h$ (d) $h = 2.9$ cm

Chapter 7

Exercise 7.1

3. (i) $f(1.6) = 5.8$ (ii) 2.6 **4.** (i) $f(0) = 1$ (ii) $a = 3$
6. (i) $x = 0$ (ii) Axial symmetry in the y-axis **7.** (i) 10^9
(ii) 20^6 (iii) 7^8 (iv) e^5 (v) 4^5 (vi) e^{-3} (vii) -5^7
(viii) 10^{36} (ix) e^4 (x) e^{25} **8.** (i) -3^3 (ii) 2^{20}
(iii) -5^{19} (iv) 3^3 (v) 4^{12} (vi) -1 (vii) -6^3 (viii) 6^3
9. (i) $\frac{1}{8}$ (ii) $\frac{1}{49}$ (iii) $\frac{1}{16}$ (iv) $\frac{1}{81}$ (v) $\frac{4}{81}$ (vi) $\frac{1}{8}$ (vii) $\frac{1}{32}$
(viii) $\frac{1}{200}$ (ix) $\frac{1}{10}$ (x) $\frac{1}{6}$ (xi) $\frac{1}{2}$ (xii) $\frac{1}{27}$ (xiii) $\frac{1}{4}$ (xiv) $\frac{1}{243}$
10. (i) 7 (ii) 3 (iii) 2 (iv) 2 (v) 1 (vi) 6 (vii) 3
(viii) 2 (ix) 11 **11.** (i) 2 (ii) 3 (iii) 10 (iv) 4 (v) 6
(vi) 4 **12.** (i) -2 (ii) -4 (iii) -10 (iv) 2 (v) 2 (vi) 2
13. (i) 1,000 (ii) 25 (iii) 32 (iv) 27 (v) 27 (vi) 256
(vii) $\frac{1}{125}$ (viii) $\frac{32}{243}$ (ix) $\frac{9}{5}$ (x) $\frac{4}{9}$ **14.** (i) a^5 (ii) a^9
(iii) a^{14} (iv) $a^{\frac{1}{2}}$ (v) $a^{\frac{7}{2}}$ (vi) a^{-3} (vii) $a^{\frac{-1}{2}}$ **16.** $k = 2$
17. (i) 3×5 (ii) $3^9 \times 5^9$ **18.** (i) $36 = 2^2 \times 3^2$;
$36^{2,011} = 2^{4,022} \times 3^{4,022}$ **19.** $100 = 2^2 \times 5^2$;
$100^{1,601} = 2^{3,202} \times 5^{3,202}$

Exercise 7.2

1. (i) $x = 4$ (ii) $x = 4$ (iii) $x = 3$ (iv) $x = 2$ (v) $x = 6$
(vi) $x = -5$ (vii) $x = -3$ (viii) $x = 0$ **2.** (i) $x = 7\frac{1}{2}$
(ii) $x = 2\frac{1}{2}$ (iii) $x = 1\frac{1}{2}$ (iv) $x = 1\frac{2}{3}$ (v) $x = \frac{3}{4}$
(vi) $x = 1\frac{3}{10}$ **3.** (i) 2^4 (ii) 2^3 (iii) $2^{\frac{1}{2}}$ (iv) $2^{2\frac{1}{2}}$; $x = 4\frac{1}{4}$
4. (i) $x = 4\frac{1}{2}$ (ii) $x = 7$ **5.** 2^p **6.** (i) $x = 8$ (ii) $x = 14$
7. (i) $x = 2$ (ii) $x = 1$ (iii) $x = 3$ (iv) $x = -1$ (v) $x = 1$
(vi) $x = 2$ or $x = 1$ **8.** (i) $x = 0$ or $x = 2$ (ii) $x = 1$ or $x = 0$
(iii) $x = -2$ or $x = 2$ (iv) $x = 0$ (v) $x = -1$ or $x = 0$
9. (i) $x = 2$ (ii) $x = -1$ **10.** (i) $(3^x)^2$ (ii) $x = 2$ or $x = 1$

Exercise 7.3

1. (i) 28 (ii) 250 (iii) 20 (iv) 200 (v) 135 (vi) 400
2. (i) 4 (ii) 8 (iii) 10 (iv) 3 (v) 5 (vi) 5 **3.** (i) $2\sqrt{2}$
(ii) $3\sqrt{5}$ (iii) $10\sqrt{3}$ (iv) $2\sqrt{3}$ (v) $4\sqrt{2}$ (vi) $10\sqrt{5}$
(vii) $3\sqrt{3}$ (viii) $3\sqrt{5}$ (ix) $5\sqrt{3}$ (x) $7\sqrt{2}$ **4.** (i) $7\sqrt{2}$
5. $5\sqrt{3}$ **6.** $7\sqrt{5}$ **7.** $3\sqrt{11}$ **8.** (i) $3\sqrt{2}$ (ii) $\sqrt{7}$ (iii) $\frac{1}{2}\sqrt{2}$
(iv) $\frac{3}{5}\sqrt{5}$ (v) $\frac{2}{11}\sqrt{11}$ (vi) $\frac{3}{5}\sqrt{15}$ (vii) $\sqrt{2}$ (viii) $-\frac{2}{3}\sqrt{15}$
(ix) $\frac{1}{5}\sqrt{5}$ **9.** (i) $2 + \sqrt{5}$ (ii) $\frac{1}{2} - \frac{1}{6}\sqrt{3}$ (iii) $20 + 5\sqrt{2}$
(iv) $\frac{7}{22} - \frac{3}{22}\sqrt{3}$ (v) $-\frac{26}{23} + \frac{7}{23}\sqrt{3}$ (vi) $-\frac{43}{74} + \frac{11}{74}\sqrt{11}$
(vii) $\frac{1}{5} + \frac{1}{10}\sqrt{2}$ (viii) $-4 + \sqrt{15}$ (ix) $\frac{101}{37} - \frac{22}{37}\sqrt{21}$

Exercise 7.4

3. (i) $\frac{1}{2}$ (ii) -2 (iii) $\frac{1}{2}$ (iv) 0 (v) $\frac{1}{3}$ (vi) 1 (vii) 2 (viii) 3
4. (i) 4 (ii) 4 (iii) 3 (iv) 3 (v) 3 (vi) $\frac{5}{3}$ (vii) -7
(viii) -4 **5.** (i) 7.39 (ii) 4.48 (iii) 1.11 (iv) 1.10
(v) -1.60 (vi) 2.73 (vii) 0.81 (viii) 2.40 **8.** (i) log 10
(ii) log 5 (iii) log 6 (iv) log 2 (v) $\log\frac{p}{3\sqrt{q}}$ (vi) $\log\frac{10a^3}{\sqrt[3]{b}}$

9. (i) $x = 1$ (ii) $x = 2^9$ (iii) $x = 5$ (iv) $x = 3$ **10.** (i) $x = 29$

(ii) $x = 2$ (iii) $x = 4$ (iv) $x = 2$ **11.** (i) $x = \frac{1}{2}$

(ii) $x = \frac{1}{2}(5^{12} - 1)$ (iii) $x = 4{,}096$ (iv) $x = 25$

(v) $x = -\frac{1}{2}$ **12.** (i) $x = 5$ (ii) $x \approx 8.34$

(iii) $x \approx 7.03 \times 10^{16}$ (iv) $x \approx 1.53$

13. (i) $x = 2.32$ or $x = 1.58$ (ii) $x = 1.00$ (iii) $x = 0.70$

(iv) $x = 0.18$ (v) $x = -1.00$ **14.** $x = \log_3 2$ or $x = \log_3 4$

15. (i) $x = 0.77$ or $x = 0.63$ (ii) $x = -0.25$ (iii) $x = 0.58$

(iv) $x = 0.39$ or $x = 0.90$ (v) $x = 0.30$ **16.** (i) $x = 1$

(ii) $x = e^2$ (iii) $x = -1$ (iv) $x = \frac{1}{3}$ **17.** (i) $x = 5$ (ii) $x = 4$

(iii) $x = 2$ (iv) $x = \sqrt{\frac{e}{7}}$ **18.** (i) $x = \ln \sqrt{3}$ (ii) $x = \frac{1}{3}e^2$

(iii) $x = \frac{1}{e^5}$ (iv) $x = -\ln 7$ **19.** (i) $x = 2$ (ii) $x = \frac{7}{11}$

(iii) $x = 0$ (iv) $x = -0.34$

Exercise 7.5

1. (i) $a = 30$; $b = -\frac{1}{8}\log_e 2$ (ii) ≈ 5.30 g

(iii) 34.65 days **2.** (i) pH ≈ 4.8; Acid

(ii) pH ≈ 8.9; Base (iii) 6.0×10^{-9} moles/litre

3. (i) pH $= 7.9$ (ii) 1.0×10^{-7} moles/litre

4. (i) pH $= 6.14$; Yes **5.** (i) 14 years and 2 months

(ii) 10 years and 3 months (iii) 7 years and 3 months

6. 12 years **7.** (i) $M = 0$ (ii) $M = 6.08$ (iii) 2,512 mm

8. (i) $M \approx 5.9$ (ii) $m = 10^{26.595}$

(iii) ≈ 708 times stronger (iv) ≈ 32 times stronger

Revision Exercises

1. (i) 5^{11} (ii) 3^6 (iii) 16^4 (iv) 7^{-5} (v) $17^{\frac{3}{5}}$ (vi) $5^{\frac{1}{2}}$

2. (i) a^{10} (ii) a^{24} (iii) $a^{\frac{3}{2}}$ (iv) a^2 **3.** (i) $5\sqrt{5} + 3\sqrt{2}$

(ii) $20\sqrt{5}$ **4.** (i) $\frac{1}{8}$ (ii) (a) 2^7 (b) $2^{\frac{1}{2}}$ (iii) $2^{\frac{3}{4}}$

5. (i) $4a^4$; 2^6 (ii) $2^{\frac{9}{4}}$ (iii) $9a^5$; 3^7 (iv) 3^{11} **6.** (i) $\frac{5}{2}\sqrt{2}$

(ii) $2\sqrt{3}$ (iii) $\frac{1}{6}\sqrt{6}$ (iv) $-7 - 3\sqrt{6}$ (v) $\frac{1}{4} - \frac{1}{20}\sqrt{10}$

(vi) $2 - \frac{1}{2}\sqrt{14}$ (vii) $-\sqrt{15} - 2\sqrt{5}$ **7.** (i) $x = 6$ (ii) $x = 2$

(iii) $x = \frac{19}{4}$ (iv) $x = \frac{3}{5}$ (v) $x = 6$ **8.** (i) $x = 100$ (ii) $x = 25$

(iii) $x = 81$ (iv) $x = 3$ **9.** (a) Least value of n is 13.

(b) Largest value of n is 18. **10.** (i) $x = 3$ (ii) $x = 2$

(iii) $x = 0$ (iv) $x = \log_e\left(\frac{1}{3}\right)$ or $x = \log_e 2$ (v) $x = 9$ or $x = -3$

11. (i) $x = 3, y = 8$ (ii) $x = 2, y = 2.5$ (iii) $x = 4, y = -1$

13. (i) $a = 5$ (ii) $g(x) = 5^x$ **14.** (i) 40 dB

(ii) Range $= [10^{-8}, 10^{-7}]$ (iii) 9 trumpets **16.** (b) 5.25 g

(c) $k = 0.132$ (d) 17.4 years **17.** 91.7%

18. 83.41 minutes **19.** (b) (i) 1,020 (ii) 1,370 (d) 2008

Chapter 8

Exercise 8.1

1. a, b, d are functions; c, e, f are not functions

2. (b) (i) 3 (ii) 1 (iii) $\frac{5}{2}$ (iv) $\frac{1}{3}$ **3.** 8 **4.** 4 **5.** (i) Yes

(ii) Domain $= \{1, 2, 3, 4\}$; Range $= \{8, 9, 10, 11\}$

(iii) $x \mapsto x + 7$ (iv) 70 **6.** (i) $f(x) = x^2$ (ii) $f(x) = 4x + 6$

(iii) $f(x) = 98 - 3x$ (where $x = $ 5-min interval)

(iv) $f(x) = 10 - 2x$ (where $x = $ no. of seconds passed)

7. (i) $f: x \mapsto \frac{x}{2} + 3$ or $f: x \mapsto \frac{x + 6}{2}$ (ii) $f(4) = 5$;

$f(18) = 12$; $f(-6) = 0$ (iii) 12 (iv) $\frac{x + 18}{4}$ (v) $\frac{x + 1}{2}$

(vi) $\frac{x + k}{2} + 3$ **9.** $a = 3, b = 2$ **10.** $m = -\frac{5}{2}, c = \frac{17}{2}$

11. $a = 2, b = 3$ **12.** (i) $f(x) = 200 - x^2$

(ii) $10\sqrt{2}$ minutes (iii) 10 minutes **13.** $y = 100x - x^2$;

Domain is $\{x \mid x \in R, 0 < x < 100\}$ **14.** $l = 2\sqrt{25 - x^2}$;

Domain $= \{x \mid x \in R, 0 \leqslant x < 5\}$ **15.** (a) (i) 6 (ii) 24

(iii) 38 (iv) 78 (v) 8 (vi) 14 (vii) 24 (viii) 78

16. (a) (i) $x^2 - 2$ (ii) $(x - 2)^2$ (iii) $(x + 1)^2$

(iv) $(x - 2)^2 + 1$ (v) $(x - 1)^2$ (vi) $(x^2 - 2)^2$

(vii) $(x + 1)^4$ (viii) $x - 3$ (b) $g \circ f \circ h$ **17.** (i) $c = 2$

18. (i) $k = -5$ **19.** $a = 0$ **20.** (a) (i) $h(x) = fg(x)$

where $g(x) = x^2$ and $f(x) = x + 1$ (ii) $f(x) = pq(x)$ where

$q(x) = x^2$ and $p(x) = 2x$ (b) (i) $g(x) = a(bc(x))$ where

$c(x) = x^2, b(x) = 3x, a(x) = x - 5$ (ii) $j(x) = f(gh(x))$

where $h(x) = 4x, g(x) = x - 3, f(x) = x^2$

21. (a) (i) $f(x) = x^2 + 6$ (ii) $f(x) = 6(x - 2)^2$

(iii) $f(x) = (\sqrt{x} + 4)^3$ (iv) $f(x) = \frac{1}{4}.\sin^2 x$ (b) (i) $f = h \circ g$

where $g(x) = x^2, h(x) = x + 6$ (ii) $f = k \circ h \circ g$ where

$g(x) = x - 2, h(x) = x^2, k(x) = 6x$ (iii) $f = k \circ h \circ g$ where

$g(x) = \sqrt{x}, h(x) = x + 4, k(x) = x^3$ (iv) $f = k \circ h \circ g$ where

$g(x) = \sin x, h(x) = x^2, k(x) = \frac{x}{4}$ **22.** (i) $x = -\frac{1}{3}$ or $x = -1$

(ii) $x = -\frac{3}{14}$ **23.** (ii) $a = 2, b = 3$ or $a = -2, b = -3$

24. (i) E.g. $h(x) = \sqrt{x} + 9$ (ii) E.g. $h(x) = x - 6$

(iii) E.g. $h(x) = 2x$ (iv) E.g. $h(x) = 3x^2 - 7$

25. (i) $3x^2 + 8$ (ii) $9x^2 + 12x + 6$; No **26.** $g \circ f$

Exercise 8.2

1. (i) 7 (ii) $\frac{9}{4}$ (iii) –1 (iv) $x \geqslant 1$ **2.** (ii) 120 km

(iii) $87\frac{1}{2}$ miles (iv) [104 km, 120 km] **3.** (i) –4.5

(ii) –1.45 or 3.45 (iii) $-1.45 \leqslant x \leqslant 3.45$ (iv) 6

9. (ii) 0.25 seconds or 4.15 seconds (iii) First ball:

31.25 m, second ball: 20 m (iv) First ball: 2.5 seconds,

second ball: 5 seconds (v) 3.9 seconds (vi) First ball

10. (i) 16 (ii) 0.6 or 6.9 (iii) $0.6 \leqslant x \leqslant 6.9$

(iv) $0 \leqslant x \leqslant 0.6$ or $6.9 \leqslant x \leqslant 8$ **11.** (i) –2.6 or 0.6

(ii) $-3 \leqslant x \leqslant -2.6$ or $0.6 \leqslant x \leqslant 2$ **12.** (ii) 2 seconds

or 4 seconds (iv) 0.2 seconds (v) 1.3 m

13. (ii) 500 units (iii) €2,500 (iv) 400 units or 600 units

(v) It is more lucrative to produce 725 units;

with 725 units, monthly pay $\approx$ €2,000, whereas with

250 units, monthly pay $\approx$ €1,875. **14.** (ii) 300

(iii) €90 (iv) No

Exercise 8.3

1. (i) $y = (x - 6)^2$ (ii) $x = 6$ (iii) $(6, 0)$; $x = 6$

2. (i) $f(x) = (x + 1)^2 - 7$ (ii) $x = -1 \pm \sqrt{7}$

(iii) $(-1, -7)$; $x = -1$ **3.** (i) $g(x) = (x - 3)^2 - 25$

(ii) $x = -2$ or $x = 8$ (iii) $(3, -25)$; $x = 3$

4. (i) $f(x) = 2(x + 1)^2 - 9$ (ii) $x = -1 \pm \frac{3\sqrt{2}}{2}$

(iii) $(-1, -9)$; $x = -1$ **5.** (i) $f(x) = 3(x + 2)^2 - 8$

(ii) $x = -2 \pm \frac{2\sqrt{6}}{3}$ (iii) $(-2, -8)$; $x = -2$

6. (i) $h(x) = 4\left(x + \frac{9}{8}\right)^2 - \frac{1}{16}$ (ii) $x = -\frac{5}{4}$ or $x = -1$

(iii) $\left(-\frac{9}{8}, -\frac{1}{16}\right)$; $x = -\frac{9}{8}$ **7.** $f(x) = 5(x - 1)^2 - 17$

(ii) $x = 1 \pm \frac{\sqrt{85}}{5}$ (iii) $(1, -17)$; $x = 1$

8. (i) $g(x) = (x + 1)^2 - 4$ (ii) $x = -3$ or $x = 1$
(iii) $(-1, -4)$; $x = -1$ **9.** (i) $y = 7 - (x + 2)^2$
(ii) $x = -2 \pm \sqrt{7}$ (iii) $(-2, 7)$; $x = -2$

10. (i) $y = 13 - (x - 2)^2$ (ii) $x = 2 \pm \sqrt{13}$
(iii) $(2, 13)$; $x = 2$ **11.** (i) $h(x) = 15 - 2(x + 1)^2$
(ii) $x = -1 \pm \frac{\sqrt{30}}{2}$ (iii) $(-1, 15)$; $x = -1$

12. (i) $g(x) = 2 - (x - 2)^2$ (ii) $x = 2 \pm \sqrt{2}$
(iii) $(2, 2)$; $x = 2$ **13.** (i) $g(x) = \frac{43}{3} - 3\left(x - \frac{7}{3}\right)^2$
(ii) $x = \frac{7 \pm \sqrt{43}}{3}$ (iii) $\left(\frac{7}{3}, \frac{43}{3}\right)$; $x = \frac{7}{3}$

15. $(x - 6)^2 - 40 = 0$; $x = 6 \pm 2\sqrt{10}$
16. $(x + 6)^2 - 40 = 0$; $x = -6 \pm 2\sqrt{10}$
17. $(x + 6)^2 - 27 = 0$; $x = -6 \pm 3\sqrt{3}$
18. $2\left(x - \frac{3}{4}\right)^2 - \frac{1}{8} = 0$; $x = \frac{1}{2}$ or $x = 1$

Exercise 8.4

2. (i) $x = 2.05$ (ii) $x = 2.25$ **3.** (i) $x = 0$, $x = 1.2$
(ii) $x = -4$, $x = -0.6$, $x = 1.6$ **4.** (i) $x = -3.1$,
$x = -0.75$, $x = 0.85$ (ii) $0.2 < x < 0.85$
(iii) $x = 1.45$ **5.** (i) $x = 1.9$ (ii) $x = 1.8$
6. $x = -1.55$, $x = -0.35$, $x = 1.9$ **7.** (i) 12,000 units
(ii) 0.65 years   (iii) 0 years and 2 years   (iv) 30,000 units
8. (i) $f(1.5) \approx 4.9$ (ii) $x = -0.45$, 0.6 or 2
(iii) $x \approx -0.4$, 1.15 or 1.45   **9.** (i) 30°C   (ii) 13°C
(iii) [0.7 mins, 1.3 mins] or [3.95 mins, 4 mins]
10. (i) 1.85 years   (ii) 0.4 years or 3.8 years
11. (ii) €10,480   (iii) €1,670 per year   (iv) Yes
12. (ii) 495 cm   (iii) 2.52 and 6.86 seconds
13. (a) length = $15 - h$ (cm); width = $20 - 2h$ (cm);
height = h (cm)   (b) $(15 - h)(20 - 2h)(h)$ (cm³)
(d) $h \approx 2.9$ cm   (e) Not possible as $h < 10$

Exercise 8.5

9. $a = 6$, $b = 2$ **10.** $a = 3$, $b = 2$ **11.** $a = 2.5$,
$b = 2$ **12.** $a = 4$, $b = \frac{1}{2}$ **13.** $a = 2$, $b = \frac{1}{3}$
14. (iii) 5 days 18 hours   **15.** (i) 1 hour: 20 cm³;
2 hours: 40 cm³; 3 hours: 80 cm³; 4 hours: 160 cm³
(iii) 57 cm³   (iv) 3.3 hours   **16.** (ii) 2035
(iii) $P(x) = 15(1.25^{0.1x})$, where P is in millions.
17. (ii) 170 W/m²   (iii) 172.26 W/m²
(iv) 1.22 mm

Exercise 8.8

8. x^3 **9.** $(x - 2)^3 - 6$ **10.** (i) Shift four units to the left
and three units downwards.   (ii) $(x + 4)^3 - 3$

Exercise 8.9

6. (i) Shift two units to the left.   (ii) 2^{x-2} **7.** 3^{x-3}
8. $3(4^{x-3})$ **9.** $2^{x+2} + 3$

Exercise 8.10

4. (i) Multiply the function by 0.5.   (ii) $f(x) = 0.5 \log_4 x$
5. $y = \log_8 (x - 5)$ **6.** $y = 3\log_6 (x - 3) - 3$

7. (i) Domain $x > 1$; Range: no max., no min.
(ii) Domain $x > -1$; Range: no max., no min.
(iii) Domain $x > 0$; Range: no max., no min.
(iv) Domain $x > \frac{1}{3}$; Range: no max., no min.

Exercise 8.11

1. (i) a   (ii) c   (iii) d   (iv) b   (v) c   (vi) b
2. (iii) Is not injective, as $f(-2) = f(2) = 7$
3. (i) (a) Range = {0, 4, 8, 16}   (b) One-to-one
(ii) (a) Range = $[2, \infty)$ (b) Not one-to-one
(iii) (a) Range = $[-7, 5]$ (b) One-to-one
(iv) (a) Range = $R\backslash\{0\}$ (b) One-to-one
(v) (a) Range = $[2, \infty)$ (b) Not one-to-one
(vi) (a) Range = R (b) One-to-one
(vii) (a) Range = $[-1, 1]$ (b) Not one-to-one
(viii) (a) Range = $[0, \infty)$ (b) One-to-one   **4.** (i) a
(ii) b   (iii) d   **5.** (i) Is a function   (ii) Is not a function
(iii) Is a function   (iv) Is not a function   **6.** (i) c   (ii) d
(iii) b   (iv) a   **7.** (i) No   (ii) If $f: R \mapsto (-\infty, 2]$
8. f is not injective   **9.** f is not injective
10. f is injective   **11.** $f: N \to E: x \to 2x$
12. $f: N \to 0: x \to 2x - 1$ **13.** $f: N \to E: x \to -2x$
14. (i) Yes   (ii) No   **15.** (i) Not surjective
(ii) Not surjective   (iii) Not surjective
(iv) Not surjective   (v) Surjective   (vi) Surjective
(vii) Surjective   **17.** Yes   **18.** No   **19.** Yes   **20.** No
21. No   **22.** No   **23.** No   **24.** Yes
25. (i) Not bijective   (ii) Bijective   (iii) Not bijective
(iv) Bijective   (v) Not bijective   (vi) Not bijective
(vii) Not bijective   **26.** (i) Is a bijection
(ii) Not a bijection   (iii) Is a bijection.   **27.** Yes
28. Yes   **29.** (i) Yes   (ii) Yes   (iii) Yes   **30.** (i) No
(ii) No   (iii) No   **31.** $f: (-1, 1) \to R: x \to \tan\left(\frac{\pi x}{2}\right)$

Exercise 8.12

1. $f^{-1}(x) = \frac{x}{2}$, $x \in R$ **2.** $g^{-1}(x) = \frac{x-1}{3}$, $x \in R$
3. $p^{-1}(x) = \frac{x+4}{6}$, $x \in R$ **5.** (i) $h^{-1}(x) = \log_2 x$, $x \in R^+$
6. Is invertible   **7.** Not Invertible   **8.** Is invertible
9. Is invertible   **10.** Not invertible
11. $g^{-1}: [-5, \infty) \to [3, \infty): x \to \sqrt{\frac{x+5}{2}} + 3$
12. $f^{-1}: [0, 1) \to [0, \infty): x \to \sqrt{\frac{x}{1-x}}$
13. $h^{-1}: R^+ \to R: x \to \ln x$
14. $f^{-1}: \left[\frac{1}{2}, \infty\right) \to [0, \infty): x \to \frac{1}{3}\log_2(2x)$
15. $f^{-1}: R \to (-1, \infty): x \to b^x - 1$

Revision Exercises

1. (i) -4 (ii) -3 (iii) 96   (iv) $3x^2 - 12x + 6$
2. (i) $bb: x \to \frac{x}{1-4x} - 4$ (ii) $ba: x \to \frac{1}{x^2 - 3} - 4$
(iii) $cc: x \to x + 6$ (iv) $acb: x \to \left(\frac{1-x}{x}\right)^2 - 3$
(v) $bac: x \to \frac{1}{x^2 + 6x + 6} - 4$ (vi) $cab: x \to \left(\frac{1}{x} - 4\right)^2$
3. (i) $x = 0.04$ or -2.71 (ii) $x = \pm 0.41$

4. One real root   **5.** (i) $f(x) = \frac{x}{4} + 3$
(ii) $f(3) = 3.75$; $f(-2) = 2.5$; $f(-8) = 1$ (iii) 24
6. (i) $y = 700 - 20x^2 + 40x$ (ii) 7 minutes
(iii) After approx. 5.3 minutes   **7.** (i) 1–1 only
(ii) 1–1 only   (iii) 1–1 and onto   (iv) Onto only
(v) 1–1 only   **8.** (i) 1–1 function   (ii) Not a function
(iii) Onto function   (iv) 1–1 and onto function
9. (i) Is injective   (ii) Not injective   (iii) Not injective
(iv) Is injective   **10.** Yes   **11.** No   **12.** No   **13.** (i) Yes
(ii) No   **18.** (i) $16\pi r^2$ (ii) $18\pi r^2$ (iii) $8\pi r^3$; 729π (cm³)
19. $40{,}000(0.88)^t$ (in €)   **20.** $f^{-1} = \frac{x+3}{3}$
21. $g^{-1} = \frac{3x-1}{x}$ **22.** $h^{-1} = \frac{1}{3}(12 - 8x)$ **23.** $f^{-1} = -\frac{4}{x}$
24. $g^{-1} = \frac{7x}{4}$ **25.** (i) $g^{-1} = \frac{x}{3}$; $h^{-1} = \frac{1}{x}$; $gh(x) = \frac{3}{x}$
26. (a) (i) $[0, \infty) \rightarrow [0, \infty)$ or $(\infty, 0] \rightarrow [0, \infty)$
(ii) $[-3, \infty) \rightarrow [0, \infty)$ or $(\infty, -3] \rightarrow [0, \infty)$
(b) (i) Using f: $[0, \infty) \rightarrow [0, \infty)$: $f^{-1} = \sqrt{x}$
(ii) Using g: $[-3, \infty) \rightarrow [0, \infty)$: $g^{-1} = \sqrt{x} - 3$
27. (i) Not invertible   (ii) Not invertible   (iii) Is invertible
28. (iii) 220   (iv) 4.19 hrs   (v) $A(1.18)^x$
(vi) $P(x) = 125(1.18)^x$ (vii) 223.1   **35.** (i) –1 or 1
(ii) $x \leqslant -1$ or $x \geqslant 1$ (iii) $-1 < x < 1$ **36.** $a = -1$,
$b = -2$, $c = 4$ **37.** (i) $\frac{2}{3}$ (ii) –2, –1 or 0
(iii) One real root   **39.** (i) (a) $y = (x + 3)^2$ (b) $x = -3$
(c) $(-3,0)$; $x = -3$ (ii) (a) $y = (x + 1)^2 - 9$
(b) $x = -4$ or $x = 2$ (c) $(-1,-9)$; $x = -1$
(iii) (a) $y = 2\left(x + \frac{1}{2}\right)^2 - \frac{19}{2}$ (b) $x = -\frac{1 \pm \sqrt{19}}{2}$
(c) $\left(-\frac{1}{2}, -\frac{19}{2}\right)$; $x = -\frac{1}{2}$ (iv) (a) $y = (x + 1)^2 + 5$
(b) No real roots   (c) $(-1,5)$; $x = -1$
(v) (a) $y = \frac{1}{3} - 3\left(x - \frac{2}{3}\right)^2$ (b) $x = \frac{1}{3}$ or $x = 1$
(c) $\left(\frac{2}{3}, \frac{1}{3}\right)$; $x = \frac{2}{3}$ (vi) (a) $y = 3\left(x - \frac{2}{3}\right)^2 - \frac{7}{3}$
(b) $x = \frac{2 \pm \sqrt{7}}{3}$ (c) $\left(\frac{2}{3}, -\frac{7}{3}\right)$; $x = \frac{2}{3}$ **40.** (i) $x = 6 \pm 3\sqrt{5}$
(ii) $x = -5 \pm \sqrt{29}$ **41.** (b) (i) Codomain $= [-4, \infty]$;
Range $= [-4, \infty]$ (ii) f is bijective
(iii) Domain $= [-4, \infty]$; Range $= [1, \infty]$ **43.** $2(3^x)$
45. $a = 6$ **46.** $a = 2$, $b = -\frac{1}{4}$ **47.** (ii) Missile B
(iii) Fire missile B seven minutes before missile A.
49. (i) Year 1: €448, Year 2: €501.76, Year 3: €561.97,
Year 4: €629.41, Year 5: €704.94   (iii) Base $= (1 + i)$;
exponent $= t$ (iv) €580   (v) 0.33%
50. (i) $c(x) = 120(0.5^x)$ (iii) After roughly 1.25 days
51. (i) 9 billion   (ii) 2019   (iii) 0.4% on part (i), 0.4%
on part (ii)   **52.** (i) 72° C   (ii) At 5 mins   (iii) 32 mins
53. $\approx$2.4 mol/cm³; over first interval of 0–30 seconds
54. (ii) $F \approx 1.27$ (tonnes)   (iii) $W \approx 22\%$
(iv) $F = -\frac{7}{75}.W + 2.2$

Chapter 9

Exercise 9.1

1. (i) Triangle   (ii) Square   (iii) Every 3rd tile is a square
2. (i) Green triangle   (ii) Purple hexagon
(iii) Yellow hexagon   (iv) Hexagon; triangle

(v) $x = 2$ (vi) Purple   **3.** (i) The number of lines in each
figure is a prime number (2, 3, 5, 7, 11, 13, ...)
(ii) It is a repeating pattern (2, 3, 5, 7, 2, 3, 5, 7, ...)
4. (ii) $T_1 = 6$, $T_2 = 9$, $T_3 = 12$, $T_4 = 15$, $T_5 = 18$, $T_6 = 21$
(iii) Arithmetic   (iv) 27   (v) $3 + 3n$ **5.** (ii) $T_1 = 4$, $T_2 = 7$,
$T_3 = 10$, $T_4 = 13$, $T_5 = 16$ (iii) Arithmetic   (iv) 28
(v) $1 + 3n$ **6.** (ii) $T_1 = 6$, $T_2 = 8$, $T_3 = 10$, $T_4 = 12$,
$T_5 = 14$ (iii) Arithmetic   (iv) 18   (v) $4 + 2n$ (vi) $n - 1$
7. (i) $-7 - 4n$ (ii) -227 **8.** (i) $7n - 7$ (ii) 588
9. (i) $-5 + 8n$ (ii) 763   **10.** (i) $37 - 6n$ (ii) -89
11. 35th term   **12.** -502 **13.** (i) Base $= 200$ cm;
height $= 100$ cm   (iii) 210th triangle   (iv) 2
(v) 2nd triangle   **14.** (i) Arithmetic   (ii) Arithmetic
(iii) Not arithmetic   (iv) Not arithmetic   (v) Arithmetic
(vi) Not arithmetic   (vii) Arithmetic   (viii) Arithmetic
(ix) Not arithmetic   (x) Arithmetic   (xi) Arithmetic
15. (i) Arithmetic   (ii) Arithmetic   (iii) Not arithmetic
(iv) Arithmetic   (v) Not arithmetic   **17.** (i) Sequence C
(ii) A: 2, 4, 8, 16; B: 1, 4, 9, 16; C: 5, 9, 13, 17   (iii) 4
18. (i) $d_A = 6$; $d_B = 2$; $d_C = 3$ (ii) $m_A = 6$; $m_B = 2$;
$m_C = 3$ (iii) They are the same.   **19.** (i) $x = 7$ (ii) -3
(iii) 14   **20.** (i) 7   (ii) -4 (iii) $T_4 = 7$; $T_5 = 3$
23. 46 terms   **24.** 21 terms   **25.** 34 terms
26. The 13th term   **27.** (ii) 301   (iii) 298
(iv) Column A, Row 670   **29.** (i) 95   (ii) 2020
30. (ii) The 49th day   **31.** (ii) 1,800   (iii) 101
32. (i) $T_n = (10n - 3)^2$ (ii) $T_n = (10n)^2 - 6 \times 10n + 9$,
$n = 1, 2, 3...$

Exercise 9.2

1. (i) 1,425   (ii) 2,265   (iii) 2,895   (iv) 180   (v) 165
2. (i) 3,240   **3.** 900   **4.** 1,640   **5.** (i) 1,560   (ii) 6,320
(iii) 4,760   **6.** (i) €395   (ii) €14,850   **7.** (i) 9.25 km
(ii) 33rd week   (iii) 2,744 km   **8.** (i) 10 hours   (ii) 110 cm
9. (i) $T_1 = 21$; $d = -3$ (ii) Three terms or less OR
12 terms or more   **10.** 13 rows; 9 tins   **11.** (i) 228
(ii) 34%   **12.** (i) 27   (ii) 50   (iii) 2,650
17. $T_4 = 4$; $T_n = 2n - 4$

Exercise 9.3

1. (ii) $T_1 = 1$, $T_2 = 3$, $T_3 = 6$, $T_4 = 10$, $T_5 = 15$, $T_6 = 21$
(iii) Quadratic   (iv) 28   (v) $T_n = 0.5n^2 + 0.5n$
2. (ii) $T_1 = 1$, $T_2 = 4$, $T_3 = 9$, $T_4 = 16$, $T_5 = 25$, $T_6 = 36$
(iii) Quadratic   (iv) 64   (v) $T_n = n^2$ **3.** (ii) $T_1 = 4$,
$T_2 = 9$, $T_3 = 16$, $T_4 = 25$, $T_5 = 36$ (iii) Quadratic   (iv) 64
(v) $T_n = n^2 + 2n + 1$ **4.** (i) Quadratic; 2nd diff. constant
(ii) Exponential; terms double each time
(iii) Quadratic; 2nd diff. constant   (iv) Quadratic;
2nd diff. constant   (v) Arithmetic; 1st diff. constant
(vi) Exponential; terms triple each time   (vii) Quadratic;
2nd diff. constant   (viii) Arithmetic; 1st diff. constant
(ix) Exponential; terms double each time
(x) Exponential; terms triple each time   **5.** (i) (a) 8;
(b) 1st diff. $= 6, 10, 14$; 2nd diff. $= 4$ (c) 56, 78, 104
(ii) (a) 1; (b) 1st diff. $= 2, 3, 4$; 2nd diff. $= 1$

(c) 15, 21, 28   (iii) (a) 7; (b) 1st diff. = 9, 15, 21;
2nd diff. = 6   (c) 79, 112, 151   (iv) (a) 3;
(b) 1st diff. = 10, 14, 18; 2nd diff. = 4   (c) 67, 93, 123
(v) (a) 15; (b) 1st diff. = 8, 16, 24; 2nd diff. = 8
(c) 95, 135, 183   (vi) (a) 8; (b) 1st diff. = 4, 2, 0, –2;
2nd diff. = –2   (c) 8, 2, –6   (vii) (a) 5;
(b) 1st diff. = 2, –2, –6, –10; 2nd diff. = –4
(c) –25, –43, –65   (viii) (a) 1; (b) 1st diff. = –3, 0, 3;
2nd diff. = 3   (c) 7, 16, 28   (ix) (a) 10;
(b) 1st diff. = –6, –3, 0, 3; 2nd diff. = 3   (c) 10, 19, 31
6. (i) $T_n = n^2 + n + 1$ (ii) $T_n = n^2 - n + 1$
(iii) $T_n = n^2 + 2n + 3$ (iv) $T_n = 3n^2 - 7n + 17$
(v) $T_n = 4.5n^2 - 8.5n + 10$ **7.** (i) $T_n = 4n^2 - 4n + 20$
(ii) $T_n = -n^2 + 7n + 5$ (iii) $T_n = -2n^2 + 8n + 2$
(iv) $T_n = 4 + 3n - n^2$ (v) $T_n = 1.5n^2 - 7.5n + 19$
8. (i) 8, 21, 40   (ii) $T_n = 3n^2 + 4n + 1$ (iii) 7,701
(iv) $(3n + 1)(n + 1)$ is not prime.   **9.** (i) 3
(ii) $T_1 = a + b + c$; $T_2 = 4a + 2b + c$; $T_3 = 9a + 3b + c$
(iii) $T_1 = a + b + c = 12$; $T_2 = 4a + 2b + c = 16$;
$T_3 = 9a + 3b + c = 23$ (iv) $T_n = 1.5n^2 - 0.5n + 11$
(v) 1,346   **10.** (i) 125, 216, 343   (iii) 3rd differences
are constant   **11.** (ii) 2nd differences are constant
(iii) 127   **12.** (ii) $T_5 = 66$; $T_6 = 91$
(iv) Quadratic: 2nd differences are constant.

Exercise 9.4

1. (i) $r = 2$; $T_n = 2^{n-1}$ (ii) $r = 2$; $T_n = 5(2)^{n-1}$
(iii) $r = 3$; $T_n = 7(3)^{n-1}$ (iv) $r = \frac{1}{2}$; $T_n = \frac{1}{2^n}$
(v) $r = \frac{1}{2}$; $T_n = 2^{6-n}$ (vi) $r = -2$; $3(-2)^{n-1}$
2. (i) 3, 9, 27, 81   (ii) 6, 12, 24, 48   (iii) 20, 200,
2,000, 20,000   (iv) 1, 5, 25, 125   (v) 2, 6, 18, 54
3. (i) 2, 4, 8, 16, 32   (ii) 2   (iii) 24
4. (i) Geometric   (ii) Not geometric   (iii) Geometric
(iv) Geometric   (v) Not geometric   **5.** (i) 765   (ii) 97,656
(iii) 1,275   (iv) 6,560   (v) $\frac{510}{512}$ **6.** (i) $T_1 = \frac{1}{1,032}$; $r = 4$
(ii) 21,675.99   **7.** (i) $\frac{1}{4}$ (ii) 287.93   (iii) 0.06
8. (i) $x = 2$; $y = 4$ (ii) 438   **9.** 32,769   **10.** $T_1 = \frac{1}{2}$; $r = 2$
11. $-\frac{1}{2}$ **12.** 24.67253   **13.** $S_n = \frac{8}{3}\left(1 - \frac{1}{4^n}\right)$; $n > 3$
14. 8.4932   **15.** Approx. 10 years   **16.** 15 years
17. $r = \pm \frac{3}{\sqrt{5}}$; $T_2 = \frac{10\sqrt{5}}{3}$ or $-\frac{10\sqrt{5}}{3}$ **18.** (i) 1.4%
(ii) 2006: 134,025; 2011: 143,674   (iii) 1,241,038
19. (i) €18.06   (ii) €17.41   **20.** (i) 42.875 mg
(ii) ≈12 hours   (iii) ≈100 mg

Exercise 9.5

1. (a) (i) 3   (ii) $\frac{4}{3}$ (iii) $\frac{5}{6}$ (iv) $-\frac{1}{3}$ (v) $\frac{13}{15}$ (b) (i) 3   (ii) 2
(iii) $\frac{5}{2}$ (iv) 3   (v) 3   **2.** (i) $\frac{2}{5}$ (ii) 4   (iii) $-\frac{13}{15}$
(iv) Limit cannot be found.   (v) $\frac{4}{7}$ **3.** (i) 0   (ii) 0   (iii) 3
(iv) 1   (v) $\frac{8}{5}$ **4.** (i) $\frac{7}{25}$ (ii) $\frac{17}{25}$ (iii) $\frac{1}{12}$ (iv) 12   (v) 5
5. (i) 6   (ii) 3   (iii) $\frac{1}{6}$ (iv) 2   (v) $\sqrt{3}$ **6.** (i) $\frac{n^2 + n}{2}$ (ii) $\frac{1}{\sqrt{6}}$

Exercise 9.6

1. (i) 1   (ii) $\frac{9}{14}$ (iii) $\frac{25}{4}$ (iv) 6   (v) $\frac{16}{21}$ **2.** (i) 2   (ii) $\frac{16}{15}$
(iii) $\frac{21}{4}$ (iv) $\frac{1}{3}$ (v) $\frac{2}{3}$ **3.** (i) $1 - \frac{1}{2}\sqrt{2}$ (ii) $2 + \frac{3}{2}\sqrt{2}$ (iii) 1
(iv) $\frac{10}{99}$ (v) $\frac{25}{126}$ **4.** (i) $\frac{5}{3}$ (ii) $\frac{2}{3}$ (iii) 2   **5.** $r = \frac{1}{2}$
6. 8, 4, 2, 1 or 24, –12, 6, –3   **7.** $T_1 = \frac{2}{2 + \sqrt{2}}$ or $\frac{2}{2 - \sqrt{2}}$;
$r = \frac{2 \pm \sqrt{2}}{4}$ **8.** (i) 1   (ii) $\frac{1}{3}$ (iii) $\frac{16}{9}$ (iv) $\frac{28}{9}$ (v) $\frac{697}{9}$
(vi) $\frac{904}{900}$ **9.** (i) $\frac{37}{30}$ (ii) $\frac{415}{90}$ (iii) $\frac{736}{90}$ (iv) $\frac{827}{90}$ (v) $\frac{311}{90}$
(vi) $\frac{72}{99}$ **10.** (i) $\frac{826}{99}$ (ii) $\frac{12}{99}$ (iii) $\frac{612}{99}$ (iv) $\frac{342}{99}$ (v) $\frac{65}{99}$
(vi) $\frac{2,931}{990}$ **11.** (i) $|x| > 1$ (ii) $|x| < \frac{1}{2}$
(iii) $-1 - a > x > 1 - 9$ **12.** $S_\infty = \frac{4x}{x^2 - 4x + 9}$
13. (i) $T_1 = \frac{2}{3}$, $T_2 = \left(\frac{2}{3}\right)^2$, $T_3 = \left(\frac{2}{3}\right)^3$, $T_4 = \left(\frac{2}{3}\right)^4$, $T_5 = \left(\frac{2}{3}\right)^5$,
$T_6 = \left(\frac{2}{3}\right)^6$ (ii) Geometric sequence   (iii) Yes   (iv) 0
14. (i) $0 < x < 1$ (ii) $x > \sqrt{6}$ or $x < -\sqrt{6}$

Revision Exercises

1. (i) $2 + 4n$ (ii) 42   (iii) 22nd pattern
(iv) 1,920 matchsticks   **2.** (ii) $T_1 = 5$, $T_2 = 9$, $T_3 = 13$,
$T_4 = 17$, $T_5 = 21$ (iii) Arthmetic   (iv) $4n + 1$ (v) 33
3. (i) 40   (ii) $\frac{1}{4}$ (iii) $\frac{37}{64}$ **4.** (i) 1 7 21 35 35 21
7 1; 1 8 28 56 70 56 28 8 1   (ii) Arithmetic; $T_n = n$
(iii) Quadratic; $T_n = 0.5n^2 + 0.5n$ **5.** (i) –4, –1, 2, 5
(ii) $\frac{n(3n - 11)}{2}$ **7.** (i) (a) 16; (b) 1st diff. = 1, 2, 3;
2nd diff. = 1   (c) $T_n = 0.5n^2 - 0.5n + 16$ (d) 4,966
(ii) (a) 1; (b) 1st diff. = 2, 3, 4; 2nd diff. = 1
(c) $T_n = 0.5n^2 + 0.5n$ (d) 5,050   (iii) (a) 12;
(b) 1st diff. = 2, 3, 4; 2nd diff. = 1
(c) $T_n = 0.5n^2 + 0.5n + 11$ (d) 5,061
(iv) (a) 1; (b) 1st diff. = 5, 9, 13, 17; 2nd diff. = 4
(c) $T_n = 2n^2 - n$ (d) 19,900   (v) (a) 8
(b) 1st diff. = 1, –1, –3; 2nd diff. = –2
(c) $T_n = 5 + 4n - n^2$ (d) $T_{100} = -9,595$
8. (i) $T_1 = 1$, $T_2 = 5$, $T_3 = 25$, $T_4 = 125$, $T_6 = 625$
(ii) 5   (iii) $\frac{1}{4}(5^n - 1)$ (iv) 4.5^{998} **9.** (i) $T_n = (2n - 1) \log_e 3$
(ii) 18 terms   **10.** $\frac{22}{3}$, 9, $\frac{32}{3}$ **11.** (i) $\frac{521}{99}$ (ii) $\frac{8}{9}$ (iii) $\frac{252}{99}$
(iv) $\frac{103}{33}$ **12.** (ii) $a = 2.5$, $b = 4.5$, $c = -6$
13. $P_n = a^n r^{\frac{n^2}{n}}$ **14.** (i) Quadratic   (ii) $T_n = 4n^2 - 3n + 2$
(iii) 3,512   **15.** (i) 2   (ii) $T_1 = a + b + c = 3$;
$T_2 = 4a + 2b + c = 7$; $T_3 = 9a + 3b + c = 13$
(iii) $T_n = n^2 + n + 1$ (iv) 931   **16.** (i) 3
(ii) $\sqrt{3}$ (iii) $\frac{4}{7}$ **17.** (i) $S_n = \frac{4n^2 + 4n}{2}$ (ii) $\sqrt{\frac{2}{3}}$
18. (i) $6\left(1 - \left(\frac{5}{6}\right)^n\right)$ (ii) 6   **19.** (i) $\frac{5n^2 + 5n}{2}$ (ii) $\frac{1}{\sqrt{2}}$

Chapter 10

Exercise 10.1

2. €4,999.95   **3.** €12,244.47   **4.** €4,829.76
5. (i) Year 1: €18,867.92; Year 2: €17,779.93; Year 3:

€16,792.39 (ii) −€1,539.76 (iii) No **6.** As NPV > 0, this is a good proposal **7.** Project A is more profitable **8.** (i) Restaurant area is more profitable (ii) Amusements area is more profitable **9.** Invest, as the NPV > 0 for the project

Exercise 10.2

1. €27,204.19 **2.** €3,104.84 **3.** €137,130.62
4. €16,325.87 **5.** €35,513.69 **6.** €10,429.21
7. €173,830.60 **8.** €130,877.14 **9.** €1,418,299.58
10. €8,821.33 **11.** €1,958.82 **12.** €99,749.07
13. €14,002.66 **14.** €12,000 **15.** (i) €56,044.36
(ii) €58,764.46 **16.** €369,600.48 **17.** €16,177,050
18. €3,934.01 **19.** (i) €18,200 (ii) €231,065.97
(iii) €16,026.40 **20.** The first option will cost less.
21. €9,563.09 **22.** €6,333.85 **23.** 3.09%
24. 3.23% **25.** B (10-year bond) **26.** 3.58%
27. 25.89 years **28.** 3 years **29.** 4 years
30. 7.57 years **31.** 6.07% **32.** 1.13%
33. The 10-year bond offers a higher AER
34. 1.47% **35.** (i) 3 years (ii) The loan for €16,000 was cheaper (iii) 0.63% (iv) No

Exercise 10.3

1. (i) €180,000 (ii) €783,009.38 (iii) €47,494.85
(iv) €19,555.73 (v) €15,372.14 (vi) €14,173.48
(vii) €3,796.88 **2.** (i) €166,000 (ii) 15%
(iii) €109,724.07 (iv) 3.5% (v) €15,372,139.84
(vi) €21,260.22 (vii) 25% **3.** €9,830.40
4. 150,859.81 m^3 **5.** €60,000 **6.** ≈€979,100
7. 5 years **8.** 4 years **9.** (i) €150,663.52
(ii) 5 years (iii) 2003 **10.** The vehicle is not due for a change; it has 1 year of usage remaining.
11. 6 months more **12.** 18% **13.** 24.34%
14. 87.91%

Exercise 10.4

1. €11,265.95 **2.** €6,662.46 **3.** €8,941.42
4. €9,959.35 **5.** €8,488.89 **6.** €5,861.53
7. €43,942.09 **8.** €3,577.36 **9.** €3,968.06
10. (a) €862.74 **11.** Yes **12.** €448.13
13. €3,544.66 **14.** €123.87 **15.** €122,077.73
16. €$\left(\frac{200}{i}\right)$, where i is the annual interest rate (in decimal form) **17.** (i) €11,485.57 (ii) €944.22
18. €226,423.91 **19.** €56.74 (payments made at start of each month) **20.** (a) €19,417.48 (b) €$\left(\frac{20,000}{1.03^t}\right)$
(c) €358,710.84 (d) (i) 0.002466 (ii) €$[P(1.002466)^n]$
(iii) 390.16 (iv) €618.29 **21.** (a) 2nd: A(1.04);
3rd: A(1.04)^2; 4th: A(1.04)^3; 26th: A(1.04)^{25}
(b) A$\left(\frac{1.04^{26}-1}{0.04}\right)$ (c) $485,199
(d) (ii) n^{th} payment: €$\left(\frac{485,199(1.04)^{n-1}}{(1.0478)^{n-1}}\right)$
(iii) $11.5 million (e) 31.3% **22.** (a) 0.0846836%
(b) €333,408.52 (c) ≈€1,968.08

Revision Exercises

1. (i) €194,444.44 (ii) €126,886.57 (iii) €25,215.42
(iv) €304,003.88 (v) €352,897.24 **2.** €12,879.37
3. (a) 1st year: €113,207.55; 2nd year: €106,799.57;
3rd year: €100,754.31 (b) €280,761.43 (c) Yes, as NPV is positive **4.** Project B **5.** (a) €1,632,062.94
(b) €37,514.69 **6.** €190,426.99 **7.** €98,493.84
8. 6.536% **9.** 1.353% **11.** (i) 132,000 (ii) 13%
(iii) 219,448.14 (iv) 3% (v) −18% **12.** €67,704.07
13. €822,800 **14.** 6 years **15.** 10 years
16. €28,164.88 **17.** €21,926.69 **18.** €17,584.58
19. (a) 0.2263% (b) €467.38 **20.** €1,536.42 is a fair price **21.** (i) 2nd: $\frac{A}{(1.025)^1}$; 3rd: $\frac{A}{(1.025)^2}$; last: $\frac{A}{(1.025)^{20}}$
(ii) $\frac{A\left(1-\left(\frac{1}{1.025}\right)^{21}\right)}{\left(1-\frac{1}{1.025}\right)}$ (iii) €6,630.84

Chapter 11

Exercise 11.1

1. (i) 55 (ii) 385 (iii) 2,046 (iv) 20 **2.** (i) 20
(ii) 55 (iii) 873 (iv) 322 **3.** (i) $\sum_{r=1}^{6} r^3$
(ii) $\sum_{r=n}^{r=n+5}$ or $\sum_{r=n}^{n+5}$ or $\sum_{r=1}^{6} 5$ (iii) $\sum_{r=1}^{5} 3^r$
(iv) $\sum_{r=1}^{5} 5^r$ **4.** (i) $\sum_{r=1}^{5} r$ (ii) $\sum_{r=5}^{n} r^2$ (iii) $\sum_{r=3}^{n} r!$ (iv) $\sum_{r=1}^{n} 3r$
6. (i) 7x (ii) x + y (iii) y − x (iv) 3y + 2x

Exercise 11.2

10. (i) f(1) = 1, f(2) = 5 (ii) a = 2, b = 3

Exercise 11.3

3. (i) 14 **4.** (i) 5

Exercise 11.4

6. (iv) 700^2, 3^{700}, 701!

Revision Exercises

1. (i) 180 (ii) 3,528 (iii) 46,230 (iv) 2,058 **2.** (i) 210
(iii) 8,200 **3.** (i) $\sum_{r=1}^{n} 1,000 (1.0575)^r$ (iii) €13,776.12
4. (i) $\sum_{r=1}^{n} 10,000 (1.0425)^r$ (iii) €318,614
8. (i) $\sum_{r=1}^{n} 2,000 (1.0325)^r$ **9.** (i) $u_2 = \frac{5}{2}, u_3 = \frac{5}{3}, u_4 = \frac{5}{4}$
(ii) $u_n = \frac{5}{n}$

Chapter 12

Exercise 12.1

1. (i) 10i (ii) 9i (iii) 5i (iv) 6i (v) 11i (vi) 8i
2. (i) 2√2i (ii) 7√2i (iii) 3√5i (iv) 10√3i (v) 2√3i
(vi) 5√5i **3.** (i) ±3i (ii) ±2i (iii) ±5i (iv) ±7i

(v) $\pm\sqrt{7}i$ (vi) $\pm\sqrt{17}i$ (vii) $\pm\sqrt{14}i$ **4.** (i) $-i$ (ii) -1 (iii) i (iv) 1 (v) i (vi) $-i$

5.

A	i^4	$2i^3$	$i^8 + i^3$	i^{98}	$3(i)^2$	$i^4 - i^8$	$(2i)^7$	$i^4 - i^7$	$(4i)^3$	$5i + 4i$
B	1	$-2i$	$1 - i$	-1	-3	0	$-128i$	$i + 1$	$-64i$	$9i$

6. (i) $\frac{3}{8}$ (ii) $\frac{1}{8}$

Exercise 12.2

3.

$-2 - 2i$	$2 + 4i$	$-2 + 4i$	$-3 - 2i$	$2 + i$	$2 - 2i$	$5i$	$-1 + i$	$-1 + 3i$	$2 - 2i$	$3 + 0i$
T	C	H	A	I	K	O	V	S	K	Y

4. $3 + 4i$, $3 - 4i$, $4 + 5i$, $4 - 5i$, $3 + 5i$, $3 - 5i$, $3 + 0i$, $4 + 0i$, $5 + 0i$, $0 + i$, $0 - i$, $3 + i$ **5.** (i) $\sqrt{5}$ (ii) $2\sqrt{2}$ (iii) $\sqrt{10}$
(iv) $\sqrt{11}$ (v) 3 (vi) 7 (vii) $\sqrt{2}$ (viii) $\sqrt{109}$ (ix) 4 (x) 5 **6.** ± 3 **7.** ± 5 **10.** $1 - \frac{1}{2}i$, $1 + 2i$

Exercise 12.3

1. (i) $5 + i$ (ii) $2 + 4i$ (iii) $-4 - 2i$ (iv) $14 + 17i$
(v) $7 - i$ (vi) $-8 - 3i$ **2.** (i) $5 - 3i$ (ii) $4 + 0i$ (iii) $-2 + 3i$
(iv) $1 - i$ **3.** (i) $1 + i$ (ii) $2 + 2i$; $\dfrac{\text{stretching of factor 2}}{\text{dilation by factor 2}}$

(iii) $3 + 3i$; $\dfrac{\text{stretching of factor 3}}{\text{dilation by factor 3}}$ (iv) $4 + 4i$; $\dfrac{\text{stretching of factor 4}}{\text{dilation by factor 4}}$

(v) $5 + 5i$; $\dfrac{\text{stretching of factor 5}}{\text{dilation by factor 5}}$ **4.** (ii) $-12 + 24i$;
dilation by factor $\frac{1}{2}$ (iii) $-8 + 16i$; dilation by factor $\frac{1}{3}$
(iv) $-6 + 12i$; dilation by factor $\frac{1}{4}$ (v) $-4 + 8i$; dilation
by factor $\frac{1}{6}$ **5.** (ii) $z_1 + w = 3 + 4i$, $z_2 + w = -1 + 6i$,
$z_3 + w = 0 + 5i$ (iv) Translation of distance $\sqrt{2}$ units
in north-east direction. **6.** (ii) $z_1 + w = 4 + i$, $z_2 + w$
$= 0 + 3i$, $z_3 + w = -2 + 4i$ (iv) Translation of distance
$\sqrt{2}$ units in south-east direction.

Exercise 12.4

1. (i) $41 + 11i$ (ii) $-18 + 13i$ (iii) $-15 + 16i$ (iv) 13
(v) 25 (vi) $-12 + 6i$ (vii) 2 (viii) $30 - 5i$ (ix) 8
(x) $9 + 17i$ **2.** (i) $\frac{5}{8} + \frac{5}{8}i$ (ii) $\frac{2}{5}$ (iii) $\frac{37}{1760} - \frac{43}{220i}$ (iv) $\frac{1}{2}$
(v) $\frac{43}{150} + \frac{73}{180}i$ (vi) 7 (vii) 88 (viii) $7 + \sqrt{6}i$
(ix) $15 + 7\sqrt{3}i$ (x) 27 **3.** (i) $-1 + 3i$
(iii) A 90° rotation anti-clockwise about the origin.
4. (i) $-2 - 3i$ (iii) A 90° rotation anti-clockwise about
the origin. **5.** (i) $4 + 3i$ (iii) A 90° rotation clockwise
about the origin. **6.** (i) $-3 + 2i$ (iii) A 90° rotation
clockwise about the origin. **7.** (i) $(1 + 0i)(i) = 0 + i$,
$(1 + 1.5i)(i) = -1.5 + i$, $(1 + 3i)(i) = -3 + i$,
$(2 + 1.5i)(i) = -1.5 + 2i$, $(2.5 + 3i)(i) = -3 + 2.5i$
(iii) A 90° rotation anti-clockwise about the origin.
8. (i) $(1 + 0i)(-i) = 0 - i$, $(1 + 2i)(-i) = 2 - i$,
$(1 + 4i)(-i) = 4 - i$, $(2 + 0i)(-i) = 0 - 2i$,
$(2 + 2i)(-i) = 2 - 2i$, $(2 + 4i)(-i) = 4 - 2i$
(iii) A 90° rotation clockwise about the origin.
9. (i) $)(2i)(1 + 2i) = -4 + 2i$, $(2i)(1 + 1.5i) = -3 + 4i$,
$(2i)(2 + i) = -2 + 4i$, $(2i)(3 + 2i) = -4 + 6i$
(iii) A dilation of factor 2 combined with a 90° rotation
anti-clockwise about the origin. **10.** (i) Blue (ii) Green
(iii) Red: $1 + i$, $1 + 2i$, $2 + i$, $2 + 2i$; Blue: $6 - i$, $6 + 0i$,
$7 - i$, $7 + 0i$; Green: $1 + 6i$, $0 + 6i$, $1 + 7i$, $0 + 7i$

Exercise 12.5

1. (i) $-6 - 9i$ (ii) $-12 - 4i$ (iii) $\frac{1}{5} - \frac{1}{5}i$ (iv) $0 - \frac{11}{4}i$
2. (i) $3 - i$ (ii) $3 - 2i$ (iii) $1 + 3i$ (iv) $1 - 2i$ (v) $2 + i$
3. (i) $1 - 3i$ (ii) $3 + 3i$ (iii) $5 - i$ (iv) $4 - 3i$ (v) $\frac{1}{2} - \frac{1}{2}i$
(vi) $2 - \frac{1}{2}i$ (vii) $-\frac{9}{2} - \frac{1}{2}i$ **4.** (i) $a - bi$ (ii) $c + di$
(iii) $(a + c) + (d - b)i$ (iv) $(a + c) + (b - d)i$
(v) $(a + c) + (d - b)i$ **5.** $-\frac{4}{5} + \frac{3}{5}i$ **7.** (i) $2 - 3i$
(ii) $|z_1| = \sqrt{221}$, $|z_2| = \sqrt{17}$

Exercise 12.6

1. $-2 \pm 3i$ **2.** (i) $-3 - 4i$ (ii) $-2 + 4i$ **3.** $1 \pm 3i$
4. $4 \pm i$ **5.** $-3 \pm 4i$ **6.** (i) $48 - 14i$ (ii) $-98 + 14i$
7. $6 \pm 2i$ **8.** $-5 \pm 3i$ **9.** (i) $1 \pm i$ (ii) $4 \pm 3i$ (iii) $-1 \pm 4i$
(iv) $-2 \pm 6i$ **10.** (i) $\pm 4i$ (ii) $\frac{3}{2} \pm 2i$ (iii) $\frac{1}{3} \pm \frac{2}{3}i$
(iv) $4 \pm 3i$ **11.** (i) $3 + 2i$ (iii) $3 - 2i$

Exercise 12.7

1. (ii) $5 - i$ **2.** (ii) $-3 + 4i$ **3.** (ii) $-1 - i$ **5.** (i) $n = 3$
(ii) $1 + 3i$ **6.** (i) $k = 39$ (ii) $2 - 3i$ **7.** (i) $a = 2, b = -10$
(ii) $z - 2$ (iii) $k = 10$ (iv) $z - 2$ (v) $-1 \pm 2i$ **8.** (i) 20
(iii) $z^2 + 4z + 5$ (iv) $z = 4, -2 + i, -2 - i$ **9.** (i) $z = -1$
or $z = 3$ (iii) $z = \pm i$ **11.** (i) $z_1 = 1 + \sqrt{3}i$ or
$z_2 = 1 - \sqrt{3}i$ (iii) $x^3 - 4x^2 - 4x + 16 = 0$
12. (i) 4 (ii) $-4, -2, 1$ (iii) The fourth root occurs
between -2 and -1. (iv) $z = -1.5$ **13.** (ii) $1 \pm 2\sqrt{6}i$
(iii) 25 (iv) $z^2 - 8z + 400 = 0$ **14.** (i) z_1 is also a root.
(ii) 3 (iii) 64 (iv) $z^2 + 3z + 64 = 0$
15. (i) z_1 is also a root. (ii) $z = 2 \pm 2\sqrt{15}i$, $z_1 + \overline{z}_1 = 4$
(iii) 64 (iv) $z^2 - z + 4 = 0$ **16.** (i) $b_1 = 1, b_2 = -2, b_0 = 2$
(ii) $a_2 = -7, a_1 = 12, a_0 = -10$

Exercise 12.8

1. (i) $2\sqrt{2}\left(\cos\frac{\pi}{4} + i\sin\frac{\pi}{4}\right)$ (ii) $2\left(\cos\frac{\pi}{3} + i\sin\frac{\pi}{3}\right)$
(iii) $\sqrt{2}\left(\cos\frac{3\pi}{4} + i\sin\frac{3\pi}{4}\right)$ (iv) $4\left(\cos\frac{11\pi}{6} + i\sin\frac{11\pi}{6}\right)$
(v) $5\left(\cos\frac{\pi}{2} + i\sin\frac{\pi}{2}\right)$ (vi) $2(\cos\pi + i\sin\pi)$
(vii) $3(\cos 0 + i\sin 0)$ (viii) $1\left(\cos\frac{3\pi}{2} + i\sin\frac{3\pi}{2}\right)$
(ix) $\sqrt{2}\left(\cos\frac{5\pi}{4} + i\sin\frac{5\pi}{4}\right)$ (x) $4\sqrt{3}\left(\cos\frac{7\pi}{6} + i\sin\frac{7\pi}{6}\right)$
(xi) $4\left(\cos\frac{3\pi}{4} + i\sin\frac{3\pi}{4}\right)$ (xii) $2\sqrt{3}\left(\cos\frac{11\pi}{6} + i\sin\frac{11\pi}{6}\right)$
2. (i) $4 + 4i$ (ii) $-3 + 0i$ (iii) $0 + 2i$ (iv) $\sqrt{3} - i$

(v) $-100 + 0i$ **3.** (i) $\frac{3\pi}{4}$ (ii) $-\frac{3\pi}{4}$ (iii) $-\frac{5\pi}{4}$

5. (i) $6\left(\cos\frac{5}{24} + i\sin\frac{5}{24}\right)$ (ii) $50\left(\cos\frac{3\pi}{10} + i\sin\frac{3\pi}{10}\right)$

(iii) $3\left(\cos\frac{\pi}{16} + i\sin\frac{\pi}{16}\right)$ (iv) $3\left(\cos\frac{\pi}{14} + i\sin\frac{\pi}{14}\right)$

6. (ii) $-2\sqrt{3} + 2i$ **7.** (i) $\frac{23\sqrt{3} - 14}{2} + \left(\frac{-23 + 14\sqrt{3}}{2}\right)i$

(iii) $\arg(z) = \frac{2\pi}{3}$, $|z| = 1$ (iv) $\cos\frac{2\pi}{3} + i\sin\frac{2\pi}{3}$

9. (i) $1\left(\cos\frac{\pi}{4} + i\sin\frac{\pi}{4}\right)$ (ii) $1\left(\cos\frac{3\pi}{4} + i\sin\frac{3\pi}{4}\right)$

(iii) $a = \frac{-1}{\sqrt{2}}$, $b = \frac{-1}{\sqrt{2}}$

Exercise 12.9

1. (i) $\frac{1}{\sqrt{2}} + \frac{1}{\sqrt{2}}i$ (ii) $\frac{1}{\sqrt{2}} + \frac{1}{\sqrt{2}}i$ (iii) $\frac{1}{2} + \frac{\sqrt{3}}{2}i$ (iv) $1 + 0i$

(v) $15{,}625 + 0i$ (vi) $-4 + 0i$ (vii) $-\frac{81}{2} + \frac{81\sqrt{3}}{2}i$

(viii) $\frac{1}{2} - \frac{\sqrt{3}}{2}i$ **2.** (i) $\frac{\pi}{6}$ (ii) 2 (iii) $2\left(\cos\frac{\pi}{6} + i\sin\frac{\pi}{6}\right)$

(iv) $512 - 512\sqrt{3}i$ **3.** (ii) $\arg(z) = \frac{7\pi}{4}$, $|z| = \sqrt{2}$

(iii) $\sqrt{2}\left(\cos\frac{7\pi}{4} + i\sin\frac{7\pi}{4}\right)$ (iv) $16\sqrt{2}\left(\cos\frac{7\pi}{4} + i\sin\frac{7\pi}{4}\right)$

4. (i) $\frac{3\pi}{4}$ (ii) $\sqrt{2}$ (iii) $\sqrt{2}\left(\cos\frac{3\pi}{4} + i\sin\frac{3\pi}{4}\right)$

(iv) $z^5 = 4\sqrt{2}\left(\cos\frac{7\pi}{4} + i\sin\frac{7\pi}{4}\right)$,

$z^9 = 16\sqrt{2}\left(\cos\frac{3\pi}{4} + i\sin\frac{3\pi}{4}\right)$ **5.** (i) $4{,}096 + 0i$

(ii) $256 + 0i$ (iii) $\frac{1}{2} + \frac{\sqrt{3}}{2}i$ (iv) $-\frac{1}{\sqrt{2}} + \frac{1}{\sqrt{2}}i$ (v) $1 + 0i$

(vi) $-1 + 0i$ (vii) $-8{,}192 + 8{,}192i$ (viii) $64 - 64i$

6. (i) $\arg(z) = \frac{\pi}{4}$, $|z| = 1$ (iii) $\cos\frac{\pi}{4} + i\sin\frac{\pi}{4}$ (iv) $0 - i$

(v) $n = 8$ **7.** (i) $\alpha = 3\theta$ (ii) $\alpha = 3$ (iv) Period $= \frac{2\pi}{3}$,

Range $= [-1, 1]$ **8.** (i) $B = 4A$ (ii) $m = 4$

(iv) $A = \frac{\pi}{8} + \frac{n\pi}{4}$, $n \in Z$

Exercise 12.10

1. (ii) 2 (iii) $2\left[\cos\left(\frac{5\pi}{3} + 2n\pi\right) + i\sin\left(\frac{5\pi}{3} + 2n\pi\right)\right]$

(iv) Two (v) $n = 0$: $z = \frac{\sqrt{6}}{2} - \frac{\sqrt{2}}{2}i$; $n = 1$: $z = \frac{-\sqrt{6}}{2} + \frac{\sqrt{2}}{2}i$

2. (i) $n = 0$: $z = \sqrt{2} + \sqrt{2}i$; $n = 1$: $z = -\sqrt{2} - \sqrt{2}\,i$

(ii) $n = 0$: $z = -\frac{\sqrt{2}}{2} - \frac{\sqrt{6}}{2}i$; $n = 1$: $z = \frac{\sqrt{2}}{2} - \frac{\sqrt{6}}{2}i$

(iii) $n = 0$: $z = \frac{\sqrt{6}}{2} + \frac{\sqrt{2}}{2}i$; $n = 1$: $z = -\frac{\sqrt{6}}{2} - \frac{\sqrt{2}}{2}i$

(iv) $n = 0$: $z = -\frac{\sqrt{3}}{2} - \frac{1}{2}i$; $n = 1$: $z = \frac{\sqrt{3}}{2} - \frac{1}{2}i$

(v) $n = 0$: $z = 2$; $n = 1$: $z = -1 + \sqrt{3}i$; $n = 2$:

$z = -1 - \sqrt{3}i$ (vi) $n = 0$: $z = \frac{1}{2} + \frac{\sqrt{3}}{2}i$; $n = 1$:

$z = -1 + 0i$; $n = 2$: $z = \frac{1}{2} - \frac{\sqrt{3}}{2}i$ (vii) $n = 0$:

$\sqrt{2}\left(\frac{\sqrt{3}}{2} - \frac{1}{2}i\right)$; $n = 1$: $\sqrt{2}\left(\frac{1}{2} + \frac{\sqrt{3}}{2}i\right) n = 2$: $\sqrt{2}\left(-\frac{\sqrt{3}}{2} + \frac{1}{2}i\right)$;

$n = 3$: $\sqrt{2}\left(-\frac{1}{2} - \frac{\sqrt{3}}{2}i\right)$ (viii) $n = 0$: $z = 0 + 4i$;

$n = 1$: $z = -2\sqrt{3} - 2i$; $n = 2$: $z = 2\sqrt{3} - 2i$

3. (i) $\alpha = 64\left[\cos\left(-\frac{\pi}{2} + 2n\pi\right) w+ i\sin\left(-\frac{\pi}{2} + 2n\pi\right)\right]$

(ii) $n = 0$: $z_1 = 2\left(\cos\frac{\pi}{12} + i\sin\frac{\pi}{12}\right)$;

$n = 1$: $z_2 = 2\left(\cos\frac{\pi}{4} + i\sin\frac{\pi}{4}\right)$;

$n = 2$: $z_3 = 2\left(\cos\frac{7\pi}{12} + i\sin\frac{7\pi}{12}\right)$;

$n = 3$: $z_4 = 2\left(\cos\frac{11\pi}{12} + i\sin\frac{11\pi}{12}\right)$;

$n = 4$: $z_5 = 2\left(\cos\frac{5\pi}{4} + i\sin\frac{5\pi}{4}\right)$;

$n = 5$: $z_6 = 2\left(\cos\frac{19\pi}{12} + i\sin\frac{19\pi}{12}\right)$

(iv) $30°$ (v) Hexagon **4.** (ii) $z_2 = -1 + \sqrt{3}i$, $z_3 = -1 - \sqrt{3}i$

5. (i) $2^{\frac{1}{4}}$ (ii) $z_2 = 2^{\frac{1}{4}}\left(\cos\frac{7\pi}{12} + i\sin\frac{7\pi}{12}\right)$,

$z_3 = 2^{\frac{1}{4}}\left(\cos\frac{13\pi}{12} + i\sin\frac{13\pi}{12}\right)$, $z_4 = 2^{\frac{1}{4}}\left(\cos\frac{19\pi}{12} + i\sin\frac{19\pi}{12}\right)$.

By rotation of preceding root 90° anti-clockwise about

the origin. **6.** (ii) $z_2 = 1 - \sqrt{3}i$, $z_3 = 1 + \sqrt{3}i$

7. (iii) Three **8.** $(z - 1)(z - z_2)(z - z_3)(z - z_4)(z - z_5)$

Revision Exercises

1. (a) (i) $12i$ (ii) i (iii) $-i$ (b) (i) $17 - i$ (ii) $10 + 3i$

(iii) $\frac{13}{5} - \frac{9}{5}i$ **2.** (ii) $z_1 + \theta = 3 + 2i$, $z_2 + \theta = -2 + 3i$,

$z_3 + \theta = -4 + 3i$ (iv) A translation of $\sqrt{2}$ units in

length in the direction of north-west. **3.** (i) $\frac{11}{37} - \frac{8}{37}i$

(ii) $|z_1| = \sqrt{5}$, $|z_2| = \sqrt{37}$ **4.** (a) (i) $z^2 = 0 + 2i$,

$z^3 = -2 + 2i$ (b) $z^4 = -4$, $z^8 = 16$, $z^{12} = -64$, $z^{16} = 256$

(c) Positive (d) 2^{20} (e) $2^{20} + 2^{20}i$ (f) $2^{20.5}$

5. (ii) $-1 + \sqrt{3}i$ or $-1 - \sqrt{3}i$ (iii) $2\left(\cos\frac{2\pi}{3} + i\sin\frac{2\pi}{3}\right)$ or

$2\left(\cos\frac{4\pi}{3} + i\sin\frac{4\pi}{3}\right)$ **6.** (i) $z = 7$ (ii) $z - 7$

(iii) $z^2 + 4z + 5$ (iv) $-2 \pm i$ **7.** (i) $z_2 = -5 + 4i$

(iii) A 90° clockwise rotation about the origin.

9. (ii) 2 (iii) 44 (iv) $z^2 - z + 11 = 0$ **10.** (i) i

11. (i) $z_1^2 = 16 - 30i$, $10z_1 = -50 + 30i$ (ii) z_1

(iii) $-5 - 3i$ (iv) $z^3 + 12z^2 + 54z + 68 = 0$

12. (i) $\frac{\pi}{3}$ (ii) $\frac{2}{\sqrt{3}}$ (iii) $\frac{2}{\sqrt{3}}\left(\cos\frac{\pi}{3} + i\sin\frac{\pi}{3}\right)$

(iv) $-\frac{1}{2}\left(\frac{4}{3}\right)^{10} + \frac{\sqrt{3}}{2}\left(\frac{4}{3}\right)^{10}.i$ **13.** (i) $n = 0$: $z = 2 + 2\sqrt{3}i$;

$n = 1$: $z = -4$; $n = 2$: $z = 2 - 2\sqrt{3}i$ (ii) $2 + i$ or $2 - 3i$

14. (i) $\beta = 32\left(\cos\left(\frac{\pi}{4} + 2n\pi\right) + i\sin\left(\frac{\pi}{4} + 2n\pi\right)\right)$

(ii) $n = 0$: $z_1 = 2\left(\cos\frac{\pi}{20} + i\sin\frac{\pi}{20}\right)$;

$n = 1$: $z_2 = 2\left(\cos\frac{9\pi}{20} + i\sin\frac{9\pi}{20}\right)$;

$n = 2$: $z_3 = 2\left(\cos\frac{17\pi}{20} + i\sin\frac{17\pi}{20}\right)$;

$n = 3$: $z_4 = 2\left(\cos\frac{5\pi}{4} + i\sin\frac{5\pi}{4}\right)$;

$n = 4$: $z_5 = 2\left(\cos\frac{33\pi}{20} + i\sin\frac{33\pi}{20}\right)$ (iv) $72°$

(v) The shape formed is a pentagon.

15. (a)(i) $2\left(\cos\frac{2\pi}{3} + i\sin\frac{2\pi}{3}\right)$ (ii) $n = 0$:

$z = \frac{\sqrt{2}}{2} + \frac{\sqrt{6}}{2}i$; $n = 1$: $z = -\frac{\sqrt{2}}{2} - \frac{\sqrt{6}}{2}i$ (b) (ii) $k = \frac{1}{2}$

16. (a) (i) $\sqrt{2}\left(\cos\frac{7\pi}{4} + i\sin\frac{7\pi}{4}\right)$ (ii) $16 - 16i$ (b) (ii) $\frac{5\pi}{6}$

Chapter 13

Exercise 13.1

1. (i) 2 (ii) 2 **2.** (i) 3 (ii) Does not exist **3.** (i) 4

(ii) Does not exist **4.** (i) 7 (ii) 25 (iii) 8 (iv) 0 (v) 12

5. (i) $\frac{4}{3}$ (ii) $\frac{6}{7}$ (iii) $\frac{2}{15}$ (iv) $\frac{2}{5}$ (v) $\frac{3}{4}$ **6.** (i) 5; continuous

(ii) -3; continuous (iii) $\frac{3}{0}$; not continuous

(iv) $\frac{0}{0}$; not continuous (v) $\frac{9}{0}$; not continuous

7. (i) 1 (ii) 1

Exercise 13.2

1. (ii) $f'(x) = 3$ (iii) $f(x)$ is a linear function so has a constant slope. 2. (ii) –6 3. (i) $6x$ (ii) 6 (iii) $y = 6x – 3$
4. (i) $2x + 2$ (ii) 6 (iii) $y = 6x – 4$ 5. (i) $3 – 2x$ (ii) 1
(iii) $x – y + 3 = 0$ 8. (i) $6 – 4x$ (ii) $(–2,–19)$

Exercise 13.3

1. (i) $8x + 2$ (ii) $12x^{11} + 9$ (iii) $9x^2 + 8x – 3$ (iv) 3 (v) –2
(vi) –1 (vii) 0 (viii) 0 (ix) 0 2. (i) $2x – 2$ (ii) 198
3. (i) $3x^2 – 2x$ (ii) 85 4. (i) $2 – 4x$ (ii) –6
(iii) $y = –6x + 13$ (iv) $(0,13)$ 5. (i) $3x^2 + 10x + 5$
(ii) 5 (iii) $y = 5x + 1$ (iv) x-axis: $\left(–\frac{1}{5},0\right)$; y-axis: $(0,1)$
(v) $\frac{1}{10}$ units^2 6. (i) $2 + 6x – 3x^2$ (ii) 2 (iii) $y = 2x + 1$
(iv) x-axis: $\left(–\frac{1}{2},0\right)$; y-axis: $(0,1)$ (v) $\frac{1}{4}$ units^2 8. $(3,2)$
9. (i) $x^{\frac{1}{3}}$ and $\frac{1}{3x^{2/3}}$ (ii) x^{-1} and $-\frac{1}{x^2}$ (iii) $2x^{-\frac{1}{2}}$ and $-\frac{1}{x^{3/2}}$
(iv) $5x^{-3}$ and $-\frac{15}{x^4}$ (v) $x^{\frac{3}{2}}$ and $\frac{3\sqrt{x}}{2}$ (vi) $-3x^{-\frac{5}{2}}$ and $\frac{15}{2x^{7/2}}$
10. (i) $3 + x$ (ii) $\frac{3\sqrt{x}}{2} + \frac{1}{2\sqrt{x}}$ (iii) $-\frac{2}{3x^{5/3}} - \frac{1}{2x^{3/2}}$
(iv) $\frac{2}{3x^{1/3}} - \frac{1}{3x^{4/3}}$ 11. (i) 1 (ii) $2x + 1$ (iii) $2x – 1$
(iv) $3x^2 + 4x + 4$ 12. $a = 3, b = –4$
13. $c = 4, d = -\frac{1}{2}$ 14. (i) $\frac{3}{2\sqrt{x}} + \frac{2}{x^3}$ (ii) $-\frac{2}{x^3} + \frac{3}{x^4} - \frac{4}{x^5}$
(iii) $-\frac{1}{x^{3/2}} + \frac{1}{3x^{4/3}}$ (iv) $-\frac{15}{x^4} + \frac{1}{2\sqrt{x}}$ (v) $3\sqrt{x}$ (vi) $\frac{1}{\sqrt{x}} + 2x$

Exercise 13.4

1. (i) $9(3x + 1)^2$ (ii) $6x(x^2 + 7)^2$ (iii) $(6x^2 – 12x)(x^3 – 3x^2 + 2)$
(iv) $24(8x + 3)^2$ (v) $6x^2(x^3 – 25)$ 2. (i) $6(3x + 1)$
(ii) $–4(3 – x)^3$ (iii) $20(4x – 5)^4$ (iv) $6x(x^2 + 1)^2$
(v) $21(2 + 3x)^6$ 3. (i) $–18(2 – 6x)^2$ (ii) $\frac{4x^3}{\sqrt{2x^4 – 5}}$
(iii) $-\frac{2x}{(x^2 + 3)^2}$ (iv) $\frac{6x^2}{\sqrt{4x^3 – 5}}$ (v) $-\frac{1 + 14\sqrt{x}}{4\sqrt{x}(\sqrt{x} + 7x)^{3/2}}$
4. (i) $\frac{6x}{(8 – x^2)^{3/2}}$ (ii) $\frac{3x^2 + 6}{(x^2 + 6x)^{4/3}}$ (iii) $\frac{3x}{2(2 + x^2)^{1/4}}$ (iv) $\frac{6x}{(4 – x^2)^4}$
(v) $-\frac{7x^6}{2(x^7 – 6)^{3/2}}$ 5. (i) $-\frac{1}{8\sqrt{x}(6 – \sqrt{x})^{3/4}}$ (ii) $-\frac{1}{2x^2\sqrt{1 + \frac{1}{x}}}$
(iii) $\frac{2(x^4 – 1)}{3x^3\left(x^2 + \frac{1}{x^2}\right)^{2/3}}$ (iv) $-\frac{x + 2}{2x^2\sqrt{x + 1}}$ (v) $\frac{4x – 3}{\sqrt{4x^2 – 6x + 9}}$
6. (i) 2 (ii) $y = 2x – 1$ (iii) $\frac{1}{4}$ units^2 7. (i) $y = –10x + 11$
(ii) 1 (iii) $y = –10x + 1$ (iv) $\frac{10\sqrt{101}}{101}$ units (v) 6 units^2
8. (ii) –1.5 (iii) $\frac{2x + 3}{2\sqrt{x^2 + 3x}}$ (iv) $y = \frac{5}{4}x + \frac{3}{4}$ 9. –0.32
10. $\frac{25}{4}$

Exercise 13.5

1. (i) $15x^{14}$ (ii) $15x^{14}$ (iii) $24x – 7$ (iv) $2x$ (v) $5x^4 + 10x$
2. (i) $10x^{\frac{3}{2}} + 6x$ (ii) $\frac{35}{2}x^{\frac{5}{2}} + 9x^2$ (iii) $18x^2 – 10x + 4$
(iv) $\frac{9}{2}x^{\frac{1}{2}} + x^{-\frac{1}{2}} + 7$ (v) $3x^{\frac{1}{2}} + \frac{17}{2}x^{-\frac{1}{2}} + 11$ 3. (i) $6x^5$
(ii) 1 (iii) $12x^3 + 1$ (iv) 1 (v) $2x – 3$ (vi) $15x^4 – 1$
4. (i) $30x + 11$ (ii) $15x^2 – 4x – 5$ (iii) $–4x^3 – 15x^2 – 4x + 5$
(iv) $3\sqrt{x} + \frac{2}{\sqrt{x}}$ (v) $48x^3 + 3x^2 + 22x + 17$
5. (i) $-\frac{1}{(7x + 2)^2}$ (ii) $-\frac{13}{(9x + 1)^2}$ (iii) $\frac{1 – x^2}{(x^2 + 1)^2}$
(iv) $-\frac{2(x^2 + x + 5)}{(x^2 – 5)^2}$ (v) $-\frac{1}{(x + 2)^2}$ 6. $-\frac{7}{9}$
7. (i) $40x^3 – 21x^2 – 26x + 13$ (ii) 5.8125
(iii) $y = 5.8125x – 2.0859375$ 8. (i) 5 (ii) 5 (iii) $y = 5x$

9. (i) $\frac{3}{2}\left(\sqrt{x} + \frac{1}{\sqrt{x}}\right)$ (ii) $\frac{x^{5/2} + 9x^{3/2} + 3\sqrt{x} + \frac{3}{\sqrt{x}}}{2x(x + 3)^2}$ (iii) $\frac{1}{2}$
10. (i) $15x^4 – 68x^3 + 93x^2 – 42x$ (ii) $\frac{3}{8}$
11. (i) $(90x^2 – 20x)(3x^3 – x^2)^9$ (ii) $-\frac{84x^4 + 18x^3 – 360x^2 + 80x}{(3x^3 – x^2)^{11}}$
12. (i) –1 (ii) 1 (iii) –1.6875

Exercise 13.6

1. (i) $\cos x – \sin x$ (ii) $–3 \sin \theta$ (iii) $\cos \theta$ (iv) $4 \cos \theta$
(v) $–2 \sin x – 3 \cos x$ 2. (i) 0 (ii) 1 (iii) 0 (iv) $–\sqrt{2}$ (v) 1
3. $y = –\theta + \left(3 + \frac{\pi}{2}\right)$ 4. (i) $2[\cos x – x \sin x]$
(ii) $x(x \cos x + 2 \sin x)$ (iii) $x \sec^2 x + \tan x$
(iv) $\frac{\sin x – x \cos x}{\sin^2 x}$ (v) $\frac{4(\cos x + x \sin x)}{\cos^2 x}$ 5. (i) $5 \cos(5x)$
(ii) $–9 \sin(3x)$ (iii) $35 \sec^2(5x)$ (iv) $6 \cos(3x) – 10 \sin(2x)$
(v) $2 \sec^2(2x) + 3 \sec^2(3x)$ 6. (i) $2 \sin x \cos x$
(ii) $2 \tan x \sec^2 x$ (iii) $–15 \cos^2(5x) \sin(5x)$
(iv) $2 \sin 4x – 3 \sin 6x$
(v) $12 \tan^3(3x) \sec^2(3x) + 20 \tan^4(4x) \sec^2(4x)$
7. (i) $\cos x – x \sin x$ (ii) $y = \left(\frac{3\pi}{2}\right)x – \left(\frac{3\pi}{2}\right)^2$
8. (i) $\sec x \tan x$ (ii) $\sec^2 x$ (iii) $–\text{cosec}^2 x$ 9. (i) $\cos 2x$
(ii) $y = -\frac{1}{\sqrt{2}}x + \frac{1}{\sqrt{2}}\left(\frac{11\pi}{8} + \frac{1}{2}\right)$
(iii) $y = \frac{1}{2\sqrt{2}}\left(1 – \frac{11\pi}{4}\right)x + \frac{(11\pi)^2}{24\sqrt{2}}$
10. (i) $\frac{\cos x + \sin x – \sin x \sec^2x}{(1 + \tan x)^2}$ (ii) $y = x$
11. (i) $y = (\pi – 1)x – \pi(\pi – 1) + 1$ 12. $\sqrt{2}\left(\frac{3\pi}{4} + 1\right)$
13. (i) $\cos 3\theta + 3\cos \theta$ (ii) $a = 4, b = 3$
14. (i) $\frac{2 \cos t}{(1 – \sin t)^2}$ (ii) $\frac{2\left(1 – \tan^4 \frac{t}{2}\right)}{\left(\tan \frac{t}{2} – 1\right)^4}$ 15. $\cos(2\theta)$ 16. $t + t^3$

Exercise 13.7

1. (i) $\frac{1}{\sqrt{9 – x^2}}$ (ii) $-\frac{1}{\sqrt{16 – x^2}}$ (iii) $\frac{5}{25 + x^2}$
(iv) $\frac{1}{\sqrt{49 – x^2}} + \frac{1}{\sqrt{81 – x^2}}$ (v) $\frac{1}{\sqrt{64 – x^2}} – \frac{1}{\sqrt{121 – x^2}}$
2. (i) $\frac{x}{\sqrt{1 – x^2}} + \sin^{-1} x$ (ii) $-\frac{x + 4}{\sqrt{9 – x^2}} + \cos^{-1} \frac{x}{3}$
(iii) $\frac{4(x^3 + 1)}{x(16 + x^2)} + \frac{2x^3 – 1}{x^2} \cdot \tan^{-1} \frac{x}{4}$ (iv) $\frac{1}{x\sqrt{4 – x^2}} – \frac{1}{x^2} \cdot \sin^{-1} \frac{x}{2}$
3. (i) $\frac{1}{x^2\sqrt{1 – x^2}} – \frac{2\sin^{-1} x}{x^3}$ (ii) $-\frac{1}{(x – 1)\sqrt{4 – x^2}} – \frac{\cos^{-1} \frac{x}{2}}{(x – 1)^2}$
(iii) $\frac{1}{(x^4 – 1)(1 + x^2)} – \frac{4x^3 \tan^{-1} x}{(x^4 – 1)^2}$
(iv) $\frac{1}{(x^2 + 1)\sqrt{9 – x^2}} – \frac{2x \cos^{-1} \frac{x}{3}}{(x^2 + 1)^2}$ 4. (i) $\frac{2}{\sqrt{1 – 4x^2}}$ (ii) $\frac{2x}{\sqrt{1 – x^4}}$
(iii) $\frac{2}{1 + (2x – \pi)^2}$ (iv) $\frac{5}{\sqrt{1 – \left(5x + \frac{\pi}{2}\right)^2}}$ 5. (i) $\frac{4\sqrt{455}}{455}$ (ii) $\frac{75}{34}$
(iii) $-\frac{8\sqrt{7}}{7}$ (iv) $-\frac{3\sqrt{5}}{10}$ 6. (i) $\frac{1}{\sqrt{x}(1 + x)}$ (ii) $y = \frac{1}{2}x – \frac{1}{2}(1 – \pi)$
7. $y = \frac{\pi}{4}$ 9. (i) $F(x) = \tan^{-1}\left(\frac{1 + x}{1 – x}\right)$ (ii) $\frac{2}{(1 – x)^2}$ (iii) $\frac{1}{1 + x^2}$
10. (ii) $\frac{1}{x\sqrt{x^2 – 1}}$ (iii) $-\frac{1}{x^2\sqrt{x^2 – 1}} – \frac{1}{x^2} \sin^{-1} \frac{1}{x}$
11. (i) $\tan^{-1} \frac{x}{1 + x}$ (ii) $\frac{1}{(1 + x)^2}$ 12. (i) $f'(x) = \frac{2}{4 + x^2}$;
$g'(x) = -\frac{2}{4 + x^2}$ (iii) $\frac{\pi}{2}$

Exercise 13.8

1. (i) $2e^{2x}$ (ii) $5e^{5x}$ (iii) $4e^{4x}$ (iv) $–2e^{–2x}$ (v) $–e^{\cos x} \sin x$
(vi) $5e^{5x- 4}$ (vii) $2(x + 1)e^{(x + 1)^2}$ (viii) $\sec^2 x \, e^{\tan x}$
2. (i) $\frac{3}{3x + 2}$ (ii) $\frac{2x}{x^2 – 8}$ (iii) $\frac{4}{4x – 5}$ (iv) $\cot x$ (v) $\frac{4x^3}{x^4 – 5}$

(vi) $\frac{2}{x-1}$ (vii) $\frac{2}{\sin 2x}$ (viii) $-\frac{4}{1-4x}$ (ix) $-\frac{3x^2}{3-x^3}$ (x) $\frac{1}{x}$

3. (i) $1 + \ln x$ (ii) $e^{2x}(1 + 2x)$ (iii) $x^2(1 + 3 \ln x)$

(iv) $x(x + 2)e^x$ (v) $x^3(3x + 4)e^{3x}$ (vi) $3x^2$ **4.** (i) $\frac{(2x - 1)e^{2x}}{x^2}$

(ii) $\frac{2(1 - x \ln x)}{xe^x}$ (iii) $\frac{e^x - 3e^{2x}}{e^x + 1}$ (iv) 0 (v) $\frac{e^{x^2}(2x^2 - 3)}{x^4}$

(vi) $\frac{1 - x}{e^x}$ **5.** (i) $-\frac{1}{x}$ (ii) $\frac{1}{5x}$ (iii) $\frac{9}{3x + 9}$ (iv) $\frac{3}{3x + 2} - \frac{2}{2x - 3}$

(v) $\frac{5}{2(5x + 2)}$ (vi) 5 **6.** (i) $3^x \ln 3$ (ii) $2^x \ln 8$ (iii) $\frac{4^x \ln 4}{8}$

(iv) $\frac{5^x \ln 5}{2}$ (v) $\left(\frac{7}{8}\right)^x \ln\left(\frac{7}{8}\right)$ (vi) $15^x \ln 15$ **7.** (i) $\frac{108}{155}$ (ii) 0

(iii) 0 (iv) 3 (v) $-\frac{1}{e}$ (vi) 2 **8.** $\frac{2}{x(x^2 + 1)}$

Revision Exercises

1. (i) 6 (ii) 4 (iii) Limit does not exist   **2.** (i) 42 (ii) $\frac{1}{5}$

(iii) 6 (iv) -3 **3.** (i) $2x - 3$ (ii) 1 (iii) $y = x - 4$

4. (i) $-2x$ (ii) $y = -4x + 5$ **5.** (i) 2 (ii) $-6x$ (iii) $2x$

(iv) $2 - 2x$ **6.** (i) $4x + 12$ (ii) $30x + 10$ (iii) $4x^3 - 19$

(iv) $21x^6 - 24x - 4$ (v) $12x^2$ **7.** (i) $3x^2 - 3$ (ii) 3.75

(iii) $y = 3.75x - 4.75$ (iv) x-axis: $(1.26,0)$; y-axis: $(0,-4.75)$

(v) 3.0083 units^2 **8.** $y = 5.75x - 25$ **9.** (i) $24x + 18$

(ii) $\frac{9}{(5x + 2)^2}$ (iii) $\frac{21(x - 4)^2}{(x + 3)^4}$ (iv) $9x^2 - 4x - 15$

10. (i) $\frac{5}{(8x + 1)^2}$ (ii) $-24x^3 + 36x^2 + 58x - 6$

(iii) $-\frac{2(x^2 + 1)}{(x^2 - 1)^2}$ (iv) $-\frac{12(x + 5)^{11}(x^2 + 10x - 3)}{(x^3 + 3)^{13}}$

(v) $\frac{-3x^2 + 2x + 15}{(x^2 + 15)^2}$ **11.** (i) $2x(2 \cos x - x \sin x)$

(ii) $2x \sin x + (x^2 + 1)(\cos x)$ (iii) $\frac{\cos x + x \sin x}{\cos^2 x}$

(iv) $2 \cos 2x$ **12.** (i) 0 (ii) 0 (iii) 0 (iv) 0

13. (i) $\frac{9\sqrt{x}}{2} - \frac{11}{2\sqrt{x}}$ (ii) $-\frac{2}{(2x - 3)^2}$ (iii) $\frac{2t - 1}{5(t^2 - t + 1)^{4/5}}$

(iv) $\frac{2}{(x^2 + 1)^{3/2}}$ **14.** (i) 4 (ii) $-\frac{5}{e}$ (iii) $-\frac{1}{e^3}$ (iv) 4 (v) 0

15. (i) $f =$ blue graph; $f' =$ red graph   (ii) $4e^{4x}$ (iii) $e^{4x} + 9$

16. (i) $\frac{3}{3x + 1} - \frac{2}{2x - 5}$ (ii) $\frac{17}{12}$ **17.** (i) 0.1482 (ii) 8

(iii) -1.5271 (iv) -0.05 **18.** (i) $2x^{\frac{3}{2}} - x$

(ii) $15x^4 - 4x + 3\sqrt{x} - 1$ **19.** (i) $\frac{2}{1 + \cos 2\theta}$

20. (ii) $\sqrt{13} \cos(3x + \alpha)$ (iii) $\sqrt{13} e^{2x} \cos(3x + \alpha)$

(iv) $x = \frac{1}{3}\left(\frac{\pi}{2} - \alpha + 2n\pi\right)$ or $x = \frac{1}{6}(3\pi - 2\alpha + 4n\pi)$, where n is an integer.

Chapter 14

Exercise 14.1

1. (i) 4 (ii) $36x^2$ (iii) $810x^8 - 756x^5 + 12x^2$

(iv) $276x^2 - 1092x - 32$ (v) $-\frac{6(4 - 9x^2)}{(3x^2 + 4)^3}$ **2.** (i) $-\sin t$

(ii) $-\frac{4x}{(4 + x^2)^2}$ (iii) $\frac{4\pi}{3}$ (iv) $-\frac{1}{t^2}$ (v) $2e^x \cos x$ **7.** $m = -3$

8. $k = \frac{\ln 32}{60}$ **9.** (i) Velocity is the rate of change of displacement with respect to time.   (ii) Acceleration is the rate of change of velocity with respect to time.

(iv) $\frac{\sqrt{3}}{2}$ m

Exercise 14.2

1. (i) (a) $[0.1, 1.1]$ (b) $(0.1, 1.1]$ (c) N/A   (ii) (a) $[0, 2]$

(b) N/A   (c) $(0, 2)$ (iii) (a) $R\backslash\{2\}$ (b) N/A   (c) $R\backslash\{2\}$

(iv) (a) $R\backslash\{3\}$ (b) $R\backslash\{3\}$ (c) N/A   **2.** (i) (a) $[-4, 3.6]$

(b) $(-4, 2]$, $(2, 4]$ (c) $(-2, 2)$ (ii) (a) $[0.2, 2.1]$ (b) $(0.1, 1.5)$

(c) $(1.5, 2.1]$ (iii) (a) R (b) $(-\infty, 0)$ (c) $(0, \infty)$ (iv) (a) R

(b) $\left(\frac{5}{3}, 5\right)$ (c) $\left(-\infty, \frac{5}{3}\right)$, $(5, \infty)$ **3.** (i) $f': A \to R$:

$x \to 6x^2 - 90x + 216$ (ii) $[1, 3)$, $(12, 16]$ (iii) $(3, 12)$

(iv) f is not injective. Reason: You can draw a horizontal line that cuts the graph of f more than once.

4. (i) $f': B \to R: x \to 3x^2 - 10x + 3$ (ii) $\left(\frac{1}{3}, 3\right)$ (iii) $[0, \frac{1}{3})$,

$(3, 5]$ (iv) f is not surjective. Reason: No $x \in [0, 5]$ gets mapped to, say, $1,000$ by f.   **5.** (i) (a) $(3, 9]$ (b) $[1, 3)$

(ii) (a) $[0, 3)$ (b) $(3, 5]$ (iii) (a) $[1, 5)$ (b) $(5, 6]$ (iv) (a) $[0, 6]$

(b) N/A   **6.** (i) (a) $(4, 7)$ (b) $[3, 4)$, $(7, 8]$ (ii) (a) $[3, 5)$, $(8, 9]$

(b) $(5, 8)$ (iii) (a) $(-\infty, -1)$, $(2, \infty)$ (b) $(-1, 2)$ (iv) (a) $(-2, 11)$

(b) $(-\infty, -2)$, $(1, \infty)$ **7.** (i) The slope of the tangent to the graph of f is everywhere negative on $R\backslash\{1\}$.

8. (i) The slope of the tangent to the graph of f is everywhere positive on $R\backslash\{1\}$.   **9.** (i) $f': R \to R$:

$x \to 3x^2 + 12x + 15$; $f': R \to R: x \to 3[(x + 2)^2 + 1]$

Exercise 14.3

1. (i) $(-1,-9)$ (ii) $(-4,-4)$ (iii) $(3,63)$ or $(-3,-45)$ (iv) $(1,2)$

2. (iii) $(2.5,-8.25)$ **3.** (iv) Min. $(5,-250)$; Max. $(-5,250)$

4. (i) $a = 3$ (iii) $(3,8)$ **5.** (i) $a = 5$ (iii) $(5,28)$

6. (i) $x = \pm2$ (iii) $A(-2,16)$; $B(2,-16)$

7. (i) Min. $(3,-71)$; max. $(-2,54)$ **8.** (i) Min. $(-1,0)$;

max. $(1,4)$ (ii) x-axis: $(-1,0)$ or $(2,0)$; y-axis: $(0,2)$

(iv) $(-1, 1)$ **9.** (i) Min. $\left(\frac{\pi}{3},-0.685\right)$; max. $\left(\frac{5\pi}{3},6.968\right)$;

min. $\left(\frac{7\pi}{3},5.598\right)$ (ii) ≈9.4 (iii) 3π (≈9.425)

10. (ii) $\left(\frac{1}{e},-\frac{1}{e}\right)$ **11.** A   **12.** A   **13.** D   **14.** (ii) Max. at $x = 0$;

min. at $x = 8$; point of inflexion at $x = 4$ (iii) $x = \frac{2b}{3a}$ (min.);

$x = \frac{b}{3a}$ (point of inflexion)   (iv) $a = 1$, $b = 12$

(v) Max. $(0,0)$; point of inflexion $(4,-128)$; min. $(8,-256)$

15. (ii) Local minimum   **17.** (i) $f'(x) = 2xe^{x^2}$;

$f''(x) = 2e^{x^2}(1 + 2x^2)$ (ii) $(0,1)$ (iii) Local minimum

18. (iii) e^π

Exercise 14.4

1. (ii) Area $= 100x - x^2$ (iii) $x = 50$ m   (iv) $r \approx 31.83$ m

(v) $3,183$ m^2 (vi) Circular   **2.** (ii) $150x - \frac{3}{2}x^2$ (iii) $x = 50$ m

(iv) $7,500$ m^2 **3.** (ii) $8x - 3.57x^2$ (iii) $x = \frac{400}{357}$ m,

$y = \frac{400}{357}$ m   **4.** $x = y = 40$ **5.** $x = y = 50$

6. (i) $R(x) = 440x - 0.3x^2$

(ii) $P(x) = -0.8x^2 + 440x - 6,000$ (iii) 275 (iv) €$54,500$

7. (i) $h = \left(\frac{1,000}{\pi}\right)r^{-2}$ (ii) $r = \left(\frac{500}{\pi}\right)^{\frac{1}{3}}$ mm; $h = 2\left(\frac{500}{\pi}\right)^{\frac{1}{3}}$ mm

9. (iv) 10 cm   **10.** (i) $2\sqrt{3}$ (iii) $4\sqrt{3}x - 2\sqrt{3}x^2$ cm^2

(iv) $2\sqrt{3}$ cm^2 (v) 50% **11.** (i) Longer side $= 5x$

(iii) $6,075$ cm^3 **12.** (ii) $\frac{x}{v_1\sqrt{x^2 + d^2}} - \frac{(a - x)}{v_2\sqrt{(a - x)^2 + c^2}}$

14. (i) $p^m(1 - p)^{n - m}$ (ii) $p = \frac{m}{n}$

15. (i) $a(t) = 0.001190547t^2 - 0.055040784t + 7.1963$

(ii) Velocity: 70.55 m s^{-1}; acceleration: 6.76 m s^{-2}

(iii) Max. 19.16 m s^{-2}; min. 6.56 m s^{-2}

16. (i) $R(x) = 1,200x - x^2$ (ii) $P(x) = -3,500 + 1,180x - x^2$

(iii) 590 (iv) €$344,600$ (v) €610

Exercise 14.5

1. (i) $f'(V)$ is the rate of change in weight with respect to the height (of the tree). (ii) Positive, as taller trees weigh more, other things being equal. (iii) kg/m
2. (i) $h(x)$ is the speed of the rock after falling 5 m. (ii) $h'(x)$ is the acceleration of the rock after falling 5 m.
3. (i) $f(5)$ is the temperature of the bread 5 minutes out of the oven. (ii) Negative, as the temperature drops with time. (iii) °C/min **4.** (i) Positive, since infants get heavier with time. (ii) At seven months, the infant's weight is 7.65 kg. (iii) kg/month **5.** (i) 16 m (ii) 25 m (iii) $2t$ m/s (iv) 8 m/s **6.** (i) 35 m (ii) $h'(t)$ = rate of change in displacement with respect to time; this is defined as the speed. (iii) $40 - 10t$ m/s (iv) 0 m/s (v) 4 seconds (vi) 80 m **7.** (i) $-1.2t + 0.67$ °C/day (ii) -2.93 °C/day (iii) $t \approx 13$ hours **8.** (i) $n = 3$ (ii) $m = 6, n = 2$ (iii) The length x is decreasing with respect to time. (iv) 1,200 cm³/min (v) 480 cm²/min
9. (i) $V = \frac{4}{3}\pi r^3$ (ii) $S = 4\pi r^2$ (iii) $r'(t)$ is positive, as the radius is increasing with time. (iv) 576π cm³/s
(v) 96π cm²/s **10.** (i) $8\pi r$ cm² cm⁻¹ (ii) 144π cm² s⁻¹
11. (i) 2π cm cm⁻¹ (ii) $2\pi r$ cm² cm⁻¹ (iii) $\frac{1}{r}$ cm cm⁻²
(iv) 2 cm s⁻¹ **12.** (i) $\frac{dP}{dx} = 6$ cm cm⁻¹; $\frac{dA}{dx} = 4x$ cm² cm⁻¹
(ii) $\frac{3}{2x}$ cm cm⁻² (iii) 12 cm s⁻¹ **13.** (i) 32 m³
(ii) -10 m³ hr⁻¹ (iii) $T = e^{3.2}$ hrs **14.** (i) 1:3
15. (i) $\frac{4}{\pi}$ m min⁻¹ (ii) 2 m² min⁻¹ **16.** (i) $x = \frac{r}{\sin\theta} - r$
(ii) $-\frac{1}{10\sqrt{3}}$ rads/hr **17.** (i) 450 m (iii) 2 ms⁻¹
(iv) $P = \sqrt{1.5625x^2 + 1,675x + 452,500}$ metres
(v) $\dfrac{1.5625x + 837.5}{\sqrt{1.5625x^2 + 1,675x + 452,500}}$ m m⁻¹ (vi) ≈ 2.499 m s⁻¹

Revision Exercises

1. (i) $3x^2 + 6x + 4$ (ii) $3x^2 - 4x + 4$ (iii) $\frac{x^2 - 8x - 8}{(x-4)^2}$
(iv) $\frac{2x^3 - 18x^2 + 48x + 64}{(x-4)^2}$ **2.** (i) 0 (ii) 0
(iii) $12 \tan(6x) \sec^2(6x)$ (iv) 0 **3.** (i) $\frac{21(x-4)^2}{(x+3)^4}$
(ii) $\frac{12(y+5)^{11}(3 - 10y - y^2)}{(y^2 + 3)^{13}}$ (iii) $\frac{2t - 1}{5(t^2 - t + 1)^{4/5}}$
(iv) $\frac{2x^2}{(x^2+1)^{3/2}} - \frac{2}{\sqrt{x^2+1}}$ **4.** (i) $\frac{1}{\sqrt{16-x^2}}$ (ii) $\frac{2}{4+x^2}$
(iii) $-\frac{1}{(x-1)\sqrt{-x}}$ (iv) $\frac{10}{\sqrt{(x-2)^2 - (3x+4)^2(x-2)}}$ **5.** (i) $2xe^{x^2}$
(ii) e^2 (iii) $\frac{3}{x}$ (iv) $1 + \ln x$ (v) $-\frac{6}{(x+4)(x-2)}$
(vi) $2e^x[\frac{1}{x} + \ln x]$ **6.** (i) $f''(x) = 18x + 4$; $f''(-3) = -50$
(ii) $f''(x) = 30x$; $f''(-3) = -90$ (iii) $f''(x) = -18x$; $f''(-3) = 54$
8. (i) $2x - 12\sqrt{x} + 16$ (iii) (4,17) and (16,1)
(iv) (4,17) max.; (16,1) min. **9.** (i) 9 m s⁻¹ (ii) 9.375 m s⁻¹
(iii) 13.75 m s⁻¹ (iv) 16.$\dot{6}$ m s⁻¹ (v) 17.5 m s⁻¹
(vi) [0.4, 0.5] (vii) Average speed $= \dfrac{s(t+h) - s(t)}{h}$
(viii) Speed at t seconds $= \lim\limits_{h\to 0} \dfrac{s(t+h) - s(t)}{h}$ **10.** (i) cm/s
(ii) Radius $= a$ cm (iii) $33\frac{1}{3}\%$ (iv) $\frac{4a^3c}{27}$ cm/s

11. (i) 13.197 cm (ii) 30 cm (i.e. form one circle)
12. (i) kg/months (ii) At 3 months, the calf's weight is increasing at a rate of 4 kg/month. **13.** (i) πr^2 (ii) $24\pi r$
(iii) 10 cm/s (iv) By the Chain Rule (v) 500π cm²/s
14. (ii) N/m (iii) 10 N (iv) -2 N/m **15.** (i) 100θ metres
(iv) $-\dfrac{200\cos\theta}{\sqrt{5 - 4\sin\theta}}$ (v) $\frac{7\sqrt{15}}{4}$ m s⁻¹ **16.** (i) Variables: F, θ;
constants: μ, W (ii) $-\dfrac{\mu w(\mu\cos\theta - \sin\theta)}{(\mu\sin\theta + \cos\theta)^2}$
(iii) $-\dfrac{\mu w}{(\mu\sin\theta + \cos\theta)^3}[-\mu^2(1 + \cos^2\theta) + 2\mu\sin\theta$
$\cos\theta - 1 - \sin^2\theta]$ **17.** (a) 100 cm (b) 400 seconds
(c) 680 cm³ s⁻¹ (d) 216.32 cm s⁻¹ (f) 0.6
18. (b) $h = 2$, $h \approx 7.83$ (c) ≈ 294 cm³
(e) The middle cup (radius 4.43 cm, height 7.83 cm) is most suitable for use as a conical cup. The other cups are much too wide and shallow to hold. (f) $\approx 177°$
19. (i) $60 + \frac{169}{4}\sqrt{3}$ cm² (ii) Length: $5\sin\theta + 12\cos\theta$ cm;
width: $12\sin\theta + 5\cos\theta$ cm (iii) $\frac{169}{2}\sin 2\theta + 60$
(iv) 45°; 144.5 cm² (v) Sinéad is incorrect.

Chapter 15

Exercise 15.1

1. (i) $\cos x$ (ii) $-\sin x$ (iii) $\sec^2 t$ (iv) $\frac{1}{t}$ (v) e^x **2.** (i) $\sin x$
(ii) $\cos x$ (iii) $\tan t$ (iv) $\ln t$ (v) e^x **3.** (i) $-2\sin 2x$
(ii) $9\cos 3x$ (iii) $2xe^{x^2}$ (iv) $\frac{2}{x}$ (v) $2^x \ln 2$ **4.** (i) $\cos 2x$;
$\cos 2x + 5$ (ii) $3\sin 3x$; $3\sin 3x - \pi$ (iii) e^{x^2}; $e^{x^2} + \sqrt{3}$
(iv) $2\ln x$; $2\ln x - 7$ (v) 2^x; $2^x + e^2$ **5.** (i) $-\dfrac{1}{\sqrt{16 - x^2}}$
(ii) $\dfrac{1}{\sqrt{25 - x^2}}$ (iii) $\dfrac{6}{36 + x^2}$ (iv) $-\dfrac{3}{\sqrt{1 - 9x^2}}$ (v) $\dfrac{4}{1 + 16x^2}$
6. (i) $\cos^{-1}\frac{t}{4} + \pi$ (ii) $\sin^{-1}\frac{t}{5} - \ln 2$ (iii) $\tan^{-1}\frac{t}{6} + \sqrt{3}$
(iv) $\cos^{-1} 3t - 11\sqrt{7}$ (v) $\tan^{-1} 4t + 5$ **7.** (i) x^r
(ii) $\frac{x^{r+1}}{r+1} + 17$ **8.** (i) $\frac{x^3}{3} + c$ (ii) $\frac{x^4}{4} + c$ (iii) $\frac{x^2}{2} + c$
(iv) $\frac{2x^{3/2}}{3} + c$ (v) $\frac{2x^{5/2}}{5} + c$

Exercise 15.2

1. (i) $\frac{x^3}{3} + c$ (ii) $\frac{x^4}{4} + c$ (iii) $\frac{x^2}{2} + c$ (iv) $4x + c$
2. (i) $\frac{x^5}{5} + c$ (ii) $\frac{x^6}{6} + c$ (iii) $\frac{x^9}{9} + c$ (iv) $\frac{x^{n+1}}{n+1} + c$
3. (i) $\frac{5x^3}{3} + c$ (ii) $\frac{3x^2}{2} + c$ (iii) $2x + c$ (iv) $\frac{ax^4}{4} + c$
4. (i) $\frac{x^3}{3} + x^2 + x + c$ (ii) $\frac{x^5}{5} - 6x + c$ (iii) $\frac{x^4}{4} + x + c$
(iv) $\frac{x^4}{4} + x^3 - \frac{x^2}{2} + 2x + c$ **5.** (i) $\frac{x^2}{2} + \frac{x^3}{3} + c$
(ii) $\frac{x^4}{4} + \frac{8x^3}{3} + 8x^2 + c$ (iii) $x^4 - \frac{9x^2}{4} + c$
(iv) $\frac{x^5}{5} + \frac{x^4}{4} - \frac{x^3}{3} - \frac{x^2}{2} + c$ **6.** (i) $\frac{25t^6}{6} + 6t^5 + \frac{9t^4}{4} + c$
(ii) $\frac{y^4}{4} + y^3 + \frac{3y^2}{2} + y + c$ (iii) $\frac{x^4}{2} + \frac{x^3}{3} - 2x^2 - 3x + c$
(iv) $\frac{x^2}{2} - x + c$ **7.** (i) $413\frac{2}{3}$ m s⁻¹ (ii) $20,263\frac{1}{3}$ m
8. (i) If up is the positive direction, then the acceleration of the ball is towards the earth (negative direction) and of magnitude 9.8 m s⁻². (ii) $16 - 9.8t$ m s⁻¹
(iii) 0 m s⁻¹ (iv) $\frac{80}{49}$ seconds (v) $16t - 4.9t^2$ m
(vi) ≈ 7.294 seconds **9.** (i) $y = 4x^2 - x^3$ (ii) (0,0) or (4,0)

10. (i) $0.1t^2 - \frac{t^3}{750}$ (ii) Five whole words
11. (i) $10 + 9t - 0.45t^2$ (ii) 55 m s⁻¹
(iii) $10t + 4.5t^2 - 0.15t^3$ m (iv) 11.81 seconds
12. $y = \frac{3x^2}{2} - 5x - 1$ 13. $s = ut + \frac{at^2}{2}$

Exercise 15.3

1. (i) $3e^{3x}$ (ii) $\frac{1}{3}e^{3x} + \pi$ 2. (i) ae^{ax} (ii) $\frac{1}{2a}e^{2ax} + \sqrt{5}$
3. (i) $e^x + e^{-x} + c$ (ii) $\frac{1}{2}e^{2x} - \frac{1}{6}e^{6x} + c$ (iii) $\frac{1}{3}e^{3x} + x + c$
(iv) $e^x - x + c$ 4. (ii) $\frac{1}{y \ln a}$ (iv) $\frac{1}{\ln a}a^x + c$ 5. (i) $\frac{2^x}{\ln 2} + c$
(ii) $\frac{3^x}{\ln 3} + c$ (iii) $\frac{5^x}{\ln 5} + c$ (iv) $\frac{7^x}{\ln 7} + c$ (v) $5e^{2x} + c$
(vi) $\frac{x^3}{3} + \frac{4^x}{\ln 4} + c$ 6. (i) e^t (ii) te^t (iii) $te^t - e^t + c$
7. (i) $-ate^{-t}$ (ii) $-ae^{-t}(t + 1) + c$ 8. (i) $y = \frac{x^3}{3} - e^{-x} + 1$
9. (i) $\frac{1}{x}$ (ii) $\ln x + c$ (iv) $Q(t) = 2.8 \times 10^8 \times 0.99835^t$
(v) ≈46.728 kg

Exercise 15.4

1. (i) $-\frac{23}{12}$ (ii) $270\frac{3}{5}$ (iii) $62\frac{11}{12}$ (iv) $10,784\frac{2}{7}$ 2. (i) $2\frac{1}{2}$
(ii) $170\frac{1}{3}$ (iii) $682\frac{1}{2}$ (iv) $\frac{1}{11}$ 3. (i) $2e^{2x}$ (ii) $\frac{1}{2}[e^2 - 1]$
4. (i) $e^2 - e$ (ii) $\frac{1}{3}\left(e^{12} - \frac{1}{e^3}\right)$ (iii) $\frac{1}{2}\left(1 - \frac{1}{e^{10}}\right)$
(iv) $\frac{1}{5}\left(\frac{1}{e^5} - \frac{1}{e^{25}}\right)$ 5. (i) 1 (ii) −1 (iii) $\sqrt{3}$ (iv) $\frac{\sqrt{3}}{2}$ 6. (i) $\frac{\pi}{2}$
(ii) $\frac{\pi}{2}$ (iii) $\frac{\pi}{3}$ (iv) $\frac{\pi}{4}$ 7. (a) Area ≈ 0.4914 units²
(b) Area ≈ 0.63 units²; answer to part (b) is larger.
8. (a) Area ≈ 90 units² (b) ≈79.625 units²; answer to art (b) is smaller. 9. (i) The interval [0, 1] is one unit wide, and n rectangles are drawn; therefore width of each rectangle is $\frac{1}{n}$. (v) $\frac{1}{6}\left(14 - \frac{3}{n} + \frac{1}{n^2}\right)$ (vi) As $n \to \infty$, the rectangles become narrower and narrower, and so the sum of their areas → the area under the graph of $f(x)$.
10. (i) The interval [0, 1] is one unit wide, and n rectangles are drawn; therefore width of each rectangle is $\frac{1}{n}$. (v) $\frac{1}{4}\left(17 - \frac{2}{n} + \frac{1}{n^2}\right)$ 11. $22\frac{2}{3}$ units²
12. 18 units² 13. $\frac{\sqrt{3}}{2}$ units² 14. 4 units²
15. $17\frac{1}{3}$ units² 16. (i) $p = 1, q = 8$ (ii) $3\frac{3}{4}$ units²
(iii) $11\frac{1}{4}$ units² 17. (i) 1 unit² (ii) $\frac{\pi}{6}$ 19. $\left(\frac{4}{\sqrt{3}}, 32\right)$
20. (i) (0,1) (iii) 1 unit²

Exercise 15.5

1. $\frac{1}{48}$ units² 2. 4.5 units² 3. (i) (3,6) (ii) 4.5 units²
4. (i) $P(-2,-8)$; $Q(2,8)$ (iv) 8 units² 5. (i) $N(-2,0)$; $P(2,0)$
(ii) 32 units² 6. (ii) $\alpha = 0.416$ units²; $\beta = 2.6$ units²

7. (i) $y = 8x - 16$ (iii) $5\frac{1}{3}$ units² (iv) $\frac{64}{3}$ units²
8. (i) $b - a$ (iv) 7.34 units² (v) Overestimates
(vi) $7\frac{1}{3}$ units² (vii) 0.09% 9. $38\frac{1}{2}$ units²
10. (i) 41 units² (ii) 50 units² (iii) 42 units²

Exercise 15.6

1. (i) $5\frac{2}{3}$ (ii) $5\frac{5}{12}$ (iii) $5\frac{1}{3}$ 2. (i) 33 (ii) $30\frac{3}{4}$ (iii) 30
3. (i) $6\frac{2}{3}$ (ii) $-7\frac{5}{12}$ (iii) $22\frac{1}{5}$ (iv) $31\frac{1}{2}$ 4. (i) $\frac{2}{\pi}$
(ii) $2\frac{8}{15}$ (iii) $\frac{1}{4}(e^4 - 1)$ (iv) $\frac{4}{\pi}$ 5. $\frac{3 \pm \sqrt{5}}{2}$
6. ≈3.634°C or $\left(10 - \frac{20}{\pi}\right)°C$ 7. (i) $\frac{3m}{2} + 3$ (ii) $a^2 + 2$
(iii) $\frac{2^n}{n + 1}$ (iv) $\frac{e^4}{3} - \frac{e}{3} + \frac{25}{2}$ 8. ≈149,426
9. (i) ≈46.855 km/hr (ii) 247.29 m 10. (i) 70 (ii) 76.05
(iii) $55\frac{5}{6}$ 11. (i) $6\frac{2}{3}$ m/s² (ii) $\frac{t^3}{150} - 0.9t^2 + 25t$ m/s
(iii) $151\frac{1}{24}$ m/s (iv) $\frac{t^4}{600} - 0.3t^3 + \frac{25t^2}{2}$ m (v) $3,776\frac{1}{24}$ m
(vi) $3,776\frac{1}{24}$ m

Revision Exercises

1. (a) (i) $2\cos 2x$ (ii) $-2\sin 2x$ (b) (i) $\cos 2x + c$
(ii) $\sin 2x + c$ (iii) $\frac{\sin 2x}{2} + \frac{\cos 2x}{2} + c$
(iv) $\frac{3\sin 2x}{2} - \frac{\cos 2x}{2} + c$ (c) (i) 0 (ii) $\frac{1}{2}$ (iii) 0
2. (i) $\frac{1}{\sqrt{a^2 - x^2}}$ (ii) $\frac{\pi}{2}$ 3. (i) $4\frac{1}{3}$ (ii) $47\frac{5}{6}$ (iii) $877\frac{1}{2}$
(iv) $\frac{61}{66}$ 4. (i) $e^2 - e$ (ii) $\frac{1}{5}\left(e^{20} - \frac{1}{e^5}\right)$ (iii) $\frac{1}{3}\left(1 - \frac{1}{e^{15}}\right)$
(iv) $\frac{1}{2}\left(\frac{1}{e^2} - \frac{1}{e^{10}}\right)$ 5. (a) $a\cos ax$; $-a\sin ax$; $a\sec^2 ax$
(b) (i) $\frac{1}{5}$ (ii) $\frac{1}{3}$ (iii) 1 (iv) 0 6. (i) $\frac{\pi}{2}$ (ii) $\frac{\pi}{6}$ (iii) $\frac{\pi}{6}$ (iv) $\frac{3\pi}{16}$
7. (i) $\frac{2}{5\pi}$ (ii) $\frac{74\sqrt{2}}{21}$ (ii) $\frac{1}{3}(e^4 - e)$ (iii) $\frac{4}{\pi}$ 8. 10.7072°C
9. (i) Interval width = 1 unit; therefore, each rectangle has width $\frac{1}{n}$ units (v) $\frac{1}{6}\left(2 + \frac{3}{n} + \frac{1}{n^2}\right) + \frac{1}{2}\left(1 + \frac{1}{n}\right) + 1$
10. (i) 6 (ii) $y = 3x^2 - 2x^3 + 1$ 11. (iv) $21\frac{1}{3}$ units²
12. $2\frac{2}{3}$ units² 13. (i) 1 a.m. (ii) $8(1 - e^{-t} - te^{-t})$ kWh
(iii) ≈7.677 kWh (iv) ≈0.0998 kWh 14. (a) $\ln x$
(b) $10\log_e 5 - 8$ units² 15. (i) 17.5 units²
16. (i) $A(-2,0)$, $B(2,-4)$, $C(4,18)$ (ii) $\frac{148}{3}$ units²
17. (a) (i) $\frac{x^4}{4} - x^3 + 3x + 5$; $\frac{x^4}{4} - x^3 + 3x - 2$; $\frac{x^4}{4} - x^3 + 3x + 7$ (iii) $\int(x^3 - 3x^2 + 3)$ $dx = \frac{x^4}{4} - x^3 + 3x + c$ (b) (i) $1 + \ln x$
(ii) $x\ln x - x + c$, where c is an arbitrary constant
18. (ii) ≈6.559 m/s (iii) ≈91.828 m (iv) 2 m/s²
19. (a) (i) 0 (b) (ii) 36.864 m (iii) 12.48 seconds
(c) (ii) 3 hours 51 minutes 20. (a) (5,37), (−1,7)
(b) 36 units²